T5-AWI-750

DATE DUE

OCT. 2 1 '92		
NOV 2 4 '92		
MAY 2 4 1993		
JUN 1 5 1993		
DEC 3 0 1993		
JAN 3 1 '94		
AUG 3 0 1994		
MAR 2 8 1995		

HIGHSMITH 45-220

CHINESE EDUCATION
Problems, Policies, and Prospects

REFERENCE BOOKS IN
INTERNATIONAL EDUCATION
(VOL. 20)

GARLAND REFERENCE LIBRARY
OF SOCIAL SCIENCE
(VOL. 585)

Reference Books in
International Education

Edward R. Beauchamp
General Editor

1. *Education in East and West Germany: A Bibliography, by* Val D. Rust
2. *Education in the People's Republic of China, Past and Present: An Annotated Bibliography, by* Franklin Parker and Betty June Parker
3. *Education in South Asia: A Select Annotated Bibliography, by* Philip G. Altbach, Denzil Saldanha, and Jeanne Weiler
4. *Textbooks in the Third World: Policy, Content and Context, by* Philip G. Altbach and Gail P. Kelly
5. *Education in Japan: A Source Book, by* Edward R. Beauchamp and Richard Rubinger
6. *Women's Education in the Third World, by* David H. Kelly and Gail P. Kelly
7. *Minority Status and Schooling, by* Margaret A. Gibson and John V. Ogbu
8. *Teachers and Teaching in the Developing World, by* Val D. Rust and Per Dalin
9. *Russian and Soviet Education, 1732–1988: An Annotated Bibliography, by* William J. Brickman and John T. Zepper
10. *Early Childhood Education in the Arab World: A Source Book, by* Byron G. Massialas and Layla Jarrar
11. *Education in Sub-Saharan Africa: A Source Book, by* George Urch
12. *Youth in the Soviet Union, by* Anthony Jones
13. *Education in Israel: A Source Book, by* Yaacov Iram
14. *Arab Education in Transition: A Source Book, by* Byron G. Massialas and Samir A. Jarrar
15. *Education and Cultural Differences: An International Perspective, by* Deo H. Poonwassie and Douglas Ray
16. *Contemporary Perspectives in Comparative Education,* edited by Robin J. Burns and Anthony R. Welch
17. *Education in the Arab Gulf States and the Arab World: A Select Annotated Bibliographic Guide, by* Nagat El-Sanabary
18. *The International and Historical Roots of American Higher Education, by* W.H. Cowley and Don Williams
19. *Education in England and Wales: An Annotated Bibliography, by* Franklin Parker and Betty June Parker
20. *Chinese Education: Problems, Policies, and Prospects,* edited, with an introduction, by Irving Epstein

CHINESE EDUCATION
Problems, Policies, and Prospects

edited, with an introduction, by
Irving Epstein

GARLAND PUBLISHING, INC. • NEW YORK & LONDON
1991

Library of Congress Cataloging-in-Publication Data

Chinese education : problems, policies, and prospects / edited and
with an introduction by Irving Epstein.
    p.   cm. — (Reference books in international education ; vol.
20)   (Garland reference library of social science ; vol. 585)
    Includes bibliographical references and index.
    ISBN 0-8240-4382-0
    1. Education—China. 2. Education and state—China. I. Epstein,
Irving, 1951– . II. Series. III. Series: Garland reference
library of social science ; v. 585.
LA1131.82.C544   1991
370'.951—dc20   90-21938
                                                    CIP

Printed on acid-free, 250-year-life paper
Manufactured in the United States of America

SERIES EDITOR'S FOREWORD

This series of reference works and monographs in education in selected nations and regions is designed to provide a resource to scholars, students, and a variety of other professionals who need to understand the place of education in a particular society or region. While the format of the volumes is often similar, the authors have had the flexibility to adjust the common outline to reflect the uniqueness of their particular nation or region.

Contributors to this series are scholars who have devoted their professional lives to studying the nation or region about which they write. Without exception they have not only studied the educational system in question, but they have lived and travelled widely in the society in which it is embedded. In short, they are exceptionally knowledgeable about their subject.

In our increasingly interdependent world, it is now widely understood that it is a matter of survival that we understand better what makes other societies tick. As the late George Z.F. Bereday wrote: "First, education is a mirror held against the face of a people. Nations may put on blustering shows of strength to conceal public weakness, erect grand façades to conceal shabby backyards, and profess peace while secretly arming for conquest, but how they take care of their children tells unerringly who they are" (*Comparative Method in Education*, New York: Holt, Rinehart & Winston, 1964, page 5).

Perhaps equally important, however, is the valuable perspective that studying another education system provides us in understanding our own. To step outside of our commonly held assumptions about schools and learning, however briefly, and to look back at our system in contrast to another, places it in a very different light. To learn, for example, how the Soviet Union handles the education of a multilingual society; how the French provide for the funding of public education; or how the Japanese control admissions into their universities enables us to understand that there are alternatives to our familiar way of doing things. Not that we can often "borrow" from other societies; indeed, educational arrangements are inevitably a reflection of deeply rooted political, economic, and cultural factors that are unique to a society. But a conscious recognition that there are other ways of doing things can serve to open our minds and provoke our imaginations in ways that can result in new approaches that we would not have otherwise considered.

Since this series is designed to be a useful research tool, the editors and contributors welcome suggestions for future volumes as well as ways in which this series can be improved.

Edward R. Beauchamp
University of Hawaii

CONTENTS

ILLUSTRATIONS   ix

PREFACE   xi

INTRODUCTION
by Irving Epstein   xiii

CHAPTER ONE
POST-MAO REFORMS IN CHINESE
EDUCATION: CAN THE GHOSTS
OF THE PAST BE LAID
TO REST?
by Suzanne Pepper   1

CHAPTER TWO
THE EARLY CHILDHOOD EDUCATION OF
THE
ONLY CHILD GENERATION IN URBAN
CHINA
by Delia Davin   42

CHAPTER THREE
THE "CRISIS" IN CHINESE SECONDARY
SCHOOLING
by Heidi Ross   66

CHAPTER FOUR
THE TAPESTRY OF CHINESE HIGHER
EDUCATION
by Ruth Hayhoe   109

CHAPTER FIVE
CHINESE ADULT EDUCATION
IN TRANSITION
by Jianliang Wang and Nat Colletta   145

CHAPTER SIX
MINBAN SCHOOLS IN DENG'S ERA
by Jean Robinson — 163

CHAPTER SEVEN
SPECIAL ECONOMIC ZONES AND EDUCATION
IN CHINA: BOLD REFORM OR
TIMID EXPERIMENT?
by John N. Hawkins and Bruce Koppel — 172

CHAPTER EIGHT
EDUCATING CHINA'S DISADVANTAGED
YOUTH: A CASE OF MODERNIZATION
AND ITS DISCONTENTS
by Irving Epstein — 196

CHAPTER NINE
REFORMING TEACHERS:
THE ORGANIZATION, REPRODUCTION,
AND TRANSFORMATION OF TEACHING
by Lynn Paine — 217

CHAPTER TEN
CHINESE MEDICAL SCHOOLING:
GLOBAL SCIENCE,
LOCAL SCHOOLS
by Mary Ann Burris — 255

CHAPTER ELEVEN
BEYOND 'STUFFING THE GOOSE': THE
CHALLENGE OF MODERNIZATION AND
REFORM FOR LAW AND LEGAL EDUCATION
IN THE PEOPLE'S REPUBLIC OF CHINA
by Sharon K. Hom — 287

CHAPTER TWELVE
MILITARY EDUCATION AND TECHNICAL
TRAINING IN CHINA
by Richard J. Latham   316

CHAPTER THIRTEEN
GENDER AND EDUCATION
by Beverley Hooper   352

CHAPTER FOURTEEN
AN ORGANIZATIONAL ANALYSIS OF
CENTRAL EDUCATION ADMINISTRATION
IN CHINA
by Zhixin Su   375

CHAPTER FIFTEEN
THE INSTITUTIONAL ROOTS OF
STUDENT POLITICAL CULTURE: OFFICIAL
STUDENT POLITICS AT BEIJING
UNIVERSITY
by Corinna-Barbara Francis   394

CHAPTER SIXTEEN
POLITICAL EDUCATION AND STUDENT
RESPONSE: SOME BACKGROUND FACTORS
BEHIND THE 1989 STUDENT
DEMONSTRATIONS
by Stanley Rosen   416

BIBLIOGRAPHY   449

NOTES ON CONTRIBUTORS   491

Index   495

ILLUSTRATIONS

TABLES

2.1	*Only Children as a Percentage of Pupils in the Fuxue Hutong Primary School*	58
4.1	*Fields of Study: 1955-1985 (Higher Education)*	124
5.1	*Adult Literacy and General Education*	148
5.2	*Adult Higher Education Statistics*	153
7.1	*Labor Force Educational Level: Shenzhen*	180
7.2	*Secondary Vocational Enrollments and Specializations: Shenzhen*	186
7.3	*Vocational and Technical Education Comparisons: 1985-1987 (Shenzhen)*	187
10.1	*Biomedical Curriculae in China: 1912-1989 (Required Hours)*	269
13.1	*Female Percentage of Total Students*	354
16.1	*Reasons for Friends Joining the Communist Party*	423
16.2	*Reasons why People Lack Interest in Marxism*	424
16.3	*Student Attitudes Concerning Difficulty in Determining Right From Wrong*	425
16.4	*Student Attitudes Concerning Cheating on Exams*	425
16.5	*Student Attitudes Concerning Couples Who Fall in Love and Decide to Live Together Without Marrying*	426
16.6	*Reaction to Case of a Student Volunteer Who Loses a Leg on the Vietnamese Border*	427

16.7   *Should One Offer Help to a Student Who Studies Hard But Has a Poor Foundation?*   428

16.8   *Student Responses to Various Philosophical Statements*   429

16.9   *Beijing University Student Interest in Various Activities*   432

16.10   *University Students in Beijing and Party Membership*   433

16.11   *Views of University Students in Beijing About Party Work Style*   434

16.12   *Views of Graduate Students in Beijing Regarding Ideas of Fang Lizhi*   434

16.13   *Desire of Political Work Cadres in Universities in Beijing to Continue in Their Work*   437

16.14   *Reasons Why Respondents Do Not Want to Spend Their Lives Engaged in Political Work*   438

FIGURES

4.1   *Three-Tiered Administrative Structure of Chinese Higher Education: 1985*   120

14.1   *Organization of the Ministry of Education: 1977*   378

14.2   *Educational Administration in China: 1977-1985*   382

14.3   *An Incomplete Learning Process*   383

14.4   *Organization of the State Education Commission: 1985-1988*   387

14.5   *A Complete Learning Process*   389

PREFACE

The decision to compile an edited volume of essays which would uniformly address Chinese education issues, arose from the conviction that such a project could provide the interested reader with a comparative perspective which was both comprehensive and informative. Given the inherent diversity within the Chinese educational system, and the rapidity with which policy changes have occurred, there are limits which mark the degree to which these goals can be achieved. Nonetheless, it is hoped that the volume will be useful in providing the reader with an appreciation for many of the salient characteristics which are representative of that system.

To that end, the volume is roughly divided into three parts. Chapters one through five provide an historical overview and proceed to analyze issues common to basic structures and sectors: primary, secondary, higher and adult education. Chapters six through twelve discuss specialized educational programs in rural and commercial geographical areas, programs for disadvantaged youth, and education in the professions (teacher preparation, medical, legal and military education). Chapters thirteen through sixteen conclude the volume by examining specific policy issues: gender and education, administrative organization and student politics.

A project of this size requires the cooperation of many colleagues and friends. In addition to the contributors, whose patience and professionalism has been laudatory, the editor is indebted to the assistance of the staffs of the Lafayette College Skillman Library and Academic Computing Center, particularly Susan Leopold, the Lafayette College Committee on Advanced Study and Research, Marie Ellen Larcada of Garland Publishing, and series editor Ed Beauchamp.

INTRODUCTION

by Irving Epstein

This is a book about educational change. It seeks to place Chinese educational policies within the broader social context of Chinese development and modernization imperatives by analyzing issues germane to specific educational sectors and structures. At the same time, it attempts to inform the reader of larger policy issues which affect the educational system as a whole and speak to more global concerns: the nature of Chinese student activism, the persistence of gender inequality, rural-urban disparities and the existence of educational inequity, the possibilities for educational empowerment and autonomy, the influences of market forces upon educational reform, and the growth of professionalism as part of the country's modernization ethic.

The Tienanmen Massacre of 1989 and its ensuing repression, which continues to harshly affect the Chinese academic community at this time, have argued for a reconsideration of the terms under which Chinese education has developed since 1976. Suzanne Pepper's chapter offers penetrating historical insight which explains the growth of an independent political culture that oversaw the resuscitation of an elitist educational system, designed to protect and reproduce those in possession of a shared value orientation, from 1977 onward. Chapters by Ruth Hayhoe, Mary Ann Burris and Sharon Hom also use an historical perspective to analyze continuities and disparities in higher education, medical education, and legal education sectors. However, it is useful to look specifically at issues of class and the state from a *theoretical perspective* as a means of clarifying the nature of that continuing political and social conflict which expressed itself with such vehemence during the spring of 1989. The first part of this introductory essay will attempt to address that need. Afterwards, it will highlight a number of the salient themes which are explored in various chapters of the volume.

A brief summation of the western scholarship which has sought to evaluate Chinese educational trends since 1949 reaffirms the importance of seeking new conceptual frameworks to interpret change and conflict in Chinese educational circles. Through the 1950s and mid-1960s, the best of western scholarship which addressed educational issues relied upon formal policy documents, issued by government and party officials, as a prime source for analyzing the nature of policy and its impact upon practitioners and constituents.[1] Given the lack of access to the very participants and constituents who shaped and were affected by official policy, the reliance upon primary source documents was understandable and necessary in spite of obvious limitations.

By the mid-1970s, foreign travelers and invited academicians were able to observe selected Chinese classrooms on a first hand basis. Occasionally, short-term delegation visits produced valuable insight into curricular and pedagogical methods practiced at China's better schools.[2] Their work supplemented more comprehensive views of educational practice, chronicled by those who spent significant periods of time teaching in China.[3] Again though, limited access made it impossible to generate comprehensive conclusions based upon single case scenarios.

During the late 1970s, refugee interviewing in Hong Kong was used extensively to gain new awareness of class conflict within educational environments[4] and Red Guard factionalism[5]. The best of these works relied upon interview data which was internally consistent and complemented the interviews with a judicious use of Red Guard publications.[6] Our understanding was further enhanced through the use of these methodologies to describe urban rustication policies[7]. Further attempts to redefine higher education access issues and re-establish elitist hierarchies during the later years of the Cultural Revolution and the early years of the post-Mao Era were similarly analyzed using both the informant interview and primary source publication.[8]

Since the early 1980s, western scholarship has benefited significantly from improved access to Chinese policy-makers and administrators and their institutions. The opportunity to conduct lengthy fieldwork in China resulted in important contributions which described in great detail university admissions procedures,[9] debates over key school policies,[10] changing attitudes and values of youth,[11] and the growing importance of individual and institutional networking with the world academic community.[12] At the same time, as the Chinese press itself became more open and the number, quality, and type of publications proliferated, Western scholars were able to take advantage of increased press pluralism and analyze internal conflict with respect to policy and public opinion in clearer terms.[13]

Nonetheless, the search for inclusive conceptual frameworks which can more elegantly contextualize empirical research findings continues. Two studies have sought to relate issues of class conflict to educational and social policy with mixed results.

Julia Kwong's *Chinese Education in Transition* sought to analyze educational policies from 1949-1965 within a neo-Marxist structuralist framework, linking economic developments directly to their educational counterparts.[14] Kwong's use of the Altusserian notion of overdeterminism, which postulates that economic relations are mirrored in superstructure, was applied directly to the Chinese case. A more recent effort, which benefited from extensive fieldwork, chronicled the application of Taylorism and capitalist management skills aimed at maximizing profit, to university life during the mid 1980s.[15] In this case though, she was able to successfully link the two domains without using the theoretical model which dominated the previous study.

Richard Kraus offered the most penetrating analysis of Chinese notions of class and class conflict in his work *Class Conflict in Chinese Socialism*. Kraus was the first to document how changing ideological notions of class served various interests, were ultimately unsuccessful in ameliorating conflict, and in fact perpetuated it. He argued that competing views of class, as representing political behavior (class consciousness) or caste (associating class solely with family background), were used to serve the interests of antagonistic groups who attempted to used their class labels to facilitate their upward mobility (often through the educational system). The irresolution of this conflict in ideological terms influenced the outbreak of the Cultural Revolution.[16] During the post-Mao Era, an imposed stratification system served to protect the interests of those closely aligned with the state, as the vocabulary of social class affiliation was excised from official ideological pronouncement. It should be noted that Kraus's work was written too early to address the economic impact of commodification socialism, with its freer market, upon a stratification system borrowed from the 1950s. His more recent efforts, however, address the relationship between market and western influences upon social norms more directly.[17]

As has been noted, Ruth Hayhoe's scholarship has similarly linked Chinese educational reform with China's opening to the West, a process which has had numerous historical resonances but which also highlights the potential for increased regional diversity and experimentation as well as educational inequality and growing international cooperation and/or dependency. One of the chief benefits of Hayhoe's work is that it forces the reader to place the Chinese state in a global context. If we are to directly address issues of class and class conflict as they relate to educators, students, academicians, and members of the Chinese intellectual community, though, it may be useful to look at historical antecedents, review some of the western literature which speaks to issues of class affiliation, and then place the events of Tiananmen within a broader theoretical framework.

Jerome Grieder has argued that Confucian education was synonymous with self-cultivation and self-realization whose function was to guarantee the continuation of humane governance. Social inequality was assumed to be reflective of natural social order, with those who were capable of performing difficult mental tasks charged with the responsibility for preserving social order. Thus, the traditional role of the intellectual was one of upholding the moral authority of the state, and the costs of expressing individually autonomous beliefs included political estrangement.[18] The official role of civil servant-literati did not allow for pluralistic expressions of opinion deviating from accepted norms. Although the potential ramifications were severe, intellectuals often were willing to express their autonomy as a matter of moral conviction, in order to protect the welfare of the state. Thus, Merle Goldman and Timothy Cheek argue that intellectuals in the twentieth century have continued to perform roles which offer service to the state while also serving as moral critics of the country's leadership when they believe circumstances compel them to do so. However, in the early part of this century, Chinese intellectuals were exposed to western values of professionalism, which specifically emphasized the importance of autonomy and the protection of individual free expression. Since 1949, Goldman and Cheek claim that intellectuals have played three distinct roles: ideologue, member of a professional and academic elite, and critic. In recent decades, intellectuals have performed multiple roles and the three roles must be seen as individually distinctive without having been mutually exclusive. However, the type of role portrayed must be understood in relation to the power of the state at any particular time.[19]

Historians Benjamin Elman and R. Kent Guy have documented the growth of a professional ethic, indigenous to Confucian traditionalism, which sought to redefine scholarly norms in the study of texts during the Qing dynasty. The importance attached to verifying broad claims through empirical research based upon rigorous textual criticism had the effect of questioning basic canons of neo-Confucian orthodoxy, the basis for the *k'ao-cheng* movement. Yet ultimately, the long term impact of the *k'ao-cheng* movement was limited by the appearance of growing social conflict and rebellion during the late eighteenth and early nineteenth centuries, which argued for a rejection of the movement's apoliticism.[20]

Fascination with western modes of professionalism during the Self Strengthening and May Fourth Movements must also be seen within the context of a weakened state. It has been noted, for example, that John Dewey's pragmatism, which was so enticing to many May Fourth intellectuals, assumed a degree of social structure and political stability which was characteristic of selected democracies but was sorely lacking in Republican China.[21] As Pepper's and Hayhoe's chapters document, under such conditions it is not surprising that an alternative construct, Marxism, which invited a transfer of loyalty from the authority of Confucian culture to the authority of the Chinese state, now redefined to encapsulate the former, eventually won out. Thus, the re-emergence of the strong state, alternatively relying upon bureaucratized institutions and mass mobilization techniques, as a means of promoting social cohesiveness and inclusivity, was a defining characteristic of the Maoist legacy.

During the post-Mao Era, the ideological legitimacy of the state has dissolved in reaction to the abuses of state power under Maoism and the introduction of a limited free market under the pretext of creating commodity socialism. Events such as the Tiananmen massacre expose a patrimonial regime, clinging to power through a spasmodic use of coercion; intellectuals, who have accepted their roles as members of an academic, and the professional elite, who are also expected to express moral criticism of political abuses, continue to fall victim to the regime's authoritarian excesses.

Any analysis of the relationship between the Chinese intellectual community and the state must include a discussion of educational structure, policy and practice, which speaks directly to the formation of that relationship. It is thus not surprising that educational pluralism has been most evident when state power has been diffused. Hayhoe, for example, has deftly chronicled in her chapter here and elsewhere, the eclectic borrowing of western higher educational models during the Republican Era and their visible re-emergence during the post-Mao Era. As Pepper and Hayhoe note, the use of Stalinist educational patterns during the 1950s, with their association of technical expertise with manpower needs and their emphasis upon elitism and curricular specialization, can also be viewed within a political context where statism predominated. Alternative modes of educational practice, which competed with their formal counterparts for legitimacy, can be viewed as representing the legacy of the *shuyuan*, the non-formal academy popular in previous centuries, as well as some of the tenants of progressive education discussed in the 1920s by Dewey and his followers. During periods of political conflict when formal state institutions were subjected to intense criticism (such as the Cultural Revolution), non-formal educational alternatives received official sanction.

We have referred to the post-Mao Era as a period where the power of the state has been reasserted *sans* the ideological legitimacy of Maoism, which rationalized overt political control over everyday life. In educational terms, policy has had the effect of reintroducing an elitist structure, borrowed from the 1950s, which has allowed for the exercise of selective autonomy in its most prestigious sectors. The goal has been one of attempting to coopt intellectual expertise for national modernization goals. When one examines the effect the reintroduction of limited market forces as a means of encouraging commodity socialism has had upon different sectors within the educational system, it is clear that distinct winners and losers have arisen.

For those who have been able to position themselves at the apex of the educational ladder, for example, market forces have maximized opportunities for consultancies, increased personal freedom of movement, overseas travel, etc. (at least before the Tiananmen massacre). At the lowest end of the educational ladder, market forces have overpowered attempts to provide basic educational services. Education is viewed as an ineffective means of guaranteeing upward social mobility resulting in severe rural dropout and ensuing exploitation of child labor, increased illiteracy, teacher abuse, staffing shortages and resource insufficiency. As Beverley Hooper's chapter suggests, increased gender inequality has been an additional negative byproduct. For those educators in the middle or near the upper end of the ladder, a freer market has meant erosion of basic services traditionally guaranteed to academicians and university staff (e.g. housing) and a sharp decrease in earning power as inflation severely harmed those on fixed incomes. The anomaly of taxi cab drivers earning higher wages than university professors certainly perpetuated the frustration with academic life which encouraged the events leading to Tiananmen.

It should be noted that adherence to commodity socialism has had distinctive curricular repercussions as expressed through the growth of commercial, technical, and vocational education and private educational ventures, popular in those areas where market forces have been particularly influential, less popular where the economic gains of such policies are less apparent. The chapters by Heidi Ross, Ruth Hayhoe, John Hawkins and Bruce Koppel, and Mary Ann Burris speak directly to this phenomenon, while Jean Robinson's piece demonstrates the futility of attempts to refit the *minban* or work-study school concept with the current commodification ethic.

Certainly the lines of stratification within the educational system correspond to urban and rural, gender related, and sectoral inequalities (key vs. non-key schooling, research institute and university vs. primary or secondary schooling). Given this characteristic, it is important to address questions concerning the homogeneity of the intellectual community. Does the Chinese educational system create such disparity that the situation for example, of a primary level teacher employed in a poorly funded rural school no longer deserves comparison with that of the academician working for the Academy of Sciences regardless of obvious income and quality of life differentials? Are the experiences of these two actors so different that they represent antagonistic interests and value claims? And, if the answer is affirmative, what are the implications for modernization and political change?

The work of Eric Olin Wright may be useful in attempting to discover a framework which can clarify the means through which one would begin to seek answers to these questions. Wright has argued with reference to advanced capitalism that it is useful to analyze class structure by conceiving of "some positions as occupying objectively contradictory locations within class relations." Under his scheme, the modern university researcher would occupy a contradictory location between the petty bourgeoisie and the working class, possessing at least some autonomy over the conditions of one's work, what is produced and how it is produced, yet removed from the physical means of production. Even within a particular class, different groups possess varying degrees of autonomy and semi-autonomy, as their position becomes closer or farther removed from that of distinct social classes. The analogy that Wright offers is the difference in social location between the research scientist, in charge of his own grants, hiring his own personnel, and operating semi-autonomously, almost as an individual entrepreneur, and the lab technician, who maintains significant but limited control over the nature of his own work.[22]

Returning to the case of Chinese education, we have argued that autonomy exists in varying degrees as one moves up the educational ladder, a non-accidental occurrence. One of the prices to be paid for encouraging research and development effort, a key to modernization, is allowing practitioners to engage in what Polyani describes as "independent initiatives, combined towards an indeterminate achievement," although the practitioners will adhere to strict scientific tradition and authority in pursuing their efforts.[23]

China's leadership has also respected scientific authority, viewing it as a developmental and politically non-threatening necessity, and has tolerated the necessary autonomy and freedom of inquiry which the privileged members of the scientific community demand. That tolerance, at least before the spring of 1989, was expanded to include academicians involved in the social sciences and humanities, disciplines which had been formerly discredited, due to their susceptibility for overt political manipulation during periods of ideological stridency (it is not surprising that in the aftermath of Tienanmen, humanities and social science departments, faculty and students have been disproportionately selected for retaliation). At the same time, a growing acceptance of academic professionalism influenced attempts to upgrade the educational qualifications of party and military personnel (see Richard Latham's chapter) as well as the initiation of fields of study such as journalism and law (see the chapter by Sharon Hom).

The professional autonomy afforded the typical school teacher, consigned to teach to a pre-determined standardized curriculum which is examination driven, has been another matter. Lynn Paine, in her chapter, speaks of efforts to promote the social standing and economic condition of teachers as evidence of the state's recognition of the need to increase their authority and status although she is appropriately circumspect in assessing the impact of these initiatives. Heidi Ross mentions efforts in Shanghai to create alternative assessment mechanisms which would free students and teachers from their forced participation in traditionally mandated, externally driven pedagogical rituals emphasizing rote memorization. With the growth of vocational programs at the secondary level, Ross argues that a significant degree of curricular diversity had in fact been achieved by the late 1980s. Yet, it is arguable whether such reforms have had significant success in altering the fundamental nature of teacher work or the student-teacher relationship.

Certainly, structural differences exist concerning the specificity of knowledge communicated, the size and nature of clientele, and the conditions under which educators throughout the Chinese educational system operate. However, the concept of autonomy as applied to one's working conditions within the educational ladder is important in the Chinese case if one is to address larger issues concerning political inclusivity, the degree to which political protest represents the shared conviction of disparate educators, intellectuals, and students and the extent to which the educational system as a whole has contributed to pressure for social and political change.   If one follows Wright's framework, it would seem clear that the educational bureaucracy has encouraged the growth of contradictory and perhaps antagonistic locations within the social strata which contain the essence of the country's intellectual community.

The application of a theory of contradictory location within and among social classes in advanced western capitalist states to a Third World context such as that of China must be rigorously qualified. Autonomy, as an operational term, should be understood to exist in concert with other powerful social relations: patronship and clientship, and horizontal as well as vertical personal ties which influence mobility, positioning, and power.   It has been argued, for example, that the Chinese work place promotes organized dependency because of the informal means with which power and status are typically negotiated.[24] Without belittling the continued importance of personal connections within Chinese society, it may be useful to examine the specific conditions under which they are most effective.   And, in hierarchically structured, elitist systems such as that of education, it is conceivable that clientship, patronage and personal association might be less important influences in restricting one's behavior and expression of opinion if one's individual autonomy is insured by the nature of one's work. Similarly, the negative impact of market forces upon educational practice is probably experienced in those situations where educational activity is conceived as being generically non-empowering.   The use of Bourdieu's notion of habitus, or the internalization of one's relationship to an external social environment, as an important factor which determines one's perception of the chance to succeed is quite important here.[25]   In any event, it is our contention that, while certainly non-explanatory in a totalistic sense, the use of work autonomy as a theoretical construct in determining position and location within the educational community has value for the Chinese case.

How then would the differential allocation of autonomy within an academic community affect pressures for political and social change? The work of Ivan Szelenyi, with reference to Eastern European socialism, is particularly instructive here.   Szelenyi argues that the new dominating class in Eastern European countries is the intelligentsia, including both bureaucratically inclined party aparatchiks and, in more recent years, highly trained technocrats.   Eventually, with the growing popularity of rational scientific planning and with an increase of autonomy in civil society, the technocrat takes over completely. His interesting conclusion is that class conflict between intelligentsia and workers is a much more likely outcome of the political changes to date, but conflicts between party members and the intelligentsia, while holding temporary significance, are more easily resolved in the long term.[26] In order to apply such a model to the China case, one would have to explain why the pressures for political change in China have been successfully contained by a party gerontocracy using an enormous amount of repression, while also addressing the repercussions of such containment for China's future.

When one analyzes the expression of significant political protest in China during the past decade, three distinct periods are apparent. The Democracy Wall Movement in 1979-1980 was dangerous to the party leadership insofar as its leaders were disaffected party members, former Red Guards who rebelled against the reimposition of institutionalized authoritarianism in the early years of the post-Mao Era. The threat to party orthodoxy came from within.[27]

As Stanley Rosen's chapter indicates, in 1986, student protest was led by the beneficiaries of an elitist educational system now in place, who had rejected ideological orthodoxy in toto. Spurred on by intellectuals who performed traditional roles as moral critic (Liu Binyuan) and respected professional scientist (Fang Lizhi), this protest was contained through the creation of a compromise solution which included the sacking of Party Secretary Hu Yaobang, the initiation of a limited spiritual pollution campaign aimed at reforming the attitudes of cynical students, the ascendancy of Zhao Ziyang as Deng's likely successor, and the imposition of stringent controls upon Zhao's liberal economic policies.

The events of 1989, which can be understood in global terms as reflective of the failures of the 1987 solutions, were remarkable for a number of reasons. Unlike other student movements, the students displayed extraordinary organizational skill while demonstrating an ability to channel spontaneous impulse into non-violent protest. They additionally showed a surprising degree of technological sophistication, utilizing fax machines, computer networks, and the electronic media to their advantage. They were aware of the international character of their audience and certainly played (some would argue overplayed) to world opinion. Finally, by articulating essentially reasonable demands for the establishment of a free press and an end to government corruption they were able to gain popular approval for their cause, among urban workers and certain non-elites.

The vehemence with which the central leadership crushed the student protest is graphically illustrative of the schism between party and intellectual elites, which is much wider in China than in other socialist countries amenable to reform from within. As Suzanne

Pepper's chapter notes, China never had a Stalinist "cultural revolution" where bureaucratic and technocratic elites were allowed to merge. In fact, the shared belief in a political culture that views the proper role of the intellectual as legitimate moral critic encouraged widespread support for the students on the one hand yet made a patrimonial geriatric leadership feel extremely threatened by their peaceful activities.

And, as painful as the events of spring 1989 were, it is clear that China's current leadership will be eventually replaced, and when that occurs, Szelenyi's prediction will have to be addressed. Will new technocratic elites be able to gain power in China, and, once having gained power, will they be able to keep it? As beneficiaries of an educational system which grants individual autonomy and free expression to only its most privileged practitioners, will they have or be able to maintain the popular support of those who have been disenfranchised by that same system? It may be that shared traditional assumptions concerning the power of the intellectual's voice will continue to be salient, certainly when the alternative is corrupt and illegitimate accession to positions of influence based upon patronage. But this will not always be the case. Although it is conceivable that the Chinese educational system will be able to produce enlightened, intellectually capable leadership, it remains an open question as to whether the leaders will be able to speak to the concerns of a mass audience that is not nearly so privileged or well educated. Issues of autonomy and equity may have intrinsic significance to our understanding of Chinese education, but there are other important themes in this volume as well. One of those themes concerns the relationship between modernization and institution building. The chapters by Robinson and Epstein, for example, argue that *minban*, reformatory and special education schools, operate with weak organizational arrangements which limit their institutional effectiveness. Their authority is derived ideologically, from their symbolic mission of offering disadvantaged students the promise of social and economic inclusivity, even when that promise is grossly unrealistic. As Jean Robinson notes with particular reference to *minban* schools, their presence rationalizes the existence of continued educational disparity in the name of diversity even after their original goal of offering opportunities for community participation and empowerment has been completely abandoned.

Certainly modernization efforts are impeded when institution building is weak. But what makes for a strong or weak institution? In the Chinese case, one is forced to examine the extent to which existing institutions are addressing or failing to address the diverse educational needs of a large population. In many instances, rhetoric exceeds performance. This can be explained to a certain degree, by a continued reliance upon authoritarian structures popularized in the 1950s. But issues of institutional conservatism as opposed to innovation and renewal are open ones.

Corinna-Barbara Francis' chapter, for example, documents the similarities between student political organizations at Beijing University in 1986 and their formal counterparts in the State and in the Communist Party, concluding that their inherent authoritarian nature has placed severe limits upon student understanding of and commitment to democratic process and procedure. Stanley Rosen and to some extent, Ruth Hayhoe argue, on the other hand, that it was the very failure of traditional political arrangements in the aftermath of the student demonstrations of 1986-87 which led to a genuine, grass-roots call for democratic reform in 1989.

An examination of the prospects for institutional innovation and renewal in other areas leads to the exploration of the relationship between education and the market, another important theme in this volume. Has the creation of a freer market encouraged institutional creativity within educational sectors? For John Hawkins and Bruce Koppel, the response is one of qualified optimism with respect to the special economic zone case of Shenzhen. Yet as has been noted in this introduction and will be reiterated throughout this volume, China's rural responsibility system has had some harsh negative effects upon rural education. In addition, an excessive preoccupation with profit has raised serious concerns with regard to the compromise of fundamental educational aims. Heidi Ross's chapter aptly documents the dual edged results market forces have inflicted upon secondary education, while Mary Ann Burris observes similarly ambiguous outcomes in medical teaching and practice. In various degrees, at both the secondary and higher education levels, the search for short-term financial profit, made necessary by limited funding from government authorities but also encouraged by the ethic of commodity socialism, has both liberated and severely harmed educational policy and practice. The inevitable conclusion -- that weak institutions are susceptible to pressures of external economic demand -- is not surprising.

Another important theme in this volume, though, is that such susceptibility is equally important when one analyzes institutional responses to social and cultural forces such as those which define and perpetuate gender inequality within the society. In the chapters by Beverley Hooper and Heidi Ross, it is clear that traditional social prejudices, reinforced through discriminatory employment policies, are given further legitimacy through upper secondary and higher education admissions practices and the channelling of females into less prestigious curricular disciplines. Prevailing attitudes which evoke gender bias are not only unofficially sanctioned within school walls but are mediated and reproduced in distinct curricular and pedagogical forms through the perpetuation of differential perceptions of academic achievement and ability based upon assumed biological difference and codified in sex education materials.

Issues of gender and education implicitly raise even larger questions concerning the efficacy of all socialization patterns within schools. How effective are Chinese schools, as secondary socialization agents, in their efforts to not merely reflect external social trends but to create distinct patterns of student behavior which conform to specific normative value claims? The chapters by Delia Davin, Heidi Ross, and Richard Latham speak directly to socialization issues, and all three authors voice some skepticism concerning the effectiveness of school socialization efforts. For Delia Davin and Heidi Ross, Chinese teachers themselves express uncertainty over their own ability to positively shape their students' behavior. Davin argues that pre-primary and primary-level instructors are asked to offer instruction to children from single-child families, whom they perceive as being overindulged yet severely pressured by their parents to exhibit successful academic achievement. Their criticism of the one-child family policy is based upon the teachers' own moral panic, as a result of their uncertainty about their ability to influence student behavior in an age where moral certainty can no longer be clearly expressed or guaranteed. In Heidi Ross's interviews with secondary teachers, similar discomfort is expressed as teachers feel conflicted in the contradictory demands placed upon them to create an educational experience, relevant to the pressures of the market and the open door yet respectful of moral as well as critical thinking imperatives.

For Richard Latham, the use of military education in schools as an effective socialization mechanism for the purpose of instilling a sense of patriotism is extremely questionable, particularly after the Tiananmen Massacre. Latham notes though, that doubt as to the efficacy of military education for socialization purposes has been voiced in larger comparative contexts outside of China too.

A final theme concerns the growth of professionalism and its contribution to modernization imperatives. Chapters by Lynn Paine, Mary Ann Burris, Sharon Hom, and Richard Latham, in particular, emphasize the fact that contemporary Chinese definitions of professionalism exclude the degree of independence with which we have typically associated western professions and professional disciplines. The influence of the open door upon medical and legal education as well as teacher training is quite visible. And, for all of these sectors, discussion continues concerning the optimum mix of technical as opposed to general education to be offered within the professional disciplines. As one might expect, China's emerging professions are marked by their lack of gender neutrality, a characteristic common to the western professional disciplines as well.

I believe that one of the strengths of this volume is its diversity of perspective. Many of the authors represented in these pages rely upon the traditional social sciences for their analytical tools. One notes a consistent appreciation for historical context and the perceived continuities and discontinuities of the current Chinese educational system. But the tools of the political scientist are also used to analyze survey data and Chinese public opinion or view the operational dynamics of organizational structures within student political associations. Sociological perspectives place existing educational practice within the broader social context of predominant modernization imperatives. The work is additionally strengthened by chapters which chronicle valuable personal experience through author participation in a literacy campaign, work within the State Education Commission, and the teaching of law in China as a Fulbright scholar. It is a hope and expectation that together, the chapters will shed some light upon a variety of issues which will continue to characterize the world's largest educational system for the foreseeable future.

Notes

1. See, for example, Stewart Fraser, *Chinese Communist Education: Records of the First Decade* (Nashville, Tennessee: Vanderbilt University, 1965); Leo Orleans, *Professional Manpower and Education in Communist China* (Washington, D.C.: U.S. Government Printing Office, 1961).

2. See William Kessen, editor, *Childhood in China* (New Haven: Yale University, 1975).

3. See R.F. Price, *Education in Modern China* (London and Boston: Routledge and Kegan Paul, 1979).

4. See Susan L. Shirk, *Competitive Comrades* (Berkeley: University of California, 1982); Jonathan Unger, *Education Under Mao* (New York: Columbia University, 1982).

5. Stanley Rosen, *Red Guard Factionalism and the Cultural Revolution in Guangzhou* (Boulder: Westview, 1982).

6. In Professor Rosen's work, for example, over a hundred different interviews were conducted with informants.

7. Thomas P. Bernstein, *Up to the Mountains and Down to the Villages: the Transfer of Youth from Urban to Rural China* (New Haven: Yale University, 1977).

8. See Suzanne Pepper, "Education and Revolution: The 'China Model Revisited'," *Asian Survey* 18, no.9 (1978):847-890; Suzanne Pepper, "Chinese Education After Mao: Two Steps Forward, Two Steps Backward and Begin Again?," *China Quarterly* 81 (1980):1-65; Suzanne Pepper, "China's Universities: New Experiments in Socialist Democracy and Administrative Reform," *Modern China* 8, no.2 (1982):147-204; Suzanne Pepper, *China's Universities: Post-Mao Enrollment Policies and Their Impact on the Structure of Secondary Education* (Ann Arbor: University of Michigan Center for Chinese Studies, 1984).

9. *Ibid.*

10. Stanley Rosen, "Obstacles to Educational Reform in China," *Modern*

China 8, no.1 (1982):3-40; Rosen, "Recentralization, Decentralization and Rationalization: Deng Xiaoping's Bifurcated Educational Policy," *Modern China* 11, no.3 (1985):301-346.

11. Stanley Rosen, "Prosperity, Privatization and China's Youth," *Problems of Communism* (March 1985):1-28.

12. See Ruth Hayhoe, "A Comparative Analysis of the Cultural Dynamics of Sino-Western Educational Cooperation," *China Quarterly* no. 102 (December 1985); Ruth Hayhoe, "Shanghai as a Mediator of the Educational Open Door," *Pacific Affairs* 61, no.2 (1988): 253-284; Ruth Hayhoe and Marianne Bastid, editors, *China's Education and the Industrialized World: Studies in Cultural Transfer* (Armonk, N.Y.: M.E. Sharpe, 1987); Ruth Hayhoe, *China's Universities and the Open Door* (Armonk, N.Y.: M.E. Sharpe, 1989).

13. Stanley Rosen and David S.K. Chu, *Survey Research in the People's Republic of China* (Washington, D.C.: United States Information Agency, 1987).

14. Julia Kwong, *Chinese Education in Transition: Prelude to the Cultural Revolution* (Montreal: McGill-Queens University, 1979).

15. Julia Kwong, "In Pursuit of Efficiency: Scientific Management in Chinese Higher Education," *Modern China* 13, no.2 (April 1987):226-256.

16. Richard Kurt Kraus, *Class Conflict in Chinese Socialism* (New York: Columbia University, 1981).

17. See Richard Kurt Kraus, *Pianos and Politics in China* (New York: Oxford University, 1989); Richard Kurt Kraus, " China's Cultural 'Liberalization' and Conflict Over the Social Organization of the Arts," *Modern China* 9 no.2 (April 1983):212-227.

18. Jerome Grieder, *Intellectuals and the State in Modern China* (New York, Free Press, 1981).

19. Merle Goldman and Timothy Cheek, "Introduction: Uncertain Change," in Merle Goldman, with Timothy Cheek and Carol Lee Hamrin, editors, *China's Intellectuals and the State: In Search of a New Relationship* (Cambridge: Harvard University Contemporary China Series, 1987):2-20.

20. Benjamin Elman, *From Philosophy to Philology: Intellectual and Social Aspects of Change in Late Imperial China* (Cambridge: Harvard University, 1984); R. Kent Guy, *The Emperor's Four Treasuries: Scholars and the State in the Late Chien-lung Era* (Cambridge: Harvard University, 1987).

21. Barry Keenan, *The Dewey Experiment in China: Educational Reform and Political Power in the Early Republic* (Cambridge: Harvard University, 1977).

22. Erik Olin Wright, *Classes* (New York: Schocken, 1985):19-104; Erik Olin Wright, *Class, Crisis and the State* (London: Verso, 1979):61-96.

23. Michael Polyani, "The Republic of Science: Its Political and Economic Theory," in Edward Shils, editor. *Criteria for Scientific Development: Public Policy and National Goals* (Cambridge: Massachusetts Institute of Technology, 1968):1-20, particularly p.18.

24. Andrew Walder, *Communist Neo-traditionalism: Work and Authority in Chinese Society* (Berkeley: University of California, 1986).

25. Pierre Bourdieu, *Reproduction in Education* (Beverly Hills: Sage, 1977).

26. Ivan Szelenyi, "The Intelligentsia in the Class Structure of State-Socialist Societies" in Michael Burawoy and Theda Skocpol, editors, *Marxist Inquiries: Studies of Labor, Class and States* (Chicago: University of Chicago, 1982):287-326.

27. See Stanley Rosen, "Guangzhou's Democracy Movement in Cultural Revolution Perspective," *China Quarterly* no.101 (March 1985):1-31.

Chinese Education

CHAPTER ONE

POST-MAO REFORMS IN CHINESE EDUCATION:

CAN THE GHOSTS OF THE PAST BE LAID TO REST?[*]

by Suzanne Pepper

Western students of China usually are of two kinds: they concentrate either on the pre-1949 past or on the post-1949 present. The former are mostly historians; the latter become social scientists; rarely do the two interact after the first year of graduate school. These kinds of distinctions may make sense academically and professionally where the modern disciplinary approach necessitates such a division of labor, but they can also create major obstacles to understanding present-day China.

This is because 1949 is a political date, the year the Chinese Communist Party (CCP) finally won national power and declared the inauguration of the People's Republic. Thus, some important political implications are built into the seemingly apolitical academic division. For example, the tendency of those who study only the post-1949 period to treat everything that happened before as pre-history, and the year 1949 as the beginning of Chinese time, was reinforced by the new Communist regime intent on convincing everyone that it was creating

---

[*] This chapter is a revised version of a Universities Field Staff International Report (no.10 Asia, 1986) [SP-1-'86]. An expanded and updated version of the chapter will be appearing under the title, *China's Education Reform in the 1980s: Policies, Issues and Historical Perspectives*, China Research Monograph no. 36, University of California, Berkeley (forthcoming).

1

a totally "new China." The near-impossibility of gaining access to the country, except through official publications, also made it difficult to prove or disprove the claims. For all of these reasons, then, the pre-1949, pre-Communist past seemed increasingly irrelevant for an understanding of the present and was left primarily in the historians' domain.

More recently, however, the year 1976 has become almost as significant as 1949. This is because the most powerful of Communist China's leaders, Mao Zedong, died in 1976. Since then, a great deal of what he and the Communist Party tried to do to change China after 1949 has been turned on its head. In many policy areas, moreover, post-1949 developments have been overturned to reveal remnants of the pre-1949 past still surviving beneath the surface, at the same time that our improved access makes it easier to observe and verify them. This has sent many social scientists back to their history books, and there we have found some fascinating precedents and parallels. It is tempting, if somewhat presumptuous, to try to use these now to predict the future. More pertinent, perhaps, given the sweeping patterns of change they seem to clarify, is the explanatory background such patterns provide for both the Maoist innovations and the post-Mao reforms that have reversed them.

One important issue area where these historical roots can be traced to provide many such insights is education. In few sectors did the Maoist innovations receive wider publicity; and in few sectors have they been as totally overthrown by the successor administration under the leadership of China's current most powerful leader, Deng Xiaoping. The developments in Chinese education are thus relatively well-known. They are also decidedly antagonistic. We hear nothing good about the Maoist "line" from its opponents who are the advocates of present policies, whereas the greatest detractors of the present "line" were those of the Maoist persuasion. Each side has concentrated on promoting its own strong points and maligning its opposition. It has therefore only been with the passage of time and change of Chinese administrations that we have been able to piece this story together while trying to corroborate the claims and counter-claims. It turns out, for example, that in the post-1949 era this direct competition between the logic and aims of the two lines over education, and in other sectors as well, has been developing since the early 1960s.

In broad outline, the education controversy might be portrayed as follows:

The Maoist educational innovations aimed at quantity over quality as conventionally defined. They aimed to expand the base of the educational pyramid with mass education at the expense of the elite and tertiary-levels. They were concerned also with equalizing the content and quality of education available to everyone. This is another way of saying that they tried to reduce the social inequalities that education helps to reproduce. And they aimed to break the power of Chinese "intellectuals" or the educational professionals over education.

One of the reasons for this effort was the "bourgeois" or non-proletarian background of China's educated minority in a society ruled by a newly-victorious Communist Party which still took seriously its proletarian objectives. Another reason for wanting to break the continuing influence of the educated elite was to remove the obstacles they were creating--indeed had always created --to radical innovations in education. These latter developed off and on over a period roughly from 1958 until Mao's death in 1976.

Meanwhile, the Maoists were contending with opposition on almost every point. That opposition has been in the ascendancy since 1976, however, reversing all the Maoist priorities as its strength has grown. Hence, power has been restored to professional educators, and elite education has become the overriding focus of attention. This is done in the interest of economic development while social inequalities are now allowed to develop unobstructed as an inevitable cost of the overriding aim.

The contention between these two sets of educational priorities in China, however, is not a contemporary phenomenon. Indeed, this particular competition has been developing in one form or another since the early decades of the present century. This report, therefore, looks backward in time to try to pick up the strains of the relevant controversies. Limitations of space mean that those strains will have to be painted with fairly broad brush strokes, but in some ways, this particular subject may benefit from the "sweeping themes of history" approach, since it helps to highlight trends that might otherwise be obscured by the multitude of events and interests surrounding them.

The Pre-1949 Past

The crucial years of the pre-1949 period are the 1920s. A number of key critical themes emerged during that decade around the basic issue of educational development. One reason these themes can be traced down to the present day is that no satisfactory solutions have yet been devised for many of the underlying problems that inspired them in the first place.

The dilemmas and disruptive consequences of trying to establish a formal educational system where one has not previously existed are certainly not unique to China. For a number of reasons, however, they have been more intense and long-lasting there than in many other countries. Yet the nature of the challenge has been essentially the same for all, namely, to devise forms of education that are (1) acceptable to the society and its leaders, (2) economically feasible, (3) appropriate to the existing level of technology, (4) yet also capable, when the target area is a predominantly rural non-Western society, of introducing the advanced knowledge and international standards now associated with the urbanized industrialized West including both its communist and capitalist variants.

In China, the themes that emerged in the 1920s were part of the critical questioning that followed the first enthusiastic embrace of Western learning after 1905. It is not yet clear why these particular themes developed as they did in the 1920s. Earlier resistance to Western learning had been part of the more general and continuing opposition to the military-political intrusion of the West, and educated Chinese remained sensitive to the dislocations which accompanied the fairly rapid growth of Western-style schooling during the first two decades of the century.

THE "TRADITIONAL" PAST[1]

Acceptance of modern, which initially meant Western learning, did not come easily to nineteenth-century China. Actually, it was not accepted at all until a succession of humiliating military defeats and encroachment by the Western powers forced change upon the self-confident Chinese empire. But change, when it finally came, was massive in scope. It reflected the close relationship between traditional Confucian learning and the imperial bureaucratic state. The two collapsed almost simultaneously, suggesting that neither could have long survived the demise of the other.

The state's direct involvement with education was confined essentially to administering the civil service examinations. These were used for selecting officials to staff the imperial bureaucracy from the county (*xian*) level upward. The content of these examinations was fixed and limited by tradition to the Confucian canon. This ensured the perpetuation of the latter not only as a source of traditional learning and values, but more immediately as the only course of study leading to the most prestigious occupation in the land. Study for these examinations was, then, a sort of integrated, academic-vocational training course, prerequisite for acquiring at a minimum the status of scholar-gentry. This status was achieved by all who passed the basic level prefectural (comprising several counties) examinations. Passing the provincial examinations was the next step and the minimum requirement for actually holding bureaucratic office. At the highest level were the metropolitan examinations held in the imperial capital, with the emperor himself presiding over the final round. The civil service examinations thus played an immensely important role in maintaining the political and intellectual continuity of the imperial system as a whole.

There were, of course, many privileges that set this class apart from everyone else. The boundary between gentry and commoner was clearly drawn once a man had passed the first of the three examination levels. Women were not permitted to compete. Successful examination candidates at the prefectural level thereafter were not to engage in degrading occupations, which included manual labor. Traditionally, a stigma had also been attached to commerce, but that was breaking down by the nineteenth century. Among the other material, legal, and symbolic privileges which set these lucky few apart was their exemption from the corvee, or labor service, and its tax equivalent. The gentry also were exempt from the corporal punishments administered for lesser offenses and were treated differently from commoners for major ones. They were entitled to wear special clothing and certain other luxury items forbidden to others. In terms of the local power structure, those who had passed the basic level examinations enjoyed a status comparable to that of government officials, while the commoners were subordinate and inferior. In addition to these formal privileges, the gentry were able to exploit their status to a variety of economic advantages in their local communities.

This was basically an open system and in one sense was becoming more so over the centuries. For example, the sons of people in demeaning occupations, such as prostitutes and entertainers, could not compete in the examinations. But the number of such occupations was declining. Originally, the bans had included even the sons of merchants and artisans, but these had been removed early in the seventeenth century. Thus, upward mobility was possible. Newcomers could move up the ranks of the elite either by passing the examinations or, increasingly in the troubled nineteenth century, by buying their results. In practice, of course, the long series of examinations imposed upon those who sought to achieve and retain scholar status ensured that only families with a certain amount of surplus wealth could support such a pursuit by one or more of its male members. Literary achievement and official appointment were clearly dependent upon and facilitated by wealth.

The evidence indicated, moreover that the sons of higher-level officials tended to achieve better results on the examinations and in the subsequent competition for actual appointment. Appointments were said to depend on literary achievement and having the right "connections." A study of 915 higher degree holders spanning the entire 350 years of the last Qing Dynasty, and going back five generations in each case, showed that only 13 per cent were from "newcomer" families whose ancestors had never managed to qualify for gentry status by passing the prefectural examination.[2] To summarize: because of the dominant role played by office-holding and the examinations in defining elite status, China's traditional ruling class was not, strictly speaking, hereditary; nor was its structure rigidly stratified, despite the clear tendency for officials' sons to follow in the footsteps of their fathers.

The numbers of people involved were significant. In the latter half of the nineteenth century, there were some 900,000 "regular" gentry members, or those who had advanced at least through the prefectural examinations. The number of purchased "degrees" at that same level had risen, bringing the total figure of "gentry" to about 1.4 million. Of this total, approximately 200,000 had risen above that level to qualify for bureaucratic appointments. Since only the immediate families--children, wives, and concubines--enjoyed the privileges and protection of gentry status, this class has been estimated at 7.2 million, or about 2 per cent of the total population of 377.5 million, in the late 1800s.[3]

Education in traditional China, as might be expected under the circumstances, was dominated by the civil service examinations. The only formal schools above the elementary level were the academies or *shuyuan*, and these were oriented almost exclusively toward the content and schedules of the exams. Academies became famous in direct relation to their students' skills at writing mock examination essays and to the success they ultimately achieved on the actual examinations.

Elementary education was almost entirely an informal and local affair. Children of the more affluent were usually taught at home by a family member or tutor. This was also virtually the only way that young girls might receive instruction. Another alternative was for extended families or groups of villagers to hire a teacher jointly. Expenses were not great, confined essentially to the teacher's salary. Supplies and furnishings were provided by the parents, and classes were held in a temple or spare room. Occasionally, a teacher might set up a tuition-paying school in his own home.

Teachers were drawn from the relatively large pool of advanced students and gentry--probably about three million--that existed as an important cultural by-product of the examination system in both urban and rural areas. Only a small percentage of the county-level candidates actually achieved gentry status by passing the prefectural exams, and only a small proportion of these ever qualified for public office. That left, in the late nineteenth century, approximately one million "unemployed" gentry among the successful prefectual scholars. The pool of candidates who passed the preliminaries at the county level, but failed to attain formal gentry status, has been estimated at about two million. For these men, particularly those of modest means, teaching was one of the few "honorable" ways to earn a living.[4]

The result of all this activity, however, was a bureaucratic elite highly educated in the Confucian classical tradition, superimposed upon a base of mass illiteracy. Relatively few of the estimated 40 million boys in the age group seven to fourteen years could aspire to the "higher" learning that would have allowed them to compete in the examinations. The conventional estimate is a 20 per cent literacy rate for the population as a whole. One scholar has concluded that no more than 10 per cent of all women were literate, with the figure reaching 30-45 per cent for men. Her estimates, however, are based upon a definition of literacy which included knowledge of only a few hundred Chinese characters. Such people today, when the standard is 1,500 characters, would be classed as semi-literate at best.[5]

THE COLLAPSE OF THE IMPERIAL SYSTEM

As noted, the changes that brought about the collapse of this structure--of traditional learning, the examination system, and the imperial bureaucratic state--were forced upon China by the West's intrusion into Chinese territory. And even as they were forced to yield space to the unwelcome foreigners, the Chinese refused to concede anything else. They had for millennia regarded themselves as the social and intellectual superiors of their neighbors. Hence, China's self-confidence took more than half a century of direct confrontation with the West to break.

The memory of the ensuing national humiliation is still very much alive today. At one point during the tense 1982-84 negotiations with the British for the return of Hong Kong, Deng Xiaoping declared that the Chinese had to take back the colony in 1997 because he had no intention of emulating his predecessors, the imperial officials of a hundred years ago who had lost Hong Kong to the encroaching foreigners in the first place.

As it happened, Western learning was introduced to China in schools founded by Christian missionaries. They were not able to embark seriously upon the task of establishing modern schools until after 1842, the year Britain defeated China in the "First Opium War," which resulted in the first of what the Chinese still refer to as the "unequal treaties" imposed upon them by foreign powers. The 1842 treaty forced China not only to cede the island of Hong Kong, but to open up five "treaty ports" to foreign trade and residence. Yet it would not really have mattered how they came; educated Chinese would still have dismissed the Christian schools for what they were: instruments for promoting the Christian faith. It was said at the time, and later, that the mission schools couldn't develop "because Chinese looked down on the missionaries as barbarians!"[6]

Even when they were not offered by the missionaries, the schools and the education that developed in the treaty port cities were held suspect. Such schooling was broadly viewed as tainted by the base motives of collaborators willing to make their lives among the foreigners. Chinese officialdom and the scholar class in general remained as antagonistic to the intellectual intrusion as to the military and political interventions that were making it possible. Under these circumstances, the influence of Western learning remained peripheral to the traditional education system until the end of the nineteenth century.

During those decades, official educational reforms followed a limited course. They were promoted not by the imperial government but by a few "progressive" officials. These found themselves in an uncertain position, balancing precariously between the prevailing antagonism and their own perceptions of China's changing needs. The popular view of China's needs, however, was expressed almost exclusively in terms of military and diplomatic defense against the foreigners. Several quotations that emerged from this period, roughly 1860 to 1895, are still used today whenever the occasion seems appropriate. One example is the quote from a modernizing official in the 1860s: "What we have to learn from the barbarians is only the one thing, solid ships and effective guns."[7] Later, in the 1890s, the famous motto was "Chinese learning for the essence: Western learning for use." This summed up the "self-strengthening" efforts to preserve China's traditional culture while trying to modernize its technology only.[8]

Motivation for change, then, was clear: the Western barbarians were able to force themselves on China because they were rich and powerful. Their superiority, manifested in weapons of war, was due to their more advanced technical learning. Given this reasoning, it followed that successive military defeats should inspire even more insistent demands for educational change, which is essentially what happened. It was not until the war with Japan in 1895, however, that the wall of hostility and indifference was finally breached on a significant scale. China's defeat, not by Western power, but by one of its "inferior" Asian neighbors, was widely interpreted as a failure of its self-strengthening efforts, which were initiated in the 1860s at roughly the same time as a similar movement began in Japan. This final humiliation seemed to ignite a sudden craze for Western learning. The Emperor himself was said to be studying Western science. Even old Confucian scholars enrolled in the "despised" missionary schools.

Well-known events then followed in rapid succession. The imperial court-sponsored reforms of 1898, anticipating, among other things, radical changes in education, were aborted by the Empress Dowager leading to a conservative reaction. Its force culminated in the anti-foreign Boxer Rebellion of 1900, leaving many of the new modern schools in north China destroyed in its wake. The rebellion then provoked another humiliating round of foreign retaliation. Thereafter, the die was finally cast.

Between 1901 and 1905, the court issued a series of education reform decrees. The old academies that had supported the civil service examinations were to be reorganized. Upon their foundations was to be built a modern school system with primary, secondary, and college levels patterned on Western models. The Japanese school system was the primary reference point, since it had already created what seemed to be a successful adaptation of those models for a non-Western society. The examinations, still the route to public office, were increasingly criticized as an obstacle to the development of the new schools, diverting attention and patronage from them. The examinations were therefore abolished in 1905, marking the end of an institution that had survived for a thousand years. Their demise preceded by only six years that of the Qing Dynasty and indeed of the imperial system itself. Both were overthrown by the Revolution of 1911, and a republican form of government was established in its wake.

So complete was the collapse of the old system that the efforts of the "self-strengtheners" to preserve the "essence" of Chinese tradition soon became a target of derision for the new Chinese intellectuals. These emerged within only a few years time as the "modern" twentieth century re-incarnation of the old Confucian scholar-gentry. It was an ironic, almost unnatural end for what had been so unyielding and glorious a tradition. Everything was abandoned in the full-scale shift to Western models--everything, that is, except some Confucian assumptions about a number of things including the role of education as a prerequisite for the acquisition of personal as well as public wealth, prestige, and power.

THE RUSH TO MODERNIZE

In the meantime, Japan had also defeated a Western nation, Russia, in the War of 1905. The Chinese now could not be deflected from their conclusion that Japan owed its growing strength to Western learning. This, as well as the abolition of the imperial examinations that same year, led to an exodus of Chinese students to Japan. The numbers increased from 2,400 in early 1905 to 15,000 by the end of 1906.[9]

It was this sudden change, after 1895 but especially after 1900, that shocked veteran "China-watchers" of that time out of their long-standing pessimism. The Western press began giving China rave reviews. A society that had been "dead and stagnant," they reported, was now "alive and in motion." At long last, China seemed ready to join the rest of the modern world. Historian Mary Wright, in her account of that period, has cited a number of such press accounts. Her essay has been re-read many times since 1976 to discover the parallels between China's sudden opening to the West today and its antecedent at the turn of the century.[10]

It seemed to China-watchers, then, that a series of massive hurdles had finally been overcome by Chinese officialdom and the educated class as a whole:

(1) the memory of centuries of unchallenged supremacy in East Asia;

(2) a self-conscious conviction that Chinese civilization, with its Confucian tradition, was not just more powerful, but intellectually and morally superior to all others;

(3) resentment over the political and military violations of Chinese territory which had served as the vehicle for introducing Western learning;

(4) the practical threat to the positions, prestige, and power of China's ruling class that Western learning represented.

In another parallel with the 1980s, people at the turn of the century had begun to speculate as to why Japan and China had responded so differently to the Western intrusion, which occurred about the same time in both countries. A major hypothesis in those days was that the fault lay at least in part with the Chinese intellectual-ruling class. Its interests were so integral to the imperial bureaucratic system, and so strong was its commitment to Confucian learning as the source of power within that system, that many decades of dithering and military defeat were necessary before that ruling class could bring itself to accept the fundamental changes required.

In their enthusiasm over the reality of change in China after 1900, however, foreign observers failed to gauge its depth. The old assumptions about Chinese superiority and the mid-nineteenth century preoccupations with ships and guns were indeed evolving into their more modern, twentieth century equivalents of nationalism, cultural pride, and economic development. But underlying this evolution there remained much of the old logic. For example, still clearly identifiable was the mid-nineteenth century assumption, now transformed almost into an article of faith, that Western learning could make China rich and powerful like the West. China's traditional learning was responsible for China's backward state; Western learning would somehow set things right.

In summary, then, the key educational components with which China entered the twentieth century were, first, a base of mass illiteracy tempered with a tradition of informal schooling which reached, in a limited way, a considerable minority of the male population both urban and rural. Secondly, there was superimposed upon the mass base a highly educated intellectual-bureaucratic ruling class, suddenly robbed of its birthrights. Finally, having been deprived in this manner, the ruling class ultimately did a swift about-face, at least superficially. It embraced Western learning as a panacea for China's ills. From that time to the present day, it has remained a commonplace within Chinese intellectual and ruling circles (although the argument has taken different forms over the years) that the science and technology of the West are the keys to national wealth and power.

During the first three decades of this century, thousands of Chinese went overseas to study: to Japan, the United States, and Europe. When they returned home, they moved rapidly into positions of leadership and began to build carbon-copy images of the educational systems they had seen in other countries. Yet their basic uncertainty about how to proceed was clearly evident as they went about this task. Western learning may have become the accepted formula, but it came in many different varieties; there were many choices to be made; and no one seemed to know for certain how to make it produce the quick results desired. Hence, China's education system went through a continuous series of reforms and readjustments between the turn of the century and the early 1930s.

China's first modern school system, formally promulgated by imperial decree in 1903, was modeled on that of the Japanese. After the Qing Dynasty was overthrown in 1911, the new Republic decreed a new education system more in tune with world trends. This was in deference to the progressive ideas being promoted by graduates returning from Western countries. By the early 1920s, the influence of students returning from the U.S. was at its height. Most prominent for a time were those trained at Columbia University's Teachers College. They brought John Dewey and others to China on well-publicized lecture tours, and their influence predominated when the national education system was again reorganized in 1922. Later, around 1927, there was a brief flirtation with a French model, followed by more revisions under the new Nationalist Government in the late 1920s and early 1930s, to cite only the high points.

THE BACKLASH

Between 1915 and 1920, however, a critical reaction began to set in against this frenetic search for the right Western formula. As noted, what inspired this reaction is not entirely clear, but it had to do with a growing awareness that the creators of China's modern eduction system seemed more sensitive to changing fashions abroad than to the realities of life at home. Much has been written about this period; here it is necessary only to reiterate the following.

The critical reassessment did not emerge suddenly full-blown in the 1920s. It appeared to derive from several sources, including the undercurrents of conservative dissent and modern liberal criticism which co-existed with the dominant enthusiasm for the new learning from its inception. The events of the years 1915-1920, known as the May Fourth Period, intensified existing intellectual concerns and introduced new political conflicts in a society as yet un-reconstructed after the collapse of the old order. Thus, the national political scene and hopes for democratic representative government devolved into the militarism of the warlord era, while the new receptivity to intellectual challenge culminated in the "new culture" movement. Inspired by the ideas Chinese students were bringing back with them from abroad, the intellectual content of the movement was sweeping in scope. For a time it went far beyond science, technology and education. It included philosophy, political thought, literature, and a skeptical attitude toward all traditional Chinese ideas, customs, and institutions.

Not surprisingly, such intellectual and cultural activism could not long remain isolated from politics. For one thing, the Russian revolution inspired a new interest: the economic and political alternatives suggested by Marxism. Then, at the end of World War I, the Western democracies sanctioned the transfer to Japan of Germany's interests in the northern Chinese province of Shandong. This appeared to legitimate Japan's aggressive intentions in China, apparent since at least the 1895 war, and the entire "unequal treaty" system that no Chinese, whether modern or traditional, was able to accept. The old grievances against foreign encroachment on Chinese soil were reborn, now in more potent form as the new nationalism of the May Fourth era. The student protest on May 4, 1919, over the Shandong question thereafter gave its name to this period of Chinese intellectual and political re-awakening. In fact, the events of 1919 marked the culmination of the movement committed to the creation of a totally new culture. During the years that followed, its adherents split as only Chinese intellectuals can; new political commitments grew; and the Communist Party was born.[11]

In this climate began a critical reappraisal of the recent devotion to all things foreign, inspired now by the growing currents of post-World War I disillusionment, nationalism, and anti-imperialism. The new skepticism which followed hard upon the heels of the new culture--as a backlash against it--reinforced the ongoing arguments of conservatives and spread doubts widely among the pro-West modernists. Everyone, or almost everyone, set out upon the task of reappraisal. Students returning home with their privileged status and new foreign learning became objects of satire.[12] One of the returned students from Columbia University Teachers College expressed the new mood. In trying to explain why educators had grown much more critical in recent years, he said that at first they had "sacrificed everything old for the new"... then they had come to realize that "the old is not necessarily bad and the new is not necessarily good."[13]

By the 1920s, the reappraisal had already acquired the more radical contours it would retain, in one form or another, for at least the next fifty years. Despite the widely differing political inclinations of its contributors, the critique of Western-style learning had revolved around a common denominator of key concerns:

(1) The creation by the new schools and by education abroad of an urban-oriented elite divorced by its learning and life-style from the rest of Chinese society.

(2) The uncritical acceptance by those new intellectuals of the Western educational models to which they were indebted for their learning and status.

(3) The formalistic as well as elitist nature of those models when transplanted into the alien Chinese environment.

(4) The need to devise appropriate forms and find the necessary sources of teachers and money to promote mass education, especially in the countryside where the vast majority of China's people lived.

These concerns remained unchanged and unresolved until the Japanese invasion in the late 1930s turned war into the more immediate priority. Such issues were then essentially put on hold until 1949, since Japan's defeat was followed immediately by the civil war between the Communists and the Nationalist Government.

Some elaboration upon these concerns may help to explain their significance. The first point to make is that by the early 1920s they were already in the air and people of all political inclinations were beginning to think of ways to combat the perceived problems. The idea that the elitism of the intellectuals was an inheritance from the recent Confucian past ran through most of the proposals. Hence, most of them contained specific provisions that intellectuals must engage in manual labor. This was to break the legacy as symbolized in the old exemption of the scholar-gentry from corvee labor service. Probably the first major product to incorporate the novel idea that mental and manual labor should not be separated was the work-study program for sending

Chinese students to France during World War I. It began in 1915, to coordinate with the war effort. Among its advocates was European-educated Cai Yuanpei, the first Minister of Education under the Republic and later head of Beijing University.

There was also the Hunan Self-Study University, set up by the young Mao Zedong and his friends in 1921. Mao was then only a provincial activist and at most a nascent Marxist. His idea was to combine the best traits of modern schools with those of the old academies that had prepared students for the civil service examinations. Mao envisaged his new university to have one feature that both the new and old schools lacked: the element of populism. Other schools, whether traditional or modern, treated learning as a special, privileged commodity and limited access to it. They were also expensive, so poor people could not attend. This, Mao observed, created the absurd division between the intellectual class and the uneducated commoners. His experimental university aimed to eliminate that distinction.[14]

Another developing Marxist, Li Dazhao, had formulated his demands for an "intellectual youth to the countryside" movement in early 1919. The "peasant problem" was also already in the air at that time, but Li was apparently the first to project it into the limelight of national intellectual discourse. Later in the year, he declared that "intellectuals who eat but do not work ought to be eliminated together with the capitalists. The condition of China today is that the cities and the villages have been made into two opposite poles and have almost become two different worlds."[15]

An American-educated liberal, Tao Xingzhi, returned to China to become head of the pro-American Chinese National Association for the Advancement of Education. He wrote that his own personal "moment of awakening" came in 1923, and he "rushed back to the way of the common people." After that, he devoted himself increasingly to mass education and non-formal schooling. Literacy training, especially peasant literacy, became Tao's primary preoccupation.

Another major effort inspired by similar ideals was that of James Yen, the Yale-educated YMCA worker who pioneered mass education for illiterates among the Chinese laborers in France during World War I. Back in China after the war, Yen began his famous rural reconstruction project at Ding county in northern Hebei province.[16]

Balancing off the leftists and pro-American liberals was cultural conservative Liang Shuming. By the early 1920s, he too was exploring the causes of China's apparent demoralization. He concluded that it was due to Western influence. Previous reform efforts had been led by intellectuals in imitation of the West, primarily as a means to match its wealth and power. They had failed in that objective, Liang argued, and had destroyed China's culture in the process. Wealth and education had gravitated toward the cities, while the countryside was ignored. He especially blamed the new Western-style education system which was "educating people for another society" but was inadequate to meet China's own needs. Liang's most famous attempt to put his ideas into practice was a rural reconstruction project centered in Zouping county, Shandong province, between 1931-37.[17]

By the late 1930s, when the Japanese invasion put an end to everyone's experiments, the Nationalist Government, the missionaries, and even the Rockefeller Foundation had all jumped on the rural reconstruction bandwagon. Education was always a major part of their projects. The Rockefeller Foundation's response was especially interesting. In deference to the widespread demands in China for nationalistic forms of education with practical application, the Foundation re-directed its funding in the mid-1930s away from missionary schools and education abroad. The reports accompanying these decisions reflected the increasingly critical consensus that had hardened around these issues. The standards of missionary schools were judged mediocre. Equally harsh was the judgement on the Peking Union Medical College, which had received the bulk of Rockefeller investment in China since 1913 (US $33 million of a total of $37 million). Despite the high standards of modern medicine it had introduced into China, a Foundation report concluded, the achievements were not commensurate with the investment. This was because its "stereotyped medical education" was not meeting China's medical and public health needs. The most scathing criticism, however, was reserved for education abroad and the returned students. Degrees from foreign universities, as tickets to academic positions in China, appeared to be the students' dominant ambition. Ability and productivity were secondary concerns.[18]

The verdict of the League of Nations report on Chinese education, compiled in 1931, was identical. The European authors concluded that the mechanical imitation of foreign educational institutions had many adverse consequences. The net result was a disjointed system emphasizing schools of higher standard while mass education was neglected. This was creating an "enormous abyss between the masses of the Chinese people, plunged in illiteracy, and not understanding the needs of their country, and the intelligentsia educated in luxurious schools and indifferent to the wants of the masses.[19]

If the first point to note was that people at all states of the political spectrum were contributing to the critique of the formal education system, then the last point to emphasize is that reforms inspired by the critique never progressed much beyond the pilot project stage. According to historians who have studied these efforts, the immediate cause of failure in each case was usually something dramatically political--if not the intransigence of the government, then ultimately the Japanese invasion. But the historians' typical focus on individual reformers obscures the larger picture, in which blame for the failure of the reform efforts lay not just with politicians and militarists but with the intellectuals themselves. Individual reformers gained recognition *because they were exceptions to the rule*, not representatives of it. Such reformers had to take their experiments outside the established school system because there was no place for them within it.

The "returned students" from the West, with their new learning, emerged even for some of the reform projects themselves as major impediments. Certainly they were not as a whole in the vanguard of reform, at least not the kind anticipated by the growing critical consensus of the 1920s and 1930s. Throughout the period, and especially after the Nationalist Government came to power in 1927, those who had been educated abroad monopolized all of the leading administrative and academic positions, including those in the Ministry of Education, the provincial education bureaus, and in higher education. The most prestigious positions, whether in government administration or in the universities, went to students returning from abroad rather than to graduates of the new Chinese colleges. Upon returning to China, the former congregated near the centers of national power, first in Beijing, before 1927, and then in the Shanghai-Nanjing area after the new Nationalist Government moved the capital south. This explained the disproportionate development of colleges, set up by returned students, in those two urban centers, respectively, before and after 1927.[20] In fact, the education system that proved so impervious to reform was the creation of these Western-trained intellectuals who used the power and prestige of their positions to maintain that system in accordance with their own interests and commitments.

What the critics and reformers were trying to say--indeed, what they did often say directly--was that the same intellectual class was running the new education system as had dominated the traditional one. The new system was, moreover, being run in the same manner and toward the same ends. The initial demands for educational change had come not from an industrializing middle class, but from a few government officials. Their demands were therefore statist; and they sold them to the traditional educated class on that basis. This was the origin of the idea that science and technology had created the power of the West and could do the same for China. The goals were, in other words, Western education for national and personal wealth and power. The new learning had been adapted to play the same function as the old, as qualification for the new equivalent of scholar-official status. Science and technology became slogans, honored in the abstract, but much less in terms of concrete application.

Without actually acknowledging this ancient tradition that was reproducing itself in modern guise, the League of Nations report noted regretfully that "the ambition of most Chinese university students is a career in the public service, central or local, and failing that, a post as a teacher." The report also lamented the related "hypertrophy of legal, political and literary studies" to the neglect of science and technology.[21]

It had obviously been assumed that, just as Confucian learning both epitomized the state and controlled access to the most prestigious occupations, so Western learning would do the same. In reality it did neither, at least not in the manner assumed. But decisions based on these outdated assumptions continued to influence the new education for decades. Its clientele as a whole --including students, parents, and educators--retained the traditional attitudes toward education. The products of the new learning, with their advanced degrees in political science and education, may have been new-style intellectuals in the sense that their Western learning had prepared them for specialized occupations in the modern sector, but they were not wholly modern professionals because their career aspirations remained essentially unchanged from those of their Confucian predecessors.

Critics such as Liang Shuming were undoubtedly correct to deride the Western transplant as being neither Chinese nor Western, while having lost the best of both. Vocational and practical training was so alien to this academic environment that it could not survive even in the American comprehensive-school format which was also tried for a time. The separate vocational school seemed the only solution, but the trend invariably was to upgrade its status by imitating the "regular" academic schools, if only in the pretensions of its graduates. Formal schooling marked the route upward, and everyone had hoped to use it toward that end. A secondary school education thus became the modern equivalent of passing the basic level prefectual examinations under the traditional system. Those who did so moved automatically into the intermediate, expectant status between the commoner and elite, identifying thereafter with the lifestyle of the latter.

Manual labor was beyond the pale; practical and vocational training was treated as an inferior version of "real" education.

A major problem remained: while the inherited assumptions about the function of learning were largely unchanged, a very real change in the political power structure had developed. The unified hierarchy of political power and learning had been broken. A modern education did not guarantee access to government and its bureaucracy. On the contrary, military men had "usurped" political power, to quote a frequent lament of the new intellectuals in the post-imperial China of the warlords.

In that environment, therefore, China's modern intellectuals were being projected into a potentially vulnerable position. Having lost their monopoly over government power, which had assured their status at the top of the traditional social hierarchy, they were nonetheless using the new schools to reproduce old elitist pretensions. Thus, the ground was being laid for the charge that the new educated class was becoming "an unproductive clique enclosed within the narrow bounds of its own interests."[22]

Meanwhile, the critique was building up around the system it had created, based on a growing awareness of the need for forms of education that could more appropriately serve all of Chinese society, both in its contemporary condition and in its future aspirations. Demands arose for an educational system that would be (1) technologically appropriate, yet modern; (2) China centered; (3) non-elitist; and (4) mass based for a largely rural population. The major question in 1949, then, was how the new Communist Government would respond to this challenge it was inheriting from the past.

The 1949-1976 Era

Communist leaders were not only familiar with the old reformers' critique, but had themselves contributed to it, as indicated by Mao Zedong's self-study experiment in 1921. More significant were the Communist Party's education reforms 20 years later, designed for areas of the north China countryside that came under its rule during the war against Japan. These reforms were presented as the result of a disagreement. On one side were said to be those who favored the development of a conventional educational system patterned on foreign models such as existed elsewhere in China. On the other side of the argument were those who advocated more practical forms of schooling adapted to the needs of the largely rural population in the Communist-controlled areas. The latter carried the day, and new education policies announced in the early 1940s indicated that at least some Party leaders were interested in promoting the logic of the old reformers' critique beyond the pilot project stage.[23]

Once the Party moved out of the countryside and won national power, however, it would be more difficult to implement such policies for the society as a whole, even if political leaders still wanted to do so. This was because the experience of all past reform efforts had taught that while political support may have been a necessary condition, it was not sufficient to achieve the reformers' aims. In addition, some way would have to be found to retain the expertise of the educated elite while simultaneously breaking the interests and commitments of this same group of people who had created and maintained the nation's school system - with all its faults - for half a century. And that, of course, is what the Chinese Communist Party (CCP) spent most of the next 30 years trying unsuccessfully to do.

THE 1950s: "LEARNING FROM THE SOVIET UNION"

In the context of the pre-1949 controversy over foreign influence, it is difficult to explain how the Chinese Communists could have charted a course so similar to the one they had criticized their predecessors for following. The official rationale was that since the best of Western science and technology had already been absorbed by the Russians, the most efficient way was to acquire it directly from them. Perhaps there was an initial, unspoken assumption that copying from a socialist ally was not the same as imitating the capitalist West. In any event, the movement to "learn from the Soviet Union" was pursued with all the enthusiasm that had characterized the foreign borrowing process in earlier decades. As with the earlier exercises, virtually no concern was initially shown for the particular features of the Chinese environment in which the Soviet model was being transplanted. Thus, the entire national education system was first reorganized to conform to it. Then, as the incongruities became almost immediately apparent, remedial measures were introduced, launching the entire system on yet another round of adjustments and reforms. In this respect, the 1950s seemed like a socialist re-play of the previous experience.

One important difference between China and the Soviet Union was the less developed state of Chinese education. Fully half of all Russian children were already attending school when the Soviet Union came into being in 1917. This contrasted with only one-quarter of the school-aged group in China in 1949. Equally important, the Soviet Union had concluded its own class-conscious, anti-intellectual "cultural revolution" a full 20 years earlier and had therefore long since ended the conflict between the new "proletarian" and old "bourgeois" intellectuals.[24] Yet it was the conservative "Stalin model," based upon that "integration" of new and old, and deliberately designed to meet the imperatives of industrialization, that the newly victorious Chinese revolutionaries set out to copy. Hence, the old problems that some Chinese Communist leaders had chosen to remember from the pre-1949 reformers' critique remained insoluble under a rigorous application of the Soviet model.

In fact, as the end of the First Five Year Plan approached in 1957, Chinese education still looked remarkably like its pre-1949 past. The Soviet-style system of higher education, like the one it replaced, still rested on a base of mass illiteracy. In 1956, only about half the school-age children of China were attending elementary school. Only seven million were enrolled in secondary schools, by contrast with the 64 million at the primary level. Yet, there were more than 150 million young people in the elementary and secondary age groups.[25]

The need to improve quality to meet the demands of modern science and technology could only be achieved at the cost of reducing the number of students and slowing the rate at which teachers were being trained to instruct them. Alternatively, the only way to establish a school in every village was to revert to the old wartime philosophy from the 1940s rural base areas, which meant not worrying much about quality and uniformity of standards, which could only be achieved in a fully state-supported system staffed by properly trained teachers.

Especially at the elite level, the new demands for specialization according to the Soviet model made quality increasingly imperative. This ensured the perpetuation of the existing educated elite, since the early goal of high worker-peasant college enrollment could not be fulfilled if academic plans and standards were to be met. The working class composition of college students was only about 20 per cent when the unified college entrance examinations were introduced in 1952. Informal recruiting of adult worker-peasant Communist Party members had only just begun and was soon halted in order to meet the standards set by the exams. This meant that the regular senior secondary schools remained the chief source of college students. This further meant that the existing educated elite--with its less than sympathetic orientation toward "proletarian culture"--would remain essentially unchanged. For example, even after the attempt to enroll large groups of adult worker-peasant Party members was no longer operative, "rightist" students in May 1957 were said to have criticized as unfair the moderate admissions policy. The prevalent policy gave preference to five kinds of candidates - workers and peasants, army personnel, children of "revolutionary martyrs," national minorities, and Overseas Chinese - when their qualifications were otherwise competitive. In fact, according to official statistics, during the 1956-57 academic year, only 34 per cent of all undergraduates in tertiary institutions were of worker-peasant origin. The figures for worker-peasant graduate students in these institutions and at the National Academy of Sciences were 17.46 and 5.92 respectively.[26]

Despite much rhetoric to the contrary, then, the gaps between the elite-mass and urban-rural cultures that had been the focus of so much concern during the early decades of the century were little changed by the Soviet model. The heavily working-class membership of the CCP (69 per cent peasant and 14 per cent worker), however, indicated the shift in political power that had occurred, and the direction from which the impetus for change would continue to come. Certainly, it represented the absolute low-point for the educated class in its progressive descent from political power that began with the abolition of the civil service examinations in 1905. Yet within their own professional sphere, as educators and intellectuals, the influence of the educated elite remained intact.

Another important change had taken place by the end of the Soviet-style First Five Year Plan in 1957. This was the apparent disillusionment with the Soviet model. Once again, the Chinese began to criticize themselves for attempting the ready-made, foreign-transplant solution. They would spend the next 20 years trying to devise a more original version, capable of merging the conflicting imperatives at the top and bottom of the educational pyramid into a single integrated system.

China therefore turned away from the Soviet model of the 1950s to experiment with different variants that we have since come to call "Maoist" after their chief promoter. These Maoist experiments progressed through the Great Leap Forward of 1958 and the Cultural Revolution decade of 1966-76. In the process, it would become increasingly clear that their goals for education, at least, were similar to those earlier critical themes dating back to the 1920s. One distinction, however, was that they had graduated from isolated pilot projects outside the system to become part of a nationwide radical platform to promote education that would be technologically appropriate, China centered, mass based, and non-elitist.

MAO'S EXPERIMENTS

The educational reforms of 1958 were introduced as part of a comprehensive new strategy of mass mobilization for economic development which Chinese leaders named the Great Leap Forward. This movement thus created the larger economic and political parameters within which the new round of educational changes occurred, influencing both their initial "success" and their subsequent "failure." In education, the aim was to end the continuing influence of such old "pre-revolutionary" ideas as "education can only be led by experts" and "the separation of mental and manual labor." Recent policies were criticized for having paid insufficient attention to politics, productive labor, and Communist Party leadership.

To strengthen Party leadership as a prerequisite for all the rest there were several new measures. For example, universities were to fill both academic and administrative leadership positions with Party members. This was one of the least popular and most long-lived of all of the changes introduced at this time. The outpouring of dissident opinions when the Party asked for criticism in 1956-57 indicated the general lack of sympathy for the Party's overall performance that existed in intellectual circles.[27] Even worse, Party members assigned to university work often did not have a higher education, which increased antagonistic feelings on both sides.

Furthermore, in order to break the continuing domination of the "bourgeois" academic professionals, several "mass line" measures also were introduced at this time. Productive labor was to become part of the curriculum in all schools at all levels. In addition, quantitative goals were as extravagant for education as for the economy. Within five years, illiteracy would be eradicated, primary schooling would be universal, and there would be a secondary school in every village. Within 15 years, college education would be available for everyone with the necessary qualifications who wanted it; raising the quality of higher education would then be pursued during the 15 years thereafter. Many different forms of schooling would be used to create this system of mass education: schools run by the state and by collectives, general education and vocational training, full-day schools, work-study schools, and spare-time schools.

More specifically, the task of rapidly universalizing education for the masses was given to the half-work/half-study schools. This was because these schools could be run on a self-supporting basis without financial aid from the state. They also did not need a professional staff, but could rely on "whoever could teach." Directives stipulated, however, that some of the already established regular schools should have the responsibility to maintain a complete curriculum and pay attention to raising the quality of their own academic work.[28]

It was said, moreover, that "some comrades" and "some bourgeois educators" objected to the extent and speed of educational change as anticipated in the Great Leap reforms. Such people advocated one type of school system only, run and funded by the state, with regular schools, professional teachers, and conventional methods of instruction. But these "erroneous suggestions" were overridden. Mao's strategy of "walking on two legs" was adopted instead because it was the only means of popularizing education among the worker-peasant masses within a reasonable period of time--given the huge burden of state expenditure that would otherwise have been necessary.[29]

Nevertheless, as with all other limited attempts at educational reform in earlier decades, Mao's earlier reforms essentially failed, and the reasons were similarly complex. They were due partly to the larger political parameters and partly to the obstacles raised by the professional intellectual establishment. The political parameters were defined by the Great Leap reforms of which education was only a part. When that movement collapsed due to its excesses, most of the component parts went with it. Essentially, it was a forced-march attempt to achieve both communism and economic development simultaneously, in accelerated tempo. The ensuing disruptions to agriculture and industry cost the country three years of severe economic depression. During that time, many but not all of the innovations that were supposedly to have expanded availability of education at the mass level were reversed.

More important was the inherent flaw built into the educational reforms themselves, at least from the perspective of their ideals. The flaw is best explained through the slogan of "walking on two legs." In education, the "two legs" meant the irregular, locally financed and staffed, work-study schools for the masses, while the regular, state-financed system continued with its elite "key" school stream to ensure quality. The result made a mockery of the Great Leap's proclaimed goals. Indeed, even the reformers of old would have found their ideals compromised by the end result.[30]

The "irregular" work-study options might have functioned well enough in the rural environment where they were originally designed, but when they were grafted onto a modern, regular school system, still run by and for academic professionals, no amount of political tinkering and ideological reform could change the system into anything other than the divided, elitist structure it was. To assign the "irregular" work-study system the task of educating the rural-peasant and working-class sectors, while the "regular" system imparted quality education to those most in a position to benefit from it, merely provided a new means of reinforcing all of the old cleavages at once. Rather than accept this result, Mao decided to try again. His final solution was to destroy altogether the divided system that had developed during the 1960s, together with the power structure that sustained it. And that, among other things, is precisely what the Cultural Revolution intended to do.

Even with the Cultural Revolution, however, a case can be made for a kind of indirect influence from the Soviet Union. This is traced back to an event of the same name initiated apparently by Stalin in the late 1920s. The Chinese Cultural Revolution seems to have had a clear precedent in that earlier Soviet experience, since it was similar in many details. Both episodes were intended to perform comparable functions as radical attempts of recently empowered Communist parties to prevent bourgeois influence from reproducing itself through the educated elite. The aim in both cases was to reinforce the destruction of bourgeois economic and political power by destroying bourgeois influence in the cultural realm as well.[31]

There were of course, important differences between the two. Mao's Cultural Revolution was more comprehensive in aim and systematic in implementation. And Stalin himself had called a halt to his Cultural Revolution after three years, whereas Mao's endeavor ended only with his death a full ten years after the movement was launched in 1966. Mao's tenacity was also rooted in China's longer and more self-conscious tradition of cultural reform. Despite the grandiose vehicle of cultural revolution and class struggle within which it was now embedded, the "education revolution" component of the 1966-76 decade still represented a search for solutions to the issues that had challenged Chinese cultural reformers since the 1920s.

The fascination with foreign models was apparently still there, unless we assume that Mao's Cultural Revolution was truly original and that the similarities with Stalin's adventure of the same name were purely coincidental. The Cultural Revolution, like the Great Leap before it, grew out of the need to devise Chinese formulas adapted to the specifics of the Chinese environment. The urban-oriented elite was continuing to reproduce itself well into the second decade of Communist rule, provoking resentment among at least some sectors of the new revolutionary leadership. The countryside also remained the disadvantaged sector. Mao's Cultural Revolution strategy was national in scope and promised solutions on all counts.

The key features of the Cultural Revolution are, of course, well known. At the start was the destructive Red Guard phase. Young people throughout the country were mobilized first to attack old ideas and customs. Then the tempo accelerated rapidly as the target was broadened to include "people in authority" who were "going the capitalist road." These people--in governmental, economic, and social organizations throughout the country--were then replaced by a new or at least thoroughly chastened set of leaders. These people would presumably be more amenable than their predecessors to Maoist policies and solutions.

"Cultural Revolution" thus applied to the entire 1966-76 decade, not just to the early Red Guard phase. It was first a mass movement, with the Red Guards and rebel youth in the role of mobilized masses. It was also a power struggle, with Mao using those masses against his opposition, or all the people in positions of authority throughout the system who disagreed with his views. Finally, the Cultural Revolution was the culmination of Mao's effort to change Chinese society and create a successor generation who would continue to implement that effort after he had passed from the scene.[32]

In educational institutions, the Cultural Revolution was implemented to break the power of the existing educational bureaucracy, the professional academics, and any Party leaders who supported them. This represented a final solution to the obstacles the Chinese intellectual establishment had always thrown up against radical reform of the education system as a whole. This solution was then supposed to ease the reintegration of that entire system on the basis of those same anti-elitist, work-oriented norms that had before 1949 been applied only in pilot projects, and after 1949 only to the rural and working class sectors.

The net result of the policies that were implemented during the Cultural Revolution decade was to expand the availability of mass education; to emphasize local relevance and practical learning; and to eliminate all the most glaring manifestations of elitist education, including the "keypoint" college preparatory stream that had been institutionalized during the early 1960s. The problem of insufficient jobs for urban, educated youth was addressed by sending such people into the rural areas to live and work. As for the costs of these Cultural Revolution policies, they led to a general lowering of academic standards, particularly in that elite, college preparatory stream. As a result of the experimentation in that area, the content of college curricula on the average was probably reduced by about half. The policy of sending city youth to the countryside also produced many millions of dissatisfied young people who could not adjust to life there. And in particular, the "class struggle" method of implementing the reforms produced many disillusioned and embittered intellectuals of all ages.[33]

Limitations of space prevent examination of Cultural Revolution education policies in greater detail, but their content will become clear when we consider the backlash against them that has occurred since Mao's death in 1976. The opponents he had tried to disinherit, now led by Deng Xiaoping, began immediately to reassert their right to the succession. They declared the Cultural Revolution formally over within a year and set about revoking the policies and unseating the personnel Mao had sought to establish. Within a few more years, his opponents had succeeded in formally "negating" the Cultural Revolution and re-christening the entire period a "decade of disaster." They dismantled not only the Maoist experiments, but also policies, institutions, and alliances that had in some cases had a history under Communist rule going all the way back to its beginnings in the early 1950s.

Mass movements have now been repudiated, as have class struggle and the whole elaborate set of class and political categories into which all Chinese were divided after 1949. These had then served as the basis for allocating all of life's benefits and punishments under the new revolutionary order. At the same time, virtually all of the old "rightists" have been rehabilitated. That was the label placed on the many thousands of people, mostly university trained professionals, who were already conspicuous by their lack of enthusiasm for Communist rule when they spoke out against it in 1956-57.

In other words, if we grant the education policies of the Cultural Revolution the status they deserve as only the most recent and ambitious in the long line of such efforts that date from the initial reform critique of the 1920s, we have to conclude that, like virtually all the others, Mao's final effort failed also. It failed, moreover, in the same ways that all the others did. On the one hand, the immediate reasons were political: the overall backlash against the political and class warfare which had become, in Maoist eyes, the prerequisite for achieving reform of the education system as a whole. On the other hand Mao's efforts failed also because the intellectual and professional establishment would not buy that particular reform package. And the reasons are now clear.

That package, in its Maoist variant, as in all others before it, was critical of the intellectual establishment's elitism; yet that establishment still regarded itself as an intellectual and social elite. The Maoist reforms worried about urban-rural disparities, while the intellectuals remained unashamedly urban based. The fate of the Maoist program for sending millions of educated city youth "down to the countryside" provides ample testimony to that bias. Manual labor and practical learning have been similarly dispensed with. The Maoist reforms also retained the old ambivalence toward foreign borrowing and sought formulas adapted specifically for the Chinese environment. But for the educated class as a whole, the West continued to represent the highest authority of learning and achievement. Once they regained control of the education system, the educational professionals set out to purge it of every policy and program that was designed to achieve the Maoist reform goals.

The Post-1976 Present

Administratively, the Cultural Revolution changes did indeed break the power of the professionals over education and displace (although not eliminate) the impediment they had always represented to such radical reforms. This had been accomplished by temporarily closing down the Ministry of Education, transferring its powers to national political leaders, and further by "de-professionalization" throughout the system. This meant increasing the power of local Communist Party leaders over education. It also meant including outsiders or local people with no previous educational experience on school leadership committees. Since 1976, all of these changes have been reversed and professional educators have regained leadership over education. They are still under overall Party control; but within their own sphere, they now enjoy greater preeminence than at any time since the early 1950s.

Of even greater historic significance for the intellectuals, however, are the new efforts to upgrade the professional competence of government and Party officials. The goal, already being implemented, is that a college-level education is to be a prerequisite for all officials, including county-level leaders. There is nothing earth-shaking about this by contemporary Western standards. In China, however, it has historic implications. It means that the old unity of learning and political power first broken with the abolition of the civil service examinations of 1905--and all but obliterated in the name of a newly victorious worker-peasant revolution--is now being re-created in a modernizing Communist bureaucracy. What is currently underway, then, is not just the professional vindication of an educated elite, but the political reintegration of China's intellectuals within the ruling class.

With this historic reconciliation, it is perhaps to be expected that the new policies devised for education in the post-Mao era also contain some distinct echoes of a much more distant past. The "new" rationale has been clearly stated by Deng Xiaoping himself: the key to modernization lies in science and technology and the key to these lies in education.[34] The tertiary level of education is therefore once again the favored sector.

Since the West, and especially the United States, has developed science and technology to its most advanced state, so China must once again look to the West as a source of this expertise. Given the complexity of China's past relationships with things foreign, however, such a course is not without political hazards. Hence, Deng Xiaoping has also had to reaffirm repeatedly that China will follow a policy of opening to the outside world while resisting the temptations of bourgeois life. This has led to a curious revival of the now century-old dilemma of how much Chinese society must be changed so that Western science and technology can fulfill their promise of prosperity.[35] By 1983, the Education Minister found it necessary to caution against the old habits of "mechanically imitating" the West. The analogy with the distant past was drawn directly, as in the article praising the even earlier formula of "learning from the barbarians to overcome the barbarians" in order to build a rich and powerful nation.[36]

The post-Mao Administration is also openly critical of its predecessor's social and egalitarian ideals. As noted, these had been promoted in many ways. But as the new leaders explain it, the logic of materialism and economic development decree that quantitative goals must to some degree be sacrificed to quality, since China cannot afford the luxury of promoting both simultaneously.

The changes have therefore been both drastic and deliberate. At the secondary level, Cultural Revolution policies are now said not only to have tried to universalize schooling prematurely, but also to have tried to unify the kind of education provided in a manner inappropriate to China's development needs. The new policies have therefore reversed the "equalization" of quantity and quality that had occurred due to those policies. By 1982, total secondary enrollments had been cut by over 20 million. The cutbacks have been most severe at the senior secondary level, and have occurred in both the cities and the countryside. The rationale is that a senior secondary education is essentially a college-preparatory exercise, and since so few students can go on to college, senior high school need not be made universal. The reduction in junior secondary enrollments has occurred primarily in the countryside.[37]

Together with these qualitative cutbacks is a "new" qualitative reorganization. The Cultural Revolution policies were concerned about the social implications of the mental-manual labor distinction and aimed to devise forms of schooling that would moderate those implications. The result was a uniform schooling that offered work-study combinations of some kind for everyone. Now, the objectives are all in the opposite direction. The idea is to reorganize the system to serve the immediate needs of economic development. It is argued that this can best be done by deliberately exploiting the existing divisions of labor in society. Consequently, all rural schools, from primary upward, are now directed to teach agriculture-related subjects. All ordinary or general middle schools in the cities must introduce vocational courses, while the key schools stand alone as the main college-preparatory stream once more. Conventional wisdom among Chinese educators themselves holds that it is the children of intellectuals and officials who now enjoy the easiest access to the restored key schools, but the social distinctions between the vocational and academic streams are not acknowledged as a relevant policy concern.

At the primary school level, the quantitative declines are at least more derivative than deliberate, but it is the rural sector that has been allowed to absorb the loss. For a number of reasons, an attitude of benign neglect has replaced the active promotion of rural schooling which began in the early 1970s. The main adverse influence, however, has come from the new individual responsibility system in the countryside. At first, the only apparent influence on education was the rising drop-out rate as children left school earlier to participate in the newly legitimate, individual family, money-making activities. But by 1983, press reports began to reveal a more fundamental problem growing out of the new order in the countryside. With the dissolution of collective agriculture, the collectively funded local health, education, and welfare networks seemed to be dissolving, as well. The new challenge, in any event, is to rediscover a reliable source of local leadership and financial support so as to guarantee the maintenance of rural schools.

The most recent officially sponsored idea is that state funding should essentially be withdrawn from all rural primary schools outside the county towns, leaving rural communities to rely totally on their own resources.[38] Since the new rural township governments are still in a transitional take-over state from the old communes, however, it remains unclear as to how this new idea can be made to work. At present, the new local authorities still lack the powers of taxation and administration necessary to ensure the general success of such a plan for the rural areas as a whole, which still contain almost 80 per cent of the total population. In the meantime, the officially recommended expedients are of truly ancient origin. Local officials are advised to solicit contributions from wealthy benefactors such as the new-rich peasants; to revive the old tradition of private and family-supported schools; and to encourage the revived custom of Overseas Chinese contributing to schools in their home districts. These were the means used in imperial and early Republican China to maintain local schools although they were never sufficient to serve more than a small minority of the school-age population.

In any event, it now seems clear that the logic of the Chinese political struggle which culminated in the negation of the Cultural Revolution has removed the old reform ideals more effectively from the educational realm than at any time since they were first raised more than half a century ago. Just as the Cultural Revolution education policies sought to universalize those ideals throughout the system, the repudiation of the Cultural Revolution has removed them totally from that system. All of the old concerns have essentially been banned from the field of official policy and public discourse. How this will work in practice over the long run is another matter.

This last consideration returns us to the subtitle of this essay with its question as to whether those old concerns really can (or even should) be laid to rest. The formal education system that has been recreated since 1976 appears curiously disembodied of its on-going twentieth century critique, but indications are that those issues have not disappeared at all, only retreated inward. Official policies have been re-designed to exclude them, and all related public controversy has been more or less effectively suppressed. The concerns are still there, however, beneath the surface and "in society," to use the Chinese term for public opinion.   Gradually, the policy-makers of the post-Mao Administration are being forced on some points to acknowledge the underlying concerns and complaints to which the new policies have given rise.

For example, the worry about mechanically copying from the outside world is as much alive as the inclination to do just that.   The revival of the old controversy escalated briefly into the officially-sponsored campaign against "spiritual pollution" in 1983.   That campaign was almost immediately scuttled because of the threat it created for the supporters of the new Administration's policies.   Yet an analogy raised then is still used by Chinese officials to illustrate the continuing problem the campaign addressed: it is often said that when a window is opened, a few flies usually come in along with fresh air. Similarly, "spiritual pollution" is an unwelcome side-effect of the opening to the outside world.   "Pollution" is, in this case, a code word for China's old dilemma.   The 1983 campaign therefore deserves more attention than it has received as a contemporary revival of China's century-old concern over what to take from the outside world and how much to compromise Chinese ways in the process.

The literature accompanying that campaign tried to define acceptable limits of foreign influence, to strike a balance between those who advocated a return to "national seclusion" and others who wanted to "imitate and copy foreign things."   Technological equipment could be copied intact; literature, art, ideas, and ideological systems could not. The campaign fretted, in particular, over the "alienation" of Chinese youth from both the pre-revolutionary and revolutionary traditions, leading by default to "blind imitation" of foreign culture.[39]   People were too easily "dazzled" by the economic successes of foreign countries, and their self-doubt turned into "indiscriminate worship of foreign things."[40]

This spiritual pollution campaign had to be aborted within a few months because so many people were so willing to jump on its bandwagon.   In the process, they began to threaten the coalition of interests necessary for the success of the current Administration's policies toward students abroad, potential foreign investors, Hong Kong capitalists, Christian believers, and even new-rich peasants.   The issues raised are far from being resolved.   Chinese society *as a whole* has clearly not yet reached the stage attained by some of its constituent parts (for example, Hong Kong and Taiwan) and sectors (for example, Western educated intellectuals and Overseas Chinese communities). Therefore, it cannot indiscriminately adopt foreign ways and means without suffering considerable qualms of nationalistic and cultural conscience.

Another indicator of the critical concerns aroused by the new policies has been the continuing undercurrent of opposition to the restored college preparatory key (or keypoint) schools. The old issue of elitism is also still alive and was officially acknowledged, although again only briefly, in a flurry of critical press commentary in 1981.[41] This was soon suppressed, but has been followed by several attempts to adjust and tone down the elitist nature of these schools. These measures have been more superficial than substantial, but the issue of elitism in Chinese education is still very much a cause for public concern.

The opposite side of the coin, moreover, has been the acknowledged "universal" rejection of strictly vocational education.[42] Everyone has tried to resist the official effort to exclude vocational courses from the college preparatory stream. That stream now offers prospects so greatly enhanced by comparison with the limitations built into the vocational alternatives that the key schools dominate the entire education system to a greater degree than ever before. Students, parents, teachers, and administrators, have all in their own ways opposed the directives to transform all general academic, non-key secondary schools into vocational equivalents. The reason is that, with the change-over, the students are then automatically excluded from the competition for college, while the schools and teachers automatically lose "face" and status. Incentives are also further reduced, given the practical difficulties always inherent in devising vocational curricula that actually prepare students for the jobs they are likely to find after graduation. The Chinese reforms have not been able to avoid this "classic" vocational school problem.

The quantitative reduction in enrollments has also come under critical fire, indicating concern in some quarters for what has happened to mass education since 1976.[43] This is the reason for the recent directives calling for eventual nine year (six years of elementary and three of junior high) universal compulsory education. An additional reason, however, is the new sensitivity to the outside world where thousands of Chinese have now gone to study and many thousands more just to have a look. There they have discovered that universal mass education is a mark not of Maoist excess but of modernity. Hence, a new compulsory education law went into effect, as of July 1, 1986.[44] But the law does not stipulate how compulsory education is to be achieved for the majority who live in the countryside, especially since the measures of recent years have just closed down the collectively-run junior high school classes and stipulated that only one junior high school should be maintained in each commune (or its equivalent territory). This will make attendance virtually impossible for the majority of China's youth. Even the means for achieving universal primary schooling are now more problematic in the countryside than they were a decade ago.

In answer to the question with which this essay began, then, the ghosts of the past obviously have not yet been laid to rest. Given their continuing presence within Chinese society, the post-Mao Administration may well have erred in treating those concerns strictly as planks in a radical platform that deserved to be totally discredited. The Maoist program did indeed incorporate them as its own. But they also had roots extending far back into the pre-1949, pre-Communist past and extending throughout Chinese society itself. All of these issues grew up simultaneously with the development of Western learning and Western-style schools in China during the early decades of the twentieth century. Certainly, none of them came into being as the exclusive property of the Chinese Communist Party, much less of any one faction within it. Just as pre-1949 adherents could be found at points all along the political spectrum, so those same concerns remain widespread today as "opinions in society."

A major difference between today and the pre-1949 past, however, is that the concerns have been drawn into the factional struggle within the ruling Communist Party. To express sympathy with them now is to invite automatic charges of loyalty to the out-of-power and out-of-favor Maoist line. In continuing to play out the logic of the two-line struggle in this way, the post-Mao Administration has therefore projected a difficult road for itself. Under the circumstances, it would probably have been better advised to follow a course of more direct compromise, since the underlying problems cannot be solved in the foreseeable future. These are the still under-developed state of China's rural economy and the great differences that still exist between China and the international standards to which it aspires. So long as those basic conditions remain, the concerns and issues that have grown up around them will not dissipate; they are too integral a part of China's twentieth century history. The "ghosts" will thus be around for many years to come.

As to how this past might continue to haunt the future, there seem to be three principal possibilities, any one of which might dominate Chinese education. One possibility, of course, is that currently being pursued by the present administration. Despite the challenges it has already had to acknowledge, the assumption obviously remains that the old concerns can be neutralized without actually allowing them back into the arena of open political discourse. In education, as in other sectors, this present course places its hopes almost entirely on the economics of modernization. All other perceived distractions must be removed from the arena in deference to that overriding aim. It is not clear whether this alternative really refuses to acknowledge those distractions as legitimate or simply wants to treat them that way as a temporary expedient to facilitate economic development which, if successful, will eventually erode many of those old concerns (as has occurred in the richer Chinese communities of Taiwan and Hong Kong).

A second possibility is the worst of all, so far as the present policy line is concerned. Yet the current attempts to contain and suppress the old concerns might, in turn, provide another backlash in the direction of the Maoist ideals they are trying to obliterate. Certainly, in the near future, before the current strategy has had a chance to register significant economic gains, the Administration will count itself lucky if it can find ways to keep the old concerns from contributing fuel to the fires of a political backlash.

A third possibility is some sort of compromise solution. For instance, a deliberate attempt might be made by a new team of leaders to extract the old concerns from the logic of the national power struggle in which they are still embedded. It might then be possible to come to terms more openly with the on-going and still unresolved questions about foreign borrowing, elitism, fair opportunities, mental versus manual labor, appropriate versus advanced technology, and a re-integration of the rural areas into the national mainstream.

However the future possibilities develop, the current policy-makers and the rehabilitated educational establishment will not be able to keep this past from haunting them in one way or another. Even if the Maoist backlash or compromise solutions do not occur, the ever present challenges and "opinions in society" against various points along the current policy line for education bear witness to the continuing reality of the old concerns.[45]

Notes

1. The literature on China's Confucian past is voluminous. The brief summary here is based largely on the following: Chung-li Chang, *The Chinese Gentry* (Seattle: University of Washington, 1955); John K. Fairbank, ed. *Chinese Thought and Institutions* (Chicago: University of Chicago, 1957); Wolfgang Franke, *The Reform and Abolition of the Traditional Chinese Examination System* (Cambridge: East Asian Research Center, Harvard University, 1972); Ping-ti Ho, *The Ladder of Success in Imperial China* (New York: Columbia University, 1962); Johanna M. Menzel, editor, *The Chinese Civil Service* (Boston: D.C. Heath, 1963); Ichisada Miyazaki, *China's Examination Hell: The Civil Service Examinations of Imperial China* (New Haven: Yale, 1981); Karl A. Wittfogel, *Oriental Despotism* (New York: Vintage, 1981).

2. P'an Kuang-tan and Fei Hsiao-t'ung, "City and Village: the Inequality of Opportunity," in Menzel, *The Chinese Civil Service*, p.15.

3. Chung-li Chang, *The Chinese Gentry*, *op. cit.*, pp. 97-113, 137-141.

4. China's greatest twentieth century satirist, Lu Xun, left a memorable short story portraying the plight of one such failed aspirant scholar ("*Kung I-chi*," translated in *Selected Stories of Lu Hsun*; (Peking: Foreign Languages Press, 1972): 19-24.

5. Evelyn Sakakida Rawski, *Education and Popular Literacy in Ch'ing China* (Ann Arbor: University of Michigan, 1978): 33-43, 66-80, 183-186.

6. Lu-dzai Djung, *A History of Democratic Education in Modern China* (Shanghai: The Commercial Press, 1934):167.

7. Ssu-yu Teng and John K. Fairbank, editors, *China's Response to the West: A Documentary Survey, 1839-1923* (New York: Atheneum, 1963):53.

8. On the self-strengthening efforts of the late nineteenth century, see

William Ayers, *Chang Chih-tung and Educational Reform in China* (Cambridge: Harvard University, 1971).

9. Y.C. Wang, *Chinese Intellectuals and the West, 1872-1949* (Chapel Hill: University of North Carolina, 1966):64.

10. Mary Claubaugh Wright, "Introduction: the Rising Tide of Change," in Mary Wright, editor, *China in Revolution: the First Phase, 1900-1913* (New Haven: Yale University, 1968).

11. The classic account of this period is Chow Tse-tsung, *The May Fourth Movement* (Cambridge, Harvard University, 1960).

12. Lu Xun immortalized this phenomenon as well. In the most famous of all his stories, the exalted "returned student" becomes the "false foreign devil" who prevents the hero--a poor illiterate Chinese everyman--from joining the revolution."The True Story of Ah Q," translated in *Selected Stories of Lu Hsun* (Peking: Foreign Languages Press, 1972).

13. From a 1923 statement by Chinese educator Tao Xingzhi, quoted in Barry Keenan, *The Dewey Experiment in China: Educational Reform and Political Power in the Early Republic* (Cambridge: Harvard University, 1977):91.

14. Mao Zedong, "Hunan zixiu dazue chuangli xuanyan" (Announcement on the Founding of the Hunan Self-study University),1921, in *Mao Zedong Ji* (Works of Mao Zedong) vol. 1 (Hong Kong, 1975):81-84.

15. Quoted in Maurice Meisner, *Li Ta-chao and the Origins of Chinese Marxism* (Cambridge: Harvard University, 1967):87.

16. Barry Keenan, *The Dewey Experiment in China, op. cit.*, pp. 81-110; Shirley S. Garrett, *Social Reformers in Urban China: the Chinese YMCA, 1895-1926* (Cambridge: Harvard University, 1970):155-156; Sidney D. Gamble, *Ting Hsien: A North China Rural Community* (New York: Institute of Pacific Relations, 1954).

17. Guy S. Alitto, *The Last Confucian: Liang Shu-ming and the Chinese*

Dilemma of Modernity (Berkeley: University of   California, 1979).

18. James C. Thompson, Jr., *While China Faced West: American Reformers in Nationalist China, 1928-1937* (Cambridge: Harvard University, 1969), chapter six; also, Mary Brown Bullock, *An American Transplant: the Rockefeller Foundation and Peking Union Medical College* (Berkeley: University of California, 1980), chapters six and seven.

19. The League of Nations' Mission of Educational Experts, *The Reorganization of Education in China* (Paris: League of Nations' Institute of Intellectual Cooperation, 1932):21.

20. Y.C. Wang, *Chinese Intellectuals and the West, op. cit.* pp. 366-67. For a fuller treatment of the intellectuals' political role, see Jerome B. Grieder, *Intellectuals and the State in Modern China* (New York: The Free Press, 1981).

21. The League of Nations' Mission of Educational Experts, *The Reorganization of Education in China, op. cit.*, p. 151 and pp. 139-158.

22. *Ibid.*, p.21.

23. See Peter J. Seybolt, "The Yenan Revolution in Mass Education," *The China Quarterly* no. 48 (October-December 1971); and Michael Lindsay, *Notes on Educational Problems in Communist China, 1941-47* (New York: Institute of Pacific Relations, 1950).

24. Mervyn Matthews, *Education in the Soviet Union* (London: Allen and Unwin, 1982):2; Sheila Fitzpatrick, editor, *Cultural Revolution in Russia: 1928-1931* (Bloomington: Indiana University, 1978).

25. New China News Agency-English (Peking, June 20, 1956) in *Current Background*, No. 400 (1956):21; State Statistical Bureau, *Ten Great Years* (Peking: Foreign Languages Press, 1960): 192; *New China News Agency* (Peking, March 22, 1959), in *Survey of China Mainland Press*, No. 1985 (April 3, 1959):

26-27; and Robert D. Barendsen, *Half-Work Half-Study Schools in Communist China* (Washington, D.C.: U.S. Department of Health, Education and Welfare, 1964): 1,7.

26. State Statistical Bureau, *Ten Great Years, op. cit.*, p. 200; *Renmin Ribao* (People's Daily), (Beijing, July 6, 1957), translated in *Current Background*, no. 467 (July 15, 1957):11.

27. On this episode, see Roderick MacFarquhar, editor, *The Hundred Flowers* (London: Atlantic Books, 1960).

28. *Renmin Ribao* (People's Daily), (Beijing, September 20, 1958).

29. Lu Ting-yi, "Education Must Be Combined with Productive Labor," *Hongchi* (Red Flag), No. 7 (Sept. 1, 1958) in *Current Background*, No. 516 (Sept. 2, 1958):4.

30. On Chinese education after the Great Leap, see, Robert D. Barendsen, "The Agricultural Middle School in Communist China," *The China Quarterly* No. 8 (October/December 1961), and an updated version by the same author, *Half-Work Half-Study Schools in Communist China* (cited above); Susan Shirk, *Competitive Comrades* (Berkeley: University of California, 1982); Stanley Rosen, *Red Guard Factionalism and the Cultural Revolution in Guangzhou* (Boulder, Colorado: Westview, 1982): part I.

31. Sheila Fitzpatrick, editor, *Cultural Revolution in Russia, 1928-1931* (cited above); and Sheila Fitzpatrick, *Education and Social Mobility in the Soviet Union, 1921-1934* (Cambridge: Cambridge University Press, 1979).

32. The interpretation is my own. Among the many books available on the early years of the Cultural Revolution are: Stanley Rosen, *Red Guard Factionalism* (cited above), part II; David Milton and Nancy Dall Milton, *The Wind Will Not Subside* (New York: Pantheon, 1976); Gordon Bennett and Ronald N. Montaperto, *Red Guard* (Garden City, New York: Anchor, 1972); William Hinton, *Hundred Day War* (New York: Monthly Review Press,

1972); Hong Yung Lee, *The Politics of the Chinese Cultural Revolution* (Berkeley: University of California, 1978).

33. See, for example, Thomas P. Bernstein, *Up to the Mountains and Down to the Villages: the Transfer of Youth from Urban to Rural China* (New Haven: Yale, 1977); Jonathan Unger, *Education Under Mao* (New York: Columbia University, 1982).

34. See *Deng Xiaoping wenxuan* (Deng Xiaoping's Selected Works). (Beijing: Renmin chubanshe, 1983), especially the essays entitled, "A Few Opinions on Science and Education Work," and "Respect Knowledge Respect Talent."

35. For a discussion of this dilemma in education, see for instance, Zhang Wei, "Xiqu waiguo jingyen bixu cong wo guo shiji chufa" (The absorption of foreign experience must start with our own country's realities), *Renmin jiaoyu* (People's Education), (Beijing) No.5, (1980):21-23.

36. *Xinhua* (New China) *News Service* (Beijing) (May 30, 1983), in *Foreign Broadcast Information Service* (June 2, 1983): K-13; *Guangming ribao* (Beijing) (July 27, 1983).

37. *Zhongguo baike nianjian, 1980* (China Encyclopedic Yearbook, 1980) (Beijing and Shanghai, 1980): 536; *Zhongguo baike nianjian, 1982* (China Encyclopedic Yearbook, 1982) (Beijing and Shanghai):568. *Zhongguo tongji nianjian, 1983* (China Statistical Yearbook, 1983) (Hong Kong: Economic Information and Agency, 1983):511-512.

38. The proposal is discussed at length in Hubert O. Brown, "Teachers and the Rural Responsibility System in the People's Republic of China," *The Asian Journal of Public Administration* vol. 7, no.1 (June 1985): 2-17.

39. For example, *Guangming ribao* (September 24, 1983):1.

40. *Renmin ribao* (November 16, 1983): 5.

41. This controversy is discussed in Suzanne Pepper, *China's Universities: Post-Mao Enrollment Policies and Their Impact*

on the Structure of Secondary Education (Ann Arbor: Michigan Monographs in Chinese Studies, No. 46, 1984): 27-30. See also, Stanley Rosen, "Restoring Key Secondary Schools in Post-Mao China: the Politics of Competition and Educational Quality," in *Policy Implementation in Post-Mao China*, David M. Lampton, editor, (Berkeley: University of California, 1987):321-353.

42. *Renmin ribao* (October 29, 1983).

43. Song Jian, "Population and Education," *Ziran bianzhengfa tongxun* (Journal of the Dialectics of Nature) (Beijing) No. 3, (June 1980):1-3, translated in *Joint Publications Research Service*, 77745/China/PSM/178 (April 3, 1981).

44. *Xinhua* (New China) *News Service-Chinese* (Beijing) (April 17, 1986), translated in *Foreign Broadcast Information Service* (April 22, 1986): K-19.

45. Additional useful references on Chinese education not cited in the notes above include the following: Theodore Hsi-en Chen, *The Maoist Educational Revolution* (New York: Praeger, 1974); Theodore Hsi-en Chen, *Chinese Education Since 1949: Academic and Revolutionary Models* (New York: Pergamon, 1981); John N. Hawkins, *Education and Social Change in the People's Republic of China* (New York: Praeger, 1983); Ruth Hayhoe, editor, *Contemporary Chinese Education* (Armonk, New York: M.E. Sharpe, 1984); Ronald F. Price, *Marx and Education in Russia and China* (Totowa, New Jersey: Rowman and Littlefield, 1977); and R.F. Price, *Education in Modern China* (London and Boston: Routledge and Kegan Paul, 1979); Robert Taylor, *China's Intellectual Dilemma* (Vancouver: University of British Columbia Press, 1981). Another useful source is *Chinese Education: a Journal of Translations*, edited by Stanley Rosen, published by M.E. Sharpe, Armonk, New York.

CHAPTER TWO

THE EARLY CHILDHOOD EDUCATION OF THE ONLY CHILD GENERATION IN URBAN CHINA

by Delia Davin

Since 1979, Chinese couples have been very strongly urged to limit their families to a single child. The policy has been implemented with particular force in the cities where very few permissions for a second child are issued.[1] Moreover, as will be explained below, various factors make the idea of a small family more acceptable in the cities; indeed, even before the advent of a strict limit on the number of children per family, many urban couples limited themselves to two and some chose an only child.[2] Thus, in the cities of the People's Republic, most children under ten have no brothers or sisters. The education of these children at home, in kindergartens, and schools has given rise to much discussion in China. Parents, teachers, experts, and the media all tend to emphasize the character development of the only child as being problematic, and complaints about the generation of "little emperors," *xiao huangdi*, abound in the press.

Only children are supposed in all societies to be different from their coevals with siblings. Where a whole generation is dominated by only children, one can clearly expect many interesting changes and pressures which will force a careful consideration of practice both in education and in childrearing. In this chapter, I will discuss the way in which the socialization of children and early childhood education has been affected by the arrival of the only child generation. For reasons of space and also because the one-child family policy has had far greater impact in the towns, I will only look at urban children. My research is based on interviews with parents, kindergarten staff, teachers

42

and officials carried out in Beijing, Shenyang, and Chengdu in the autumn of 1987 and of course, printed sources.[3]

In my chapter, I will briefly review the ways in which the state became involved in the socialization of children during the first decades of the People's Republic of China, to provide a backdrop against which current developments may be viewed. I will then discuss the education of the young child at home, in kindergarten, and at primary school, focusing on what seems to be perceived as the problems and needs of only children. All three institutions are viewed by the state as agents of socialization. Its attempts to influence and guide practice within them are a clear assertion of its interest in the quality and character of the younger generation. In my final section, I return to the problem of why early childhood education seems to have become a matter of such concern to parents, teachers and the state in post-Mao China. The first section of the chapter summarizes the effects of the one-child family policy in urban China which has so altered the whole context of child socialization.

The One Child Family Policy in Urban China

In societies throughout the world, urbanization tends to be associated with lower birthrates. Old values and aspirations are transformed, the status of women improves, child rearing becomes more costly, the short-term economic value of children is reduced, infant mortality declines and people appear to wish to invest in quality rather than quantity where their children are concerned.

Such patterns broadly hold good for urban China. There is a severe housing shortage in the cities. Most families live in one, two, or if they are lucky, three small rooms. Large families exacerbate overcrowding and lower the quality of life of the rest of the family. Many urban people look forward to receiving pensions in old age; in addition, they expect to receive some help from their children but do not expect to become absolutely dependent upon them.[4] As urban men earn more on average than urban women, they may be better placed to provide help. However, urban women, unlike their rural counterparts, do retain close links with their natal families and often support or care for their elderly parents. The pro-natalist pressure of son preference is therefore less strong in the cities. It is common for both parents to work an eight hour day six days a week. They naturally wish to reduce the domestic work burden and to concentrate the time they have to spare for family life on fewer children. Paid child care, a necessity for many working couples, may cost a third of an adult's wage per child in a kindergarten and far more if private help is engaged. Other costs associated with childrearing are high and have risen sharply in recent years, not the least because greater prosperity and smaller families themselves altered perceptions of what children "need." More is spent on education, clothes, toys, and other consumer goods for children and standards of nutrition have risen. Taken together, these factors explain why the urban birthrate fell steeply years ago and why a substantial number of urban couples decided on an only child even before the introduction of the single child policy.

The policy was introduced in 1979, and its elaborate range of incentives and penalties was developed in the following years. The government hoped this extreme measure would avert a population explosion that threatened to block economic development. The factors that had encouraged urban couples voluntarily to limit their families also made them more receptive to the new policy. A couple who had only wanted two children and were not too concerned about whether they were boys or girls, would obviously be softer targets than peasants who hoped for three or four children with at least two boys. Moreover, the government exerts more control over most city people than over peasants. It can punish those who refuse to conform by docking their wages and by limiting their access to child care, schools, and the best medical care for their children. Those who pledge to have only one child enjoy a monthly allowance for the child. Their children receive priority access to all services and enjoy subsidized child care and health care. A climate has been created in which it is economically and socially difficult to have a second child. Even those who have twins (thus involuntarily failing to conform with the policy), and therefore miss out on the privileges of the one-child family, complain that their standard of living is thereby harshly reduced.[5] It is understandable that in the larger cities at least, the great majority of the under tens, are now only children.

The Socialization of Chinese Children in Historical Perspective

In Chinese culture, there is a long tradition of consciously using the socialization of children to try to produce an adult person who is "good" according to the tenets of the dominant ideology, a person who will fulfill an appropriate, socially allocated role.[6] This was the case, of course, in Confucian China and it was equally true of the early years of the People's Republic of China. Reading material, directed at children in Confucian China, stressed obedience, duty, hard work and above all, filial piety.[7] Communist literature for children also emphasizes hard work and duty but glorifies patriotism and a willingness to serve the people rather than filial piety. Whereas in Imperial China, the state contented itself with a general championing of Confucian education, otherwise leaving the socialization of children to the family, in Communist China, the state became much more active in the attempt to build the model citizen.

There were some official attempts to influence family socialization, but the state was also able to affect the socialization of children on a scale hitherto unprecedented in China through a great range of non-family agents. These included extensive pre-school care, an education system that drew in the vast majority of urban children, and the Communist children's organization, the Young Pioneers. A new "children's culture" also developed in the 1950s, sustained by children's books and magazines, radio programs made for the young, and later, by television. Peer group activity assumed a new prominence. Children were organized to carry out simple forms of manual labor such as sweeping the streets. They played a major role in hygiene campaigns; when the attempt was made to eliminate flies, each child had a quota to kill. When the unhygienic habit of spitting in public places was under attack, the Young Pioneers were mobilized to educate their elders. They were supposed to call after any offending adult, "Auntie, uncle, please don't do that, it spreads disease." They carried chalk so that for added emphasis, they could draw a circle around the globule. At the Qing Ming festival, traditionally the day when Chinese sweep their family graves, school children were taken to sweep the graves of those who had died in the Revolution. Despite all this, the family remained immensely important. It is true that children learned that their elders were not always right and that they were encouraged to put loyalty to the country and the Party above loyalty to their parents. Some unfortunate children whose parents got into political trouble had to make hard choices. Yet, on the whole, the government valued the institution of the family, recognizing it as a stabilizing social influence and a unit within which both children and the elderly could be provided care. Family reform was directed toward modifying its authoritarian structure and improving the position of women within it rather than destroying it.

State interest in child socialization was, of course, underpinned by a strong ideology and a clear idea of what the model citizen should look like. Children were taught to "love China and the Communist Party" and to be willing to do all they could to serve both. As the Maoist leadership's anxiety about the future of the revolution intensified in the 1960s, more and more emphasis was placed on the politicization of the younger generation or "revolutionary successors," *geming jiebanren*, as they began to be called.[8] There were children who were constantly told that Chairman Mao had said, "The world is yours, as well as ours, but in the last analysis it is yours... The world belongs to you. China's future belongs to you."[9]

Socialization in the Post-Mao Family

Today's young parents were children during the Cultural Revolution. The youngest are too young to have any memory of it, the oldest were themselves participants. This gap in life experience does not seem to be reflected in great differences in their aspirations for their children, which very generally include their maintaining good health and obtaining a good education, pursuing their talents and achieving success, landing a good job and acquiring prosperity.[10] Less commonly mentioned is having a happy life. Some talk about desirable character traits for their children: they should be good, unselfish, and hardworking. Few mention such things as being patriotic, being useful, or making a contribution to society. Their goals are very much for their children as individuals in striking contrast to the high ideals of their own childhood days.

The material conditions of childhood have changed very sharply too. Urban parents report spending from 25%-50% of their joint incomes directly on their single child. This seems very plausible after looking around their homes. Tiny apartments are often dominated, not by one huge doll or teddy bear but by several. Even in low-income families, the only child is likely to own many toys, sometimes piled neatly in a corner, sometimes carefully arranged on a shelf. Tricycles and children's bicycles have become commonplace. Most city children are also well dressed. Parents who as children during the Cultural Revolution wore patched clothing, often by choice, and scorned leather shoes as bourgeois, now replace their children's clothes as soon as they show signs of wear and will not buy them cloth shoes if they can afford leather. Perhaps the oddest piece of conspicuous consumption by today's parents is the piano. So many were purchased in the mid-eighties that their price, already equal to a year's average salary, was significantly raised to reduce demand. This had little effect. If they can possibly afford it, even parents who live in one room with their child, will squeeze a piano in among the other large items like the double bed, the refrigerator-freezer, and the sofa.[11]

From its first days, the infant's progress is watched with anxiety by the parents. Nearly all the parents I asked were able to recall the exact age at which the child had said its first words and had taken its first steps. Parents are quick to seek advice or consult books on child care and development if they think they detect anything abnormal.[12] There is a considerable audience for new magazines directed at the parents of young children and for radio and television programs that give advice on child care.[13] The organizers of a drop-in child guidance clinic in Beijing operated by the Women's Federation, told me that most of the cases brought to the pediatricians on staff there reflected parental anxiety rather than real problems.

Another source of advice is the *jiazhang xuexiao* or parent craft class. *Jiazhang* is used here in the sense of "parent or guardian" and the classes are open to grandparents as well as parents. Indeed, some of the class organizers seemed to regard combating old-fashioned, unscientific ideas held by the older generation as a major part of their task. Factories put on such classes for their employees and they are also organized by residents' committees, kindergartens, and schools. The Women's Federation offers advice on the classes, produces materials for them, and sometimes runs them itself. Subjects which are taught include family education, child development, immunization, nutrition, and fostering the child's imagination, creativity and moral character (*pinde*).[14] Although I was frequently told about such classes and once observed one in operation, I never met anyone socially who had attended one. This may have been partly because they were very new, but I suspect also that they are primarily intended for less-educated parents who are thought unlikely to have become familiar with child rearing ideas through reading. Parents can get time off work to attend the classes, which are said to be compulsory, although more educated parents appear to be under no pressure to attend.

In China, as is true elsewhere, the problem of day care is a major worry for working parents. In earlier decades, the working mother had 56 days paid maternity leave after the birth of a child. When this was over, the baby might be cared for by a grandmother or less often by an elderly neighbor or taken to a nursery, *tuoersuo*, specializing in the care of children under three years of age. Enterprises with a significant number of female employees ran their own nurseries on the premises, and mothers got time off for breast-feeding.

During the 1980s, one of the great rewards to mothers who accept the single-child pledge has been an enhanced maternity leave entitlement of six months. The care of the baby after that period remains for most, a source of anxiety. Some parents still use nurseries, but there are not enough places to meet demand. Moreover, parents now have doubts about institutional care for the very young infant. They feel that their precious only child should not be exposed to infection through contact with other babies at an age when it is still so vulnerable, and they fear that the care may not be of a high enough standard. As women workers retire early, a grandmother may be available to look after the baby, and most will do so willingly. Some babies are even taken hundreds of miles to grandparents in other cities or in the countryside, although this means separation from their parents for the first years of their lives. But if grandmothers live too far away, are too frail, or have too many other responsibilities, another solution has to be sought. Some parents employ a young girl from the countryside, *xiao aiyi* (little auntie), while their child is small. If the family still has rural connections, a relative is preferred on the grounds that she will be more reliable. A maid's wages will take up a high proportion of one parent's salary and living space must be found for her in already cramped quarters. There seem to be considerable tensions in the employer-maid relationship. Young parents are full of complaints about the greed, unreliability and bad habits of these young women. Sensational rumors circulate about maids being involved in kidnapping gangs, doubtlessly reflecting parental anxiety rather than common reality, but also contributing to negative perceptions of *xiao aiyi*.

Parents who have arranged for their child to be looked after by a grandmother or a *xiao aiyi* often become critical of the way the child is being raised. Grandparents are most frequently accused of spoiling and giving the child wrong items to eat. This is of particular

concern because after all the publicity about spoiled only children or
xiao huangdi (little emperors), parents are very sensitive to signs that
their children may be spoiled. Sometimes advanced age or lack of
education is seen as preventing the elderly from offering the stimulation
the child needs. *Xiao aiyi*, who are usually from the poorest regions of
the Chinese countryside, come in for harsher criticism. They are
accused of neglecting their charges, leaving the children to cry, giving
them sweets to shut them up, consuming food purchased for the
children, being too ignorant to instruct them properly, and so on.

Although parents spend long working hours away from their
small children, most of their leisure time is spent with them. As in
other Chinese societies, small children are taken visiting, on trips, or
to restaurants, and it is not customary for parents to arrange to go out
together without them. Great patience is shown toward small children.
If they cry or get angry, then an adult will pick them up and be
prepared to spend time consoling or distracting them. They are made
to be a center of attention by visitors or other adults from outside the
family, who will generally ask them a few questions and try to get them
to talk. On such occasions, even the shyest child will be kindly but
persistently required to greet the strange adults, addressing them as
"auntie" or "uncle." They are constantly and carefully supervised and
often corrected for doing anything which seems dangerous to the carer,
or for failing to greet someone or not putting a toy away. With small
children, the tone used is usually gentle and indulgent.

As the child grows older, much more is expected of him or
her and the patience and indulgence shown to younger children begins
to fade. A failure to live up to expectations is more likely to be
formally punished, though some parents prefer to try and change the
child's behavior by expressing their own disappointment and disapproval.
The official line in China is strongly against corporal punishment.
Teachers are forbidden to hit pupils. The advice in child care manuals
and in parent craft classes is that children who have been hit at home
will think it is alright for them to hit smaller children. It is also argued
that beating tends to cause splits in families. Children look for
protection from the adult who appears to disapprove of beating, and this
gives rise to quarrels that are themselves bad for children. Nonetheless,
the majority of adults whom I interviewed admitted to hitting their
children, although they all would have known that it is against expert
advice. Some expressed regret. One mother told me that she wanted
her little girl to learn to play a large accordion which the child found
exhausting. When the child put it down, her mother hit her to make
her play. Then the girl said, "Mummy, I'm longing to grow up so that

I can hit you." She had not struck her child since this incident. Most parents, however, seemed to believe that they had to hit their children. The reasons given were that the child wouldn't do homework, played too much, was disobedient, or, most commonly of all, received low grades in school. A Beijing teacher who surveyed her class of thirty found only one who had not been beaten. School authorities regarded this as a problem but did not have a consistent line on it. Some said they could take no action, others stated that they would discuss it in the parents' meetings.

The longing for children to achieve academically is often accompanied by an intense desire to foster their artistic talents. Toddlers are taught to recite Tang poetry; they are far too young to understand the lines they are uttering, but this does nothing to dampen the enthusiasm of their proud parents. A few privileged children pursue after-school activities at children's palaces. Many parents pay private teachers for music and art classes. "Piano mania" leads parents to drive their children to practice for long hours. One woman told me how unrealistic such parents are, recalling a newspaper story of a boy who had chopped up his piano with an ax because he was so fed up with practicing. Yet she had forced her own seven year old girl to practice for three hours a day until friends advised her to reduce it to two hours a day. When I asked how the little girl felt about this, she admitted that her daughter had said that the best place in the world must be one without a piano. I asked her if she wasn't repeating the mistake of the parents whose son had chopped up the piano. "Oh no," she said. "It's different. My daughter has real talent."

The strong desire that the child should succeed is, of course, understandable. The education of many of today's parents was disrupted by the Cultural Revolution. Some have managed to compensate for lost time, generally through years of struggle.[15] Others still feel handicapped by it. All are determined that their children should make full use of what they see as the much better chance offered to them. Parents can concentrate their whole attention on their only child, and they feel that everything depends upon him or her. In post-Mao China, people are constantly urged to work hard, not depend on the state, but make themselves rich through their own efforts, and so on.[16] Inflation, unemployment, and the loss of the job security enjoyed in the past, have eroded confidence about the future. The pressure that people place on their children no doubt reflects all of these factors.

Kindergarten Education

Unlike primary education in Chinese cities, kindergarten education is not offered on a universal basis. Nationwide, in 1986, 173,376 kindergartens provided places for 16,290,000 children and by 1989, the figure was 20 million. This is said to be about 25% of those of the appropriate age.[17] The proportion of children who attend kindergartens in cities is higher, with most children spending at least some time in kindergarten between the ages of three and six or seven, when they enter primary school. Some parents and more grandparents worry about sending three year olds off to kindergarten. Sometimes, especially where the child is looked after by a grandmother, entry into kindergarten may be deliberately delayed for a year. On the whole, however, kindergarten education is very much sought after. Parents who worry about the methods through which grandparents or *xiao aiyi* have been caring for their child, turn with relief to the kindergarten, to sort any problems out. Some of the parents I interviewed even felt that they, themselves, spoiled their children and that the kindergarten would be good for them.

It is also recognized that the kindergarten offers a useful preparation for school. Children who have attended a good kindergarten will more easily attain a place in a key primary school. Consequently, despite the higher fees charged at the best kindergartens, places are difficult to secure. There are entrance "exams" designed to test coordination, verbal development, simple counting and the recognition of shapes. Parents are excluded from the room during the test. The family coaches the child for the exam, and the outcome is awaited with anxiety. Even long afterwards, it is clear from the way parents speak of the occasion that the experience was perceived as a considerable ordeal. Despite the existence of formal selection procedures, access to connections, *guanxi*, or a "back door" may also help with entry into a good kindergarten.

The elite kindergartens are operated by the local education bureaus. These serve as models of "good practice" for ordinary kindergartens and are used both for training new teachers and giving short courses to serving teachers. Factories, companies, schools, universities, and government offices all operate nurseries for their own employees. Their quality varies, depending in part on the nature of the unit to which they are attached. University kindergartens, for example, are renowned for their standards and they are hard to enter. Their teachers tend to be well trained and interested in child development theory. Whatever the perception of their quality, however, closeness to the work place and opening hours coordinated with the working day make enterprise kindergartens a convenient choice.

Both of these types of kindergartens frequently offer boarding facilities so that the child may be away from home from Monday morning to Saturday afternoon. In the past, parents who were highly committed to their careers, such as Party and government officials or university teachers, often sent their children to institutions with boarding facilities. Their families tended to be small so the boarding fee did not pose too great a problem. Boarding now seems to be declining in popularity, and some kindergartens are cutting their boarding places. Where there is only one child, the child care burden is limited, and parents feel that they do not wish to be separated from their children for so long. Some experts now argue that the separation boarding entails may be unduly stressful. A recent arrangement whereby children who are eventually going to board may attend the kindergarten on a daily basis for the first month, reflects an approach generally more sympathetic to the child's feelings.

The majority of urban kindergartens are run by the residents' committees. These provide day care only. Their equipment is simpler and their staff less highly trained than in the elite establishments. They give the impression of being concerned more with basic care and less with child development. They receive some government subsidies and are subject to external inspection. Finally, as encouragement was given to private enterprise in the 1980s, some private nurseries were established. These are usually very small undertakings, operated by retired primary or kindergarten teachers, who conduct classes from their own homes. They are inspected by an official from the Women's Federation who decides how many children may be supervised, with an upper limit of three children to one teacher.

Kindergarten teachers can be quite eloquent about the characteristics of only children. They confirm that children are spoiled, but while parents tend to blame the spoiling on grandparents, teachers blame it on the family in general and the parents in particular. It is a teachers' cliche that the only child's trouble is that he or she has the complete attention of six adults: two parents and four grandparents. In fact, this can not be literally true of very many children, given the fact that some grandparents will no longer be alive or live far away, and most have more than one grandchild in any event. But, it does convey the point that the current generation of children receives more adult attention than has any previous one. Teachers are quick to admit that some of the results of the attention are positive. They say that only children know a lot, even at age three, and that they are bright and are quick to learn. Their language is well developed and they are articulate and ready to speak. They are not shy of strange adults. Some teachers think they cry less than children did in the past. Their physical health is generally good, they are better fed; they are taller, stronger, and less susceptible to infectious diseases.

Teachers comment critically that in contrast to their level of general knowledge, only children tend to have acquired few practical skills. They have to be taught to feed and dress themselves and brush their own teeth at kindergarten. They want an adult to help them go to the lavatory. Parents presumably would find this unremarkable. Of those I questioned, very few expected that children would be able to do any of these things before they were three years old, and some thought that four or five were the usual ages for such behavior.

Teachers also observe that only children tend to be very possessive. In their homes, all the toys belong to them and it is hard for them to grasp that this is not true of the kindergarten situation. They are slow to learn to share and take turns. Several also commented that the children are now much harder to amuse or distract. If you show them a mechanical toy, they may well turn away saying, "I've got one of those at home." In Beijing, in the mid-1970s, my own daughter's kindergarten teacher expected her entire class to watch quietly while she operated a clockwork toy. They were not permitted to touch it. Things have progressed since those days.

Only children are also said to be extremely picky about their food. An unwillingness to eat vegetables is mentioned especially often. Again, teachers regard parents as the culprits. They say that in the family, children are not only allowed to eat what they like and leave what they like, they are filled up with snacks and sweets between meals. Most day nurseries supply breakfast, lunch, and the early evening meal. Between meal snacks are strictly limited and often consist of a piece of fruit. Teachers complain that parents buy the children things to eat at the end of the day after collecting them, and that the children, knowing that this will happen, don't eat the meal supplied at the kindergarten. Parents are often warned against this at parent craft classes. Obesity is said to be on the increase among children. As Chinese traditionally favor plump babies, *pang wawa*, parents are not easily convinced that this is a problem. In one residents' committee kindergarten class I visited in Beijing, the head asked a rather slender girl to stand beside a slightly pudgy boy. I thought she would make a point about parents stuffing their only children with food, but in fact she said, "You see, some children eat well and grow properly and others don't, so they are stunted." I couldn't resist commenting that heredity might be a factor too, a point which she conceded. In fact, teachers' disapproval of children's eating habits seems to relate to character development as much as to nutrition. They themselves grew up when food was less plentiful, and waste was strongly condemned from a moral standpoint. The material situation has now changed, but waste still inspires a feeling of moral outrage in many.

Kindergarten activities have undergone significant change in the last decade. The popularization of a national kindergarten syllabus has produced a surprising degree of similarity in the children's day and in teaching methods used in kindergartens all over the country.[18] The subjects taught include language, arithmetic, general knowledge (*chang zhi*), music, art and physical education. The learning through play approach is much better established than in the past. As one head put it, "We now emphasize interesting the children and getting them to understand. If we can do that, there is no need to make them learn by rote." The youngest children have few formal lesson periods but even for the "big class," there is a growing emphasis on learning through play and through role play. Simple construction toys are used and the children can play at owning shops, working in hospitals, portraying hairdressers, and experiencing other real-life situations. Such games are intended to help them learn to make and answer enquiries politely, to use and count money, and so on. Although the best nurseries are obviously better equipped for this sort of approach, and their staff are better trained, progress appears to have been made in quite ordinary establishments. They have more trained staff than in the past, and new ideas about infant education are clearly filtering down.

Such progress is all the more impressive because the status of kindergarten teachers has not risen very much since the days when the majority of staff were kindly but uneducated elderly women. Today, the trained staff are usually called *laoshi*, teacher, as a mark of respect, rather than the familiar address form of *aiyi*, auntie, used in the past. However, their wages are poor, and kindergarten training tends to be taken by those whose grades are not good enough to get into any other college. A friend of mine, urging a nine year old girl to work harder, probably reflected general attitudes when he said,

> You must get higher marks, you must do well. If you write even one wrong character you can lose marks. If you don't do well you won't get into a good higher middle school when you are sixteen.

Then you'll have to train as a kindergarten teacher.
You'll have to get up at six a.m. every morning and
be a kindergarten auntie all your life. How will you
like that? You must work hard and get into a good
school.

Curriculum changes are not always popular with the parents. The national curriculum does not require the children to start to learn to write Chinese in kindergarten. Some kindergartens that did teach writing to the children in the top class in the past have now cut this out or reduced the number of characters taught. The teachers argue that there is no point in cramming them with things which are featured in the first year of the primary school curriculum. The parents are not so sure. While the teachers argue that it will be difficult for the primary teacher to handle a class in which some children can write more than others, parents would be happy to see their own children start out with an advantage.

There is a different attitude to the fostering of artistic talent, at least in the best kindergartens which have the facilities. Children can start the violin as young as three. Those who show an aptitude for this or the ubiquitous piano or for any other instrument are given special coaching. Those who are good at painting or drawing get the same treatment. These little prodigies are always brought out to display their attainments to visitors. In the past, there was more emphasis on collective performances, and these still prevail in ordinary kindergartens.[19]

Moral and ideological education in the kindergarten has changed a great deal in the years since Mao's death. In the past, the children heard words like revolution, socialism, communism, and Chairman Mao's thought all the time. These terms appeared in songs, stories, and teachers' homilies. Significantly, these words now figure only in one small part of the curriculum.

(Children should) learn from the good qualities of the
veterans of the revolution, the heroes and model
figures, and respect and love them.
(and should) love China's Communist Party, love the
Chinese People's Republic and love the People's
Liberation Army.[20]

The section of the curriculum devoted to moral and ideological education is short, compared with sections on "habits of hygienic living," general education, music, and art. Furthermore, little of this section deals with overtly political goals. The children are taught to be modest, unselfish, tidy, and polite. They must learn to distinguish between good and bad, care for their environment, and help one another.

In comparison with the past, labor, *laodong*, occupies only a small part of the curriculum. It is no longer actually called labor nor categorized as ideological and moral education as it once would have been. It differs little from the sort of "work" which would be expected of pupils elsewhere in the world. Children in the small class (three- and four-year-olds) learn to tidy up after themselves and look after their own things. Older children are supposed to serve the collective, for example, by looking after the classroom. Where possible, children are allowed to grow things and look after goldfish, insects, or other small living things.

The Socialization of the Only Child at Primary School

In many ways, the move from kindergarten to primary school is still the biggest step the child takes. Children start primary school when they are seven or often six in the big cities and remain there for six years. In Chinese tradition, seven is the age at which the child can be expected to understand things, *dongshi*. This underlies the tendency within the family to move from indulging children and expecting little of them when they are small to requiring a high standard of good behavior and great diligence as they reach school age. Children are then seen as old enough to take responsibility for their own behavior, and when they fail to live up to that standard, they are punished. Clothes help mark the transition the child is making. Kindergarten children are dressed in riotously bright clothes, and the dresses of little girls tend to be very fussy. Like adults, primary school children have abandoned the uniform blue cotton of Maoist China, but their clothes are still far plainer than those of smaller children. However, an attempt to impose a track suit uniform has been only partially successful. Some parents oppose it on the grounds that it is unsuitable during China's hot summers and cold winters of the north.

Primary classes are large, the atmosphere is formal, and discipline is quite strict. Children are no longer required to sit with their hands clasped behind their backs as they were in the 1970s, but they sit in straight rows, stand up to answer the teacher, and recite much of what they are required to learn in unison. Most parents seem to believe that children need to complete a lot of homework if they are to do well enough at school to succeed in life. They therefore accept the fact that children as young as seven or eight will do two to three hours of work a night. Some teachers complain of pressure from parents to give more homework than the child should be asked to complete. However, if they refuse to give homework, the parents complain that the teachers are lazy. A small minority of parents take a contrary view and complain that the excessive burden of homework deprives the child of time to spend outdoors, engage in leisure pursuits and even sleep. They argue that teachers place too much pressure on the children because they get a bonus if their pupils do well enough on tests. It seems to be accepted and ever expected that parents will help their children with homework. Some parents felt that this put impossible demands on their time in the evening, while others worried that they didn't know enough to help. In Shenyang, I was told of a peasant couple who paid an urban intellectual's family to bring up their son. Apparently, they hoped to expose him to the educational advantages that they themselves were unable to offer. Obviously this was an exceptional case, yet it indicates the high level of anxiety many parents feel about their child's education.

The curriculum dictates that 40 per cent of class hours should be devoted to the study of Chinese (including reading, writing, composition, and speaking). Mastering Chinese characters is of course, time-consuming, and it is also worth recalling that standard Chinese is the home language of a minority. Most children start to speak it for the first time when they attend primary school. In junior classes, the local dialect may be used for some lessons. A further 24 per cent of class hours go to arithmetic. The remaining class hours are absorbed by physical education, music, art, natural science, politics, geography, history, and from the third grade onward, labor (this ranking represents in descending order, the time allocated to the various subjects). Where resources exist, a foreign language is taught.

Like kindergartens, primary schools are now dominated by only children. In 1987, the Fuxue Hutong Primary School in Beijing's Eastern District reported the following figures:

Table 2.1

**Only Children as a Percentage of Pupils in
Fuxue Hutong Primary School**

Class	Implied year of birth	Only children as a percentage of all pupils
6	1975	52.1
5	1976	60.8
4	1977	60.9
3	1978	70.5
2	1979	87.8
1	1980	94.9

In the school as a whole, 70.7 per cent of the 931 children were only children. The high percentage of only children, even in the upper years, is partly the result of the policy of spacing births, in force during the 1970s. This required couples to wait three to five years after a first birth before having a second. Couples whose first child was born in the latter years of the decade were thus caught by the prohibition of having second children, which was initiated at its close. The impressive degree of compliance with population policy indicated by these figures probably reflects a rather high status catchment area. Figures for the Xuanwumen District may be more representative of Beijing as a whole, and these statistics show that in 1986, 43 per cent of primary school children in the district were only children. In the top classes, the proportion fell as low as 20-30 per cent. However, 87 per cent of the children in the first year of primary school had been only children in 1986, and this figure rose to 90 per cent in 1987. Kindergartens give priority to singletons for admission, and their enrollment figures accordingly show an artificially high proportion of only children, whereas figures for only children in primary school give a real indication of the success of the one child policy. It is difficult to know how typical of other urban areas Beijing's response may be, for the capital's population contains a high proportion of officials, teachers, administrators, and others who could be expected to readily comply with the one child demand. On the other hand, its prosperity and importance as a trading center attract private traders, contract workers, and people running family businesses. As such people do not depend on the state for a living, they are not as susceptible to its controls. Furthermore, many have come from areas outside the capital where the limits on family size are less strictly applied. Figures from other big cities seem to indicate that in the first year of primary school, around 90 per cent are usually only children. It is likely that the rate is a little lower in smaller towns.

Primary school teachers make the same positive observations about the only child as do kindergarten teachers. They are more advanced than other children and are quick to learn. Their parents are willing to buy them books and stationery and anything else they need for school. Unlike earlier generations, most of them have their own table, chair and lamp at home, which gives them a suitable homework environment.

Primary school teachers also make the familiar criticisms of the only children, although they observe that children who have spent several years in kindergarten tend to have fewer problems. Only children tend to be self-centered and find it hard to get along with other children. They are careless with property; collections of lost property at school are now said to include books, brand new clothes, and even watches. No one comes to claim them, and when children are brought to look at the items which have been found, they are unable to identify their own possessions.

The children's practical abilities are said to be underdeveloped. They can't peel oranges, fold quilts or even tidy their things, because at home someone does it for them. Teachers notice this most when they take the children away on trips. One said she had showed the children how to wash their clothes and hang them out to dry. Then, they didn't think to collect them, so she brought everything in and told the children to pick out what was theirs. Some of them couldn't even do that. In earlier generations, children were encouraged to do some of their own laundry at home. Now, this custom seems to be dying out. The teachers identified this as yet another manifestation of the spoiled only child, but no doubt it is also related to the increased use of washing machines.

School children are expected to take quite a lot of responsibility for their school. They clean it once a week and are organized so that each class has its own particular job. This work counts as the "labor education" mentioned in the curriculum. The teachers try to give the children the responsibility for organizing and overseeing the work by appointing monitors. Several commented that it was not easy to give boys such jobs because in primary school, girls were more efficient and conscientious. Another difficulty was the interference of family members. One head complained that when the children had outdoor sweeping duties, many grandparents arrived early to fetch them, hoping to get the chance to relieve them of the sweeping. In another school, family members were indignant that the children had been asked to carry coal for the boiler into the school courtyard. Parent craft classes were used to explain the need for children to learn to do ordinary work and children were encouraged to report to their classes what help they had offered at home.

Several teachers remarked that there had always been a certain number of only children in schools, but they had caused no particular problems. They offered the explanation that in the past, only intellectuals had one child and they brought them up sensibly. This reflected a feeling which seemed to be shared by many educated people that the real problems of spoiled children came from families with little education and too much money.

Child Socialization and Moral Panic in Post-Mao China

Is the modern Chinese child a monster? To the outside observer who spends a great deal of time looking at children, the answer must be no. Small children seem to be indulged to a significant degree, much as they have always been. In their family groups, older children seem perhaps a little more assertive than in the past, but most still study hard, are helpful, and accept parental authority easily. Quite a different impression is given by the Chinese press, teachers, and even parents. It is clear that the socialization of the only child has been officially recognized as a major problem, and considerable effort has been expended in an effort to deal with it. Official anxiety has struck a chord in the community. Parents lack confidence about the way they are raising their children and seek out help and advice. Why is child socialization the subject of so much concern both to the government and the ordinary people in China today?

As this chapter has made clear, an important factor is the single child family policy. Couples who have only one child are able to devote more resources and more attention to the infant which inevitably affects his or her development. There has long been an awareness in China that today's children will determine the country's tomorrow. Chairman Mao wanted revolutionary successors. Today's leaders are concerned that children should grow up to be healthy and well educated enough to contribute to China's modernization, but they are also concerned for their moral development. Even though enterprise and individual self-reliance are now encouraged, it is recognized that if society is to function properly, China's future citizens will need some sense of obligation to others as well as a sense of public duty.

The government is also aware of the implications of the greying of the population, itself a consequence of fertility decline. The Chinese are proud of their tradition of caring for the elderly. However, the low life expectancy and large families of the past have combined to produce a population structure dominated by the young, in which the old are a small minority. Adults whose aged parents are still alive to care for, usually have siblings to share the duties, or at least the cost of their care.

For the generation born in the 1980s and 1990s, the care of the old will pose a far bigger problem.[21] Life expectancy in China is now high for a developing country. This, together with the strictness of current population policies, means that the population will age rapidly during the working lives of today's children. The support of the aged would be an immensely expensive burden for the state to take on, and it shows no inclination to do so. Far from extending the system of retirement pensions, to which at present, only state employees are entitled, the government has recently been insisting that pensions should in the future be financed through contributions from either the employer or the worker. With the growth of private enterprise, increasing numbers of urban people will have no pension. The social expectation that anyone with a family will be supported by the children in old age has the legal backing of the marriage law, which explicitly states that both sons and daughters are legally obliged to support their aged parents.[22] The new inheritance law also illustrates the state's preoccupation with the support of the aged.[23] It provides that an heir who has failed to support the deceased when he/she needed help, may forfeit rights to inheritance, while an heir who gives help may receive extra compensation. It also encourages citizens to leave legacies to non-relatives who care for or support them during their lifetime.

Although the single-child family is important, other factors contribute to the public concern about the way today's children are growing up. Confucianism once supplied an ideology that told people how to live, how to organize society, and how to distinguish good from bad. China's modern history produced a crisis of faith in Confucianism. Much of China's educated elite, the very group which had once propagated Confucian doctrine and attempted to live by it, now came to believe that it had to be abandoned if China was to survive in the modern world. Later, after years of uncertainty, Marxism-Leninism seemed for a time to offer an effective alternative ideology. However, the Cultural Revolution began a process of disillusion with Marxism-Leninism which has since gathered pace. In China today, the old certainties are gone. There is a certain residual agreement on the qualities which make a good human being and which should be nurtured in the child. When new developments seem to threaten the survival of those qualities even in children, people are naturally disturbed.

Many of the complaints about today's children reflect changing standards of living and changing values; in other words, they are the product of modernization. The sort of generation gap long familiar in the West has begun to emerge. Parents and grandparents brought up in an era when poverty, scarcity, and ideology combined to impose extreme economy in consumption, feel uneasy at the amount their children now own and at their relaxed attitudes to spending and waste. Yet there is a certain ambivalence here for it is often the same adults who lavish all that they can on their children, buying them more than they really need.

Children are growing up in a new world and are being pushed in quite different directions. At school, they are urged to be frugal and unselfish, but from the television, they learn that to get rich is glorious and that happiness can be achieved through consumption. They are told to serve the collective, yet they can see that good grades in school are the way to please their parents. At home, the only child is the center of family life. Care, attention, material goods, and food are heaped upon them. Such children develop a strong sense of their own importance which school and kindergarten experience can do no more than modify. The children's confident and individualistic behavior and their lack of deference, alarm some adults who see the new type of child as yet one more departure from the moral certainties of the past. This has engendered a sort of moral panic about the "Little Emperors" and "Little Empresses." Like other moral panics, China's anxiety about the younger generation has complex roots and is incomprehensible if taken at face value. Contemporary China's obsessive search for the right way to educate her children reflects the much more general uncertainty with which she now faces the future.

Notes

1. For details on the one child family policy, see E. Croll, D. Davin and P. Kane, editors, *China's One Family Policy* (New York: St. Martins, 1985).

2. See E. Croll, "The Single-child Family in Beijing" and P. Kane, "The Single-child Family Policy in the Cities," in Croll, Davin, and Kane, editors, *China's One Child Family Policy, op. cit.*, pp.190-232, 83-113.

3. I am grateful to the British Academy which financed my research and to the Chinese Academy of Social Sciences, the Liaoning Academy of Sciences and the Sichuan Academy of Sciences for hosting me and to my colleagues in these institutions for their kindness and help.

4. See Deborah Davis Freedman, *Long Lives: Chinese Elderly and the Communist Revolution* (Cambridge: Harvard University, 1983).

5. Interview with the parents of twins, Beijing, September 1987.

6. For some other discussions of the traditions of Chinese socialization and the modern context, see D. Dooley and C. Ridley, *The Making of a Model Citizen in Communist China* (Stanford: Stanford University, Hoover Institution, 1968) and Roberta Martin, "The Socialization of Children in China and on Taiwan: An Analysis of Elementary School Textbooks," *China Quarterly* no.62 (June 1975):242-262.

7. This is above all, true of the *Xiao Jing* (Classic of Filial Piety), translated by James Legge in *Sacred Books of the East, Vol. 3* (Oxford: Clarendon Press, 1879).

8. For some interesting accounts of socialization in this period, see Anita Chan, *Children of Mao* (London: Macmillan, 1985).

9. Mao Zedong, "Talk at a meeting with Chinese students and trainees in Moscow," November 17, 1957. This quotation from the talk appeared in the *Little Red Book* and was thus known to everyone in the Cultural Revolution generation.

10. Unless otherwise stated, the material in this section was gathered in interviews and questionnaires conducted during my research trip to China in 1987.

11. Richard Kraus, *Pianos and Politics in China* (New York: Oxford University Press, 1989). This work provides a fascinating social history of the piano in China.

12. There is an impressive range of such books. The most comprehensive I have seen is the five volume *Jiazhang Shouce* (Parents' Handbook), edited by the Children's Work Committee of the All-China Women's Federation (Beijing: Changzheng Publishing House, 1987).

13. Among the many magazines concerned with family life, *Fumu Bidu* (Indispensable Reading for Parents) is the most clearly targeted at parents. Television directed at parents in Beijing in one week in September 1987, included programs as varied as "How to Make Your Child Intelligent," "Preventing Rickets in Children," "Teaching Children to Play the Electronic Keyboard." Sichuan has a broadcasting correspondence school for parents.

14. Parent education committee of the Gulou District, Fuzhou City, *Jiazhang Xuexiao Cankao Ziliao* (Reference Materials for Parent Craft Classes) (Fuzhou: date unknown). Interviews in Beijing, Shenyang and Chengdu indicated that parent craft classes teach very similar subject matter in all three cities.

15. See, for example, Zhang Xinxin and Sang Ye's story of Li Xiaochang in "Wenping," in *Beijing Ren* (Shanghai: Shanghai Arts Publishing House, 1986):414-421, translated as "Diploma" in W.J.F. Jenner and D. Davin, eds., *Chinese Lives* (New York, Pantheon, 1987):55-61.

16. Orville Schell, *To Get Rich Is Glorious: China in the 1980s* (New York: Pantheon, 1984)

17. State Statistical Bureau, *Zhongguo Tongji Nianjian*, (Statistical Yearbook of China), 1987, p.784 and *China Daily*, November 30, 1989. The 25 per cent claim, made quite frequently in

China, is probably an optimistic claim. See Martin King Whyte and William L. Parish, *Urban Life in Contemporary China* (Chicago: University of Chicago Press, 1984):169, 60. The authors suggest that this claim may be intended to refer only to the proportion of *urban* children in kindergartens, but that percentage still would not correspond to the totals given in the *Statistical Yearbook*. It may be the case that Whyte and Parish look at the entire 0-6 age group and fail to distinguish between *tuoersuo* (nurseries), where enrollment would be considerably lower than 25 per cent of the eligible age group and *youeryuan* (kindergartens), for which the 25 per cent claim is usually made.

18. An English translation of the 1981 curriculum may be found in Rita Liljestrom, et al., *Young Children in China* (London: Multilingual Matters, 1982):243-262.

19. William Kessen, *Childhood in China* (New Haven: Yale University, 1975) contains descriptions of visits to kindergartens in the 1970s.

20. Liljstrom, *Young Children in China, op. cit.* pp. 250-251.

21. See Judith Bannister, *China's Changing Population* (Stanford: Stanford University, 1987), chapter 10.

22. *Zhonghua Renmin Gongheguo Hunyinfa* (The Marriage Law of the People's Republic of China) in *Zhonghua Renmin Gongheguo Zhongyao Falu Xuanbian* (Selected Major Laws of the People's Republic of China) (Shanghai: People's Publishing House, 1986). The English translation was published by the Foreign Languages Press in 1982.

23. *Zhonghua Renmin Gongheguo Jichengfa* (Inheritance Law of the People's Republic of China) in *Zhonghua Renmin Gongheguo Zhongyao Falu (Selected Major Laws of the People's Republic of China)*, (Shanghai: People's Publishing House, 1986).

CHAPTER THREE

THE "CRISIS" IN CHINESE SECONDARY SCHOOLING[1]

by Heidi Ross

Introduction: The World of Fan Shaobao

In 1988 Deng Xiaoping underscored a wide-spread perception that China's schools were in a state of crisis by identifying neglect of education as the gravest policy error of the post-Mao era.[2] Deng's pronouncement served as the epilogue to a decade of appraisals attributing educational failure to the "overly egalitarian" and "irrational" structure of education that emerged during the Cultural Revolution.[3] Ailing schools would henceforth be treated as more than a legacy of inherited bad management. Consequently, and with tragic irony, 1989 was proclaimed the Year of Education in the People's Republic of China.

Secondary education has come under special scrutiny as the most problematic and crisis-prone level of Chinese schooling. This conclusion derives in part from successful reform. The stultifying curricular and pedagogical uniformity of schools during the 1970s has been transformed by remarkable efforts at diversification and local control. The sharp decline in secondary school enrollment that accompanied post-Cultural Revolution policy has been reversed.[4] The economic and political reforms of the open door have led to unprecedented collaboration between Chinese and foreign researchers and between Chinese schools and enterprises.

Unfortunately, invigorated teaching and leadership in predominantly urban centers of excellence are accompanied by persistent shortfalls in educational provision in less-developed rural areas where ninety per cent of secondary schools fail to meet national standards for such basic facilities as chairs, desks, and safe drinking water.[5] A "book drought," brought on by printing costs that have quadrupled since 1984, threatens existing programs.[6] Nearly 29 per cent of Chinese boys and over 36 per cent of Chinese girls come to school malnourished.[7] The deaths of students in condemned school buildings and the deaths of teachers at the hands of irate clients and local thugs make newspaper headlines across the country.[8]

These crisis indicators have directed State Education Commission officers to issue stern admonitions to parents and local officials that "education needs modernization and modernization needs education." Unfortunately, this mantra for national development has exacerbated China's crisis in secondary schooling. Educational modernization has become embodied in a school responsibility system in which increased autonomy and experimentation are overwhelmed by an unending quest for economic efficiency and profit.

The profit-driven school has become necessary as state funding to secondary schools fails to keep up with teacher salaries and material costs. Although Chinese educators have resisted equating educational quality with output measures, the qualitative dimensions of schooling--the nature and worth of what is really taught and learned, to and by whom, have been preempted by economic concerns.[9] Financing formulas designed by local bureaus of education to encourage individual schools to initiate profit-making schemes are remarkably widespread.[10] As a result, school-run services and enterprises currently engage three-quarters of all China's primary and secondary school students.[11]

A principal of a municipal key school in Shanghai reports that he spends one-third of his time "borrowing" local workers for the purpose of managing his school's four workshops that generate almost one-third of his total budget. While he calls efficiency "the most detestable word in an educator's lexicon," he admits to a sense of satisfaction that after 25 per cent of the profit he generates is distributed by the district education bureau to poorer schools, remaining funds can be directed toward improving teachers' bonuses and school facilities.[12] Another administrator of a Shanghai key school calls the removal of a portion of his school's wall so as to "open shop," a painfully ironic symbol of educational reform.[13] He had tried for years to metaphorically tear down walls, enliven classes, engage students in the affairs of the world. Instead, the wall disappeared only when teachers became buyers and sellers. "This is not," the exasperated principal declared, "what a commodity economy should mean." The vision of schools selling their playgrounds to the highest bidder or gouging students with arbitrarily high fees for textbooks, make-up sessions, and school uniforms also infuriates teachers.[14] From their perspectives, students and the purposes of education are corrupted by commodity consciousness (*shangping yizhi*). Students pay more articulate classmates to write their political essays on socialist ethics or sell their lunch for profit.[15] Parents pay students for grades, stuffing the New Year *hongbao* a little thicker when a child brings home high marks. Merit pay schemes honored by national leaders reward teachers not for superior instruction but for the perceived importance of the discipline and the students who are taught.[16] Such "commodification of schooling" not only subverts the educator's obligation to cultivate well-rounded students but disenfranchises concerned colleagues.[17] As efforts to "stream-line the school's organizational structure" lead to the dismissal of out-spoken teachers,[18] slogans exhorting educators to "believe in education, not in money" (*xin jiao buyao xin qian*) seem hypocritical indeed.

Efforts to introduce "competitive mechanisms" into the classroom unintentionally perpetuate perceptions of teachers and students who abhor roles in which they feel trapped and betrayed (*xuesheng yan xue, jiaoshi yan jiao*).[19]   These images are further reinforced by educators who have adopted the vocabulary of crisis that has dominated international discourse on secondary schooling.[20]   Deng Xiaoping's counsel to point education in the "three directions" of modernization, the world, and the future even now justifies this practice of gauging success in increasingly international terms. In an ironically international use of nationalist fervor, principals and deans of Chinese secondary schools quote from *A Nation at Risk* to justify their own sense of uncertainty and loss of mission.[21]

China's media have popularized educational crisis through portraits of confused, self-indulgent adolescents and vacillating, dejected educators. In a television mini-series, "The Teacher's Soul," a frustrated vocational school instructor, Fan Shaobao, painfully discovers that his work is by definition peripheral to the lives of his students.[22] Devastated by self-doubt, Fan attempts in vain to quit his profession, to disentangle himself from the sullen, dispirited students he both loves and despises. In the end of the series, Fan reconciles himself to the shared disappointments and dreams that bind him to his pupils. Precisely because his sentimental journey back to student and profession undercuts the show's radical premise, Fan Shaobao provides a compelling metaphor for the world of Chinese secondary schools. As his name suggests, it is a constrained and impervious world, yet not without unsettling waves of change that have the potential for challenging traditional institutional inertia and individual powerlessness.

The Purpose of Secondary Education: The Contest Between Popularization and Diversification

Two major thrusts in secondary school reform, outlined in the CPC Central Committee's 1985 decision on *Reform of China's Educational Structure*, serve as our starting point for examining the shape of this "crisis" in secondary schooling.[23] The first involves a significant redefinition of basic schooling in China. Linking the success of modernization policies to a skilled workforce, the decision advocates the extension of compulsory education from six years of primary school to three years of junior secondary school for all Chinese children.

Educators have been partially successful at achieving this goal. In large cities, particularly along the east coast, where junior secondary school has been universalized for two decades, as many as 40 per cent of junior secondary school graduates now go on to some form of senior secondary school training. Expectations for universalizing junior secondary schooling in China's least advantaged counties, however, have been scaled back in the face of declining state funds. Local officials, told to expect minimal help from the state, are advised to "use diversity as creatively as possible while improving access to education." Whether local initiative alone will be successful in the 33 per cent of China's counties that have not yet achieved universal primary education is questionable. The national average rate of entrance into China's junior secondary schools hovers just below 70 per cent, placing it 80th among 139 countries and regions of the world. Nearly 7 per cent of the 38,380,000 students who do attend, drop out.[24] Yet, while the task of making possible and desirable for all children the now constitutionally-guaranteed right to a junior secondary school education is daunting,[25] external studies of Chinese schooling express cautious optimism about the likelihood of achieving a nine-year compulsory system without massive increases in material commitment.[26] In addition, the policy of universalized junior secondary schooling has strengthened China's

definition of minimum basic schooling, making its organization and structure of basic knowledge strikingly similar to that in Taiwan.[27]
The 1985 decision's second major assignment for secondary schools was their continued diversification and institutional tracking at the senior secondary level.[28] Vocational schooling was identified in the report as the "weakest link in China's education as a whole," necessitating a closer alignment of formal schooling with the employment options of the majority of Chinese youths. The one-track college-preparatory curriculum, long derided as the pedagogical equivalent of "forcing 1,000 troops and 10,000 horses across a one-plank bridge,"[29] was to be further vocationalized from the 36 per cent at the time of the report's publication to 50 per cent by the end of the decade.[30] China has come close to meeting this goal. 5,807,000 students, or 44.8 per cent of China's 12,970,000 senior secondary school students, attend vocational and technical senior secondary programs.[31] The expanding employment opportunities in major metropolitan centers such as Shanghai have made vocationalization efforts so successful that as many as 60 per cent of senior secondary school students are enrolled in technical-vocational programs.[32]

Despite these figures and five years of marching to the tune of what one Shanghai administrator refers to as "vocationalized diversity," the culture of Chinese secondary schooling can seem pervasive and unchanging. The day begins behind high school walls with the raising of the national flag. Adolescence is secured and defined by the gathering of students into closely-knit homeroom groups (*ban*) for lessons, meals, calisthenics, eye exercises, and labor. The 22-week semester is punctuated by the symbol and sentiment of state and traditional celebration. Young people light lanterns and sweep graves and lose their Young Pioneer scarves and childhood in the ritualized performances of a collective fourteenth birthday. Adult power is distributed in nearly every institution among three interlocked, hierarchical units, consisting of the administration, the CCP (Chinese Communist Party) branch, and the workers union.[33] Teachers construct lesson plans and discuss matters of national import in their departmentally-based teaching and research groups (*jiaoyanzu*). The formal purpose of all this activity is ubiquitously defined by students and teachers as the cultivation of Mao Zedong's morally, physically, and intellectually well-rounded individual.

Nevertheless, diversification and stratification have altered the old portrait of Chinese schooling where students in Beijing, Shanghai, Xian, and Xiamen were reciting the same foreign language passage on the same week of the same semester. Schools are encouraged to cultivate special identities or school climates (*xiaofeng*), which are embodied in unique eight-character exhortations displayed on school walls and entrance ways. Formulaic, centralized control of curriculum and financing is being replaced by local and regional planning. Most importantly, the formal school experience of a particular group of students, teachers and administrators is determined, more than ever since 1949, by its school's ranking in a school hierarchy that runs in descending order of power and privilege from municipal key secondary schools to technical and specialized secondary schools to vocational and regular academic schools. Indeed, a very bleak school climate confronts a seventeen-year-old who defines herself a "sub-student" attending a "nonsense school" in the last category:[34]

> The sight of my school simply depresses me--a grey
> building squeezed like a scapegoat in-between a bright-
> yellow one and a snow-white one. No one in the world
> would like my school. To be in it is my ill fortune.
> Even the teachers feel this way. They are assigned to
> work here, only because they are the losers of a
> competition or victims of fate. In us students they find
> their young counterparts. What do you get when you
> throw big losers and small losers altogether? In class a
> weird expression often shadows our teacher's face--a
> kind of disgust at the kids. We, being what we are,
> seem to have put *them* to shame.

The simultaneous effort to increase access to and stratify educational opportunity underscores how secondary schools in China, like their counterparts around the globe, have become a socially and politically convenient locus for mediating the nation's most deeply-rooted and sensitive social contradictions.[35] Chinese secondary schools must balance the demands for socialist equality and fair play with the requirements of rapid but efficient modernization. Their curricula and teaching methods must support state ideological interests *and* the values of a public whose standards of living and social expectations have become remarkably divergent as a result of market socialism and the open door. In short, China's crisis in secondary schooling is an inevitable consequence of the inability of schools to resolve these competing, sometimes mutually exclusive, social and political demands.

Academic Secondary Schooling: The Incantation
of the Golden Hoop

The utter lack of commitment and esteem evoked by China's self-proclaimed "sub-students" are declared "unbelievable" or "irrational" or "stupid" by privileged, college-preparatory students who appear to be the singularly-directed, exam-bound pupils portrayed in so many studies of Chinese schooling. As winners in primary school they "know that school works." They submit to its confining cycle of study and examination, delightfully described by Shen Baoliang as the incantation of the golden hoop used by Tripitaka in *Journey to the West* to keep Monkey under control.[36]

Municipal and district key schools are particularly adept at lassoing their students' attention and energies. Despite a decade of debate about the social and political consequences of concentrating scarce resources in highly selective institutions, keys continue to exude permanency and assuredness of purpose. They thrive in an era of diversity, buoyed by their ability to provide exceptional teaching and learning in designated areas of expertise (*xue you techang, jiao you tese*). In addition, key schools dominate the creation and distribution of secondary school knowledge. Their best teachers are not only called upon to write and grade national examination test papers, they are publishing researchers who set the terms of secondary school debate through their domination of district education bureau publications. Some keys are affiliated with overseas alumni associations that are the source of prestige and hard currency. Such schools embody China's modernization goal of defining success in relationship to international standards.[37]

"Standards" in the everyday life of Chinese schools means testable subject matter proficiency, of which Chinese, mathematics, and English (or Russian) form the triangular mainstay. Each of these "three fundamental" subjects are taught for six years and together account for well over one-half of the total hours students spend in the classroom.[38] Pupils also participate in physical education and political studies each year of secondary school. Political study, currently undergoing extensive evaluation and reform, has consisted during the past decade of political ideology and morality, the history of social development and dialectical materialism, political and legal knowledge, political philosophy, political economy, and review during the senior year. In addition, students study five years of physics, four years of chemistry and biology, three years of geography and history, and two or three years of art and music. Many schools now teach typing in the second year of junior secondary school and basic computer literacy and programming in the first year of senior secondary school. These courses are gradually being introduced in all academic schools as used equipment, textbooks, and desks from resource-rich keys are distributed by local education bureaus to non-key schools.

Because key schools are successful at shaping this curriculum into a powerful credential, they serve as gatekeepers to elite colleges in China and abroad,[39] perpetuating a "syndrome" of ever-increasing pressure on children to gain admission to the best of the best secondary schools. Applications are on occasion accompanied with family bribes that may involve the donation of thousands of dollars or even a new school car. Exhausted key junior secondary pupils who are but twelve or thirteen express nostalgia for their lost youth. "I've used up all my energy," replied a girl who was asked to justify poor examination results. "There's simply too much pressure, too many tests, too many bossy teachers and critical parents." This student's homeroom teacher nodded sympathetically at her pupil's response. "It's ironic that even though more and more of the city's senior school students can go to college, the pressure's gotten worse. It's like *taiqiquan*--boxing back and forth, back and forth, at shadows between students and the grade, between students and the test."[40]

The State Education Commission and local bureaus of education have attempted to reduce student work-loads by banning excessive examinations, stipulating the number of hours secondary school pupils must sleep each night, restricting homework during winter holidays, and preventing merit pay for instructors who teach solely "to the top" (*yousheng zhongxinhua*).[41] Many charge that while key schools are justified to the public as sources of pedagogical innovation their vision of excellence has in fact become, with a few important exceptions, an intractable obstacle to reform. The principal of one of Shanghai's most prestigious and maverick key schools struggled to reform teaching and assessment policies against tremendous protest from parents, veteran teachers, and university advisors who were loath to see success disturbed. The smugness with which most keys staunchly resist any change that might disrupt their power enrages reformers who consider their incarcerated students convicts of knowledge.[42]

As long as their prestige is conferred by the colleges for whom they train students, most academic secondary schools will offer a pedagogy and curriculum circumscribed by the golden hoop. However, active teaching approaches, the subject of numerous studies for a decade, continue to be developed.[43] Pedagogical reform has received particular attention by seven regional curriculum planning groups which are replacing China's nationally-devised textbooks and teaching outlines.[44] Some academic schools have set language textbooks aside and asked their students to read classical Chinese novels, such as *Water Margin* and *Dream of the Red Mansions*. Foreign language lessons may be based upon foreign folk music or short stories. In both cases, however, national or regional texts are not completely neglected. They are quickly reviewed to insure that students will be successful at answering questions on text-based, unified entrance examinations.

"Co-curricular" activities, which Chinese teachers have begun calling "the second classroom," have also received increased attention. Such reforms may call for nothing less than a comprehensive restructuring of all teaching and school activities so the interests of students provide the core of every formal learning experience. However, some of these activities do not originate from individual student interest but involve significant efforts to shape students in the nation's image. The most elaborate program of this type is the senior secondary student's social practice (*shehui shijian*) experience of military drill, rural labor, and urban sociology.[45]

The most influential reform in academic or regular secondary schooling is the implementation of competency tests.   Seeing pedagogical experimentation doomed to failure if it is perceived to lower a student's chances to advance up the academic ladder, educators have attempted to reshape the golden hoop. No longer justified as an admittedly narrow but essentially meritocratic sorting procedure, the college entrance examination is criticized as an overly-centralized, pressure-laden, docility-provoking, and exclusionary device that effectively "colonizes" secondary education. For example, students in the last two years of senior secondary school have been divided during most of the past decade into humanities and science tracks, paralleling the two specialties tested by the entrance examination.   Humanities students studied foreign languages, history, and geography, while science students concentrated their efforts upon physics, chemistry and biology. This early specialization has been blamed for a premature narrowing of intellectual pursuit and is being phased out nationally.   Competency examinations in each subject are advocated as a more well-rounded assessment of all students' achievements as well as a means to counter the pressure on schools to pretzel their teaching around the college entrance examination.

The   State   Education   Commission   has   honored   the implementation of Shanghai's senior secondary competency examinations (*huikao*) as a "pioneering" effort in test reform.[46] Municipal competency examinations, fully implemented since 1988, are credited with improved educational quality and balanced attention to the teaching of both humanities and sciences. While it is still unclear how well such reforms will work throughout China, the system is touted nationwide and is currently being used in some form in the provinces of Hunan, Zhejiang, Guangxi, Hainan, and Guangdong.

In the Shanghai system, a total of nine competency examinations are given during the three senior secondary school years. Examinations are based on information contained in full-day regular secondary school teaching guidelines and are normally taken during the final year a particular subject is studied.[47] Senior one students take one examination in history. Senior two students sit for examinations in Chinese, geography, and biology. Senior three students have by far the most grueling schedule of examinations in politics, mathematics, foreign languages, physics, and chemistry. Each examination is graded on a 100-point scale and students receive grades curved from "A" to "E."[48] Students throughout the municipality take each test at the same time, and results become a matter of public record. Students who pass all nine classes receive a "Shanghai Senior Secondary School Competency Certificate", and are eligible for applying to take the college entrance examination.[49]

As we have seen, a major justification for competency tests is that they require students to do well in all subjects not just those included in the college entrance examination. Prior to the implementation of competency tests, college entrance examinations consisted of the "three fundamental" subjects--Chinese, mathematics and English--and politics for all students in addition to geography and history for humanities students and physics, chemistry, and biology for students specializing in science, engineering, agriculture or medicine. Shanghai's students are now evaluated on the basis of their competency test results, their performance in elective classes and extracurricular activities, any awards they have received, as well as their entrance examination scores in four subjects which include Chinese, mathematics and English (or another foreign language), and either politics, history, geography, physics, chemistry, or biology.[50] Encouraged by the results of Shanghai's experiment, the State Education Commission hopes to implement by 1993 a national entrance examination consisting of Chinese, mathematics and two subjects of the student's choice.

The additional hope that competency testing would reduce student examination pressures remains unfulfilled. In fact, officials and teachers agree that three years of constant testing has generated ever greater obsession with high marks.[51]   Key school students are not only expected to pass but to do so with flying colors.   A pupil in one Shanghai municipal key school was nicknamed by her classmates "Doctor Donald Duck" because of the three D's she received on her competency examinations that caused the panicked girl to run hundreds of miles away from home.

Extreme reactions to the pressures of testing are particularly common in key schools whose students have the most to gain from the system.   A direct entrance (*zhisheng*) system allows a tiny number of such students who achieve superior examination results to enrol directly in a designated post-secondary institution without sitting for the college entrance examination.[52]   Key universities allot several positions (*minge*) to appropriate key secondary schools, and students to fill them are normally selected by a school administrator and the student's homeroom teacher in consultation with the student and his or her parents.   This process is extremely competitive except for students who choose to enter institutions, such as normal colleges and universities, which have trouble attracting highly-qualified students.   Seventy per cent of Shanghai Normal University's class of 1991 took no college entrance examination.

Because fortunate *zhisheng* students do not receive their test results until late spring, they are spared from only two months of anxious study.   They spend their final year with the rest of their classmates pouring over last year's competency and college entrance examination questions, which are paradoxically published in handbooks designed to alleviate the psychological pressure of testing.[53]

That benefit can not be obtained as long as students are confronted by the complex cost-benefit analyses entailed by filling out their applications for the college entrance examination.   Students must not only rank their choice of college and major but whether they wish to be considered as contract or fee-paying students.   During the last five years the system for both admitting students into tertiary institutions and assigning them jobs upon graduation has undergone tremendous reform, permitting both increased choice and the possibility of unemployment upon graduation.   Recent reassertion of political control of education, coupled with the rejection of students by numerous employers,[54] has created an environment of insecurity that reaches down to junior secondary school students.   Should they focus on sciences because their chances of college acceptance might be greater?[55]   Should they risk applying for positions in "hot" or politically controversial specializations such as international economics and foreign languages?   Or should they play it safe and take advantage of the monetary incentives such as interest-free loans and full tuition used to attract students into unpopular majors such as teaching, agriculture and geology?[56]

Competency tests may eventually free secondary schools from some of the top-down control that both constrains and legitimates their heavily-academic curricula. They may also help teachers clarify their educational goals and enliven discussions about the purposes of secondary schooling. It is unlikely, however, that they will soon remove from students the incantation of the golden hoop, that cycle of fever and despair symptomatic of what educators in Taiwan call the "disease" of students who are in their last years of junior and senior secondary schooling (*guosanzheng, gaosanzheng*).

Vocational and Technical Education: Integrating the Worlds of Work and School

The 5,800,000 students in China's increasingly diversified and decentralized vocational and technical senior secondary education programs (VTE) experience the pressures of achievement and possible failure very differently. Although they begin their senior secondary school experiences, like their regular school counterparts, as the "semi-finished products" of a nine-year general education program," they end it "polished into specialized personnel."[57] They take a different set of examinations and are barred from both the pain and the privilege of taking the college entrance examination.[58]

Full-time senior secondary school programs are commonly classified into specialized technical and teacher-training schools, technical and pre-service skilled worker schools, and, the largest sector, vocational and agricultural schools.[59] The most prestigious VTE programs are offered by over 4,000 specialized schools that train middle-level technical personnel and kindergarten and primary school teachers.[60] These institutions, developed in the mid-1950s and directed by technical ministries as well as the State Education Commission, are managed directly by education, technical, and labor bureaus at the local, district, county, and provincial levels. Entering students are increasingly junior secondary school graduates who are selected through competitive state examinations administered by bureaus of higher education. Programs of study, which generally last for four years, include ten broad specializations: architectural, chemical, and materials engineering and communications (*gongke xuexiao*); agriculture, forestry, and horticulture (*nonglin xuexiao*); finance, business and banking (caijing); hygiene and nursing (*weisheng*); the fine arts (*yishu*); politics and law enforcement (*zhengfa*); physical education (*tiyu*); teacher-training (*shifan*); in-service, vocational training for adults (*zhigong zhuanye*); and a miscellaneous category that includes everything from the training of Buddhist monks and nuns to flight attendants.[61]

Less prestigious than specialized schools, technical schools are run by education bureaus and industrial units and train technicians for a variety of positions in steel, textile, petroleum, pharmaceutical, agricultural and botanical enterprises, as well as middle-level workers in law, finance, health, art and physical culture.[62]   These primarily three-year institutions recruit junior middle school graduates who are assigned to them by labor and personnel bureaus on the basis of entrance examination results and preferred choice of specialty.[63]   They are more successful than specialized schools in forging close and flexible ties with specific enterprises, because their enrollment and curriculum are not controlled by national ministries. They share with specialized schools, however, the advantage of high demand since students receive employment upon graduation.

Key and non-key vocational and agricultural schools and classes,[64] normally managed at the district and county level,[65] have offered the least prestigious VTE programs because their graduates have not enjoyed secure employment opportunities and because graduates from these three-year programs are classified as skilled workers rather than technicians.   In-coming students are selected by entrance examinations prepared and administered by local bureaus of education. School curricula, which vary widely from school to school and are hampered by a shortage of teaching materials, follow guidelines written by the State Education Commission and offer both general and vocational training.[66]

Vocational and agricultural schools rival regular academic schools with poor reputations as the last chance for students who hope to pursue senior secondary schooling and have the highest levels of dropouts, reaching 8.8 per cent.[67]   Government pronouncements involving the rapid "vocationalization of senior secondary schooling" suggest the difficulties, especially during the first half of the 1980s, in making these schools legitimate alternatives to more prestigious academic or technical institutions.   Regulations for middle school students reminded students to "cherish one's own vocations by mastering theoretical knowledge and technical skills."[68]

Vocational and agricultural key schools in relatively developed regions of China have apparently managed to compensate for the lack of formal employment mechanisms by powerful local contacts with surrounding enterprises and economic demands for skilled labor. Job security in turn has raised the confidence of the public in such schools, which are attracting increasingly well-trained junior high school graduates. While the informality and ad-hoc nature of such schools may have generated public skepticism about their utilitarian value in the past, such flexibility is enhancing their potential for tailoring training to the needs of local economies in ways that may increase their popularity.[69] Precisely because vocational schools have been forced to work so hard to recruit students, they have been most active at forging linkages to local enterprises.

Yet, serious problems continue to obstruct the successful implementation of secondary vocational training throughout much of China. Vocational programs in agriculture and forestry have yet to overcome the perception that they offer a "second-class" education for the least qualified pupils.[70] In addition, while continued decentralization of funding, bottom-up planning, and the creation of linkages to local enterprises may provide "large-scale, flexible, and relatively low cost" vocational training attractive to Chinese youths, this seems to be occurring primarily in China's more developed regions.[71] Here, positions in non-key regular senior secondary schools have gone begging while specialized and technical institutions are swamped with student applications. Apparently, students assume either that their training will fail to prepare them well enough to pass the college entrance examinations, that a tertiary education is irrelevant to financial security, or that an expensive college education will not be able to gain them employment commensurate with their training or interests.[72] In some areas, the regular senior secondary school has become so unpopular that educators express fear that college-preparatory programs will "wither away."[73]

VTE programs are also nearly twice as expensive to operate per pupil as traditional general senior secondary schools[74] and have been plagued by excessively narrow yet time-consuming and overly-centralized curricula and a debilitating shortage of trained teachers. In 1988, for example, 238 students graduated from vocational-technical normal schools in Hubei Province. Of the 199 students for whom data was available only 75 (36 per cent) became teachers in vocational schools. Of the 82 1988 graduates of the province's one Agricultural College Education Department, only 14 became teachers. The remaining students took posts in various governmental departments and stations, companies or factories.   Less than one qualified teacher is available for each of the province's 360 vocational school specialized classes, instead of the 2 or 3 required by the State Education Commission.[75]

Finally, what senior secondary school students in such institutions are and should be learning is fraught with conflict and debate.   Some educators believe that modernization can be most effectively supported by a completely vocationalized senior secondary school system.   Others argue that vocational programs are inherently discriminatory and divert the secondary school from its major task of providing a basic equal education to all students, regardless of their future careers.[76]   Still others advocate the elimination of institutional streaming in favor of a comprehensive high school model.[77]   The scope of such debate leaves numerous educators with the impression that the "structure of VTE in China is in a state of chaos."[78]

Diversity and Disparity in Access to Secondary Schooling

The impact of China's policy of school diversification on equality of educational opportunity has been complex and contradictory. Government pronouncements that diversification "does not advocate everyone advancing to the next level, but encourages the development of everyone's talents,"[79] reflect ambivalence regarding how individual and social needs should be balanced in the process.

Studies indicate that regional disparities in access to general, vocational, agricultural, technical, and specialized secondary schooling have decreased during most of the past decade, while stratification of secondary school training within many regions has increased.[80] Likewise, at the same time junior secondary school attendance has expanded to meet the compulsory schooling law, dropout rates have risen in some schools to nearly 20 per cent, primarily, although not exclusively, in prosperous coastal regions where from 10-20 per cent of employees in rural enterprises are under sixteen years of age.[81]   The poorest of China's counties are so behind in secondary school provision that the dropout problem is hardly yet an issue.   Social class background, coupled with the local economy in which a school is situated, is crucial to explanations of whether particular groups of students attend junior and senior secondary schools.[82]   Yet the identification of a pupil's father as cadre, intellectual, or peasant alone fails to help us understand whether a student might attend a key, general, or agricultural secondary school. Conflicting responses to surveys suggest that parents and students weigh carefully and in unpredictable ways the benefits of participating in various levels of secondary schooling.

Keeping in mind the caution that studies of participation in Chinese secondary schooling belie simple generalizations regarding discrimination, we can say with assurance that policies advocating secondary school diversification, efficiency, and stratification have had unintentionally damaging consequences for educational participation among rural youths and girls. The problems faced by secondary schooling in less-developed regions of China have recently gained nation-wide attention with the implementation of China's prairie fire program, an effort to infuse educational excellence into rural school programs. Overcoming the negative consequences for female students of equating educational effectiveness with "efficient" use of resources, however, has yet to be championed by a national campaign.

The Prairie Fire Program: Educational Excellence for Rural Schools

3.8 per cent of China's rural population had attained a senior secondary school cultural level by 1987, a proportion identical to the number of urban Chinese who had attained a college education. Official illiteracy rates of rural youths between the ages of twelve and nineteen were three times the level of their urban peers.[83] While such figures might well make the case that schooling in rural China is in desperately short supply, the problems of rural schooling, in fact, have been boiled down to one epigram that has come to stand for China's educational crisis: formal schooling is useless (*dushu wuyong*).

The perception that rural schooling is a meaningless route to a life of agrarian poverty (*chule xiaomen, jinle nung men, zhifu wu men*) has been aggravated by the production responsibility system and the failure of local funding initiatives and curricular reform to address the economic conditions of rural household enterprises.[84] The State

Education Commission has attempted to redress these problems through a nationwide rural development program called "prairie fire."[85]   Alluding to Mao Zedong's philosophy of grass-roots social change ("a single spark can start a prairie fire"), prairie fire centers are rather like "a thousand points of light" for the countryside, designed to train scientific and technical personnel and thereby improve the spiritual and material culture of rural areas.

The implementation of such centers since 1988 has inspired a number of innovative secondary school programs suited to diverse local economies.   Shanghai municipality has launched a three-stage program for the development of vocational and technical education especially suited to its rural townships.   Ten demonstration townships (*shifanxiang*) with twenty to thirty demonstration schools form the nucleus of the experiment.   Educational programs developed in these institutions are eventually to be expanded to 150 schools, and finally to all of the municipality's 234 rural villages and towns.[86]   In Guangdong's Xinhui County linkages between schools and local enterprises have led to significant reform of school administration.   The school principal acts as general manager; a vice principal, with the help of a dean, is responsible for academic affairs; a second dean is in charge of production, in cooperation with the company's manager; and a third dean acts as the school's general affairs officer.   In regions such as Jilin, where local economic conditions and educational levels are substantially lower than in Shanghai or Guangdong, prairie fire programs focus upon basic literacy.   In Hebei Province, prairie fire centers are being used to support in-service training programs that are supposed to transform the status of rural teachers from "Mr. Poverty to New Sage."[87]

Prairie fire projects around the country are designed to encourage local schools to "seek facts, seek liveliness, seek high standards" (*qiu shi, qiu huo, qiu gao*).   While this aim has encouraged effective collaboration between urban and rural educational initiatives, it has not served to redistribute educational capital, now as in the past located in primarily urban centers where "the typical Chinese industrial and political leader of the future will have grown up in an intellectual or cadre family, gone to one of the best primary and secondary schools, and from there directly to the university."[88]

Gender and Chinese Secondary Schooling

Exploring the connections between Chinese schooling and gender defined here as the ways in which a particular culture (through its parents, teachers and students) give meaning to biological difference] is complicated because, on the one hand, so much seems so familiar. Schooling in China is central, as is true worldwide, to the social construction of concepts of intelligence, identity, and success. Women in China have struggled valiantly and often in vain to embrace these concepts as competing cultural demands, specifically those involving interpersonal and family obligations, are separated from and discounted in dominant images of excellence.[89]

On the other hand, the term "gender" (*xingbie*) in Chinese usually refers solely to biological difference. Thus, examinations by Chinese educators of the relationship between gender and academic achievement commonly begin with the assumption that "the special needs of girls" distinguish female education from an established (male) norm. Because Chinese educators do not adopt what many of their North American counterparts identify as "feminist" perspectives on schooling, the reader is reminded that they would neither necessarily agree with nor find relevant the following discussion, which assumes that gender is a political, socially-constructed category of analysis.

Definitions of educational excellence in China are often, if unintentionally, based upon assumptions about human development and learning that work against female students. The prevalent perception of Chinese teachers that many girls fail to achieve excellence in higher levels of schooling, including senior secondary school, nicely illustrates this pattern of biologically-determined gender discrimination.

Sociable and nurturing "by nature," a girl is thought to excel in the primary school grades where verbal skills honed through early social interaction are rewarded. A female student's descriptive capabilities enhance her ability to memorize basic information, in short, to be a good student. However, being a good student becomes equated with getting good grades (to please the teacher) rather than understanding (to please themselves). Thus, a girl's capacity to think logically and abstractly remains underdeveloped. Finally, her propensity to care for others rather than herself comes to an inevitable fruition during puberty. Bound by her physiology to a holistic, "unfocused" view of the world, a girl is turned away from the intellectual and leadership arena of males.

Two lessons from recently-published sex education materials for secondary school pupils (discussed below) reflect the ways in which girls are seen to behave "naturally."[90] The first, "Inferiority complex--the defeat of adolescent girls," sends an oddly contradictory message about a female junior secondary school graduate who, it is implied, overestimates her intellectual abilities, applies only to one key senior secondary school, fails to get in, and winds up in a vocational school.[91] Her fall from grace fills her with self-doubt and envy. Her male classmates who never excelled in junior school are now in key senior secondary schools, destined to attend college and obtain an opportunity to study abroad. Left behind, she is only able to catch the smile of clerks. Accepting her fate, she gets involved with "Little Tan" (the equivalent of a beach bum) at a swimming pool and lets her school work slide. The story ends with the girl twice damned. First her arrogant over-confidence, then her petty inferiority complex dash a promising future. The story sounds the warning that this girl should swallow her pride and take her new "vocation" seriously.

In a chapter of a widely-used sex education textbook entitled "Happily Accept your Sex," students are told to properly understand the "natural" differences between boys and girls that lead boys to be drawn to the abstract, girls to the descriptive.[92] Boys are analytical, logical, and spatial; girls are sensitive, imaginative, people oriented. Despite such characterizations, students are told their development is equal, that what students must do in developing their identities and strengths is to help each other. Subtle messages refute this bid for equity, however. Asserting that what boys can do, "most" girls can do, the author puts forward the guideline that the dominant value for males is strength, while for females nurturing gentleness (*nan gang nu rou*) is the ideal. Quoting Marx and alluding to Chinese tradition, the author contends that both nurturing female and powerful male are necessary for human completeness. Reading selections admonishing boys to define identity in terms of heroic strength and girls to define beauty as both physical and spiritual reaffirm these distinctions.

Chinese educators attempt to refute the pervasive logic of such lessons not by denying its validity, which could be done by a review of entrance examination results,[93] but rather by encouraging female pupils, "What boys can do girls can do" (*nan tongxue keyi zuodao de, nu tongxue ye keyi zuodao*). Ironically, teachers reinforce the message that areas of achievement are biologically fixed with their own pedagogy of nurturing female strengths and overcoming female weaknesses (*yang qi suo chang, bu qi suo duan*).[94] Specialized nursing and normal schools, "naturally" the domain of young female professionals, do just that by promoting the "four selves of female education" (*funu sizi jiaoyu*): self-respect (*sizun*) or self-love (*ziai*), self-confidence (*zixin*), independence (*zili*), and strength (*ziqiang*). In fact, such slogans do little to remove the powerful obstacles faced by female students in their efforts to continue study or begin a career. Efforts at maximizing productive efficiency in the home, at school and in the work place have coupled with long-standing perceptions of female talent and a backlash against the Cultural Revolution model of the strong, "unfeminine" woman to reinforce discriminatory practices in educational entrance requirements and employment requirements.[95] Such discrimination is perpetuated by school administrators who tolerate disproportionate enrollment of males in senior secondary schools and colleges, because work units consider women inefficient (because of their family obligations) and therefore undesirable workers. Training women for positions reserved for their male classmates would not only exacerbate educational inefficiency but mislead female students about their future options.

This message is received by girls barely into their teens. Their difficulties in entering schools and finding and retaining employment steer them toward "safe, feminine" paths. This is not to suggest that their teachers do not recognize how female students respond to schooling increasingly stratified by material resources and educational purpose. However, because they lack a political vocabulary for articulating how a decade of economic and educational reforms based on efficient management of resources have met the aspirations of women and men inequitably, they rarely challenge views of adolescent development that demand that female students achieve higher scores before being accepted into secondary and tertiary institutions. Instead, they blame the under-representation of girls in rural secondary schools or the fact that 80 per cent of China's seven million school dropouts are girls, on a vague notion of "feudal" influences or a lack of respect for education in general.[96]

Moral Education and the Open Door:
Redefining Chinese Adolescence

Adolescence is a concept, like gender, that varies greatly from culture to culture.[97] Despite differences in how the life stages of individuals are socially and politically construed and constructed, Chinese educators agree that puberty, called in Chinese the spring of youth (*qingqunqi*), is a universal touchstone of the human experience.[98] While Chinese educators reject that adolescence is a period of crisis (*weijiqi*)[99], some even waxing sentimentally about an intellectual, psychological, and physical golden age (*huangjin shidai*),[100] practicing teachers eschew idealized versions of youth.

How teachers view their own role as moral educator in this context reflects how socially constructed a concept adolescence is. Teachers who experienced the Cultural Revolution as children or youths, members of China's "modern" generation, are often sympathetic to the concerns of their students, even envious of their precocious abilities "to see through the system." An earlier generation, brought up or educated in the heady days of the 1950s, are perplexed or even angered by a "younger" or "post-modern" generation that refuses to bow to a collective will. These veteran teachers, themselves likened in educational literature to flowers that grew at the treeline, hardy, capable of withstanding hardship, see their naughty, conscience-free charges as greenhouse plants, "pearls in the palm," or little emperors and empresses, polished, pampered, demanding.[101]

Both these generations of teachers express dismay at what they label the "4-2-1" consequences of China's one-child family policy, that is, the financial and psychological resources of four grandparents and two parents focused upon the needs and desires of one arrogant and spoiled child.[102] They also acknowledge that despite the intrusive mechanisms at their disposal for insuring student alignment with the reified knowledge of the school and society, controlling adolescence has become increasingly difficult as alternate paths to social advancement undercut the school's ability to direct socialization. Except, perhaps, in prestigious key and technical schools where academic success on adult terms still holds out clear rewards, teachers must compete with an influx of foreign ideas, a privatization of values, and a diversifying economy to capture their students' attentions. They understand that just as the secondary school must simultaneously forge socialist community and divide a workforce, it must also resolve tensions between the social and economic pressures of diversity and the political demand for ideological conformity.   In short, teachers are the "front-line" professionals called upon to face the question of Chinese adolescence and, by extension, of China's crisis in values head on.   This unenviable charge of charting a moral course for a commodity culture is predefined and handed down to schools and teachers by the State Education Commission.   New rules of conduct (*richang xingwei guifan*) issued for secondary school students in 1988 provide a typical example.[103]   These forty regulations are divided into five sections emphasizing self-respect and bearing, friendship and courtesy, respect for order and diligent study, frugality and filial respect, and a sense of socialist ethics and self-discipline.   They caution students to treat foreigners and country folk with respect, and advise them that appropriate dress and hairstyle include no long hair for boys and no perms, make-up, or high heels for girls.   Smoking, drinking, cursing, littering, gambling, jay-walking, praying to false gods, reading other peoples' diaries and mail are out, while honesty, decorum in museums and before state symbols, conservation of water and electricity, speaking *putonghua*, and respecting the special concerns of women, the elderly, and the infirm are in.   A videocassette for middle school students is even available for those who need reminders.

Programs designed to help teachers make these rules "live in the lives of students" also derive from the state.   A "four haves" movement to accompany the new regulations has been developed for teachers to assist students define socialist ethics in terms of ideals (*lixiang*), morality (*daode*), culture (*wenhua*), and discipline(*jilu*).   While such programs are offered as assistance, they are publicized with criticisms that schools and teachers have neglected moral training, according it at most lip service and at worst, particularly during the rush of examinations, no consideration at all.[104]   Teachers are chastised for their "mistaken perspective" that moral training is only feasible when the atmosphere in society is first conducive to it.   The distance teachers must cover between the reality of teaching and national policy is reflected in their wry comments about the futility of the journey. "The day Mr. Business entered the school, was the day Mr. Morality came to grief," they complain.   "Lei Feng has emigrated."[105]

A change in the way secondary schools are accommodating to the concerns and desires of their students is reflected in the increasingly important connection in the formal school curriculum between morality and puberty.   While North Americans may find puberty in China "heavily masked"[106] by cultural and social mores, Chinese educators and parents talk regularly about the physiological changes and quest for

independence (*nao duli*) of adolescents.   In addition, discussions about
moral education, by both teachers and researchers, have been grounded
not in politics but in human development and psychology.[107]   Events
since the summer of 1989 notwithstanding, explicit socialization in
Chinese schools has become increasingly "psychologized."

The introduction of sex education in junior and senior
secondary school is the clearest indicator of this trend.[108]   Supporters
of sex education, euphemistically called puberty education (*qingqunqi
jiaoyu*), claim that information about sexual development is crucial for
the healthy development of children, particularly in an increasingly
complex and urban society.   The State Education Commission's position
is that sex education promotes a healthy spiritual civilization by
challenging both feudal traditions that treat sexuality as a closed topic
and western ones that promote sexual openness, identity confusion, and
teenage pregnancy.[109]

The lack of support for such programs among parents is
indicated by the enlistment of the popular media in promoting the
necessity of sex education.   Sometimes such efforts are indirectly
related to the school curriculum as in the case of the most recent
justification for sex education--AIDS.[110]   Most media support, however,
complements formal school programs.   In the summer of 1989,
Shanghai Television, under the direction of the municipality's
Committee on the Protection of Youth, aired public service
announcements showing an all-female class of junior secondary school
students listening solemnly as a teacher explained two charts of the
human reproductive systems.   No words were audible over the soft
music which played in the background.   Beijing has even initiated a
"reveal your heart" hotline (*zhixin dianhua*) designed to assist confused
students.

Formal sex education is normally incorporated into junior and
senior secondary school biology as biology and hygiene education
(*shengli weisheng jiaoyu*).   However, healthy sexual development is
understood as a comprehensive process that must be the on-going
concern of all political studies and homeroom teachers.   A vice-
principal of an all-female secondary school explained that the content
of sex-education is:

> wide-ranging and encompasses all aspects of a
> student's physical development, hygiene, morality, and
> interpersonal relations, with a special emphasis on
> developing an understanding of the difference between
> friendship and premature romantic attachments
> (*zaolian*).   Students must understand how correct

political thinking is linked to sexual matters. At our school this is especially important. Parents want to keep their girls safe, as well as well-educated.

A certain irony is apparent in these parents' fears when placed in juxtaposition with the preface of their daughters' sex education textbook, which encourages them to "be your own master."[111] Girls, in particular, are told that the feudal adage of equating ignorance with purity is a tactic of oppression. Several of their lessons depict a gritty world of pain and suffering. Daughters are physically abused by parents, seduced by scoundrels and material wealth, spiritually polluted by pornography.

Most of the text, however, emphasizes the dangers of early sexual relationships and romantic attachments. In sentimental stories such as "*After Receiving the Love Letter*" students are depicted as half-adult, half-child (*chengren you buchengren*). The heroine of "*Love Letter*," Little Wang, is an academically talented girl (*nu caizi*) who receives a love letter from the boy next door. For the first time in her life she cannot sleep. Nonplussed, she confides in her homeroom teacher who tells her the story of a gifted young woman whose chances at entering college were destroyed by a ruffian who wooed and then left her. Wang considers this story and agrees with her teacher that she is young and needs to study hard. Clearly expecting this answer, the teacher softens, advising Wang that the boy next door is pure of heart. Wang must write him a letter of friendship, letting him down without hurting his feelings. Wang does so, pledging to treasure his friendship on the long road ahead. "Let's bask in the light of youth," she writes, "and go down the road of knowledge together as friends."

The gap between these formal school lessons and the popular (sometimes international) culture into which Chinese pupils and their youngest teachers are participating is widening. At the same time the forty regulations of behavior prohibit students from frequenting nightclubs and listening to suggestive music, Shanghai television airs a prime time special entitled "*Songs of Youth*" (*qingqun geshou*) in which local secondary school students sing love songs on a stage made up to look like a bar.[112] The program's perky, young hosts would have been (with different costumes) at home on the set of MTV. Teachers now append to the "three merits" of all-round education the fourth merit of beauty (*mei*), implying a new sensibility for the 90s, or as one veteran teacher of mathematics put it, "simply the ability to choose proper entertainment when you see it." That young people have such choices illustrates the contradictory values Chinese secondary schools must mediate as well as the increasingly difficult task of their administrators to control the values of China's younger generations.

Conclusion: A Reevaluation of Crisis for the 1990s

Far from the moral vacuum they are currently feared of becoming, Chinese secondary schools are contested terrains where competing values lay claims to the allegiance of China's future "thinking generation." On the one hand, the state will continue to orchestrate programs for schools that urge pupils to study Lei Feng[113] or his counterparts for the 90s, such as the currently celebrated fourteen year-old martyr, Lai Ning, who died fighting a forest fire in Sichuan Province.[114] Educators will continue to negotiate between symbols of ideological rectitude and the pressures to develop a pedagogy appropriate to an era of the open door.

In the summer of 1989, officials at the Shanghai Education Bureau identified three major problems for secondary education. The first two, financial insecurity and shortages of qualified, motivated teachers were said to hinge on the third, encouraging the young to consider the teaching profession as a future career. "The issue is larger than money. We have no educational successors. Young people see the sacrifices their teachers have to make and shake their heads, 'There's no way I will become a teacher.'" This demoralization of the educational profession was described as a pervasive institutional malaise, a spiritual problem. We can say it has arisen as numerous economic and social forces converge, but it pervades everything--the hope for curricular reform, for teacher training reform, for respect of vocational knowledge, for a live curriculum, not a dead one. How we counteract this avalanche will be the legacy we pass to the next generation.

Envisaging a secondary school system that can forge a socially non-threatening plurality of excellence plagues young teachers who, like Fan Shaobao, turn readily to a vocabulary of despair. The irony is that at the very moment they have lost the power and the confidence to define and influence educational success, they have been placed more squarely in the position of mediating China's most sensitive social contradictions.

On May 18, 1989, senior secondary students at a prestigious key school in Shanghai received notice that three student hunger strikers at Beijing Normal University had died. The students, angry and upset, wore white flowers and black arm bands. After consultation with a delegation from another key school in the district, the students made up their minds to join thousands of college students in the city's streets in protest. They organized their homeroom monitors to approach the school administration for approval of their plan, expecting (and getting) an uphill battle against both a municipal announcement banning secondary school students from participation in street demonstrations as well as their parents, some of whom had warned both their children and the school to stay clear of trouble.

It is to the credit of these pupils *and* their teachers and leaders that after long deliberations the school's senior secondary students were allowed to protest on several conditions.[115] While students were asked to discard their black armbands and white flowers and throw away their "give us back our students" posters in the absence of any substantiated report that hunger strikers in Beijing had died, they were allowed to proceed with their plans to march to Shanghai's People's Square. A statement articulating why the students felt so compelled to demonstrate as well as a list of slogans would have to be provided to school authorities. Explained one administrator, "The school could not support empty activism, the students out there yelling whatever came into their heads."

In the end, the students decided their feelings came down to their love of China. Hadn't they been told by their teachers to look beyond their own petty concerns, to take their duties as citizens seriously? Gratified, if dismayed, that their students could express their beliefs so independently and with such fearless initiative, the school administration defied both municipal and parental concern and approved the students' plans. Students were accompanied on their march by homeroom teachers and the school's chief administrators who stopped short of giving official approval to the students' actions but felt obliged to lend, quite literally, their moral support.

The consequences of the students' demonstration symbolizes the dilemma Chinese educators face in doing right by their pupils. Independent thinking is a pedagogical aim that the government encourages through its rhetoric. The educators who take it seriously in practice are now in the uncomfortable position of questioning the wisdom of such commitment. Teachers who decry the impact of commodity consciousness on learning and support their students' sincere and articulate engagement in politics are ironically blamed for not establishing a set of behavioral ethics to counteract the dark side of a commodity economy and an open door. In short, such schools and their teachers have become both convenient scapegoats and solutions for China's cultural crisis.

Notes

1. Increased diversification and local control of secondary schools have resulted in a complex school nomenclature. Secondary schooling in China is typically divided into two levels, junior and senior secondary school. Although experiments throughout the country offer alternative twelve-year school structures (including 4-4-4, 7-5 and 5-4-3 programs), junior secondary schools commonly offer three years of training and enroll eleven-or twelve year-old students who have completed five or six years of primary schooling. General academic senior secondary schools and senior secondary schools that offer vocational, specialized, technical and teacher training, generally recruit junior middle school graduates who are fifteen or sixteen years old. Secondary schools include general full-time academic junior and senior secondary schools, specialized secondary and normal schools (*zhongzhuan*), worker training schools, agricultural secondary schools, and vocational secondary schools. As a result of a recent bulge in the primary school population, secondary schools in metropolitan regions temporarily house preparatory junior secondary school sixth-grade classes (*chuzhong yubeiban*), for which Chinese, mathematics, and English examinations have been designed to select socially and academically mature students.

2. Educational spending as a percentage of China's total national budget declined during the second half of the 1980s. China devotes a smaller share of its GNP to education than many other developing nations. See World Bank, *China: Issues and Prospects in Education, Annex 1: Long Term Development* (Washington, D.C.: The World Bank, 1985).

3. A diversified, "two-track educational system" for "two kinds of labor" characterized secondary school policy before the Cultural Revolution. By 1965 52.1 per cent of all secondary school students were enrolled in a variety of full and part-time vocational, technical, and agricultural schools. The remaining 47.9 per cent were studying in academic full-time programs. During the Cultural Revolution this "bourgeois tracking system" was criticized, and secondary technical schools, workers' training schools, and agricultural and vocational schools were closed or dismantled. For a review of secondary schooling before and after the Cultural Revolution, see Stanley Rosen,

"New Directions in Secondary Education" in Ruth Hayhoe, editor, *Contemporary Chinese Education* (Armonk: M.E. Sharpe, 1984):65-92; Theodore Hsi-en Chen, *Chinese Education Since 1949* (New York: Pergamon Press, 1981); John Hawkins, *Education and Social Change in the PRC* (New York: Praeger Press, 1983); and Suzanne Pepper, "Education and Revolution: 'The Chinese Model Revisited'," *Asian Survey* 18, no.9 (September 1978):847-90.

4. *Achievement of Education in China, Statistics 1949-1983* (Beijing: Peoples Education Press, 1985). Secondary school enrollment ballooned to 67 million by 1977, up from 14 million in 1965. Post-Cultural Revolution reforms precipitated a drop in the gross enrollment ratio of students in Chinese secondary schools from 46 per cent in 1977 to 30 per cent in 1983. Transition rates from primary to junior secondary school dropped from 83 per cent in 1979 to 65 per cent in 1983; the rate between junior and senior secondary school dropped from 37 per cent to 24 per cent. Reinstated specialized secondary, agricultural, and vocational schools gained less than 2.5 million students in the first half of the 1980s, while general secondary school enrollment decreased by 8 million students. Regular senior secondary school graduates dropped from 7.2 million in 1979 to less than 2 million in 1986. However, total senior secondary school enrollment, currently at about 20,000,000, is expected to expand during the next decade to a gross enrollment ratio of 55-60 per cent nationwide, up from 10 per cent in 1989. See Jacques Lamontagne, "Educational Development in China" (paper presented at the Comparative and International Education Society Annual Conference, Atlanta, Georgia, 1988); The World Bank, *China: Issues and Prospects, op. cit.*

5. *Zhongguo Jiaoyu Bao* (China Education News) (September 15, 1988); (March 18,1989).

6. *Zhongguo Jiaoyu Bao* (November 1, 1988).

7. *Zhongguo Jiaoyu Bao* (January 19, 1989).

8. *Zhongguo Jiaoyu Bao* (December 31, 1988); *Beijing Review* (May 22-28, 1989).

9. This happens by choice and through the acceptance of money from international agencies that have their own definitions of appropriate development to which China must react if not conform. The evolution of the concept of education as a productive force whose capital must be rationally managed has been inextricably linked to China's membership in the World Bank since 1980. For a discussion of this connection see Jurgen Henze, "Educational Modernization as a Search for Higher Efficiency" in Ruth Hayhoe and Marianne Bastid, editors, *China's Education and the Industrialized World*, pp. 252-270. For an example of how the vocabulary of human capital theory and resource planning dominates educational discourse see *Zhongguo Jiaoyu Bao* (March 9, 1989).

10. Local bureaus of education have developed de-centralized school funding formulas that rely on a combination of state funds (*cai*), taxes on local enterprises (*shui*), student fees for books and tuition (*fei*), profits from school-run enterprises, (*chan*), scholarships and municipal merit awards (*ji*) received by outstanding teachers (*shi youxiu yuanding jiang*), and funds raised by providing services to local units (*she*). This last category includes renting out school facilities during winter and summer vacations for spare-time training (*yeyu xuexiao*). This material was obtained through an interview conducted with officials at the Shanghai Bureau of Education, July 28, 1989. Interviews for this study were conducted in Shanghai during December, January, July, and August 1989 and were supported with the generous assistance of the Faculty Research Council of Colgate University. Individuals and institutions remain anonymous.

11. *Zhongguo Jiaoyu Bao* (November 17 and 22, 1988); (March 18, 1989). In 1988 72% of Chinese secondary and primary schools had part work, part study programs. The total value of production of goods in such programs, which include fruit orchards and bicycle factories, has increased four-fold since 1982, reaching 10,000,000,000 yuan.

12. This ratio differs slightly from guidelines generated by the municipal bureau of education that suggest that those profits left to the school should be 30 per cent for equipment, 30 per cent for bonuses for teachers and workers, and 40 per cent to be funneled back into the school factory or enterprise.

13. *Zhongguo Jiaoyu Bao* (January 12, 1989).

14. *Zhongguo Jiaoyu Bao* (September 24 and November 1, 1988). This practice has become so pervasive that offices have been set up in cities and counties with hot-lines for parents and students with complaints.

15. For a typical critique of the infiltration of commodity consciousness into schools, see Yao Jiaqun and Liu Lian, "Wei shangpin jingji zhengming" (Justifed by a Commodity Economy) *Shanghai Jiaoyu* (Shanghai Education) (May 1989):14-15.

16. *Zhongguo Jiaoyu Bao* (September 13, September 27, and December 6, 1988). Teachers who are responsible for preparing students for examinations in Chinese, mathematics and English receive the highest salaries.

17. *Zhongguo Jiaoyu Bao* (September 17 and September 27, 1988).

18. "Optimization: Reform or Not?" *Beijing Review* 32, no.9 (February 27-March 5, 1989):12-13.

19. Disillusionment is usually measured by dropout rates for both students and teachers. The official junior secondary school dropout rate is 6.9 per cent. "Drop-out teachers" are normally in search of more lucrative careers. Although the annual average salary for teachers rose from 582 to 1,423 yuan during the past decade, it has not kept up with inflation. See *Zhongguo Jiaoyu Bao* (February 16, March 11, and March 18, 1989).

20. Philip Coombs, *The World Crisis in Education* (New York: Oxford University Press, 1985).

21. *A Nation at Risk* (Report from the National Commission on

Excellence in Education, Washington, D.C.: 1983).

22. *Zhongguo Jiaoyu Bao* (March 4, 1989). The surname Fan connotes both the modelling of a teacher and the setting of limits, while Shaobao alludes to small ripples of change.

23. *Reform of China's Educational Structure--Decision of the CPC Central Committee* (Beijing: Foreign Languages Press, 1985).

24. *Zhongguo Jiaoyu Bao* (December 31, 1988 and March 16, 1989); State Statistical Bureau, "Education and Reform," *Beijing Review* 31, no.45 (November, 7-13, 1988):31-32.

25. Universal attendance would be reached in economically developed areas of China, which include about one-quarter of the Chinese population, by 1990. Less-developed regions of China, accounting for nearly one-half of China's population, were to accomplish this task by 1995 and the remaining areas by the year 2000.

26. Harold Noah and John Middleton, *China's Vocational and Technical Training* (Washington, D.C.: World Bank, 1988).

27. *Educational Statistics of the Republic of China* (Taipei, Taiwan: Ministry of Education, 1988). In Taiwan nine years of compulsory basic education (*guomin jiaoyu*) was introduced in 1968-69. Senior secondary education (*gaoji zhongdeng jiaoyu*) is divided into academic training in regular senior secondary schools (*gaoji zhongxue*) and vocational training in vocational secondary schools (*gaoji zhiye xuezxiao*). Normal secondary schools have been upgraded to colleges and are considered part of the higher education system. Over two times as many students are enrolled in vocational schools than general academic programs.

28. State Statistical Bureau, "Education and Reform," *Beijing Review* 31, No.45 (November 7-13, 1988):31-32. This trend began in earnest in 1980 when 18.9 per cent of China's senior secondary school students attended technical and vocational schools. This number had risen to 40 per cent by 1988. From 1978 to 1987

8,643,000 students graduated from technical secondary schools, 1.7 million more than during the period from 1949-1978.

29. Xi Xinxiong, et al., editors, *Shanghaishi zhongdeng zhiye jishu xuexiao minglu* (A List of Shanghai Secondary Vocational and Technical Schools) (Shanghai: Shanghai Secondary Specialized Education Research Publishers, 1986).

30. Qian Jinfang and Huang Kexiao, "On the Contemporary Reform of Secondary Education in the Eighties," *Canadian and International Education* 16, no.1 (1987):90.

31. *Renmin ribao* (Peoples Daily) (February 22, 1990).

32. The three cities of Beijing, Tianjin, and Shanghai have experienced especially rapid increases in enrollment in secondary technical schools. See Lamontagne, "Educational Development in China," 1988.

33. A school principal and one or two vice principals are in charge, respectively, of academic (*jiaoxue*) and student affairs (*xuesheng gongzuo*). The responsibilities of deans are divided into general, political, and pedagogical work, the last area linked to the departmentally-based teaching and research units (*jiaoyanzu*) to which all faculty belong. While political and pedagogical concerns are separated by two parallel organizational structures, persons holding positions of authority in each almost always overlap. The principal is commonly the CPC secretary (*dangzongzhishuji*), while vice principals and deans are members of the CPC branch committee (*dangzongzhi weiyuan*). The CPC branch coordinates its operations with the affairs of the school's workers' union, which is responsible for the benefits, bonuses, vacations, and general livelihood of all of a school's adult members. The union's director is often a CPC member as are other members of the union committee (*gonghui weiyuan*).

34. Translated by Hu Mengjie from Chen Danyan, "Seventeen in Shanghai," *Xinning wanbao* (September 19, 1987).

35. For discussions of the contested terrain of secondary schools world-

wide, see David Labaree, *The Making of an American High School* (New Haven: Yale University Press, 1988); Torsten Husen, *The School in Question* (New York: Oxford University Press, 1979); Philip Coombs, *The World Crisis in Education, op. cit.*

36. Shen Baoliang, "Gaibian jinguzhou jiefang ku haizi" (Transform the Incantation of the Golden Hoop and Liberate Exhausted Children), *Shanghai Education* (May 1989):7.

37. Qian and Huang, "On the Contemporary Reform of Secondary Education in the Eighties," p. 96; *Zhongguo Jiaoyu Bao* (September 24, 1988).

38. For sample teaching and curricular plans, see Stanley Rosen, "New Directions in Secondary Education," pp. 77-78; Heidi Ross, *Making Foreign Things Serve China* (unpublished Ph.D. dissertation, Ann Arbor: The University of Michigan, 1987).

39. Sister schools abroad provide networks for admission to preparatory schools, which serve as stepping stones to foreign universities. In Shanghai the average 1988 mathematics entrance examination score for students of municipal keys was 112.32, compared to 96.86 for students of district keys and 68.04 for pupils of regular academic schools.

40. The fierce competition that marked entrance into colleges after the reinstitution of the entrance exam in 1977 has decreased markedly. 1 out of 1.7 to 1.8 of Shanghai senior secondary school graduates could go on to some form of post-secondary school training in 1989.

41. *China Exchange News* 16, no.3 (September 1988):19; Deng Yuhong, "New Road for Secondary Education," *China Reconstructs* 36, no.8 (August 1987):20; Hu Shi-ming and Eli Seifman, *Education and Socialist Modernization* (New York: AMS Press, 1987): 160-162.

42. Shen Baoliang, "Gaibian jinguzhou jiefang ku haizi," *op. cit.*

43. Chen Zicheng, "*Tansuo jiaoxue guilu tigao jiaoxue zhiliang*"

(Explore Educational Laws and Raise Educational Quality), *Jiaoyu keyan lunwenxuan* (A Selection of Educational Research) (Shanghai: Changning District Education Bureau Educational Research Office), 1985; Qian and Huang, "The Contemporary Reform of Secondary Education in the Eighties," *op. cit.*

44. Curricular reform groups have been established in the provinces of Guangdong, Sichuan and Zhejiang as well as with the Shanghai Education Publishing House, the Peoples Education Publishing House, Beijing Normal University Press, and a coalition of eight other normal universities. National full-day textbooks and teaching outlines for all secondary school subjects are published under the auspices of the State Education Commission. The detailed information contained in each pamphlet-sized outline forms the basis of daily lesson plans and competency and matriculation examinations. Outlines in current use were published in 1986 and 1987.

45. Senior one students take part in military drills (junxun) for ten days in August. Organized by district education bureaus the students' instructors are Peoples Militia or PLA officers. In schools with better than average facilities, physical training is accompanied by video cassettes that illustrate proper drill form. Elaborate assemblies glorifying self-sacrifice and perseverance and banquets for participating soldiers complete the activities. Military drills are used not only to extol the role of the army but to build a sense of solidarity in each new senior one homeroom classroom (*ban*). By far the most popular "social practice" from the student point of view is the senior two ten-day countryside stay (*xiaxiang laodong*). This trip normally takes place during the autumn harvest months and is facilitated by the district bureau of education. Students are accompanied by teachers and administrators and live together in large rooms. The sentimental recollections of participating sixteen year-old pupils contrast sharply with the senior three students' experience of social investigation (*diaocha*). This week-long process is carried out in homeroom groups in August and often consists of simple service projects such as cleaning streets.

46. *Zhongguo Jiaoyu Bao* (October 25, 1988). These examinations

were first initiated in 1984 by the Educational Testing Center and the Municipal Higher Education Student Recruitment Office. For a useful summary of the examination procedure see Shanghai Educational Testing Center, *Shanghaishi gaozhong huikao* (The Shanghai Senior Secondary School Competency Examination) (Shanghai: East China Normal University Press, 1989).

47. The exception is Chinese language and literature, which is taught during all six years of secondary schooling.

48. An "A" is received by approximately 10 per cent of students, a "B" by 20 per cent, and a "C" by 30 per cent; "D"'s and "E"'s are considered failing scores.

49. Senior secondary school graduates who apply to specialized and technical schools are also selected by these results.

50. Individual tertiary institutions may also require further assessments such as an oral examination for foreign language students.

51. *Zhongguo Jiaoyu Bao* (January 10, 1989).

52. The only students in Shanghai ineligible for direct enrollment are those who are not permanent residents of the municipality. They must return home to take the college entrance examination.

53. For an example volume of examination questions, see Shanghai Educational Examination Center, *Shanghaishi gaokao yingyu shiti pingxi, 1985-1987* (An Analysis of Questions on the Shanghai English Language College Entrance Examinations, 1985-1987) (Shanghai Foreign Language Press, 1988).

54. *Zhongguo Jiaoyu Bao* (February 2, 1989). In 1987 5,000 of China's 360,000 college graduates were rejected by assigned employers.

55. According to the Shanghai Higher Education College Recruitment Office, minimum college entrance scores in 1989 for humanities majors were 435 (480 for key universities) compared to 392

(and 475) for science majors. This is out of a perfect score of 600 on four examinations.

56. *Zhongguo Jiaoyu Bao* (September 22, 1988) and (October 4, 1988). From 1988 candidates in Beijing, only one student was a first-choice candidate for Beijing University's Geology Department. No students requested a first choice admittance into Qinghua University's Water Conservancy Department. At Peoples University, nine specializations in finance and economics had more first choice applicants with the exceptionally high score of over 500 than there were available positions. By contrast the university's philosophy department had no applicants. Neither East China or Northeast China normal universities met their quotas for Beijing students, and none of the ten students admitted to Shenyang Agricultural University were first choice candidates.

57. Ying Junfeng, "The Structure of Specialized Personnel and the Reform of Vocational-Technical Education," *Canadian and International Education* 16, no.1 (1987):104. Because gradual universalization of nine years of schooling is occurring at a time when high school enrollments are being contained, some educators express the fear that an increasing number of school leavers will be unprepared for jobs. In response to this concern, some vocational training is offered in junior secondary schools, resulting in the revision at some schools of the largely academic content of China's basic nine-year curriculum. Such efforts to develop a vocational education prior to senior secondary schooling are minimal, however, and this analysis will focus on vocational training offered in senior secondary schools.

58. Dai Shujun, "Vocational Universities in China," *Canadian and International Education* 16, no.1 (1987):172-180. Students may apply for recently-established two-or three year vocational university programs that are run regionally, enroll graduates from regular secondary and secondary vocational and technical schools, are self-financing through student fees, and do not guarantee employment.

59. For detailed discussions of the various structures and institutions

that comprise China's secondary VTE, see Xi Xinxiong et al., *Shanghaishi zhongdeng zhiye jishu xuexiao minglu, op. cit.*; Noah and Middleton, *China's Vocational and Technical Training, op. cit.*

60. In 1988 2,051,700 students attended China's 4022 specialized schools. 1065 of these schools were teacher-preparatory institutions.

61. Specialized schools actually include both full-and part-time institutions and have admitted senior secondary school graduates as well as offered in-service training to working adults. Senior secondary school graduates study in one-and-one-half to two year programs, and adults study for two to three years. 73.2 per cent of the 776,400 new students in specialized senior secondary schools in 1988 were junior middle school graduates.

62. The growth of technical schools has varied greatly across specialties. Finance and economics programs have developed extremely rapidly throughout the 1980s, while specialties in forestry and agriculture, for example, have been much less popular. See Lamontagne, "Educational Development in China," *op. cit.*

63. Like specialized schools, technical schools have taken senior middle school graduates for 1 to 2 year training programs but are discontinuing this practice.

64. Some vocational classes are housed in regular academic schools.

65. In 1988 8,954 independent vocational and agricultural schools were operating in China, enrolling a total of 2,793,700 students.

66. Curricula vary from program to program. While specific lesson plans were not available for this study, interviews with school administrators suggest that vocational students spend two-thirds to three-quarters less time in language classes and one-half to two-thirds less time in mathematics classes than their regular academic school counterparts. See Noah and Middleton, *China's Vocational and Technical Training, op. cit.*; *Zhongguo Jiaoyu Bao* (December 8, 1988).

67. *Beijing Review* (July 17-23, 1989). Especially in urban areas where

trained workers are in reasonably high demand, application to enrollment ratios suggest that non-vocational, non-key secondary schools are the least popular alternative for senior secondary school pupils.

68. Hu and Seifman, *Education and Socialist Modernization, op. cit.*, p. 27.

69. Noah and Middleton, *China's Vocational and Technical Training, op. cit.*, p. 37.

70. *Zhongguo Jiaoyu Bao* (November 15, 1988).

71. Noah and Middleton, *China's Vocational and Technical Training, op. cit.*

72. In one county in Hebei Province 250 students applied for 500 positions in an academic senior secondary school. 70 per cent of junior secondary school graduates held back during their last year of junior secondary school requested the additional year so they could try again to enroll into a specialized high school. *Zhongguo Jiaoyu Bao* (October 18, 1988).

73. *Zhongguo Jiaoyu Bao* (October 25, 1988).

74. World Bank, *China: Issues and Prospects in Education, op. cit.*; Noah and Middleton, *China's Vocational and Technical Training, op. cit.*

75. *Zhongguo Jiaoyu Bao* (January 31, 1989).

76. *Zhongguo Jiaoyu Bao* (February 2, 1989).

77. Qian and Huang, "On the Contemporary Reform of Secondary Education in the Eighties," *op. cit.*; Ying, "The Structure of Specialized Personnel and the Reform of Vocational-Technical Education," *op. cit.*

78. Ying, "The Structure of Specialized Personnel and the Reform of Vocational-Technical Education," *op. cit.*, p. 105.

79. *Zhongguo Jiaoyu Bao* (December 10, 1988).

80. Lamontagne,"Educational Development in China," *op. cit.*; Stig Thorgensen, "China's Senior Middle Schools in a Social Perspective: A Survey of Yantai District, Shandong Province," *China Quarterly* (March 1987):72-100. Regional differences in access still remain high. 50 per cent of Shanghai senior secondary school graduates can enter college as opposed to a national average of one in six and a ratio in Sichuan of one in nine.

81. *Zhongguo Jiaoyu Bao* (October 6, 1988); *Beijing Review* (July 25-31, 1988) and (December 26-January 1, 1989).

82. Stig Thorgensen, "China's Senior Middle Schools in a Social Perspective," p.87 has suggested of Yantai that, "The big winners in the admission game are children of cadres, and to a lesser degree intellectuals, who between them held 60 per cent of the seats in the two general middle schools." Jaccques Lamontagne, in "Educational Development in China", has also found that peasant children are over-represented in agricultural schools and under-represented in county key and normal schools.

83. *Beijing Review* (July 17-23, 1989).

84. *Zhongguo Jiaoyu Bao* (October 10 and 15, 1988 and March 18, 1989).

85. *Beijing Review* (May 8, 1989 and February 12-18, 1990).

86. *Zhongguo Jiaoyu Bao* (February 18, 1989).

87. *Zhongguo Jiaoyu Bao* (January 5 and January 7, 1989).

88. Thorgensen, "China's Senior Middle Schools in a Social Perspective," p.100.

89. For an engaging treatment of the difficulties facing women in contemporary Chinese society see, Emily Honig and Gail Hershatter, editors, *Personal Voices* (Stanford: Stanford University Press, 1988).

90. Cang Gong and Cheng Yuanti, editors, *Qingshaonian ziwo baohu*

(The Self-protection of Youth) (Shanghai: Shanghai Translation Press, 1988); Yao Peikuan, editor, *Qingqunqi changshi duben* (A Reader on Sexual Development) (Shanghai: Shanghai Peoples Press,1987).

91. Cang and Cheng, *Qingshaonian ziwo baohu, op. cit.*

92. Yao, *Qingqundi changshi duben, op. cit.*

93. Despite the commonly held view that female educational achievement declines throughout senior secondary school, in Shanghai, female secondary school graduates receive higher entrance examination scores than their male classmates. According to the municipal Educational Examination Center, this is because "girls study hard and boys play."

94. Han Shizhen, *Bangzhu nusheng saochu chengcai daolushang zhangai de shiyan* (An Experiment to Help Female Students Remove Obstacles to Achievement) (Shanghai: Changning District Education Bureau Educational Research Office, 1985).

95. *Xinmin Wanbao* (Xinmin Evening News) (August 13 and 22, 1989). Two-thirds of the municipality's junior secondary school graduates who were refused entrance into senior secondary school were girls. See John Burns and Stanley Rosen, editors, *Policy Conflicts in Post-Mao China, A Documentary Survey with Analysis* (Armonk: M.E. Sharpe, 1986):302-304; Emily Honig and Gail Hershatter, editors, *Personal Voices, op. cit.*; Lu Yun, "New Challenges to Women's Employment," *Beijing Review,* 31, no.44 (October 31-November 6, 1980):18-21; "Discussion on Women and Work," *Beijing Review* 31, no.33 (August 15-21, 1988):38.

96. Stig Thorgensen, "China's Senior Middle Schools in a Social Perspective," *op. cit.; Beijing Review* (March 27-April 4, 1989).

97. Ann-ping Chin, *Children of China* (New York: Alfred Knopf, 1988); Anita Chan, *Children of Mao* (Seattle: University of Washington Press, 1985).

98. Song Chongjin, "Guanyu zhongxuesheng qingqunqi jiaoyu de

diaocha," (An Investigation into Sex Education for Secondary School Students) *Jiaoyu keyan lunwenxuan* (Shanghai: Changning District Education Bureau Educational Research Office, 1985):39-46.

99. Chen Zicheng, "Tansuo jiaoxue guilu tigao jiaoxue zhiliang," *op. cit.*

100.Song, "Guanyu zhongxuesheng qingqunqi jiaoyu de diaocha," *op. cit.*

101.Cang Gong and Cheng Yunti, editors, *Qingshaonian ziwo baohu* (Studies of the Only Child), *op. cit.*; *Beijing Review* 31, no.42 (October 17-23, 1988):12; "Teaching Students Practical Skills," *Beijing Review* 31, no.30 (July 25-31, 1988):40.

102.*Zhongguo Jiaoyu Bao* (February 2 and March 9, 1989).

103.*Zhongguo Jiaoyu Bao* (September 1 and 3, 1988).

104.*Zhongguo Jiaoyu Bao* (January 17, 1989).

105.*Zhongguo Jiaoyu Bao* (March 2 and 4, 1989).

106.Tani Barlow and Donald Lowe, *Teaching China's Lost Generation* (New York: Praeger Press, 1987).

107.*Zhongguo Jiaoyu Bao*, (November 5 and December 13, 1988 and January 17, 1989).

108.In 1988 sex education classes were held in 6,000 secondary schools in thirteen provinces. *Beijing Review*, (May 29-June 4, 1989).

109.*Zhongguo Jiaoyu Bao*, (January 12, February 2, and March 2, 1989).

110.*Beijing Review*, (May 29-June 4, 1989). Note the date of this essay, which ironically begins with a quote from Jean-Jacques Rousseau.

111.Yao, *Qingqundi changshi duben*, *op. cit.*

112.This program was broadcast on Shanghai Television on July 29, 1989 from 6:00-6:30 p.m.

113.*People's Daily* (January 11 and Feb 27, 1990).

114.*Beijing Review* (January 15-21, 1990); *People's Daily*, (March 2 and March 6, 1990).

115.Junior students could protest only within the school walls. Selected senior students would have to stay behind and participate in these demonstrations with their younger classmates.

CHAPTER FOUR

THE TAPESTRY OF CHINESE HIGHER EDUCATION

by Ruth Hayhoe

Contemporary higher education in China is the result of a series of historical experiments that combined various foreign models of the university, with a rich Chinese scholarly tradition, and some remarkably iconoclastic efforts at building revolutionary institutions of higher learning over the modern period. The main task of this chapter will be to provide an overview of the higher education system in the late 1980s, with a focus on its structure, curricular patterns, student selection, and job assignment mechanisms, and the effects of both growing foreign influences and internal economic and societal changes. My analysis will be limited to the formal higher education system and will not touch upon non-formal adult higher education or the specialist forms of higher education administered by the Communist Party. In this introduction, I will briefly characterize some of the major models that have contributed to the threads now interwoven in the present system.

While foreign models have been a part of the Chinese reform debate, ever since early in the century, China differs from post-colonial societies in that it was never forced to react to a dominant foreign model that was introduced as a result of colonial rule. Rather, some of the values and patterns of China's own rich scholarly tradition have remained as a basis for educational development. These have been challenged and modified both by internally generated reformist and revolutionary efforts and by foreign models selected for emulation at certain periods.

What are the basic patterns of Chinese tradition that have continued to exert fundamental influence? I see a polarity between opposite types of institutions, neither of whose values coincides with the academic freedom and university autonomy that became central to the values of the European tradition. At the dominant pole, the traditional civil service examinations organized by official schools, from the Hanlin Academy and the so-called imperial university (*taixue*) down, were characterized by intellectual authority and a scholarly monopoly of the entire imperial bureaucracy. The mastery of authoritative classical texts, whose interpretation and application were regulated by the Hanlin Academy, qualified the scholar to become a part of officialdom, after climbing an examination ladder of incredible rigor and competitiveness.[1] At the opposite pole were the private academies or *shuyuan*, which typically abjured the examination race and created a context for informal study with outstanding independent scholars, the building of great libraries, essay writing on a range of topics and debates, and discussions that often touched critically upon the principles and practice of good government.[2] If these latter institutions experienced a broader intellectual freedom than the more discipline-bound academic freedom of the European university, their autonomy was fragmentary and fragile, and they were constantly subject to efforts at either coaptation or closure by an imperial bureaucracy that tolerated little dissent.[3]

The tension between these poles of China's scholarly tradition persisted within modern efforts to create new style higher institutions, and a recognition of its presence is important for an understanding of the struggle in higher education development over the twentieth century. In such revolutionary schools as Cai Yuanpei's patriotic school (*aiguo xueshe*), early Fudan,[4] and the Shanghai university established by the Communist Party in the twenties,[5] as well as in some of the revolutionary institutions of the Yenan period,[6] one can see aspects of the *shuyuan* tradition, with its emphasis on a nonformal teaching and learning style, free discussion and debate on a wide range of issues, and the transformation of canonical knowledge by an openness to heterodox literature. On the other hand, there has been a strong tendency for establishment political leaders, both Nationalist and Communist, to select foreign models that would perpetuate in a modified form, the patterns of central control and doctrinal orthodoxy that characterized the imperial examination system. This was clearly the motivation of moderate reformers early in the century, who saw in Japanese patterns, the possibility of serving a renovation that preserved intact Confucian social and political values. Nationalist leaders, who adopted European patterns in the late twenties and thirties and invited European advisors for their reform process, were also attracted to the state-centric, control-oriented possibilities of these patterns. Finally, the selection of the Soviet model by Communist leaders in 1952 as the pattern for a total reorganization of the higher education system so as to serve socialist construction, had the clear advantage of promising an organizational structure that ensured tighter political control than any other model, through the regimentation of knowledge and personnel within the system.

Foreign models, likely to be subversive of these dominant values of the Confucian tradition, surfaced during periods of political disarray. For example, Cai Yuanpei selected von Humboldt's model of the university for Beijing University in 1917 with a combination of knowledge areas intended to foster free academic debates, and strong support for good scholars of all ideological persuasions. This had explosive consequences in the May 4th Movement of 1919.[7] Subsequently, the introduction of American pragmatic approaches to knowledge through the leadership of American-returned Chinese educators as well as through missionary colleges in the twenties encouraged both lively debates over socio-political questions and sustained political activism. It is my contention that the more open and emancipatory approaches to knowledge represented by these models combined rather well with aspects of China's *shuyuan* tradition to form a substructure of critical thought and questioning that has plagued establishment political leaders throughout the century. Revolutionary institutions from the Communist Party's schools of the twenties, through the Yenan period to the revival of these models in the Cultural Revolution period, were a kind of "pure Chinese" version of knowledge for practical, social and material problem-solving while models such as Beida during May 4th and Fudan during the anti-Japanese struggle were an interesting amalgam of progressive tendencies from China and the West.

There has always been some ground for scholars and students to stand on outside of establishment control, a reason for the political leadership to be constantly vigilant, especially when student organizations flourish and communicate with one another around the nation. This was the case, in the student movements of the twenties and thirties, and under rather different circumstances, during the very early Cultural Revolution days. While the content of student demands during the protests of 1986-7 and the April 26th patriotic democratic movement of 1989 was different again from that of the Cultural Revolution period, there were striking parallels in form. In spite of political and emotional naivete, the intellectual sophistication with which students articulated their demands for democratic change and an end to corruption clearly resulted from a broadening and opening up of the higher curriculum between 1978 and 1988, that was more profound than at any other period since the twenties and thirties. The tragedy of the brutal military suppression of this movement in June of 1989 highlights the unresolvable tension between the absolute regimentation of knowledge for political control, and the need, recognized even by the present leadership, for an open approach to knowledge if the economic goals of modernization are to be met. Caught within this tension and as deeply frustrated with the problems of economic reform as the aborted attempts at political structural reform, students and younger intellectuals have no alternative at present but to bow to demands that they "unify their thoughts" with those of the Party elders. Thinly veiled threats in the official press make it clear that there is no space for open expressions of resistance or critical thought. However, this submission is unlikely to go beyond the necessities of form.

The Political-Economic Context of Higher Education Reform

In the following section, I will discuss those political and economic factors that provide a needed context for understanding the higher education provisions of the 1985 reform document and the developments that have followed subsequent to the reform initiative.

On the political side, efforts to bring about institutional reforms that would encourage socialist democracy within a legal and constitutional framework affected higher level institutions, particularly at the level of elections for county people's congresses. Direct elections and the possibility of multiple candidates stimulated lively participation by students and faculty on university campuses, constituents who in many cases form an important segment of the local electoral community. The student protests of 1986-87 were closely linked to student dissatisfaction over the interference of university party authorities in the electoral process. Students and faculty were also deeply involved in the debates over reform of the political structure that preceded this protest movement. Thus the movement toward the separation of Party and State and greater democratic participation in representative state institutions, was an important part of an external milieu that sparked demands for more democratic administration within universities and aroused considerable interest among students and faculty in broad socio-political issues.[8] It is still too early to assess the political consequences of the culmination of these concerns in the democratic movement of April-May 1989. But clearly, the fall of reform-minded Party Secretary

Zhao Ziyang, the removal and even imprisonment of many of his aides, and the flight of others into exile represent a serious setback to political reform.   On the economic side, the Decision of the CCP on the Reform of the Economic Structure, adopted by the 3rd Plenary of the 12th Central Committee in October of 1984, promised much greater autonomy to urban enterprises, paralleling the earlier establishment of a rural responsibility system, and stressing the need for a reformed management group who should be educated in "advanced methods of management, including those of developed capitalist countries that conform to the laws of modern socialized production."[9] This affirmation of moves toward greater economic autonomy and accountability for enterprises, led in subsequent years to a redefinition of Chinese socialism as a socialist commodity economy, and an awareness of the importance of scientific, technical and management knowledge as a commodity for which enterprises should be prepared to pay through research and training contracts with higher level institutions.   At the same time, as higher institutions have found new opportunities for enhancing their income through such "horizontal" linkages with productive enterprises, they have also been affected by the rising inflation that has dogged the socialist commodity economy,[10] reducing the value of their state appropriations and placing faculty and administrative personnel under severe economic stress, as their limited incomes fall behind the commodity sectors of the economy.   While full professors in Chinese institutions made around 200 Chinese yuan in 1988, including cost of living subsidies and bonuses of various types, drop-out students who found openings in joint ventures in the large coastal cities made starting salaries of four to six hundred yuan, and street peddlers and small entrepreneurs were not far behind them.[11]   The kinds of pressures these escalating economic inequalities are bringing to bear on campus life can be well imagined.

The third contextual feature that has been even more closely linked to higher education reform is the reform of the science system.   In March 1985, a national science conference laid down principles for reform that have led to the establishment of a science fund for the support of basic research, to which research institutes of the Chinese Academy of Sciences and universities may apply on an equal basis for research funding, with all applications judged by a peer review process. For applied research, institutes and universities are officially encouraged to seek support through contracts with productive ministries and enterprises in addition to traditional allocations available within the national plan.[12]   This enhanced flexibility and opportunity for the exercise of initiative has made possible a more significant research role for higher level institutions, whose primary responsibility had been the training of experts under the Soviet patterns adopted in 1952.

The Policy Context: The Reform Document of 1985

The educational reform document of 1985 gives insight into both the new aspirations for higher education and what was viewed as being problematic in a higher education system restored along lines very close to the Soviet patterns of the fifties after the end of the disastrous Cultural Revolution decade in 1978. In the document, higher level institutions are depicted as being responsible for two main tasks: "training advanced personnel," essentially the same role as was prescribed in the fifties, and "developing science, technology and culture," a new, more open-ended agenda that calls for new research initiatives direct involvement in economic and social reform.[13]

The problems of the past were seen as resulting from "excessive government control," which was to be eliminated in favor of "extending the decision-making power of the colleges and universities... under the guidance of unified educational policies and plans of the state." This expanded decision-making included freedom and positive encouragement to strengthen "ties with productive units, scientific research institutions and similar sectors," so that they will have "the initiative and ability to meet the needs of economic and social development." It may be significant, however, that no mandate for political involvement or responsibility for political development was included in the document.

The promised new autonomy was to take concrete form in a number of different ways according to the provisions of this document. Enrollments were now no longer to be entirely restricted to state allocated quotas set in accordance with national planning, but universities were allowed to enroll additional students whose expenses are paid through contracts with enterprises as well as private students, who would find their own funding and would be expected to pay fees. Likewise, job assignment policies were to be relaxed, with private students responsible for finding their own jobs, contract students being allocated positions by the subsidizing enterprise, and universities themselves playing a greater role in the deliberations over job assignments for regular students. In developments subsequent to the reform document, it was decided that job assignment by unified national planning would be totally phased out by 1991 and replaced by a system of local and interregional negotiations that involved students, university administrators, local higher education authorities, and employing enterprises.

Possibly the most significant new freedom promised to universities in the reform document was much greater jurisdiction over their curricula. Universities were assured power to "redefine the goals of different specialties, draw up teaching plans and syllabi and compile and select teaching materials." This was a dramatic change from a situation in which all teaching plans, course outlines and textbooks were nationally standardized and universities were simply responsible to see that these authoritative materials were faithfully transmitted to students in each of the many narrowly defined specializations.

In addition to affirming greater freedom and discretion over the content and process of teaching itself, the document stated certain overall directions for curricular reform. First, the ratio of enrollments between natural and social sciences was to be changed in favor of a considerable social science increase, particularly in those areas seen as vital to economic reform efforts. Second, the over-specialization of curricular definition, which resulted in a proliferation of ever more narrowly defined specializations over the years, was to be remedied through a redefinition of traditional specializations in broader terms and the introduction of new cross-disciplinary and frontier fields. Third, the ratio between short-cycle non-degree programs and regular four year programs was to be changed with the goal of significantly expanding the number of short-cycle programs. These programs were intended to reach half of all undergraduate enrollments and were geared toward the forming of mid-level technical personnel rather than high level academic and professional personnel.

Finally, the financial autonomy of universities was to be strengthened by granting institutions greater jurisdiction over the use of state funds to be allocated for capital construction and complete discretion over the use of "funds collected by themselves, for educational and academic exchanges with other countries." Together with this increased autonomy came greater accountability, in terms of regular assessment of academic quality and the accompanying threat of reorganization or dissolution for unsuccessful institutions. For students, financial autonomy has involved accepting responsibility for personal living expenses, which used to be covered by bursaries for everyone, engaging in competition for scholarships awarded on the basis of academic merit, or competing for bursaries reserved only for those with serious economic problems. In addition, since the reform document was distributed, it was decided that modest fees would be gradually introduced for all students.

How have these reform directives been expressed in concrete developments over recent years? In the rest of this chapter, I will endeavor to answer this question by looking at the structure of the higher education system, curricular change directions, changes in student life and aspirations, and, finally, the various dimensions of the open door. While it is still too early to assess, in any comprehensive way, the consequences of the military repression of students in June 1989, I will offer some preliminary comments on the situation in the final section.

The Structure of the Formal Higher Education System

The formal structure of traditional Chinese higher education was marked by the three levels at which civil service examinations were administered: the lowest level was county or prefectural, where the *xiucai* examinations enabled aspirants to become enrolled as government students (*shengyuan*). The second level, that of the province, administered the *juren* examinations every three years, and successful contestants were qualified either for lower-echelon bureaucratic posts or to advance to the capital examinations in the following year. Their successful completion led to the granting of the highest degree, that of *jinshi*. It is interesting, and not entirely fortuitous, that the same three levels of administration for modern higher institutions emerged in the twentieth century and were standardized under Nationalist legislation that defined three types of institutions in accordance with their administrative identity: national institutions (*guoli*), provincial institutions (*shengli*) and city institutions (*shili*). In the development of higher education since 1949, the same three levels have come into play in an interesting sequence: the period between 1952 and 1957 was a time for reorganizing and expanding national-level institutions; the Great Leap Forward period saw a proliferation of provincial-level institutions and even the devolution of some national institutions to provincial or local control; and the period since 1978 has seen the emergence and growth of new-style vocational universities, which are administered and funded entirely by city governments and are intended to meet the manpower needs of urban enterprises. The reform document of 1985 delineates these three levels in a way that parallels Nationalist legislation of the 1930s. A second important aspect of the structure of the higher education system is the concept of a division of institutions along sectoral lines for the service of specific sectoral needs. This tendency can be seen as early as the later nineteenth century in China when navy-yard and military schools were founded.[14] It can be seen also in the early republican period when a small number of institutions were created for specific service of such key economic development sectors as the railway system. However, it was only in the full-scale adoption of Soviet patterns in 1952 that the sectoral principle became an important structural feature of the higher education system. Soviet reforms of the late twenties and early thirties led to the creation of highly specialized institutions under such production ministries as metallurgy and machine-building as well as such sectoral ministries as agriculture and health,[15] in an adaptation of a type of institution whose historical roots are probably in the *grandes écoles* of eighteenth-century France.[16] There may have also been some influence from American Fordism and Taylorism in the Soviet reforms of the time. In 1952, Chinese leaders adopted these Soviet patterns, with each of their major ministries setting up its own system of higher institutions at national and provincial levels, intending to serve the specific national and local needs of each sector in a focused way.

There were thus three types of institutions, characterized by three different approaches to knowledge, that came out of the 1952 reorganization of higher education in China. First, there were a small number of comprehensive universities with departments in the classical arts and science disciplines of the European tradition as well as six national normal universities that had additional departments of education, fine arts and music, established with the intention of training academic teachers for the secondary and tertiary level. The basic organizing principle was the European one of clearly demarcated disciplines, each with an academic authority limited to its disciplinary boundaries. The second organizing principle of knowledge was one rooted in the Marxian concept of polytechnical education, a broad exposure to the applied sciences, as exemplified in a range of production techniques that were to contribute to both human development and scientific understanding. This was the pedagogical principle behind the great polytechnical universities as Qinghua and Jiaotong, with the broad range of engineering sciences included in their curricula.   All of these institutions, in addition to a small number of foreign language institutions, were directly administered by the Ministry of Higher Education, a ministry patterned closely on its Soviet counterpart and existing between 1952 and 1957, when it was amalgamated with the Ministry of Education. The third organizing principle of knowledge and the curriculum was one which the Chinese now call " product definition." The specialist kinds of knowledge needed to build railway systems, to advance steel production, serve petroleum development etc. were bundled into narrowly defined "specializations" designed to train advanced personnel for each of these sectors.   This approach was in turn, extended beyond production-related knowledge to a wide range of service areas, including public health, which administered all medical institutions, finance, which administered institutions of finance and economics, justice, which administered institutes of political science and law, etc.[17]

The structure of higher education was thus intimately linked to a specific structuring of knowledge areas that drew much more on European and Soviet academic traditions than either the emancipatory principles of Marx's concept of polytechnical education or American pragmatic approaches to knowledge.   Using Basil Bernstein's terminology, I have defined this as an extremely strong classification of knowledge, exacerbated by an approach to teaching and learning that was characterized by even stronger framing. This structuring of knowledge, embedded as it was within a rigid set of institutional patterns, was one of the factors that aroused such intense contradictions in both the late fifties and the early Cultural Revolution decade.[18] Equally, recent attempts to modify classification and framing and redefine the boundaries of disciplines and specializations have significant political implications--a point that I will address in more detail in the next section.

The third important aspect of the structure of Chinese higher education is that relating to the regional distribution of higher level institutions, a sensitive issue throughout the twentieth century.   The distribution of intellectual resources in traditional China was often imbalanced in favor of particularly wealthy regions, most notably Jiangnan, in certain periods.   Yet this distortion was never the result of external economic forces.   Furthermore, during the Qing dynasty, particular attention was given to maintaining a fair, regional participation in imperial intellectual life, through a system of regional quotas for the all-important civil service examinations.   With the advent of western imperialist influences in the nineteenth century, economic development was inevitably skewed toward the great coastal cities, and modern higher institutions tended naturally to be concentrated in a few highly developed urban centers. Concern over this problem can be seen as early as the first decade after the 1911 Revolution, when a whole series of reform documents suggested the adoption of a French-inspired university district system, which would ensure the presence of one university and also one normal college and one agricultural college in each major region.[19]

In 1927-28, the newly established Nationalist government attempted to implement a university-district system under the National Universities Council headed by Cai Yuanpei, but it proved an impossible task.[20] The League of Nations Mission of Educators who came in 1931 made a special point of criticizing the serious geographical imbalances in higher education, with a large concentration of higher level institutions located in the two cities of Beijing and Shanghai and entire provinces and regions that had none.[21] Although educators and politicians of all political persuasions supported plans for geographical redistribution, this was only achieved, in some measure, by the disruptions of the Sino-Japanese War. In the late thirties and forties, many coastal universities moved inland and laid the foundation for modern intellectual life in hinterland regions that had been entirely excluded up until that time.

One of the most significant achievements of the new Communist government in the early fifties was to bring about the geographical rationalization that had been so long an aspiration of all concerned with higher education development. China was divided into six major geographical regions: the Northeast, East China, North China, Central China, the Northwest and the Southwest, each with three to six provinces or autonomous regions. From 1951 to 1954, there was an educational bureau overseeing each region, and it cooperated with the central administration in seeing that each region had an appropriate distribution of comprehensive universities, normal universities, polytechnical universities, and specialist institutions, suited to the practical development sectors of the region. In some cases, the very names of national institutions reflected their primary regional responsibility. For example, the six normal universities were named for their regions (East China, North East, South West, Central China, etc.) and the six institutions of political science and law were distributed in precisely the same way.

The structure of the Chinese higher education system is thus a complex one, with three basic echelons or levels, three approaches to curricular organization expressed in comprehensive, polytechnical, and sectoral institutions, and a distribution pattern that has been consciously established to ensure fair access in each of the six major geographical regions. The following figure indicates the echelon spread of higher institutions in 1985.[22]

Figure 4.1
Three-Tiered Administrative Structure
of Chinese Higher Education: 1985

National level	Provincial level		Local Level
State Education Commission	Other ministries and commissions	Provincial/ municipal higher education bureaus	City higher education bureaus
38 institutions (29 keypoint)	285 institutions (59 keypoint)	510 institutions (8 keypoint)	181 institutions (no keypoint)

Source: Adapted from *Zhongguo jiaoyu nianjian 1982-1984* (Changsha: Hunan Education Press, 1986)

The idea of keypoint or priority institutions was first introduced in the late fifties, in attempts to raise academic standards by strengthening the resources of institutions intended to exercise intellectual leadership. It was abolished during the extreme populism of the Cultural Revolution decade and re-introduced after 1978. The present distribution of keypoint institutions gives an indication of prestige, with 76 per cent of all national level comprehensive, normal and polytechnical universities being keypoint, 20 per cent of all national level sectoral institutions and a mere 1.5 per cent of provincial institutions being keypoint. There are no local keypoint universities.

The strategy of expansion in the 1980s has emphasized the non-priority local echelon, with the majority of new institutions falling into two categories: two-three year short-cycle institutions (*zhuanke daxue*), many of which are normal colleges whose purpose is to train primary school teachers or specialist colleges that train mid-level technical personnel in specific areas, and two-three year vocational universities (*duanqi zhiye daxue*), which are an entirely new type of institution, having a broad and flexible set of curricular patterns, oriented to the changing manpower needs of their respective environments. These institutions are funded and administered entirely by city governments and their existence and resources reflect the relative prosperity of their regions. For example, the prosperous east coast region had a total of 47 such institutions in 1987, 17 in Jiangsu Province alone, while the remote and less developed northwest and southwest regions had only 6 in each region.[23]

A few statistics will illustrate the present situation. By 1987, there were 1,063 higher level institutions in China, 602 of them being four-year degree granting institutions that remain strictly regulated by the standards set by the Academic Degrees Committee set up in the State Council in 1979 and by central control over the quality of entrants to the places established by national quota and those available for contract or private students. In addition, there were 339 short-cycle specialist colleges and 122 short-cycle vocational universities, with the latter all newly established since 1980.[24] Since they are not degree granting, these institutions are subject to much less strict academic control. Their proliferation has been encouraged both in order to meet rising social demand and in order to produce the mid-level technical personnel greatly needed to balance the higher level professional-academic personnel coming from degree-granting institutions. Also permitted and included in these figures are a small number of private colleges and colleges operated by professional or mass associations, which usually focus on commercial or technical fields and operate at the non-degree level. By 1987, there were 1.28 million students enrolled in four year degree granting programs and another 680,920 in short-cycle, non-degree programs. New intakes for 1987, however, indicated a gradual equalization of the two levels of enrollment, with 332,365 students entering four-year programs and 284,457 entering short-cycle programs.[25]

Off-setting this steady expansion in short-cycle higher education enrollments has been a revival of postgraduate education at the upper end of the spectrum, and its developments exceed by far the parameters of China's earlier historical experience. Before 1949, there were a few graduate programs in some of China's best universities, but the peak enrollment in 1945 was 464, and all of these students were enrolled at the masters level. In the fifties, Soviet patterns for postgraduate education were not followed with the same precision as was true of the undergraduate programs. An informal system of graduate study allowed outstanding students to remain as apprentices to established professors in universities and senior researchers, in institutes of the Chinese

Academy of Sciences. By 1962, there were 6,139 graduate students, a figure that dropped to 3,409 in 1966 and to zero during the Cultural Revolution decade. No degrees were given for either graduate or undergraduate education in this period.

Since the establishment of the Academic Degrees Committee under the State Council, graduate programs have been rapidly developed along lines similar to those of North America, with a two-three year masters degree program and a three year doctoral program. Strict academic control has been maintained through a system whereby academic departments have to be approved by the Academic Degrees Committee before they can enroll masters students, and only individual professors of high academic standing are accredited to supervise doctoral students. While expansion has been extremely rapid at the masters level, there has been much greater caution at the doctoral level. Graduate enrollments have grown from 21,604 in 1980 to 120,000 in 1987, with 106,185 students studying in 394 higher level institutions and the rest studying in institutes of the Chinese Academies of Sciences or Social Sciences. Of the total in higher level institutions, 6.9 per cent are in doctoral programs, 86.9 per cent are in masters programs, and 6.2 per cent are enrolled in two year non-degree programs. A total of 1,000 doctoral degrees and over 65,000 masters degrees have been awarded since 1980.[26]

This overview of the structure of the higher education system indicates an interesting combination of features drawn from Chinese tradition and from foreign models: an echelon spread out that mirrors traditional patterns and offers entry into professional or intellectual life, precisely at the level of the institution's own milieu, be it national, provincial, or local; a sectoral division drawn from Soviet socialist planning patterns that has created networks of professionals within each of the major sectors at national and provincial levels, and finally, a geographical distribution among six major regions that has ensured relatively fair geographical access and the physical presence of intellectual institutions throughout the nation.

The structural dimension of greatest interest to this writer is that related to knowledge area and emphasis. It can be seen that greatest prestige is accorded to the comprehensive and polytechnical universities where there is at least the possibility of some interaction among different knowledge areas, and it is here that some of the critical ferment has been concentrated in recent years. This ferment might be seen as arising from the combination of genuine Marxist critical thought, progressive aspects of German and American knowledge traditions that

have been introduced historically in different per
values of the Chinese shuyuan tradition.

The other level where broad and im
development has been possible is that of the shc
universities. They represent a challenge on a differer
in which the structuring of specialist knowledge rein   ....onal
barriers established for the purposes of regimentation and control.
While students of these institutions have had much less involvement in
the student movements, there may be a fundamental undermining of
dogmatic forms of political control in the ways they are educated in
response to local needs.

Curricular Patterns in Higher Education

My personal sense of the reforms of the decade between 1978
and 1988 is that curricular changes have been one of the most important
and least noticed aspects of change, also that these changes both lie
behind the increasing student activism and constitute an important
pressure on the political leadership for concrete policies of
democratization in China's political and social institutions. While this
is true for many developing nations and often has had as much to do
with expanding enrollments as with curricular change, the Chinese case
is somewhat special because of China's long history of rule through the
regimentation of knowledge. I have suggested earlier that persisting
values of this tradition oriented both Nationalist and Communist political
leaders toward European and Soviet patterns that made possible a strict
regimentation of knowledge under the guise of high academic standards.

As a backdrop for understanding the significance of the
relaxation of control over curricular content, which was noted as an
important clause in the 1985 reform document, I'd like to sketch out
the patterns for control put into place in 1952 and persisting to a large
degree up to the present. First of all, curricular knowledge was divided
into clearly demarcated specializations defined either in terms of
disciplines or specific professional fields. By the early sixties, there
were 627 different specializations, with 295 of them being in
engineering and this number had proliferated to 1,037 and 537
respectively by 1980. The following table gives a picture of the growth
of specializations in all fields of study between 1955 and 1985.[27]

Table 4.1 Fields of Study: 1955-1985

Year	Total	Engineering	Agriculture	Forestry	Medicine	Normal	Humanity	Natural Science	Finance/ Economy	Politics & Law	Part Time	Fine Arts
1955	249	137	18	4	5	15	25	15	14	2	1	13
1965	601	315	37	3	11	30	72	55	25	1	5	40
1980	1039	537	69	22	29	40	60	158	54	8	8	63
1985	823	368	53	16	22	46	62	125	45	11	12	63

Each specialization had a teaching plan nationally standardized and fixed by the responsible bureau within the first and second departments of higher education in the State Education Commission (formerly the Ministry of Education), with the first department having bureaus responsible for 1) humanities, 2) finance and economics, politics and law, 3) foreign languages, 4) science in comprehensive universities, 5) humanities and science specializations in normal universities and 6) fine arts; and the second department having bureaus overseeing 1) engineering 2) agriculture and forestry and 3) medicine and pharmacy. Teaching plans were devised by the bureau in consultation with leading academics in each field. They designated clearly the purpose of formation in the specialization, the organization of time, the structure of all required courses (there were no electives), and the arrangement of the teaching environment. In addition, detailed course outlines specified the content of the courses, which were divided into four types: common courses, mainly constituted by political study and foreign languages, foundation courses, specialist foundation courses and specialist courses; there was a progression over four years toward more and more specialist courses.[28]

Students in each specialization formed a cohesive group and rarely had any close contacts outside of their specialization, even with the other specializations in the same department. Faculty were divided even more narrowly, with several teaching and research groups for each specialization, responsible for the different types of courses being offered. Those teaching foundation courses tended to have lower prestige than those teaching specialist courses. Members of the same teaching and research group were even likely to have housing in the same part of the university's faculty residences, just as students of the same specialization lived in the same dormitory rooms, making substantial opportunities for mutual surveillance.

Knowledge boundaries have thus been extremely rigid and paralleled the institutional organization of faculty and students in teaching/research groups and specializations respectively. The most powerful figures were the secretaries of the Communist Party branches in each academic department and it was their task to ensure that Party policy was carried out in all teaching and research activity. Their work was extended by political instructors responsible for politics courses, the one field of knowledge seen as broad and integrative, including Marxist-Leninist philosophy, the history of the Chinese Communist Party, and political economy. Political advisors reinforced the teaching of orthodox theory through forms of personal supervision, which included a process whereby all faculty and students were expected to report on their political and ideological progress in writing, every six months. This report was commented upon by political advisors and often kept in the individual's personnel file for future reference. The most important decision of most students' lives was that relating to job assignment at the end of their university years, as it has usually been a once-in-a-lifetime decision, and departmental Party personnel have had the most important jurisdiction over it. They determined how individual students were to be fitted into the job assignments offered to the department by the state planners. This has meant a very strong incentive for conformity on the part of students and even various kinds of ingratiation with those controlling this all-important decision.

At the macro level, there has also been quite a remarkable structure for control in the enrollment quotas for each of the specializations. Those fields of knowledge likely to be most sensitive, the social sciences that guided and defined overall political and economic development, have had severely limited enrollments until recently, while there was a tremendous expansion in enrollments in all other areas, most notably the engineering areas needed for heavy industrial development. Under Soviet influence, the social sciences were defined in two general categories: politics and law, finance and economics. People's University, the center for Soviet political and intellectual influence in the fifties, set the parameters for all programs in these two areas, trained or retrained the faculty, and also instituted the general political education courses that were obligatory for all students. Under the People's University were regional institutes for politics and law, finance and economics, in each of the major geographical regions.

Enrollments in political science and law, dropped from 24.4 per cent in 1947 to 1.0 per cent in 1950, .3 per cent in 1959 and back to .8 per cent in 1965. In finance and economics, they dropped from 15.4 per cent in 1949 to 1.2 per cent in 1958, then back to 3.5 per cent in 1965.[29] In politics and law, there were never more than one or two specializations, while there was a somewhat broader range in finance and economics. The basic macro structure was one in which Party cadres and specialists in these fields, strictly defined according to Soviet canons of orthodoxy, controlled and regulated the application of this specialist knowledge to all areas of political and economic development. No space was left for the creative intellectual participation of students and faculty, and there was every incentive for them to conform to the patterns laid down for them by political authority.

I have developed in some detail elsewhere my perception that some of the violence of the early Cultural Revolution, most notably that against the People's University and the institutes of politics and law, has to be understood in relation to the deadlocked combination of knowledge regimentation and political power described above, which united Confucian and Soviet cultural patterns in ways that became intolerable. I have further argued that the attempts to transform curricula in the Cultural Revolution decade, a romantic and unrealistically broad agenda, can be understood as the counter image to the narrow specialist regimentation of the Soviet patterns, an image that was to empower the "masses" of worker, peasant, soldier representatives to take their political and economic destiny into their own hands.[30] My sense is that there are interesting parallels with the Cultural Revolution decade in the curricular reforms that have gone on since 1978, though the process has been a gradual and much more effective one.

If we look at the macro situation first, there has been striking readjustment in favor of the social sciences, with a growth in enrollments in finance and economics to 9.2 per cent of the total, while politics and law have grown to 2.3 per cent. Humanities, in comprehensive universities, have grown to 5.8 per cent of the total, and there has been a revival of such areas as sociology and anthropology, alongside of history, philosophy and literature. In addition, there are large teacher education enrollments in the humanities, which reached 13 per cent of the total in 1987. If we add up all of the humanities and social science enrollments, the total percentage reached 30.8 per cent in 1987.[31] Some interesting new thinking in the eighties suggests that all of these areas should be regarded as humanities, as such fields as history, literature, philosophy, sociology, psychology, and politics are seen as foundational humanities, while fields such as law, management, economics, and finance are viewed as applied humanities. Although the major quantitative expansion has occurred in the applied fields, foundational fields are seen as the vital basis, essential to "the reform and progress of our political system, our economy and our cultural life."[32]

These macro changes in enrollment patterns and the reconstitution of social science and humanities specializations, have been reinforced by a whole series of micro changes in higher-level institutions. The credit system has been widely adopted, which has ensured that all undergraduates have the opportunity to select courses in areas outside their own specialization. These courses are often in interesting new areas of the humanities and are offered as often in specialist engineering and agricultural universities as in comprehensive universities. In addition, some universities have introduced a double degree program that allows talented students to enroll in two specializations at once, often one in the natural sciences and the other in the humanities, such as chemistry and journalism, or demography and mathematics.[33]

While in most institutions, the structure of specializations and teaching and research groups has reflected earlier depicted patterns, there have been some interesting experimental efforts to change these patterns. For example, in Jiaotong University in Shanghai, specializations have been broadened so as to coincide with departments, giving students a much broader exposure to courses outside their specialist area during their first two years. The abolition of teaching and research groups and their replacement with informally organized disciplinary groups (xueke zu) structured around the teaching and research interests of faculty and sometimes crossing departmental boundaries has paralleled attempts to broaden disciplinary specialization.[34]

Another important area of change was in the reform of political education, toward a less doctrinaire approach that takes into account the moral and psychological needs of students as well as their political orientation. Political instructors became more professionalized and were awarded academic ranks parallel to those of regular faculty, a controversial step that was necessary in order to attract young people to what is viewed as a rather undesirable job. Graduate programs that specialize in the training of these instructors were established at a number of prestigious universities.[35]

It is not possible to elaborate on these curricular reforms within the scope of this chapter but suffice it to say that the regimented patterns of the fifties had been modified in such a way that by 1988, there was a much larger cohort of students in foundational and applied humanities than ever before, and students enrolled in basic scientific and professional specializations were also able to take elective courses that stimulated their interest in general political and societal issues. In addition, the old patterns of political education had been modified in ways that offered somewhat more respect to the individual, though the hold of Party authorities over the destiny of students and faculty had only begun to be challenged.[36]

In this more open climate, where knowledge was seen less as canonical and specialist than broad and critical, it is no wonder that students and faculty became motivated to participate in political activism. The protests of 1986-87 called for more democratic administration within universities as well as the implementation of plans for political structural reform long under discussion. After the relatively mild suppression of this round of protest in early 1987, the focus turned to the economic discontent of what was defined in the fall of 1987 as the primary stage of socialism or the socialist commodity economy. In universities, this found expression in rising enrollments in commercially desirable fields such as management, international trade, foreign languages, and law. Interest in graduate study in academically demanding fields dropped off to such a degree, that quotas for some programs remained unfilled and faculty were concerned as to where younger successors to established scholarship would arise. The two dominant obsessions among young people in the major national universities were going abroad or finding an entry into the commodity sector of the economy upon graduation. This was in striking contrast to their attraction to government and academic careers in the past.

Given the situation, political educators had to think through rather carefully the role of political education under commodity socialism. In a fascinating discussion on the subject in early 1987, three different views were put forward. The first affirmed the influences of the commodity economy on the political and moral realm, suggesting that the principle of equal exchange for equal value would foster egalitarian and democratic thinking among young people. The new attitudes toward time and efficiency, stimulated by the competition of the commodity economy, should be encouraged by political educators, it was suggested. The second view was that the commodity economy would have negative as well as positive effects on youth behavior, and such negative effects as the tendency to seek personal advantage and adopt a hedonistic lifestyle and the unwillingness to submit to national planning directives in such matters as job assignment should be countered through improved political education. The third view was that the commodity idea should be strictly confined to the economic realm and that socialist morality had nothing to do with equal exchange for equal value but was a matter of correctly regulating relations between the state, the collective, and the individual according to ideological principles. From this perspective, the old patterns of political education should be reinvigorated to prevent ideological corrosion.[37]

It is hard to know which of these views prevailed, but clearly the kinds of political education that wen on through 1988 and early 1989 had some connection with the remarkable revitalization of the movement for democratic reform that took place in the spring of 1989 around preparation for the 70th anniversary of May 4th and the untimely death of Hu Yaobang. What seems most striking was the extensive involvement of Party members and even the Party leadership within universities as well as strong citizen and worker support, especially in Beijing. Clearly the young activists were dwelling on themes of wide concern, and a common remark by university leaders before June 4th was, "The students have given us back hope in our future as a nation."[38] The Party elders, however, chose to see things differently. Subsequent to their use of military force to put down the movement, they are calling for the reinstatement of the old dogmatic forms of political education. They are also attempting to turn back the curricular changes described here, particularly those in the social sciences.

Entry Examinations, Job Assignment and Student Life Under Commodity Socialism

The restoration of national standard higher education entry examinations in 1977 marked an important turning point for both secondary and higher education, away from the revolutionary rhetoric and concern with social practice of the Cultural Revolution decade. Concern with academic and professional standards of knowledge, essential to the service of the four modernizations, came to the fore. In the early years of these nationally standardized entrance examinations, competition was intense, due to a hugely expanded secondary school population during the Cultural Revolution decade and a backlog of academically competent youth who had been disqualified for higher education because of their unfavorable family backgrounds. However, between 1978 and 1985, the consolidation and streamlining of upper secondary schools and the diversification of programs toward a much stronger vocational emphasis reduced the competition from an examination success rate of 4.5 per cent in 1980 to 16.6 per cent in 1983 and 34.4 per cent in 1985.[39] Clearly the beneficiaries of this process have been the young people able to gain entry to the better urban schools, especially keypoint schools, which direct their main efforts toward ensuring a high rate of examination success.[40] In addition, the desire of keypoint universities to ensure the best possible quality in their yearly intake of students has led them to establish special relations with particular keypoint secondary schools and help raise their already high standards as well as assuring entry to a small number of outstanding students who are selected even before they have taken the examinations.

Off-setting this elitism are regional quotas that remain operative and require that places in national institutions be made available to students from all provinces and that the majority must still be selected on the basis of examination results. Special terms also exist for those willing to select less favored and popular fields such as education, agriculture, and certain fields of engineering, with somewhat lower examination results being acceptable for entry and bursaries offered to all students. In some cases, these enrollments are specified as "oriented training" (*dingxiang peiyang*), with candidates required to sign an agreement whereby they will return and serve the region from where they have come upon graduation. Generally however, young people in rural secondary schools and non-keypoint county or urban schools have only a slim hope of succeeding in entrance to formal higher education, a reality that has resulted in increasingly high drop-outs and poor morale outside of keypoint institutions.[41]

The regional politics of higher education entry are complicated by a number of issues. National institutions, especially those directly administered by the State Education Commission, have the highest degree of prestige and should be able to attract the best qualified students from around the nation. This is certainly the case for students in less favored regions who see enrollment in a good national university in a major center as the entry point into a whole new set of life possibilities and welcome the opportunity of national job assignment upon graduation. For students who live within the major centers, however, the situation is somewhat different, as they risk being assigned a job in a less favorable region upon graduation. Even though recent policy has been to allocate jobs on the principle of "returning to where you come from," some students from major cities may have to accept assignments in less desirable regions. All students, however, have the opportunity to apply for graduate school and the assurance that there are still job assignments for postgraduates within the major cities.

Research conducted in Shanghai in 1987 indicated that the national plan was still assuring a substantial outflow of graduates from Shanghai to other regions, yet there was some slippage due to large numbers of entrants to postgraduate education.[42] As for Shanghai students themselves, the only way they can assure permanent residence in Shanghai is to forego admission to nationally prestigious universities in favor of local universities, especially new style vocational institutions that do not undertake to assign jobs for their graduates. No statistics were available to indicate the numbers making this kind of choice, but there has clearly been a trend in this direction.

New policies of job assignment were intended to devolve decision-making to the local level and harmonize student interests and abilities with national and regional manpower needs. In reality however, this has resulted in each major city protecting its own interests and keeping available places open largely to students from its own constituency. Labor immobility, which is a problem in all sectors of the Chinese economy, has thus been exacerbated. Another result of the loosening up of the job assignment process in 1987 and 1988 was the creation of a situation where students in some commercially desirable fields were able to negotiate their own positions in enterprises, in some cases in return for a generous "donation" from the enterprise to the student's university. On the other side, enterprises or units that did not welcome the students assigned to them under the plan felt free to send them back. This was a particular problem for women graduates, viewed by many work units as a burden, since child-rearing is likely to occupy the first five years of their employment.

In the new conditions following the "turbulence" of June 1989, it seems likely that centrally planned job assignment will be reasserted and that all new graduates will be assigned for their first year to a grassroots level unit before being given postings to government or academic institutions. This policy was actually put forward in 1985 but never seriously implemented. There is now evidence that it may be implemented retroactively for all who have graduated from regular higher level institutions since 1985.

While these policies are clearly intended as a reassertion of central political control, the economic pressures facing universities are such that they will still depend heavily on horizontal economic linkages to enterprises. Students are likely to be even more assiduous in seeking job opportunities in the commodity sector of the economy outside of direct government control. The trend already evident in 1987 and 1988 for students to drop out early in favor of such jobs is likely to increase.[43]

Universities, for their part, will be even more driven to augment their incomes through contract training of personnel and contract research arranged by direct horizontal linkages to productive agencies. While such contracts are regulated by central academic authorities if they lead to degrees, there is no limit on what a university can earn through short-term non-degree oriented training. The income generated by these activities is valuable, probably an essential subsidy to increasingly limited government allocations---but it creates other problems. Academic faculty may be kept extremely busy with kinds of teaching and training that have little academic or professional significance but are purely money-making exercises. By the same token, research contracts with industry may distract research personnel toward routine and scientifically uninteresting concerns. By an ironic twist, this commodification of knowledge has the potential not only to undermine political control but also to jeopardize academic standards and test the strength of the university's commitment to advancing basic knowledge.[44]

We are thus facing a situation in Chinese higher education where the old familiar patterns of knowledge regimentation and political control that I have suggested go back much farther than the decision of Communist leaders to adopt Soviet patterns in 1952 are being fundamentally challenged on two rather different fronts. On the one hand, curricular reforms toward a more open and flexible knowledge system have led to an ongoing ferment of political activism among students and faculty in higher education; they are more able to think for themselves and explore broad concerns for China's future development through their academic work. On the other hand, the new economic dynamics that have accompanied commodity socialism are undermining the political control in rather different ways by a whole new set of values and aspirations, inculcated in students through the opportunities and trends of commodity socialism. These new orientations are not only undermining the political legitimacy and authority of the Party on the campus but may also be antithetical to genuine academic development needs. As a result, there has been a recent decline in entrants to graduate education and a shortage of younger researchers and teachers able and ready to take the mantle from middle aged and older scholars, the backbone of university teaching and research.[45]

How far are these internal problems being exacerbated by the open door and the many channels of interaction that have opened up between Chinese universities and their counterparts abroad in recent years? The answer to this question is somewhat different after the military suppression of June 1989.

The Open Door and Chinese Higher Education

There are two important ways in which the open door impinges on Chinese higher level institutions: (1) the pull for both faculty and students to go abroad as it becomes more and more evident in Chinese society that experience abroad and the acquisition of a foreign degree is highly regarded and may open up new career possibilities in China and (2) the contribution made by returning scholars and students as they settle back into professional life in China and seek to adapt what they have learned abroad to Chinese needs and circumstances. Quite a lot more is known about the first issue than the second, but recent research gives some insight into the kinds of contributions made by returning scholars and the problems they face.

First of all, who is going abroad for study, under what circumstances, and in what numbers? China's most recent official figures stated that over 80,000 students and scholars had gone abroad since 1978, and about 33,000 had already returned by the end of 1989.[46] The figure for those going abroad is almost certainly much higher, as a considerable number are able to go entirely as self-funded students and arrange their documentation through local public security offices without any report being made to national or local education authorities. It is thus impossible to say for sure how many students and scholars are abroad and, indeed, how many of these are genuine students or scholars. For example, in 1987 and 1988, over 30,000 young people were issued student visas to go to Japan under private auspices, most of them from Shanghai and other large coastal cities. Ostensibly they were going to study, but actually they traveled so they could earn valued foreign currency through various kinds of illegal labor.[47] This group had very little to do with the higher education system in either China or Japan.

Of the genuine students and scholars, a certain percentage are undergraduates who either have the sponsorship of relatives abroad or scholarships that enable them to complete their undergraduate studies started in China at a foreign university. In the late seventies, the Chinese government sent a small number of students at this level, but since 1982, official support has been given only to graduate students going for masters and doctoral degrees and to visiting scholars. Since 1986, with the expansion of Chinese masters programs, the focus has been on doctoral study or visiting scholar programs alone. Students enrolled in Chinese masters degree programs are not allowed to apply for study abroad and are required to work for two or three years after graduation before they are given permission to study abroad even at their own expense. In fact, the pull factor is so great that many masters degree students drop out of their programs before graduating in order to get around this obligation and go abroad for study at an earlier point. Naturally, of course, this situation exists predominantly in large cities and on nationally prestigious campuses, on which students have the contacts and the know how to apply for scholarships abroad.[48]

When it comes to students and scholars who are going abroad with some kind of financial assistance officially approved or provided, the situation is closely monitored by the personnel office of each university. Funding possibilities for such scholars include national quotas established by the State Education Commission, some of which are part of national level exchange agreements, quotas established by provincial governments or provincial level exchange agreements, opportunities through a university's own linkages abroad, and finally, all kinds of projects sponsored either multilaterally through the World Bank and various UN agencies, or bilaterally, through such agencies as the Deutscher Akademische Austauschdienst, the British Council, the United States Information Agency, the Canadian International Development Agency, etc.[49] In addition, Chinese universities seek to persuade their faculty going abroad on scholarships they have gained themselves to accept the status of unit sponsored scholars, which means their position is kept open for them in China and their salary is paid for at least the first year they are abroad.

In the early years of exchange, the kinds of opportunities delineated above were available almost exclusively to scholars in large national universities with comprehensive and polytechnical universities under the State Education Commission having the best opportunities and sectoral institutions following next. However, from the mid-eighties, the combination of efforts by provincial governments to open up opportunities for scholars in provincial level institutions and efforts by foreign agencies from the World Bank down to involve provincial and local level institutions in their projects has gradually changed this situation. For example, among the 183 Chinese higher-level institutions involved in World Bank projects, 69 are provincial institutions and another 17 are locally administered vocational universities. All are able to send some of their faculty abroad using project funds.[50]

Personnel management offices in Chinese universities, which regulate the selection of candidates for a varied array of opportunities for study abroad, face several important questions. Probably the most pressing is which age group should be given preference. Some institutions have chosen to focus on younger teachers, many of whom now have Chinese masters degrees and are eager to gain doctoral degrees abroad. In most cases, they are funded only for one year and are expected to find their own funding through scholarships abroad to complete their degree program. Other institutions see this group as being potentially high risk, since the number of returning doctoral graduates has so far been very modest, while mid-level scholars who go abroad for one or two years as visiting scholars can be counted on to return and make a contribution to the institution within a reasonable period of time.

A recent research project on the returning scholars carried out in Shanghai included three local universities and five national ones, and statistics collected indicated that only one local and one national university, out of a total of eight, had chosen the high risk venture, where a strong emphasis was placed upon sending young scholars for doctoral degrees. The other six had put greater emphasis on the mid-level group, who attended foreign universities as visiting scholars. Of the 1,500 persons who had already returned in these eight universities, only 35 were doctoral degree holders and another 15 had earned masters degrees abroad. In the short-term, therefore, it is clear that the main contribution of the open door is being made by this mid-level group, most of whom are engaged in research and teaching, many of whom have also undertaken such leadership responsibilities as chairing academic departments and research institutes.[51] Most have been promoted on return, following fairly rigorous review procedures established since 1978. However, some question remains as to how far genuine academic achievements are weighted against the mere prestige of spending a period abroad. Clearly, some scholars have made important advances and a real contribution at the international level while abroad, but others have used the time for recreation while exercising the opportunity to acquire desirable consumer goods. In any case, only those who have gained doctoral degrees abroad have become fully integrated into western academic life both in terms of scholarly and socio-economic orientation. They are the ones whose return holds promise for fundamental innovations in Chinese academic life with both the possibilities and the problems this may entail.

With the military repression of the student movement in June of 1989, the situation changed dramatically. Many of these graduate students abroad decided not to return. The loss of highly qualified doctoral graduates, some of whom have been trained at Chinese expense, is likely to be quite severe. Even though it is more difficult for older, visiting scholars to establish professional careers abroad, some of them have also decided not to return. The outrage in the West over Chinese government action in the violent suppression of the students has led to unparalleled political concessions toward these Chinese citizens in North America and Europe.

In China, the political climate has become extremely tense with the arrest of large numbers of intellectuals, including members of Zhao

Ziyang's various think tanks and leading activists among the students and young faculty on university campuses. It now seems hard to believe that only a few months ago it was possible to cite the relative freedom of activity of such well-known dissidents as Fang Lizhi as evidence of a maturing of China's political system that finally made possible open debates over different political visions for the future. With those intellectuals most committed to a new political vision now either in prison or in exile in the West, intellectual exchanges are bound to be affected, especially in social science areas.

On the economic side, commodity socialism has suffered a considerable setback through efforts to recentralize the economy and reassert national planning mechanisms. These may limit the worst excesses of corruption and inflation but are unlikely to touch the fundamental problems of economic reform. It is yet to be seen how they will be harmonized with the continued commitment to economic openness to the capitalist world, epitomized by the appointment of the politically conservative yet economically outward looking Shanghai leader, Jiang Zemin to the position of General Secretary of the Communist Party in late June, 1989.

It appears that the new leaders are set on a course of economic modernization within the parameters of a rigidly repressive political regime, a course for which they may find inspiration from some of their repressive yet economically successful Asian neighbors. The consequences for higher education policy represent a turning back on many of the achievements depicted above. University enrollments for 1989 were reduced by 30,000, nearly 5 per cent, with the majority of the cuts being in the social sciences, affecting the 36 comprehensive and polytechnical universities directly administered by the State Education Commission most heavily [52] (these institutions, of course, played a leading role in the movement). New policies on sending scholars abroad, announced by Vice-Minister He Dongchang of the State Education Commission in August 1989 made it clear that the number of graduate students sent abroad for doctoral study will be greatly reduced in favor of visiting scholars going for relatively short periods who can be expected to return on time and "achieve quick academic results."[53] As for fields of study, these will be carefully set in direct relation to the needs of the State. It seems unlikely that the State will need many social scientists in the present climate, unless it be in narrowly technical fields. This policy is thus likely to reinforce the pressures on social scientists that will result from reduced enrollments.

Most crushing of all to the universities is the revival of traditionally dogmatic forms of political education and the purging from

Party ranks of all those Party members who signed petitions and involved themselves in the movement in other ways. It has been noted earlier that one of the unusual features of this movement, in contrast to those of 1985 and 1986, was the overt Communist Party support it gained, especially in the universities. There is thus likely to be considerable resistance and real problems with implementing central directives for a purge within the Party on university campuses.

Will the present regime be able to go forward with policies of economic modernization within these stringently repressive political conditions? Will it be able to turn back the clock in such a way that universities revert to the modalities of the fifties, turning out highly qualified specialists who have been educated to raise no awkward political or social questions? It is certainly easy to understand why this course is a more appealing one than the task of building a new socialist morality and polity that incorporate the kinds of openness and commitment to democratic participation called for by young activists. However, my own sense is that the fortress of Confucian-Soviet patterns for control and regimentation has already crumbled beyond restoration in face of the sweeping economic forces of commodity socialism and the changes in consciousness that have arisen from the liberalization of knowledge and information over the past decade. A foundation has been laid in the realm of consciousness and culture that awaits visionary political leaders who know how to build upon it. The universities, as important repositories of this new thinking, should be able to weather a storm whose ideological vapidity and blatant orientation toward the preservation of power and privilege make it, in the end, less threatening than earlier, more ideologically persuasive campaigns.

Notes

1. Ichisada Miyazaki, *China's Examination Hell: The Civil Service Examinations of Imperial China* (New Haven: Yale University, 1981).

2. John Meskill, *Academies in Ming China* (Tucson, Arizona: University of Arizona Press, 1982).

3. Ruth Hayhoe, "Chinese, European and American Scholarly Values in Interaction," *London Association of Comparative Educationists*, Occasional Paper 13, 1984.

4. Ruth Hayhoe, "Towards the Forging of a Chinese University Ethos: Zhendan and Fudan 1903 to 1919," *China Quarterly* No.94 (June 1983):323-341.

5. Huang Meizhen, Shi Yuanhua and Zhang Yun, editors, *Shanghai daxue shiliao* (Historical Materials on Shanghai University) (Shanghai: Fudan University Press, 1984).

6. Wang Hsueh-wen, *Chinese Communist Education: the Yenan Period* (Taipei: Institute of International Relations, 1978).

7. William Duiker, *Ts'ai Yuan-pei: Educator of Modern China* (University Park and London: Pennsylvania State University, 1977).

8. Suzanne Pepper, "Deng Xiaoping's Political and Economic Reforms and the Chinese Student Protests, "*University Field Staff International Reports* no.3, Asia (Indianapolis, 1987); Ruth Hayhoe, "China's Intellectuals in the World Community," *Higher Education* vol. 17, no.1 (1988):121-138.

9. *Xinhua* (New China News Agency), October 22, 1984 (special issue).

10. Gao Shangquan, "Develop Theories on the Socialist Commodity Economy in the Course of Deepening Reform in All Fields," *Renmin ribao* (November 18, 1988) in *Foreign Broadcast Information Service-Daily Report China* (hereafter *FBIS*), No. 22 (December 5, 1988):58.

11. This information comes from a study of returned scholars conducted in Shanghai in November 1988. Interviews with 42 scholars indicated a pretty consistent income for academics in different fields. However, reports on the incomes of university drop-outs or graduates working in joint ventures and street peddlers are based only on hearsay.

12. "Revamping China's Research System - Excerpts from Premier Zhao Ziyang's March 6 Speech at the National Science Conference," *Beijing Review*, No. 14 (April 8, 1985):15-21. See also, Richard Suttmeier, "China's Science and Technology Reforms: Towards a Post-socialist Knowledge System," *China Exchange News* Vol. 16, No.4 (December 1988):7-13.

13. *Reform of China's Education Structure: Decision of the CPC Committee* (May 1985) (Beijing: Foreign Language Press, 1985):13-18.

14. Knight Biggerstaff, *The Earliest Modern Government Schools in China* (Ithaca, New York: Cornell University, 1961).

15. Sheila Fitzpatrick, *Education and Social Mobility in the Soviet Union* (Cambridge: Cambridge University, 1979):184-205.

16. F.B. Artz, *The Development of Technical Education in France:1500-1850* (Cambridge, Massachusetts, and London: Society for the History of Technology and MIT Press, 1966).

17. For a Chinese depiction of the higher education system after the reorganization of 1952, see Tseng Chao-lun, "Higher Education in New China," in Stewart Fraser, editor, *Chinese Communist Education: Records of the First Decade* (Nashville: Vanderbilt University, 1965). For a discussion of the nature and extent of Soviet influence, see R. Price, "Convergence or Copying: China and the Soviet Union," and L.A. Orleans, "Soviet Influence on Chinese Higher Education," in R. Hayhoe and M. Bastid, editors, *China's Education and the Industrialized World: Studies in Cultural Transfer* (New York: M.E. Sharpe and Toronto: OISE Press, 1987): 158-198.

18. Ruth Hayhoe, *China's Universities and the Open Door* (Armonk

New York: M.E. Sharpe, 1989):9-28.

19. Chen Qingzhi, *Zhongguo Jiaoyu Shi* (History of Chinese Education) (Shanghai: Commercial Press, 1936): 671.

20. Allen Linden, "Politics and Education in Nationalist China: The Case of the University Council 1927-28," *Journal of Asian Studies* Vol. XXVIII, No.4 (August 1968):763-776.

21. C.H. Becker, et al., *The Reorganization of Education in China* (Paris: League of Nations Institute of Intellectual Cooperation, 1932):175-177.

22. Hayhoe, *China's Universities and the Open Door*, *op. cit.*, p.174.

23. State Education Commission Planning and Finance Bureau, editors, *Zhongguo jiaoyu tongji nianjian 1987* (Chinese Yearbook of Educational Statistics, 1987) (Beijing: *Beijing Gongye daxue chubanshe*, 1987):114. See also, Dai Shujun, "Vocational Universities in China," *Canadian and International Education* Vol. 16, No.1 (June 1987):172-182.

24. These statistics were provided by Huang Shiqi, retired director of the Information and Documentation Unit, State Education Commission and Vice-President of the Chinese Educational Association for International Exchanges, in a recent unpublished paper titled, "Higher Education in the P.R.C."

25. *Zhongguojiaoyu tongji nianjian, 1987, op. cit.*, pp.26-27.

26. Huang Shiqi, "University Research in China," paper presented at the International Seminar on Current Policies of Higher Education Reform, Beijing, June 21-25, 1988.

27. *Achievement of Education in China Statistics: 1949-1983* (Beijing: People's Education Press, 1984):56; *Achievement in Education in China: 1980-1985* (Beijing: People's Education Press, 1986):21.

28. R. Hayhoe, *China's Universities and the Open Door*, *op. cit.*, pp.35-36.

29. *Achievement of Education in China Statistics:1949-1983, op. cit.*, pp.54-55.

30. R. Hayhoe, *China's Universities and the Open Door, op. cit.*, pp.21-29.

31. Zhonguo jiaoyu tongji nianjian 1987, *op. cit.*, pp.28-29.

32. Wang,Hao and Chen, "On Strengthening Humanities in Higher Education," *Jiaoyu yanjiu* No.8 (1981), translated in *Chinese Education*, Vol. XIX, No.1 (1986); R. Hayhoe, "Knowledge Categories and Chinese Educational Reform," *Interchange*, Vol.19, (Autumn/Winter 1988-89).

33. R. Hayhoe, *China's Universities and the Open Door, op. cit.*, pp.60-85.

34. *Ibid.*, pp.54-55.

35. *Ibid.*, pp.54-55.

36. Kathlin Smith, "Red, Black and Yellow Paths: New Choices for Young Scientists," *China Exchange News* Vol.16, No.4 (December 1988):14-15.

37. *Zhongguo jiaoyu bao* (January 24, 1987):3.

38. The author spent the month of May 1989 conducting a research project that involved extensive interviews with university administrators in six Chinese universities in the North China region and was in an excellent position to observe the development of the movement and the attitudes of university authorities.

39. These transition rates are calculated from statistics on upper secondary graduates and higher education entrants in *Achievement of Education in China Statistics:1949-1983* and *Achievement of Education in China Statistics: 1980-85*.

40. For a comprehensive study of the re-instatement of entry examinations, see Suzanne Pepper, *China's Universities: Post-*

Mao Enrollment Policies and Their Impact on the Structure of Secondary Education (Ann Arbor, Michigan:Center for Chinese Studies, University of Michigan, 1984).

41. Stanley Rosen, "Restoring Key Secondary Schools in Post-Mao China: the Politics of Competition and Educational Quality," in D. Lampton, editor, *Policy Implementation in Post-Mao China* (Berkeley: University of California, 1987); Stanley Rosen, "The Impact of Educational Reforms on the Attitudes and Behavior of Chinese Youth," *Interchange* Vol.19, No.3/4 (Fall/Winter, 1988):60-75.

42. R. Hayhoe, "Shanghai as a Mediator of the Educational Open Door," *Pacific Affairs* Vol.61, No.2 (Summer, 1988):253-284.

43. Zhang Hua, "End Business Fever Among College Students," *China Daily* (August 1988):4; "University students 'craze for schooling' declines," *Xinhua* (in Chinese) (August 25, 1988) in *FBIS* (August 29, 1988):24-25.

44. See the article by Zhou Tongyun in *Zhongguo gaodeng jiaoyu* (May 1988):30-31.

45. In my interviews with returned scholars in six Shanghai universities in November of 1988, this was the issue most often raised as a serious obstacle to their research work.

46. *Xinhua* (in English) (July 6, 1990). See also, *China's Scholars Abroad* No. 10, (November 1988): 9, and Zhang Yan and Shen Yong, "Chinese Students' Study Abroad - A Perspective," in *Liaowang* (Overseas Edition) No.12, (March 21, 1988):4-6, translated in *FBIS* No.73, (April 15, 1988):27-30.

47. "Shanghai Students Protest Japanese Visa Delay," *Kyodo* in English (November 9, 1988) *FBIS*, No. 218 (November 10, 1988):13.

48. For an overview of policy, trends, and research, see R. Hayhoe, and Zhan Ruiling, editors, "Educational Exchanges and the Open Door," *Chinese Education* Vol. XXI, No.1 (Spring 1988).

49. R. Hayhoe, *China's Universities and the Open Door, op. cit.*,

pp.134-156.

50. *Ibid.*, pp.157-190.

51. R. Hayhoe, "China's Scholars Returned from Abroad: A View from Shanghai: Parts I and II," *China Exchange News* Vol.17, Nos. 3 and 4, (September and December 1989):3-8, 2-7.

52. *China News Analysis*, No.1390 (July 1989):6.

53. *China Daily* (September 2, 1989):4.

CHAPTER FIVE

CHINESE ADULT EDUCATION IN TRANSITION
by Jianliang Wang and Nat Colletta

Since the 1920s, China has relied heavily upon adult education to promote desired changes in political ideology, socio-economic relations, and human productive capabilities. The belief in the power of education in general and adult education in particular to create a "new socialist person" and construct a "new social order" has at times reached religious proportions. The cyclical shifts in ideology and the accompanying shifts in socio-economic development strategies, from the "Great Leap Forward" to the "Four Modernizations," have been mirrored by the different emphases placed upon investment in agricultural versus industrial development, small-versus large-scale technologies, mass versus elite education, particularly child-versus adult-centered learning, and formal versus non-formal education. Even within a particular sector such as adult non-formal education, the focus has continually shifted between peasants and workers from offering specialized skill training and knowledge dissemination to offering programs with rough equivalence to their formal counterparts, accompanied by enhanced certification power.[1]

The historical development of adult non-formal education in the People's Republic of China has been recounted in a number of published works.[2] This chapter will provide an update on recent developments and pose hypotheses concerning future challenges facing adult educators in China. Nonetheless, a brief historical overview is presented for the purpose of presenting current policy issues within an appropriate context.

145

Historical Overview

From 1949-1981, the term "adult education " was non-existent in China. Until a study team from the International Council for Adult Education visited China, adult education was called worker-peasant education, and the top administrative agency for adult education, located under the Ministry of Education, was similarly known as the Worker-Peasant Education Bureau. However defined, adult education in China has undergone three stages: the initial post-liberation and Great Leap Forward periods of 1949-1965, the Cultural Revolution from 1966-76, and the current post-Mao Era from 1977-present.

In 1949, 80 per cent of China's five hundred million people were illiterate. The new regime's response was to convene the first National Conference on Worker-Peasant Education in September 1950, at which worker-peasant literacy was positively associated with economic reconstruction.

By 1955, over two million workers had participated in various kinds of literacy workshops and classes while approximately 14 million peasants attended spare time schools in rural areas. During the winter, enrollments reached as high as 42 million people, an extraordinary accomplishment. Spare time schools and night schools operated on 6-2 (six hours of work and two hours of study) and 4-4 (four hours of work and four hours of study) schedules, while some schemes allowed for selected students to participate in an education program on a full-time work release basis for a maximum of three years. Formal classroom instruction, distance instruction through correspondence, and radio instruction were utilized as almost all enterprises, government agencies, factories, production brigades as well as schools and administrative organizations were involved in providing literacy training.[3]

It is no exaggeration to conclude that the entire nation was fully mobilized for this first literacy campaign, launched by the government. It was not uncommon to find husbands and wives teaching one another, or children teaching parents, and neighbors establishing community learning centers. One of this chapter's authors, as an elementary school student, was not only an active member in the teaching force of the literacy campaign but also served as a tutor for his mother. As a result of their efforts, his mother graduated from a literacy class.

By 1956, about 62 million peasants had attended different types of literacy classes, representing about 30 per cent of the age group of fourteen years and over from the country's rural population. Spare-time secondary educational programs were initiated in 1953 in urban areas, and spare time higher education programs began in 1955. It should be noted that although the "Great Leap Forward" caused significant economic hardship to the Chinese people, it was successful in providing further impetus to literacy efforts.[4]

Adult education suffered during the Cultural Revolution (1966-76), in the sense that it was largely ignored and was negatively influenced by the general politicization of the country's educational system. After ten years of neglect, the central government issued its first document regarding adult education on November 6, 1978, titled "Directives on the Issues of Literacy." The document called for the eradication of illiteracy among workers and peasants throughout the country and reiterated basic literacy criteria first enunciated in the 1950s. These standards included the ability of peasants to master 1,500 Chinese characters and of workers to master 2,000 characters; the capacity to read a newspaper; the ability to write simple letters and complete applications and appropriate forms; and, the ability to complete a simple test measuring the above mentioned skills. [5] It is interesting to note that mastery of 3,000 characters is considered to be a minimum level of proficiency for primary school graduates.

40-50 per cent of China's population was judged illiterate by the end of the Cultural Revolution. Formal schooling was confronted with teacher shortages, poor facilities and buildings, and an increasing number of children waiting to be educated. Adult education was thus considered to be the second leg of the policy of "walking on two legs" as a means of solving China's education problems.

Current Adult Education Programs

COMBATTING ADULT ILLITERACY

Adult education during the post-Mao period can be characterized by the restoration and re-establishment of institutions neglected or abolished during the Cultural Revolution, a shift from secondary level course work with an academic focus to secondary level technical education and an expansion of higher educational opportunity for adults.

1977 to 1983 was considered to be a period of restoration and re-establishment for adult education. During this time, most of the suspended institutions that sponsored adult training were restored while new ones were created. Administrative structure at all levels of adult learning was correspondingly restored and in some cases, initiated. In 1983, enrollment in adult educational institutions of all kinds amounted to 22 million people. In addition, there were about 20 million workers who participated in various learning activities offered by their employers, local communities and mass organizations such as the Women's Federation and trade unions. There was an even larger number of peasants who participated in various short-term technical training courses.[6]

Table 5.1
Adult Literacy and General Education (1985)

	Number of Institutions	Enrollment (,000)
Literacy classes	176,076	5,190
Adult Primary schools	100,337	3,148
Academic Secondary schools	45,133	4,123
Technical Secondary schools	4,189	1,347

Source: *Achievement of Education in China* (Beijing: People's Education Press, 1985)

More recently, the gradual shift from a centrally planned economy to an economy that incorporates elements of a free market has had a tremendous impact upon Chinese educational programs of all types, including those that address the needs of adults.

The "job responsibility system" in rural areas has had the effect of neatly reinforcing a compelling economic rationale for peasant parents to pull their children out of school. The decentralization of responsibility for financing elementary and secondary education has further resulted in many schools raising tuition for elementary and secondary students. As a result, many students are dropping out of school because of cost.[7] Not only are dropouts involved in small business and trade, sometimes acquiring sizeable sums of money in spite of their illiteracy, but schools have reacted to inflationary pressures by using playgrounds and classrooms as restaurants, grocery stores, department stores, and small factories. Teaching has thus become a secondary priority.[8]

In 1988, 4,280,000 students dropped out of primary school, while 2,870,000 lower secondary students dropped out.[9] Although the government admits to the existence of some 260 million illiterates, this statistic only includes the number of illiterates from age twelve to forty. Illiteracy is a growing problem which is directly affecting adult education efforts.

Illiteracy is gender related and it is largely a rural phenomenon. 69 per cent of the 220 million illiterate peasants are women. 21 per cent of the male population over twelve is illiterate, 49 per cent of the female population is so designated. 91 per cent of all people designated as being illiterate reside in rural areas.[10] The following eight approaches have been taken by central as well as local governments in an attempt to address the problem.

The Establishment of Administrative Offices and Appointment of Full-time Literacy Administrators.

The State Education Commission now includes an adult education department as do provincial, autonomous regional, municipal, and county-level education commissions, departments and bureaus. 50,000 full time cadres have been given the responsibility of administering peasant education in rural areas.[11]

The Use of Professional and Non-professional Teaching staff to Promote Literacy Training.

Most of those who participate in rural literacy training are spare-time workers. Primary and secondary school teachers, retired teachers and government employees, technicians, and educated youth have all been invited to teach. Even some senior primary school pupils have been appointed as "little teachers." One incentive measure that has been adopted to increase teacher participation in literacy efforts in Shandong's Wulian county links bonus pay with the number of students in one's class, along with one's ability to make students complete the

assigned curriculum and raise their reading and writing abilities to a required level.[12]
    Teachers and cadres, who are charged with the responsibility of promoting literacy and live in townships, are trained at the county level while those who reside in the village are trained in the township. They discuss teaching materials and methods, exchange teaching experiences, and are given instruction concerning standard government policies.

Solicitation of Mass Support for Finances.

    Schools attempt to collect funds from those who are wealthy enough to donate financial support, and they often organize work-study programs to increase their income. Local governments also offer some subsidies.

Implementation of Official Policies that Encourage Further Study.

    The Chinese constitution stipulates that the State develop educational facilities of various types in order to wipe out illiteracy and provide political, cultural, scientific, technical and professional education for workers, peasants, state functionaries and other working people. It encourages people to become educated through self-study. Technically, all illiterates aged twelve to forty, with the exception of those who are disabled, must be educated. Those who finish their study in the required time are given their education for free, while those who refuse to study though they are able to do so or fail to become literate within the required amount of time, are forced to pay compensation fees that are placed in an "illiteracy fund." They can not be hired as workers or promoted.

Making Teaching Material More Practical.

    To meet the demands of modern rural life, students are learning not only how to read and write but also to study agricultural techniques, general knowledge, basic law, and current events. Subject matter relevance is critical for the program to be successful. It is directly related to the motivation of the participants. In order to attract and maintain drop-outs, the curriculum needs to be adapted to local and rural needs. Thus provision of more relevant and practical materials helps to motivate and retain the participants. Therefore, many rural schools and literacy programs have added to their curricula, courses such as agronomy, horticulture, pesticide, agro-technique, animal husbandry, livestock and poultry, and arts and crafts. For example, females of the Miao nationality in Guizhou Province traditionally learn singing and embroidery from childhood. These are required skills useful for adult life. In order to attract Miao students, adult educators have opened an embroidery class for illiterate females and have invited two folk artists to work as instructors, teaching them these skills in addition to focusing upon basic reading and writing skills.

Using Flexible and Varied Teaching Methods.

Classroom size varies according to housing patterns. Where there are large numbers of illiterates who live in close proximity, large classes are held; those who are separated from one another study in small groups or individually. More classes are held during slack farming seasons than during the busy seasons, and most of the classes are of a spare-time nature.

Universalizing Primary Education.

It is recognized that illiteracy can not be successfully combatted until drop out rates in primary and secondary schools decline. As primary education has become universalized, some areas have issued the "three permissions" to school-aged children, in an attempt to promote school attendance. These especially apply to girls from poor families and include permission to attend school while bringing younger brothers and sisters to school premises, permission to arrive at school late and leave early, and permission for pupils from full and part time schools to join each others' classes and transfer to each others' schools.[13]

Long Range Plans and the Creation of Standards in Support of the Elimination of Illiteracy.

The State Education Commission plans to eliminate illiteracy by the middle of the 1990s in developed areas and the late 1990s in less developed and remote areas. It has been stipulated that the twelve to forty year old age group must be the priority target for eliminating illiteracy, and that minimal literacy rates must be set at 85 percent in the countryside, and 90 percent in urban areas. The eradication of illiteracy in remote and mountainous areas, as well as in those areas where substantial numbers of minority nationalities reside, remains especially difficult.

ADULT HIGHER EDUCATION

The 1980s witnessed a radical expansion of higher adult education institutions, as economic policies affected this sector as well. Promotion and employment are now more directly linked to one's academic rather than political background, increasing the demand for a college diploma. Because of the restrictive admissions policies of formal higher educational institutions, the vast majority of high school graduates seek non-formal higher education training. In 1988, China's 1075 formal higher education institutions enrolled a total of 2,065,900 students while alternative adult higher educational institutions numbering 1,420 enrolled 1,855,000 students.[14]

For the most part, adult higher education has developed to its present level over the past five to ten years. Eight hundred of the adult higher education institutions are workers' colleges that are factory operated. Their quality varies enormously and many lack appropriate facilities, faculties, a well-designed curriculum, and qualified administrators. Many of these institutions do not even have one full time faculty member and rely totally upon adjunct instructors. The background of the students who enter these programs is also uneven. Because there has never been a centralized accreditation system sponsored by the government, which could monitor the quality of these programs, the government decided in early 1989 that no new adult higher education institutions would be allowed to register, and those that fail to meet minimum requirements would be abolished.[15]

In addition to workers' colleges, non-formal higher education alternatives include radio and television universities, correspondence courses offered by formal colleges and universities, in-service training institutes offered to administrators, in-service teacher training institutes (often called institutes of education) and peasant colleges. A short description of these offerings follows.

Radio/Television Universities.

The radio/television university system was created in February 1979. The Central Radio/T.V. University offers basic course work in general and specialized subjects. By 1986, almost all of the country's provinces had established their own provincial radio/television universities. Their enrollment is the largest of all adult higher education institutions, as Table 5.2 attests.

Table 5.2
Adult Higher Education Statistics (1985)

Type	Number of Institutions	Enrollment (,000)
1. Radio/TV universities	29	637.0
2. Workers' colleges	863	260.0
3. Peasant colleges	4	0.9
4. Administrator institutes	102	40.3
5. Institutes of Education	216	247.1
6. Independent correspondence colleges	2	9.9
7. Evening colleges and classes	-	493.0

Source: B. Yu and H.Y. Xu. *Adult Higher Education: A Case Study of a Workers' College in the People's Republic of China*(Paris: IIEP, 1988).
    Students are enrolled in radio/tv universities for three years and are most often released by their employers, with full salary, in order to pursue their studies. The university offers programs in the sciences and engineering, the humanities, and economics. Currently, 50 courses in five science and engineering specialties and 40 courses in seven economics specialties are available. Upon graduation, students receive a diploma from their local television university. Although the diplomas are officially supposed to be equivalent to those offered by formal universities, which require their students to complete four years

of training, the comparison represents a flawed sense of accomplishment given the disparate academic background of the two student population groups.[16] The Central Radio/TV University is jointly administered by the State Education Commission and the Ministry for Radio and Television. The Central Radio/TV University supervises the local radio/television universities which are run and managed by provincial or municipal departments. So far, with the exception of Tibet, all the provinces have established their own radio/television universities. A radio/television educational network has virtually covered the entire country with radio/t.v. units, local affiliated schools, teaching centers and tutorial classes. In 1986, the network started to use manmade satellites as a means of transmission.

Job allocation for graduates of these institutions is based on the principle of "where from, where to." Under such rules, the majority of graduates will return to their original place of residence. Admission, training and job assignment form integral parts of a coherent plan: planned enrollment, planned training according to needs, and planned job allocation. Students are recommended by their work units to take the entrance examinations. If they meet the requirements, they will be admitted to the radio/television universities. These students will be released from their institutions, firms, companies and factories with full pay for three years. Expenses related to their study are included in the budget of their own employers under the item of "staff training." After graduation, the students are required to return to their original work units. Their qualification will be normally respected and hence their posts and salaries adjusted, as if they were graduates from regular universities. However, it is not uncommon to discover that some or many of the graduates from these programs will attempt to move to other "white collar" positions with relatively higher social prestige.

Correspondence and Evening Classes.

Most of China's formal colleges and universities operate correspondence studies and evening classes. These classes often generate extra revenue for the college, and instructors and professors can obtain extra income for themselves by participating in these programs.

Correspondence and evening classes fall within two categories: those which only offer certificates in a single area or specialty such as English, engineering, forestry or agriculture and those that offer a diploma. These programs last from three to four years; they enroll students who usually have full time occupations. In 1983, 378 formal universities had established correspondence departments and evening colleges, and by 1985, the number of institutions that offered correspondence and evening programs increased by 64 percent to 591.[17]

Workers' Colleges.

Workers' colleges include full-and spare-time colleges. The latter evolved from the "July 21 Workers' College", created during the Cultural Revolution. Administratively speaking, workers' colleges are operated by three types of organizations and work units: local education departments or workers' unions, which operate regional workers' colleges; non-educational ministries and local industries, and individual enterprises.

Students are required to be under thirty years of age with two years of job related experience. The duration of these programs varies from four to five years; students are not given release time from their regular employment. The government requires that workers' colleges operated by industries and enterprises must have an enrollment of more than ninety students in order to be accredited by the State Education Commission, and many of these colleges fail to meet that standard.

In 1981, the mission and institutional purpose of workers' colleges was redefined by the Ministry of Education. These colleges were to be viewed as institutions offering higher education for workers with the specific aim of training skilled personnel. Curricular programs in workers' colleges would follow the same three-year programs taught in regular colleges, although a few workers' colleges might also offer degree courses. In 1983, the Ministry of Education specified the qualifications that should be acquired by graduates of workers colleges, arguing that they should include " ...mastery of fundamental theories, the main body of knowledge and major technical skills necessary in respective fields, with the ability to analyze and solve technical problems in respective specialties and the ability to use one foreign language in reading books and journals in their own specialties."[18]
Thus, all workers' colleges now have the same educational objectives as specialized colleges regardless of their specific size, structure and conditions under which they operate. Both workers' colleges and specialized colleges now are part of the same stratum within China's higher educational system.

While undergraduate students in regular higher education institutions are required to study for four or five years depending upon the nature of their specialization, and students of specialized colleges are required to study for two or three years, the situation in workers' colleges is more complicated. Because the latter include full-time, part-time and spare-time formats, there is no uniform pattern of course duration. In 1983, a few workers' colleges operating under optimum conditions, such as the Shanghai Workers' Spare-time College, began to offer degree courses. After four years of full-time study, the graduates of these colleges acquired qualifications that were formally equivalent to those who received degrees in the same major from regular colleges.

Diploma courses offered by workers' colleges are also similar to those offered by regular, three-year specialized colleges, insofar as both institutions attempt to train technicians and engineers in areas that allow them to integrate theory and practice. Full-time students are required to study for three years and part-time students, four years. The Ministry of Education laid down guidelines that required full-time students in science and engineering to complete 2,000-2,200 periods in theory, and liberal arts students to complete no less than 1,600 periods. Part-time and spare-time students majoring in science and engineering are required to complete 1,800 to 2,000 periods in theory; liberal arts students face the same period requirements as their full-time counterparts. Curricular programs are standardized in all cases so as to enable the graduates of workers' colleges to attain the same level of proficiency as do graduates of regular colleges.[19]

In 1982, the Ministry of Education introduced standardized evaluation procedures in workers' colleges. All applicants to workers' colleges are required to complete a unified examination, organized by the respective local education departments. In 1982, 86,000 students applied to 494 workers' colleges, administered by 21 provinces, municipalities, autonomous regions and two non-educational ministries, and 25,000 were admitted for study. Most of the provinces select four or five basic courses that are subject for testing. Upon completion of the required courses, students must complete graduation projects (or theses) and participate in the graduation examination held by the respective colleges. In 1983, the Ministry of Education issued standardized procedures governing registration, student records, student status, examination and grading, graduation, transfer students, repeat students, drop-outs, suspensions, attendance, awards, appropriate student conduct and discipline.[20]

Independent Study Through Examination Committee.

This type of certification system is uniquely Chinese. Adult students (most of whom are in their mid-twenties and have failed the national college entrance examination) undertake self-study, based upon a curriculum designed by provincial committees. Each year, the National Examination Committee will create tests, administered by local committees. Students can apply to take these examinations without having acquired previous course credit. Students who pass the examinations for four year degree courses receive a bachelor's degree; those who pass three year courses or single courses are issued certificates.

The approach was first piloted in three major cities and one province in 1981 and was extended nationwide in 1983. At present, most of the provinces, municipalities, and autonomous regions have set up their own local committees for self-study examinations, whose specializations include the liberal arts, science, engineering, agriculture, finance, economics, politics, and law.

During the first half of 1983, more than 73,000 applicants sat for examinations in Beijing, Tianjin, Shanghai and Liaoning, and during the second half of the same year, the number of examinees increased to 188,000. More than 115,800 single-course certificates have been issued. In 1985, there were over a million applications for single-course certificates, and in 1986, bachelor's degrees were conferred on successful applicants for the first time. Thirteen examinations have been conducted over the past six years in Beijing, certifying over 200,000 applicants.[21]

The special feature of the self-study examination approach to adult education is, of course, its openness in admission. The official regulation stipulates that "any citizen of the People's Republic of China may apply." There is no restriction whatsoever with regards to occupation, age, or educational background, nor are there subject area restrictions. Although the general impression that independent study is the most painstaking among all approaches to adult education continues to persist, this is the only case of higher education in China to date, where admission is unconditional.

In-service Training for Administrators and Teachers.

Two types of adult education institutions have been established for providing in-service training to administrators and teachers. Administrator institutes are designed to upgrade the skills of those who reside at a management level but lack management skills or training. They are attended by cadres who have been mainly promoted because of political background and connections. In-service teacher training institutes have been charged with the responsibility of upgrading the skills of over 50 percent of China's unqualified teachers, who work in the country's primary and secondary schools.

Challenges

Non-formal adult education is confronted with a number of problems and challenges that have unexpectedly arisen in the wake of the implementation of changing economic policies. Literacy training is not receiving sufficient funds, and when programs are started, they are almost always based upon local initiatives. Literacy training and non-formal primary education receive official lip service, as being important, but substantive commitments are lacking. To use a Chinese saying, "it is like cooking without the necessary ingredients." When policies are formulated at the higher levels, policy makers fail to consider local conditions. Producers and users of literacy programs are not highly motivated, as linkages to future prosperity are far from visible. Learners calculate their opportunities in immediate terms.

It can be concluded that literacy programs and peasant education, generally, have lost momentum. If new programs are not created in the near future and new sources of funding for these programs are not discovered, illiteracy will continue to increase dramatically. Since the vast majority of rural students terminate their education at the elementary level, post-primary and post literacy programs are important agenda items for a government attempting to prevent the growth of illiteracy. However, these programs are not sufficiently available throughout the country, particularly in those areas that would benefit most from their presence.

At the secondary level, technical and vocational programs are now more popular than academic programs as their participants can link the skills they have mastered from exposure to these programs, to immediate economic return. The main problem confronting secondary adult technical education is that it is urban oriented and limited in availability of teaching materials, textbooks, qualified personnel, and other resources. Adult secondary technical training, and academic programing are viewed as important in rural areas, only insofar as they are seen to positively affect agricultural productivity.

As long as formal higher education continues to be free and as long as admission to formal universities is highly selective, the demand for adult higher education will continue to grow. These programs will mainly be concentrated in urban areas and while the urban elites are benefiting from their presence, rural populations will be forced into learning limited yet marketable skills or skills that will improve their productivity. Adult higher education will experience substantial expansion in the next decade with respect to enrollment. It is the government's desire to control program quality and guard against diploma disease as it supervises this expansion.

Conclusion

It is not surprising that ideology continues to dictate educational priorities within both formal and non-formal sectors in contemporary China. The current emphasis upon modernization, through expertise in science and technology, has foreshadowed the rise of secondary and post-secondary technical training, which characterizes adult education in urban population areas. At the same time, rural populations have experienced an erosion of basic skills and a worrisome increase in illiteracy. The rural responsibility system is a prime culprit, because in its commitment to increase economic productivity, the policy has subtly undermined the perceived importance of basic level education. Dropouts and non-attenders seek to contribute to family income in the short run, rather than commit themselves to schooling. The zealous quest for obtaining the short-term benefits of economic development may have the effect of creating the "dual economy" and "dual society" reminiscent of modern India. It would be a shame if China, so renowned historically for its progressive work in combating ignorance and illiteracy, should surreptitiously enter the twenty-first century competing with India for the unadmirable status of possessing the largest number of illiterates of any of the world's nation states.

Notes
1. N.J. Colletta, "Worker-Peasant Education in the People's Republic of China", World Bank Staff Working Paper No. 527 (Washington, D.C.: World Bank, 1982).

2. Colletta, "Worker-Peasant Education," *op. cit.*, J. Lofstedt. *Chinese Educational Policy* (Stockholm: Almquist and Wiskell, 1980); S. Pepper, "Education and Revolution: The Chinese Model Revisited," *Asian Survey* vol.18, no. 9 (1978):847-890; S. Shirk, "Educational Political Backlash: Recent Changes in Chinese Educational Policy", *Comparative Education Review* vol. 23, (1979):183-217.

3. J.L. Wang, *Literacy Campaigns in China's Rural Areas* (Paris: IIEP, UNESCO,1982).

4. Wang, *Literacy Campaigns, op. cit.*

5. Wang, *Literacy Campaigns, op. cit.*

6. *Achievement of Education in China* (Beijing, People's Education Press, 1985).

7. *People's Daily* (September 24, 1988).

8. See *People's Daily* (January 16, 1989) where it was reported that in Shanghai about 189 primary schools tore down their school walls and fences and opened businesses.

9. *People's Daily* (February 15, 1989).

10. Department of Adult Education, State Education Commission, *Create a New Situation for Peasant Education* (Beijing, Educational Science Press, 1984).

11. *Ibid.*

12. "Resolution of the Central Committee of the Chinese Communist Party Regarding Reform of the Educational System," (May 27, 1985).

13. State Education Commission, "Report on Peasant Education in

China," *Education Information* no.26 (December 20, 1984).

14. Department of Planning and Financing, State Education Commission, *Report on Educational Statistics* (Beijing: State Education Commission, December 16, 1988).

15. B. Yu and H.Y. Xu, *Adult Higher Education: A Case Study of a Workers' College in the People's Republic of China* (Paris: IIEP, 1988).

16. *Ibid.*

17. *Ibid.*

18. *Ibid.*

19. *Ibid.*

20. *Ibid.*

21. *Ibid.*

CHAPTER SIX

MINBAN SCHOOLS IN DENG'S ERA
by Jean Robinson

The price of socialist reform is high. We have witnessed over the past several years the dizzying costs of such reform: turmoil among the political leadership, civil strife, inflation and unemployment, violence, and disruption. Although short term, these phenomena undoubtedly exert long term pressures on the polity of any socialist-minded state. But deeper and more profound are the psychological dislocations and material consequences of the shift from a socialist welfare state to a more market-oriented laissez-faire political economy. These strains and stresses are clearly evident in the recent history of popular education in China since the modernization and reform program began there ten years ago.

In this brief survey, I will examine the fate of *minban* schools in China's rural areas. Long an heir to the Chinese communist tradition of self-reliance and autonomous development, *minban xuexiao* or popularly-run schools have a history going back to the early days of the Ya'nan Era. In the turbulent history of Chinese Communist public education, the popularity and legitimacy of *minban* schools have waxed and waned, congruent with the advent and demise of the radical or Maoist line in policy formulation. But like a phoenix, popularly-run schools keep reemerging, often seen as a solution to otherwise insoluble problems of public school financing.

As the preceding paragraph intimates, the past forty-five years of *minban* education reveal a radical shift in justification and legitimation. Originally *minban xuexiao* had both an ideological and a pragmatic function. They were designed, as I have argued elsewhere[1], to convince poor uneducated peasants that they could exert control over their lives and their communities, that they had power, if they cooperated together, over the wealthy educated landowners and officials in their villages. Furthermore the establishment of *minban* schools in remote villages performed a secondary ideological role in demystifying literacy and education. No longer, it was hoped by Communist cadres, would peasants obey others simply because the latter claimed literary superiority.

Practically of course, people-run schools, which also meant people-financed schools, helped the Communist Party fulfill its promise to educate and enrich the poor, without costing the Party or the fledgling revolutionary government excessive amounts of scarce capital. Instead, the Chinese Communist Party (CCP) used the slogan of self-reliance to claim credit for schools that were organized, financed, and managed by members of the local community. These schools in the 1940s were simple literacy projects. Books were few, teachers barely literate, curricula elementary. Students were taught basic characters, using texts that also delivered political messages about the leadership of Mao Zedong and the CCP, the empowerment of the Chinese peasantry, and the evils of landlords and feudalism. Arithmetic skills and scientific concepts were taught as they could be applied to local agricultural production. Travelling propaganda drama troupes shared songs and stories about the value of education, the collective power of peasants, and the patriotism of the Red Army and the CCP. Farmers and soldiers were brought to these village schools to share their wisdom and experiences in the revolution.

From the perspective of the 1950s, when the educational system was professionalized and modernized, *minban xuexiao* had served an important political and social function in the 1940s that was now superceded by Soviet-style industrialization and modernization. Yet even the most vocal critics of the *minban* system, if it deserves to be called a system, given the lack of planning and *ad hoc* nature of the schools, maintained that they remained a necessity in certain backward parts of the country until China's wealth grew. *Minban xuexiao* were relegated to the dusty corners of China's interiors, where they continued to be the only hope for basic education in much of the countryside.

In the 1960s and early 1970s, *minban* schools came into their own again, as Maoist criticisms of key schools and elite education surfaced again and held sway. For want of funding and from a deep belief in the logic of basic peasant-based education, *minban xuexiao* were widely promoted by education and political officials alike during the period of the Cultural Revolution. But by the time of Deng Xiaoping's era of Four Modernizations, there no longer existed in

Beijing a sufficiently influential band of supporters for people-managed schools as an ideological principle.   Instead, *minban* schools were a stopgap measure until the time that the state could afford to fund all primary education at a level commensurate with the prestigious key schools in China.

Thus the continued existence of people-managed schools in China has been rationalized and legitimated not by reference to the importance of self-reliance, local autonomy, and popular participation but solely because there are not enough funds available in the capital for the support of education.

The Chinese government's retreat from investment in rural local education was to have been offset by local funding, derived from the new wealth created in the countryside. Even before the retreat from experimentation with market socialism in 1988, however, such a plan faced considerable problems.

The state's decision to require funding by local communities of these schools has not been complemented by a "hands-off" approach to regulating curriculum, staffing, and decision-making.   Rather, there has been an unprecedented increase in state control over the *minban* school network, precisely in those areas once left to community discretion.   Thus as state demands for local financing of schools have increased, there has been no concomitant rise in local control over the schools.

What follows is a brief survey of the state of *minban xuexiao*. It is suggestive rather than definitive, for there has been a concerted decrease in the news coverage of *minban* schools in the Chinese media over the last several years. Plans to do further field research on the schools in summer 1989 were aborted because of the Tiananmen massacre in May 1989.

Minban Xuexiao in the late 1980s

In 1985, the CCP Central Committee on Education Structural Reform called for the formulation of a compulsory education law. Within one year, the State Council (SC) and the State Education Commission (SEC) submitted the "Compulsory Education Law (Draft) of the People's Republic of China"[2] to the Fourth Session of the Sixth

National People's Congress in April 1986. The new legislation called for nine years of compulsory education for all Chinese children beginning on July 1, 1986 and for the development of primary and secondary schools to meet China's needs. Recognizing the varying level and quality of educational systems in China, the legislation stipulated a gradual implementation of the program, designed to erase illiteracy and "promote the cultural and scientific qualities of the people" by the end of the century.[3] The focus of the initial law and subsequent policies and reports issued by the SC and the SEC[4] was three-pronged: standardization of educational systems throughout the country, improvement of teacher training and effectiveness, and increased funding for education.[5]

In all these areas, *minban* schools appear to have been significantly affected. The Compulsory Education Law demands a formidable reform of the entire nation's schools and educational organization that was (and is) characterized by different types of systems for primary and middle school education. These include, formally, the "6-and-3" (6 years for primary school and 3 years for middle school), "5-and-4", "5-and-3", and a 9-years system. The "5-and-3" system predominates in the rural areas where *minban* schools are located. Usually at best the *minban* schools offer 5 years of schooling. Most children attending *minban* primary schools do so irregularly and without the benefit of well-trained, well-educated teachers. Thus despite the recognition of SEC officials that standardization is a "complex" issue[6], this remains an understatement. Primary school education is not yet universal, despite the longterm presence of *minban xuexiao* in the countryside. Indeed reliance on *minban* schools to provide basic education in the "mountain areas and minority regions" (*shanqu he shaoshu minzhudiqu*)[7] may have contributed to the low standard of education now so prevalent in China's rural areas. The schools offer basic character instruction, simple political instruction and propaganda, and math and science as it can be applied to work in the local community and production. They do not intend to prepare students for further education or for vocations different from those of their parents. The success of these schools is also questionable, given the continuing and even increasing levels of illiteracy in remote and rural "mountainous areas."

The number of *minban xuexiao*--and here we are speaking only of primary schools although there may be middle schools that are "people managed" as well[8]--is unreported by Chinese authorities. There has never been an accurate accounting of the schools, partly because they are *ad hoc* and temporary creations. But there is another reason as well. The schools are an embarrassing reminder to the state and the citizens of the continuing inability of the Chinese government to provide equal educational opportunities to all its citizens. No one denies that *minban* schools serve poor backward villages; no one denies that the quality of education is rudimentary at its best. The potential for empowerment through this education is minimal given the lack of respect accorded *minban* schools by the state, the community, and the teachers and pupils themselves. Still we have some indication of the large numbers of *minban xuexiao* in rural China. Recent issues of *Renmin Jiaoyu* (People's Education) imply that the number of *minban* schools is quite large. In Yunnan province, for instance, there are over 46,000 *minban* school teachers in primary education, although many of these are not full time teachers.[9] In Fujian province, in 36 "mountainous areas," there are 32,100 *minban* teachers.[10] There are occasional and very casual figures available for other provinces; if the past is any indicator (and it may not be), there are equally high numbers of teachers in most rural marginal provinces.

Over the past 36 months, the state has expressed very rarely any attention to *minban xuexiao*. The only concern over *minban* schools seems to be the way the population treats the teachers. Apparently, they are snubbed and abused by both local residents and at times pupils; teachers are apt to want to become farmers or engage in economic activities rather than teach.[11] Concurrently, with the state's new emphasis on quality, all *minban* as well as what are referred to as "public" (*gongban*) teachers must pass the examinations certifying that they have obtained a sufficient level of knowledge and proficiency.[12] Since most *minban* teachers are almost wholly uneducated, they face a major hurdle in these exams. But if they do not pass, the government is stymied. Reliance on *minban xuexiao* is one of the ways the state and its educational arm, the SEC, hope to achieve the compulsory education goal of nine years of education for every child by the end of the century.

The implementation of compulsory education has created severe problems, primarily because it focuses both on the quality of education (a perennial issue in the critique of *minban* schools) and on increasing the number of schools. The consequence has been one of increased stress for teachers who wonder why they should stay in what they consider to be thankless, extremely low-paid, and difficult jobs[13]; anxiety on the part of local authorities who rely on inexpensive teachers to ensure that schools exist at all; and perhaps (although there is only sketchy evidence of this) anger on the part of local parents. If parents follow the compulsory law and send their children to school, they may lose out on several years of child labor, labor that has become more important over the past decade as the household responsibility system became the major contract mechanism for agricultural production. The state furthermore has warned parents not to keep children out of school and particularly has expressed opposition to parents employing children before they are educated. Indeed Articles 11 and 15 of the Law on Compulsory Education state that parents must ensure their children attend school and that no organization or individual may employ school-age children.[14] On the other hand, parents who do send their children to local *minban xuexiao* may be perturbed that their children are not receiving the quality of education promoted by the authorities. One wonders what parents' reaction is to official statements that tell them the state does not have enough money to invest in education throughout the country and that poor backward areas will just have to wait their turn.[15] In other words, will the money ever trickle down that far?

Kathlin Smith[16] asked in her report on education funding whether the funding will trickle up?; from the peasants' point of view, this is an impossibility. Recently from the point of view of the state, it is also a problem. If the state is relying on locally generated funds to pay for education beyond the local *minban* school, the plan for widespread reform of the education is in jeopardy.

The low quality of buildings in which *minban* schools are housed is attested to in the press by reports of roof collapses, freezing classrooms, and rickety if existent furniture.[17] So too, teachers' salaries in *minban xuexiao* are markedly low, despite nationally commanded raises in May 1986. Local funds must be used to bring the *minban* schools up to the level dictated by the new policies issued in the wake of the Law on Compulsory Education. Yet given the slowdown in China's economic situation, and the general poverty that obtains in many parts of rural peripheral China, it is highly unlikely that any extra funds will be found to pay for additional schools and to generate investment in regional or national education plans.

This has been especially true since the Tiananmen Massacre of May 1989, which among other things, signified a serious retrenchment in both production and consumption. Provincial plans, like that of Jiangxi Province, which would tax group purchases of 29 consumer items to subsidize education, will likely fall apart given the growing economic crisis.[18] Educational surcharges approved by the SC in 1986 will also be less profitable than expected. These were to have been a boon to local school systems, since the "surcharges collected by local governments [were to] be kept and used locally."[19] It is unlikely then that massive doses of money will be infused into any local school system in the near future: *minban xuexiao*, the poorest cousin of all, will be hit the hardest.

Given these characteristics of weakness, it is not surprising that there has been little reportage on *minban xuexiao* in the national or even regional press in China over the past few years. The one exception to this has been a recent series of articles in *Renmin Jiaoyu* published under the title "Everybody should be concerned about *minban xuexiao* teachers" (*Dajia doulai guanxin minbanjiaoshi*). The series focused on the similarities and differences between *minban* and public (*gongban*) teachers, claiming the former were as valuable as the latter; articles reporting on the heavy reliance on *minban* school teachers to accomplish educational goals of primary education, and the necessity to allow *minban* teachers to do their work without interference from abusive parents.[20]

The thrust of this slight media attention to *minban* education is to emphasize to the public and to teachers the importance of all types of educational systems to a successful compulsory education program. The *minban xuexiao* are not touted however as final answers to the need to educate peasants nor are they presented as institutionalized processes through which local authority, that is citizen authority, can be exercised. As is evident even from the rough outline of the condition of *minban* schools in a modernizing China presented above, decisions about the quality of teachers, the funding of schools, and the implementation of compulsory education plans are the province of the authorities. *Minban* schools are not intended to and do not currently reflect any effort at parental participation or true popular-management save for the accumulation and investment of funds into school systems. These local-based systems, from all evidence, remain accountable only to authorities in Beijing and provincial capitals not to the local community. The original intent of *minban xuexiao*--to empower citizens while providing education--has been completely obscured and has apparently failed on all measures.

Notes

1. See Jean C. Robinson, "Decentralization, Money and Power: The Case of People-Run Schools in People's China," *Comparative Education Review* 30, no.1 (February 1986): 73-88, and Jean C. Robinson, "State Control and Local Financing of Schools in China," in Mark Bray and Kevin Lillis, eds., *Community Financing of Education: Issues and Policy Implications in Less Developed Countries* (Oxford: Pergamon Press, 1988): 181-195.

2. The text of the Compulsory Education Law can be read in English in *Joint Publications Research Service: China* (hereafter *JPRS: China*) (April 22, 1986): K-17, as translated from *Xinhua* (Beijing) (April 17, 1986).

3. See *Xinhua* (Beijing) (April 17, 1986) translated in *JPRS: China* (April 24, 1986): K-10.

4. See, for example, *Xinhua* (Beijing) (September 25, 1986) as translated in *JPRS: China* (September 29, 1986): K-21. .

5. See Li Peng's explanation of the Education Law in *Xinhua* (Beijing) (April 17, 1986) as translated in *JPRS: China* (April 24, 1986): K-10 - K-17.

6. *JPRS: China* (April 24, 1986): K-12.

7. *Renmin Jiaoyu* 300 (March 1989):19.

8. See *Foreign Broadcast Information Service: China* (hereafter *FBIS:China*), 88-170 (September 1, 1988):48.

9. "Guanyu minban jiaoshi de jige wenti," *Renmin Jiaoyu* (hereafter *RJ*) 300 (March 1989):16.

10. "Tigao minban jiaoshi daiyun de youxiao tujing," *RJ* 299 (February 1989): 14.

11. *China Daily* [*CD*] (December 12, 1988); (April 6, 1989).

12. "Guanyu minban jiaoshide jige wenti," *RJ* 300 (March 1989): 19-20.

13. "Xiang minban jiaoshi zhijing," *RJ* 298 (January 1989):15.

14. "Compulsory Education Law of the People's Republic of China," *Xinhua* (Beijing) (April 17, 1986) as translated in *JPRS: China*, (April 22, 1986): K-17.

15. See *Xinhua* (Beijing) (February 21, 1987) as translated in *JPRS: China* (February 25, 1987): K-14.

16. Kathlin Smith, "Funding China's Education: Will Trickle-up Work?," *China Exchange News* 17, no.2 (June 1989): 8.

17. *CD* (April 15, 1989); (April 18, 1989), and (February 26, 1983).

18. *CD* (January 3, 1989).

19. *Xinhua* (Beijing) (May 7, 1986) as translated in *JPRS: China* (May 8, 1986): K-4.

20. See *RJ* issues of January-April 1989.

CHAPTER SEVEN

SPECIAL ECONOMIC ZONES AND EDUCATION IN CHINA: BOLD REFORM OR TIMID EXPERIMENT?

by John N. Hawkins and Bruce Koppel

As Chinese leaders attempt to reassure the world on the continued policy of the "economic open door" while at the same time tightening their grip on the polity, those who have been intrigued with the phenomenon of special economic zones (SEZs) are watching places like Shenzhen, Zhuhai, Xiamen and Shantou with great interest. This is because it has been in the SEZs that the greatest efforts have been made to adopt flexible policies toward the outside world with respect to trade, production, joint ventures and a whole group of economic experiments. It has also been in the SEZs that some of the most interesting educational experiments have also taken place, experiments at all educational levels but particularly with respect to the transition from school to work within the context of rural-urban linkages. The burgeoning and at times chaotic economic expansion in the SEZs has created a high demand for skilled labor, socialized in new ways to accommodate to the rapidly changing economic environment. China's conventional schooling pattern was ill equipped to meet this demand, and thus a variety of educational reforms has also been a hallmark of China's experiment with SEZs. In this chapter we will explore the general nature of SEZs, focusing on basic educational goals and objectives and then narrowing in on specific issues related to education and work within the context of rural-urban linkages. In some respects, China's experiences with SEZs highlight the expansive transformation that has occurred throughout China, particularly in terms of diversification within areas as well as linkages between rural areas and the urban sector. Rural transformation and the relationship with training

172

and skill development may be two of the most significant and lasting features of SEZs in China.[1]

The processes involved are not entirely unique to China. Similar processes have been seen in East Asia (Korea, Japan, and Taiwan) and can be seen today throughout South and Southeast Asia. To better understand the Chinese case, however, it helps to recognize characteristics of rural transformation processes elsewhere in terms of scope, rate, causes, and consequences.

Throughout Asia, the relative contribution of agriculture to gross domestic product (GDP) is declining while the relative contributions of manufacturing, trade, and service activities are increasing. In fact, by 1983, agriculture accounted for more than half of GDP in only two Asian countries, Bhutan and Nepal. However, across South and Southeast Asia, conventional national statistics report that the agriculture sector's share of the total labor force continues to substantially exceed one-half. What these statistics directly reflect is the fact that the majority of Asia's people still live in areas classified as "rural," an attribution routinely assumed to be equivalent to the dominance of agricultural economic activities. Labor force participation, however, is not the same as productive employment. Despite significant increases in land productivity, average annual growth of agricultural output per worker in Asia's agriculture continues to be below 2 percent in the 1980s, not nearly enough to provide productive employment in agriculture for an expanding rural labor force and hence hardly enough to significantly reduce continuing problems of rural poverty and inequality.[2]

Awareness of these issues has generated increased interest in productive rural employment outside of agriculture.[3] However, several problems have placed constraints upon the ability to document the existing scope and rate of growth of nonagricultural rural employment. Most of what is known, particularly in South and Southeast Asia, comes from income and expenditure surveys. These reveal that large proportions of farm household income (estimates of 30 percent-40 percent are common) are being attributed to off-farm sources.[4]

However, interpretation is complicated by evidence throughout Asia of declining real wage rates in agriculture. Such statistics do not distinguish between wage, self-employment, and family enterprise income sources, an especially crucial point given evidence that female and child labor may be dominant in rural self-employment activities.[5] This certainly seems to be the trend in China's SEZs.

What information there is reveals numerous issues about the structural changes characterizing rural Asia, including China and the Shenzhen area. For example, linkages among wages, employment and output appear to vary at regional and even village levels throughout rural Asia. How wide is this variation and what are the primary underlying socioeconomic conditions that account for it? Oshima and others have pointed to the seasonality of demand for agricultural labor, especially in Asia's tropical monsoon climates, as a principal cause of variability of rural labor markets.[6] They suggest that seasonality has a primary influence on the evolution and performance of rural labor markets for *both* agricultural and non-agricultural activities, and, in fact, it is the major reason why South and Southeast Asia might not replicate the non--farm employment experiences of Japan, Korea, Taiwan, and the shifts that have occurred in Shenzhen. While recognition of the importance of increasing employment, labor productivity, and income in rural Asia is high, the context in which these problems are defined and the means generally advocated to address the problems may be too narrow. What is needed is more explicit attention to the broader structural changes characterizing rural Asia and their relationships to rural work.

The broader dimensions of Asia's rural transformation include the relationships of socioeconomic change in rural areas with processes of urbanization, industrialization, expanded international trade in rural natural resources, and technological change in agriculture. The consequences of these processes are reflected in the changing social organization of agriculture, the growing significance of secondary and tertiary urban centers for rural socioeconomic life, the increasing importance for national economic development of international trade in rural natural and human resources, the rising importance of non-rural and nonagricultural economic power in rural economic life, and the burgeoning complexities, capacities, and ambitions of contemporary national administration, communication and political systems.

These examples reflect three significant longer-term characteristics of rural transformation in Asia. First, the transformation process is uneven in terms of which individuals, groups, institutions, and social, economic, and political relationships are affected, when, and how. It is not clear at all--from historical experiences in East Asia or contemporary experiences in South and Southeast Asia--that the transformation process can proceed without significant social costs. However, to this point, Asia's rural transformation has involved two processes that historically have not always worked in tandem: (a) an *evolution* of the structure, composition, and functions of traditional rural socioeconomic institutions; and (b) an *imposition* of relationships, structures and processes that can significantly modify and ultimately displace existing patterns of rural resource management, economic development, social mobility and political determination.[7]

Second, there is a subtleness in the unevenness of Asia's rural transformation because of the coexistence but not necessarily the correlation of numerous transformations. Consequently, equating rural transformation with only one process--when transformation is described purely as a non-market to market transition--agriculture to industry or rural to urban transition, discounts many other processes that are also occurring such as political assimilation and mobilization, social differentiation and integration, and cultural innovation, revitalization, and suppression. These omissions are crucial, because they deflect attention from the richness of the heterogenous transformation patterns present.[8]

Third, Asia's rural transformation may well represent the emergence of a new form of socioeconomic organization, neither urban or rural as conventionally defined but rather the product of increasingly intense interaction between urban and rural socioeconomic activities. Within these zones of more intense economic interaction (e.g., the Jakarta-Bandung-Bogor triangle in Java; Central Luzon in the Philippines, Guangdong Province, including the SEZs, in China), one already sees an increase in nonagricultural activities (trading, transportation, services, and industry), high population mobility, and intense mixtures of land use with agriculture, cottage enterprises, industrial establishments, and a wide variety of trade and service activities coexisting side by side.[9] If there is a "new" socioeconomic form emerging, then what variabilities (for example, in characteristics of rate, structure and impacts) is this form displaying and why? These are just some of the issues that comprise the complex environment of political, economic, and social change that is occurring in Asia in general and in China's SEZs in particular. The role of education and training in this transformation will be discussed below.

Evolution and Development of SEZs

The policy of identifying distinctive regions in China specifically for the purpose of attracting foreign investment dates back to the late 1970s and was clearly inspired by efforts in other countries (often referred to as export-processing zones or trade platforms). The areas immediately around Hong Kong and Macau seemed natural candidates for such zones and in 1979 the State Council and Central Committee of the Chinese Communist Party (CCP) announced that such a zone would be established at Shekou, slightly Northwest of the New Territories in Hong Kong and Southwest of the City of Shenzhen--both areas accessible by rail and sea lanes. Politically, decisions were made at the top levels of the Chinese government by Deng Xiaoping and Yang Shangkun to authorize such zones at four sites: Shenzhen, Zhuhai, Shantou, and Xiamen. Other areas including the "open cities" have since been added to the list. The evolution of these areas from "industrial and/or export zones" into special economic zones (SEZs) was a natural development driven to some degree by the more complex interaction that developed between the different export zones, thus requiring a more comprehensive administrative structure. Thus, SEZs in China are characterized as areas with more extensive territory and larger populations than the typical export zone, which tends to be an enclave with few connections to the rest of the local economy. The SEZs in contrast, encompass not only industry but also agriculture, animal husbandry, tourism, education, science, services, and commerce. By 1980, the concept of a somewhat autonomous SEZ with broad political and economic goals was solidly entrenched in the power structure in Beijing, linked to overall national modernization goals, and attracting a significant amount of foreign attention.[10]

What appeared to be the rather abrupt development of SEZs seemed to some outside observers as unsupported by previous PRC economic development policy. Despite the criticism of the "self-reliance" model of prior political periods, China's reluctance to engage foreign economic networks is longstanding. However, a spatial re-deployment had been taking place since the mid-1950s and when viewed from this perspective the special treatment given to selected coastal areas is not surprising. Rather, this development was a gradual movement from the interior to the coast, from isolation and self-reliance to a more open door, from a more egalitarian economic system to a more market-oriented and differentiated one, from highly centralized management to a more decentralized, competency based system, and from an appropriate technology model to a sustained drive for "socialist modernization" of which the SEZs are the most dramatic experiment. The linkages between China's coastal regions and the thriving Pacific Rim was also clearly an important spatial factor. Thus, from a spatial perspective, China's SEZs can be viewed as a small area demarcated within a country's territory and suitably insulated for adopting special and flexible policies in external economic activities to attract and encourage foreign investments".[11]

The case of Shenzhen is illustrative of the striking scale of change that has taken place since its designation as a SEZ. Basically a sleepy village/town with a population of 72,000, Shenzhen consisted in 1979, of an urban area of only two square kilometers, a poor infrastructure of roads, buildings, and support facilities, surrounded by agricultural land. Within about four years it had grown to over 110 square kilometers of urban space and a total of 327.5 square kilometers when business sectors are included. The population has increased about 30 percent since then drawing on labor from the surrounding countryside as well as in the interior of China.[12]

Growth in SEZs, especially Shenzhen, has been significantly driven by investment from and linkages with Hong Kong-based enterprises. Estimates are that Hong Kong's subcontracting system alone has created 220,000 direct employment opportunities in more than 3,000 factories and has attracted 260,000 people from other parts of China. These linkages have evolved less in sales and more in terms of fabrication and assembly of garments, textiles, and especially electronic semi-manufactures. In 1986, for example, Shenzhen's electronic industry accounted for 46.5 per cent of the city's GVIO and 45.8 per cent of Guangdong's GVIO. In Shenzhen, there is a greater concentration of linkages involving completed garments than seen in the other SEZs, but this reflects the greater availability of foreign exchange in the Shenzhen SEZ and greater familiarity with and access to the Hong Kong market.[13]

However, there have been problems, which have, in turn, influenced the nature of Shenzhen's impact on surrounding rural areas. Significant problems in material and labor quality have limited the scope of linkages, especially in the garment and electronic industries. In response, many foreign companies are providing some form of training and technical support, especially to deal with issues of quality control, but as is discussed below, these strategies have had only limited success in addressing quality problems. One result is that much of the enterprise development seen in the SEZs is "footloose," i.e., it does not represent a significant investment in terms of facilities and technology. These enterprises that could be shifted elsewhere if need be.

Despite the scale of activities, therefore, the impact of Hong Kong's subcontracting linkages on the rural economy of Guangdong has been limited mainly to the actual subcontracting zones in the Pearl River Delta. What is changing in rural-urban relations, however, are two points that reflect the wider and more intense forms of interaction unfolding between Hong Kong and the SEZs: the movement of larger numbers of people at a faster rate over a wider area and the expansion of the scope and content of market interactions.

The first point, increased movement of people, is having effects on land use and services, and, as we shall see, on education. Urban-like services and land use patterns are appearing in corridors that separate the SEZs and Hong Kong. The second point, expanding markets, is affecting the sources of income for rural households as well as resource allocation within many enterprises outside the SEZs.

Thus, while it was clear from the start that SEZs would be "open" economically, allowing greater flexibility with respect to investment and management matters, it was also clear (though not much discussed) that they would not be open politically, or, as one scholar put it: "...it has been quite clear that the SEZs in China are not 'special' in the context of the state apparatus despite their more open policy in economic matters. The administration remains politicized both in structure and function."[14] This point is important considering the 1989 events in Beijing. The bureaucracy that was established to support the structural functions of the SEZs was politicized from the beginning with all top government posts held by top CCP leaders of the cities in which the SEZs are located. Some prominent features of this politicization are: state and CCP conflicts with respect to administrative power in the SEZs (the CCP dominating); regularized interference by the CCP in areas supposedly under state jurisdiction; multiple reporting relationships facilitating communication between state agencies and CCP officials.

Some efforts to depoliticize the bureaucracy over the past two years have been launched. For example, some state-owned enterprises have moved to local elections of managers rather than passively accepting the CCP nominee or complaining to Beijing or to a prominent central official. Enterprises are also utilizing economic rather than political criteria to assess a manager's performance and have made use of local media to critique CCP interference in SEZ matters. Despite these efforts, progress toward de-politicization has been slow. Some suggest that the dilemma of a politicized bureaucracy is imbedded in Chinese tradition and has little to do with the various revolutions since the turn of the century. In this view, China's bureaucracy will always seek to protect its vested interests, and if this means a slowing down of modernization, so be it. The events in Tiananmen Square lend credence to this view.[15] Nevertheless, certain favorable factors peculiar to the SEZs are present that encourage a more depoliticized bureaucracy. They include the large number of foreign investors involved in the enterprises thus making political interference more difficult and costly, the emphasis on consumer goods and foreign markets to drive economic growth in the SEZs, and the policy of inviting ethnic Chinese from Southeast Asia, Hong Kong, and other countries to participate at all levels in SEZ development.

Thus, although the development of SEZs seemed abrupt, in fact they evolved in a gradual manner and focused on central economic change with minor political adaptation. The spatial linkages between the interior and coastal regions were critical as were the linkages with neighbors on the Pacific Rim. Having moved in this direction, however, one of the first major obstacles to the success of the zones was the quantity and quality of labor available. Each zone, without exception, faced serious labor problems. The overall strategy of the SEZs, and particularly Shenzhen, was to provide two of the three factors of production (land and labor) to combine with external capital. It was quickly realized that as the population of the SEZs grew--particularly because of labor imported from surrounding rural areas and interior regions--the level of technical skills along with basic education was lower than desired. While the overall educational level of the labor force in Shenzhen, for example, was much higher than during the 1960s, it is still insufficient for the level of technical skills required by the rapid economic expansion that has occurred and will occur in the future.

Table 7.1
Labor Force Educational Level: Shenzhen

	1964	1982
Primary or above	48.31	77.51
Primary	37.06	31.60
Junior secondary	7.51	25.93
Senior secondary	3.11	17.99
Tertiary	.54	2.03
Illiterate (aged 12 or above)	23.34	9.05

Source: *Renkou Yanjiu* (Population Studies) Vol. 2, 1984, p.29 in R.Y.W. Kwok, "Structure and Policies in Industrial Planning in the Shenzhen Special Economic Zone," *China's Special Economic Zones* (1986).

There are still far too few graduates of senior secondary schools and the tertiary level. Furthermore, among those educated up to the senior secondary level, preparation in functional vocational and technical skills is deficient, leading one scholar to comment: "The relatively low quality of human capital revealed in the statistics does not appear to *be* compatible with advanced technology production, or high-level services."[16] In the early period of the SEZs, temporary workers were imported to solve the human capital problem, and plans were made to make major financial commitments and educational reforms to solve the problem for the future. In the remainder of this chapter we will outline some of those plans and assess their feasibility and progress.

Sez Educational Policies and Prospects

In keeping with the notion of an "open" economic system, educational policy in the SEZs has also been characterized as open, a window to the outside through which fresh new ideas, pedagogical practices, and important knowledge can flow. Of course, early on, it was also recognized that "unhealthy elements" would also gain access through the window and therefore educational officials must be vigilant and follow principles of "opposing pollution." While principally following the general educational pattern of China's inland educational system, educational policy in the SEZs has distinct characteristics and has been in a state of continual change.

At a broad level, a major goal of education in the SEZs is to provide all recipients of any form of education (from early levels to adult education) with three types of knowledge and skills: knowledge of socialist economic and political theory, knowledge of capitalist economic and political theory, and a thorough understanding of the specific characteristics of the SEZ area. Special courses are offered at each level to introduce students to these areas of knowledge, but it would appear that the primary emphasis is on the character of the zone itself.

Teacher compensation and status is another area of reform in the SEZs. General salaries have been raised, job titles adjusted to reflect actual work performed, bonuses paid for superior performance, and benefits increased (including overtime pay) for teachers at all levels. The procedure for initiating and completing capital construction projects for educational facilities has also been reformed. Such projects are more locally controlled with less state involvement in planning and approval procedures. The hope is that educational facilities can be constructed more quickly, efficiently, and geared toward specific educational needs.

A comprehensive reform of secondary education has occurred in most SEZs. The emphasis here has been on introducing more vocational-technical courses, including the establishment of demonstration centers, to provide the research and development base for further reforms. Unlike the situation in the interior where vocational-technical education is almost solely school-based, linkages have been formed with employers in the SEZs to provide hands-on instruction and ease the transition from school to work. Other reforms have been in the areas of political and ideological work (to combat "foreign corrosion"), teaching reform (experimenting with elicitation method, unit teaching, self-taught efforts, and a variety of curriculum design and teaching content revisions), and alternative methods of financing education (seeking funds from a variety of local sources as well as overseas Chinese in Hong Kong and Macau). One of the most dramatic reforms, however, has been in the area of adult education. As the technological level of the SEZs has grown more complex through joint ventures and the importation of new equipment from outside the region, so has the need for higher levels of technical skill grown. Short-term training classes in literacy, finance, information science, industry and commerce have been offered through both educational and enterprise sources. Additional instructors from adjacent regions (such as Hong Kong and Macau) have been invited to the zones to provide new teaching methods and up-to-date knowledge regarding technical and business skills. Students study in the zone, and then some go on to fieldwork in the adjacent area. Related to these efforts in adult education is the introduction and promotion of educational media through the use of television, language laboratories, video-tapes, and other audiovisual aids.

Finally, a concerted effort has been made to introduce the notion of "educational science" and research. In Shenzhen, a Municipal Institute of Educational Science has been established with the difficult task of determining how to introduce the most advanced pedagogical concepts from outside and mold them into an educational form that maintains "a unique Chinese character." The Institute is moving up the educational ladder, studying first the primary and secondary sectors and then the tertiary level.[17]

While the above points illustrate the broad features of educational policy in the SEZs, other analysts have linked education in the SEZs with certain specific economic sectors such as construction. Although building the physical plant for SEZs has been a top priority since 1979, the poor quality and quantity of the labor force have limited an effective response. One result has been major educational reform to transform a largely rural-based labor force into an educated urban construction force with higher level technical skills than are required in the interior.

Arguing that investment in education was the key to development in the West and Japan, policy-makers in Shenzhen and Shantou have outlined an ambitious plan to transform first primary and secondary general education (to lower the illiteracy rate below the current 16 percent in Guangdong) and provide a base for more specialized worker training. The principal thrust for the transformation of education in various zones, however, is on secondary vocational education and specialized college training for specific sectors such as construction. Here Chinese analysts are drawing a direct line between vocational-technical education and pre-employment training leading automatically to further economic growth and development. There is little awareness of the complexity of this educational sector, the costs involved (in Germany, for example, where it is heavily subsidized) or the lack of fit between training and actual work that often characterizes these programs. Yet they are moving ahead and a variety of programs have been established including specialized training programs at Shenzhen University.

Perhaps more promising, however, is the emphasis on adult education and on-site training. Again, citing numerous foreign examples (Japan, Soviet Union, Sweden), policy-makers have promoted the concept and practice of adult education in several enterprises in the zones. In the case of the Shantou Supersonic Company, literacy classes, specialized training, and general culture classes were initiated from 1978 to 1982 coinciding with a rise in labor productivity and earnings. This led authorities to conclude that, "These increases convincingly prove the cost-effectiveness of promoting adult education among employees."[18] Regardless of the real cause of increases in these two indices, further investments in adult education are likely to pay off for SEZ leaders if they are kept at a low cost and are enterprise supported. The program will be particularly useful for those workers coming from the rural sector where educational opportunities have been lacking and general skill levels are low. If the SEZs are going to continue to rely on the surrounding countryside as *a* source *of* labor for expansion within the zones, then a vigorous adult education program linked directly to specific enterprises will be critical.

The section above has sketched out the principal features of education and development in the context of rural-urban transformation in special economic zones. Despite China's other economic difficulties, the SEZ's seem to be in a continual state of development. The most advanced of these zones, as already noted, is the Shenzhen zone. In the section that follows, a more detailed picture of both vocational and technical as well as adult education in this SEZ will be outlined. It is *these* two areas that account for the bulk of skill-training that occurs, making them *so* essential for the economic transformation *of* the region.

CASE STUDY: SHENZHEN SPECIAL ECONOMIC ZONE

As has been noted above, Shenzhen has been transformed from a quiet village to a bustling urban area under great stress in order to continue the current rapid pace of development. Essential to its current success in transforming not only its own population but newly arrived workers from surrounding rural areas has been its developing vocational and technical education program and, by extension, its adult education program. Each has contributed enormously to supplying the kind of skilled manpower necessary to staff the new enterprises that have emerged as a result of more open economic policies. Although many shortcomings exist (and these will be discussed below), basically the system has moved ahead as economic development has taken place. While the formal educational system has grown considerably (44 kindergartens, 66 elementary schools, 19 middle schools, 2 universities), efforts to strengthen vocational-technical and adult education have also advanced.[19]

Once called an "educational desert," Shenzhen has in the past eight years increased its educational funding to over half a billion yuan. The average annual increase has been over 50 percent and in 1988, educational investment was 14 percent of the total financial expenditures of the city. This compares to a national average for similar sized cities of 11 percent. The funding supports 52 middle schools, 257 elementary schools throughout the entire Shenzhen area, and 17 middle schools and 36 elementary schools specifically within the zone. There are two universities and a variety of vocational-technical and adult education enterprises (see below).[20] Enrollments are high throughout the system, ranging from almost 100 percent at the elementary level to 87 percent at the junior high level. Administratively, Shenzhen has adopted the "principal responsibility system." Principals hold their positions for three years upon approval of the SEZ and local work units in the case of vocational-technical and adult education.[21] Financing of education in the Shenzhen SEZ follows a diversified pattern. A mix of central and local government support is combined with "collective funding" (government collectives and private enterprises), donations from overseas Chinese (donations of about 15 million yuan in 1987), school-run enterprises (factories and farms which brought in 400,000 yuan in 1986), and tax revenues from both local Chinese and foreign firms operating in the Shenzhen SEZ (3 percent is added to other tax levies and collected by the Shenzhen tax department although those enterprises already running part-time schools are exempted). The mix of funding and efficiency in collection and allocation has spurred overall educational development in the zone.[22]

The general approval process for establishing workers' and vocational schools follows a route from the relevant local government office or work unit to final approval by the National Commission on Education, the related department of the State Council, and finally the National Committee on Workers' Education. In fact, the process is quite decentralized as far as SEZs are concerned; although all of the above mentioned steps are taken, the latter central level approvals have been pro forma.[23] This may change as the PRC tightens up the educational system as a whole and indeed there are already signs of a re-centralization. General guidelines for these schools have also existed since 1982 and are entitled "Methods for Trial Implementation on Running Workers' Secondary Vocational Schools."[24] Applicants to such schools are expected to have the equivalent of a junior middle school level of education, two years of work experience, and be under thirty-five years of age. They need to have approval of their work units and be examined both in terms of academic content and subjective criteria (to be "morally, intellectually, physically" sound). The content of the formal examination focuses on Chinese, mathematics, elementary physics, chemistry, political studies (likely to be taken more seriously in the future), either history or geography. The specific details of the examinations have been determined at the local level by the Shenzhen Educational Bureau (SEB).

The SEB also determines the cycle for formal vocational-technical education, whether it runs the full three years or is shortened to a two and one-half year cycle. In general, the average number of teaching hours per week range between 26-30; for those workers who are part time, the number of teaching hours are reduced although the total time to finish the program is lengthened. The teaching staff has been recruited from the region as well as from other provinces in China. Both full-time and part-time teachers are utilized although there has been a preference recently for hiring full-time teaching staff with college level education and training in their background. The specific schools in Shenzhen as is true elsewhere are highly specialized, as can be seen in Table 7.2.

Table 7.2
Secondary Vocational School Enrollments and Specializations
Shenzhen

School	Specialization Grade	10	11	12
Cuiyuan	English	50	54	51
Wenjin	Secretarial		61	51
Yijing	Auto repair	97	53	
Guiyuan	Clerk/Banking	210	104	229
Gangxia	Electronics/Computer	312	380	350
Shekou	Electronics/Computer	40	30	28
Tielu	Transportation	43		
Shahe	Home Electrical Repair	40		
Huaqiang	Electronics		104	100
Luohu	Banking/Foreign Trade	111	111	
Xingzhi	Practical Arts/Cloth Design	61	120	29
Total		985	1013	821

Source: Shenzhen Educational Bureau, Statistics Department 1987-88
Academic Year (9/24/88)

The larger enrollments and number of specializations are clustered in the fields of electronics and the clerking/banking areas but range through English, auto repair, and "practical art." Enrollment ratios between general high school and the vocational technical level can be seen in Table 7.3. As Table 7.3 indicates, substantial numbers of students have been enrolled in this sector, and enrollments have steadily increased each year since 1985.

Table 7.3
Vocational and Technical Education Comparisons: 1985-87

School Category	Enrollments	Percentage of Secondary
	1985	
General High School	1779	63.56
Vocational/Technical	1020	36.44
	1986	
General High School	2210	57.85
Vocational/Technical	1610	42.15
	1987	
General High School	2334	55.36
Vocational/Technical	1884	44.64

Source: Shenzhen Education Bureau 9/24/87

Overall, formal vocational-technical education has grown and expanded as the Shenzhen SEZ has developed. It serves the basic needs of the zone but falls far short of providing the quantity and quality of skilled human resources necessary for the continued expansion of the region. It is recognized that in order to realize the principal goal of the zone--the attraction of foreign capital--a high quality work force is a necessity. Thus, since its designation as a SEZ, Shenzhen *has* promoted an extensive adult education network comprised of many *levels* and a variety of specializations. It is estimated that the formal vocational - technical sector can provide only about 10 percent to 30 percent of the needed skilled human resources necessary for continued modernization of the zone down to 1990. The remainder must be supplied through the adult education program. To this end, the SEB established a sub-bureau called the Shenzhen Adult Education Bureau. The Bureau monitors and supports not only the Shenzhen adult education enterprises but also those established by foreign enterprises. The latter assist the zone to serve as a "window" (*chuangkou*), allowing Shenzhen residents and officials to observe, introduce, and transmit foreign knowledge, science, technology and investment to the interior.[25] A variety of adult educational modes have been established since Shenzhen was designated as a SEZ. A general principle in the establishment of these programs was that they should not be modeled on the spare-time, part-work, part-study programs of the interior. Specifically, the management and administration of the adult programs is designed to utilize more central authority (the SEB) to collect data, monitor quality and keep records while delegating internal management of the schools to the schools themselves.[26]

Critical to the rural transformation that is taking place in the Shenzhen region is the lack of skills required by the move from single farm production to more organized agricultural and nonagricultural production geared toward export. There is an increased emphasis on moving from grain production to fresh fruit and vegetables and animal husbandry. By the mid-1980's Shenzhen had run more than three hundred poultry farms, vegetable land had reached 30,000 mu (fifteen mu equals one hectare), fruit farms had developed 85,000 mu, and aquaculture had developed 60,000 mu of land. A corresponding economic and industrial infrastructure has developed to support the processing and sales of the produce thus further requiring a higher level of skill than possessed by most in the surrounding farm area. With rural reforms came more prosperity in the Shenzhen area. In 1982 the average annual income in rural Shenzhen was 840 yuan, and about 20 percent of the rural households had surpassed the "ten thousand yuan" level while four villages had been designated "ten thousand yuan" villages (every household earning about 10,000 yuan per year). Over 80 percent of the peasant families owned televisions and tape recorders, and "many" were reported to have built new homes.[27] While such figures should be viewed with caution, they do reveal very large gaps between low and high incomes and other resources.

The adult programs for peasants consist of special courses on import training focused on the new import technologies associated with the shifts in production referred to above. Peasants with relatives in Hong Kong and Macau are offered support to attend special courses in those areas geared to the import-export business, housing costs are kept low since family homes are used, and the skills learned are directly applicable to new agricultural industries. The use of educational television for the purpose of transmitting agricultural techniques to farmers in outlying areas near Shenzhen has also been utilized and shown to be effective.[28]

Thus, a variety and range of educational reforms and educational levels have been introduced into the Shenzhen area, linked to economic change, and reflective of the demand placed upon the system by changing patterns of relationships between the rural and urban sectors. In some respects, Shenzhen has become a model for the other SEZs to emulate, particularly with respect to educational change. A number of SEZ educational conferences have been held in the region and the Shenzhen Educational Bureau has served as a training site for educators from the other zones.

Conclusion

In the broad context of rural transformation in Asia, the experiences of the SEZs in China are somewhat unique. Where the transformation has been evolutionary and to some degree ad hoc in the rest of Asia, it has been planned with respect to China's SEZs. Where there have been severe dislocations between rural and urban populations, lack of fit between economic needs and labor force skills, and governmental inaction in many Asian nations, these issues have been less problematic in China. Yet, despite the differences, the principal rural transformation characteristics discussed earlier in this chapter form the conceptual context in which to view development in general and educational development in particular in China's SEZs.

China's SEZs have served the purpose of supplying various factors of production and attracting outside capital and expertise. Previously rural areas are now an interesting mix of urban and rural development with a diversified labor force. Large numbers of people formerly engaged in agriculture have now been transformed into urban worker/technicians through a system of non-formal adult education. The notion that the SEZs would serve as a "window" to the outside through which could come foreign capital and expertise has proven to be a workable concept despite the fact that it also allowed "undesirable elements" to come in.

The "window" analogy has been extended to education, and as we have seen, a variety of innovations have been introduced. Overall educational quality has improved, secondary educational reforms have been carried out, a wide-ranging effort to provide adult and continuing education for the large force of workers (and former farmers) has been initiated, and educational linkages with contiguous areas outside China (principally Hong Kong) have been established.

In Shenzhen quantitatively great advances have been made by the educational system in responding to the labor skill needs of the growing economy. The adult educational system is sufficiently different from that of the interior so that it can serve as an experimental model, allowing change back into China proper. All of this has been achieved in a relatively short period of time even given the long, evolutionary period that preceded the formation of the SEZs.

How bold or how timid has this experiment been? Certainly on the economic front the position of the central authorities in Beijing has been firm and in that sense bold. There is almost a frontier quality to the development in Shenzhen and a sense of entrepreneurial zeal among individuals conducting business in the region. Both local and central authorities continue to seem supportive of the free-wheeling economic climate of the SEZs. The fragility of all of this, however, is clearly visible when one looks closely at both social and political structures. Here we see a long-standing reluctance, particularly from Beijing and high level officials in the Guangdong provincial government, to allow for more than a modicum of political reform to take place. The timidity of China's current political leadership to take the next step in conducting a real experiment--namely to allow political reforms to follow economic reforms--was apparent even before the events of June 4, 1989. The failure to make this link--between the economic and political sectors--has sent all the wrong signals to the very foreign interests the SEZs were established to attract. This is particularly true of Hong Kong.

The dismissal of the President of Shenzhen University was a clear sign that educational reforms and their reformers could also be halted. While it is too early to assess the vitality of the educational efforts discussed above, there is some evidence that the SEZs are beginning to experience a "brain drain" of their best educators both to Hong Kong and the West.[29] If the educational infrastructure begins to slip, further economic expansion, requiring as it does "high quality human resources," will be problematic.

Thus, it appears there are elements both of boldness and timidity in the SEZs. The fragility of the economic reforms becomes apparent, however, as China stagnates politically. Unless political and economic reforms are linked, one must worry about the continued success story of China's SEZs and the educational advances that have been obtained thus far.

Notes

1. Although international assessments of the SEZs have varied from those who laud its successes to those predicting total failure, in 1988 SEZs in China had their best year ever with industrial output value up 52 percent over the previous year: Lowell Dittmer, "China in 1988: the Continuing Dilemma of Socialist Reform," *Asian Survey* Vol.XXIX, no.1 (1989):15; see also, "Austerity Program Skirts Shenzhen," *Journal of Commerce Special Report* (April 5, 1989):5a; an earlier pessimistic analysis can be found in Patrick L. Smith, "China's Economic Zones: An Experiment that Failed," *International Herald Tribune* (September 11, 1986):1. For a more detailed discussion of rural transformation and its educational implications, see Bruce Koppel, "Beyond Employment to Work: Asia's Rural Labor Skill Challenge of the 1990's," in Bruce Koppel, editor, *Rural Transformation: Issues for Policy, Planning and Project Development* (Tokyo: Asian Productivity Organization, 1989):37-72 and John N. Hawkins, "The   Transformation of Education for Rural Development in China," *Comparative Education Review* no.3, (1988):266-281.

2. Azizur Rahman Khan and Eddy Lee, editors, *Poverty in Rural Asia* (Bangkok: International Labor Organization, 1985).

3. See Bruce Koppel, "Beyond Employment to Work," *op.cit.*, pp.37-72; R.T. Shand, editor, *Off-Farm Employment in the Development of Rural Asia, Vol. 1 and 2* (Canberra, Australia: Australian National University Center for Development Studies, 1986).

4. These surveys tend to concentrate upon households that are primarily engaged in agricultural activities. If other households (such as landless families and households residing in market towns and villages) were appropriately sampled, it is likely that estimated proportions of total rural household income coming from non-farm sources would even be higher.

5. Examples include Gillian Hart, *Power, Labor and Livelihood* (Berkeley: University of California Press, 1986); Noeleen Heyzer, *Working Women in Southeast Asia: Subordination and Emancipation* (Philadelphia: Open University Press, 1986);

Diane Wolf, *Factory Daughters, Their Families and Rural Industrialization in Center Java* (Doctoral dissertation, Cornell University, 1986).

6. Harry T. Oshima, *The Transition to an Industrial Economy in Monsoon Asia* (Asian Development Bank Staff Paper Number 20) (Manila:Asia Development Bank, 1983); Harry T. Oshima, *The Significance of Off-Farm Employment and Incomes in Post-War East Asian Growth* (Asian Development Bank Staff Paper Number 21) (Manila: Asian Development Bank, 1984); Samuel P.S. Ho, *The Asian Experience in Rural Nonagricultural Development and its Relevance for China* (Washington: D.C., The World Bank, 1986).

7. See Fu-Chen Lo, Kamal Salih and Mike Douglass, "Rural Urban Transformation in Asia," in Fu-Chen Lo editor, *Rural Urban Relations and Regional Development* (Singapore, Maruzan Asia, 1981):7-43.

8. J. Harriss and M. Moore, editors, *Development and the Rural-Urban Divide* (London: Frank Cass, 1984).

9. Norton Ginsburg, Bruce Koppel and Terry McGee, editors, *The Extended Metropolis in Asia: A New Phase of the Settlement Transition* (Honolulu: University of Hawaii, 1990).

10. Thomas Chan, et al.,"China's Special Economic Zones: Ideology, Policy and Practice," in Y.C. Jao and C.K. Leung, editors, *China's Special Economic Zones: Policies, Problems and Prospects* (Hong Kong: Oxford University Press, 1986).

11. C.K. Leung, "Spatial Redeployment and the Special Economic Zones in China: An Overview," *China's Special Economic Zones* (1986):10.

12. Tim Williams and Robin Brilliant, "Shenzhen Status Report," The *China Business Review* (1984):29.

13. Chi Kin Leung, *Industrial Organization and Spatial Economic Relations Between Hong Kong and China: A Linkage-*

Interaction Approach (Doctoral Dissertation, University of Hawaii, 1989).

14. C.Y. Chang, "Bureaucracy and Modernization: A Case Study of Special Economic Zones in China," *China's Special Economic Zones* (1986):105.

15. C.Y. Yang, "Bureaucracy and Modernization...," *op. cit.*, p.119.

16. R.Y.W. Kwok, "Structure and Policies in Industrial Planning in the Shenzhen Special Economic Zone," *China's Special Economic Zones* (1986):57.

17. Shenzhen Municipal Education Bureau, "Overview of Educational Development in Shenzhen Special Economic Zone," and Wu Weiliang, "A Task of Strategic Importance to the Zhuhai Special Economic Zone--Development of Human Resources," *Chinese Education* no.3 (1988):7-24;42-57.

18. Huang Shaozeng, "Construction and Education in a Special Zone," in *Shenzhen Tequ Jiaoyu Yanjiu* (Wuhan: Wuhan University, 1985) translated in *Chinese Education* No.3 (1988):34-41.

19. Huang Shaozeng, "Construction and Education...", *op. cit.*, pp.34-41.

20. *Renmin Ribao* (January 24, 1989):4.

21. *Zhongguo Jiaoyu Nianjian* (Beijing: China Encyclopedia Press, 1986).

22. Personal communication with Mr. Xia Deqin, Director of the Shenzhen Education Bureau, October 1987.

23. Shenzhen Education Bureau, Internal Document, August 1986.

24. Shenzhen Education Bureau, Internal Document, August 1986.

25. Liao Yuangeng, "Jianshe Shenzhen Chengren Jiaoyu Jidi Chuyi," *Shenzhen Tequ Chengren Jiaoyu Wenxuan* (Shenzhen Adult Education Bureau, 1986) and Yuan Hui, "Luetan Tequ

Chengren Jiaoyu De Chuangkou," *Shenzhen Tequ Chengren* (1986).

26. Yuan Hui, "On the Development and Management of Shenzhen Adult Education," *Shenzhen Tequ Chengren Jiaoyu Luanwenxuan* (hereafter *STCJL*) (Shenzhen: Shenzhen Adult Education Association, 1985).

27. Yang Yinjie, "Guanyu Shenzhen tequ fazhan nongmin jiaoyu de tantao," *STCJL* (1985):4-9.

28. Yang Yinjie, "Guanyu Shenzhen tequ fazhan nongmin jiaoyu de tantao," *STCJL* (1985):4-9.

29. Personal correspondence from the academic personnel office at Shenzhen University and recent applications from professors for positions in the United States indicate a significant level of dissatisfaction with current conditions in higher education in the SEZs.

CHAPTER EIGHT
EDUCATING CHINA'S DISADVANTAGED YOUTH:
A CASE OF MODERNIZATION AND ITS DISCONTENTS

by Irving Epstein

Few events have been more graphically illustrative of the precarious nature of China's modernization commitments than those that involved the Tiananmen massacre of June 4, 1989 and the ensuing political repression that continues unabated at this time. This chapter will attempt to explore the limitations of those commitments within an alternative domain: the education of disadvantaged children and youth. It will compare treatments of delinquents and physically or cognitively disabled children for the purpose of analyzing those social characteristics which are indicative of a broader ambivalence toward modernization. The work assumes that the social treatment of deviance with respect to definitional and labeling procedures, specific institutional responses, and related welfare policies can provide evidence for a society's willingness to foster social integration through institutional means. It can elucidate the degree to which policy formation and implementation occur according to universalistic rather than particularistic criteria, and it can shed light upon the extent to which the individual interests of those who are so labeled are protected. All of these factors, it is argued, can enhance modernization tendencies; in post-Mao China though, their positive resolution has been easily arrested.

The respective treatments of delinquents and the disabled are comparable because in both cases, the roles of the targeted populations have been socially constructed. However, the nature of their roles has also been defined according to pervasive social labeling and, in certain cases, overt ostracism. The social construction of specific categories of disadvantage can create a rationale for using institutional mechanisms to foster social integration. However the informal use of labeling and stigmatization practices impedes efforts at achieving that goal. Furthermore, the institutions created to serve the needs of delinquents and the disabled are relatively weak and have proven incapable of successfully confronting external social pressures.

The Juvenile Delinquency Case

The social construction of deviance is easily observed throughout the forty year history of the People's Republic. During the first two decades of Communist rule, criminality, for example, was consistently defined in overtly political terms. Because it was deemed ideologically inconsistent to admit to the existence of crime in a socialist state, successful campaigns aimed at eliminating criminal deviance (such as anti-gang and anti-prostitution campaigns in Shanghai) were lauded as positive examples of the regime's commitment to create a new society.[1]

Even by the late 1950s and early 1960s, when instances of delinquency involving urban and rural theft, fighting and poor school discipline were mentioned in the press, their existence was supposedly caused by counter-revolutionary elements, and their significance was inherently associated with a political illegitimacy that could never exist in a purely socialist state.[2]

By the late 1950s and early 1960s, model reformatories and work-study schools had been constructed or refurbished in major cities and provinces. In some ways, the construction of permanent institutions designed to address delinquency activity can be viewed as a positive step, for their presence represented a tacit admission that such behavior occurred with consistency, and there were benefits to treating it with a degree of regularity and standardization. The nine reformatories constructed or rebuilt in 1957 were specifically intended to separate delinquents from adult prisoners.[3] As an alternative to the spontaneous creations and responses to social deviance that occurred through the use of mass mobilization techniques, early reformatories and work-study schools represented more measured and thoughtful social policy. Yet these were institutions were still heavily influenced by ideological considerations.

Because reformatories were conceived as production units, it was argued that inmate labor would be used to make them self-sufficient and that in time, they would contribute to the socialist economy as a whole. Precedent for this view was established in Ya'nan, where labor camps were operated according to the same assumption. The Yan'an experience was also influential for its use of lenient work-release programs, which allowed petty criminals to gain freedom in return for their cooperation in fighting the Japanese. The basic association of productive labor with the reform of criminal behavior, has its roots here.[4] By the late 1950s, the creation of *minban* schooling re-emphasized the importance of productive labor within regular educational settings too. Through engaging in productive labor, the children of peasants and workers could acquire an appreciation for the hardships their parents endured in successfully liberating the country. At the same time, minban schooling represented an alternative to formal educational structures patterned after Soviet models with an emphasis upon state control, the acquisition of specialized knowledge separated from practice, and the promotion of hierarchy and elitism.

The connection between character building and productive labor not only had generic populist overtones, but the use of productive labor within a reformatory setting had special importance for the treatment of delinquents. Other coercive institutions also consigned their inmates to production tasks. Reformatories were supposedly different though, in that youthful offenders were thought to be less culpable for their actions due to age, inexperience, and lack of moral education. Productive labor thus possessed inherent educational value for the delinquent, because its use would facilitate an understanding of right and wrong, a pre-condition to character reform. Productive labor under these circumstances became intimately associated with moral education and was officially viewed as being both therapeutic and redemptive rather than punitive. Under these terms, one could hypothetically conceive of the reformatory as performing rehabilitative rather than retributional functions.

In reality though, it never shed its normative-coercive purpose. The conditions under which offenders were taken into custody, the imposition of forced family separation, indeterminate lengths of stay, and the reliance upon forced confession of misdeed belied the non-punitive institutional aims that reformatories ideologically embraced. To be sure, penal institutions of all types are presented with conflicting expectations that express social uncertainty concerning the utility of punishment and the desirability of rehabilitation. Because reformatories were supposedly created as alternatives to the labor camp and prison, one might have expected that, in practice, they would have emphasized rehabilitative aims. In fact, although their physical conditions have always been less harsh than those of re-education and reform through labor camps, given the publicity that accompanied their construction and their designated status as model institutions, their practices have differed little from their institutional counterparts within the penal system.[5]

Work-study schools for delinquents, on the other hand, were established during the late 1950s in urban areas for those guilty of less serious delinquent activity. They also emphasized the importance of offenders participating in productive labor, although expectations for institutional self-sufficiency were no longer expressed. During the Cultural Revolution, the work of both reformatories and work-study schools was disrupted, as reformatories were viewed as overly coercive, and work-study schools were dismissed as ineffective and were shut down completely.[6]

The Cultural Revolution era thus represented something of a throwback to previous mass mobilization efforts, insofar as delinquency institutions were discredited and deviance again was associated with counter-revolutionary activity outside of the realm of ordinary behavior within the socialist state. The costs of labeling deviance solely in terms of its political illegitimacy and its lack of conventionality included an unwillingness to address its growth as expressed by increased intra-family violence, more theft and minor criminal activity pursued by sent down youth who surreptitiously returned to their urban homes and increased unruliness in middle schools, caused by a perceived break in the linkage between educational attainment and future occupational opportunity.[7] As the existence of delinquency was officially dismissed or trivialized, in reality, it increased.

It is not surprising that during the early years of the post-Mao Era, juvenile delinquency was openly admitted to be a major social problem, for such an admission only reiterated known fact. Once again however, the nature of the problem was defined and reconstructed in such a way so as to avail the regime of political capital. The Cultural Revolution was blamed categorically for the rise in delinquency; occurrences before that time were not admitted or were categorized as of minor significance, always effectively controlled. One scholar, for example, argued that during the 1950s and 60s, juvenile delinquency only increased by 20-30 per cent, while during the Cultural Revolution, the percentage increase was 60-70 per cent.[8] In 1981, the Deputy Director of the Beijing Municipal Bureau of Public Security argued that delinquency consisted of only 20 per cent of all criminal activity before the Cultural Revolution, but 80 per cent of all offenses recorded from

1977-1980.[9]   In this environment, public reporting of delinquency activity allowed the government to distinguish itself from its predecessor without taking immediate responsibility for its causes.

By the mid-1980s, more sophisticated rationales were employed to explain the presence of delinquency as the growing time lag made it increasingly implausible to blame Cultural Revolution excesses alone for continuing deviant behaviors. Some of China's social scientists associated delinquency with the country's increasingly successful modernization drive, while others, touching upon latent xenophobic attitudes, viewed pernicious Western influences as contributing to the problem.[10]   The tone of the 1982-83 spiritual pollution campaign, for example, can be viewed in that vein.

Regardless of the contextual explanations that sought to rationalize the existence of delinquency activity, the fact that its continuing presence was again admitted necessitated an institutional response, that took the form of resurrecting the work-study school and reformatory concepts. As one might expect, the contradictions which plagued these institutions prior to the Cultural Revolution have remained largely unresolved to this day.

Both institutional types have been criticized for the coercive tactics employed by the political cadres who staff the facilities. They have been attacked for providing a venue where gang members meet one another and plan criminal behavior upon their release. It has been further argued that the use of peer surveillance, through "jiti jiaoyu" or collectivist education is counterproductive, as offenders present pro forma confessions of misdeed to authorities and one another but fail to seriously reform their unhealthy dispositions.[11] During the crime wave of 1983, these institutions were criticized for allowing offenders to escape and were often bypassed altogether because youth were summarily rounded up and sent directly to labor camps unless the crimes were judged heinous enough to merit immediate execution.[12]

It is interesting to note that the use of productive labor as a character-reforming device, was not been abandoned during the 1980s, although some work-study schools, located in distinct urban settings, have emphasized the importance of teaching vocational skill mastery in a more specialized sense. But it is safe to conclude that the formal goals of productive labor are more circumspect than those of the late 1950s, as the expressed expectation is one of offenders reintegrating within normal social environments rather than directly contributing to the construction of a new social order. To be sure, the public display of offenders performing heavy construction and manual labor tasks is in evidence. But the purpose of such public displays is supposedly to speak to the offenders' capacity to successfully reintegrate into the normal social fabric only.

As has been true of western settings, certain calls for broad educational reform have actually originated among practitioners and experts engaged in criminology study. Calls for teaching sex education in an open, honest fashion within public school settings were voiced as early as 1982.[13] These authors also criticized authoritarian teaching methods and joined the national debate in opposition to ability grouping in 1981-82, arguing that such practices also contributed to delinquency activity.[14] And, concern was also expressed for the need to strengthen moral education in schools, with some effort paid to the teaching of basic law as a part of political study.[15] More general social criticism attributed delinquency growth to youth unemployment and problems of socializing youth to normal disciplinary expectations within factories as well as poor parenting.[16] Given the willingness of scholars studying delinquency issues to express social criticism, it is not totally surprising that Yu Haocheng, one of the co-authors of China's most important published volume on juvenile delinquency, is reportedly under arrest at this time in the aftermath of the Tiananmen massacre.

It is clear that in the post-Mao Era, authorities have recognized the need to create and strengthen institutions as a means of combatting juvenile delinquency. This recognition implies some acceptance of the problem as long term. This position is in direct contradiction to efforts during previous decades that denied delinquency occurrence was a part of the normal social fabric or stridently associated presumed successes in combatting delinquency with the construction of a new socialist order. Certainly, current views of delinquency contain their due amount of political capital. But this author contends that a reliance upon institutional solutions to delinquency prevention and occurrence is inherently flawed as long as the respective institutions are incapable of resolving the defects that led to their initial demise during the Cultural Revolution. Not only were they created when everyday life was more heavily politicized, but reformatories and work-study schools have additionally suffered from an inability to dissipate the strong negative social labeling tendencies that accompany offender incarceration. In fact, a number of specific institutional policies exacerbate those pressures.

The removal of youth from normal family environments can be stigmatizing, regardless of specific cultural norms. In the Chinese case, the traditional importance attached to the primacy of the family, with children and parents performing reciprocal obligations and responsibilities, and the corresponding importance attached to group affiliation--in school, work unit, and residence committee--make the effects of institutional separation even more extreme.

Parental visitations are never prescribed on a regular basis, and even though in some less restrictive work-study environments, offenders are allowed to return home periodically, an overwhelming fear of abandonment remains. Since guilt by association is strong in China, parents fear visiting their children just as wives have been traditionally forced to formally divorce husbands who have been sent to labor camps lest they lose their own job security. The fear of being shunned upon release has led to early, ill-advised marriages on the part of some released offenders, and the possibilities for employment upon their release are severely restricted.[17]

The indiscriminate manner in which youth are sent to the institutions in the first place, e.g., for being at the wrong place at the wrong time and unknowingly drawing attention to patterned deviant behavior, and the often-indeterminate length of stay there reinforce the power of informal stigmatization. Not only have females been held in work-study and reformatory settings for reasons of sexual promiscuity only (as authorities uphold a double standard in their treatment of offenders), but it has been argued that some work-study schools hold females whose only offense is pregnancy.[18]

What male and female offenders do share, however, is a deep fatalism about their futures. The use of drill and militaristic ritual within institutional settings reiterates loss of individuality as well as separation from normal lifestyles, and the cursory display of offenders completing production tasks in public view further reinforces the stigma and ostracism.

Neither the required confession of misdeed nor the persistence of peer surveillance within institutional walls can be viewed as policies that communicate a sincere belief in the successfull reintegration into normal social environments. Indeed, this author was informed during a visit to Guangdong Province's Shijing Reformatory in 1983 that when offenders turned eighteen, they were simply sent to labor camps without having the benefit of case review.

Delinquency institutions are as guilty of errors of omission as well as commission in their failure to confront the external social prejudice directed toward offenders. Work-study schools and reformatories have no systematic counseling system; offenders are lumped together regardless of their specific offense and few preparations are made to facilitate their readjustment after their release. Communications with their local residence committees and public security bureaus are initiated on an informal basis, and no effort is made to systematically follow up offender progress subsequent to release. Indeed, released offenders are not only subject to increased surveillance themselves but are required to make periodic contact with public security officials, offering information about gang and deviant activity in their immediate surroundings. The increased mobility that has resulted from the growing use of contract labor and self-employment has probably made the maintenance of social control through peer surveillance more difficult in recent years. Nonetheless, the expectation that released offenders perform this role continues to be inherently stigmatizing.

It is admitted that offenders are often "educational losers," yet the quality of education provided at delinquency institutions is often substandard, in terms of curriculum and pedagogy, and the educational qualifications of the instructors are suspect. During a time when day to day life has become increasingly depoliticized, reformatories and work-study schools are still viewed, correctly in my opinion, as essentially coercive, political institutions. To the extent that they are considered valuable, their value is assessed within a broad comparative perspective whose overall assessment of the penal system is negative. Reformatories may therefore be viewed as a better alternative than the labor camp; work-study schools, whose inmates include a large percentage of cadre children, are considered less coercive and intrusive than the reformatory.

The existence of these institutions demonstrates official concern with delinquency behavior but because the number of institutions remains small and because of their continued association with the public security apparatus, reformatories and work-study schools have found it difficult to gain popular acceptance for their efforts. Thus, while there is little evidence to suggest that the actual physical treatment of offenders is overly harsh, the pain that results from their stigmatized social roles can be severe, and these institutions have been unable to decrease that stigma.

The Special Education Case

An analysis of the social context in which the education of disabled children has developed presents a number of similarities to the delinquency case. Institutions that cater to the needs of the disabled attempt to aid their clients in overcoming traditional stigma and social ostracism.   While the establishment of schools for the physically disabled dates to the late nineteenth century (constructed with missionary assistance), institutional expansion proceeded moderately until the Cultural Revolution, and has increased substantially since its aftermath. Overall though, schooling for the disabled remains in its infancy, and serious questions remain concerning its effectiveness.

As is true for many societies, disability has been associated with shame and denial for centuries in China.   During the Shang Dynasty, its existence was thought to show evidence for the disruption of ties between the living and their ancestors; illness was a curse placed upon the living, and physical infirmity further cast doubt upon the ability of one's ancestors to protect the living.[19] Certainly, disability was an obstacle in achieving harmony with one's physical as well as social environment.   The traditional expectations concerning reciprocity of obligations between children and parents, of which we have previously spoken, had to be tempered, resulting in parental responses that ranged from hiding the child from public view to infanticide. Shame continues to exert an important influence in determining how the needs of the disabled are addressed in contemporary China, and traditional parental attitudes have proven difficult to reform.

The first generically Chinese school for the blind and deaf was established in 1927 in Nanjing, and by 1937 forty schools were operating according to the Nanjing model, which by 1932 had extended its curricular offerings to include training at middle school, vocational and normal school levels.[20]   After 1949, institutional commitments to educate the disabled were reaffirmed in general terms, in a 1951 document published by the Ministry of Education.[21] Those commitments were implemented in a moderate and irregular fashion until recently, however.   Thus, between 1953 and 1963, the number of schools for blind and deaf students increased from 64 to 253. That number reached 319 by 1983 and 350 by 1985, with a total student enrolment of 37,989. At that time, there was at least one school for blind and deaf-mute students in every province, major city and autonomous region within the country with the exception of Tibet. [22]

Schools for retarded children date from as late as 1979, and numbered 90 by 1987; 587 special classes for retarded children, attached to regular primary schools, were also functional by the end of 1987. Altogether, best estimates indicate that 504 schools employ 14,400 special education teachers and staff, who currently serve 52,800 children. Still, only 6 per cent of China's six million children and youth who suffer from disability are enrolled in any type of educational programming as demand far exceeds supply.[23]   It should be noted though that limited non-formal educational offerings are given to retarded children at social welfare institutes and occupational therapy stations (under the jurisdiction of mental hospitals).[24]

A number of factors explain the growing trend toward institutional expansion in the special education sector.   As was true with the juvenile delinquency case, changing ideological priorities have played an important role, although distinctions are less clear cut than was true of the former example.   One could argue that glorified images of the "new socialist man," prevalent during periods of ideological stridency such as the Cultural Revolution, precluded candid admissions of the existence of significant disability among the population or of the need to treat it.   Even after the Cultural Revolution ended, social bias toward the disabled has continued and was codified in a set of university entrance regulations which discriminated against applicants with poor eyesight and flat feet, not to mention those with serious infirmities [25] (these regulations were amended only in 1983).   One notes that appeals to eugenics campaigns have periodically arisen in the post-Mao era, as some have argued that the country's gene pool needs to be purified.[26]   The forced sterilization of the retarded is a common response within a number of provinces.   Although concern has been expressed over the large number of congenital birth defects in evidence in the population, it is the large percentage of infants who suffer from post-natal infirmity that is impressive according to western observers.[27]   Thus, there is no scientific rationale whatsoever for the continued appeals to eugenics practices, which must be viewed as a reaffirmation of the longstanding social prejudice conducted toward the disabled.   This thinking is noteworthy for its categorical dismissal of institutional treatments that might facilitate the social integration of the disabled. The official policy of the central government is to promote educational expansion of special schooling--an effort which is supported by attempts to redefine heroic imagery so as to include the accomplishments of the disabled.   Examples of those who have achieved personal success in spite of their physical infirmities such as the limbless artist or the blind musician were propagated as instances of heroism during the early 1980s in an effort to consciously promote values of individualism rather than collectivism in youth literature.[28]   At the same time, disabled athletes who have successfully competed in special Olympics competitions have received praise for their efforts, which are seen as having strengthened the country's international standing.

Long term trends such as decreases in infant mortality and increases in life expectancy have improved the chances of physically disabled children to survive.[29] At the same time, certain technological advancements have increased the circumstances under which disability may occur--vehicular accident, industrial danger, etc. Certainly the efforts of Deng Xiaoping's disabled son, Deng Pufang, who is a visible if controversial political figure in his own right, have influenced official policy. One can conclude that a number of convergent factors have compelled policy makers to recognize the need to educate China's disabled children in spite of continuing expressions of social bias.

The education of students with special needs is occurring as corollary efforts have been made to improved the general condition of the disabled: tax breaks are offered to welfare factories employing the mildly disabled or to disabled individuals who operate their own enterprises. The China Welfare Fund specifically pays supplemental stipends to teachers who work with special students and facilitates efforts to hire the disabled as well.[30] However, there is no substantive commitment to occupational mainstreaming, in large part because employment practices continue to use *guanxi* networks that are not always available to the disabled.

It is within an ambiguous social environment that educational policies are shaped, often with mixed results. For the most part, special schools offer a basic, primary level education, which stresses mastery of survival skills along with those manual skills traditionally performed by adults with specific disabilities. Blind students learn handicraft skills as well as finger massage; deaf children are initially given audio training and are then taught vocational skills such as handiwork, tailoring, porcelain carving and the filling of false teeth. Standardized primary textbooks used in regular classroom environments have now been translated into braille, and the State Education Commission has published teaching guidelines for instructors who work with the blind and the deaf.[31] Special textbooks and materials that directly address the needs of these students have yet to be completed though.

It was previously noted that discriminatory college admissions regulations have been rescinded, and it is now claimed that approximately 800 disabled students a year are attending some form of post-secondary education.[32] Keypoint institutions such as Beijing Normal and East China Normal Universities have established special education majors and teacher training institutions catering specifically to the training of special education teachers have been established in Jiangsu, Liaoning, Shandong, Heilongjiang, Jilin, Henan, and Hunan. One of the more famous special education programs was established at Chengchun University, which enrolls 150 disabled students in five special education curricular specializations.[33]

The significant progress in extending educational opportunities for the disabled should not be underestimated. However, it is important to note that in most cases, institutional growth has not been accompanied by commitments to pursue educational mainstreaming. Few disabled students who are lucky enough to be admitted to higher level institutions, for example, will pursue study in disciplines not directly related to their disability.

The segregation of disabled students from regular school experiences begins much earlier, of course. There are few primary or pre-primary classes available to disabled children at all, for even in a province such as Sichuan whose efforts to expand special education have been publicly lauded only 47 per cent of blind and deaf students attend school.[34] When children with special needs are placed in special settings, the placement occurs because of teacher or parental referral on an informal basis. Because the initial diagnosis of disability is conducted with a large degree of imprecision, it is probable that incorrect placements often occur, but once a student is placed in a special setting, there is little chance of his/her ever returning to a regular school environment.

The overwhelming impresssion this author received during a visit to a school for retarded children in Hangzhou in 1988 reaffirmed the impact of leveled expectation upon curricular and instructional behaviors. One was able to observe in this setting, low student-teacher ratios, a significant amount of group work, and a variety of activities designed to improve students' physical coordination and motor development that blended academic work and play. At the higher grade levels, students were able to operate machines and begin to simulate the work experiences they might hope to perform in the welfare factory located next to the school after their graduation. The teachers showed a remarkable tolerance for divergent student behavior, yet they failed to recognize the possibility that each student had particular needs that could be met by using an individualized curricular and instructional approach. Many of the activities students were expected to perform were of a traditional nature that one would ordinarily observe in a regular Chinese pre-school or early primary level classroom--unison singing or collective dancing to a common melody or theme, tasks that required memorization of gesture in sequence (a similar set of activities has been described at a school with a similar focus in Wuhan[35]). Although most of the students followed teacher commands with varying degrees of irregularity, they were always encouraged to keep trying.

It is interesting to note that this school, like most of the special schools for disabled children, follows a work-study structure. Unlike juvenile correctional institutions, however, the purpose of the work experiences in these settings is to teach socialization and survival skills. Character reform is not an important issue within these surroundings. Still, to borrow Basil Bernstein's terminology, both types of institutions convey a preference for weak classification schemes, where disciplinary boundaries are often indistinctly formed according to loose collection codes.[36]   Classroom rituals appear to be more expressive than instrumental, although where children are expected to be able to successfully use job related skills upon their graduation, rituals become more instrumental in orientation (e.g. work-study schools for mildly delinquent youth, advanced classes for the retarded). Bernstein has argued that in the British context, curricular classification schemes paralleled changes in framing, or the pedagogical relationship between teacher and student. Framing certainly is tighter within correctional institutional settings, where the authority of the staff is visible and unquestioned. In the special-education setting, framing is looser than would normally be expected, given the occasional use of small group instruction and smaller student-teacher ratios, although in most cases, basic pedagogic authority remains visible and unchallenged. I have argued elsewhere that the tolerance for weak classification systems belies the lowered set of teacher expectations in these situations.[37] Because it is assumed that their educational achievement will be dramatically less than their "normal counterparts," there is less importance ascribed to the subject matter students are taught or the specific methods used to convey the information.

It has been noted that the work-study organizational structure has been utilized for different purposes as authorities attempt to address the needs of clients as diverse as those of delinquents and the disabled. Although the particular meanings attached to the work experiences differ for each institutional setting, work is generally viewed as a positive influence, indicative of one's capacity to constructively participate in shared social experience. It has been further argued that within these settings, there is a reluctance to radically individualize instruction to cater to the specific needs of different students. The unwillingness to recognize individual learning differences may be explained, to a certain degree, by a lack of training and experience on the part of special education teachers and correctional institution staff. It is my contention, however, that the reluctance to individualize instruction is indicative of a deeper epistemological orientation, which has traditionally viewed all children above the age of infancy as possessing the inherent ability to comprehend truth. It has been argued that such a belief explains important differences in parental attitudes toward children, as a change from over-indulgence to strict authoritarianism is commonly observed when the "infant" becomes a "child." It is argued that once children have reached the stage where they are deemed capable of making informed judgments, they begin to be treated as miniature adults.[38] Traditional expectations concerning the inherent ability of students to acquire knowledge and commit to self-improvement have also been offered as explanations for the academic success of Asian students in cross-cultural comparisons. Achievement motivation is encouraged when parental/teacher expectation is uniformly high.[39]

In the cases we have examined, however, it is possible that the opposite result occurs, as the fundamental exceptionality of the children's conditions remains unrecognized in a pedagogical sense. In their refusal to recognize cognitive ability and behavioral differences among these children, teachers of the disadvantaged fall back upon traditional teaching methods, which fail to directly address their students' needs. The result is lowered achievement which further results in teachers' lowered expectations for their future progress.

Within the special education sector, new issues concerning testing demonstrate that although some traditional assumptions are being challenged, the means through which conflicting premises are resolved are indicative of an inconclusive commitment to change.

As has been true of higher education in general and health related services in particular, the special education sector has been affected by increased international contact with western specialists. UNICEF has begun to play an important role in subsidizing school construction, offering grants for teacher training and research. The demands for a re-professionalization of medical practice have had a corollary effect upon special education as evidenced by an increased commitment to pursue ability testing. Components of Weschler and Ravens Matrix IQ tests have been translated into Chinese, supposedly for use as diagnostic tools. However, the use of such tests is occurring without regard to regional and local norms, which have yet to be compiled, and in some instances, Japanese versions have been used. In the Hangzhou school for retarded children that this author visited, for example, children were given the tests only after they were placed in the school setting, and there was no concrete evidence to suggest that instructional methods were altered after the students were tested. Indeed, the school's principal admitted that after the tests were administered, the results were summarized and then put away for storage. Clearly, a pro-testing ideology is growing in China without reference being made to the implications of testing.

It should be additionally noted that special schools are proliferating at the same time that various social welfare services have been commodified and expanded, particularly in urban and wealthier rural areas.[40]   One cannot discuss special education in China without mentioning access issues, since the demand for services far exceeds supply. It can be assumed that a small contingent of wealthier, better educated parents, who are able to contribute to school fees for their children's care and who view these schools as enhancing their children's opportunities for self-sufficiency, would be most supportive of special education efforts. In this author's interviews with staff at the school for retarded children, it was specifically stressed that parents demonstrated more support for this school and concern for their children's progress than was true of their contact with their other child's school. For most Chinese parents with disabled children, however, the lack of a viable institutional option dictates that their children either attempt to blend in with other members of the community or directly confront the social ostracism of which we have spoken. The condition of their disability continues to be negotiated according to informal means.

Conclusions

It should be noted that China does not have a history of institutionalized commitments to social welfare issues, as it was traditionally expected that family and clan members would resolve such issues internally as they arose. From a comparative perspective, the social attitudes that the Chinese express toward disadvantaged youth today are quite typical of those voiced in other parts of the developing world. And, it has been perceptively noted, that as post-Mao China moves from its revolutionary antecedents to a commitment to social reintegration, a reliance upon institutions that continue to reflect their revolutionary origins may impede this effort.[41]

Furthermore, this chapter has assumed that enhanced institutionalization would necessarily promote the social integration of China's disadvantaged youth, an assumption which is not supported by the Japanese experience. In that case, the institutional expansion of special educational programming has seemed to rationalize and codify students' social separation.[42]

Still, even with these caveats kept in mind, China's commitments to the education of its disadvantaged youth are instructive for what they fail to include. Although the rhetoric of functionalism and human capital theory has been used to justify creeping elitism within the social structure, for example, similar arguments have not been invoked to justify rehabilitating delinquents or educating students with special needs. The argument that in order to guarantee a productive future the country needs the expertise of its disadvantaged youth is never consistently expressed. Instead, policy makers bear the burden of convincing competing interests that in a country with scarce resources, it makes sense to direct some of those resources toward targets whose chances of success are prejudged to be slim at best.

In the United States, child advocacy with particular reference to juvenile justice and special education issues, has associated itself with the protection of children's rights and the preservation of their best interests. Special education legislation, in particular, relied heavily upon the precedents established during the civil rights movement. Not only is it extremely questionable as to whether similar constituencies have any influence in effecting policy in China, but basic institutional procedures which would enunciate a firmer commitment to protect the interests of disadvantaged children and their parents are not in place. Indeed, Chinese authorities are in violation of a number of articles of the United Nations Convention on the Rights of the Child, adopted (but not yet ratified by individual states) by the General Assembly on November 29th, 1989. The assumption of innocence until one is proven guilty, the guarantee of access to legal assistance and continuous contact with family members, provisions for alternatives to institutional care and periodic review of institutional placement, and the guarantee that all disabled children receive special care and training so as to facilitate their self-sufficiency are specific provisions of the Convention that are not enforced in contemporary China.[43] These omissions may not be as egregious as was the use of naked aggression to squash legitimate political protest in June 1989. However, both examples are illustrative of the restricted capacity of political and social institutions in responding to the very pressures for change that modernization efforts unleash. Although it is too early to prejudge the ability to reform institutions that cater to the disadvantaged, the record of the first decade of the post-Mao Era does not give rise for future optimism.

Notes

1. Xiang Bo, "Jiefang chu Shanghai liumang gaizao jilue," *Shehui* no.2 (May 1982):29-32; Zhou Yinjun, Yang Jiezeng and Xue Suzhen, "Xin shehui ba guibien chengren: yi Shanghai gaizao changji shi hua," *Shehui* no.1 (October 1981):46-51.

2. "Rascals and Juvenile Delinquents Rampant in Shanghai," *SCMP* no. 1576, (July 24, 1957):30-31; "Don't Overlook the Work Concerning Teenagers," *SCMP* no. 2675 (February 9, 1962):18-19; "Don't Let Your Children do Small Business," *SSCMP* no.105 (March 14, 1963):44-45.

3. Jerome Alan Cohen, *The Criminal Process in the People's Republic of China:1949-1963* (Cambridge: Harvard University Press, 1963):595.

4. Patricia Peck Griffin, *The Chinese Treatment of Counter-revolutionaries* (Unpublished Ph.D. dissertation, University of Pennsylvania, 1971):121-139.

5. Cohen, *The Criminal Process, op. cit.*, pp. 592-593 reprints the Law on Reform Through Labor which stipulated reformatory procedures and environmental conditions.

6. *Amnesty International Report on Political Imprisonment*, (London: Amnesty International Publishing Company,1978):90, 38.

7. Thomas Bernstein, *Up to the Mountains and Down to the Village* (New Haven: Yale University Press, 1977):93, 261, 313-314; Jonathan Unger, *Education Under Mao* (New York: Columbia University Press, 1982):171-187; Fu Gaoxian and Xu Jian, "Dangqian qingshaonian fanzui xinxing tai yu dingfang yanjiu," *Faxue* no.11 (1981):21-25.

8. Xu Jian, "Qingshaonian fanzui wenti yanjiu," *Shehui Kexue* (Shanghai) no.11 (1980):82.

9. Wei Min, "Reforming Criminals," *Beijing Review* (February 23, 1981):22.

10. Yi Ronghua, "Jiating huanjin yu qingnian de weifa fanzui," *Faxue*

Yanjiu no. 5 (1982):48-49; Ma Jie, "Guanyu qingshaonian fanzuixue," *Beijing Zhengfa Xueyuan Xuebao* no.3 (1981):32-36; Yin Jiabao, "Shilun wo guo dangqian qingshaonian fanzui de tedian," *Beijing Zhengfa Xueyuan Xuebao* no.3 (1981):38; Zhang Youyi, "Du qingshaonian fanzui yanjiu tongdi," *Qingshaonian fanzui yanjiu* no.1 (1983):2; "Fanzui yu dianying," *Faxue Zazhi* no.4 (1981):21-23.

11. Fang Bo, "Lun fanzui lixing chengde yuanyin," *Faxue Zazhi* no.4 (1981):43; Jinanshi jianchayuan, "Tamen weishemme zuo shang fanzui dao luge?" *Faxue Jikan* no.1 (1982):62; Shangdong sheng fang laogai zhidui jingyan jiehe, "Ba laogai changsuoban gaizao fanzuide xuexiao," *Qingshaonian fanzui yanjiu* no.1 (1983):20.

12. Amnesty International, *China: Violation of Human Rights* (London: Amnesty International Press, 1984)

13. Cheng Yingfa and Zhao Haiyan, "Zhongxuesheng weifa fanzui wenti shixi," *Beijing Zhengfa Xueyuan Xuebao* no.2 (1982):72.

14. Cheng Yingfan and Zhao Haiyan, "Zhongxuesheng weifa fanzui wenti shixi," *op. cit.*, p.72; see also Jinanshi jianchayuan, "Tamen weishemme zuo shang fanzui dao luge?" *Faxue Jikan* no.1 (1982):62.

15. Cheng Yingfan and Zhao Haiyan, "Zhongxuesheng weifa fanzui wenti shixi," *op. cit.*, p.71; Zhang Mingguang, "Qingshaonian fanzui yige zhongyao yuanjin fameng," *Minzhu yu Fazhi* no.8 (1980):6-7.

16. Jinanshi jianchayuan, "Tamen weishemme zuo shang fanzui dao luge?" *op. cit.*, pp.60-61; Zhao Jian and Lin Qingshan, "Hunyin jiating wenti he qingshaonian fanzui," *Shehuixue zazhi* no.2 (1983):32-34.

17. Irving Epstein, "Children's Rights and Juvenile Correctional Institutions in the People's Republic of China," *Comparative Education Review* 30, no.3 (August 1986):371.

18. Beverley Hooper, *Youth in China* (Victoria: Australia, Penguin Press, 1985):117.

19. Paul U. Unschuld, *Medicine in China: A History of Ideas* (Berkeley: University of California Press, 1985):24-28,54-56.

20. Irving Epstein, "Special Educational Provision in the People's Republic of China," *Comparative Education* 24, no.3 (1988):365.

21. *Education in China* (Beijing: Ministry of Education, 1981):111.

22. *Achievement of Education in China: 1949-1983* (Beijing: People's Education Press, 1984):236; *Statistical Yearbook of China: 1986* (New York: Oxford University Press, 1986):659.

23. *People's Republic of China Yearbook: 1988/1989* (Hong Kong: Xinhua and NCN L+D, 1988):430; "Wo guo teshu xuexiao yiyou 504suo," *Renmin Ribao* (Overseas edition) (March 2, 1988):8; "Teshu jiaoyu youer jiaoyu shoudao zhongshi," *Zhongguo Jiaoyu Bao* (January 2, 1988):1; "Duo zhong tujing jiakuai fazhan canjiren jiaoyu," *Renmin Ribao* (Overseas edition) (March 12, 1988):1; "Li Tieying Meets Special Educators," *FBIS-CHI-88-226* (November 23, 1988):32.

24. Tao Kuo-Tai, "Mentally Retarded Persons in the People's Republic of China: Review of Epidemiological Studies and Services," *American Journal on Mental Retardation* 93, no.2 (1988):197.

25. Suzanne Pepper, *China's Universities: Post-Mao Enrollment Policies and Their Impact on the Structure of Secondary Education* (Ann Arbor: University of Michigan Press, 1984):54-59.

26. Epstein, "Special Education Provision," *op. cit.*, p.366.

27. Tao Kuo-tai, "Mentally Retarded Persons in the People's Republic of China," *op. cit.*, pp. 195-198.

28. Stanley Rosen, "Prosperity, Privatization and China's Youth," *Problems of Communism* (March-April 1985):1-28.

29. Gail Henderson, "Issues in the Modernization of Medicine in China" in Denis Fred Simon and Merle Goldman, editors, *Science and*

Technology in Post-Mao China (Cambridge: Harvard University Press, 1989):203.

30. Epstein, "Special Education Provision," *op. cit.*, pp. 367-368.

31. *Ibid.*, pp.367-368; *People's Republic of China Yearbook: 1988, op. cit.*, p.430.

32. *Ibid.*, p. 430.

33. *Ibid.*, p. 430; "Canjiren shang daxue," *Renmin Ribao* (February 18, 1989):3; "Duo zhong tujing jiakuai fazhan canjiren jiaoyu," *Renmin Ribao* (Overseas Edition) (March 12, 1988):1.

34. "Commentator Urges Education for Handicapped," *FBIS-CHI-88-230* (November 30, 1988):45-46.

35. Wu Lili and Hu Zhide, "Cong Wugang dizhi ertong fudubande diaocha kan dizhi jiaoyu," *Jiaoyu Yanjiu* no.8 (1987):69-72.

36. Basil Bernstein, *Class, Codes and Control, Vol.3* (London: Routledge and Kegan Paul, 1975)

37. Irving Epstein, "Critical Pedagogy and Chinese Education," *Journal of Curriculum Theorizing* 9, no.2 (1990).

38. David Y.F. Ho, "Continuity and Variation in Chinese Patterns of Socialization," *Journal of Marriage and the Family* 51 (February 1989):149-163.

39. Chuansheng Chen and David H. Uttal, "Cultural Values, Parents' Beliefs, and Children's Achievement in the United States and China," *Human Development* 31, (1988):351-358.

40. Deborah Davis, "Chinese Social Welfare: Policies and Outcomes," *China Quarterly* no.119 (1989):557-597.

41. Tang Tsou, *The Cultural Revolution and Post-Mao Reforms* (Chicago: University of Chicago Press, 1986). See especially chapter 5, "Back from the Brink of Revolutionary -'Feudal' Totalitarianism."

42. Irving Epstein, "Special Education in Japan and China," *Curriculum and Teaching* 4, no.2 (December 1989):27-38.

43. Kay Castelle, *In the Child's Best Interest: A Primer on the U.N. Convention on the Rights of the Child* (New York: Foster Parents Plan International and Defense for Children International-USA, 1989)

CHAPTER NINE

REFORMING TEACHERS:
IE ORGANIZATION, REPRODUCTION, AND TRANSFORMATION OF TEACHING[1]

by Lynn Paine

Introduction

The 1980s witnessed a period of unprecedented worldwide reform of the teaching profession. In the United States, the United Kingdom, and France, structural changes reversed decades of institutional arrangements and bureaucratic authority. China was no exception. The post-Mao years in Chinese education have been distinguished in part by efforts to reform the reproduction of teachers and reshape their profession.

Often in educational discourse "reform" is used to refer to revision of policy. In the case of China's teachers and their social relations, reform conjures up a more physical image of molding and shaping. Seeing teachers as people to be molded (or re-molded) has a tradition in contemporary Chinese history, as the Cultural Revolution perhaps best demonstrated.[2] In the 1980s reforms were aimed not only at changing individual teachers, but were intended to change the shape of the profession--its size, its composition--and to alter its location in relation to the rest of society.

The attempts to reform teachers and teaching in China are connected to a global process of educational rationalization and specialization as well as to China's own education, economic, and social

217

developments. The many issues associated with reforming teachers--increasing their numbers and quality, introducing a system of credentials, revising the structure of rewards, and encouraging different practices--were closely related to broader goals of national development in the post-Mao era.

An examination of teacher education, its reform, and reforms aimed at the teaching profession highlights the centrality of teachers to China's post-Mao modernization strategy as well as their vulnerability. This chapter considers the teaching profession as it has been formed in recent history, is shaped by the production of teachers through teacher preparation, and is being transformed by state-initiated policies of reform.

Teachers in the post-Mao years, like teachers of earlier periods,[3] hold complex and ambiguous roles. They occupy sensitive positions in society and the polity that have made them vulnerable to dynamic conflicts outside of education. Over the years since Liberation, teachers have either been prized or suspect, placed on pedestals or denounced. The typical story line of the history of contemporary teaching, given by either Western or Chinese accounts, puts teachers in the role of passive actors, victims of State and Party control. While popular lore emphasizes this vulnerability (and I find evidence to support this description), teachers also influence policy. The post-Mao agenda for reforming teachers tells us much about teachers and the goals of education but also is instructive about the education bureaucracy within a fragmented state and the limits of State/Party power.

We can view teachers of elementary and secondary school students as an occupational group, one defined largely by its collective social history and by the various political roles it has been given at different points in time.[4] Even with restricting this discussion to precollegiate teachers, analyzing teachers as a group poses some difficulties. Teachers in China represent a large and diverse group; in 1987 they numbered 8.7 million and differed greatly in their professional preparation, quality, and contexts of practice.[5] The regions and communities in which teachers work often have had quite different educational histories which affect their contemporary experiences (perhaps the most noteworthy contrasts are between urban and rural settings). The position and work of teachers vary significantly by the level of school in which they work (elementary, junior high, or senior high), the type of school (academic, vocational, specialized-technical), and the school's administrative base. They may work in state-run or community-run (*minban*) schools, and, in the state sector, in schools administered by the district, city, or province. Their status and experience vary also with the formal status of the school--whether it is some version of a "key" school or non-key. In addition, teachers' experiences often also differ widely according to the subject matter they teach. Because of these and other factors, teachers vary in the salary and benefits available to them, the degree of autonomy they enjoy in curriculum development and professional practice and their ability to engage in rewarding activity.

While these represent important differences, for the analysis of professional reform it is the similarities that are of greater relevance. Chiefly most teachers have shared as a group certain pivotal relations--their relationship to other occupational groups, their relationship to the State and to class position defined by the Party, and their role vis a vis students and a hegemonic curriculum determined by the State.

In this chapter I describe the factors that influence the formation of teachers, then analyze efforts at professional reform. Data come from educational texts and journals (popular and scholarly), policy statements, and the media as well as my field research in teacher education colleges and school classrooms. That field work involved an intensive two year participant observation study based largely on one teacher education institution, with shorter periods of interviewing and observation at 34 schools and colleges in 1982-84. Subsequent shorter data collection trips in 1986 and 1987 included follow-up visits to several of these institutions and additional interviews and observations at three other schools.

The Transformation of Teachers

How are teachers formed? Entry into teaching in the post-Mao years was shaped in many ways by history. History influenced not only who decided to become a teacher but also the conceptions they held of teaching and the teacher's role, as well as the sorts of experiences and knowledge they gained in the process of entering the profession.

In a setting in which official ideology has been the focus of conflict, teachers, as transmitters of state ideology, hold sensitive positions. The economic reproductive function of teachers, embodied in their charge to give useful knowledge and skills to students, adds to the delicate nature of the Chinese teacher's job, as controversies have raged about technical knowledge and its connection to power and politics. Over the past 40 years, many of China's debates have centered over defining ideology and knowledge; this complicates the work of those who labor in these areas. China's teachers, like all teachers, have had to be qualified to serve as the bearers of state power and as representatives of technical expertise. The experiences of Chinese teachers are distinguished from those of their counterparts in other countries, however, because the relationship between these two functions of teachers has changed so often and with such force. To meet both qualifications (ideological and technical) has put teachers under great scrutiny; it also means that at any one point in time teachers have been subject to suspicion or criticism on at least one dimension.

The Legacy of History

Since 1949, teaching has often been referred to as a glorious vocation; its nobility and value to society and the State have been stressed in much official rhetoric. Yet in fact Liberation brought an odd mixture of persistent problems left over from the Imperial and Republican eras and new difficulties inspired by re-conceptualizations of the role of teacher. Teachers' proletarian class position was officially defined and the link between teachers and proletarian politics stressed early after the founding of the People's Republic.[6] The chief textbook for teachers of the 1950s emphasized teachers' political role: teachers were "the basic implementors of the educational policies for the socialist nation. Their social function is to give education, training and instruction in the Communist spirit to the young generation."[7] This new class position and role required a new kind of teacher, but the urgency of the task in the early 1950s precluded relying only (or chiefly) on newly trained teachers. Instead, veteran educators had to be used, though tempered through involvement in land reform projects, thought remolding campaigns, and other political education. To augment their numbers, other new teachers had to be brought in untrained.

In the first decade of socialist construction, transforming an initially capitalist educational system to a socialist one implicitly involved a special burden for the teacher. It was in the ways students learned and behaved that socialist ideals were to be expressed. The political demands were great for the teacher, but, significantly, the teacher during this period often came from a bourgeois background. Teachers were claimed as part of the working class, but the educational expectations of them in these transitional first years meant that the ideally qualified teacher had enjoyed the privilege of higher education in a college system that remained fundamentally elitist. Simple redefinition of their position alone without substantially altering the rest of the system made teachers' situations precarious.

In addition, the expansion of schooling and teachers, most notably the creation of community-run schools, brought to the teaching profession large numbers of poorly trained teachers.[8] Those critics then and later who were prone to underestimate teaching had more cause to see it as a dead-end profession, one offering little promise, attracting people unable to venture down other career routes. Thus, changes in this regard left teachers particularly susceptible to technical critiques of competency.

By the end of the first decade of the People's Republic the ground was laid for attacks that would be made against the teaching profession--in the early 1960s, the Cultural Revolution decade, and in the backlash that followed. These attacks--of elitism and incompetence--further weakened the teachers' position and morale.

This legacy of the 1950s, exacerbated by the criticism and abuses of the 1960s and 1970s, left teaching in a weak position for the post-Mao years. Morale and prestige have been low, despite periods of official support for teaching, since early in the PRC. Traditionally the position of the ordinary school teacher (in contrast to the great scholar persona) was to be avoided if at all possible (literally, according to the proverb, "if there's rice in the house").[9] This disdain for teaching persisted after Liberation. One newspaper article in 1959, for example, lamented:

> Why are there still people who look down on teaching as a profession and some secondary and elementary school teachers who look down on their own vocation? In the final analysis, it is old thinking and old perspectives left over from the old society that have not been thoroughly eradicated. There are some among these people who today still consider teaching to be work that has no future.[10]

The negative view of teaching was reinforced by the political scrutiny to which teachers in the new regime were subjected. While periods of the 1950s and 1960s offered respites from criticism, teachers interviewed who had worked during those years recalled teaching as being buffeted by one political movement after another. The result of this accumulated collective memory has been a profession with low morale and a history of poor economic rewards, political status and social prestige. Many still consider teaching as having "no future."

The Social Construction of Teachers

The teaching profession in the years after Mao's death has been directly affected by this history. The impact is visible in patterns of individual entry to the profession and in the institutions that mediate that process.

INDIVIDUAL ENTRY

The most intellectually able or most promising students typically have selected not to go into teaching. Instead, other, often weaker students are attracted to teacher education by the special stipends given to teacher education students, by traditional gender constructions and notions of appropriate work, or by low exam scores that made teacher training their only choice for higher education.

In interviews I conducted with 83 undergraduates at a teacher preparation college, almost a quarter of the students (24 per cent) explained that they were attending their university primarily because of their entrance examination score [11] (in fact, this was one of the most frequently given explanations). Many others explained that they were influenced by others (26.7 per cent). Of that group, several, especially women, explained that they were "suited" to be a teacher, that it was an "appropriate" career for one of their temperament and personality. Among those students (34 total) who listed the school as their first preference, four were were veteran teachers and were therefore to attend a teacher education college; others did so only after their scores were announced.[12] Strikingly absent were people who actively chose to attend a teacher education institution out of an interest in teaching as a career. Very few (only 8 per cent) cited wanting to teach as the reason for their going into teacher education. These patterns at one institution are typical of a national trend decried by many educators.[13] Students blame the lack of interest in teaching on the low social, political, and economic condition of teachers. Thus, the social history of teaching affects teachers' socialization long before they even enter formal training.

INSTITUTIONAL MEDIATION

Official responsibility for preparing teachers for their profession is given to teacher education institutions. There were 1,319 such pre-service programs in 1987. They varied by the level of teaching for which they prepared their students: teacher training colleges (that is, tertiary institutions) are charged with preparing secondary school teachers and teacher training schools (at the secondary level) with preparing elementary teachers.[14] Not all teachers enter teaching by way of formal teacher preparation.[15] Yet to understand the teaching profession and attempts at its reform, we should consider the sorts of knowledge and conceptions of teaching these institutions offer beginning teachers.

Those students who by choice or chance end up in teacher education institutions enter a socialization process notably affected by external policy shifts and the related precarious and frequently shifting balance in the institution's missions. Over the years teacher education institutions, initially disadvantaged by low prestige, have suffered further in social, financial, and academic standing. They receive comparatively weaker funding, facilities, faculty, and students than those found in peer institutions.

Teacher education institutions are characterized by a tension between goals that reflect divergent conceptions of teachers and their roles. Post-Mao teacher education programs are a product of layers of reforms implemented at different political periods. Each layer represents a "solution" that later was viewed as a "problem" that prompted additional, sometimes radical "solutions." Teacher education institutions have been pulled, often abruptly, between political and technocratic models of education.[16] The current configuration of teacher education curriculum and programs reflects these tensions.

The prospective teacher encounters these layers in several ways. Teacher preparation occurs in teacher education institutions, organizationally separated from other higher education or secondary education, which reflect a rational model of specialization borrowed from the Soviets. Specialization is mirrored in the narrowness of the student's program of study. In the teacher education college, 60-70 per cent of a B.A. student's time (and 75 per cent of a 2-3 year A.A. or *zhuanke* student's) is devoted to one discipline (their major). Prospective teachers have few choices about their courses or what they will learn. The curriculum, with its relative dearth of elective courses, is rigid. It reflects the techno-rational models and teacher education's shortage of material and faculty resources. The proportionally small role for professional course work (chiefly, courses in education and psychology)--only 5 per cent for B.A. students, 5-8 per cent for A.A. students, and approximately 16 per cent for teacher training school students--represents the technocratic model's preference for subject matter knowledge as well as the political model's suspicion that education and psychology are bourgeois disciplines.[17]

The prospective teacher's out-of-class experiences, like the course work, stand as reminders of earlier debates. At the teacher education college, a thesis requirement, a relatively new addition advocated by supporters of teacher education's technical mission, is juxtaposed with labor and political theory requirements, which--though their relative time allotment has varied--reflect periods of the political model's dominance. Finally, the construction of the student teaching experience reflects the conception of teaching as a moral/political act. Even though the experience lasts only six weeks and provides few opportunities (often only 4 to 10 classes total) for instruction, the message about teacher's political and moral role is emphasized, particularly by the collective approach to practice, the thrust of orientation lectures and summary sessions, and the assignment of each teacher candidate to serve as a temporary class advisor (*banzhuren*).[18]

After four years of formal preparation, the prospective secondary school teacher has had extensive but narrow exposure in one area, very limited experience with teaching and learning as it occurs in schools, and few opportunities to design his/her program. Teacher education programs reproduce people prone to maintain conventional teaching practices (which are dominated by concerns regarding the subject matter and not individual learners). Similarly the teacher education curriculum's emphasis on preparing teachers to know and rely on government-produced textbooks encourages the new teacher to accept the hegemonic curriculum. This formal program of teacher preparation builds on prospective teachers' earlier conceptions of teachers constructed during their "apprenticeship of observation"[19] as students; long before beginning formal teacher education, these students saw teaching dominated by an orientation to transmitting knowledge. Teacher education programs strengthen these conceptions.

TRANSITION TO TEACHING

Graduates of college-based teacher education programs in the 1980s have tried hard to avoid assignment to teaching posts. Only 4 per cent of the students I interviewed said they wanted to be a high school teacher, and the majority hoped to use their undergraduate teacher education studies towards some other goal. One student I interviewed put it bluntly: "I'd rather be a toilet cleaner than a high school teacher." A survey done by Chinese colleagues in another region of China reports similar tendencies, with only 22.6 per cent of the teacher training college students surveyed wanting to be high school teachers.[20] Reading between the lines of recent praise for teacher preparation programs that send the majority of their graduates to teaching, it appears that many of these students manage to escape teaching. A vice-commissioner of the State Education Commission claims, in fact, that the 1980s witnessed a decline in the proportion of teacher college graduates going to precollegiate teaching positions.[21]

For those who complete teacher preparation and enter classroom teaching after teacher preparation, however, there have been messages along the way, below the formal text of praise for teaching, about teaching's few rewards, low status, and conservative orientation. Once assigned to a school, the messages continue. The distribution of teachers to work groups structured around norms of collegiality and seniority encourages the new teacher to conform to current practices of the school and discourages individual innovation. The division of teacher labor reinforces hierarchical distinctions that set some apart from others; special-grade teachers (*teji jiaoshi*) and class advisors (*banzhuren*) differ from other teachers in the work, distinction and material compensation they receive. The practice in urban schools of assigning new teachers lighter loads and arranging for them to apprentice under an older mentor is another common differentiation among teachers that represents the conservative, reproductive orientation of the work place. Finally, the centrality of the entrance examination system and state-authorized texts that support it define authoritative knowledge and foster a text-centered (as opposed to a learner-centered) approach to teaching.[22]

In reviewing the formative influences on teachers, particularly the historical tendencies, the professional socialization of teacher education, and the organization of teachers' work, it is not surprising that China's teaching contingent suffers from uneven quality, low standards, and poor morale.[23] The post-Mao leadership responded to what were seen as weaknesses in teaching with a range of efforts to transform the profession: notably, to control quality, upgrade standards, improve morale, and support a new conceptualization of teaching. Together these efforts represent the newest in a long series of attempts to re-make teachers. The current process and its mixed success tell us something about the intractable nature of some of these problems and the limits of State reform.

THE TRANSFORMATION OF TEACHING

Since 1978, the State and Party have relied on two major avenues for teacher reform: regulation and allocation (or re-distribution). These have included a range of reforms of pre-service and in-service teacher education and of the teaching profession. The State's efforts to regulate teacher knowledge and standards through teacher education reform and the introduction of professional certification is one example. State attempts to "stabilize" the teaching profession through distribution of rewards and welfare benefits represent another example. The State has been partly successful in its control efforts, but lower level actors have exerted significant influence. In distributing goods to teachers, the State has made limited gains. The story of that effort illustrates teachers' potential for influence as well as the limits of the education bureaucracy's power in a fragmented state.

Regulating Quality

Since the 1978 3rd Plenum of the Eleventh Party Congress, improving the quality of teaching and the general standards of the teaching profession has been a frequently stated goal of the central government, one explicitly linked to the goals of modernization and development.[24] The State has directed its energies to both pre-service and in-service education for teachers as well as to incentive programs of various kinds that encourage and reward higher standards. Here I focus on several State initiatives intended to improve the quality of teacher preparation and regulate standards for practicing teachers: the efforts to recruit stronger students to teacher education, to strengthen teachers' professional training, and to establish a system of teacher testing and credentials. These reforms have met with mixed success in re-shaping teaching, and along the way they have themselves been shaped by the participation (passive and active) of educators.

RECRUITING STRONG TEACHERS

One of the major constraints on improving the quality of the teaching force has been the people who enter the profession.[25] As discussed earlier, the historical treatment of teachers has discouraged the most capable students from entering teaching, and the relative academic weakness of teacher education students, combined with their weak commitment to teaching, has limited what professional preparation programs have been able to do. With this in mind, the Ministry of Education (now the State Education Commission, hereafter referred to as the SEdC) has tried a range of experiments to recruit stronger students into teaching.

When the nationally unified entrance exam was re-instated in 1977 (provincially administered in 1977, nationally administered in 1978), teacher education colleges had what they believed was a more objective basis for decision making about prospective teachers. But teacher education institutions were at a disadvantage in recruiting the academically most talented students. While teacher educators championed the goal of setting higher standards for their students'

academic level and "professional attitude," normal colleges have had
little success in achieving it despite a variety of approaches.
For example, in an effort to improve the teacher education
programs' ability to attract outstanding students, the SEdC gave normal
universities "first pick" of students with top exam scores. A non-key
teachers university was allowed to join key universities in the first
round of student selection for admissions. Yet because the final
selection decisions reflect a matching of a student's ranking of
university preferences with a university's ranking of students it prefers,
the advantage given the teacher education college meant little. Very
few high-scoring students ranked teacher education as their first choice,
ranking instead comprehensive universities or engineering schools ahead
of it. The normal university has had to turn to lower scoring students
to fill its admissions quota.

Public relations efforts to persuade students to choose teacher
education have also not worked. In the early 1980s the Ministry of
Education allowed schools to distribute recruiting materials to high
schools and information offices. But teacher training colleges found
themselves unable to advertise or present themselves in new, attractive
ways. While other types of universities have developed appealing
posters, this has been difficult for teacher education. Administrators at
the case study school, for example, described their school's poster as
"plain," since the campus "doesn't have great buildings or laboratories"
and since the school's specializations are self-explanatory. The school
seemed baffled in its public relations efforts to reform its image, nor
did it feel able to make this effort.

More recent reforms include early admissions for teacher
education applicants and the continued use of stipends to teacher
training students despite the elimination of stipends in much of the rest
of higher education.[26] Both of these were seen as possible means to
attract stronger students. It was hoped, for example, that the
opportunity to secure college admission early would lure academically
more able students to teacher education. Officials from the SEdC,
provincial Bureau of Education, and university admission offices in
interviews said this approach was effective in attracting a stronger
student to teacher preparation, yet all noted its limits. As one
university official explained in 1986, the candidates were "not the best,
but (academically) upper-middle students." And results from the most
recent college admissions cycle are discouraging to those concerned
about teaching. While news accounts praise the success of teacher
education institutions in some areas (such as Tianjin and Beijing) in
having large proportions of students list teacher education as their first

choice, more common are the woeful reports from places like Hubei and Jiangsu where teacher education programs have not been able to fill their quotas.[27] In one particularly gloomy example, a provincial teacher training college that had set an admissions quota of 147 students had only one student list it as a choice.[28]

The problems are clear, and state initiatives have had limited success in countering longstanding and continued disinterest and disdain for teaching as a career. The university admissions reforms may well have been exploited by those who use them for their own goals--students, for example, who enter teacher education but do not go into teaching. A recent survey in Shanxi found that 71.4 per cent of the students questioned said outright that they had come to their teacher education programs in order to achieve other goals, and 57.9 per cent were unwilling to become a teacher.[29]

Perhaps the *dingxiang* (fixed destination) program best illustrates the irony of state-initiated programs being re-interpreted or captured by their participants. That program, introduced nationally in 1983, is designed to guarantee that more teachers with professional training will be posted to rural and remote areas. Given urban graduates' resistance to rural teaching assignments, the Ministry designed the program as a means of filling rural teaching positions with rural graduates. Applicants agreeing to go to rural schools after university may be given special consideration in admissions and admitted with scores below the specified minimum. Although the program officially commenced in 1983, interviews in 1984 with 11 department chairs at one teacher training college revealed a range of interpretation of the policy and its implementation. Some department chairs described plans to implement the policy; others assured me that they were not planning to do so, while one leader said that he did not know what the policy was.

According to one university-level administrator interviewed, poor publicity and limited information left both applicants and administrators bewildered. In the 1983 university entrance examination registration form, which doubled as a preliminary application form, one line simply asked, "Do you agree to be *dingxiang*?" 90 per cent of those students coming to the case study university agreed, yet in the view of a college administrator interviewed about this, they probably agreed more from fear of rejection from university than out of some understanding and acceptance of the *dingxiang* conditions. Furthermore, added the respondent, "students may feel the policy will change by the time they graduate" and thus believe their agreement is not binding. A recent survey from another teacher training college confirms these early

suspicions: at that school, 96.17 per cent of the students had come
from rural areas, but very few were willing to return.   Students,
according to the reporters, did not "understand" the policy of fixed
destinations for teacher education graduates.   Whether or not this is a
question of understanding, it was clear to the researchers that not one
student was willing to support the *dingxiang* policy.[30]

STRENGTHENING THE CURRICULUM

The government also tried to raise the standards of those going
into teaching by revising the teacher education curriculum.   Like some
of the admissions reforms, these efforts suggest a high degree of local
interpretation and mutual adaptation.

As early as 1978 the teacher education curriculum was targeted
for reform.   Central leaders like Hu Yaobang, then General Secretary
of the Party, claimed that teachers needed knowledge of subject matter
and pedagogy as well as moral qualities.[31]   Improving the curriculum to
provide such knowledge became important.   Formally the changes
appeared to be controlled by the SEdC.   Teacher education colleges are
good examples.   In 1978 and 1980, the Ministry (SEdC) published
teaching plans (*jiaoxue jihua*) for eleven departments in teacher training
colleges.   They also issued teaching outlines (*jiaoxue dagang*) for 140
courses offered at normal colleges (the plans list courses and placement
in a student's program, while the outlines specify the topics and their
sequence for each course).   Both the plans and outlines, however, are
"reference" (*cankaoxing*) documents that serve as guidelines rather than
as regulations.   There has been some measure of institutional autonomy.

In general, teacher education programs early in the post-Mao
years tended to expand their academic curriculum.   Programs varied in
what they were able to do, but the trend was for significant additions
to be made to the curriculum: more courses were offered, more course
hours required and more specialization within students' programs.   The
goal was to compensate for the Cultural Revolution's effects on
scholarly training in academic disciplines by strengthening the
curriculum in "specializations" or academic majors.   Similarly, the
redistribution of the curriculum was intended to achieve the goal of
higher academic standards.   Electives were added as was a senior thesis
requirement and laboratory work for science majors.   As a result, other
parts of the curriculum atrophied: general course requirements in politics

and professional requirements in education course work were reduced as was time spent in student teaching.

Alteration of the central policy subsequently occurred in ways that demonstrate the somewhat interactive quality and mutual adaption that has characterized much of recent teacher education reforms. In a 1980 National Teacher Education Conference, Gao Yi used a keynote address to respond to the experimentation of local institutions and to warn against an overly academic curriculum.[32] Soon after, a slight though significant re-orientation of teacher education curriculum took place. Department chairs report that some departments reduced their electives and others shifted course content away from theoretically advanced work to "fundamentals." The core sequence in political theory was strengthened, a new course in moral education required, and an extra year of physical education was added.

Over several years, the reform policies to strengthen teacher education took on different meanings at different times. Though relatively weak and with limited power to influence policy, teacher educators re-cast policy in their own and their unit's interest. At one college, for example, each department interpreted the central government's stated goal of "higher quality teacher education" as encouragement for expanding its own course hours and offerings. In the end, university plans that called for strengthened preparation in education and more advanced course work in the student's major field produced an increase in specialized disciplinary study at the expense of professional training in education. In one university's 1980 plan, for example, education courses represented only 2.7 per cent-5.8 per cent of a student's course hours, in contrast to an earlier 10-20 per cent. The recent history of college curriculum change suggests that lower-level units deflect and interpret decisions in ways they find congenial.

Throughout the period of the post-Mao reforms, the broad objective and principles of strengthening professional standards have not changed. Yet the process of central government policy announcement, local experimentation, and subsequent mutual adaptation by the central government and individual education programs continually redefined the boundaries of acceptability. Reformulation and tinkering with the curriculum continued throughout the 1980s.

There are ironies to these curriculum reforms aimed at strengthening teaching. Time directed at professional issues and the contexts of practice has been significantly reduced; time for student teaching was cut in half at the case study institution during the post-Mao years, and throughout teacher education institutions, education and psychology have come to be given limited time and attention. Teachers responsible for the pedagogy and psychology courses viewed this decrease in education hours as a hardship, yet they appeared resigned to it. As one pedagogy faculty member noted, the situation "is not suitable" but "it's got to be this way for now." Similar concerned resignation was heard from university-level administrators who lamented the fact that, in the spirit of reform and strengthening, the university had expanded its requirements so that students now had little time to study or think on their own. At the case study institution, between 1980 and 1983 the average total hours of course work required for graduation rose from 2835 to 3139, with the elective courses' role in the overall study program of a study actually dropping from 11.3 per cent to 8.3 per cent. Students in the mid-1980s were often taking course loads of 20-30 class hours a week. And while university officials complained, the territorial claims of each department fueled course expansion in the interest of upgrading standards.

ESTABLISHING STANDARDS FOR TEACHING IN SCHOOLS

        Efforts to reform teaching through recruiting stronger candidates and revision of teacher education curricula have been mediated by students and teacher educators. These reforms have not been wholly successful, nor could they solve what the central government views as the full extent of the problems of teaching quality in China's schools. As a result in the mid-and late 1980s, the State tried to directly re-shape the teaching force through a system of teacher examinations and credentials. The push for certification shows the State trying to control change in the teaching profession. The push also hints at the limits to what this regulation can achieve.
        Unlike the United States and many countries, the PRC traditionally has had no system of teacher certification. Rather, it was assumed that teachers were qualified by the professional training they received in their teacher education program. The reality of China's teaching force, particularly in the aftermath of the dramatic influx of untrained teachers in the Cultural Revolution decade, is that large numbers of teachers have not received pre-service preparation and have no claim to technical qualifications (recall that in 1987 approximately 37 per cent of elementary teachers and 71 per cent of secondary teachers were deemed unqualified in terms of their degrees). The

government's interest in credentials can be seen as serving several purposes: clearly emphasizing the centrality of technical knowledge (i.e., subject matter and professional knowledge) to the definition of the teacher's role; monitoring the standards of those teachers already in the system, and providing education authorities with legitimacy when they make distinctions that favor some teachers and disadvantage others; extending concerns for degrees and certificates to adults in professional areas; and using internationally common symbols of educational rationalization and specialization.

The 1986 Compulsory Education Law specifically discussed teacher testing and certification, and while the program remains in an early phase, there are several noteworthy aspects.[33] In this system, the government has mandated tests for all teachers who lack appropriate degrees for their current positions (that is, elementary teachers who do not have a teacher training school degree or equivalent and secondary teachers who do not have a teacher training college degree or equivalent). Teachers are endorsed as "qualified" (and awarded certification) when they successfully complete the test for the level at which they teach. The official estimate has been that approximately 2.4 million teachers need such certification. The formally stated goal is that, by motivating teachers to study on their own and in in-service programs the professional and subject-specific knowledge they lack, the system will "raise the professional character of teachers and the level of education and teaching."[34]

Whether or not the credential system can achieve these goals is uncertain, but the introduction of the system certainly produced anxiety for teachers. The education bureaucracy had to spend some time responding to their fears and complaints, and there has been much discussion of how this system does or does not dovetail with previous in-service training programs.[35] The pass rate on these tests has, to date, been quite low. In an experimental version of the test tried out in six provinces, autonomous regions, and municipalities in 1987, only between 22 and 27 per cent of the 430,000 secondary school teachers passed.[36] In 1988, with 900,000 teachers taking the examination in cultural and professional knowledge, the rate was about 15 per cent higher but still below 50 per cent: 42.13 per cent of senior high teachers, 39.62 per cent of junior high teachers, and only 34.40 per cent of elementary teachers passed.[37]

The examinations are standardized for secondary teachers by the central government, while examinations for elementary teachers are the responsibility of each province. The system has a potentially powerful impact as it was designed to be coordinated with teacher ranking and salaries from 1989 on. For both elementary and secondary teachers, this represents a new level of penetration of state authority in their work lives. The low pass rate, coupled with the difficulties the SEdC has had in moving beyond an experimental phase, may suggest passive resistance on the part of teachers weary of an interventionist state involved in their work.

Allocating Benefits

Through changing who goes into teaching, what they study in preparation, and how their qualifications are monitored, the State has been active in trying to remold the profession of teaching. The results so far--with students avoiding teaching, teacher educators taking advantage of curriculum reform, and the majority of candidates failing to qualify--recommend that we re-examine the ways in which we think of the relationship between teachers and the State in China. Certainly the State has been active. Yet no one could call it successful.

The State has not been limited only to regulatory measures to reform teaching. Operating with assumptions about teachers as rational actors, the State and Party in the post-Mao years have tried to allocate benefits to teachers in ways that will win the support of teachers for State policy, strengthen the commitment of teachers to educational policies and teaching, and stabilize a teaching force that has been badly damaged by teacher attrition and low morale.

Recall that the profession of teaching, by the end of the Cultural Revolution, had fallen prey to waves of shifting policy campaigns. Teachers had been criticized alternately for their elitism or incompetence, and the majority of policies aimed at teaching had directly or indirectly punished teachers for their collective sins. With changes in the economy and society after the fall of the "Gang of Four," teachers had relatively few avenues for improvement compared with more prestigious technical and scientific intellectuals (whose support for modernization policies was highly sought by the Party and State), workers whose labor was directly rewarded by industrial reform policies, or individuals working in new areas made possible by the encouragement of entrepreneurial activity. Throughout the post-Mao years teachers remained among the lowest paid professionals.[38] Their political and social position--never high---was very low. As a group they appeared poorly trained and demoralized. Retention problems exacerbated the recruitment crisis mentioned earlier, as large numbers of teachers gave up the security of their job (and often their residential registration or *hukou*) to leave the field.[39] Particularly disturbing to education officials and policy planners was the high proportion of strong, experienced, middle-aged teachers, known as "backbone teachers" (*gugan jiaoshi*) among the leavers. Principals estimated that of the teachers left after attrition, only 37.5 per cent are qualified.[40]

What has been the State and Party response in the face of these crises for the teaching profession? Government leaders call the tendencies in the profession an obstacle to education reform. In an effort to reverse these trends and re-build the profession, in particular by encouraging both stronger candidates to enter the field and persuading able teachers to remain at their posts, the State and Party have undertaken a series of policy gestures directed first at social position, then political support, and finally, only when these were insufficient to quell teacher malaise, economic improvement. But, as the narrative below suggests, achieving gains in these areas has required growing disaffection and passive resistance from teachers as well as coordination across different sectors of the government. While teachers have not been organized in ways that permit collective action or bargaining, they have been able to make a case for themselves by their ability to withhold support for State policy in education. At the same time, their ability to improve their conditions has been limited by the sector of the State authorized to mediate their concerns, which bureaucratically has been too weak to bring about the changes most needed by teachers. A review of social, political, and economic efforts, though not exhaustive, demonstrates these problems.

Social Work in the Post-Mao Era

White argues that CCP leaders from the beginning have believed that they had both the responsibility and ability to "manipulate the relative prestige of specific social groups and strata."[41] The CCP has used a variety of direct and indirect means to influence--positively or negatively--the social position of teachers. White shows that over the years teachers have been able to receive recognition and blunt policies that might damage their already weakened social position. Party and State efforts since Mao certainly suggest that leaders have continued to assume that they can influence teachers' social standing. But these efforts have had limited impact in a decade when economic profit has significantly contributed to one's social position.

It is common to attribute many of the problems of the teaching profession to social position. The lack of prestige and respect, as well as repeated instances of violence and abuse against teachers, is seen as evidence of unfavorable social attitudes toward teachers. They were among the State and Party's first targets for transforming teaching.

For example, the State instituted a national Teacher's Day to celebrate and honor teachers. Inaugurated on September 9, 1985, the message in each year's celebratory stories, reports, poems, and photographs of the day is clear: the teacher's role is socially valued, supported by the country's top leaders, and appreciated by ordinary people.[42] Similar chords are struck in other socially oriented reforms, including the "respect teachers, love students" (*zunshi aisheng*) campaign, the 1986 Compulsory Education Law's stipulation to prosecute assaults on teachers, and the creation of a professional merit system (with honors for "models" and "special grade" teachers).[43]

The central government has relied on the media as an inexpensive way to promote and imply change. Symbolism has been the chief currency of these efforts. But data suggest that such symbolic gestures have had limited power for both teachers and the public. My interviews indicate that while these symbolic efforts have been somehow comforting to "backbone teachers," they have offered little comfort to new teachers and little incentive to enter the profession.[44] Cryptically and cynically, teachers noted that these social reforms were "not hard to carry out." Talk was cheap, they argued.

The limits of this talk have been underscored by the continued evidence of abuse even after the establishment of policies to improve the treatment of intellectuals. In the 1980s teachers have been beaten, killed, and publicly humiliated.[45] The Chinese Education Union reported that in just the first months of 1987, there were several hundred reported instances of serious physical attacks on teachers.[46]

Improving Teachers' Political Status

A second area of relatively early attention, often discussed in connection with social efforts, centered around political gestures directed at increasing what White calls teachers' "formal political power."[47] These efforts have required broader cooperation, have necessitated going beyond symbolic action, and have proven more difficult.

The goal of these efforts has been to confer political legitimacy on teachers, something particularly needed after teachers were the target of the political campaigns of the Cultural Revolution and "Gang of Four" years and consequently placed in antagonist relations to the Party and masses. Of the range of efforts, most important has been the attempt to incorporate teachers into the dominant political organization, the Chinese Communist Party (CCP). The Party's recruitment efforts, however, have had limited success.

It is especially noteworthy that the Party's lack of success with regard to teachers has come at a time of active recruitment of intellectuals.[48] Local CCP leaders have even been encouraged to go to schools to recruit strong candidates. But despite this policy, there are reports of local resistance to the political legitimation of teachers. In one 1984 survey 15.7 per cent of the teachers complained of being denied Party membership despite years of testing, and some schools had stopped altogether the recruiting of teachers as new Party members.[49] More recently, 62.5 per cent of rural teachers surveyed in Ningxia and Inner Mongolia identified inadequate support from the Party as a key concern.[50] The experience of political efforts demonstrates the difficulties encountered in implementing non-symbolic aspects of the policy and highlights the education bureaucracy's limits in overseeing compliance.

Distributing Economic Benefits

In reviewing the history of the teaching profession's material situation, White notes that:

The nature and level of teachers' material conditions
have been a recurring bone of contention between the
teaching profession and the Party since 1949. In their
desire to increase their wages and welfare provisions
and improve their working conditions, teachers have
faced political authorities whose decisions on such
matters have been constrained by egalitarian scruples
and concern about the political implications of material
relativities between occupational groups. Moreover, the
desire to reserve state funds for high priority sectors,
notably economic construction and the national defense,
has imposed strict limits on educational spending.[51]

In the post-Mao years these limits have been seen by policy makers,
teachers, and prospective teachers alike as negatively affecting the
teaching profession. In my 1984 interviews with future teachers at one
teacher training college, material conditions--that is, wages, bonuses, and
housing--were offered as the key explanation for people's unwillingness
to be teachers by 27.5 per cent of the respondents, second in frequency
only to teachers' social position. In a different survey, Chinese
researchers found that 55.2 per cent of teacher education students
sampled gave economic and material reasons for not wanting to be
teachers.[52] And in explaining the departure of veteran teachers from
their classrooms, education officials interviewed regularly claimed that
economic troubles were a major cause.

If the State was to show itself supportive of teachers, win their
allegiance, and guarantee some stability in its professional ranks,
distributing better or new economic and material benefits to teachers
was essential in the 1980s, a decade of rapid economic reform
nationally. State efforts in this regard can be grouped into several
major categories: housing, health, family economic security, and
income. In each there have been certain patterns to the policy reform
process: SEdC difficulty in procuring resources, the reliance on local
initiative, and the need to persuade other sectors to join in these efforts.
Also, in this area of professional life, one notes important differences
in the avenues for teacher redress, the alliances teachers have been able
to strike, and the force teachers have been able to bring to gaining their
interests. While all teachers have felt inadequately treated to material
benefits, urban and rural teachers, and particularly state-employed
teachers and *minban* teachers, have differed in the focus of their
concerns.

As an example, consider the issues of housing and health care.
Housing has been a source of particular concern for urban primary and

secondary teachers. Unlike workers in factories, enterprises, and government offices, urban teachers typically have not been provided apartment and dormitory housing by their work units. In 1985 32.3 per cent of urban elementary and secondary teachers were estimated as lacking housing.[53] It is striking that, despite much ballyhooed gains in housing in the years since then, a 1989 government report to a national conference on the topic estimated that about 33 per cent of school staffs still lacked adequate housing.[54]

The government's approach to improving the housing shortage, which accounts for much of the current instability in the urban teaching force, has been to encourage provincial, municipal, and local initiatives to solve the problem. A SEdC vice-minister in 1986 explained that while the central government can contribute something, teachers "need to rely chiefly on local areas."[55] Although national meetings have been held to discuss the housing problem for teachers, they tend to publicize individual success stories of cities, districts, and schools.[56] A typical local solution is illustrated by Jinzhou, held up nationally as an example, where 2 per cent of the annual city and town housing investment was directed to construction of housing for elementary and secondary teachers, the housing of teachers who leave was returned to the provincial Bureau of Education (rather than to other departments), schools' factory income was used to buy housing, and schools relied on their staff's spouses' housing allocations.[57] The State has been explicit in its view that supplying housing is a means to gain teachers' trust, make them more willing to teach and to take on the responsibilities assigned them by the State.[58] Yet the message for teachers may well be that the proper recipient of their commitment and trust should be not the State but their local, personal connections as individuals or as a school faculty.

While teachers criticize the State for its material treatment of their profession, educators have turned to low level bureaucrats and advocates close at hand for support. In the post-Mao economic climate, entrepreneurial opportunities and bargaining by school leaders with other units have become important means by which teachers' housing needs have been addressed and their cooperation secured. In my high school interviews I encountered administrators who had bargained with a nearby factory to admit a set of its workers' children in exchange for both construction and money, and other administrators had agreed to exceed their student enrollment quota to admit local students with lower entrance examination scores for a 2,000 *yuan* per pupil fee. Part of this income went to teachers' housing.

These contractual arrangements and informal bargains highlight the value of personalized ties for teachers. The increase in entrepreneurial solutions to teachers' problems also illustrates the need for negotiation with organizations outside of education and the importance of Party policy in legitimating the bureaucratic methods. Certainly the heavy involvement of school principals in "creating income" as a solution to the teaching profession's difficulties is only possible through its congruence with the Party's agenda for national reform. In that sense, the story of teacher housing reminds us of the vulnerability of teachers to Party policy; yet the centrality of local connections to whatever successes have occurred suggest that in the 1980s teachers had ways of pleading their cases locally through traditional patronage systems.

While the specific focus of the rural *minban* teachers' concerns are different from their urban counterparts, we see in both cases the vulnerability of teachers to State/Party attention and possibilities for influence of local solutions. In the era of post-Mao reforms and strengthening the teaching ranks, there had been consideration of transforming the profession by eliminating *minban* teachers, who are not state employees and tend to have weaker qualifications than the state-hired teacher, through educational upgrading (into state-hired teacher status) and attrition. But in 1989 more than 3 million such teachers remain, and their existence at least in the near future is now implicitly guaranteed by the State's acknowledged inability to get teacher education graduates to assume rural teaching posts.[59]

The *minban* teacher's worries differ from those of state-hired teachers. Paid by the local community, their incomes tend to be significantly lower than those of state-hired teachers; the Gansu Provincial Education Commission estimated, for example, that the *minban* teacher earns one half or even one third of what the state teacher does.[60] Recent increases in health care costs are especially worrisome for the *minban* teacher, given their lack of guaranteed insurance. Yet here patterns of bureaucratic action are similar to those found in the housing reforms for urban teachers: the central government encouraged reforms, but local areas were expected to provide the resources and action.[61]

There are some noticeable differences, however, in the ways in which teachers and the State have interacted. Urban teachers increasingly turned to school leaders for support for their grievances, while the State and Party--particularly their central representatives--have played perhaps a less critical role in addressing their concerns than in the past. In the 1980s central leadership has chiefly been significant for its symbolic support for teachers and for legitimizing certain kinds of activities, even if it has been up to local actors to take advantage of this situation. The support of urban teachers and the need to maintain their ranks have been important enough to the State to encourage it to take symbolic leadership in tackling the housing problem. The ranks of rural *minban* teachers, on the other hand, have been targeted in the 1980s for major transformation--through their becoming state-hired teachers. Their vulnerability to State policy has been softened chiefly by the reluctance of state-hired teachers to take over their posts. As teachers hired by local communities, they have looked to central or provincial government support to overcome local inequities in ways that mirror the urban teachers' reliance on local advocates to help them address inequities caused by central and provincial policies.

While housing, health care, retirement benefits, avenues for family support, and other issues have all received extensive discussion by teachers, their advocates, and education policy makers, certainly the most controversial issue in the economic treatment of teachers has been the reform of their wages and bonuses. This issue has been at the heart of the discussions about the relationship between the teaching profession and the State; it also has been the costliest but most significant area in which leaders have labored to revitalize the teaching profession and garner teacher support. Unlike many other areas, this issue could not be handled with symbolic gestures, the delegation of authority, or the publicizing of success stories. The education bureaucracy's efforts alone have been insufficient, and cooperation with other sectors of the government has been essential.

The need to address directly teachers' economic complaints was clear from the beginning of the post-Mao era and several actions have been taken. There have been three wage increases in the ten years between 1977 and 1987 for most elementary and secondary teachers.[62] The 1985 reform of the wage system also resulted in higher wages, by replacing the previous rank-based system with a wage determined by the sum of a basic wage, a wage for years of employment (*gongling*), and a special "teachers' years of service" wage (*jiaoling*), which is provided only to teachers and computed on the basis of years of service in education. Finally, as in the industrial sectors, teachers in the 1980s were the beneficiaries of bonuses, but bonuses--despite their variance in size and allocation pattern by school--represent a smaller proportion of the total income for teachers than for industrial workers.[63]

These reforms in wages, wage structure and bonuses are in keeping with the general State policy aimed at transforming the profession; they reward teaching and provide incentives for joining and staying in the profession. But the effectiveness of these measures has been very limited. Teachers I interviewed complained that their recent wage increases, ostensibly aimed at redressing inequities, had been followed almost immediately by comparable or even greater increases in wages for workers and others. Even the teachers' union, prone chiefly to transmitting state policy in top-down fashion, was critical in assessing the problem: "In recent years when teachers had their salaries raised a level, soon after other fields would also raise theirs a level, and the disparity in incomes which had just been reduced was once again created."[64] The expanded possibilities for bonuses for workers made teachers' salaries drop further in comparison.[65] For example, bonuses in 1986 represented 13.4 per cent of the total earnings of staff and workers in state-owned units but contributed only 3.4 per cent and 3.2 per cent to the income of secondary and elementary teachers in 1988.[66] Opportunities for supplementing wages with outside income, one feature of the 1980s reforms, have been quite limited for teachers; in Beijing, for example, teachers rank lowest of twelve occupational group for outside income generated.[67]

Teachers' wage changes have also failed to keep pace with inflation in the mid and late 1980s. "With price increases in recent years the real standard of living of teachers has not only not risen but actually declined."[68] Hence, any gains made in teachers' living conditions tended to disappear with the combined impact of inflation and the relative increases in the wages, bonuses, and outside earnings of workers in other sectors. In 1987 the average income of teachers ranked 11th out of 12 occupations.[69]

In response to growing frustration by teachers and concern by the education bureaucracy, a teacher-specific wage hike, this time for 10 per cent across the boards for teachers, was announced in 1987. That increase, although initially called for by the SEdC, required agreement between the SEdC and Ministries of Finance and Labor. As one SEdC official explained, the SEdC did not have the power to do this on its own. It had to approach the other ministries and persuade them of the importance and of resource availability. Together the three groups wrote the proposal for submission to the State Council.

The SEdC's eventual success in negotiating this raise was influenced by several factors. The partial success of the social campaigns and political reforms had done little to solve and had possibly highlighted the problems of teachers. It is likely that the persistence of frustration among teachers about wages, the increasing sense of relative deprivation, and subsequent flight from teaching all contributed to the sense of necessity associated with the wage increase. Certainly, the passing of the Compulsory Education Law added legitimacy, specificity, and urgency to the policy of revitalizing the teaching force. Finally, the SEdC's case was strengthened because the broader education reform policies and, by extension, much of the modernization strategy, depended on recruiting and retaining good teachers in schools.

The wage increase policy change is significant for what it tells us of the limits of the teaching profession's bureaucratic leadership--the SEdC--and its need to persuade and make common cause with other sectors of the State that may not share the same interests. The story of the wage increase may in fact tell us more about bureaucratic weakness than it does State power. The wage increase, for all the official praise it received, may be simply one more symbolic gesture. Although announced in 1987, the distribution of the increase by late 1988 was still locked in provincial and county-level debates.[70] Even when distributed, the increase is small, since it is based on a percentage of an already low wage. Given inflation rates of that year over 10%, the increase represents an actual decline in standard of living.[71] And as provincial level delays slow distribution, the actual value of the wage increase declined still further.

The wage policy change is also important for what it may suggest about the ability of teachers as constituents of State power to plead their case or apply pressure from the grassroots--even if through negative action. Teachers' avenues for positive political participation have been relatively restricted in the post-Mao era, despite the official language of support for teaching and its key role in modernization--but traditions of passive resistance have continued in the 1980s to serve teachers in making their points. Teachers' power in relation to the State comes from what White sees as their "distinct occupational role: as transmitters of the social values and expertise crucial to China's socialist modernization."[72] They do not have access to the same degree of power that more prestigious intellectuals do, yet the wage situation suggests that teachers have been able, if only slowly and to a small extent, to extract from the State tangible resources that go beyond the symbolic exchanges that have characterized most of the State-teacher interaction.

Summary

The People's Republic of China has a long history of efforts to redefine teachers' roles and re-shape their ranks. In the post-Mao era, teachers have formed their conceptions of teaching and their approaches to practices in large part as the result of earlier State and Party policies that have affected the definitions of teachers, the institutions that prepare them, and those that house their work. This historical and social construction of teachers has produced a teaching profession that in its numbers, quality, and orientation to teaching poses problems for a state committed to its version of modernization.

In response, the State has used regulatory and distributive measures to bolster the teaching profession; improve its character, numbers, and conditions; and garner support for the State's political and education agenda. The results of this reform process do not suggest a wholesale transformation of the teaching profession. Instead, the combined weakness of the State's bureaucratic capacity and the actions of teachers have led to mixed results: teachers at the end of the 1980s were somewhat better educated, better categorized, and better rewarded than they were a decade earlier. Yet their situation as a group still represents a major challenge for State and Party leaders and a potential obstacle to educational reform. In its efforts, the government has relied on rational models of organization and motivation, but practices have favored traditional forms of practice and traditional networks of interaction.

Teachers in China are not cohesive as an interest group.[73] The divisions that cut across teaching as well as the organizational structures and norms within which teachers must operate work against teachers being able to voice collective interests. Teachers are deeply divided by location, employer, and level at which they teach. But just as Connell found for a divided teaching force in Australia, "that does not mean that teachers are either powerless as a group or immobile. On the contrary, their collective practice has clearly played an active role" in the shaping of current social and economic relations in China.[74] Though not commonly thought of as powerful, teachers exert much control of significant institutions through their daily practice in classrooms. The State's reform efforts, weak though they have been in their support of teachers, signify the State's recognition of this.

The irony in the most recent efforts at transforming teachers is that the teaching profession's power to influence State policies rests in large part on the State's conceptualization of the teacher's role. In the most recent period of suppression following the 1989 democracy movement, as the teacher's moral and political role once again gains prominence in public discussions of education, we must wonder about the new directions the transformation of teaching will take and the ability of teachers to influence that process.

Notes

1. An earlier version of this chapter was presented at the UCLA
    Conference on Education in Modern China, January 27, 1990.
    The author wishes to acknowledge the support of the
    Committee for Scholarly Communications with the People's
    Republic of China and Michigan State University for making
    possible the field research on which this chapter is based. I
    also appreciate comments from David M. Lampton, Kenneth
    Lieberthal, and other participants in the ACLS sponsored
    conference on The Structure of Authority and Bureaucratic
    Behavior in China, as well as the help from Brian DeLany,
    Ma Liping, and Zhang Naihua in gathering data and
    commenting on versions of this work.

2. One example of this history of concern for remolding teachers (and
    the apparent difficulty of that task) is reflected in a Cultural
    Revolution-era radical group's statement that "Remolding
    teachers is like pressing a rubber ball under water. Press hard
    and it goes under, but as soon as you let go, it pops up again."
    Gordon White, *Party and Professionals: The Political Role of
    Teachers in Contemporary China* (Armonk, NY: M.E. Sharpe,
    1981): 88.

3. For more on teachers in earlier periods, see *Ibid.*, pp. 1-109.

4. Because university and college teachers differ significantly from
    the less-prestigious precollegiate teachers in their social history,
    their   roles, their current social position and avenues for
    economic reward, and the degree of autonomy available to them
    in their work, they will   not be considered in this analysis.

5. Guojia Jiaoyu Weiyuanhui Jihua Caiwuju, editors, *Zhongguo jiaoyu
    tongji nianjian 1987* (*Chinese Education Statistical Yearbook
    1987*) (Beijing: Beijing   Gongye Daxue Chubanshe, 1988): 5.

6. *Renmin Ribao* (hereafter RMRB) (November 2, 1949).

7. Kailuofu, *Jiaoyuxue* (*Pedagogy*), trans. Shen Ying (Beijing: Renmin
    Jiaoyu Chubanshe, 1952): 451.

8. J. Kwong, *Chinese Education in Transition: Prelude to the*

Cultural Revolution (Montreal: McGill-Queens University Press, 1979); and Zhao Tian   and Liu Xingwei, "Yao ba shifan jiaoyu wei zhengge jiaoyu de zhanlue zhongdian jia yi zhongshi, jiaqiang he fazhan" ("Pay Attention to, Strengthen, and Develop Teacher Education as a Key Point to All of Education") in *Jiaoyu yu Sihua jianshe: Lunwen xuanji* (Liaoning Provincial Higher Education Association: n.p., n.d.): 28-34.

9. Huazhong Shifan Xueyuan Jiaoyuxi, Henan Shifan Daxue Jiaoyuxi, Gansu Shifan Daxue Jiaoyuxi, Hunan Shifan Xueyuan Jiaoyuxi, Wuhan Shifan Xueyuan Jiaoyu Jiaoyanshi, editors., *Jiaoyuxue* (*Pedagogy*) (Beijing: Renmin Jiaoyu Chubanshe, 1982): 319.

10. *Guangming Ribao* (hereafter *GMRB*) (February 24, 1959): 2.

11. These interviews included students from 3 arts and 3 science departments.   For more on the sample and process of interviewing as well as more background on the field research generally, see L. W. Paine, *Reform and Balance in Chinese Teacher Education* (Ph.D. diss., Stanford University, 1986).

12. In various provinces in various years students received their exam results before applying/registering for college, while at other times and places applicants have had to register college preference without knowing how they had fared on the standardized entrance exam. In my sample there were students from both types of situations.

13. Gu Mingyuan, "Gaige shifan jiaoyu de jidian yijian" ("Several Opinions on the Reform of Tertiary Level Teacher Education"), *GMRB* (December 2, 1983):3; Billie L.C. Lo, "Teacher Education in the Eighties," in Ruth Hayhoe, editor, *Contemporary Chinese Education*, (Armonk, NY: M.E. Sharpe, 1984); Fan Gongrong, "Gongtong nuli, banhao Fujian Shida" ("Work Hard Together to Run Fujian Normal Well"), *Shifan Jiaoyu Yanjiu* 1 (1983): 6-10; *Beijing Ribao* (February 4, 1986): 1.

14. While I use the Chinese approach of describing a two-tiered system, distinguishing between teacher education institutions that are

higher education institutions and those at the secondary level,
within the tertiary level there are two distinct institutional types-
-the *gaodeng shifan yuanxiao* or 4 year college or university
preparing senior high school teachers and the *shifan zhuanke
xuexiao*, typically offering a 2-3 year *zhuanke* or Associates
degree for junior high teachers. Given this, Lo (pp. 169-172)
describes Chinese teacher education as having a three-tiered
structure. Of the total of pre-service institutions in 1987, 73
were 4 year colleges and universities granting a B.A. for
secondary school teachers, 187 were 2-3 year colleges offering
the *zhuanke* degree, and 1,059 were secondary schools training
elementary teachers (Guojia Jiaoyu Weiyuanhui Jihua Caiwuju,
Zhongguo jiaoyu tongji nianjian 1987 pp. 5, 22). Additional
teacher education institutions, not described in this analysis, are
responsible for in-service or continuing education for practicing
teachers.

15. While official statistics do not clarify what percentage of new
    teachers in any one year have been exposed to formal
    professional training, we do know that of practicing teachers,
    only 68.2 per cent of elementary and 35.6 per cent of junior
    high teachers in 1987 and 39.6 per cent of senior high teachers
    in 1985 had the recommended preparation for their posts
    (*Zhongguo Jiaoyu Bao* (hereafter *ZGJYB*) (December 31,
    1988):1; State Statistical Bureau, Social Statistics Section,
    editor, *Zhongguo shehui tongji ziliao 1987* (China Social
    Statistics Data 1987) (Beijing: Zhongguo Tongji Chubanshe,
    1987): 161.

16. For a fuller description of this geneology and the ways in which
    these contrasting models have affected teacher education, see
    Paine, "Teacher Education in the People's Republic of China,"
    in E.B. Gumbert, editor, *Fit to Teach: Teacher Education in
    International Perspective*, Lecture Series, no.8   (Atlanta:
    Georgia State University Center for Cross-cultural Education,
    1990): 135-142.

17. Figures for tertiary level teacher education programs are based on
    Dongbei Shifan Daxue Jiaowuchu, *Dongbei Shifan Daxue
    jiaoxue zhidaoshu (Benke) (Northeast Normal University
    Teaching Guide (Undergraduate Program))* (Changchun, 1985),

and Ministry of Education draft plans, in Dangdai Zhongguo Congshu Jiaoyujuan Bianjishi, editors, *Dangdai Zhongguo gaodeng shifan jiaoyu ziliaoxuan (Selected Materials on Contemporary Chinese University-level Teacher Education)* vol. 1. (Shanghai: Huadong Shifan Daxue Chubanshe, 1986): 781-795, 802, 820-909. The figure for prospective elementary teachers comes from one case study (Cheng Wing-chung, "Primary Teacher Education in China: The Case of Harbin," *Canadian and International Education* 16 (1987): 146-161), but given the centralized plan for teacher training schools and secondary education more generally, we can assume that this figure is fairly representative of the broader pool of teacher training schools.

18. L. W. Paine, "The Teacher as Virtuoso: A Chinese Model for Teaching," *Teachers College Record* vol. 92, no.1 (1990):50-81.

19. Dan C. Lortie. *Schoolteacher: A Sociological Study* (Chicago: University of Chicago Press, 1975): 61-67.

20. Zhuang Mingshui, "Gaoshi xuesheng zhuanye sixiang jiaoyu cuyi" ("Some Comments on the Education of Normal College Students' Professional Thinking"), *Fujian Shida Xuebao* 1 (Part 2), (1983): 55-62.

21. Liu Bin, "Jiaqiang hongguan guanli tigao jiaoyu zhiliang" ("Strengthen Macro-management, Raise the Quality of Education"), *Renmin Jiaoyu* 1 (1986): 5-8.

22. Paine, "The Teacher as Virtuoso," *op. cit.*

23. At simply the level of qualifications, the situation is alarming. 1987 estimates, for example, found only 62.8 per cent of elementary and 29.2 per cent of secondary teachers qualified in terms of degrees. *ZGJYB* (July 9, 1987), p. 1; *ZGJYB* (November 10, 1989), p. 1; *ZGJYB* (December 26, 1987), p. 1, and *ZGJYB* (December 31, 1988), p. 1.

24. For examples of stated policies and goals, see selections in *Jiaoyu gaige zhongyao wenxian xuanbian (Important Selected*

Documents on Education Reform) (Beijing: Renmin Jiaoyu Chubanshe, 1986).

25. Gu, p. 3; Lo; Paine, "Reform and Balance in Chinese Teacher Education," *op. cit.*

26. See, for example, *GMRB* (January 13, 1985): 1; *Foreign Broadcast Information Service Daily Report: China* (hereafter *FBIS*) (July 28, 1986): R1; Liu Bin, *ZGJYB* (July 12, 1986): 1; *ZGJYB* (June 1 and 6, 1987): 1; Xue Daohua, "*Shifan yuanxiao zhaosheng tiqian dandu luquhao*" (A Separate Early Admissions for Teacher Training Institutions is Good), *Gaojiao Zhanxian* 5 (1986): 34-35.

27. *ZGJYB* (October 7, 1989): 1; *ZJGYB* (June 1, 1987): 1; *ZGJYB* (June 6, 1987): 1; *ZJGYB* (April 30, 1988): 1; and *ZJGYB* (August 2, 1989): 1. One explanation for this success in Tianjin and Beijing is students' desire to go to schools that keep graduates in those cities. Municipality-administered teacher training colleges in those cities are now in high demand for that reason.

28. *ZGJYB* (November 9, 1989): 1.

29. *ZGJYB* (July 25, 1989): 4.

30. *ZGJYB* (July 25, 1989):4.

31. *FBIS* (June 29, 1980): L1.

32. Gao Yi, "Banhao shifan jiaoyu tigao shizi shuiping wei sihua jianshe peiyang rencai zuochu gongxian" ("Run Normal Education Well, Raise the Level of Teachers, Train Talent to Make a Contribution Towards the Construction of the Four Modernizations"), *Jiaoyu Yanjiu* 4 (1980): 6-12.

33. *Jiaoyu gaige zhongyao wenxian xuanbian*, pp. 15-28; *GMRB* (October 2, 1986): 1.

34. *ZGJYB* (August 18, 1988): 1.

35. *ZGJYB* (July 9, 1987): 2; *ZGJYB* (December 17, 1988): 1.

36. *ZGJYB* (November 10, 1987):1.

37. *ZGJYB* (December 17, 1988): 1.

38. Central Committee Document Research Section, editors, *Zhishifenzi Wenti Wenxian Xuanbian* (*Selected Documents on the Problems of Intellectuals*) (Beijing: Renmin chubanshe, 1983); *ZGJYB* (September 6, 1988):1.

39. *ZGJYB* (November 23, 1985):1. In Liaoning, for example, more than 6,300 teachers left or retired during 1979-84, and about half of these were "backbone teachers." Between 1980-84 one small city in the province had more than 2,000 teachers leave the field. See Zheng Guanjian, "Wending jiaoshi duiwu de yixiang genbenxing cuoshi" ("A Basic Measure to Stabilize the Teaching Force"), *Liaoning Shida Xuebao* 6 (1984): 25-30. More recently in Hunan 3,850 "backbone teachers" changed jobs or were transfered out of the classroom. See *FBIS* (June 27, 1986): P5. In just the Dongcheng district of Beijing, already 103 of the newly assigned graduates have left their teaching jobs. See Chen Siyi, "Zhongxue jingfei he shizi duanque youwu chulu?" ("Are there Solutions to Secondary School Funding and Teacher Shortage Problems?"), *Liaowang* 32 (1988): 30-31.

40. "Zhongxue xiaozhang zuotanhui" ("The Headmasters' Panel Discussion"), *Keji Daobao* 5 (1988): 22-24, in *Fuyin baokan ziliao* 3, 11 (1988): 13-18.

41. White, *Party and Professionals, op. cit.*, p. 18.

42. See, for example, selections from *FBIS*, (September 10, 1984): K1-8; *FBIS* (September 11, 1985): K1-5; and *FBIS* (September 12, 1985): K1-5.

43. Cai Hangcui, "Sichuan caiqu shiji cuoshi qingzhu jiaoshijie" ("Sichuan Takes Concrete Steps to Celebrate Teachers' Day"), *Shifan Jiaoyu* (October, 1985): 8; Chinese Education Yearbook Editorial Group, editor, *Zhongguo jiaoyu nianjian 1949-1981* (Beijing: Zhongguo Dabaike Quanshu Chubanshe, 1984): 200.

44. Paine, "Reform and Balance in Chinese Teacher Education," *op. cit.*

45. See, for example, *RMRB* (May 31, 1984): 3; *FBIS* (August 20, 1985): 1; Chinese Education Yearbook Editorial Group, ed. *Zhongguo jiaoyu nianjian 1982-84* (Changsha: Hunan Jiaoyu Chubanshe, 1986): 351; *ZGJYB* (October 24, 1987): 1; *ZGJYB* (April 19, 1988) 11; and *ZGJYB* (December 31, 1988): 1.

46. *ZGJYB* (December 31, 1988): 1.

47. White, *Party and Professionals*, *op. cit.*, p. 60.

48. *Jiaoyu gaige zhongyao wenxian xuanbian*; Zheng Guanjian, "Wending," *op. cit.*, pp.25-30.

49. He Bin, "Dui jiaoshi de kunao yu xuyao de diocha fenxi" ("A Survey and Analysis of Teachers' Troubles and Needs"), *Jiaoyu Lilun yu Shijian* 1 (1985): 16-22.

50. Ma Denghai, Wang He, & Chen Wentai, "Nongcun zhongxiaoxue jiaoshi jingsheng yu wuzhi xuyao de diaocha" ("A Survey of the Spiritual and Material Needs of Rural Elementary and Secondary School Teachers"), *Ningxia Jiaoyu Xueyuan Xuebao* 1 (1987): 31-34. For additional examples, see *GMRB* (March 25, 1984); *RMRB* (July 10, 1984); Zu Shanji, "'Zuo' de bianjian neng defu jiaoshi rudang jiu bu nan" ("If the Leftist Influence Can Be Overcome, It Will be Easy for Teachers to Join the Party"), *Jiaogong Yuekan* 2 (1985): 8-9; *Jiaoshibao* (June 29, 1986); and *Jiaoshibao* (July 7, 1986).

51. White, *Party and Professionals*, *op. cit.*, p. 47.

52. Zhuang Mingshui," Gaoshi xuexsheng zhuanye nixiang jiaoyu cuyi," *op. cit.*, pp.55-62.

53. Li Kegang, "Lun jiaoshi de laodong baochou" ("On Teachers' Work Rewards"), *Jiaoyu yu Jingji* 1 (1985): 34-37, 46.

54. *ZGJYB* (October 17, 1989): 1.

55. *Jiaoyu Tongxun* (June 1986): 16.

56. See, for example, the report by Zhang Hongju, "Jiejue jiaoshi

zhufang wenti dayou xiwang" ("Great Hopes for Solving Teachers' Housing Problems"), *Renmin Jiaoyu* 2 (1985): 5-6.

57. *Jiaoyu Tongxun* (June 1986): 7.

58. *ZGJYB* (November 16, 1989): 1.

59. *ZGJYB* (October 28, 1989): 1.

60. Gao Xiandong, "Cong jiejue shiji wenti rushou" ("Solving Real Problems"), *Renmin Jiaoyu* 9 (1989): 43-44.

61. See, for example, Wang Fengxiong, "Dui jiejue minban jiaoshi de jidian kanfa" ("Some Views on Solving the Problems of Minban Teachers"), *Renmin Jiaoyu* 7-8 (1989): 26-27; *ZGJYB* (September 7, 1989):1; *ZGJYB* (September 1 and 26, 1989):2; "Liaoning jiejue jiaoshi gonfei yiliao baogan wenti" ("Liaoning Solves the Problem of Responsibility for Teachers' Health Insurance") *Jiaogong Yuekan* 10 (1985): 5; "Minban jiaoshi dao gongren yiliaoyuan liaoyang" ("Locally Hired Teacher Goes to Convalesce at Workers' Sanitorium") *Jiaogong Yuekan* 9 (1985): 23.

62. These occurred in 1977, then 1978, then 1980 or 1981. Wage increases to teachers have typically been given to categories of teachers, such as all those in a certain professional grade range. "China Education Almanac," *Chinese Education* (Fall 1986):90

63. This seniority bonus of *gongling* is worth 0.5 *yuan* for each year of work, up to a total of 20 *yuan*, while the *jiaoling* is worth 5 *yuan*/month for people having taught 5-9 years, 7 for 10-15 years, and 9 for more than 15 years of teaching. Xiang Yaonan, "Dui jiaoshi gongzi zhidu gaige de yixie shexiang" ("Reflections on the Reform of the Wage System for Teachers"), *Jiaoyu Yanjiu* 2 (1989): 15-17, reports however, that some provinces have not complied with the policy of distributing bonuses for experience.

64. Zhu Yuanxing, "Yao tigao jiaoshi jingji daiyu he shehui diwei"

("Teachers' economic and social position needs improvement"), *Jiaogong Yuekan* 2 (1985): 20-23.

65. Zhang Hongju, "Jiejue jiaoshi zhufang wenti deyou xiwang," *op. cit.*, pp.5-6.

66. State Statistical Bureau Social Statistics Section, editor, *China: A Statistical Survey in 1987, op. cit.*, p. 101; Wang Li, "Lun jiaoshi laodong baochang" ("On Compensation for Teachers' Labor"), *Zhongguo Shehui Kexue* 4 (1988): 83-95.

67. Xiang Yaonan, "Dui jiaoshi gongzi zhidu gaige de yixie," *op. cit.*, pp. 15-17. The result is that teachers' income is often one third that of workers. See Wei Dianhua, "Qieshi tigao zhongxue jiaoshi de shehui diwei," ("Raising Secondary School Teachers' Social Status") *Jiaoyu Yanjiu*, 1 (1985):17-21.

68. Yuan Liansheng, "Lun woguo jiaoyu jingji kuique" ("On the Shortage of China's Educational Funds: An Analysis of the 1977-87 Educational Investment"), *Jiaoyu Yanjiu* 7 (1988):25.

69. *Ibid.*, p.25.

70. *ZGJYB* (September 6, 1988):1.

71. He Daofang, Duan Yingbi, Yuan Zongfa, "Lun woguo tonghua pengzhang de facheng jizhi he jiegou biaoxian" ("On the Development Mechanism and Structural Manifestation of our Country's Recent Inflation"), *Jingji Yanjiu* 1 (1987): 21-28.

72. White, *Party and Professionals, op. cit.* p. 90.

73. P. Ferdinand, "Interest Groups and Chinese Politics," in D. Goodman, editor, *Groups and Politics in the People's Republic of China* (Cardiff: University of Cardiff, 1984):10-25.

74. R.W. Connell, *Teachers' Work* (Boston: George Allen and Unwin, 1985): 200.

CHAPTER TEN

CHINESE MEDICAL SCHOOLING: GLOBAL SCIENCE, LOCAL SCHOOLS[1]

by Mary Ann Burris

Medicine is the most applied of all sciences. Therefore, it gives us a particularly fine opportunity to see how scientific knowledge is translated into social practice. Schools give us the same opportunity. By definition, schooling has to do with knowledge and its applications. Schools create and inherit knowledge, and then "reproduce"it: they pass it on to people who will, in one way or another, use it in their societies. Because much of scientific medicine is imported knowledge in China, and because modern universities are also, in some ways, imports, Chinese medical universities connect the global to the local in most compelling ways.

There are few things as basic to the human condition as health, but that does not make medicine a simple or non-contentious enterprise. The fabric of relationships between knowledge, power, and schooling that directs medical education in China is a rich and complex one. In my contribution to this book, I am going to unravel a few of its historical threads so that we may better analyze them. Then, by so doing, we can weave a more informed understanding of today's most modem Chinese version of doctors and their schooling.

---

[1] The author wishes to acknowledge the support of the Committee for Scholarly Communications with the People's Republic of China for offering financial assistance which contributed to the completion of the field research upon which this chapter is based.

Medical education in China is of unprecedented size, complexity, ambition, and duration. Today, China's medical schools graduate 200,000 individuals each year in a pagoda of many levels. They encompass two distinct science traditions, and have very ambitious goals toward service and science which they attempt to meet with limited resources. Medical training boasts almost as long a continuous history as all else Chinese, so we could begin our study of the passing on of medical knowledge with the sage emperors and the family apprentice system. But we shall focus more squarely on medical colleges, the knowledge that they pass on, and their relation to the state. Throughout post-revolutionary times, Chinese medical schools have been affected by political winds from international, national, and local directions.

There are few things Chinese that have not been profoundly affected in recent days and years by the "open door." Universities are not among the few. Health is not one of those few nor is medicine. Today's "open door" is sometimes understood as China's second, but the door is more usefully recognized as having always been open, one way or the other. Over time the door has sent out gales of influence, and let in winds of affect--depending on the "health" of the Chinese nation-state, its place in the world, and its relationship with its people. In medicine today, technology, personnel, educational models, medical specialties, research agendas, foreign languages, medical textbooks, health care strategies, and foreign exchange certificates are brought in through that door, influencing the medical profession and having an impact on medical training. In medicine today, the outward drafts are the weaker ones; yet, China has been credited with the export of rural health care strategies and the existence of useful indigenous medical therapies. If outsiders today are aware of any two things about Chinese medicine, those are likely to be "barefoot doctors" and acupuncture.

It helps to put things in context. Health is an appropriate context for medicine and medical training, but disease and death are easier to define. In the late nineteenth century, China was "the Sick Man of Asia" in more than metaphorical ways. China was sick in literal ways, and continued to be sick into the middle of the twentieth century. In 1949, one baby in four died during its first five years. In 1989, 95.5 per cent survive to the age of five.[1] In the 1940s, Chinese people suffered almost every known form of infectious and nutritional disease in record-setting numbers. Venereal diseases, cholera, leprosy, tuberculosis, typhus, smallpox, meningitis, plague, relapsing fever, encephalitis, and the host of parasite-born diseases added to the league of illnesses caused by malnutrition--osteomalacia, pellagra, scurvy, beriberi--to make China a very unhealthy place. Dr. Sze Szeming estimated in 1943 that his country had 4 million "unnecessary deaths" each year.[2] In 1989, there were also unnecessary deaths, but fewer of them were due to disease. Though some diseases are on the rise, most are not. Chinese people are more likely to be healthy of body today than they were fifty to sixty years ago.

In most people's opinion, this lessening of disease since 1949 is due more to food and shelter than it is to doctors and hospitals, but doctors and other health workers are undeniably important to China's health. Today, China has one of the largest medical training systems in the world. Yearly, it graduates roughly 200,000 health workers--50,000 of them doctors trained at the post-secondary level. In 1949, there were twenty-two medical colleges, none specializing in Chinese Medicine.[3] In 1989, there were 129 medical universities and colleges, twenty-eight of them specializing in Chinese Medicine. Since 1949, China has established primary, secondary, and tertiary level medical schools and varied courses in continuing education. Between 1949 and 1986, formal health schools graduated 6,893 graduate students, 586,000 undergraduates, 1,245,000 middle school students, and 564,000 nurses.[4] Today, approximately 12% of the total enrollment in higher education is in medicine, third after engineering and teacher-training. Still, China "needs more doctors."[5]

But, there is more to this than numbers. Medicine and medical training in China are the connection between the sick Shensi grandfather and international development agencies. They are the connection between science and society, nation and health. Medical schools and the health care systems of which they are a part have everything to do with whether the Shensi fellow gets moxibustion treatments for his headache or a CAT scan for further diagnosis. If he is admitted to the provincial teaching hospital for this headache, they determine whether his doctor writes in his chart in Chinese or in English, whether that doctor has had appropriate training, and whether s/he feels obliged to help him. The system that this sick peasant looks to for help determines the answers to other questions, as well. Can this old wheat or coal producer afford the treatment his doctor suggests? Does this treatment make him and his society healthier?

Medicine and the State

The ages-old Chinese verb *zhi* still means both to heal and to govern.[6] Early Chinese political philosophy clearly connected the health of the state to the health of the people. In theory, the moral state ensured a stable and healthy society. In practice, the realization of this ideal was inconsistent.[7] Today, the post-revolutionary Chinese state's role in providing for the people's health is even more clearly enunciated, but practice is still inconsistent. Medical universities, even in their modern visages, are at the nexus of both governing and healing. Medical education policy, like other state policy, is a piece of the national development agenda now calling for modernization. Because medical training is controlled by the government, it connects the state to the people. State personnel decide what medicine to teach, how to teach it, to whom, and for what purposes, but they do not make these decisions in a vacuum.

TRADITIONAL LEGACIES: FAMILIES, STATES AND THE CONFUCIAN DOOR

Looking to the past enriches our understanding of the present. China has perhaps the oldest continuous medical tradition on the globe[8] and some of the earliest records of organized medical colleges. For most of imperial China, medicine, like schooling, was largely a family affair. Families guarded their monopolies on certain potions or therapies and the knowledge requisite to applying them, and many of the earliest sages of medicine came from medical families. "Don't take the medicine prescribed by a physician from a family practicing medicine for less than three generations," warns the Confucian *Book of Rights*.[9] The earliest medical colleges, like all schools in imperial China, were family inititives interfaced with state needs. Families produced literacy--or access to classical learning, which was then the same thing. Families protected the secrets of medical practice. The state tested and employed successful sons.

It is in the early transition of the social position of healers in China from *wu*, or shamans, to *shi,* or scholars, where we find knowledge and its uses more strictly defined and women excluded.

Women practiced midwifery through the ages, but as in the case of Western medicine in Europe, medicine as scholarship and medicine as a profession in China were largely reserved for men. Consequently, the tale of medical science and its reproduction in China is largely a story of men.[10] Chinese medical knowledge was part of classical learning. This meant that the Chinese state was involved in its definition and in its institutionalization.[11] Medical theory was part of the canon, so all Confucian gentlemen were to study it. All gentlemen did not study the rich library of specialized medical texts that focused on treatment, however. Certainly, all employed officials who were successful examination-takers could not "needle" (do acupuncture) or prescribe herbal medicines. They were not likely to be professional medical practitioners because the status of a doctor was different from and lower than that of a state bureaucrat.[12] Still, the literate did understand orthodox theories of health and their connection to the body politic. And the state was thereby a shaper of both medical knowledge and medical practice.

The Chinese state has always been involved in medicine in at least two decisive ways: in its power over orthodoxy and in its interest in health--that is, in its power to define legitimate knowledge and in its efforts to control the uses to which that knowledge is put. The Confucian order which tied scholarship to state service through the examination system was successful in directing knowledge for hundreds of years. As part of Confucian orthodoxy, medical knowledge, too, was filtered through this legitimating apparatus. The imperial state's control over medical practice in the larger society was less complete, but history shows that attempts were made to assert control when threats were considered great enough. In premodern times, struggles over medical practice were often between a Confucian state and Taoist or Buddhist healers outside of that state. In 643, Buddhist and Taoist monks were forbidden to practice certain kinds of medicine. In 845, Buddhists lost control of their hospitals through state decree.[13] The Chinese state was concerned not only with protecting its hegemony over knowledge but its monopoly over the resources resulting from the application of that knowledge. In this regard, medicine was no different from art and science.

The Chinese state's power over medical knowledge had everything to do with its place in the universe of its times. Medicine as a knowledge system in China has evidently always been a geographical amalgam. The "door" has always been somehow open. The earliest extant medical classic, the *Nei Jing*, or *Canon of Medicine*, published around 400 B.C., tells us that this blending had begun long before Western medicine entered China. That is, much earlier medical knowledge was also plagiarised from here and there: "stone acupuncture came from the east... poisons from the west... moxibustion from the north... the nine needles from the south... and breathing exercise and massage from the center."[14] What is now referred to as *Zhongyi*, or Chinese Medicine, is only a fraction of the rich compendium of health practices that have existed in 3000 years of recorded history in the territories that were China. It is that fraction sanctioned by and codified in Confucian historiography and its commentaries.

As the Middle Kingdom, China could borrow from less empowered cultures and incorporate those borrowings into its own orthodoxy. The door swung in as well as out. Once the Middle Kingdom met defeat at the hands of the West, that centripetal process disintegrated. The unifying whole, the hegemony, of traditional orthodoxy was weakened. Western medicine was not incorporated into *Zhongyi*, it stood as a challenge to it. This is both because of the nature of these knowledge cultures [15] and the weakness of the Chinese state on the international scene. The old order lost its monopoly over knowledge [16] as it lost power in the market and on the battlefield. But the relationship between national power and scientific practice did not disappear; it was re-ordered. Subsequent Chinese states would step in to manage and control the uses to which Western science was put, but it could no longer have exclusive control over the definition and content of its knowledge base.

As is the case in education generally, medical examinations predated medical schools and state interests dictated curriculum, pedagogy, and practice. The state tested existing physicians for court service earlier than it trained doctors, but by the seventh century the Chinese state was in the business of both.[17] Medical universities were tied to scholarship and they were very literally tied to the health of the state. Their graduates typically served state officials; sometimes they were state officials. The educational institutional story roughly goes as follows. During the Tang dynasty (618-906), there existed a medical education institute with eight specialties and standardized examinations. By the Yuan dynasty (1260-1368), an Imperial Medical College had been established with ten departments, district colleges, and national examinations every three years. In the Ming dynasty (1368-1644), students were recruited by examination from the families who had produced physicians for generations for entrance into the Imperial Medical College which had expanded to thirteen departments.[18] Although they flourished in the early Qing (1644-1911), by the end of the last imperial dynasty, state institutions for training doctors lost funding. By 1840, the Imperial Medical College existed in name only.[19] Though there is some evidence of public health efforts of the imperial Chinese state,[20] most state medicine was concerned with scholarship and service to the officialdom and its families. Others fended for themselves. Consequently, the state's second interest in medicine, that of controlling the uses to which medical knowledge is put, was one of regulation for fiscal or other benefit at the top and not usually one of provision at the bottom.

The Confucian penchant for denigrating specialized applied knowledge functioned to curb and to complicate the organization of physicians and the shape of medical training. The inclusion of medical theory in the schooling of all "gentlemen" limited the possibilities for the organization of a medical profession based on the exclusive possession of theoretical knowledge. The hegemony of the Confucian state empowered a particular medical orthodoxy and scholarship over others, and it discouraged the organization of physicians as an independent interest group. The Confucian world view placed the responsibility for social stability on right-behaving individuals, but the state was required to intervene on the side of order and ethics. It had a moral responsibility to take the health of the people into account. In imperial times, it was the responsibility of individuals to serve the state by behaving in ways prescribed by the Confucian code of filiality, a system that placed the state, the father, at the top. It was also the responsibility of the state to look after those below. The traditional Chinese state has a variable record on fulfilling its responsibility to provide medical care to its citizens. It was more consistent in controlling medical knowledge and, when it mattered, those who possessed it.

The Chinese post-revolutionary state has also acted to contain professional prerogative, to control the profits to be gained from medicine, and to determine which medical knowledge is most empowered. The state defines the status of doctors, which has often meant that their status is low compared to doctors elsewhere. The post-revolutionary Chinese state has embraced the mandate to look after the health of its citizens in ways unequalled elsewhere, or in China before 1949. Since 1949, the dual goals of encouraging advanced medical science and its requisite institutions on the one hand and instituting a health care system with a mass orientation on the other have caused a central tension in medical education policy. In most candid conversations, medical personnel today will talk of their failures to achieve complete success in either science or service but rightly boast of the improvements since 1949 in both areas. Success or failure, therefore, must be understood in this context of somewhat polarized objectives and certainly limited resources.

MEDICAL KNOWLEDGE: SCIENCE AND EXCHANGE

The imperial order did not collapse the moment it encountered the West. Introductions preceded the apocalypse by at least three hundred years. Early scientific exchanges between China and the West were just that--exchanges. In the sixteenth century, Jesuits brought Western scientific knowledge to China and brought Chinese scientific knowledge to the West. Matteo Ricci and less famous colleagues and foes spent considerable effort translating scientific books into Chinese and relaying Chinese knowledge back to Europe. Books in European languages on Chinese acupuncture date back to the late seventeenth century,[21] and the Chinese are credited with the discovery of at least one life-saving medical technique that had a profound effect on Western medical practice, smallpox inoculation.[22]

As the power balance in this East-West relationship weighed heavily in favor of the West, so, too, did the empowerment of Western knowledge take ascendence over Chinese science. Medicine was no exception. In a more positive way than gunboats, medicine was of particular value to the evangelical enterprise of Christian missionaries and to fledgling mercantile interests in China. The Chinese state did what it could to contain it. The first hospitals of Western medicine were set up in the treaty ports of Guangzhou and Macao. As part of the Treaty of Nanking in 1842 following China's defeat in the first Opium War, China "agreed" to allow missionaries to set up hospitals in other selected locations. The Peking Peace Treaty of 1858 extended more privileges to foreigners, thereby opening more territory to missionaries. By 1892, there were 60 missionary hospitals in China. Of these, 39 enrolled students, but most enrolled only a few who were trained specifically to assist the Western experts. By 1905, there were 166 missionary hospitals, 241 clinics, and 301 missionary doctors.[23] None of these was controlled by the Chinese state. Today, all of them are.

To look at universities in any society is to look at the confluence of knowledge and power as it is formally instituted. During the last years of the past century and the early years of this one, several full-fledged medical universities were set up by outsiders to train Chinese in the science and practice of Western biomedicine. German, French, Japanese, British, and North American medicines were the most influential; not coincidentally, German, French, Japanese, British, and North American imperialistic interests were the most empowered.[24] The Chinese themselves set up their first Western medical college in Tientsin in 1881 and several others followed in the last years of the Qing dynasty,[25] but the foreign-endowed schools were the pacesetters. In the 1910s and 1920s, philanthropic organizations and foreign universities eclipsed the missionaries as the major actors who defined the institutionalization of Western medical science in China. Still, the locus of control remained outside China's borders.

Few studies of medical education in China omit mention of the Rockefeller Foundation or of Peking Union Medical College and some analysis of the times they entered China. It is a primary thread in the weave that followed. Rockefeller-funded Peking Union Medical College (PUMC), the "Johns Hopkins of China," set a standard for Western medicine in China whose legacy is still very much alive. Spending over forty-five million dollars through its twenty-two years of operation, PUMC trained 166 graduates. As an institution, it was "committed to the primacy of science." [26] Peking Union Medical College set unreachable (and many would say unreasonable) educational standards in China by basing its course of study not on the dismal health conditions of the nation at the time but on the "highest of standards" in the most prestigious universities of the West, a sort of trickle-down application of professionalism. PUMC's lengthy curriculum, taught almost exclusively in English, aimed to train medical scientists and teachers who could then go on to become the backbone of the Chinese medical profession.

But, Peking Union Medical College did that and more. PUMC official John Grant and several of his Chinese colleagues were also responsible for some of the public health practices that were later to become an integral part of post-revolutionary medicine and the legacy better known as the "barefoot doctor." One hundred miles outside of Beijing in Dingxian county, a community medicine program was set up that fit into a multi-tiered health care system resembling that of today. The Dingxian model incorporated village level health workers and by 1934 served 75 villages, maintained seven subdistrict health stations, and established a district center. The project defined a particular role for medical training as well. The Dingxian experiment, according to one of its participants, "demonstrated that it is entirely possible to correlate instruction in public health and clinical medicine in a meaningful way...

that medical education could be developed in relation to community needs."[27] This vision of medical education is in direct contradiction to much of PUMC practice, whose version of medical training and medical science was not always meaningfully grounded in the health needs of the community in which it was located.

Medicine in the first half of this century reflected tensions in many spheres, political and philosophical. Two medical sciences vied for legitimacy and at least two models of medical practice and medical training vied for implementation. China was rejecting much of its past and not in control of its present. As China sought a future, three tensions fomented struggle in medicine. The first was the conflict between *Zhongyi* and biomedicine. The second was a conflict between Western nations themselves for influence and power in the professional and educational communities of Republican China. The third was the tension between models of medicine, initially a struggle between missionary medicine and Rockefeller medicine, but more largely understood as an effort to find the best compromise between a focus on community health and one on transnational medical science. Each of these tensions has continued to the present time. Each has its foot in the open door.

PRE-REVOLUTIONARY LEGACIES

The Chinese Communist Party came to national power in 1949 with a mandate to "serve the people." Two of the ways it was to do this were to improve prospects for health and increase possibilities for education. Many of the early policy decisions in medicine and in education were attempts to combine two contradictory histories: those of the Communist base areas between 1927 and 1949, and those of foreign and Nationalist programs primarily in operation in the urban areas of pre-revolutionary China.

Medicine in the Communist base camps was shaped by poverty, war, and isolation. So was medical education, where it existed. The medical system that the Red Army built emphasized preventive medicine, the use of health workers with little formal training, mass mobilization, and a mixture of Western biomedicine with Chinese medicine. Self-reliance was not only an ideological stance, it was a practical necessity. Much of the medical effort went to treating the wounded, just as much of the organizing and educational effort went to waging the war.   The General Medical Department of the Red Army set up a public health school in the 1930s that accepted students with primary education and taught them the rudiments of internal medicine, surgery, and pharmacology.[28]   Efforts were made to improve and politicize public health.   Medicine and hygiene lessons were included in early base area literacy curriculae, and mass campaigns targeted specific public health issues.

The situation in the cities not yet under Party control was quite different.   While the Communists and their physicians and paramedics were struggling, the Chinese Medical Association was professionalizing and networking as well as curing.   Founded in the 1920s, the Association's first eight presidents were physicians educated at Yale, Cambridge, Pennsylvania, London, Harvard, and Edinburgh.[29]   As a professional organization, the Chinese Medical Association called for medical research and teaching that were competitive with international standards.   They (1700 in number in 1935) acted to censure practitioners of Chinese Medicine through restrictive licensing requirements, and they published.   By 1935, 178 medical journals had appeared in China.[30]

Several CMA members were also active in a community health movement, the first for China.   "We were greatly disturbed," writes one public health activist, "by the prevailing inertia in the medical profession concerning our country's grave health problems, and we wanted to make our citizenry more aware that the national interest in health was their own." [31]   For five years, before the war against the Japanese interfered (1932-1937), a systematic public health organization was set up in Dingxian county under the Mass Education Movement that aimed not only to provide medical care but also to "improve the health consciousness" of village inhabitants.[32] Dingxian was later to be a model for the health system put in place twenty years later by the Communist government.   Despite sporadic state support, however, this minority community medicine voice in the profession has remained the minority voice, in part, because public health has never been the priority of the medical academy at its highest levels.   Medical universities have often been more attuned to medical science as a discipline or an orthodoxy than to public health as an application.

POST-REVOLUTIONARY COMPROMISES

After 1949, conflicts existed between medical personnel and nonmedical cadres from the People's Liberation Army and physicians and educators from elite, often foreign-oriented, medical colleges. The compromises reached over these forty years have changed with the political winds. They reflect the enormous demands put on the health system in China as well as the tensions between different philosophies of medical knowledge and practice. The prerevolutionary legacy was eclectic and the postrevolutionary solutions have been a mixed bag. In general, it is the public health and populist Communist base camp model that has influenced the lower levels of medical training and mass public health campaigns. The more elite and foreign-oriented model of Nationalist and urban areas has consistently had the more influential role in shaping higher medical education. The adoption of Soviet models in the 1950s did not challenge this nor has the more recent impact of interchange with the West. Only the Cultural Revolution years can be seen as the exception to this general rule. That is the one time when a substantive challenge to the previously-accepted role of the university and the structure of its curriculum resulted in drastic changes in medical schooling at the highest levels. But, by all accounts, few of the reforms of these chaotic times were carried out in ways conducive to health, community, or education.

The pendulum swings of post-revolutionary politics have been reflected in medicine and tertiary medical schooling, but there has been a certain continuity over the past forty years as well. Chinese have continued to reinforce as high status knowledge a medical science, medical curriculum, and medical schooling pedagogy imported from outside. Despite the fact that medicine is very much a matter of public policy in socialist China, tertiary training institutions have not embraced a community medicine model.[33] This has been true even where social conditions and political rhetoric have seemingly contradicted that arrangement. Why? At least in part because of the continuing power of transnational medical science and its far reaching influence as a global model.

Today, while all policy-makers recognize the need for more health workers (particularly in the countryside), quality is of great concern, too. A well-financed effort is being made to put some Chinese medical students and medical doctor/scientists "on a par" with their colleagues in the West. The Chinese want quality science and this makes sense. In fact, the Four Modernizations approach to development was predicated on a self-criticism concerning Chinese "backwardness" compared to the Western scientific and economic communities, and a call to "catch up." Science is central to modernization and part of medicine is science. Patterning a medical system aimed at Chinese public health realities while welcoming technology, texts, and training from the West calls for opening and closing the same "door" at the same time or at least assiduously monitoring the drafts. Herein lies the greatest challenge to the truly concerned policymakers in China today. They recogize the validity of both claims on the system--the call to ensure public health and the call to participate in the higher halls of medical science. Rather than choose a single model for training and health care delivery, then, the Chinese have done their best to walk a many-legged line between several approaches, hoping to reap the useful in each. The weave, then, that has shaped and continues to shape medicine and medical schooling in the People's Republic of China is one where huge scale, limited resources, and very separate traditions have set the patterns and where policies are aimed at meeting the two sometimes-conflicting demands to serve the public and to serve science.

Medical Curriculae and Its Meanings

How have these conflicting demands been accommodated in medical curriculae in China? According to Michael Apple, "Schools allocate people and legitimate knowledge. They legitimate people and allocate knowledge."[34] To look at curriculum anywhere, then, is to look at legitimate and allocated knowledge. Medical curriculae in China over the past one hundred years have many stories to tell. One sees that today biomedicine or Western medicine is clearly the more empowered of China's two medical sciences, both in terms of representation at the university level and in terms of the accommodation in each curriculum to the other paradigm.

Curriculae in *Zhongyi* universities have accommodated Western medicine in very fundamental ways, while curriculae in Western medicine universities have typically added one required course in Zhongyi to an otherwise fairly standard biomedical course list. The curriculum of the Shensi Institute of Chinese Medicine, where this author has conducted fieldwork, is roughly typical of other tertiary

Zhongyi curriculae. Approximately 40 per cent of its curriculum is devoted to Western medicine and its basic sciences. The curriculum of Xian Medical University, a Western medicine core university also located in Shensi, requires 108 hours of *Zhongyi* in a 3415 hour curriculum, or around 3 per cent. A few weeks in the *Zhongyi* ward are part of most students' fifth clinical year. The other weeks and months are divided between surgery, internal medicine, pediatrics, obstetrics, and gynecology (none with substantial *Zhongyi* content).[35]

With the exception of the Cultural Revolution, in the forty years since 1949, there has been what was to me surprisingly little change in the fundamental arrangement of tertiary medical coursework in China. There was similarly little change over the 1949 divide. Table 10.1 [36] disaggregates medical college course hours into several broad categories. In most schools, the years of study have fluctuated between five and six, and courseloads have varied from 3500 to 5000 hours. Roughly speaking, the proportion of the curriculum devoted to general courses, basic medical science, and clinical science has remained at about one-third each. General courses (*putong jiaoyu*) include politics, foreign language, physical education, and natural science and are disaggregated in the table. Basic medical science includes all lecture and laboratory coursework (pathology, microbiology, physiology, anatomy, etc.) in the sciences specific to medicine. The clinical courses include coursework and clinical practice in the various medical specialties (obstetrics, pediatrics, surgery, etc.)

Table 10.1
Biomedical Curriculae in China: 1912-1989 (Required Hours)

	1912	1936	1942	1954	1956	1959	1959	1961	1962	1975	1977	1982	1987
Years of Study	4	6	6	5	5	5	6	5	6	3	5	5	5
Total Req. Hours	4572	5903	5750	5187	4915	4534	5336	4320	5004	4117	3972	3834	3415
Political Study: Hours % of Total	177 3.9	36 .6	36 .6	370 7.1	270 5.5	406 8.9	406 7.6	288 6.7	216 4.3	884 21.5	324 8.2	216 5.6	252 7.4
Foreign Language: Hours % of Total	144 3.1	216 3.7	270 4.7	306 5.9	270 5.5	286 6.3	288 5.4	288 6.7	324 6.5	198 4.8	288 7.3	306 8.0	432 12.7
Soc. Sci. & Hum.: Hours % of Total	-	108 1.8	140 2.4	32 .6	36 .7	-	-	-	-	-	-	-	38 1.1
Phys. Ed.: Hours % of Total	-	-	-	144 2.8	147 4.0	142 3.1	142 2.7	144 3.3	144 2.9	186 4.5	180 4.5	144 3.8	144 4.2
Nat. Sciences: Hours % of Total	324 7.9	1296 21.9	1124 19.5	516 9.9	504 10.3	486 10.7	612 11.5	486 11.3	702 14.0	72 1.7	378 9.5	486 12.7	418 12.2
Basic Med. Sci.: Hours % of Total	1296 28.3	1974 33.4	1840 32	1542 30.1	1440 29.3	1281 28.3	1764 33.0	1260 29.2	1566 31.3	709 17.2	1220 30.7	1188 31.0	1079 31.6
Clinical Medicine: Hours % of Total	2631 57.5	2273 38.5	2340 40.7	2277 43.9	2104 42.8	1637 36.1	1818 34.1	1638 37.9	1962 39.2	2068 50.2	1280 32.2	1350 35.2	1043 30.5
Zhongyi: Hours % of Total	-	-	-	-	144 2.9	296 6.5	306 5.7	216 5.0	90 5.0	N.A integrate	302 7.6	144 3.8	108 3.2

The contents of courses have changed with the scientific times and somewhat with the political times, but the essentials of this division between common coursework, basic science, and clinical science, and of their respective roles in medical training have been constant. Most medical students in China do not see a patient until their final year of study. Their studies are not specific to locale. Pedagogy and methodology have continued to be teacher centered and knowledge based.

Peculiar to the Chinese tertiary medical curriculum are three of the common or basic courses required of all medical students. Not inconsequential time is devoted to political study, physical education, and foreign language during university medical training. Chinese medical school is undergraduate school. Therefore, all preparatory and non-medicine coursework (and there is much controversy on what this should entail both inside China and outside China) must be satisfied in secondary school or during the five years of medical training. Specialization is not reflected in coursework nor is individualization. At all-important graduation time, when students are assigned jobs and futures, those who become anatomy or biochemistry teachers, gastro-enterologists, surgeons, opthalmologists, and pediatricians have all shared the same course of studies. Residencies in China vary greatly ("from non-existent to barely there," according to one outside observer), so specialized training tends to be weak after graduation, too.

Within this required course of study, politics and foreign language requirements have fluctuated somewhat in the post-1949 years. Physical education has been constant at around 150 hours (plus required daily morning exercises at 6:15 to the rasping and recorded voices of two upbeat drill sergeants). Requirements for manual labor have changed with the political times; sometimes it has involved medical labor and sometimes it has not. As Table 10.1 reveals, political study increased during the Great Leap Forward, the Cultural Revolution years, and again in the 1989-90 academic year.[37] These are times when politics has been "in command." Not revealed in the table but important to us here if we are interested in community medicine, is the fact that public health coursework at the university level in China has been consistently low. Often the course time devoted to public health studies has been around one-third of the hours devoted to foreign language. In China, public health and preventive medicine as academic specialties struggle with nearly the same low-status problems that they do in the capitalist West.

Though stronger curricular emphasis has been placed on foreign language during Modernization than at some earlier times, we can see that foreign language study has always been an important ingredient in medical studies in China.[38] Biomedicine was not conceived, nor has it largely been advanced in Mandarin. From missionary times onward, the issue of language of instruction has very much been part of the policy landscape. When Chinese has been used, course content has often been dictated by translated texts. New since Modernization, several of the best medical universities have begun a foreign language stream that separates a single class of its better students and trains them for all preclinical coursework as exclusively as possible in English, French, German, or Japanese. The purpose of this practice, according to one of its policy-makers, is to ensure that China has medical scientists who can engage in "meaningful exchange with international colleagues."

Modernization has ushered in funding, technology, personnel, audio-visuals, and educational models from the outside to medical universities and teaching hospitals in China. As happens elsewhere in the developing world, Chinese medical universities and hospitals seem to be most interested in bringing state-of-the-art technology through that open door, and urban curative medicine has been most empowered by international exchange.

In curricular terms, modernization has increased the premium put on mastering English.[39] It has differentially empowered certain medical specialties while nearly ignoring others. Official curricular recognition is given in modernizing China to discarding the former biological model of medicine and of medical training in favor of the psycho-social-biological model (*xinli shehui shengwu yixue moshi*). Though some universities have added elective courses in medical ethics, psychology, and an assortment of other social sciences and humanities, this proclamation has had as much trouble being realized curricularly in China as it has in the United States, where it was first conceived.

The latest medical curriculum policy in China is a unique attempt to reconcile the two goals we mentioned earlier: to advance medical science and to provide basic health care to the population. This plan aims to provide generalist post-secondary-trained doctors for the now underserved rural population while encouraging specialization at the core hospitals and schools, almost always in the cities. It is called the 3-5-7 Plan[40] and is a Ministry-level attempt to standardize a confused tertiary training picture, while at the same time encouraging localization. The plan, instituted two years ago, adds to the previous five-year Bachelor's program, a three-year program overseen by core medical universities to train doctors for rural service. It also adds seven-year programs to train Master's students as clinical specialists. As has been consistently true, it is at the lower levels of the training pagoda where public health and community medicine approaches are most likely to be found and where pedagogical innovation is most common. Each of the thirteen medical universities now instituting the 3-5-7 Plan is encouraged to develop its own curriculum for the three-year associate program based on local needs.[41] Those instituting the seven-year Master's programs in clinical medicine are encouraged to shape their seven-year curriculae according to the particular strengths of faculty and facilities.

To move from the three-year to the five-year to the seven-year curriculum is to move from low status to high status knowledge within the medical profession. It is also to move from rural and community applications to urban and more exclusively curative ones. What do we find? As we move from three- to five- to seven-year curriculae, the proportion of foreign language and basic science study increases and the proportion of *Zhongyi* and public health study decreases, evidence of the relative status of each within this new arrangement. That is to say, in curricular terms, public health and *Zhongyi* are low status and English and basic science are high status. In practical terms, *Zhongyi* and public health are more necessary to rural community practice than are English and physics.

Gender and Status in Chinese Medicine

Gender is also related to status in medicine but in quite a dissimilar way. While certain kinds of knowledge are awarded high status by virtue of their incorporation in the highest levels of academe, women are awarded a particular status in medicine by virtue of their perceived social value. In practice, as we move into the seven-year master's degree programs, we find it is a matter of policy to favor male applicants to graduate programs. In order to bring in the ideal of 70 percent male participation in such programs, entrance requirements for men have been made lower than those for women. Much in the same way that opportunities to go abroad in the medical sciences are skewed in favor of men,[42] educational opportunities at the highest levels of the profession within China favor males.[43] Relatively recent modernization policies that give greater power to work units for refusing those assigned to them has exacerbated this. Nearly everyone in medical circles is complaining about the "need" for more men; admissions personnel share this complaint with those responsible for job placement. Men are easier to place than women. Compared to the situation in many other countries, Chinese medicine is relatively egalitarian. Women's participation is high. But in medicine as in other professions inside and outside of China, women's participation in this occupation seems to be negatively correlated to its status in larger society.

The Modernization of Medical Schooling--Professions and Profits

How has modernization affected medicine and medical schools? Today's responsibility system policies have changed the possibilities for earning within the medical profession, and changed the provision of health care. This affects schooling, as does the outward-looking lens of scientific development. China's re-opening to the West in the 1980s has reshaped laboratories and hospitals and brought in millions of dollars in medical technology. It has put a premium on foreign languages. It has turned the best Chinese medical universities into international exchange and personnel brokers. In some ways, modernization has encouraged progress and innovation in health care delivery and medical training in China, but the system continues to be plagued by a lack of fit between schooling, practice, and health needs.

Who are the doctors and how do they live? The position of physicians in post-revolutionary China has been substantially different from their Peking Union Medical College role models and from their literati ancestors, even if the knowledge bases upon which their practice rests are similar. Medical training is no longer a family affair; it is a state affair. And, like other kinds of education (and other state affairs) in post-revolutionary China, questions in medical schooling have been struggled over. The content of the curriculum, the make-up of the student body, the power of orthodox science, the task of teachers, the assignment of work for graduates--all of these things have been decided and redecided over the forty years since 1949. Mao's call for "struggle, criticism, and transformation" has been heeded again and again, with mixed results. Yet, even the ephemeral nature of educational policy in postrevolutionary China has not fundamentally infringed upon biomedical science as a knowledge system. In part, that is because many

Chinese share the belief that science is neutral and transferable. But, the same neutrality cannot be claimed for the medical profession, which puts that knowledge into social practice. Post-revolutionary policies have had a lot to say about the lives of those in the medical profession. Modernization is just the latest readjustment in the lives of medical workers. Each has slightly redefined the power that doctors can claim.

There is a 1960s saying in China that people still quote. It points to four kinds of people with power: drivers, bureaucrats (*renshi ganbu*), shop clerks, and doctors. People agree that it is best to have good relations with at least one of each. That way, you would be mobile (especially if your driver-friend had relations with one railroad worker), you would meet open doors in the halls of power,[44] you would have more polite access to goods, and you would be taken care of when ill.

I have had several funny conversations about this saying when talking to Chinese doctors about medicine and power. They usually chuckle and then say that, really, they do not have very much power. And they are right. In many of the ways social scientists (especially those who study professions) talk about power, Chinese doctors do not have much. There is no medical lobby acting in physician's interests in China. The Chinese Medical Association and the American Medical Association are today organizations with very different kinds of power. But common sayings always have something to teach about social reality. In China, the power of physicians results more from their individual influence at the practice level than their collective influence at the policy level. They have access to scarce goods and services: health care and medicines. That awards them certain privileges. Until very recently, this access did not so readily translate into cash, but if you get sick in China, it has always been best to have some relationship to a medical worker.

Modernization has made a few Chinese people rich, but few of them are doctors. Medicine is still largely perceived as a public service, so entrepreneurial medicine has been slower to develop than entrepreneurship in other fields. In the early modernization years, the relative lack of earning opportunity in medicine was especially apparent when contrasted to business and marketing opportunities. Medical university administrators bemoaned the fact that this discrepancy was having the effect of discouraging Chinese young people from applying to or continuing in medical schools.

"Why should they study for five or six years," asked one greying dean, "if they can sell tangerines outside the school gate and make more money?" As anyone who has lived in China during the late 1980s can attest, though money is not all that matters, profits play a central role in all parts of

Chinese life. For the first time in post-revolutionary history, many medical programs (particularly at the graduate level) are underenrolled, presumably because potential students did not envision sufficient returns to their investments in schooling.[45] In the later modernization years, the responsibility system (*chenbao*) [46] was beginning to legitimate ways for physicians to increase their earnings. They, too, could receive bonuses for work done "in their spare time." Some admininstrators I spoke with in 1989 believed that students would therefore begin to want to study medicine again, particularly in those fields most positively affected by the reforms or those that offered the carrot of study abroad.

By most people's estimates, the quality of medical education, health care, and medical research have risen substantially during the past decade.[47] By most estimates, the disparities in access to this medicine across social sectors have also increased. Certainly, those who fall ill in today's China with access to the best have much more diagnostic and surgical equipment at their disposal now than they would have had five or ten years ago. They may have doctors with more schooling and hospital rooms with more amenities. Moving down the continuum to the countryside in the poorest provinces, it is not so easy to know what individuals have at their disposal. The situation is very complex. Some rural folks have lost the subsidized health care they had in the past; others have fared better because they now have the economic power to purchase medical goods that were less available to them in the past.

As the newly-established Chinese Medical Ethics Association has publicly recognized, the new commodity economy in China poses serious problems for ethical medical practice.[48] Modernization is sometimes understood as professionalization and socialism as deprofessionalization. But what does this mean for medicine? How has modernization affected the medical profession and what does socialism have to do with it? Since the provision of medical care is an economic transaction, medicine has been affected by economic reforms along with most everything else in China. The responsibility system was having a considerable impact on medical care and medical training before June of 1989. "Sideline work" was reshaping the lives of medical physicians and educators. Decentralized financial schemes were changing hospital wards and academic departments. Many medical university faculty were moonlighting or consulting--some, like surgeons and English teachers, were beginning to do very well for themselves. Others, like anatomy teachers and opthalmologists, were having more trouble figuring out ways to make extra money. Faculty administrators complained that they felt that they had to become "businessmen" under the pressure to make profits. Hospital administrators must struggle to figure out incentive schemes to prevent the distorted bonus-earning possibilities from undoing the delicate balance between wards. Radiologists with access to a CAT scanner have tremendous extra-salary earning potential (they get a substantial bonus for each use of the machine), but pediatricians do not. Other hospital administrators are more optimistic about Modernization reforms: they feel it is a step forward to have hospitals run as "efficient enterprises" where fees are more in line with actual costs. Does all of this sound like professionalization? Does it sound like socialism? I am not sure.

Conclusion: The Future?

In early 1989, the Ministry of Health was encouraging its best medical schools to adopt administrative structures that reduced the control of the Party over educational matters at medical schools. In early 1990, there seems to be increased Party control. When politics is in command as it has been since June of 1989, the Party is in command. But the Party is not a monolith and opinion within it differs greatly. To transfer administrative power from a medical university president to a Party secretary is not clearly or necessarily the ascendance of one medical model over another. It is, typically, the replacement of one man with another, both of them with histories and constituencies in the institution. The transfer is a complicated line-of-command issue. And, most importantly, it is an unresolved issue. During the current period of readjustment, Chinese medical universities are working hard to continue the substantial international connections that they have established. As with much else, Chinese medical science will seek to diversify its exchange to rely less exclusively on the United States but will not turn inward. Policy-makers and practitioners are continuing to walk the difficult line between quality and quantity demands on the medical schooling system, between international standards and very local needs. They continue to grapple with the opening and closing of that "door."

As for medical schooling in the post-June environment, politics may be in command, but science and service continued to be the struggling mandates of the day. Enrollments at some politically active medical universities were lowered by as much as 20 per cent in 1989-1990 despite the recognized need for doctors. Stricter political guidelines were established for entrance and more normative studies were required in the curriculum. Fewer graduates were expecting to go abroad, and many who graduated after 1985 were sent to rural areas for one year or more of clinical service there. Though some medical administrators deeply regret the conditions of this decision to send young doctors and teachers to rural areas against their wishes, the policy did look like one way to address the very serious problem of physician flight--both rural-to-urban and China-to-abroad--that has been a consequence of modernization strategies. Some wards in China's better teaching hospitals are reported to have lost an entire generation of young residents to the West. Increased urban employment opportunities during the past ten years had resulted in many doctors refusing their assigned posts in rural areas. Young graduates after June will have less chance to act "out-of-plan," but the plan is still in the making.

The events of June painfully underscore the volatile nature of China's modernization strategy and of the incompatibility between controlling and unleashing that is endemic to it. In medicine as in all else, when we are talking about modernization today, we are talking about changing policies and an on-going process. The medical universities I visited in early 1990 were more cautious and politicized places than they were in early 1989. On a policy level, modernization strategies for medicine and medical education were not being drastically redefined even if some of the lives of medical workers, students, and teachers had been drastically affected by recent events. People agreed that there are many questions still to be answered. What will be the long-range impact of foreign technology and international exchange on medical training and Chinese health? How will the modern de-collectivized economy provide primary health care to those who need it? Is medicine a consumer good on the market or a right to be provided by the state? How can medical universities encourage "independent learning" in their students (very much a catchword in modernizing medical education policy and journals) and still control their job assignments and work lives? How can Chinese medicine work to become an equal partner in the transnational scientific community and still shape its science for China's own public health needs?

The Chinese state, through the Ministry of Public Health, the State Education Commission, Chinese Communist Party organs, and health care institutions, still has the final say in shaping China's medical future. As we saw in traditional times, state power still influences not only what kinds of medical knowledge are sanctioned, but how that knowledge is applied to society.   The three tensions evident in Republican times between *Zhongyi* and Western medicine, between the Western powers themselves for influence over medicine, and between models of medical care and medical training are still very much a part of the weave.   The modern scoreboard now favors biomedicine, the United States, and curative hospital-based medical care and training.   At the present time, this is what is "modern."   But, as Ruth and Victor Sidel so aptly put it, "the Chinese are unashamedly pragmatic in their application of ideology,"[49] and they continue to struggle to locate a workable path for medical schooling and medical practice.   In both the distant and recent pasts, Chinese medicine (the profession, the knowledge, and its training) has been determined by both domestic and global realities.   And, I suspect, it will continue to be.

Notes

1. From 1952 until 1987, the under five mortality rate in China decreased 4.8 per cent per year. See UNICEF, *The State of the World's Children:1989* (Oxford: Oxford University, 1989):80-83.

2. Seventy-five percent of those were caused by gastrointestinal diseases, pulmonary tuberculosis, and infectious diseases in infants. Sze Seming, *China's Health Problems* (Washington, D.C.: National Institute of Health, 1972):263-268.

3. By "Chinese medicine," I refer to what others sometimes call "traditional Chinese medicine," *Zhongyi*.

4. Xu Wenbo, *Zhongguo de Weisheng Renyuan Zhiliang he Yixue Jiaoyu Gaige* (China's Health Personnel Quality and Reforms in Medical Education), (Beijing: China Medical Association, 1987):2-3.

5. The Chinese have set a target of one doctor per 1000 population. If one defines "doctor" as those people with tertiary medical training, then the doctor/population ratio in China is still below 1 per 1000. This is an average. More detailed statistics reveal that in urban areas, the ratio is 2.4 per 1000 and in the countryside, it is less than .5 per 1,000. See William Hsiao, "Transformation of Health Care in China," *The New England Journal of Medicine* no. 310 (April 5, 1984):932-936.

6. *Zhi* means to manage, to balance, to administer, to cure. To heal the physical body is to put it in balance; to govern a land is to put things in order, to control the chaos. Therefore, the times of *zhi shi* are times of prosperity and peace. Medical theory was literally the translation of an image of the national economy transferred to an understanding of the body, or vice versa. In 400 A.D., Ko Hung wrote: "Thus the body of a man is the image of a state. The thorax and abdomen correspond to the palaces and offices. The four limbs correspond to the frontiers and boundaries. The divisions of the bones and sinews correspond to the ministers, and the *qi* to the people.

Thus we see that he who can govern his body can control a kingdom." Cited in Frederick Kao, "China, Chinese Medicine, and the Chinese Medical System," *American Journal of Chinese Medicine* Vol.1, no.1 (1973):14.

7. There was an ideal of state responsibility for public health evidenced in the imperial sponsorship of medical schools and medical relief established at least as early as the Sung. By and large, however, the common people were left to fend for themselves. See Angela Ki Che Leung, "Organized Medicine in Ming-Qing China: State and Private Medical Institutions in the Lower Yangzi Region," *Late Imperial China* Vol.8, no.1 (1987):134-166.

8. Babylonian and Egyptian medicines may predate *Zhongyi*, but neither of these is still coherently practiced.

9. Cited in Cheng Zhifan, "Evolution of Medical Education in China," *Chinese Medical Journal* Vol.97, no.6 (1984):435.

10. We are speaking of folks at the top. Today, of course, there are many women in the rank and file of the medical professions and as many who are patients of doctors as there ever were, but few women are in the powerful and pace-setting positions in scientific or policy roles.

11. The power of the Chinese state to define and defend its "knowledge culture," a term I learned from Margaret Sutton, was formidable. Writes C.C. Chen, "The principles of medicine formulated by the scholar-physicians were legitimized by ancient classical thought, and in time, an attack on traditional medicine came to be regarded as an attack on the cherished national cultural heritage itself." C.C. Chen, *Medicine in Rural China: A Personal Account* (Berkeley: University of California, 1989):16.

12. The status of medicine, both as knowledge and vocation, as compared with "pure" Classical studies, which resulted in office for successful test-takers, was that of a distant, but respectable,

second or third.   Both were textual disciplines with classical
roots.   Mastery of either resulted in some status and security.
See Robert P. Hymes, "Not Quite Gentlemen? Doctors in Sung
and Yuan," *Chinese Science* no.8 (1987):9-76, for a richly
detailed analysis of the status of physicians in traditional times.

13. Paul U. Unschuld, *Medical Ethics in Imperial China* (Berkeley:
University of California, 1978) p.20.

14. Unknown authors of the Warring States period (475-221 B.C.), *Nei
Jing* (Canon of Medicine), which consists of two parts: Plain
Questions" and "Miraculous Pivot," cited in Cheng Zhi-fan,
"Evolution of Medical Education," *op. cit.*, p.435.

15. Western medical science required the repudiation of Chinese medical
science.   *Zhongyi* is based on what Paul Unschuld calls a
"pattern structure of knowledge," meaning that it can encompass
seemingly contradictory paradigms.   It does not have the
Western epistemological mandate to choose between paradigms
in an "either-or" fashion.   See Paul U. Unschuld, "The Role of
Traditional Chinese Medicine in Contemporary Health Care," in
Recent Advances in Traditional Medicine in East Asia
(Amsterdam: Excerpta Medica, 1985):16-19 for an evocative
analysis of this contrast.

16. I do not mean to imply that this monopoly was uncontested before
the West entered.   It was continuously struggled over.   As Ruth
Hayhoe and others continue to remind us, there is historical
precedent in the *shuyuan* for challenging orthodox knowledge,
even if their fate is inconsistent.   What is important to us here is
the fact that as the imperial order crumbled, so did its
stranglehold on orthodoxy, on science.

17. Paul U. Unschuld, *Medical Ethics*, *op. cit.*, p.20.

18. These thirteen departments were adult diseases, children's diseases,
women's diseases, ulcers and swelling, acupuncture,
ophthamology, oral diseases, bone-setting febrile diseases,
incisive wounds, massage, and praying cure.   See Cheng Zhifan,

"Evolution of Medical Education in China," *op. cit.*, pp.437-439.

19. *Ibid.*, p.438.

20. The Chinese state did, on occasion, pay for the printing and distribution of medical texts, conduct epidemic relief work, and fund pharmacies.

21. In 1671, the first European treatise on acupuncture was published in France by Reverend Father Harview. Many others were to follow. See Frederick F.Kao, "China, Chinese Medicine and the Chinese Medical System," *American Journal of Chinese Medicine* Vol.1, no.1 (1973):1-59, for details.

22. The varioation technique was discovered by the Chinese by the beginning of the sixteenth century, brought by Russian doctors to Turkey, and made its way to England by the beginning of the eighteenth century. See, Joseph Needham, "China and the Origins of Immunology," *Eastern Horizon* 19 (1980):6-12.

23. Cheng Zhifan, "Evolution of Medical Education in China," *op. cit.*, p.439.

24. Russia was the only major imperialist power that failed to establish a program in medical education in China. Its influence was to be felt in the 1950s.

25. Mei Renlang, Zhong Shiping, Jin Wentao, "Zhongguo Yixue Jiaoyu de Xianxing Qingkuang" ("The Current Status of Chinese Medical Education") (unpublished manuscript, 1987).

26. E. Richard Brown, "Rockefeller Medicine in China: Professionalism and Imperialism," in Robert Arnove, editor, *Philanthropy and Cultural Imperialism* (Bloomington: Indiana University, 1980):123-146.

27. C.C. Chen, *Medicine in Rural China, op. cit.*, p.97. Chen describes

in first hand detail the participation of several PUMC graduates in the public health movement of the 1930s and 1940s.

28. David Lampton, *The Politics of Medicine in China* (Boulder: Westview Press, 1977) p.12.

29. Ralph Crozier, *Traditional Medicine in Modern China* (Cambridge: Harvard University, 1968):249.

30. *Ibid.*, p.249; C.C. Chen, *Medicine in Rural China, op. cit.*, p.62.

31. C.C. Chen, *Medicine in Rural China, op. cit.*, p.47, who writes of the founding of the *Binying Society* and its *Binying Weekly*, which sought to publicize health issues and challenge the majority conceptions about scientific medicine and its best applications in China.

32. *Ibid.*, p.75.

33. Nor have medical universities in other nations for similar reasons. Community medicine is a system of care based on a particular population group. It is "that branch of medical science which is concerned with the health needs and conditions of a population, and with dealing with these by appropriate methods and inteventions. It differs from that which is present in most affluent industrialized nations, which is based on an individual doctor-patient relationship." Willoughby Lathem, *The Future of Academic Community Medicine in Developing Countries* (New York: Praeger, 1979):12.

34. Michael W. Apple, *Education and Power* (London: Routledge, Kegan Paul, 1982):42.

35. In 1985, the concern over *Zhongyi* being subsumed into Western medicine prompted the establishment of a separate administrative bureau within the Ministry of Public Health to oversee *Zhongyi* practice and training. Moves were made to

limit the percentage of biomedicine in *Zhongyi* curriculae to 40 percent. They had been higher than that in some colleges.

36. This table is a compilation of curriculae from Shanghai Medical University, Shanghai Number Two Medical University, Xian Medical University, Beijing Medical University, and national curriculum plans. The course lists of earlier curriculae are included in Mei Renlang, "Qishi Nianlai Wo Guo Gaodeng Yixue Yuanxiao Kecheng Jihua de Fazhan" (Seventy Years of Higher Medical Curriculum Development), *Medical Education and Administration* no.3 (1986):45-60. Early curriculae separated natural science from medical science, so I have done so in this table. For example, chemistry and physics would be considered a preparatory natural science, necessary for the understanding of medical science coursework to follow. Increasingly, however, there is less of a distinction here because many science courses are listed as natural science as it is applied to medicine--Medical Chemistry or Medical Math. Course content appears to have been less changeable than course titles.

37. In 1989, this has been done by adding two required courses in ideology (*sixiang jiaoyu*) of roughly 100 hours each. These courses in medical colleges are supposed to include medical ethics, up until now, an elective and professional course unto itself.

38. Russian was the language of choice in the early 1950s ("Learn from the Soviet Union" years). Otherwise, English has been the most studied.

39. At many universities I visited, residents had to pass an examination in English in order to be promoted, regardless of their specialties.

40. The idea of these three levels came initially from the Soviet Union in the 1950s, but it has never been successfully implemented. According to two Chinese researchers, the 1980 proportion of graduate, (*yanjiu*) to bachelor (*benke*), to associate level

(*zhuanke*) students in medicine was 1:39:13 (21,600 to 861,900 to 280,000). The ideal ratio, according to health planners, would be 1:2:4. Li Xuemin and Qiu Yangxing, "Youhua Gaodeng Yixue Jiaoyu Cengci Jieguo de Chubu Shexiang" (A Tentative Program for Improving the Administration of Higher Medical Education), *Zhejiang Medical University Higher Medical Education* no.4 (1986):12. To achieve this would require more attention at both the three year and the graduate studies levels.

41. Some of these three year experimental programs are a collaboration between Chinese and U.S. medical schools, using community medicine models in practice in North American and Canadian universities and attempting to adapt them to local conditions. The World Health Organization has played a role in disseminating these North American community medicine models as well. The University of New Mexico Primary Care Curriculum has one such program with Xian Medical University to help develop a community medicine training program in two locations in southern Shensi province.

42. In surveying the conditions of Chinese students sent abroad, Ruth Hayhoe has discovered that while roughly 50 per cent of the professional-level medical workforce in Chinese medical universities is female, less than 25 per cent of those in the medical sciences sent abroad have been female. A summary of Professor Hayhoe's study, which does not speak to the gender issue specifically, appears as Ruth Hayhoe, "China's Scholars Returned from Abroad: A View From Shanghai," *China Exchange News* Vol.17, no.3 (September 1989):3-8.

43. The Chinese argue that women are less likely to have as much time to devote to their work because they are usually reponsible for their families. As far as this thinking goes, it is a valid argument.

44. The *renshi ganbu* is likely to be a Party member, too.

45. This recognition was, in fact, encouraging medical universities that

had won the prestigious right to institute six year course of study to change back to five. Medical people in China continuously compared medicine to engineering, which only takes four years of schooling and yields substantially better employment and earning opportunities.

46. The responsibility system was originally conceived to make peasants and factory workers more accountable for their production by allowing them to keep the proceeds from their labors that exceeded their state set quotas. In medicine, it has been interpreted into policies that ask hospitals to begin to operate more like enterprises. As in these other fields, the responsibility system has also decentralized many budgetary practices so that departments or wards are now operating as separate subsidiaries and are in competition with other departments and wards for profits and privilege.

47. See, for example, Gail Henderson, "Issues in the Modernization of Medicine," in Fred Simon and Merle Goldman, editors. *Science and Technology in Post-Mao China* (Cambridge: Harvard Contemporary China Series, 1989):199-221.

48. At their October, 1987 meeting in Chongqing, the theme was the relationship between the new commodity economy and medical ethics. The conference concluded that new economic policies had caused medical ethics to retrograde and called for policies that both take doctors' interests into account and oversee equitable provision of health care. They also called for more emphasis on ethics in medical curriculae.

49. Victor and Ruth Sidel, *Serve the People* (Boston: Beacon Press, 1973):129.

CHAPTER ELEVEN

BEYOND "STUFFING THE GOOSE": THE CHALLENGE OF MODERNIZATION AND REFORM FOR LAW AND LEGAL EDUCATION IN THE PEOPLE'S REPUBLIC OF CHINA

by Sharon K. Hom

Introduction: Frogs at the Bottom of a Well (*Jing di zhi wa*)

Several centuries ago, the Chinese philosopher Zhuangzi observed that a frog's field of vision is much wider than a man's. But a frog sitting at the bottom of a well can see only a fraction of the sky a man sees.[1] This metaphor for limited vision and its implicit recognition of the contingency of perception are particularly useful to inform and contextualize any effort to understand modern China. As foreign observers of the contradictions and struggles in China, we are inevitably limited by partial glimpses of shifting realities. Although the focus of this essay is not the whole "sky" of China but Chinese legal education, Zhuangzi's voice from the distant past is a useful reminder that our perceptions are shaped by who and what we are and our particular vantage point.

In addition, Thomas Merton's observation that "(as) soon as one has finished saying something, it is no longer true,"[2] reminds us that our perceptions are not only contingent and partial but also perhaps never quite in sync with a changing context. This gap between descriptive accounts and the shifting realities may account for the frustration of many foreign observers who have attempted to understand the complex realities of a China struggling to give birth to its modern self. This essay is a reflection upon the potential of legal education to respond to the challenges posed by China's modernization and reform goals. It emerges from the perspective of one who is a critical practitioner in the legal education exchange field. It does not presume the expertise of a sinologist nor claim to assume the disengaged objectivity of a "China watcher" on the sidelines.[3] The discussion will first briefly outline the historical background and developing role of law in China's modernization efforts and then proceed to explore several closely interrelated issues: (1) the role of legal education in China's developing legal system; (2) ongoing policy, structural and pedagogical issues as identified by Chinese sources and foreign observers; and (3) prospects for the future.

In addition to drawing upon the existing body of literature on Chinese legal education,[4] this essay will also draw upon my teaching and legal education exchange experiences and observations. From 1986-88, I taught in a Chinese law school and worked extensively with Chinese law teachers to develop a teacher training program. The young teachers, like most of my Chinese students, were young committed individuals, struggling under depressing and difficult conditions. Yet, they continued to hold onto a hope that they might make a contribution to building the future of China. In the Beijing winters sitting in cold, dusty concrete classrooms, their pale faces peered out from bundled up, padded bodies as they tried to make some sense of the American law and alien worldviews of this strange foreigner. In any exploration of the issues facing legal education in China, it is important to remember these faces and the human dimensions and costs of what Victor Li has described as "... a vast and fascinating human experiment, trying in a short time and with only meager resources, to transform a poor and backward country into one of the major countries in the world."[5]

From the particular vantage point of a Chinese-American female law teacher in China, my perspective may be neither the vision of a frog inside the well nor that of a man outside the well. My Chinese colleagues often treated me as either a returning overseas "daughter of China" or a foreigner or sometimes both simultaneously. Perhaps experiencing China as both an insider and an outsider contributes to my consciousness of contexts and the constructed borders of our two societies. Although it is often true that we cannot escape the perspectives of our own society, "the human being in whom two cultures meet, moves, as it were, along the margins of each."[6]

Therefore, this essay inevitably also reflects one individual's pacing of the margins and borders of two worlds, hoping at moments to perhaps be able to touch both.

The Role of Law in China

An old Chinese proverb states, "It is better to be vexed to death than to bring a lawsuit." This Chinese saying reflects a deep historical ambivalence on the part of Chinese society toward law and lawyers. Yet, contrary to the notion that pre-imperial China (prior to 221 B.C.) was governed by customary law and Imperial China was ruled primarily through a bureaucratic regime,[7] evidence suggests that positive rules existed even in pre-Imperial China.[8] However, in the traditional Confucian view of the proper order of Chinese society, that is one in which the people have internalized the "rules" of proper behavior, the ruler should govern by means of virtuous example rather than through an imposed rule of law.[9] In contrast to the Confucian view of law, the Legalists advocated a system of law which was clear, easy to know, and strictly applied. In contrast to the Confucian tradition, which stressed social harmony and morality, the Legalists emphasized state power and control[10] and viewed positive rules of law as necessary to control the actions of men.[11] In the course of history, the Confucian view of law and man's basic nature prevailed in shaping and legitimating the hierarchy and patriarchy of traditional Chinese society. However, the Legalists and other schools of thought such as the Mohists and the Taoists also continued to make their influence felt.[12]

In addition to the historical legacy of conflicted views regarding the role of law in Chinese society, the practice of law itself was regarded as a dishonest pursuit in Imperial China. During the Qing Dynasty (1644-1911), the criminal law punished those who made a profit from "managing a lawsuit,"[13] and lawyers were referred to as "litigation tricksters".[14] The practice of law was viewed as a "parasitic act disruptive of social harmony."[15] Although a 1910 Qing reform statute included a role for lawyers, it was never implemented due to the collapse of the Dynasty in 1911. Therefore it is not surprising that there was no formal legal education in law until the emergence of the social,

legal and political reform movements of the Republican era (1912-1949).
   During the early part of the twentieth century, Chinese Nationalist leaders attempted to modernize Chinese law through the promulgation of new codes and the development of a legal system based in large part upon borrowing from abroad. In addition to the imperial codes and bureaucratic modes of administration, the emerging Chinese legal system during the Republican period, "assimilated or borrowed" from the French courts (prior to 1949); and Germanic codes as passed on and modified by the Japanese.[16] These legal reform efforts were supported by the belief that through modernization, China would be strengthened, foreign influence would be reduced, and economic and social development would be advanced.
   During the 1930s, in the Communist controlled areas, there were some fledgling efforts to implement land reform and marriage law reforms, but these were never developed nor implemented fully.[17] In 1949, the Communists abolished Kuomingtang laws and began to rebuild a legal system based upon the Soviet system. However, given the lack of legal specialists, they were forced to rely on those trained under the Nationalists, particularly in the judiciary and on the law faculties. New cadres were chosen for their ideological dependability and past service rendered. Tensions emerged between the legal "specialists," who viewed the establishment of a formal rule of law as important, and the "new cadres," who viewed the "rule of man" or a rule by enlightened and conscientious officials as more important than a rule of law. This "red" versus "expert" split had implications for the direction of political reform and the policy goals for the development of legal education. Between 1954-1957, in the continuing conflict regarding the extent to which class struggle was to be enforced, which found expression in movements such as the "Hundred Flowers" campaign and the Anti-Rightist backlash, law schools shifted emphasis from professional training to political training.[18]
   Despite the primacy of maintaining order and a deep Chinese revulsion to chaos (*luan*), the history of law in modern China has reflected and continues to reflect shifting political policies, campaigns and party lines, the most destructive perhaps occurring during the Cultural Revolution when libraries and law schools were closed and destroyed; thousands of law faculty were sent to the countryside cowsheds and legal research and journals stopped publication.
   Beginning with the Third Plenum in 1978 and continuing through the Thirteenth Party Congress in 1987, the role of law was once again stressed as essential to the process of promoting reform and modernization. Zhao Ziyang stated in his report to the National

People's Congress, describing what was then referred to as the first stage of Chinese socialism, "Socialist democracy is inseparable from a socialist legal system... During the whole process of reform we must go on building our legal system."[19] Chinese scholars have defined socialist law as "broad and rich," including the key concepts of the unity of citizen's rights and duties; the equality of all citizens before the law; the unity of freedom and discipline; and the concept of relying on law to govern.[20] At the same time that the Chinese leaders advocated the general principle of "making the past serve the present and foreign things serve China," Deng Xiaoping emphasized that China must

... do things in accordance with Chinese conditions and find a Chinese-style path to modernization... Departure from the four basic principles (socialism, Marx-Lenin-Mao Thought,dictatorship of the proletariat, and party leadership)... will inevitably lead to the unchecked spread of ultra-democracy and anarchism.[21]

Although the Chinese leaders were willing to reopen China's windows to the outside world, it was(is) also clear that they were(are) also intent on controlling the inevitable undesirable foreign "flies" that attempt to enter.

Han Depei and Stephen Kanter identified the following functions of this Chinese socialist legal system: to suppress class enemies; to sabotage any trouble-making activities; to regulate contradictions among the people; and to readjust the relationships between various aspects of national economic construction.[22] In addition to the ideological and social ordering functions assigned to the Chinese brand of socialist law, three motivations for China's law reform efforts since 1978 include: the "popular demand for legal protection against arbitrary behavior by Party or government officials or by other citizens; the need for clear guidelines for economic activity; and the need for a systematic network of rules and procedures in civil, economic, and commercial law to attract and protect foreign capital."[23]

Thus law continues to be viewed by the current regime as both a useful instrumentalist tool, necessary for completing the task of modernization; an effective means of building the infrastructure and stability necessary for reopening China to the outside world; and to a limited extent, a vehicle for initiating political reform in terms of addressing the problems of bureaucratic abuse and corruption.

Assessments of China's developing legal system[24] by both foreign observers and Chinese leaders have relied upon quantitative indicators such as the number of graduates from law schools; new legislation promulgated, and the increase in the number of lawyers and lawsuits. In 1980, there were only about 5,500 lawyers and by 1984, about 8,700 law students. From 1949 to 1984, the total number of graduates from higher institutes and departments of political science and law was fewer than 20,000 or only 0.62 per cent of the combined total of college graduates of the country. As late as 1984, there were less than 1,000 law teachers in the higher institutes and departments of political science and law. [25] In 1987, 3,582 students were enrolled in the science of law specialty (*faxue zhuanye*) or 3.0 per cent of the total 106,105 graduates students graduating.[26] By 1986, the number of lawyers reached 21,000,[27] and 1987 statistics show that China had more than 31,000 lawyers in more than 3,000 law firms, 15,000 notaries public in more than 2800 notary firms and 6,000 mediators in neighborhoods and work units. In 1988, courts at all levels of government handled 8,500 tort cases covering a wide range of areas: the police, city planning, customs, taxation, patent, land, forest, food and hygiene, the environment, and drug administration. Suits against the government were allowed as of 1982.[28] Between 1979 to 1986, 670,000 criminal cases were handled by the courts.[29] This apparent increase in litigation and court cases may not be surprising in light of the proliferation of new laws over the past decade.

Since 1978, the National People's Congress and its Standing Committee have promulgated approximately 80 pieces of legislation, (including a criminal code, a code of procedure, and a joint venture law all initiated in 1979, an economic contract law, an inheritance law, and the general principles for the civil code).[30] An administrative procedure law was passed in 1989, and there is underway a current effort to draft a government tort liability statute. In addition to thousands of local laws and regulations promulgated by provincial governments, the State Council, China's executive part of government, has promulgated more than a thousand rules and regulations.

But these statistics emerge from diverse sources regarding the profusion of new laws promulgated over the past decade. The increase of litigation and the expansion of the legal profession may be misleading if relied upon beyond their obvious significance as quantitative evidence of the development of a formal legal system of laws and institutions. In addition to the "public" laws promulgated, there are probably thousands and thousands of internal (*neibu*) regulations, guidelines, and policy statements that have an impact on the decision making process. These *neibu* regulations, guidelines, and policy statements may be revised, superceded, or overturned without a trace or prior notice to those responsible for implementing the old and new rules or to those who will affected. Given the highly politicized nature of law (as an ideological and modernization tool for party policy) and the discretion inherent in the existing bureaucratic decision making process, there is thus an inevitable gap between the law "on the books" and the law as implemented.

This gap between theory and practice as it were is also affected by the fact that several different generations of legal personnel, trained under different systems and approaches, are now called upon to teach, draft, or implement a system of law in which they may be neither trained nor committed. Gao Xi-Ching has identified four groups that make up the legal profession in China. Each group reflects particular social and ideological backgrounds and different views of law and expresses behavioral patterns that affect their ability to be flexible, open, and/or willing or able to cope with the demands and needs of a rapidly developing system. The "seniors/veterans," the majority of whom were Soviet trained (1950-57), are the most orthodox, cautious, and idealistic. The "juniors or mid-streamers," which include Red Guard college students, were caught in the rupture with the Soviet Union and its consequences of de-Sovietization of the Chinese legal system and the beginning of the Cultural Revolution. The "sophomores or worker-peasant-soldiers," with varying competency in terms of academic and intellectual preparation for legal work, are direct products of the direct rejection of a formal rule of law rampant during the Cultural Revolution. Finally, the "freshmen or newcomers" entered college after 1976 and are often only children or one of two children in the family. They do not feel grateful to the Communist party, and although educated in Marxist-Leninist ideology, they often had teachers who were drifting, suspicious, and confused about the changing system.[31]

In the context of the ongoing "rule of man" versus the "rule of law" discussions that echo some of the tensions and conflicts articulated more than two thousand years ago by the Confucianists and the Legalists, Shen Zongling makes the pragmatic and realistic observation that the effort to change from the "rule of man" such as was rampant during the Cultural Revolution to the "rule of law," which is the articulated goal of current Chinese leaders, cannot be accomplished overnight or easily. Shen Zongling argues that any effort to change such a fundamental aspect of the Chinese system must take into account the past, which continues to exist, and the present. This past includes men who believe in the "rule of man" and a system that continues to function at some level at the discretion of a "rule of man."[32]

In addition, the definitions of key terms in the past 40 years have shifted, making it difficult to use statistical data for comparative purposes over different time periods. For example, who is or can be a lawyer or a judge? What is the meaning of cases "handled" by the courts? In criminal cases, where individuals may be detained, possibly for months or years for "investigation," where if at all are these cases reflected in the court dispositions? How were data collected and what was the data base? For foreign scholars of Chinese law, there are the additional obstacles of obtaining access to information and *neibu* sources or attempting to complete empirical research in shifting political climates, not to mention the different approaches and legal training of foreign-and Chinese trained scholars.

Although Chinese official reference materials begin to present extensive, comprehensive, and clear statistical information,[33] quantitative information is of limited usefulness in assessing qualitative, value based, or structural concerns. "What is overlooked in quantification or the investigation of mere surfaces is the deep infrastructure which underlies all surface phenomenon." Why is this significant? Perhaps because any effort to transform culture (as China's current modernization may inevitably require) implicates these deep structures: the transformation of consciousness (linguistic, perceptual, affective, and cognitive) and institutions (linguistic, political, economic, and social).[34] Clearly, the democracy movements of the last decade and the works of the new generation of film makers, writers and artists reflect an effort to examine the existing deep structures within Chinese society and present broad and controversial critiques.[35]

Chinese law as a reflection of Chinese society's values and structures is also affected by and affects these ongoing critiques. In Chinese legal academic circles immediately prior to June 1989, the issues of modernization in a Chinese Socialist context,[36] the reform of China's legal system,[37] and the development of Chinese democracy[38] were debated and discussed widely and more openly than would have been thought possible even in the political climate existing at that time.

Outside observers of the Chinese legal system and Chinese pro-democracy activists have viewed the emerging legal system and the development of a rule of law with skepticism and concern. Human rights scholars have pointed to the lack of due process in criminal proceedings: the treatment of political dissidents, such as Wei Jingsheng, and the much publicized trial of the "Gang of Four" as evidence of an existing system of questionable legality and legitimacy.[39] Against a background of Mao's "politics in command," Chinese writers and intellectuals argued courageously but futilely for legal reforms that would protect individual rights and limit the powers of government.[40] Unfortunately, the Chinese government's violent crackdown of the protests by students and workers in June 1989 contributed to the ongoing doubts and concerns about the viability of China's legal reforms and the future of law in China. Reflecting the disappointment of many scholars and friends of China, one China expert observed,

> Westerners hoped to see stability achieved in China through legal and political institutions which had sufficiently matured to allow a smooth transition of power, yielding creative political responses to China's growing economic and social problems. That hope was dashed by the Beijing massacre and the accompanying political purge.... The entire legal system, upon which western confidence had been based, now is in doubt.[41]

The close interrelationships among law, political reform, state power, and policy making reflect the ongoing themes of modern China, which were present from the beginning of the twentieth century: the conflict between a centuries-old culture and the imperatives of modernization, a conflicted attitude on the part of the Chinese towards foreigners and foreign concepts and values; and a deep historical ambivalence toward the rule of law.

The Role of Legal Education in China's Legal System

The conflicts, themes and issues present in China's effort to modernize and reform its legal system are also played out in the development of legal education and shape the challenges facing Chinese educators and policy makers. Yet ironically, in the extensive Chinese legal literature on the issues of modernization and legal reform, there is a conspicuous absence of attention to the role of legal education which has the task of training the legal personnel who will think about, draft, teach, and practice in the existing system and any future system which emerges. The discussion that follows will outline briefly an overview of Chinese legal education and then explore the role that legal education plays and might play.

OVERVIEW OF CHINESE LEGAL EDUCATION

The beginning of modern legal education began with the Republican era (1912-49). A period of uncontrolled law school expansion occurred from 1910-1930, and by 1936, there were 16 government law schools and 17 private law schools (including *faxueyuans* at Beijing, Wuhan, Suzhou), although the standards for admission, curriculum, and faculty were quite uneven. A Chinese Legal Education Association even organized a conference in 1936 to discuss the issues of the use of foreign law textbooks, improvement of the law curriculum and legal research.[42]   Compared to this beginning period, which was characterized by strong western influence and leadership and a focus on the development of legal experts and professionals, Chinese legal education today is broadly conceived and includes the formal higher educational institutions, on-the-job (in-service) training for legal cadres, correspondence programs,[43] and, beginning in 1985, mass public education efforts.

The Chinese leaders viewed the establishment of a new socialist legal consciousness as not just a matter for specialists--it required a mass movement and included the use of newspapers, media, radio lectures, popular pamphlets, exhibits in city neighborhoods, and discussions in the street committees in the urban areas, the rural people's communes, in political study groups, in primary and middle-school classrooms.[44] Depei and Kanter argue that "this emphasis on the general distribution of legal norms and information serves as a social control mechanism, as an expedient to compensate for the scarcity of trained legal personnel, and as an expression of the theoretical ideal that law should be directly accessible and comprehensible to the masses."[45]

In terms of formal higher level institutions for law study and training, the *1987 Law Year Book of China* (*Zhongguo Falu Nianjian*) listed 109 institutions including universities, law departments, specialties, institutes, and cadre management training schools.[46]   The 1989 *Law Year Book* (*Zhongguo Falu Nianjian*) separately lists the existing institutions involved in law training: 72 higher level law schools and departments (*falu yuan, xi*), not including additional cadre management training schools and 55 research institutes and centers.[47] The reopening and expansion of the law schools appeared to be a hopeful indicator of a recovery from the Cultural Revolution. By the mid-1980s, many observers believed that China was in the midst of laying significant groundwork for the further development of its legal system.[48] However, the revival of formal legal education may also be presenting Chinese authorities with a potentially threatening aspect of an emerging professionalism: a drive to establish professional and occupational autonomy[49] that may conflict with the dominance of the Chinese communist party upon which the Chinese socialist legal system is predicated.

Curriculum planning is highly centralized and falls under the jurisdiction of the State Education Commission (the former Ministry of Education) and the Ministry of Justice. In 1980, the (then) Ministry of Education and the Ministry of Justice in an effort to strengthen the uniformity of the curriculum jointly organized a board of editors composed of law specialists to compile two sets of teaching materials including a set of thirty standardized teaching texts and ten reference books. The editors also undertook translation of foreign materials.[50]

What is taught as part of the formal legal curriculum at the university level? The four year program for both the faculties of law and the institutes of political science and law include required courses in jurisprudence, constitutional law, Chinese legal history, foreign legal history, civil law, civil procedure, criminal law, criminal procedure, criminal investigation, international law, private international law, forensic science, logic, Chinese language, basic theory of Marxism-Leninism, philosophy, a foreign language, and physical education.

However, curriculum requirements may be altered in light of political climate shifts. For example, after the June 4th crackdown, schools were required to revise military training or practical work experience requirements for their first year students. Curricular reform thus continues to reflect the ongoing tension between the practice-theory debate and the red-expert conflict, which address the appropriate balance between ideological indoctrination and professional training.

With respect to formal legal training, four years are required to obtain an undergraduate law degree; another three years are required for a masters degree with an additional two years required for receipt of the doctorate.[51] Students specialize quite early on in their studies resulting in a narrowing of their focus and the foundation of their legal training. The current law study specialties, most of which were established after 1984, include economic law, international economic law, reform through labor law, criminology, intellectual property law, theory of legal science, history of legal thought, history of legal systems, constitutional law, criminal law, civil law, procedure law, and environmental law.[52] In addition to courses of study, students are all assigned to and are monitored through political study groups.

Despite the often noisy and crowded conditions (four or six people sharing a small 8' by 10' or 10 by 12' room for most of their law study years), Chinese students retain an impressive sense of goodwill and patience toward each other. Most of them live away from home for the first time, so these students often form deep and lasting friendships with the small tight group of their roommates and other students in the same specialty and political study groups. Due to the lack of appropriate or adequate housing or different work unit assignments, it was not uncommon for many of the married students or teachers to live separately from their spouses, visiting them once or twice a year if they were in another city.

The bulk of the teaching is taught by the young teachers or assistant teachers. The young teachers also often teach the review cram courses for those taking the Lawyers Qualification Examination.[53] The full professors tend to teach the graduate level or post graduate courses or direct post graduate candidates. Lecture and memorization continue to predominate in current Chinese teaching approaches.[54] However, other teaching methods may sometimes also be used in the Chinese law classrooms and outside the schools. These include moot courts, seminar discussions and independent research and writing projects, and a semester of practical experience in courts, public security bureaus, procuratorates, judicial affairs offices, and notary offices.

ROLE OF FORMAL LEGAL EDUCATION AND METHODOLOGY

The key function of formal legal education as viewed by the Chinese is to train specialists for the courts, legal institutes and schools, and research universities.[55] More specifically, the Chinese look to the training of legal personnel who possess basic knowledge of the Marxist-Leninist Theory of Law, who are familiar with the Party's political and legal work, policies, and guiding principles, who are endowed with socialist consciousness, who have mastered the professional knowledge of the law, and who are capable of undertaking research, teaching, and practical legal work.[56] According to earlier Chinese estimates by the Supreme People's Court and the Supreme Procuratorate, China needs 186,000 legally trained personnel. If legal cadres and advisors are included, the total may be as high as a million. Deng Xiaoping has estimated that 1-2 million legal workers will be needed by the end of the century.[57]

Formal legal education thus has the difficult role of training the legal personnel to staff the present system, which is still in a formative stage of development, and also training the teachers, scholars, and lawmakers who will and can contribute to the further development of that system. Although the American legal system is also evolving and changing, the unsettled and highly politicized nature of the context, issues, and tasks facing the Chinese system results in a more radical environment of uncertainty and tension in China.

Like the larger legal system, legal education in contemporary China has been directly influenced by the authoritarian characteristics of both socialist and Confucian traditions. It is not surprising that centralized curricular decision-making has served to reinforce traditional pedagogy. In carrying out their role, Chinese universities and law schools have and continue to adopt an approach described "as traditional, extremely academic and overly theoretical,"[58] an approach that reflects and accepts the legitimacy of existing authority, hierarchy, and values. A Chinese proverb warns that the nail that sticks out gets hammered down, reflecting a deeply-held Chinese reluctance to stand out, discouraging the taking of risks, creativity, or the exploration of unorthodox approaches.

As a result of the predominance of the passive "talking textbook" teaching method in most Chinese law classrooms, the atmosphere is often characterized by a deadly, oppressive silence or simply boredom, broken occasionally by a question from the teacher. Students may be found sleeping in the back of classrooms with their heads on the desks or dreaming of an escape by studying for the English TOEFL examination.

In any efforts to introduce new approaches, teachers point hopelessly to the pressures of getting the students through the required materials and the severe limitations of existing conditions. Yet, due to the enormous volume and provisional nature of many of the new laws and regulations promulgated since 1979, and the informal aspects of the decision-making processes used by the courts, administrative bodies, and mediators, law teachers need to more effectively prepare law students to cope with the uncertainties in the Chinese legal system. Dealing with such uncertainty requires creativity and flexibility, but Chinese legal education, as it is currently structured, does not emphasize, value, or train in the areas of specific problem solving and analytical skills. If legal education is to meet the challenges facing it, it must develop and explore appropriate alternatives models.

Clearly, there is a need to train legal educators and teachers who play an important role in developing and implementing any approaches. Although there has been a rapid expansion in teacher training programs for teaching faculty in other institutions of higher learning, the focus has been on training teachers in the natural sciences and advanced technology.[59] Thus, many new Chinese law teachers, like their American counterparts, still begin teaching immediately after graduation without any formal systematic teacher training. These new teachers, often face the imposing task of getting up in front of a class of hundreds of waiting faces.[60] The development of clinical legal education in the United States[61] grew out of strong criticisms directed at the failure of American law schools to train students in the skills, professional responsibility, and theoretical dimensions of law practice, and in its effort to respond to these criticisms drew upon the work of humanistic philosophies[62] and the experiential learning theories developed by educational philosophers such as John Dewey. What is the role, if any, of these clinical experiential models? Should the approaches of Dewey be revisited as a potential source of models for China?[63] Even if there were the interest to explore these areas further is the political label of bourgeoise humanism the kiss of death for humanistic, experiential, student centered teaching approaches?[64]

The teacher training approaches relied upon in my own limited work in China, relied heavily upon these American clinical legal education approaches and western learning theories. Although this experience is too limited as a base from which to draw any conclusions about the relevance of these approaches for Chinese legal education generally, it is significant that the overwhelming responses of the Chinese students and teachers to these new approaches were first discomfort, curiosity, and then excitement and total engagement with the interactive process. Their responsiveness and openness to the exploration of new approaches was accompanied with such courage, energy, and often a wonderful sense of humor, that there appears to be an enormously unrecognized potential for these young people to play a vital role in the future of legal educational reform and development.

Although Chinese education leaders look to the increasing numbers of Chinese LLM degree holders and graduate students in the United States and other countries to return to China and reduce the shortage of teachers, since the government suppression of the pro-democracy movement of June 4th, 1989, there are serious questions whether the Chinese students and scholars now abroad are likely to return to China in the near future. Even if they were to return, questions remain concerning the feasibility of knowledge transfer and the appropriate adaptation of those legal skills, acquired in foreign environments. The simple exposure of Chinese students and scholars to American legal education through degree study or visiting scholar research visits will not necessarily train them to assess, transfer, and apply the range of American methodology in a Chinese classroom. Only by explicit, systematic, and critical study of American and other foreign legal teaching methods can Chinese teachers assess the relevance of these methods for Chinese legal education and adapt them to Chinese conditions, needs, and goals.[65]

Finally, despite the significant role of legal education, there is a surprising lack of attention by Chinese legal educators and scholars to legal education itself as a crucial institution in the legal infrastructure. It is interesting to note that there is not one entry for legal education or the legal profession in the *Encyclopedia of China* volume on Law.[66] In light of the complexity of the task facing Chinese legal education, it is important that the theoretical, institutional, and policy issues inherent in the conflicted role of Chinese legal education be put on the research and training agendas of Chinese scholars, educators, and policy makers.

Ongoing Issues: "Stuffing the Goose" in a Modern but Chinese Way

Like the emerging legal system, the goals and development of legal education have been shaped and buffeted about by both shifting political lines and an ongoing legacy of tensions and conflicted impulses reflected in China's struggle toward a Chinese vision of modernity. Although the official articulation of the goals of legal education appears to be clear, the implementation and implications of these goals appear to be less clear. Ongoing issues include the balancing of the dual goals of training of legal personnel in critical independent skills and also ensuring political reliability, the question of the appropriate content and scope of legal training for different legal tasks and functions, the development of teaching methods which encourage reflective, creative legal thinking, and the role of overseas study and training for Chinese students and scholars as well as the dilemma of and problems resulting from brain drain.

From the perspective of American legal education, American law teachers have pointed to the failure of Chinese legal education to develop "the most essential lawyering qualities, notably a healthy skepticism, intellectual curiosity, and creativeness."[67]   In addition to placing a greater emphasis upon the inherent tensions and political implications of the choices facing Chinese legal education, foreign observers point to structural and institutional obstacles. These include the shortage of trained faculty,[68] a chronic shortage of funds for new facilities, dormitories, and classrooms, and the lack of adequate materials, libraries, and books.

But even by Chinese standards, legal education is not fully responding to both quantitative and qualitative goals. These goals are of course, inextricably linked to the future of law and legal process in China. Chinese leaders have stated, "Higher education in law should be closely linked to practice, and we must lead our law teachers to develop our law and legal education from the vantage point of our country's current reality."[69]   In the aftermath of June 4, 1989 the official rhetoric in the Legal Times (Fazhi Bao) also pointed to the need to strengthen ideological and political training, thus once again exposing the close relationship between the instrumentalist function of the legal system for implementing party policy and the development of legal education. Despite the Chinese tendency to measure progress in quantitative terms, in the past decade, there appears to be a growing concern regarding the quality of Chinese education in higher education academic circles.[70] Newspaper editorials and articles have expressed criticism of the schools, including the law institutions, for failing to adequately prepare graduates for their future work, for not making the connections between theory and practice in teaching methods, and for failing to train the students' problem solving and analytical abilities. They speak of the need for improving the "efficiency of the system" and "raising the level" of the education.

Thus, the need to design and use more creative pedagogical methods appropriate for Chinese conditions and the training of future generations of lawyers, teachers, judges, legislative drafters is clear. However, Chinese law teachers interested in exploring new approaches and improving their teaching continue to face real constraints and obstacles posed by inadequate resources, the lack of adequate teacher training programs and materials, and other factors such as passive student learning habits and large classes. The lack of adequate libraries and facilities, the current low salaries and poor living conditions of Chinese teachers also have an impact on teacher morale and motivation.[71]   These obstacles all underscore the enormity of the task of building a legal system in a still very poor, developing country.

Randall Edwards notes, "the search for effective legislative techniques, lawyering skills, and law-teaching techniques has been carried to that bastion of the free-enterprise system, the United States." [72]

Yet, looking toward the west for academic and legal professional training opportunities[73] has historically been part of China's approach to the outside world: welcoming western ideas and technology on the one hand; and yet trying to reject undesirable values (unwanted "flies"). Since China's reopening to the west in 1978, there have been renewals of educational and cultural exchanges.[74] In the legal field, students, scholars, attorneys, and on the Chinese side, officials from government ministries and corporations who have gone to the United States for research, degree study, and for internships and training, primarily in the large corporate firms.

However, given the limited exposure to American law study and practice reflected in the primary focus on private law and corporate practice of legal exchanges in the past decade (with some recent development of interest in our courts, legislative drafting process, and critical legal theories), Chinese scholars, students and lawyers may not understand American law in the comprehensive and critical way that is necessary for an assessment of the relevance of the American or any foreign system for China. The scope and focus of exchanges thus need to be reassessed by participating American institutions and Chinese leaders in the Ministry of Justice, the State Education Committee, and the Chinese universities,law schools and research institutes.

Obviously there is a close interrelationship among the existing material conditions, general education research and reform thinking, politics, and the composition and worldviews of present and future generations of law drafters, teachers, judges, lawyers, and legal workers. A change in one of these domains will affect the others, but the existing conceptual frameworks also influence them.

The status and treatment of Chinese women in the law schools and the profession present additional issues that are only beginning to be addressed and acknowledged.[75] Although Hugh Chan observed in 1936 that despite the limited number of women in the law schools and the profession, "they have long gained a foot-hold, and among them are noted lawyers and jurists,"[76] the current situation of Chinese women in the profession suggests that gender discrimination is pervasive. Chinese women lawyers and law professors in the 1980s continue to be a distinct minority[77] and like women in the American legal profession[78], Chinese women may make nominal gains in terms of law student representation, but they continue to face similar hierarchical and gender tracking stereotypes in the job assignment system upon graduation.[79]

My own anecdotal and impressionistic sense of the position and role of women in the legal profession suggests that women still are a minority in terms of numbers and representation in the tenured senior ranks of law professors, with some apparent tracking occurring in particular fields and specializations. Many women students often told me of their difficulties in getting jobs after graduation in the more competitive and prestigious *danweis* (work units).

In one class, I asked my students to list the characteristics of their male and female teachers in their recent past. After protesting vigorously that there were no distinctions (the "women hold up half the sky" version of reality), they produced a list that was strikingly similar to American gender stereotypes, echoing socially constructed and media perceptions regarding the differences between men and women. Women law teachers were described as nurturing, more accessible, easier to talk with, and less rigorous and analytical. Male law teachers were described as more distant, theoretical, and disciplined. Despite the "feminist outcries" in the newly founded women's magazines; the media exposes of discrimination against women; and the emergence of women's organizations, professional societies, and study groups, my students' characterizations of their teachers still reflected popular Chinese images of men and women: "men have will power, are resolute and steadfast...women are generally rather delicate, fragile, and gentle, although they are sometimes very stubborn. Women loved to talk and exhibit sensitivity to and understanding of other people's feelings".[80] Certainly the persistence and pervasiveness of gender discrimination within the profession and law schools is a significant emerging issue, which will have to be addressed if democratic and political reforms are pursued seriously for all the members, male and female, of Chinese society.

Prospects for the Future

Harvard Law School Dean Roscoe Pound observed almost forty years ago that "...it is futile to expect to make a great people over by law. It is more likely that the people will make over the law imposed upon it that than people will be made over."[81]

Today, the role of law and legal education is defined not only by the instrumentalist visions of Chinese leaders but also by the democratic aspirations of the Chinese people. Although the present regime appears to be viewing the approach towards modernization and reform in a bifurcated manner (e.g. believing that economic modernization can be separated from political reforms in terms of priority and development), the demands for democratic reforms, the "fifth modernization,"[82] must be addressed by the Chinese leadership, if it is to maintain social stability and political legitimacy by means other than repression and brute force. In addition, the sometimes violent shifting of political agendas and party policies continues to contribute to the uncertain future of the academic legal institutions.

As China struggles to balance and reconcile the conflicting impulses toward order at all costs with the imperatives of political, economic, and social reform implicit in modernization goals, foreigners may also have a limited role to play. Foreign teachers and friends of China can continue to work to keep the doors open between China and the outside world, to remain sensitive to and respectful of China's internal processes of social change and legal reform, and at the same time be supportive critics.

The role that legal educators and legal education will play will be shaped by the extent to which they can address and resolve the tensions between education as reinforcement of existing values and structures and education as critique and creative re-envisioning of the existing legal and social order. In this difficult and challenging task, they are encumbered by the conflicted legacy of the past and the uncertainties of the present and the future. The future of the legal system and legal education also will inevitably continue to depend upon the complex political landscape and those who will inherit or grasp power after the inevitable passing away of the present regime. Yet, as Jamake Highwater stated so eloquently, speaking out of his dual cultural orientation as a traditional Blackfeet Indian and as a western trained scholar:

> Change cannot come until neither loyalty to the old
> nor fear of the new can no longer delay it. Such a
> transformation is all the more difficult because it seems
> to require the greater to be exchanged for the less.[83]

Ultimately, perhaps the greatest source of hope for future reforms and change lies within the minds and hearts of those Chinese leaders, educators, teachers, and students who continue to struggle with courage, patience, and spirit, not only with existing structural and shifting political realities and difficult material conditions but also with their loyalties and their fears.

Notes

1. The *Book of Zhuangzi* was compiled by Zhuang Zhou (369-286 B.C.), the founder of the Taoist school of philosophy, and his disciples. This story is recounted in Gao Xi-Ching, "Today's Legal Thinking and Its Economic Impact in China," *Law and Contemporary Problems* vol. 52, no.2 and 3 (Spring-Summer, 1989):89.

2. Merton is cited in Simon Leys, *The Burning Forest: Essays on Chinese Culture and Politics* (New York: Henry Holt and Company, 1986):3.

3. Simon Leys has made the characteristically cynical but sharp observation that "China watching" has been one of the safest of all occupations. "Whatever you may predict is bound to come true one day or another - all you need is a little patience." See *Ibid.*, p.211.

4. For bibliographies of English language materials on Chinese legal education, see Sharon Hom, "Legal Education in the People's Republic of China: A Selected Annotated Bibliography of English-Language Materials," *China Law Reporter* (1990):69-81; "Annotated Bibliography," *Columbia Journal of Transnational Law* vol.22 (1983):175-232; Mon Yin Lung, "Annotated Bibliography of Selected English-Language Literature on Chinese Law," *Legal References Services Quarterly* vol.6, no.3-4 (Fall/Winter 1986):95-121; and Jeanette L. Pinard, "The People's Republic of China: A Bibliography of Selected English Language Legal Materials," *China Law Reporter* vol.3 (1985):46-143.

5. Victor Li, *Law Without Lawyers: A Comparative View of Law in China and the United States* (Boulder: Westview, 1978):xxi.5.

6. Francis Hsu, *Americans and Chinese: Passage to Differences* (Honolulu: University of Hawaii, 1981):xxi.

7. See Roberto Unger, *Law in Modern Society* (New York: The Free Press, 1976): 86-105.

8. William Alford, "The Inscrutable Occidental? Implications of

Roberto Unger's Uses and Abuses of the Chinese Past," *Texas Law Review* vol. 64, no.5 (1986):915-972.

9. Li, *Law Without Lawyers*, *op. cit.*, p.13.

10. Ralph H. Folsom and John H. Minan, *Law in the People's Republic of China: Text, Readings and Materials* (Dordrecht: Martinus Nijhoff,1989):2.

11. The use of the male pronoun to refer to the whole of society is retained in this discussion when appropriate to reflect the historical context and usage of the sources cited.

12. Alford, "The Inscrutable Occidental?" *op. cit.*, pp. 940-952. Furthermore, in their historical development, although each school did reflect different values and assumptions about the role of law in society, each school also influenced each other's development and was integrated into each other's philosophy. Gu Chunde and Du Ganjian, "Zhongguo Chuantung Falu Guannian yu Xiandai Shehuizhuyi Fazhi Jianshe" (China's Traditional Concept of Law and the Creation of Modern Socialist Law), *Chuantung Wenhua yu Xinadaihua* (Traditional Culture and Modernization) (Beijing:People's University Press,1987):291-304.

13. Henry Pitney, "The Role of Legal Practitioners in the People's Republic of China," *Stanford Journal of International Law* vol.24, no.2 (Spring 1988):323-388, at p.328.

14. William Alford, "Of Arsenic and Old Laws: Looking Anew at Criminal Justice in Late Imperial China," *California Law Review* Vol.72, no.6 (December 1984):1180-1256, at p.1194, footnote 76.

15. R. Randall Edwards, "An Overview of Chinese Law and Legal Education," *The Annals of the American Academy of Political and Social Science* vol.476 (November 1984):48-59, at p.53.

16. By 1923, it was reported by the Dean of the Peking Law College that 70 per cent of the textbooks used were translated from Japanese texts. Chan also predicted that China was developing

a legal system of its own and that legal texts written by "Chinese with Chinese viewpoints" would increase. Hugh Chan, "Modern Legal Education in China," *China Law Review* 9, (1936):142-148.

17. Victor Li, *Law Without Lawyers, op. cit.*, pp.20-21.

18. Han Depei and Stephen Kanter, "Legal Education in China," *The American Journal of Comparative Law* vol.32 (1984):543-582, at p.572, footnote 89; Alison M. Connor, "Legal Education in China: A Look at Nanda," *Singapore Law Review* vol.7 (1986):181-201, at p.181; R. Randall Edwards, "An Overview of Chinese Law and Legal Education," *op. cit.*, p.53.

19. Zhao Ziyang, "Advance Along the Road of Socialism with Chinese Characteristics", *Report Delivered to the Thirteenth Congress of the Communist Party of China* (October 25, 1987).

20. Gu Chunde and Du Ganjian, "Zhongguo Chuantung Falu Guannian yu Xiandai Shehuizhuyi Fazhi Jianshe" (China's Traditional Concept of Law and the Creation of Modern Socialist Law), *Chuantung Wenhua yu Xiandaihua* (Traditional Culture and Modernization), *op. cit.*, p.304.

21. Andrew J. Nathan, "Is China Ready for Democracy?," *Journal of Democracy* vol. 1, no.2 (Spring,1990):50-61, at p.50.

22. Han Depei and Stephen Kanter, "Legal Education in China," *The American Journal of Comparative Law* vol.32 (1984):569.

23. R. Randall Edwards, "An Overview of Chinese Law and Legal Education," *op. cit.*, p.52

24. Pitney offers a concise discussion of the history of the legal profession, pages 328-332, and for additional articles on lawyers and the emerging role of law, see Hom, "Legal Education in the People's Republic of China: A Selected Annotated Bibliography of English-Language Materials," *op cit.*,p.70, footnote 6.

25. Han Depei and Kanter, "Legal Education in China," *op. cit.*, p.581.

26. *1989 China Law Yearbook* (Zhongguo Falu Nianjian) (Beijing: Law Publishing House): 11

27. Henry Pitney, "The Role of Legal Practitioners in the People's Republic of China," *op. cit.*, p.364, footnote 230.

28. Yu Mengjia, "A General Presentation on China's Endeavor to Establish and Perfect its Legal System Since 1979," *New York Law School Journal of International and Comparative Law*, Vol.10 (1989):27-30.

29. Henry Pitney, "The Role of Legal Practitioners in the People's Republic of China," *op. cit.*, p.364.

30. Alison Connor, "Legal Education in China: A Look at Nanda," *op. cit.*, p.181.

31. Gao Xi-Ching, "Today's Legal Thinking and Its Economic Impact in China," *Law and Contemporary Problems* vol. 52 (Spring 1989): 89-115.

32. Shen Zongling, " *'Fazhi,' 'Fazhi,' 'Renzhi' de ciyi Fenxi* (An Analaysis of the meaning of Law, Rule of Law, and Rule of Man) *Faxue Yanjiu* (Studies in Law) (August 23, 1989):4-9.

33. See *1989 China Law Yearbook* (Beijing: Law Publishing House): 1057-1118, which have extensive tables of statistics and information on population, disasters and deaths, civil cases organized by substantive areas, legal periodicals, law firms, law schools including departments, and training institutes.

34. Hwa Yol Yung and Peter Jung, "The Hermeneutics of Political Ideology and Cultural Change: Maoism as the Sinicization of Marxism," *Cultural Hermeneutics* vol.3 (August 1975):168.

35. See Claude Widor, editor, *Documents on the Chinese Democratic Movement 1978-89: Unofficial Magazines and Wall Posters* (Hong Kong: The Observers Publishers, 1981, 1984); Sun Lung-Kee, *Zhongguo Wenhua de Shenceng Jiegou* (The Deep Structure of Chinese Culture) (Hong Kong: Ji Hsien Publishing

House, 1983); Su Xiaokang's *River Elegy* (1988 Chinese television series).

36. Qi Benxun, "Chuantung Wenhua yu Xiandai Yantao Gaishu" (A Summary of Research and Discussions on Traditional Culture and Modernization), *Gaoxiao Shehui Kexue* (University Social Sciences) (June 1989):73-77.

37. In celebration of the tenth anniversary of the publication of *Faxue Yanjiu* (Studies in Law), formerly *Zhengfa Yanjiu* (Politics and Law Studies) established in 1954, the Academy of Social Sciences (CASS)'s Institute of Law and *Faxue Yanjiu's* Editorial office jointly organized a conference on the reform of China's legal system. The speeches of the more than forty participants are summarized in "Zhongguo Fazhi Gaige Xueshu Taolunhui Fayan Zhaiyao" (Digest of Speeches on the Reform of the Legal System of China), *Faxue Yanjiu* (Studies in Law) (April 23, 1989):10-35.

38. See for example, Yang Ruisen, "Lun Shehui Zhuyi Minzhu Jianshe" (On the Construction of Socialist Democracy), *Gaoxiao Shehui Kexue* (University Social Sciences) (August 1989):4-8.

39. See, for example, John F. Copper, Franz Michael, and Yuan-li Wu, *Human Rights in Post-Mao China* (Boulder: Westview Press, 1985): 53.

40. James D. Seymour. *The Fifth Modernization: China's Human Rights Movement, 1978-1979* (New York: Human Rights Publishing Group, 1980): 99-105.

41. W. Gary Vause, "China's Ideological Retrenchment--Can the Economic and Legal Reforms Survive?," *George Washington Journal of International Law and Economics* vol.23 (1989):111-177, at p.176.

42. Hugh Chan, "Modern Legal Education in China," *China Law Review* vol.9, (1936):142-148. at pp.142-143; W.W. Blume, "Legal Education in China," *China Law Review* vol.1 (1923):305-311, at p.309.

43. James Krause, "Legal Education in the People's Republic of China," *Suffolk Transnational Law Journal* vol. 13 (1989):75-134, at p.88.

44. Timothy A. Gelatt and Frederick E. Snyder, "Legal Education in China: Training for a New Era," *China Law Reporter* vol.1 (1980):41-60, at pp. 56-57.

45. Han Depei and Stephen Kanter, "Legal Education in China," *op. cit.*, p.564, footnote 69.

46. *Zhongguo Falu Nianjian* (China Law Yearbook) (Beijing: Law Publishing House, 1987):17-18.

47. *1989 Law Year Book of China, op. cit.*, pp.1057-1069.

48. "Chinese law and legal education are in the midst of the most rapid and significant changes in 50 years." Randall Edwards, "An Overview of Chinese Law and Education," *op. cit.*, p.49; "China is restoring legal education and expanding it on a scale unprecedented in the ... history of the People's Republic." Gelatt and Snyder, " Legal Education in China: Training for a New Era," *op. cit.*, p.43.

49. *Ibid.*, pp.58-60.

50. Some of the standardized legal teaching texts include *Basic Theory of Law, International Law, A History of the Chinese Legal System, A Course on Criminal Procedure, Private International Law, Administrative Law, Economic Law, Marriage Law,* and *Constitutional Law.* See Han Depei and Stephen Kanter, "Legal Education in China," *op. cit.*, pp.562-563. Another set contains fourteen textbooks for on-the-job training of judicial workers. See Li Ning, "Legal Education Surges Ahead," *Beijing Review,* No. 18 (May 6, 1985):23.

51. *Ibid.*, pp.22-33 at p.23.

52. *1989 China Law Yearbook* (Zhongguo Falu Nianjian), *op. cit.*, pp. 1109-1110.

53. In 1980, the National People's Congress approved the *Provisional*

Regulations on Lawyers* (Zhonghua Renmin Gongheguo Lushi
Zhanxing Tiaoli) which were entered into force January 1,1982.
In 1986, 16,000 people took the first nationwide lawyers
qualification examination. Henry Pitney, "The Role of Legal
Practitioners in the People's Republic of China," *op. cit.*,
pp.331-332.

54. James Kraus, "Legal Education in the People's Republic of China,"
    op. cit., p. 121; R. Randall Edwards, "An Overview of Chinese
    Law and Legal Education," *op. cit.*, p.54.

55. Li Ning, "Legal Education Surges Ahead," *op. cit.*, p. 23.

56. Han Depei and Stephen Kanter, "Legal Education in China," *op.
    cit.*, p.563.

57. Timothy A. Gelatt and Frederick E. Snyder, "Legal Education in
    China: Training for a New Era," *op. cit.*, p.43, footnote 23.

58. R. Randall Edwards, "An Overview of Chinese Law and Legal
    Education," *op. cit.*, p.54

59. *Education and Science: China Handbook Series* (Beijing: Foreign
    Languages Press, 1983):111.

60. The lack of formal teacher training is similar to the situation faced
    by new American law teachers, who also criticize American
    legal education on this point.   See Sharon Hom, *American
    Legal Education Methodology in China: Teaching Notes and
    Resources, op. cit.*, p.19.

61. *Ibid.* pp.77-96.

62. See Project for the Study and Application of Humanistic Education
    in Law, *Reassessing Law Schooling* (Columbia University
    Monograph, 1980).

63. Jo Ann Boydston, editor, *The Middle Works of John Dewey(1899-
    1924), Volume 13: Essays on Philosophy, Education, and the
    Orient:1921-1922* (Carbondale: Southern Illinois University
    Press, 1988).

64. In the highly sensitive area of human rights discourse, it is a hopeful note that there are Chinese scholars who argue that, despite the label bourgeoise on the concept of human rights, human rights is the most fundamental problem for all of mankind. Although its history and origin may have its roots in western countries, the concept and significance of human rights transcends national borders. Xu Bing, "Renquan Lilun de Chansheng he Lishi Fazhan (Creation and Historical Development of a Theory of Human Rights), *Faxue Yanjiu* (Studies in Law) (June 23, 1989):1-10.

65. Sharon Hom, *American Legal Education Methodology in China: Teaching Notes and Resources, op. cit.*, p.18.

66. *The Encyclopedia of China: Law* (Zhongguo DaBaike Quanshu: Faxue) (Beijing and Shanghai: Encyclopedia of China Publishing House, 1984), Vol. I.

67. Richard H. Herman, "The Education of China's Lawyers," *op. cit.*, p.804.

68. Henry Pitney, "The Role of Legal Practitioners in the People's Republic of China," *op. cit.*, p. 369.

69. Liu Fuzhi, "We Must Exert Ourselves to Create a New Situation in Legal Education," *Fazhi Bao* (January 9, 1984):1.

70. See for example, Zhou Liren, "Danggian Jiaoxue Gaige de Tedian He Qiaoshi" (The Special Aspects and Trends of Present Educational Reform), *Jiaoyu Yanjiu* (Education Research), No.2 (February 1988). Aspects and trends in pedagogical reform include making learning scientific; unifying the goals of educational reform; developing a comprehensive and systematic design for educational reform; synthesizing curriculum design; creating a multi-dimensional teaching structure including observation, analysis of thinking and operation; regulating the training of ability and intelligence; creating a variety of teaching styles; modernizing teaching tools; standardizing the evaluation of teaching; and diversifying experimentation with educational reform.

71. Sharon Hom, *American Legal Education Methodology in China:*

Teaching Notes and Resources, op. cit., pp. 12-13.

72. R. Randall Edwards, "An Overview of Chinese Law and Legal Education," *op. cit.,* p.59.

73. At the beginning of the twentieth century, Chinese legal scholars and students studied at a wide range of institutions in the United States. According to the *Youmei Tungxue Lu* (Who's Who of American Returned Students), 53 Chinese graduated with degrees in law study from schools that included Columbia University, Yale University, Cornell University, Dartmouth College, Oberlin College, University of Pennsylvania, and Wellesley College; and seven Chinese were involved in post-graduate law study in four American law schools: University of Chicago, New York University, University of Pennsylvania, and Yale University. The Chinese who returned to China came back to take up posts as teachers in government law colleges, to take government positions in the ministries, legislatures, and courts, and to practice law. *Youmei Tungxue Lu* (Who's Who of American Returned Students) (Peking: Tsing Hua College, 1917), reprinted by Chinese Materials Center, Inc. (San Francisco, 1978).

74. For some works discussing U.S.-China educational exchanges, see Thomas Fingar and Linda Reed, *An Introduction to Education in the People's Republic of China and U.S.-China Educational Exchanges* (Washington, D.C.:U.S.-China Education Clearinghouse, 1982); The Committee on Scholarly Communication with the People's Republic of China, *A Relationship Restored: Trends in U.S.-China Educational Exchanges, 1978-1984* (Washington, D.C.: National Academy Press, 1986); Leo Orleans, *Chinese Students in America* (Washington, D.C.: National Academy Press, 1988).

75. See for example,"Zhongguo Funu Shehui Diwei Diaocha 9 Yue Jinxing" (The Investigation of the Status of Chinese Women to begin in September) *Renmin Ribao* (People's Daily), August 4, 1990; Liang Jun, "Twelve Lectures on Women," Beijing Radio, (December 1988) discussing a range of topics including: middle-aged women, women's education, women university students, the double role of women, and women cadres.

76. Hugh Chan, "Modern Legal Education in China," *op. cit.*, p.146.

77. Lois Naftulin, "The Legal Status of Women in China," *China Law Reporter* vol. 2, No.1 (1982): 57-60.

78. For a comparative analysis of the American case, see James J. White, "Women in the Law," *Michigan Law Review* vol.65 (1966):1051-1122; Richard H. Chused, "The Hiring and Retention of Minorities and Women on American Law School Faculties," *University of Pennsylvania Law Review* vol.137, no.2 (December 1988):537-569.

79. James Kraus, "Legal Education in the People's Republic of China," *op. cit.*, p.128

80. See Emily Honig and Gail Hershatter, editors, *Personal Voices: Chinese Women in the 1980's* (Stanford: Stanford University, 1988):33-36.

81. Roscoe Pound, "Comparative Law and History as Bases for Chinese Law," *Harvard Law Review* vol.61, no.5 (May 1948):749-750.

82. Wei Jingsheng, "The Fifth Modernization" in James Seymour, editor, *China's Fifth Modernization: China's Human Rights Movement, 1978-79, op. cit.*, p.47.

83. Jamake Highwater, *The Primal Mind:Vision and Reality in Indian America* (New York: Meridian Books, 1981) : xiii.

CHAPTER TWELVE

MILITARY EDUCATION AND TECHNICAL TRAINING IN CHINA

By Richard J. Latham

This chapter has two objectives. The first is to describe the basic structure and scope of military education and technical training in China's People's Liberation Army (PLA). The second is to explore the extent to which military education results in a positive spillover effect for domestic economic development and socialization. Since the early 1950s, "military-in-development" writers have argued that military organizations provide a socializing experience that contributes to social cohesion, a leadership experience that helps promote development, and technical skills necessary for economic development. Not surprisingly, Chinese military leaders and institutions share this view of military training and education.[1] During China's "decade of reform" (1979-1989), there were mounting indications, however, that some political leaders viewed the defense establishment as excessively burdensome. Chinese journals and newspapers have been engaged in an occasionally candid discussion about the burdens and benefits of defense expenditures.

Some Western literature, such as Nicole Ball's *Security and Economy in the Third World*, argues that military education and training do not necessarily lead to socially useful values, attitudes, transferable skills, and human capital formation.[2] Ball suggests that many military skills are not useful in the civilian sector; the skills of some military technicians are too advanced and narrowly focused to be useful in developing economies; most soldiers are not taught economically useful skills; soldiers do not necessarily become more politically conscious or patriotic; soldiers do not necessarily acquire leadership skills that are

316

useful in nonmilitary settings; and prolonged retention in the military may preclude a useful impact in the civilian sector. In short, she concludes that writers must prove--not merely assume--that military training and education are socially beneficial.³ In this chapter I contend that military education in China has been socially beneficial--more so now than in the past. I have not challenged any underlying assumptions regarding the legitimacy of national security, nor have I attempted to show that social benefits are greater than the financial or social costs. To do the latter necessarily involves a consideration of China's defense budgets for which there are few data regarding specific programs. I explore instead the following points or issues regarding education in the PLA:

--relevance to economic development
--transferability to the civilian sector
--availability to the civilian sector in a timely manner
--contribution to the development of leadership skills
--contribution to positive socialization
--supplement to the civilian education network

Evidence from the 1980s suggests the Chinese military establishment annually educates and trains significant numbers of Chinese. Especially since 1985, the PLA has become involved in regular occupational training for people leaving military service. The army, however, has not always been an important source of civilian-use technical skills.

Generic Aspects of Military Training and Education

Military manpower requirements are complex. The PLA has more than 2000 technical job classifications and an even larger number of distinct occupational positions.⁴ Many skills and much of the military knowledge that soldiers need are not taught in civilian secondary or post-secondary institutions. These requirements range from combat to menial or nonoccupational skills to graduate level engineering and scientific research degrees. Combat skills, in particular, which are essential to military training, are not particularly transferable to the civilian sector.

Military establishments develop skills through two processes: training and education. At times they are inseparable; normally they involve different teaching methods, venues, and objectives. In this chapter training is used to describe two general military activities:

--Combat training that involves reiterative practice with an emphasis on the use of individual skills within operational units (e.g., platoon, company, battalion).

--Technical training that involves a mixture of classroom and practical training--usually noncombative--and has a comparatively high level of vocational content. Support staffs usually receive technical training.

Military education generally includes some technical training but usually places a greater emphasis on the classroom experience as it is more concerned with literacy, quantitative skills, analytic skills, cultural and social matters, and abstract knowledge.

Militaries focus mainly on repetitive combat and support training. In the main, militaries are not structured to support ambitious education programs. Since certain minimal capability is assumed at the time military service begins, in-service military education normally is of a professional nature. Exceptions exist when civilian institutions are unable to meet the unique manpower requirements of military establishments. The primary focus of this chapter is on military education, technical-vocational training rather than combat training, and, to a lesser extent, the socialization effect of the military.

Military training and education can be divided into several categories. Elements of the following seven broad categories are found in Chinese writings although the relative emphasis placed upon specific elements varies among Chinese writers.[5]

PREPARATORY EDUCATION

Modern militaries require better educated soldiers and officers than in the past. One Chinese proponent of recruiting better educated soldiers has contended that the day of the Chinese soldier who is only concerned with "groping one's way, crawling, rolling, and shooting" has passed.[6] However military services may be unable to recruit soldiers in adequate numbers or attract officers who meet specific standards. When this occurs, one solution that is often employed is preparatory education. It may take such forms as remedial in-service education courses, secondary "prep" schools, college education taken at military schools (e.g., West Point or Annapolis in the United States), or pre-commissioning courses.

PROFESSIONAL MILITARY EDUCATION

Large military establishments also provide professional military education (PME) at various career stages. The purpose of PME is to impart knowledge and sometimes practical experiences that enhance professional competence, develop problem-solving skills and interpersonal leadership. Personnel are introduced to higher levels of professional issues and problems, which focus upon tactics, strategy, technology, civil-military relations and the military threat environment. This kind of education includes Officer Training School (OTS), leadership schools, command and staff colleges, and senior service schools (e.g., the National War College in the United States).

GRADUATE EDUCATION

As military establishments increasingly rely on advanced technologies, interact with the economic sector, and work with government officials, higher education becomes more desirable if not necessary. Militaries rarely have the resources or time to maintain a separate system of military graduate schools; hence officers routinely attend civilian institutions. In China's case, nearly all graduate education for officers is offered at military academies. Instructors from civilian colleges sometimes teach at military bases but military students do not normally obtain college degrees from the civilian schools.[7]

INSERVICE TRAINING

Military establishments provide in-service training and cross-training that ranges from refresher to advanced courses. Largely vocational in nature, in-service training upgrades and refines technical skills (e.g., mechanics, aircraft engine repairmen, health care personnel, security policemen, logistics staff members). Effective war-fighting capabilities of units can be maintained only if those units that face the possibility of suffering conflict-related casualties have redundant skills and knowledge. Cross-training also stimulates job satisfaction and provides opportunities to acquire civilian occupational skills.

PRE-DEMOBILIZATION TRAINING

There is not a close correlation between most combat skills and civilian sector manpower requirements. Militaries may provide some form of training prior to demobilization, but such training is problematic for militaries: it consumes time and resources. Because conscripts who serve for only one or two years barely have time to learn combat competency, militaries are reluctant to jeopardize combat training for single-term servicemen. In some cases though, armies may be forced to endure occupational training costs to improve recruitment and morale. It is also a necessity if political policies lead to large, unplanned force reductions. Such training helps alleviate pressures in the civilian sector where returning servicemen seek jobs.

POST-MILITARY EDUCATION

Militaries may offer educational benefits as recruiting inducements (e.g., the GI Bill education entitlements in the United States), which are normally awarded after servicemen satisfy enlistment obligations. However, militaries do not benefit directly from this education since it is received after leaving the military service. The main advantage is that armies can concentrate on military training during the brief period of military service.

SOCIALIZATION

The contention is often made that military service *passively* provides a broadening socialization experience. Soldiers, it is argued, undergo a maturation process influenced by military discipline and the social experience that derives from diversity in the barracks. Critics of this view, such as Ball, contend that it falsely assumes that all militaries provide similar disciplinary and socially diverse experiences, which is difficult to demonstrate empirically or quantitatively.[8] Militaries are sometimes used as an instrument of *active* socialization outside the military communities when the military institution and values are used as a role model or to publicize social and political values, civic responsibility, and patriotism. Since the early 1980s, for example, the PLA has been involved in a joint civil-military promotion of "spiritual civilization."[9] However, the efficacy of active socialization is not easily proven.

Military Demographics and Education

The PLA consisted of about 3.03 to 3.2 million soldiers in the late 1980s which made it the world's second largest standing army.[10] The Soviet Union has 4.258 million men under arms, while the United States has 2.12 million men and women serving in the military. The Chinese military relies on a conscript force--as does the Soviet Union--and annually inducts about 400,000 to 500,000 servicemen as compulsory service soldiers (*yiwu bing*) and officer-cadets. China has a first year eligible (eighteen years) pool of about 12.3 million males, [11] while total number of males who are annually eligible (18-22 years) is estimated to be 66,225,000.[12]

This contrasts with an annual draft age pool in the Soviet Union of only 2.3 million. For China, therefore, only about 4 to 5 per cent of eligible males actually are inducted.

The PLA also has a high ratio of officers to enlisted personnel. In early 1987 the ratio was 1 to 3.3.[13] This figure was published after the PLA completed its demobilization of at least one million servicemen. In early 1990 a Chinese military attache suggested the ratio was actually closer to one to three.[14]   This is a relatively high ratio given China's longstanding commitment to a manpower-intensive ground force associated with the PLA's People's War strategy.

There are several reasons for this phenomenon. First, the PLA lacked a noncommissioned officer (NCO) corps until 1988. All soldiers with technical skills were therefore cadres (i.e., officers). Second, the PLA had no civilian employees. As a result, a large corps of technical support personnel served as officers.

In some support branches of the PLA (e.g., logistics, education, medicine, research and development), 50-60 percent of all officers were technical cadre prior to 1988.[15] Across the board, one-third of all PLA officers in 1986 were technical as opposed to line officers.[16]

After the reintroduction of ranks in 1988, the PLA sought to restructure its personnel structure as Deng Xiaoping not only criticized military manpower imbalances, but the Chinese press also acknowledged that the structure was "out of balance and irrational."[17] The creation of a NCO corps was a controversial solution because the decision meant that some officers had their officer-technician classifications changed to less prestigious NCO designations or they were required to leave the PLA.[18]

Conscription

More than passing attention is given here to China's conscription system since it heavily determines who receives military training and education, when soldiers reenter the civilian sector, and what kind of training they are likely to receive.

According to China's Military Service Law (1984), all Chinese males age eighteen to twenty-two are eligible for conscription. Females are eligible "according to the needs of the military units," although women are not required to register. Relatively few people (no more than 4-5 per cent) successfully pass the various qualifying tests.

Prior to the decade of reform conscription was far from compulsory and in reality, there was more competition than conscription.[19]   Military service was viewed as an attractive and prestigious means of social and political mobility and while there were no guarantees, especially for single-term recruits, membership in the

Chinese Communist Party (CCP) was easier to obtain than in the civilian work place since the PLA is not constrained by the party membership quotas that exist in civilian communities and work units. In addition, compulsory servicemen with outstanding records could be extended as volunteers (*zhiyuan bing*) and have access to technical training.

Recruitment of compulsory servicemen and officer-cadets follows an annual cycle unlike many Western countries where recruitment is an ongoing, flexible process. Since autumn 1989, the beginning of the "choose, educate, conscript, accumulate" cycle was moved from spring to early fall--notably after the harvest. The winter months are used to register all eligible conscripts, conduct appropriate tests, and educate potential recruits concerning military service, obligations and benefits. In the spring local conscription offices publish a final list of conscripts.[20]

The conscription of single-term servicemen currently favors rural youths. They must have at least a junior middle school education, but exceptions are made especially in minority group areas.[21] This minimum education requirement does not necessarily contradict the PLA's quest for better educated personnel. Most jobs for ground force conscripts are not demanding and since the PLA only selects about 15 percent of conscripts to continue as NCOs, it can offer secondary education opportunities to the most promising conscripts.[22] Another underlying issue, however, is social needs of local jurisdictions that oversee recruitment and post-military service job placement. There is, in fact, a specified ratio of agriculture to non-agriculture conscripts. By relying mainly on rural farm conscripts, civilian authorities in urban areas (towns, townships, and cities) are able to lend some stability to an already difficult urban employment situation. A primary reliance on rural recruits therefore provides potential training and opportunities for 60 percent of the labor force that normally has the most constrained access to secondary education. Despite the attractions of military service to many rural youths, especially in areas with large surplus labor forces, it is necessary for areas that do not have labor surpluses to offer compensation to recruits and their families to offset lost income while in the army. In other words, there is a perception in the military as well as in Chinese society that knowledge gained in the military or even colleges is not useful in making money. As one youthful Chinese cynic observed, "Knowledge is devaluated."[23] The window of age eligibility was extended by a year in 1989 for nonagricultural youths. Ostensibly this permitted the PLA to recruit more mature conscripts with higher educational levels. Since there is a mandated ratio of agricultural and nonagricultural conscripts--at least in some provinces--the PLA appears constrained as to how many urban youths it can actually induct each year.[24]   Single-term recruits--the American equivalent of "GI's"--serve for three (army) or four (navy and air force) years. The PLA and government officials are sensitive to the need not to keep conscripts out of the civilian work force too long so the PLA annually conscripts between 400,000 and 500,000 soldiers--and demobilizes a similar number.[25]   As basic recruits they fill the least technical jobs, and in ground force units they are trained to be combatants. Normally those troops are the least likely to acquire transferable civilian skills. Compared to non-conscripted rural youths, however, even minimal training as a truck driver or a small machine operator provides an enormous advantage compared to totally unskilled rural workers.[26]

Conscription is based on quotas assigned to geographical areas such as counties and cities. This area-based method results in some recruiting problems and rigidities. For instance, some areas are hard pressed to meet their quotas because the local economy absorbs most labor. In those areas conscription offices may often send substandard recruits to the PLA. In areas that have surplus labor the competition to join the army can be so intense that recruiters have sometimes accepted bribes or favors to admit certain individuals. Capable people who exceed the quota in one district cannot be counted against another district's quota. The current recruiting ratio that favors rural recruits further disadvantages urban youths who probably have a better education. Whether intended or not, the area quota system promotes some regional diversity in a country that struggles with powerful regional tendencies. The current method also ensures a dispersion of access to possible training, education and Party membership.[27]

Volunteers: Beyond Conscription

China has a small noncommissioned officer (NCO) corps that consists of volunteers. Beginning in the 1980s, the PLA began to rationalize duties and ranks and by 1988, a more clearly differentiated stratum of mid-level soldiers with NCO ranks and duties was evident. Conscripts who have become specialized or technical cadres by virtue of their training are permitted to remain in the PLA beyond the maximum five year service limit for conscripts. Their subsequent terms of service will be at least an additional 8 years and a maximum of 12 years--provided they have not passed their thirty-fifth birthday. Provisions exist for continued service based upon the needs of the military units.

The Chinese have not released statistics on the size of the NCO force, but status as a volunteer is particularly attractive. It virtually assures the service member of CCP membership, comparatively advanced technical skills, some degree of cadre or managerial status, and reentry into the civilian sector while still comparatively young. In terms of transferable skills and human capital formation, the PLA's NCO corps may represent the military's most important educational contribution to the civilian sector. These soldiers not only are the beneficiaries of extensive vocational training, but their terms of service permit them to return to the civilian sector during their most productive years.

A Large Officer Corps

A one-to-three ratio of officers to conscripts means the PLA has roughly 900,000 officers. Each year the PLA trains and educates an estimated 35,000 to 40,000 officer-cadets, and assuming a stable manpower force after the 1985-1987 demobilization, a similar number of servicemen also retire each year. Chinese writers often view the PLA officer corps as consisting of two general categories: command cadres or officers (*zhihui ganbu*) and technical cadres or officers (*jishu ganbu*). [28] Commanders are line officers whose responsibilities are to lead combatants, command ships, or command flight operations. With the PLA's relatively recent emphasis on higher officer educational attainment, line officers increasingly have acquired technical expertise or college degrees. There is, however, a pronounced difference between line and technical officers. Line officers can acquire technical experience, but technical officers are unlikely to command combatants. Indeed, until the mid-1980s, at all levels of the PLA, the average educational level of conscripts was higher than that of officers (cadres).[29]

Although technical officers generally do not become commanders of combatant units, they are the backbone of support services such as logistics, medicine, engineering, research and development, and maintenance. Their skill levels are varied. At the lower end are technicians, while the upper end includes engineers, scientists and a new breed of defense intellectuals.

And, the proportion of technically trained officers has continued to increase. In 1977, for example, only 27.8 per cent of officers consisted of technical cadres but by 1986, the proportion had increased to more than 33 per cent. Still, a Chinese author has contrasted China's ratio with a 50 per cent ratio in the Soviet Union's military.[30] The new PLA emphasis on a technically modern army partially explains the increase in technical officers. In actuality, the large demobilization after 1985, which involved the paring off of the People's Armed Police, the PLA Railway Engineering Corps and other units, had an equally important bearing on the higher proportion of technically trained officers because the latter units were heavily manned with relatively unskilled manpower.

Officer training and education take place in a variety of ways and defense reforms have placed increased emphasis on college-level education for officers. Because the PLA has an extensive system of secondary and tertiary institutions, most officers receive their advanced education at military academies. Approximately 160 military academies trained one million commanders and technical officers between 1949 and 1978. This figure represents an average of 34,000 officers per year. Since 1979 and following a 12 per cent downsizing of the military officer education system, slightly more than 100 academies have graduated 400,000 cadets and officers.[31] With fewer institutions and faculty, the yearly average was increased to 40,000. The increase apparently reflects the beginning of regular retirements due to the ageing of the pre-Liberation (1949) and Korean War era officer corps. Equally important, newly enacted laws in the 1980s set mandatory retirement ages. The advent of regularized retirements meant the PLA could begin to think in terms of a rational flow of personnel through various phases of education and training.

The educational attainment of basic level (platoon and company) officers has also risen. This is the entry level for line officers who, in most cases, are drawn from the ranks. In 1980, 56.9 percent of the basic level officers had a junior high school education or less. By 1987 this figure dropped to only 8 per cent. Conversely, officers with a high school or tertiary education rose from 34.1 to 64.4 per cent. The figure for people with "still higher education" increased from 9 to 27.6 per cent.[32] In early 1987, 97 per cent of platoon and company officers had a high school education, while one in six line officers above the grass-roots level was a university graduate.[33] A further long-term emphasis is being placed on increasing the proportion of line officers with college level educations.

These changes have been accomplished in several ways. First, the PLA has changed recruitment standards and officer selection policies. This approach alone can produce a positive upward shift in the statistical data without any expansion of PLA education programs. Second, the Central Military Commission in 1984 authorized a substantial increase in funding for military education. Because per capita funding for education is quite low in China, such funding was especially necessary to "jump start" the military education system that essentially had been moribund for more than a decade. Third, the PLA has encouraged serving military officers to pursue advanced education through evening classes, correspondence schools and self-study.[34] In terms of the relationship between educational attainment and the opportunity to become an officer, there is a significant social implication: recruits from the non-agriculture sectors with higher entry level educations (i.e., about 20 per cent of the annual conscripts) will be more likely than rural youths to become officers as long as higher education standards are emphasized. This will be an important change--if it is maintained--from the era of an officer corps that more closely reflected the social background of rural than urban China. The trend can be attenuated, of course, by giving priority to rural conscripts for further in-service education.

The PLA is seeking bright high school graduates by offering college educations at military academies prior to their being commissioned as officers. Candidates compete for limited positions in the nationwide annual college entrance examination as the PLA annually reserves about 15 per cent of its seats in tertiary military schools for direct civilian entrants. In some instances, the PLA uses direct entry quotas to attract students to majors in hard to fill fields such as marine engineering. Because there are limited opportunities to attend civilian colleges, the PLA academies represent at least a small expansion of tertiary education opportunities. Unlike many Western countries, the PLA has not faced a serious outflow of educated talent, nor has it been an unwelcome competitor for China's best and brightest. The state-controlled system of manpower distribution and a regulated compensation system reduce the civil-military competition for educated personnel. In spite of these factors though, the PLA has acknowledged that it nonetheless experiences a net outflow of college-educated talent.[35]

It is easier to enter a PLA academy after joining the military than trying to enter directly from high school. Of the 400,000 officer-cadets educated between 1980 and 1986, 320,000 were already serving in the PLA. Only 70,000 or 17.5 per cent were directly recruited from high schools. Slightly more than 1.5 per cent (5,000) entered directly from civilian colleges and universities over the six year period.[36] In 1988, the PLA accepted 5,400 high school graduates for direct entry into 48 military schools and academies.[37] Concurrently, the PLA intended to recruit 30,000 officer-cadets for additional education from within the ranks of the PLA.[38] The educational emphasis--for the policy reasons stated above--was on expanding secondary rather than tertiary education.

Overall, by 1988 the annual number of entering officer-cadets was down by one-third (35,000 officer-cadets per year) compared to the annual average (53,333) between 1980 and 1986. To continue raising the general educational level of officers, especially at the platoon and company levels, there was a policy-mandated emphasis in 1988 on priority secondary education for those officers with junior high school educations.

The PLA's Military Education Structure

The PLA has not publicly published a thorough description of its military education system. The *Military Training Handbook*, a Chinese-language publication, devotes a scant two pages to the subject and identifies only about 20 institutions.[39] The two military volumes of *The Great Chinese Encyclopedia* (1989) are even less informative.[40] Lonnie D. Henley's "Officer Education in the Chinese PLA" is the best study in English and it contains an annotated list of more than one hundred PLA educational institutions as well as a detailed description of PLA officer education.[41]

The PLA educational system is composed of two main subsystems: (1) specialized technical academies and schools and (2) command-officer schools and academies. The technical institutions--a broad use of the word--form a five-tier network:
--secondary specialized training/education
--education/training equivalent to specialized colleges

--education/training equivalent to regular universities
--graduate level education (M.A.)
--graduate level education (Ph.D.)[42]
The professional officer training or command-officer schools and academies comprise a three-tier network:
--primary command/leadership training
--intermediate command/leadership training
--higher command education
Military education does not come under rigid, centralized PLA control. Some schools are administered by the Ministry of National Defense's General Staff Department while others are subordinate to the General Logistics Department or the General Political Department. Still other schools and academies belong to the Service branches. The PLA Air Force (PLAAF), for example, has 26 such schools, but it does not control a number of major aeronautical engineering colleges that come under direct General Staff Department control.

TECHNICAL TRAINING

Education in the PLA is generally synonymous with the education of the officer corps. It is now conducted at slightly more than 100 institutions. Between 1951 and 1953, the PLA quickly established 107 schools and academies and with Soviet assistance, that total increased to more than 160 by 1958. Published Chinese sources claim that from 1966 to 1976 the system was largely inoperative. By 1979 the PLA began to revitalize its education system. Following three major work conferences on military education in the mid-1980s, the number of institutions was reduced by 12 percent to about 100 institutions; faculty and staff were cut by 20 percent. Although systemically smaller, PLA educators felt they had a more responsive and effective system.[43] Additionally, in 1984 the CCP Central Military Commission increased funding for military education (1985-1990) by US$ 320 million.

Approximately 48 military academies (*yuan*) participate in the tertiary education of officers and cadets while technical schools (*xiao*) provide largely secondary and technical (i.e., vocational) training. Sometimes a single PLA institution is responsible for in-service, secondary, and tertiary programs. The PLA has identified over 2,000 "specialized tasks" and several thousand "technical assignments." These categories, which are similar to "specialty codes" or "military occupational specialties" in the U.S. military services, are used to associate ranks with duties as well as determine the education/training requirements for jobs.[44] Since the opportunities for vocational-technical training in China are few, graduates of these technical schools traditionally have enjoyed officer or cadre status.

PROFESSIONAL MILITARY EDUCATION

Professional military education (PME) for officers consists of tri-level command training and education.[45] The purpose of these schools is to cultivate professional competence as leaders of soldiers and combat units.

The PLA officer corps formerly could be divided into three main personnel or career tracks: line officers, political officers and technical officers although western analysis has not emphasized the technical officer career track. Historically, this division was based mainly on the pursuit of separate education tracks. Today, the education of political and technical officers comes under the purview of the "technical system," while line officers are generally educated in the "command academy system." What remains unclear is the extent of assignment crossovers between the line and technical officer hierarchies. In other words, are technical officers largely excluded from command assignments? The PLA points to cases of college graduates serving as combatant commanders and pilots, but the extent to which this practice is common is unclear and the emphasis on obtaining a college education for all new officers may blur the earlier basis of distinction between line and technical officers (i.e., education).

The PLAAF Engineering College in Xi'an is PLAAF's equivalent of the U.S. Air Force Academy in terms of status. It is the PLAAF's premier officer-cadet college, but its graduates are technical officers. A majority of them will not become line officers, whereas graduates of military academies in the United States not only have technical degrees but are encouraged to seek command opportunities. Graduates of the Engineering College as a rule will not be pilots. Officer-cadets who "wash out" of pilot training can, however, complete college degrees at the Engineering College or other PLAAF schools before becoming technical officers.[46]

The three-level command-officer training system prepares officers to command troops at three different levels of responsibility during their careers. At the primary command schools the officer-students are platoon and company commanding officers (i.e., lieutenants and captains). Training emphasizes leadership and specialized and advanced combat skills.[47]

Future line promotions are now contingent upon attendance at intermediate and advanced PME schools. For the intermediate command schools the officer-students are selected from battalion level officers (majors and lieutenant colonels) and selectees must have previously attended a junior level school. Officers receive advanced professional education to prepare them for higher levels of leadership responsibility. The meld of education and specialized training is unclear, but the emphasis is on military and leadership competence.

Senior or "higher command" academies accept officer-students selected from candidates at and above the division level (colonel and senior colonel) who are offered a "comprehensive education of a higher level."[48]

The social transfer benefits of professional military education are intangible. Retired officers ideally are more informed and--to use the Chinese jargon--more likely to "understand the all around situation" than civilian cadres with no comparable leadership training. These officers can fill senior and middle management positions, but their reentry into the civilian sector normally comes well past their most productive years. Until the 1980s, with the introduction of a mandatory retirement age, reentry into the civilian work force was not a normally anticipated event. Additionally, senior military cadres were not always welcomed in civilian organizations where they were given higher level jobs than local employees who had been waiting for promotions.[49]

The National Defense University

By PLA accounts the capstone to its three-tier command-officer education system is the National Defense University (NDU) located near Beijing's Western Hills. The PLA's NDU provides military education for commanders at or above the rank of group army commander, senior

staff officer, or senior military research officer (i.e., general officers).[50]
It is different from the U.S. "senior military schools," such as the
Department of Defense's National War College (NWC) or Industrial
College of the Armed Forces (ICAF), where lieutenant colonels and
colonels attend one-year courses and general officers usually attend a
six-week Capstone Course.[51] Conversely, PLA general officers may
spend a year or more at their NDU.

The PLA's NDU opened in September 1986 with 400 to 550
student-officers. It not only teaches general officers, but the school is
one of the premier loci of research and writing about military strategy,
doctrine and key defense issues. A separate institution located near
NDU--the PLA Academy of Military Sciences (AMS)--also conducts
important policy research. Unlike the NDU, the AMS does not teach
military courses; it concentrates on matters such as policy, doctrine, and
strategy.[52]

The NDU currently has at least five functional areas or
departments: the Defense Research Department, the Basic Military
Science Department, the Refresher Course Department, the Postgraduate
Institute, and the Teacher Training Program.[53] The university is chartered
to fulfill the following objectives:

--Provide professional military education for high level military
and civilian leaders

--Maintain a curriculum of more than 100 course offerings

--Conduct policy research for the PLA and Central Military
Commission

--Offer a Masters Degree program in military science and
national security

--Publish national security research

--Train defense policy instructors for PLA academies

--Prepare a five-year military science research program[54]

The school's Scientific Research Department is its think-tank.[55]
In 1986 nearly 80 full-time researchers were working in several
subordinate institutes (e.g., Strategic Research Institute, Army Building
Research Institute, Marxism Research Institute).[56] This department has
been responsible for the publication of an influential series of books and
papers about national security and defense strategy.[57] Indeed, the
National Defense University Press rivals the People's Liberation Army
Press and surpasses the AMS Press in volume and scope of publicly
available defense-related publications.

Higher Education

PLA academies not only offer undergraduate degrees, but they have begun to confer graduate degrees, too. In 1988, for example, 22 PLA academies offered masters degrees in 212 departments or specialties. Doctorates were offered at 10 military institutions in 54 specialties and departments.[58] Still other military units have been authorized to teach courses that can be used as credit at degree-granting institutions.[59] Military involvement in postgraduate education is indicative of the "large and complete" mentality that exists throughout China, a mind-set that prompts organizations to seek autonomy and self-sufficiency. Unlike the Chinese case, most developed Western nations rely principally on civilian institutions as their sources of undergraduate and advanced academic degrees.

Reentry Education

In *Security and Economy in the Third World*, Nicole Ball challenges the popularly held view that militaries in developing countries are an important source of spillover benefits (including education) for economic development.[60] Prior to China's massive demobilization in 1985, the transferability content of PLA education and training had not been a problem since PLA academies had taught little more than political ideology. The low civilian skill content of training was irrelevant because there were minimal economic demands for technical expertise: political expertise was deemed sufficient.

As a spin-off of the CCP's decision to pursue economic modernization, attention was focused on securing reentry jobs for PLA soldiers--especially as a large-scale demobilization was becoming a reality. Chinese commentators attribute to Deng Xiaoping the initial impetus to explore ways to create transferable job skills for PLA soldiers. In December 1977, when Deng was China's de facto leader and Chairman of the CCP's Central Military Commission, he made employment and skills development for soldiers a top agenda item for the Party, government and military.[61] Since Deng's comments predated

by several years the actual 1985 demobilization, the demobilization itself
was not the catalyst for the change in policy. The employability of
returning conscripts amid the national push for economic development
was a problem in its own right. The establishment of a mandatory
retirement age for military cadre also meant that officers would reenter
the civilian economy in larger numbers and at earlier ages. Thus, the
PLA had almost no experience in planning for the *systematic* reentry of
soldiers into the civilian economy.

It is therefore not surprising that the 1985 demobilization was
difficult for the PLA as well as for civilian government agencies and
economic entities since the civilian institutions had to find jobs for
trained and untrained, demobilized recruits and officers who had been
forced to retire. The PLA discovered that the lack of planning that
accompanied the demobilization of 1985 had a backlash effect for the
criticism and comments of disenchanted "unemployable soldiers" created
problems related to recruitment, education, training and morale.

As China became more wrapped up in the spirit of reform and
economic invigoration, military service became a comparatively less
attractive option for draft age youths in some parts of China. There
were complaints that military service was less appealing from a personal
and family financial standpoint; it disrupted families and life styles;
Party membership was less relevant or useful; and the public no longer
regarded soldiers with respect. Soldiers sometimes complained that
skills learned before military service were not utilized while in the
army. Still others argued that retirement or involuntary demobilization
placed them at an economic disadvantage when they returned to civilian
life.[62]

Dual-Purpose Personnel

The PLA solution to these issues, which began to be
experimentally employed in the late 1970s, was decentralized, pre-
demobilization vocational training. Typically, it passed through several
years of experimentation. Civilian units or companies sometimes had
previously offered post-demobilization training, but civilian government
officials felt this method was inadequate. The new approach
emphasized an unprecedented element of PLA responsibility. By the
early 1980s regional programs became more standardized. Eventually
the catch-phrase became "dual-purpose personnel" (*liangyong rencai*).

The term meant that soldiers received military training as well as the opportunity to learn practical civilian skills. It was not until February 1986, however, that the State Council and Central Military Commission officially confirmed the importance of vocational job training for soldiers while they were still in the army,[63] and it was the Nanjing Military Region, that pioneered many of the practices that eventually were adopted nationwide.[64]

Chief among PLA concerns that delayed a central government endorsement of vocational training was apprehension that military training would be or was being undermined. Dual-purpose training was a contentious issue in the PLA. Only slightly less controversial was the problem of finding teaching resources, materials, funding and instructional facilities.[65]

The vocational training offered in the Nanjing Military Region was illustrative of the general PLA response to these issues. First, a distinction was made between officers and soldiers. Greater emphasis was placed on soldiers with lower educational levels who would be the most difficult to place in post-military jobs. Second, an assessment was made as to the extent of transferable civilian skills in each military job classification. As transferable content decreased, the length of civilian job training increased. Third, recruits who enlisted for longer periods (i.e., volunteers) were given proportionally more job training. Fourth, soldiers who failed to perform satisfactorily in military training were not permitted to participate in civilian job training. Finally, and quite significantly, civilian job training was given to conscripts with two and one-half years of service. They received the training during the first four months of the annual training cycle, which was when new conscripts received basic military training,[66] coming however, near the end of their tours of duty.

Military cadres (officers) usually took classes that prepared them for civilian management jobs. Although the issue is not raised explicitly in Chinese sources, some officers may have been hard to place in civilian jobs. Since a high percentage of officers had lower education levels than conscripts, they were poorly prepared to assume technical or management jobs. Concurrently, given their cadre status, they were not likely to want vocational training if it meant a loss of social status.

Statistical data about dual-purpose training are frequently cited in the Chinese press, but they are incomplete and often inconsistent. They are useful in gaining an order of magnitude idea of the scope of military vocational training however. The training is actually part of a two-stage process: vocational training in the PLA followed by placement by local Civil Affairs offices.

8,400 military training centers were established throughout the country, and civilian-run placement and service centers were established in 1,959 of China's 2,000 counties and major municipalities.[67] In 1985, 900,000 servicemen received at least one form of civilian job training.[68] However, the figure for 1986 dropped to 565,000, apparently reflecting the number of soldiers who would have been routinely demobilized that year. It also was indicative at that time of a general social trend of waning interest in education.[69] After 1986, Chinese sources published cumulative data, and in late 1989, China Daily's total figures for dual-purpose training distinguished between participants and actual graduates. Thus, six million servicemen took part in dual-purpose training between 1979 and 1989, but only 2.6 million actually received graduation certificates.[70]

Dual-purpose training was an ambitious initiative to help solve a difficult civilian labor problem. On the whole it was successful, but it also encountered problems. First, the quality of the training was not uniformly consistent. Some soldiers still needed additional post-demobilization training in the receiving units. Other soldiers simply could not be placed in suitable jobs, because they failed to acquire skills even after undergoing training. Second, the attrition rate was high. Conscripts often lacked the motivation or interest to learn technical skills. Others held the view that education was of "little value in making money."[71] In one military region one out of three participants failed to complete the training program.[72] The nationwide completion rate in 1986 was about 40 per cent, but the average rate between 1979 and 1989 was 43 per cent.[73] Third, demobilized soldiers did not necessarily use their vocational training. About one in five became local leaders (cadres) rather than practicing technicians; only about 13 percent took technical (vocational) jobs in villages and townships; and about 25 percent returned to farming.[74]

By late 1987, dual-purpose training had all the earmarks of becoming a permanent part of the PLA's training cycle. Although the content, scope and methods of the decentralized program varied from unit to unit, the PLA was committed in principle, if not fact, to an "integrated army-civilian training program" by 1987. If the program is permanently adopted, it will mean as much as a 17 percent reduction in combat training time for conscripts. Conversely, it has the annual potential to provide vocational training opportunities for 400,000 to 500,000 demobilizing conscripts and an estimated 35,000-40,000 NCO and officer retirees.

By and large, PLA and civilian officials have expressed satisfaction with the program. Military units conduct periodic surveys of former soldiers to ascertain the success of the program and its responsiveness to local needs,[75] and the prospect of vocational training for youths who otherwise would be unlikely to have access to such training has boosted recruitment in some areas. In Zhejiang's Wenzhou prefecture, for example, where recruitment has always been difficult, there were 100,000 applications in 1986 to fill the recruitment quota of 2,000 conscripts.[76] Job satisfaction among recruits while in the PLA also is said to have improved. Supporters of dual-purpose job training claim this is because soldiers are less anxious about post-military employment problems.[77] Finally, dual-purpose personnel claim it has been easier for them to obtain employment than otherwise would have been the case. In most cases the major apprehension of rural conscripts from economically backward areas is that they will have to return to traditional farming.[78]

Military Training at Civilian Institutions

China's 1984 Military Service Law mandates military training for students of schools of higher learning and senior middle schools [79] (a similar program briefly existed between 1955 and 1957). The Ministry of Education and Ministry of National Defense introduced a pilot program (1985-1987) at 69 colleges and universities and 104 senior middle schools with approximately 100,000 participating students.

There are two broadly stated purposes for introducing military training during the first two years of civilian post-secondary education. The overriding objective is to strengthen the manpower base for the army's reserve force. Some college students who show an aptitude and interest in military service may be selected to serve as officers in the PLA's reserve forces. The second objective is to develop patriotic attitudes, a sense of organization, and high standards of discipline.[80] For some Chinese the second objective was unsettling. It evoked memories of the PLA's political role in society during the early 1970s. In *Concepts for China's National Defense* the author defends the program. He cites the example of defense education and training in Switzerland for the Chinese, like Swiss citizens, he argues, should have a civic obligation to support national security.[81]

In the aftermath of the Tiananmen violence (June 1989), military training at universities drew critical comments when the training was extended to 150 campuses. In reality this action had been planned well before June 1989. Subsequently, the expansion of college level military training was incorrectly associated with martial law. The fact that Beijing University students spent the 1989-1990 year at the Shijiazhuang Army Academy further fueled doubts about the objectives of military training in college.[82] The participation of the PLA in events in or near Tiananmen Square will have a negative effect on the effectiveness of the PLA as an active agent of socialization, but the consequences for the PLA's reserve program are less evident in the near-term because the initial participants will not have graduated until after 1989.

Active Socialization: The Defense Education Campaign

When Deng Xiaoping announced that China faces a period of extended peace rather than imminent war, his comments underscored a major shift in China's strategic assumptions about the international environment. In part the reassessment of the threats to security was a maneuver to justify reduced defense spending. There was no intention, however, to undermine the legitimacy of China's defense establishment. But amid the excitement of domestic reform, senior government, PLA and CCP leaders soon faced the phenomenon of growing indifference and even criticism regarding the relevance of national security. For the first time since 1949 the PLA was faced with defending its reputation, mission, and budget. Relatively open policy debates ensued regarding the appropriate size of a large standing army, weapons procurement and defense spending.

Additionally, army commentators openly acknowledged that the growth of "apathy toward defense" was at least partially the result of a "damaged image of the army" that was self-induced.[83] Another writer for the PLA's *Liberation Army Daily* accurately noted that some of the "defense apathy" sprung from erroneously "equating the army with national defense." National defense, he observed, involves much more than the instruments of force. The analysis reflected a new sophistication that was appearing in Chinese national security debates in the 1980s.[84]

In November 1987, then Party Secretary Zhao Ziyang told the CCP's 13th National Party Congress that "national defense education should be strengthened to enhance the people's concept of national defense."[85] Zhao's call to enhance "defense education" provoked heated discussions at the Congress. The inclusion of the defense education issue in Zhao's speech seemed out of character for the leading advocate of reform. Zhao's statement conjured up images of traditional propaganda work. Reformists usually took the position that such propaganda movements detracted from economic development and subsequent interviews with PLA delegates revealed that defense education was indeed a simmering issue. In the words of one delegate, there is a "problem of a weakened concept of national defense among some people, especially youth." In his view the consequences were clear: "If no national defense education is carried out and things are allowed to take their own course, the building of the Army will suffer. So will the national construction effort."[86]

Zhao's willingness to support a defense education movement reflected a longstanding concern of Chinese leaders across a broad spectrum of views on reform. They shared a common interest in cultivating a sense of national pride and civic responsibility. Defense education was a way of focusing national attention on the need for patriotism, national interests, and social discipline without the public rejecting the message as mere Party propaganda. Zhao's support represented official CCP approval to undertake an initiative that Defense Minister Zhang Aiping had less formally advocated at least one year earlier. Noting that China still faced genuine threats to its national security, Zhang warned against "putting the weapons back in the arsenal and letting the war horses graze on the hillside."[87] Zhang, of course, was not so much worried about patriotism as he was concerned that the Chinese public should understand the enduring nature of national security.

With the Party's blessing, 1987 marked the beginning of CCP and PLA efforts to publicize the peacetime requirements of national defense. Fundamentally, defense education or awareness was a program to raise the sensitivity of the Chinese public to defense issues. Although it was not self-evident, the initiation of defense education in the public arena signaled an important change in the relationship of the army to the Chinese public. For the first time China's defense establishment had to defend its existence and effectively compete for public support: support no longer was something that could be assumed.

National defense education appears to have evolved into an annual summer propaganda campaign. Even in 1988 editorials observed that leaders in some areas had already resorted to "the old method of 'raising a big fanfare'" and then dropping the issue.[88] Initially there were positive benefits. The most obvious was publicizing new laws regarding military service, conscription, post-military employment, the new reserve system, and military welfare issues (e.g., public treatment of soldiers, housing, education, and employment for dependents). There was little evidence between 1987 and 1990 to demonstrate that national defense education visibly changed public views about national security, and if the program enjoyed initial success, the June 1989 events at Tiananmen Square were bound to dilute it. The claim of one provincial authority that national defense education was "systematic socio-engineering" was indicative of the overly ambitious aspirations of some leaders. The campaign never achieved such grandiose objectives.[89]

Conclusion

PLA leaders are pleased with the successes of their military education and training reforms. The PLA moved from the "mass classroom" approach that mainly stressed political indoctrination to a more regularized and structured system of training and education. In terms of the six central issues outlined at the beginning of this chapter, the analysis here suggests the PLA's assessment is generally accurate.

Several caveats are in order. First, many of the positive achievements are the result of changes in PLA training and education only since the early 1980s. Second, the opportunities for military education vary depending on one's status in the PLA (i.e., conscript, NCO, officer). Third, opportunities vary according to the needs of the PLA and demobilization pressures. The PLA can regulate education opportunities to meet policy (military or civilian) objectives.

This study set out to examine military education as a contributing factor in economic and social development. An underlying premise was that to be of value in a broader study of Chinese education, it is necessary to demonstrate or disprove the social and economic relevance of military education. In the case of the PLA's education system, it provides extensive training to a largely conscript force. Higher education is also provided through an in-house system of colleges. The dual-purpose training program specifically aims to teach economically useful skills to conscripts and officers (to a lesser extent). There appears to be a reasonable and timely flow of personnel back into the civilian sector. This is due to the use of a conscript system and the return of NCOs during their most economically productive years. Officers, who normally return to the civilian sector relatively late in life, are largely past the peak years when they can contribute to the economy.

The PLA is strong in imparting leadership, organizational skills, and political savvy to officers and NCOs. Because the underlying thread in management involves Party leadership methods and style, there is probably less disparity between Chinese civil and military leadership styles than is found in Western societies. It is hard to measure the success or failure of socialization. Manifestations of passive socialization, for example, are more evident among NCOs and officers than conscripts. Presumably, however, most military cadres probably demonstrated desirable social and political behavior before they were given leadership positions. It is equally difficult to assess the success of active socialization programs. They are probably most effective in disseminating information. The PLA seems to feel that such programs at least have some effect on compliance--even if actual values do not change. Finally, the PLA has shifted toward greater interaction with the civilian education system. The PLA education system supplements rather than competes with civilian secondary and tertiary schools. Perhaps the PLA's greatest educational strength is providing secondary and vocational education for rural youths who otherwise would not have the opportunity to obtain such education.

The role of education in the PLA has undergone significant changes in the last decade. There is a decided emphasis on higher educational attainment. There also is a definite intention to move away from the peasant army of the 1940s and the political army of the 1960s and 1970s. The emphasis on developing transferable civilian skills adds a new mission to the PLA. It is a mission that will continue to be a source of dissatisfaction for some commanders who feel vocational training detracts from the primary mission of training combat effective troops.

Notes

1. See "Dangdai Zhongguo" Editorial Department, *Dangdai Zhongguo Jundui Qunzhong Gongzuo* (China Today: The Mass Work of the Chinese Army) (Beijing: China Social Science Press, 1988); hereafter *China Today*.

2. Nicole Ball, *Security and Economy in the Third World* (Princeton, N.J.: Princeton University Press, 1988): 295-334.

3. *Ibid.*, pp. 148-149.

4. *Xinhua* (New China News Agency) (Beijing, August 31, 1986), in *Foreign Broadcast Information Service* (FBIS), *Daily Report: China* (Arlington, Virginia: National Technical Information Service, September 2, 1986): K8; hereafter cited as *Xinhua* and *FBIS*.

5. Mi Zhenyu, *Zhongguode Guofang Gouxing* (Concepts for China's National Defense) (Beijing: PLA Press, 1988): 169.

6. *Xinhua* (July 27, 1986) in *FBIS* (July 29, 1986): K3.

7. *China Today*, pp. 564-565.

8. Ball, *op. cit.*, pp. 325-330.

9. Jiang Siyi, editor, *Zhongguo Renmin Jiefangjun Zhengzhi Gongzuo Jiaocheng* (A Course in PLA Political Work) (Beijing: National Defense University Press, 1986): 234-250.

10. Editorial Group of the Changsha Military Engineering Academy (Hunan Military District), *Jun Xun Shouce* (Military Training Handbook) (Changsha: Hunan Education Press, May 1988): 109; hereafter cited as *Military Training Handbook*. The International Institute for Strategic Studies (IISS) estimates that the size of the PLA in 1989 was only 3,030,000. See *The Military Balance 1989-1990* (London: IISS, 1989): 145-149.

11. Central Intelligence Agency, *The World Factbook 1989* (Washington, D.C.: US Government Printing Office, May 1989):61-62.

12. *The Military Balance 1989-1990*, *op. cit.*, p. 145. The term "officer-cadet" is not used in China. It is used here to distinguish between entry level officers, some of whom are only cadets, and officer-students who are enrolled in command schools or advanced degree programs.

13. *Xinhua* (December 25, 1986) in (*FBIS*, December 29, 1986):K16.

14. Interview, Washington, D.C., January 1990.

15. *Xinhua* (June 24, 1988) in *FBIS-CHI-88-124* (June 28, 1988):24.

16. *FBIS* (September 2, 1986): K8.

17. *Xinhua* (July 27, 1986), in *FBIS* (July 29, 1986): K4.

18. *FBIS* (December 29, 1986): K16.

19. Harvey Nelson, *The Chinese Military System*, 2nd edition, (Boulder, Colorado: Westview Press, 1981):18.

20. "Questions, Answers on Military Conscription Work," *Jilin Ribao* (Changchun) (October 18, 1989): 1, in *Joint Publications Research Service: China* (Arlington, Virginia: National Technical Information Service) *JPRS-CAR-89-119* (December 19, 1989): 51; hereafter *JPRS-CAR*.

21. *JPRS-CAR-89-119* (December 19, 1989): 51.

22. PLA General Political Department, *Zhongguo Jundui: Xin Junxian Zhishi Wenda* (The Army of China: Questions and Answers about New Military Ranks) (Beijing: Changcheng Press, 1989): 11.

23. Zhong Jie, "The Dropout Phenomenon Is Disturbing," *Jiefangjun Bao* (Beijing) (November 27, 1988):1, in *FBIS-CHI-88-240* (December 14, 1988):30.

24. *JPRS-CAR-89-119* (December 19, 1989): 51.

25. Nelsen, *The Chinese Military System*, *op. cit.*, p. 21. Nelsen cites

the annual number of demobilized conscripts as 500,000 in 1981.

26. A Beijing resident related to the author the post-demobilization problems his brothers faced in the early 1980s. The younger brother, who had been trained as a truck driver, was immediately able to find work. The older and better educated brother, who was a cadre in an artillery unit, waited almost a year before being given suitable work. Family members joked that it was better to have a vocation than be a cadre (officer). Conversation with author, July 1981.

27. The concept of "dispersed access" does not necessarily mean that conscripts are intentionally assigned far from their families. Conscripts are likely to serve within the Military Region from which they were conscripted, although not necessarily near their families. It is necessary, of course, to send some soldiers to remote areas and border regions with low population densities. Dispersed access simply means that the burden--or opportunity--of military service is geographically allocated. Changing this method involves socio-political as well as defense policy issues.

28. The term "cadre" (*ganbu*) is still used by many Chinese writers interchangeably with the conventional term for "officer" (*junguan*). The use of the word cadre reflects the absence of military ranks between 1965 and 1988. In its continued usage in military circles, it connotes not only leadership but administrative status; thus writers often refer to NCOs (*shibing*) as cadres. While NCOs do not enjoy the higher status of officers, they still are accorded cadre status which is meaningful and useful outside the PLA. For a discussion of NCO duties see *Zhongguo Jundui*, *op. cit.*, pp. 13-15.

29. Yu Daqing, Wang Changlin, and Wang Xiaofu, *Junshi Rencaixue Gailun* (Introduction to the Study of Military Talent) (Hubei People's Press and Hubei Science and Technology Press, 1986):152.

30. *Xinhua* (August 31, 1986) in *FBIS*, (September 2, 1986): K8-9.

31. *Xinhua* (July 7, 1987) in *JPRS-CAR-87-140*, p. 95; Mi Zhenyu,

> *Zhongguode Guofang Gouxing, op. cit.,* p. 152. Mi cites a figure of 1,040,000 for the period 1949-1984.

32. *Xinhua* (February 26, 1987) in *FBIS* (March 2, 1987): K38.

33. *Xinhua,* (January 21, 1987) in *FBIS,* (January 29, 1987): K21.

34. Zhang Jingyi, a Senior Fellow with the Institute of American Studies, Chinese Academy of Social Sciences, claims that career military officers without college educations have generally been quite conscientious about taking evening and correspondence courses. Zhang claims PLA leaders are serious about upgrading officer educational levels. Most officers, in turn, take seriously the PLA's claim that promotions increasingly will be linked to college level and professional education. When asked if officers were "filling squares or buying degrees," Zhang claimed that in most units that he visited officers were doing better college level work than traditional undergraduates. A slightly different picture exists among conscripts and NCOs where dropout rates in spare-time educational programs are high. Interview with author, December 1989. See Zhong Jie, "The Dropout Phenomenon is Disturbing," *op. cit.,* p. 29.

35. Zhong Jie, "The Dropout Phenomenon is Disturbing," *op. cit.,* p. 30.

36. *FBIS* (March 2, 1987): K38. The figures only add up to 395,000. *Xinhua* provided no explanation for 5,000 unaccounted for officer-cadets.

37. Hu Wanzhang and Li Yuliang, "Military Academies to Recruit 5,000 Students from the Local Sectors This Year," *Renmin Ribao* (Beijing) (May 5, 1988): 3, in *FBIS-CHI-88-090* (May 10, 1988):25; *FBIS-CHI-88-088* (May 6, 1988): 25.

38. *Xinhua* (June 4, 1988) in *FBIS-CHI-88-108* (June 6, 1988):31.

39. *Military Training Handbook, op. cit.,* pp. 107-108.

40. *Junshi* (Military), Vols. I and II in *Zhongguo Dabaike Quanshu* (The Great Chinese Encyclopedia) (Beijing and Shanghai: The Great China Encyclopedia Press, 1989).

41. Lonnie D. Henley,"Officer Education in the Chinese PLA," *Problems of Communism* 36:3 (May-June 1987): 55-71; also William R. Heaton, "New Trends in China's Professional Military Education and Training," unpublished paper, International Studies Association, Anaheim, California, March 25-29, 1986.

42. *Xinhua* (June 28, 1986) in *FBIS* (July 1, 1986): K27-28.

43. *Military Training Handbook, op. cit.*, p. 107; *FBIS* (October 26, 1984):14K.

44. *Xinhua* (August 31, 1986) in *FBIS* (September 2, 1986): K8.

45. The acronym "PME" is commonly used in the U.S. military. Chinese military writers are still not fully comfortable using the term "professional" in reference to military affairs. Many PLA officers are attracted to the idea of a professionally motivated and specialized military, but the concept is unsettling for some CCP officials. They see a professional army developing an internal loyalty that may compete with loyalty to the CCP.

46. With the increased emphasis on college education for all new officers, there are different ways to earn college degrees. Since 1983 PLAAF pilots have had to earn bachelor of science degrees in military science. The four-year program *begins* with two years of college education followed by two years of flight training (academic and practical). The PLAAF Political College is a intermediate command-officer college (regiment level), but some high school students are admitted directly to earn college degrees. The PLAAF Antiaircraft College serves as both a primary and intermediate command-officer school. Additionally, it accepts high school graduates for a four-year course of study and they "become commanders." The Shijiazhuang Army College likewise provides different levels of education for officers. *Xinhua* (November 24, 1987) in *FBIS-CHI-87-229* (November 30, 1987): 21; Sun Peixian, "Air Force Political College," *Bingqi Zhishi* (Weaponry Knowledge) 2 (May 15, 1987): 19; Zhang Ping, "China's Military Academy--A Visit to

the Shijiazhuang Army School," *Xinhua* (July 31, 1986), in *FBIS* (August 1, 1986): K3-5.

47. *Xinhua* (June 28, 1986) in *FBIS* (July 1, 1986): K28.

48. *Xinhua* "Major Reform Will Be Made in the PLA's Military Command Academies," (June 10, 1986) in *FBIS* (June 10, 1986): K12.

49. Ch'i Kuan, "Armymen's Discontent in the Great Reform," *Cheng Ming* (Contending) 87 (January 1985): 22-24, in *JPRS-CPS-85-018* (February 27, 1985): 134-135.

50. *JPRS-CAR-87-140*, p. 95.

51. Apart from the National War College in the United States, each military service has a separate one-year war college program. Congressional efforts in 1989-1989 to restructure professional military education included a plan to establish at the National War College a National Center for Strategic Studies to foster grand strategists. The proposed curriculum involves extended professional education for general officers. See U.S. Congress, House Committee on Armed Services, *Report of the Panel on Military Education of the One Hundredth Congress*, 101st Cong., 1st sess. (Washington, D.C.: GPO, April 21, 1989), pp. 35-39.

52. Li Wei, "PLA Academy of Military Science," *Xinhua* (July 14, 1987) in *JPRS-CAR-87-035* (August 18, 1987): 98-100.

53. Dai Xingmin and Gai Yumin, "China's Highest Military Institution--Visiting the National Defense University," *Ban Yue Tan* (Beijing), 18 (September 25, 1986): 44-47, in *FBIS*, (October 15, 1986): K14; *Xinhua* (September 1, 1986) in *FBIS* (September 2, 1986): K10; Wang Gangyi, "National Defense University," *China Daily* (Beijing) (August 27, 1986): 1 (cites the figure of 550 students).

54. *Xinhua* (November 19, 1986) in *FBIS* (November 26, 1986):K14; *Xinhua* (December 7, 1987) in *FBIS-CHI-87-235* (December 8, 1987): 21.

55. Kai Wangmin and Tai Hsingmin, "A Visit to China's Highest Military Academy," *Ta Kung Pao* (Hong Kong) (September 2, 1986): 3, in *FBIS* (September 3, 1986): K55. Tai Hsingmin (note 52) is probably the same person as Dai Xingming. Translators appear to have used different romanizations.

56. Dai Xingmin and Gai Yumin, "China's Highest Military Institution," *op. cit.*, p. K15.

57. Kai Wangmin and Tai Hsingmin, "A Visit to China's Highest Military Academy," *op. cit.*, p. K3. For the period 1986-1991, NDU had plans to publish more than 80 works involving eight areas such as military ideology, strategy, campaigns, military systems, military mobilization, and military logistics. Military publication plans for the Military Academy of Sciences (AMS) are discussed in Fan Hao, "PLA Academy of Military Science Conducts Open-Type Research," *Liaowang* (Hong Kong Overseas Edition), 38 (September 22, 1986): 28 in *FBIS* (September 29, 1986): K18. In 1986, the AMS planned to compile works such as *The Science of Strategy, The Science of Military Systems, Essence of the Science of Campaigns, History of China's PLA, The Chinese Military Encyclopedia* and *Battles of Combined Arms Units in Brief.* AMS conferences that are possible sources of books included "China's Military Development in Contemporary Times" and "Military Management."

58. *Military Training Handbook, op. cit.*, p. 107.

59. *Xinhua* (August 25, 1986) in *FBIS* (September 2, 1986): K9. This reference indicates there were more PLA institutions in 1986 than in 1988 that could offer graduate degrees. The seeming contradiction probably stems from *authorizations* to teach courses (1986) in contrast to institutions that *actually* had degree programs (1988).

60. Ball, *Security and Economy in the Third World, op. cit.*, pp. 295-334.

61. Zhan Guoshu and Yang Huiming, "Change That Conforms with the Wishes of the Army and the People--Chronicles of the

PLA's Training of Dual Purpose Personnel," *Xinhua* (July 23, 1987) in *FBIS* (July 24, 1987): K3.

62. Hsiao Ch'ung, "PRC Faces Conscription Problem," *Cheng Ming* (Contending) 91 (May 1985): 14-16, in *JPRS-CPS-85-081* (August 12, 1985): 155-159.

63. Zhan Guoshu and Yang Huiming, "Change that Conforms with the Wishes of the Army and the People," *op. cit.*, p. K5.

64. *FBIS* (May 30, 1986): 02-3; Hu Nianqiu and Chen Xiangan, "China's Army Pays Attention to Training Qualified Personnel for Peacetime Construction," *Liaowang* (Hong Kong overseas edition) 21 (May 25, 1987): 6-8, in *FBIS* (June 3, 1987): K28-34.

65. See Wang Jusheng, *Peiyang Jundui Liangyong Rencai 100 Wen* (One Hundred Questions on Developing Military Dual-Purpose Personnel) (Shanghai: Shanghai Science and Technology Press, July 1987).

66. Hu Nianqiu and Chen Xiangan, "China's Army Pays Attention to Training Qualified Personnel for Peacetime Construction," *op.cit.*, pp. K28-34. Since 1987 the PLA has introduced specialized training regiments that do most of the basic training for conscripts. Where these training regiments have been established, regular regiments may not have the spare time they used to have during the first quarter of the training cycle. Accordingly, since 1987 it has been necessary to adjust the timing of vocational training.

67. *Ibid.*, p. K33; *Xinhua* (Beijing) (September 17, 1989) in *FBIS-CHI-87-181* (September 18, 1987):19; *FBIS* (August 1, 1986): K31. The data are slightly misleading. China had 2046 counties and 321 major municipalities in 1985. See Gao Yan and Pu Shanxin, *Zhongguo Renmin Gonghe Guo Xingzhen Quhua Shouce* (Handbook of Administrative Regions of the People's Republic of China) (Beijing: Guangming Ribao Press, 1986): 54.

68. *FBIS* (August 1, 1986): K30.

69. *FBIS* (August 1, 1986): K30; *FBIS-CHI-87-181* (September 18, 1987):19.

70. Liang Chao, "One Million Demobilized Soldiers Resettled," *China Daily* (Beijing) (September 2, 1989):1, in *FBIS-CHI-89-170* (September 5, 1989): 43.

71. This attitude seems to contradict the view that education provides greater employment opportunities and hence more income. Conscripts who felt education was of little use in making money usually displayed a spirit of entrepreneurship--legal and illegal.

72. He Jinsheng, "The Guangzhou Military Region Will Carry Out Training Which Combines Military and Civilian Skills in One Scheme," *Nanfang Ribao* (Guangzhou) (June 18, 1986):1, in *FBIS* (June 19, 1986): P4.

73. *Xinhua* (October 17, 1986), in *FBIS* (October 20, 1986): K17.

74. *Xinhua* (October 17, 1986) in *FBIS* (October 20, 1986):K17; *Xinhua* (July 29, 1986) in *FBIS* (August 1, 1986): K31.

75. *Wang Jusheng Peiyang Jundui Liangyong Rencai 100 Wen, op. cit.*, pp. 140-142.

76. Hu Nianqiu and Chen Xiangan, "China's Army Pays Attention," *op. cit.*, p. K34.

77. *FBIS* (May 30, 1986): O3.

78. Zhan Guoshu and Yang Huiming, "Change That Conforms with the Wishes of the Army and the People," *op. cit.*, p. K5.

79. For the English text of China's Military Service Law (1984), see *Xinhua* (June 4, 1984) in *FBIS* (June 6, 1984): K1-10.

80. *Xinhua* (February 7, 1985) in *JPRS-CPS-85-019* (March 1, 1985):49.

81. Mi Zhenyu, *Zhongguode Guofang Gouxing, op. cit.*, p. 143.

82. *Xinhua*, "Military Training by No Means Is Punishment Says Education Official" (October 11, 1989) in *FBIS-CHI-89-200* (October 18, 1989): 23-4.

83. "Set Strict Demands, Overcome Laxity," *Jiefangjun Bao* (Beijing) (October 29, 1988):1 in *FBIS-CHI-88-228* (November 28, 1988): 39.

84. Hu Shaowen, Zhang Dajie, Liu Quanchu, and Li Pengzhou, "There Is an Urgent Need to Develop in Practice the Theories on National Defense Education," *Jiefangjun Bao* (Beijing) (August 16, 1988): 1 and 4, in *FBIS-CHI-88-168* (August 30, 1988): 31.

85. Jiang Yonghong, "Step Up National Defense Education, Raise the National Defense Concept of the Whole People--Minutes of Discussions by PLA Delegates to the 13th Party Congress," *Jiefangjun Bao* (Beijing) (October 31, 1987):1 in *FBIS-CHI-87-216* (November 9, 1987): 27.

86. Jiang Yonghong, "Step Up National Defense Education," *op. cit.*, p. 29.

87. *Xinhua*, (July 26, 1987) in *FBIS* (July 28, 1987): K2-3.

88. Li Ligong, "Getting a Good Grasp of National Defense Education for the Whole People Is the Sacred Duty of Leading Cadres," *Shanxi Ribao* (Taiyuan) (September 27, 1988): 1 in *FBIS-CHI-88-202* (October 19, 1988): 53.

89. *FBIS-CHI-88-244* (December 20, 1988): 51; Liu Suihua and Liu Jianxin, "An Excitement and Inspiring Melody--Review of the Whole-People National Defense Education and Prospects (Part I)," *Jiefangjun Bao* (Beijing) (January 10, 1989):4 in *FBIS-CHI-89-015* (January 25, 1989): 28-30; Yao Youzhi, "The Key to Deepening National Defense Education Lies in Legislation--Review of the Whole-People National Defense Education and Prospects (Part II)," *Jiefangjun Bao* (Beijing) (January 13, 1989): 4 in *FBIS-CHI-89-015* (January 25, 1989): 30-32.

CHAPTER THIRTEEN

GENDER AND EDUCATION

by Beverley Hooper

Introduction

Gender is an important variable in education in both capitalist and socialist countries, whether developing or industrialized. Most countries have characteristically had a general pattern of higher male participation, especially at tertiary levels, strong gender variables in fields of study, and higher male earnings following graduation. While industrialized capitalist societies have been gradually correcting some of these imbalances over the past ten to twenty years, differentials are still apparent. The gender variable has been eroded rather more in Western socialist countries, for example in the Soviet Union.[1]

The issue of gender and education is significant in the People's Republic of China, particularly when viewed in the context of the constitutional guarantee of equality for females in all spheres of life: political, economic, cultural, social, and domestic. Like other socialist regimes, China's post-1949 government has consistently maintained that this equality is to be achieved basically through women's participation in the public sphere, in accordance with Engels' productivist formula: "The emancipation of women will only be possible when women can take part in production on a large, social scale."[2] While many Western women in the early and mid-1970s were impressed with the advances made by Chinese women,[3] most recent Western writers have stressed their continuing inequalities in the public, as well as in the private, sphere.[4]   Although the overwhelming majority of Chinese women are active in the work force, they still occupy positions on the lower rungs of the ladder and are clustered in jobs characteristically regarded as "women's work," from textile and clerical workers to primary school teachers.[5]

The attainment of equal educational opportunities is not, of course, a *sufficient* condition for women to achieve an equal role in the public sphere. As the experience of the Soviet Union and other socialist countries has demonstrated[6] and as Margery Wolf argues in the case of China,[7] women's "double burden" (domestic responsibilities as well as paid employment) may well be as great an impediment as inequalities in education. Equal educational opportunity is, however, a *necessary* condition for equal public participation. This chapter examines the continuing gender discrepancies in education in the PRC and the reasons for them.[8]

The Gender Imbalance

Table 13.1 presents the available statistics on the level of female participation in Chinese primary, secondary, and tertiary education since the Communist Revolution of 1949.

Table 13.1
Female Percentage of Total Students

	Primary	Secondary	Tertiary
1949	----	----	19.8
1950	----	26.5	21.2
1951	28.0	25.6	22.5
1952	32.9	23.5	23.4
1953	34.5	24.4	25.3
1954	33.3	25.0	26.3
1955	33.4	26.9	25.9
1956	35.2	29.3	24.6
1957	34.5	30.8	23.3
1958	38.5	31.3	23.3
1959	39.1	31.2	22.6
1960	39.1	31.2	24.5
1961	27.5	32.2	24.7
1962	34.8	34.1	25.3
1963	...	34.0	25.8
1964	35.0	34.1	25.7
1965	...	32.2	26.9
------	No statistics available		
1973	40.7	33.0	30.8
1974	43.7	38.1	33.8
1975	45.2	39.3	32.6
1976	45.5	40.4	33.0
1977	45.4	41.7	29.0
1978	44.9	41.5	24.1
1979	44.9	40.8	24.1
1980	44.6	39.6	23.4
1981	44.0	39.0	24.4
1982	43.7	39.2	26.2
1983	43.7	39.5	26.9
1984	43.8	40.0	28.7
1985	44.8	40.2	30.0
1986	45.1	40.7	25.5
1987	45.4	40.8	33.0
1988	45.6	41.0	33.3

Source: *Zhongguo jiaoyu nianjian 1949-1981* (Chinese Educational Yearbook 1949-1981); *Zhongguo tongji nianjian* (Chinese Statistical Yearbook, 1982-89).

These statistics reveal three basic, associated patterns.

First, there have consistently been fewer females than males both overall and at each level of education--primary, secondary, and tertiary-- throughout the history of the People's Republic. The cumulative effect of the continuing gender imbalance at the primary level, in particular, is reflected in the literacy statistics for people educated since the establishment of the PRC. For example, a survey undertaken in Anhui province in 1984-85 revealed that some 80 per cent of illiterate and semi- literate people between the ages of twelve and forty were female.[9]

Second, females have consistently constituted a declining proportion of total students as one moves up the educational ladder. Thus, in 1951, the first year for which statistics for each level are available, females comprised 28.0 per cent of primary school students, 25.6 per cent of secondary school students, and 22.5 per cent of tertiary students. In 1988 the percentages were 45.6, 41.0, and 33.3.

Third, female participation, while not reaching that of male participation, has increased over the period as a whole. Thus, while only 28.0 per cent of primary school students were female in 1951, the proportion had increased to 45.6 in 1988; for secondary school students from 25.6 to 41.0, and for tertiary students from 22.5 to 33.3. This pattern was not, however, even over the period. There was a steady increase up to the Cultural Revolution, which continued after the subsequent disruption to education (and the unavailability of statistics) until the end of the Mao era. In the post-Mao period, however, the pattern is less consistent, with a slight decline in female representation up to 1983 for primary education, 1981 for secondary education, and 1980 for tertiary education.

The overall statistics do not reveal a number of further gender variables *within* the overall framework, as comprehensive figures are not available. The female proportion of students in both primary and secondary school is generally acknowledged to have been higher in urban than rural areas, a phenomenon confirmed in literacy statistics.[10] Within the overall high school statistics, female participation at senior high school level has been lower than that at junior high school. A comparative survey undertaken in Henan province in 1985, for example, revealed that girls comprised almost half of all students in the junior high schools surveyed, but only one third to one quarter of students in the senior high schools.[11]

At the tertiary level, there have been two significant gender variables that are not reflected in the overall statistics but are readily apparent from personal visits and interviews. First, female students have been clustered in the lower status, especially "normal" (teachers) universities, with less representation at leading institutions, particularly key universities. For example, in 1982 females comprised only 16.5 per cent of students at Qinghua University, the nation's leading technological university but up to half of all students at some of the low-prestige provincial and teachers' universities.[12]   Second, females have been unevenly represented across different fields of study, playing a minor role in those areas considered of greatest importance for China's modernization. As in most Western countries and to a lesser extent in the Soviet Union and Eastern Europe[13], representation has been disproportionately low in scientific and technological areas and high in humanities and language-related subjects.[14]   For example, while women comprised appropriately 20 per cent of all students at Beijing University in 1988, their representation in the major science departments was under 10 per cent.[15]

Obstacles to Female Access to Education

In spite of the Chinese government's guarantee of educational equality for females, obstacles have existed to their equal participation at a number of levels as discussed below. The major element underlying these obstacles has been the persistence of traditional social attitudes and patterns that assign an inferior role to females.   In explaining gender discrepancies at all levels of education, Chinese spokespersons have themselves stressed the "remnant of feudal ideas" argument: that 2,000 years of traditional attitudes cannot be wiped out in a few decades.[16] Female inferiority was enshrined in the Confucian ethic "male honorable, female inferior" (*nan zun nu bei*) which prescribed a subordinate role for women and resulted in such sayings as "it is virtuous for a woman to be untalented" and "an educated woman is bound to cause trouble." Such attitudes, it is argued, have continued to be widespread, despite official efforts to eradicate them.[17]

The heritage of the past, however, goes beyond the "feudal ideas" argument. As Judith Stacey and Kay Ann Johnson have succinctly argued, the concept of female inferiority is deeply embedded in the basic social structure that persists even in the 1980s, at least in rural areas. This applies particularly to the virilocal marriage system, whereby the woman moves to her husband's village, thus reducing her value, and hence any need for her education, to her own family. Rather

than attempting to change this basic social structure, Stacey and Johnson argue, China's post-1949 government has actually reinforced it.[18]
Whether the "traditional Confucian attitudes" or the "basic social structure" explanation is stressed, the ramifications have been similar: a concept of female inferiority and even worthlessness compared with males. This concept underlies the obstacles placed at three important levels--institutional, family and personal--on female access to education.

Institutional Discrimination

Overt institutional discrimination occurs in the admission of females to both secondary and tertiary education.[19] In recent years, technical schools have been particularly active in this area, imposing quotas on the proportion of girls enrolled. For example, the female quota for admission to Shanghai's technical schools in 1984 was only 28.5 per cent of the total enrollment.[20] To attain the quotas, substantially higher entrance marks are required by girls than by boys. Thus in 1983 one Shenyang technical school required males to have 173 points for admission, but females had to have 317; the respective points the following year for a technical school in Fujian province were 194 and over 300.[21] While discrimination has been most rife at the secondary level, the highly competitive tertiary sector has not been immune, with technological institutions again being particularly discriminatory.[22]
The imposition of differential criteria in admission to educational institutions has come to be regarded as one of the major forms of discrimination against females. A poem entitled "Four Questions," published in the cartoon supplement of the People's Daily shortly before International Women's Day in 1983, included the following verse:

Times have changed,
Men and women are equal.
Then why is it that when a certain school
Admits students they are not treated equally?
To admit women they look at the score,
To admit men the score can go down.[23]

Discriminatory admission policies are justified on two basic grounds. The first is that examination marks, particularly for entrance to senior high school, are not necessarily accurate indicators of future performance. School administrators contend that, while girls mature faster intellectually than boys, they begin to fall behind at the later stage of junior middle school or in senior high school.[24]   At the tertiary level, some educators argue, girls might well do well initially but tend to fade in the third or fourth year compared with their male fellow-students.[25]

The second, and probably ultimately more important, justification for gender discrimination is the end demand for school-leavers as opposed to university graduates. With a labor surplus, potential employers can afford to be selective, and they express an overall preference for male recruits. An extreme case occurred in Tianjin in 1984 where the city's labor bureau initially stipulated that 97 per cent of the total number of new workers recruited would be men.[26] Rather than publicly declaring their preference for males, most employing organizations, like tertiary institutions, establish informal quotas by requiring females to have higher marks in entrance examinations. According to a comprehensive study undertaken in 1987 by the All-China Federation of Trade Unions, 77 businesses surveyed required an average recruitment score of 115 for men and 127 for women; the relative scores for banks were 154 and 167.[27] As a result of this "usual practice,"[28] some 60-70 per cent of unemployed young people, described euphemistically as "awaiting employment youth" (daiye qingnian) in the post-Mao era have been female.[29] Employers of university graduates have also strongly discriminated against women. Indeed, they have sometimes expressed a preference for male graduates with inferior examination grades even in occupations for which women are said to be particularly suited. In 1983, for example, a number of top female graduates of the prestigious Beijing Foreign Studies University (formerly the First Foreign Languages Institute) publicly complained that they were losing out on jobs to fellow male graduates with barely passing grades.[30] By 1985 one-third of the potential employers of graduates of Shanghai's prestigious Fudan University publicly admitted that they would simply reject any female graduates assigned to them by the state.[31]   The problem has further intensified since the mid-1980s with the decline of the state assignment system.[32] In 1988 the Beijing Foreign Studies University complained that women college graduates were "facing a higher level of discrimination than ever before"[33] and the problem of female graduate employment was provoking widespread national comment, particularly in women's publications.[34]   Preference for male employees has led to adjustments in the enrollment of females at the secondary and tertiary level, rather than to confronting the *causes* of gender discrimination in employment, and hence in education.   The first cause is what is officially labelled "distinctive female characteristics," both intellectual and psychological. Even when females are perceived as being as intelligent as males, and this is not always the case,[35] female intelligence is considered to be of a fundamentally different and often less desirable nature: verbal and tactile rather than analytical and technical.[36]   Women's distinctive personalities also ostensibly make them less suitable employees than males in many areas.   While men are said to be assertive and rational, women are labelled as passive and emotional: characteristics that allegedly do not fit them for managerial and other influential positions.[37]

The second major reason for gender discrimination in employment and hence in access to education is officially described as the "practical" one: the perceived effects of women's future biological and domestic role.   One job interviewer cited in the official Chinese women's newspaper is reported to have noted: "We would rather take in a male hoodlum than a woman. A hoodlum can be reformed, but you cannot get a woman to give up childbearing."[38]   As the newspaper commented, "harsh words tell a simple truth."[39]   Female employees, unlike their male counterparts, need to be provided with maternity leave and child care facilities; the latter are normally the responsibility of the woman's workplace.

In addition, women are considered less committed to and have less energy for their work because of their domestic responsibilities (surveys have indicated that, despite their participation in the work force, women spend around one and a half hours a day more on household chores than men).[40] A number of management level cadres interviewed by Margery Wolf in 1980, for example, implied that the "single-minded devotion with which men supposedly approach their work is not to be found ... among women after they marry."[41]   Because of their domestic responsibilities, too, women employees are considered to lack the mobility enjoyed by males.

The issue of women's biological and domestic role has become of increased significance with the economic reforms of the post-Mao era and the greater accountability of individual enterprises. As well as refusing to hire females, some individual organizations have reportedly dismissed women and employed men in their place. Females employed on contracts have been particularly vulnerable, liable to dismissal, for example, when they marry or become pregnant.[42] These factors only further encourage discrimination in the admission of females to both secondary and tertiary education.

Family Deterrents

Family attitudes and behavior also present obstacles to female education. Throughout the history of post-1949 China, the family has continued to favor the education of sons over daughters, especially in rural areas where both traditional attitudes and the virilocal family structure have been particularly strong. Girls are often withdrawn from junior high school and even primary school to assist with domestic chores, helping account for their lower participation rates in education.[43]
Once again, this problem has intensified in the post-Mao era. The structural changes in rural production have led women to assume greater responsibilities in agriculture and also become involved in sideline production, leaving little time for household chores. According to a 1986 Sichuan survey, "Some schoolgirls have to get up at five o'clock in the morning to prepare meals [for the whole family] and keep doing housework as late as nine or ten o'clock in the evening. Only then can they have time for homework, and they are often unable to fulfill school assignments."[44] Some girls simply leave school, representing a majority of the overall increased primary and secondary dropout rate.[45] A 1986-87 investigation of thirty rural primary schools in Fujian province, for example, revealed a female dropout rate of 6.7 per cent, compared with a male rate of 1.15 per cent.[46] This difference was already being reflected in illiteracy rates. In 1984, almost 15 per cent of all Chinese females aged 12 to 19 were illiterate, compared with under 5 per cent of males in the same age range.[47]
In urban areas family obstacles to female education have been less overt and probably on a par with the traditional situation in Western countries. Girls are often withdrawn from education at an earlier stage (particularly before senior high school) in order to contribute to family income. Overall, they receive less family support

than boys to continue with their education, a phenomenon especially apparent in the preparation for university entrance examinations.[48]

Female Aspirations

A major obstacle to equal participation in education is the aspirations of females themselves, a problem shared by most countries, both industrialized and developing.   Overall, female aspirations are generally regarded by both men and women as being lower than those of males.[49]   In addition, girls have continued to aspire to gender-typed occupations that are often of lower status and less well paid than those aspired to by males.   For example, a 1983 survey of over nine hundred junior and senior high school students (urban, suburban, and rural) revealed that over twice the percentage of males over females wanted to be scientific and technological personnel (16.7 per cent to 7.9 per cent), while more than twice as many females as males wanted to be teachers (14.6 per cent to 7 per cent). These preferences corresponded directly to the comparative proportions of males and females having mathematics and chemistry, versus language and history, as their favorite subjects.[50]
    As in most countries, female aspirations are a product of a number of related factors.   First, Chinese females often have a lower intellectual and different psychological self-image than males to the point of expressing the traditional notion of female inferiority. In a 1986 survey of female students in sixteen tertiary institutions in Shanghai, 62.6 per cent of the respondents regarded "female inferiority" as a major obstacle to women's advancement.[51] This notion has an impact on young women's perceived capability of undertaking a senior high school education and, more particularly, tertiary study.   Young women who do reach tertiary level are less likely than their male fellow-students to apply for entry to key universities, often limiting their aspirations to the lower status provincial teachers' colleges.[52]
    Second, female aspirations are influenced by official and media stereotypes of women's role in the work force. Although some official efforts were made during the Mao era to eradicate the gender division of labor, the recent emphasis on women's "special characteristics" has reinforced traditional stereotypes of women in "caring" and "service"

occupations,[53] and hence influenced the choice of school and tertiary subjects.   These images have been further reinforced by the media, including women's and youth magazines, which portray women as primary school teachers rather than as high school or university teachers, as assistants rather than as leaders in a field, and as textile workers rather than as technically skilled personnel.

Third, young women's educational and occupational aspirations are influenced by the attitudes of their male peers in a society in which women still tend to view marriage rather than advanced education and professional employment as a major avenue to upward social mobility. Men normally prefer to marry women of a considerably lower educational level.   In a 1983 survey of ten higher educational institutions in Beijing, for example, only 28 per cent of male students (ostensibly the most "advanced" group in the community) said they would like their wives to have a university education.[54]   A striking 50 per cent admitted they agreed with the Confucian adage: "It is virtuous for a woman to be untalented."[55]   Such attitudes only further inhibit young women from continuing their education, particularly at the tertiary level.

The issue is even more significant for potential graduate students.   A young woman who undertakes a graduate degree, especially if she spends a period overseas, may find herself unmarried in her late twenties: an age when it is difficult to find a husband even without the burden of a higher education.   A 1987 survey of ten Shanghai tertiary institutions revealed that approximately one-third of female graduate students aged 25 to 35 did not yet have a potential spouse, even though they had truly reached, and many had passed, the desirable marriage age.[56]

Fourth, young women's perceptions of their future personal and domestic roles, as wives and mothers sometimes exert a significant influence on their aspirations.   There is some evidence that young women in China, as in many countries, consciously select subjects and careers that will be compatible with their future domestic role.[57]   The unwillingness of employers to hire women for jobs involving travel, for example, is matched by the reluctance of some young women to train for such positions.[58]   Even avoidance of certain subjects of study does not always solve the problem.   Thus, 76.5 per cent of women respondents in the Beijing survey discussed above said they saw a contradiction between being successful in their future work and being able to fulfil a satisfactory domestic role.[59]   These four basic factors-- intellectual and psychological self-image, gender social stereotypes, the attitudes of male peers and the perception of one's future personal and domestic role--combine to inhibit female educational aspirations and also to influence girls and young women to enter characteristic gender-typed fields of study. Overall, they constitute a significant impediment to the achievement of male-female equality in education.

Reactions: Official, Academic and Feminist

Although Chinese officials have consistently attacked the persistence of "feudal attitudes" toward women, which they largely blame for continuing female inequalities, they have taken little action at the practical level to remedy gender discrepancies in education. The major exception occurred during the latter part of the Cultural Revolution, when some effort was made to establish female quotas, and female representation in tertiary education reached approximately 30 per cent, as reflected in Table 13.1. The "worker, peasant, soldier" (*gong, nong, bing*) students of this period, however, received a limited tertiary education and have now been largely superseded by a new cohort of university graduates with lower female representation.

The post-Mao leadership, far from taking affirmative action, has implicitly condoned and even encouraged the gender imbalance in education. This has been done by endorsing, rather than criticizing, two of the basic impediments to equal demand for women's services and to the achievement of higher female aspirations: the notion of women's "special characteristics" and the perception of their future domestic role.[60] The concept of distinctive female abilities and temperament is relayed through official statements and publications.[61] While this topic is still a controversial issue internationally, what is missing from most assessments is reference to gender stereotyping in the media and in children's and youth literature, acknowledged in the West as important determinants of aspirations and career choice.[62]

Since the late 1970s Chinese officials and the media have also stressed the burden of women's domestic roles and readily acknowledged that this interferes with their working life. As the People's Daily expressed it on International Women's Day in 1978: "Women workers, commune members and women scientists and technicians need to work hard and study, but they have to spend a considerable portion of their time tending to housework and children."[63]

In turn, women have been officially allocated a supplementary, subordinate role in the workplace in accordance with their "special personalities and abilities" and their domestic burden. No longer perceived in terms of the Maoist slogan "Anything a man can do, a woman can do too," Chinese women in the post-Mao era have been described as "the main force in logistics ... Among them are childcare and education workers, salesclerks, cooks, street sweepers, nurses, barefoot doctors and other service personnel."[64] Government policy has thus give official sanction to employing organizations' concern about women's aptitude for particular jobs and their future domestic burden, thereby implicitly encouraging employment and ultimately educational discrimination.

While the gender variable has been largely ignored by the Chinese government, it has additionally received little attention from Chinese educationalists. The topic has rarely been discussed in major educational journals such as *Educational Research* (*Jiaoyu yanjiu*) or *People's Education* (*Renmin jiaoyu*), which focus on overall developments in the educational system and curricula. Journals on youth and sociological issues have been slightly more forthcoming, with *Youth Research* (*Qingnian yanjiu*), published by the Chinese Academy of Social Sciences, playing a major role.

The leading commentator on the gender imbalance in education has been the All-China Women's Federation and its publications. As the official women's movement, in a country that has little place for autonomous women's groups, the Federation has addressed the problem at women's congresses, in its national newspaper (*Zhongguo funu bao*) and magazine (*Zhongguo funu*), and in provincial women's magazines. The Federation has consistently criticized the adoption of female quotas for admission to secondary and tertiary educational institutions and has drawn attention to the problems experienced by female graduates in obtaining employment. Suggestions aimed at ameliorating discrimination against women in the work force and hence in education have ranged from efforts to raise women's self-image to more practical suggestions that child care should be funded equally by the wife and husband's work unit. It has been additionally argued that the government rather than individual organizations should be responsible for maternity leave payments.[65]

The power of the Women's Federation is, however, limited because of its dual assigned role--not just to represent women but, more importantly, to act as a "transmission belt" for Communist Party policies toward women. As Honig and Hershatter state, the Federation has been a "top-down, government-sponsored organization, rather than one independently formed by women."[66] Indeed the Federation and its magazines have been the major vehicle for spreading the post-Mao era's changing government policies towards women's roles, basically inaugurated at the Fourth National Women's Congress in September 1978 and endorsed at the Fifth and Sixth Congresses in 1983 and 1988.[67]

Practical action, rather than rhetoric, necessary for the remediation of the reasons for the gender imbalance in education, has so far been limited. Since the mid-1980s a few all-girl schools (or classes) have been established with the aim, as in the West, of giving females the opportunity to develop intellectually and promote their self-confidence. Most often, however, they have been of a vocational nature, offering classes in such subjects as clothing design, cooking, nursing, and typing.[68] While this might help decrease the level of female unemployment, it also reinforces the concept of distinctive "women's work" and ultimately promotes discrimination against females in admission to educational institutions.

Conclusion

Although overall female participation in Chinese education has increased substantially since 1949, the improvements have been uneven, with females comprising a declining percentage of total students the farther one goes up the educational ladder. At the higher levels (senior high school and tertiary study) there have been further discrepancies in female representation at the leading institutions and also in the scientific and technological subjects in the forefront of China's modernization drive.

Obstacles to equal female participation have existed at three levels: institutional, family, and personal. Underlying these obstacles has been the persistence not just of traditional attitudes toward women but of the basic family structure in which the female was virtually worthless to her own family. Although China's post-1949 government has condemned traditional attitudes as "feudal remnants," it has not attempted to change this basic structure. And while guaranteeing equality for females in all spheres of society, it has taken only limited action to ensure their equal participation in education. Indeed, the leadership has recently endorsed, rather than attempted to ameliorate, the basic reasons for employers' rejection of females and for low and gender-specific female aspirations: the perception of distinctive "female characteristics" and the burden of their future domestic role. This, in turn, has exacerbated discrimination against females at the secondary and tertiary levels.

Certainly the gender imbalance in Chinese education has decreased since the establishment of the PRC in 1949, particularly at lower levels. While primary school statistics have approached close to equal participation, or at least over 45 per cent female and under 55 per cent male, the discrepancy is still around 1:2 at tertiary level. It would be an exaggeration to attribute the very low level of female representation at senior political and administrative levels solely to this imbalance.[69] At the same time, the 1954 constitutional guarantee of equality for women in all spheres of life cannot be met while there continues to be a gender imbalance in Chinese education.

Notes

1. Gail Warshofsky Lapidus, *Women in Soviet Society: Equality, Development, and Social Change* (Berkeley: University of California Press, 1978): 135-60.

2. Frederick Engels, *The Origin of the Family, Private Property and the State* (New York: International Publishers, 1975): 221.

3. See, for example, Claudie Broyelle, *Women's Liberation in China* (Hassocks: The Harvester Press, 1977); Ruth Sidel, *Women and Child Care in China* (Baltimore: Penguin, 1972); Sheila Rowbotham, *Woman, Resistance and Revolution* (New York: Vintage, 1974).

4. The most useful book on this subject, containing both a general discussion and translations of primary source material, is Emily Honig and Gail Hershatter, *Personal Voices: Chinese Women in the 1980's* (Stanford: Stanford University Press, 1988). See also Judith Stacey, *Patriarchy and Socialist Revolution in China* (Berkeley: University of California Press, 1983); Margery Wolf, *Revolution Postponed: Women in Contemporary China* (Stanford: Stanford University Press, 1985); Kay Ann Johnson, *Women, the Family and Peasant Revolution in China* (Chicago: The University of Chicago Press, 1983); Phyllis Andors, *The Unfinished Liberation of Chinese Women, 1949-1980* (Bloomington: Indiana University Press, 1983).

5. See Honig and Hershatter, *Personal Voices*, 243-72; Wolf, *Revolution Postponed*, 56-57, 111.

6. Lapidus, *Women in Soviet Society*, *op. cit.*, pp. 5-6, 341-2; Maxine Molineaux, "Women's Emancipation under Socialism: A Model for the Third World?" *World Development* 9, 9/10 (1981): 1019-37.

7. Wolf, *Revolution Postponed*, *op. cit.*, p.76.

8. The most useful primary source materials in English on this subject are contained in the translation series *Chinese Education* and *Chinese Sociology and Anthropology*. See, in particular, "Women, Education, and Employment," *Chinese Education* 22,

no.2 (Summer 1989). This chapter cites English translations of Chinese articles where these are available.

9. Anhui Provincial Women's Federation, Office of Investigation and Study, *"Funu chengcai yinsude tantao"* (How Women Can Become Achievers), *Shelian Tongxun* (United Newsletter of Social Sciences) 12 (1985), translated in *Chinese Sociology and Anthropology* 20, no.1 (Fall 1987): 32-38.

10. See, for example, *Beijing Review* 7 (1987): 17-19.

11. Zhao Haiyan, "Gaozhong nusheng xuexizhongde xinli zhang'ai ji jiaozheng" (Psychological Barriers of Senior High School Students in Their Studies and the Remedy), *Qingnian yanjiu* (Youth studies) 6 (1986): 17-19, translated in *Chinese Sociology and Anthropology* 20, no.1 (Fall 1987): 80-85.

12. Beverley Hooper, "China's Modernization: Are Young Women Going to Lose Out?" *Modern China* 10, no.3 (1984):320. See references at end of article for school and university interviews.

13. Lapidus, *Women in Soviet Society, op. cit.*, pp.151-55; Alena Heitlinger, *Women and State Socialism: Sex Inequality in the Soviet Union and Czechoslovakia* (London: Macmillan, 1979):151-53.

14. Personal interviews in China, September 1982, December 1984, June 1986.

15. Personal communication.

16. See, for example, Zhonghua Quanguo Funu Lianhehui (All-China Women's Federation), editors, *"Si Da" yilai funu yundong wenxuan, 1979-1983* (Selections on the Women's Movement Since the Fourth Congress) (Beijing: Zhongguo Funu chubanshe, 1983).

17. Zhonghua Quanguo Funu Lianhehui, *op. cit.*, personal interviews in China, 1982, 1986.

18. Stacey, *Patriarchy and Socialist Revolution in China, op. cit.*;

Johnson, *Women, The Family and Peasant Revolution in China,* *op. cit.*

19. For a general discussion of this issue based on personal interviews, see Hooper, "China's Modernization," pp. 323-25.

20. Chen Ziju, "Yuanyin zai nar? Chulu he zai?" (What Is the Reason and Solution for the Disproportionate Enrollment of Male and Female Students at Shanghai's Technical Vocational Schools?), *Qingnian bao* (Youth newspaper) (Shanghai), (September 14,1984): 1, translated in *Chinese Sociology and Anthropology* 20, no.1 (Fall 1987): 62-64.

21. Honig and Hershatter, *Personal Voices, op. cit.,* p. 248.

22. Personal interviews, 1982, 1986.

23. The other three questions concerned discrimination against females in employment recruitment, wages and family attitudes. Wang Fuhua, *"Si wen"* (Four Questions), *Renmin ribao manhua zengkan* (Cartoon supplement of the *People's Daily*) (March 5, 1983), translated in Honig and Hershatter, *Personal Voices, op. cit.,* 327-38.

24. Zhao, "Gaozhong nusheng xuexizhongde xinli zhang'an ji jiaozheng," translated in *Chinese Sociology and Anthropology* 20, no.1 (Fall 1987), *op. cit.,* 80-85. Personal interviews in China, 1982, 1986.

25. Personal interviews in China, 1982, 1986.

26. For this and other cases, see Honig and Hershatter, *Personal Voices,* pp. 244-45.

27. Investigative Group, Women's Work Commission, All-China Federation of Trade Unions, "Chengshi funu zai jiuye deng fangmian mianlinde xin wenti" (New Problems Confronting Urban Women in Regard to Employment), *Zhongguo laodong kexue* (Labor science in China) 5 (1988): 12-15, translated in *Chinese Education* 22, no.2 (Summer 1989): 40-49. For further

examples, see Honig and Hershatter, *Personal Voices, op. cit.*, p. 248.

28. Investigative Group, Women's Work Commission, All-China Federation of Trade Unions, "*Chengshi*," pp.12-15 translated in *Chinese Education* 22, no.2 (Summer 1989):40-49; Honig and Hershatter, *Personal Voices*, op. cit., p.248.

29. Zhonghua Quanguo Funu Lianhehui, editors, "*Si Da*" *yilai funu yundong wenxuan, 1979-1983, op. cit.*, 90; Liu Yuan, "Shilun jianli funu rencaixue de biyao xing" (On the Necessity of Initiating the Study of Female Talent), *Zhongguo funu bao* (Chinese Women's Newspaper) (February 1 1988), 3, translated in *Chinese Education* 22, no. 2 (Summer 1989): 22-33.

30. *Zhongguo funu* (Chinese Women) 6 (1983): 15.

31. Yang Xingnan, "Jushou nu daxueshengde xianxiang yingdang gaibian" (Rejection of Female College Graduates Must be Stopped), *Zhongguo funu bao* (Chinese Women's Newspaper) (February 27, 1985):1, translated in *Chinese Sociology and Anthropology* 20, no.1 (Fall 1987): 65-66.

32. See, for example, Ge Shan'nan, Hao Weijing, and Zhang Ying, "Bao-bian canbande pingjia" (A Mixed Assessment), *Zhongguo funu bao* (Chinese Women's Newspaper) (May 23, 1988): 1, translated in *Chinese Education* 22, no.2 (Summer 1989): 9-13. For details of the new job assignment system, see *Beijing Review* 44 (1988): 12-15.

33. *China Daily* (April 28, 1989).

34. See, for example, articles translated in *Chinese Education*, 22, no.2 (Summer 1989): 18-19, 28-29, 73-88, 89-95.

35. For a good discussion of this subject, see Honig and Hershatter, *Personal Voices, op. cit.*, 14-23, and Wolf, *Revolution Postponed, op. cit.*, 130-33. See also Ding Xunxiang, "Chuzhong nan nu sheng zhili chayi chuxi" (A Preliminary Analysis of the Discrepancies in Intelligence Between Male and Female Students at the Junior Middle School Level),

Shanghai qing-shaonian yanjiu (Shanghai Youth Studies) 10 (1983): 21-27, translated in *Chinese Education* 20, no.4 (Winter 1987-88): 13-30.

36. Honig and Hershatter, *Personal Voices*, *op. cit.*, pp.14-23; Wolf, *Revolution Postponed*, *op. cit.*, pp. 130-133; Ding Xunxiang, *op. cit.*, pp.21-27 translated in *Chinese Education* 20, no.4 (Winter 1987-88):13-30.

37. This is characteristic even of academic publications. See, for example, Zhongguo Shehui Kexueyuan Qingshaonian Yanjiusuo and Sichuan Renmin Guangbo Diantai (Research Institute for Youth and Juvenile Affairs of the Chinese Academy of Social Sciences and Sichuan Broadcasting Station), *Qingnian Jiuye zhi Lu* (The Road to Youth Employment) (Beijing: Broadcasting Publishing House, 1983): 90.

38. Yang Xingnan, Ye Lin, and Hao Weijiang, "Weiji, haishi shengji" (A Crisis, or a New Hope), *Zhongguo funu bao* (Chinese Women's Newspaper) (November 9,1987) translated in *Chinese Education*, 22, no. 2 (Summer 1989): 73-88.

39. Yang Xingnan, Ye Lin and Hao Weijiang, "*Weiji*, *op. cit.*, in *Chinese Education* 22, no.2 (Summer 1989):84.

40. Wang Yalin and Li Jinrong, "*Chengshi zhigong jiawu laodong yanjiu*" (Research into Urban Staff and Workers' Housework), *Zhongguo Shehui Kexue* (Chinese Social Sciences) 1 (1982): 177-90; Gansu survey reported in *Beijing Review* (October 12,1987): 24.

41. Wolf, *Revolution Postponed*, *op. cit.*, p. 72.

42. Investigative Group, "*Chengshi funu zai jiuye deng fangmian mainlinde xin wenti*," translated in *Chinese Education* 22, no.2 (Summer 1989): 40-49.

43. See Wolf, *Revolution Postponed*, *op. cit.*, pp.126, 128.

44. Wang Shuhui, "*Nuxing qing-shaonian wenhua goucheng xiajiang*" (Educational Level of Female Teenagers and Young Adults

Declines), *Zhongguo funu bao* (Chinese Women's Newspaper) (August 17, 1987): 1, in *Chinese Education* 22 no.2 (Summer 1989): 20-1.

45. Yan Weizhi and Chen Benxiang, "Changde diqu zhong xiao xuesheng shixue yanzhong" (High Dropout Rate Among Elementary and Middle School Students in Changde Prefecture), *Zhongguo funu bao* (Chinese Women's Newspaper) (May 30, 1988): 2, translated in *Chinese Education*, 22 no.2, (Summer 1989): 34-37.

46. Project Group, Fujian Education Commission, "Guanyu nongcun nu xueling ertong jieshou chudeng jiaoyu wentide diaocha yanjiu" (An Investigation of the Status of Primary Education Among Rural School-age Girls), *Jiaoyu pinglun* (Educational Review) 3 (1988): 51-55, translated in *Chinese Education* 22, no.2 (Summer 1989): 54-55.

47. *Beijing Review* 14 (1984): 23.

48. Beverley Hooper, *Youth in China* (Harmondsworth and New York: Penguin Books, 1985): 100-101.

49. Personal interviews, 1982, 1984, 1986.

50. Luo Yicun and Shen Jiaxian, "Qing-shaonian xuesheng lixiang he xingqude diaochao yanjiu," *Jiaoyu yanjiu* (Educational Research) 8 (1983): 58-63, translated in *Chinese Education* 17, no.4 (Winter 1984-85): 41-61. See also Liu Jixin, "Nuxing yuanyi gan shenme gongzuo?" (What Kind of Work do Women Want to Do?), *Zhongguo funu bao* (Chinese Women's Newspaper) (March 14 1988): 1, translated in *Chinese Education* 22, no.2 (Summer 1989): 38-9.

51. *Beijing Review* 37 (1987): 29.

52. Personal interviews in China, 1982, 1986.

53. *Beijing Review* 36 (1983):26-27.

54. *Beijing Review* 36 (1983): 26-27.

55. *Ibid.*, pp. 26-27.

56. *Beijing Review* 35 (1987) 28.

57. See, for example, Su Guilin, "Chutan nu daxuesheng fenpei ande yuanyin ji duice" (A Preliminary Probe Into the Difficulties College Women Encounter in Job Placement), *Jiaoxue yanjiu* (Research on Study and Teaching) 2 (1988): 10-13, translated in *Chinese Education* 22, no.2 (Summer 1989): 89-96.

58. Personal interviews in China, 1982, 1986.

59. *Beijing Review* 36 (1983): 26-27. The men surveyed were apparently not asked this question.

60. For a summary of changing policy on women's public and private roles, see Stanley Rosen's introduction to "Women, Education, and Employment," *Chinese Education* 22, no. 2 (Summer 1989): 3-6.

61. For a good discussion of this viewpoint, see Honig and Hershatter, *Personal Voices, op. cit.*, pp.14-23.

62. Hooper, *Youth in China, op. cit.*, pp. 106-107.

63. *Renmin ribao* (People's Daily), (March 8, 1978).

64. *Renmin ribao* (People's Daily), (September 18, 1978).

65. See, for example, Yang, Ye and Hao, "Weiji, haishi shengji," *op. cit.*, translated in *Chinese Education*, 22, no.2 (Summer 1989): 73-88; *Beijing Review* 43 (1988): 14-19.

66. Honig and Hershatter, *Personal Voices, op. cit.*, p. 320.

67. Zhonghua Quanguo Funu Lianhehui, editors, "*Si Da*" *yilai funu yundong wenxuan, op. cit.*; *Renmin ribao* (People's Daily), (September 14, 1978); *Zhongguo funu* (Chinese Women) 2 (1983): 25; *Zhongguo funu* 6 (1983): 15; *Zhongguo funu* 10 (1988): 1.

68. Honig and Hershatter, *Personal Voices, op. cit.*, pp. 322-23.

69. For example, less than 14 per cent of Communist Party members are women. See Stanley Rosen's introduction to *Chinese Sociology and Anthropology* 20, no.1 (Fall 1987): 7, and "Quanguo nu dangyuan da wubai liushiduowan" (5.6 million Female Communist Party Members in the Country), *Zhongguo funu bao* (Chinese Women's Newspaper), (October 2, 1985): 1, translated in *Chinese Sociology and Anthropology* 20, no.1 (Fall 1987): 13. For some detailed provincial-level statistics and discussion, see pages 26-43.

CHAPTER FOURTEEN

AN ORGANIZATIONAL ANALYSIS
OF CENTRAL EDUCATIONAL ADMINISTRATION IN CHINA

by Zhixin Su

On June 18, 1985, a major reorganization of central educational administration took place in China. The 11th Plenary of the Standing Committee of the People's Congress in China passed a resolution that called for the abolition of the Ministry of Education (MOE) and the establishment of the State Education Commission (SEC). Why did China make this change in its central administration? How does the SEC differ from the MOE and what were the consequences of this reform? An historical overview and organizational analysis of the former MOE will shed some light on these questions.

History and Organization

Some comprehension of Chinese values, politics and ideology is necessary if one is to understand the history and organization of the former MOE. In his sociological theory of organization, Talcott Parsons suggests that the main point of reference for analyzing the structure of a social system is its value patterns, which legitimize the organizational goals and activities of participating individuals.[1] This approach is particularly useful when applied to the analysis of organizations in

375

China, where social systems are built according to a distinct set of values, political principles and disciplines, and official ideologies.

Socialist China's values were expressed in an ideology based upon the ideas of Marx, Engels, Lenin, and Mao Zedong. They reflect both a commitment to universal norms and goals derived from Marxism and a specific application of these over-arching concepts to conditions in China. In the earlier years, after the founding of the People's Republic of China, Mao urged all organizations, especially educational institutions, to shoulder their responsibilities in ideological and political work. The primary aim of education was seen as serving the needs of politics, transforming students ideologically and enabling everyone who received an education to develop morally, intellectually, and physically, so as to become a well-educated worker imbued with socialist consciousness.

As a result, the organizational structure of education in China has been deeply nested within the Communist party, and educational administration, at all levels in China, has strictly adhered to the discipline of the Party. As Mao argued in 1938, the individual is considered subordinate to the organization, the minority is subordinate to the majority, the lower level is subordinate to the higher level, and the entire membership is subordinate to the Central Committee.[2]

The formation and evolution of the MOE was a faithful reflection of China's political ideology. Unlike the United States, where the Constitution contains no mention of the federal government's policy-making role in education, in China, legislative powers are all vested in the central authorities. It was therefore necessary to establish the MOE at the highest level of organization in educational administration shortly after 1949.

The first National Ministry of Education consisted of eight units: the General Affairs Office, the Department of Higher Education, the Department of Secondary Education, the Department of Elementary Education, the Department of Social Education, the Department of Supervision, the Commission of Higher Education and the Anti-illiteracy Campaign Commission. Once established, the MOE emphasized three tasks, in its efforts to reconstruct China's educational system. First, it attempted to redesign existing institutions of higher learning according to the Soviet model. Second, it initiated anti-illiteracy movements in the countryside, especially during winter when peasants had some time to participate. Finally, the MOE attempted to encourage Chinese students and scholars who had been studying and working in foreign countries to return to China and help with its reconstruction efforts. All three tasks were accomplished with a considerable degree of success; with respect to the anti-illiteracy campaign in particular, over ten million peasants participated in winter anti-illiteracy workshops in 1949.

In 1952, the MOE was divided into two ministries: the Ministry of Higher Education (which included departments of higher, adult, and vocational education) and the Ministry of General Education (which included departments of teacher education, secondary education, etc.). Central educational administration quickly expanded from eight units to 36 units, and by the mid-1950s, the two central education ministries discovered that they often needed to issue joint directives and announcements, and that there was considerable overlap with respect to organizational responsibility. The division of the central educational administration into two ministries had the effect of duplicating red tape at various levels rather than reducing it.

Therefore, in 1958, the two central ministries were merged into one Ministry of Education, which reduced their 36 offices and departments to 16 units. In the same year, the central government issued a directive to decentralize educational administration in China, in an effort to speed up educational development in different regions. However, the MOE maintained its authority for the administration of national planning throughout the entire country and continued to shoulder responsibility for supervising teaching and academic research, overseeing the writing, publication and distribution of textbooks and instructional materials, and regulating the different levels of schooling.

As higher education continued to expand, the central government once again felt the need to redefine the responsibilities of the MOE. In 1964, the MOE was once again divided into two ministries: the Ministry of Higher Education and the Ministry of General Education. This was the year in which China succeeded in exploding its first atomic bomb, and the central government called upon the people to contribute to the country's modernization effort through learning the works of Mao Zedong. The two educational ministries, as a result, issued numerous directives to schools at all levels, encouraging them to follow political trends.

When the Cultural Revolution broke out in 1966, leaders and senior officials of both education ministries were severely criticized, and educational administration in China was literally abolished by the Red Guards. It remained paralyzed for eight years.

A single Ministry of Education was reestablished in 1975 with only seven offices and departments: the General Affairs Office, the Department of Political Affairs, Department of Planning, Department of Higher Education, Department of Informal Education, and Bureau of

Foreign Affairs. Once resurrected, the MOE begun to reconstruct the country's educational system but was disrupted in its efforts by fierce political infighting within the central party leadership. The newly appointed, 59-year-old Minister of Education, Zhou Rongxin, for example, succumbed to anger, frustration, and physical illness, and died in 1976 after having been attacked at criticism meetings by his opponents.

As the political situation in China became more stabilized in 1977, the MOE was consolidated by the State Council. Figure 14.1 is an organizational chart of the MOE in 1977.

Figure 14.1
Organization of the Ministry of Education in China: 1977

Minister and Head of the Party Committee

General Affairs Office	Policy Research Office	Bureau of Planning	Bureau of Foreign Affairs	Bureau of Information & Documentation
First Dept. of Higher Education	Second Dept. of Higher Education	Dept. of Teacher Education	Dept. of Elementary and Secondary Education	Dept. of Student Affairs
Dept. of Vocational Education	Dept. of Physical Education	Dept. of Education for Workers and Peasants	Dept. of Education for Minority Affairs	Dept. of General Supplies and Construction

The Ministry directly reported to the State Council and received its budget through the State Planning Commission. Under each of the 15 offices, bureaus and departments within the Ministry, there were divisions performing various duties with a staff of 700. It was a very tightly coupled system, with directives flowing from top down and each level obeying and reporting to the level above it.

While a large number of staff were former officials with the Ministry before the outbreak of the Cultural Revolution, new graduates from colleges and universities were also recruited to add new blood to the organization. Although these young people knew little about the history of the Ministry, particularly its rise and demise, they would find it difficult to stay neutral between different factions among senior officials who themselves had experienced bitter factional struggles and had suffered personally during the Cultural Revolution. In addition, younger staff had to learn to cope with exorbitant bureaucratic demands consistently.

Although ideologically different from the West, most organizations in China, including the former MOE, demonstrate many of the characteristics of bureaucracy described by Western organization theorists Katz and Weber. Those characteristics include large size, specialization of work, authority residing in the office, not the person, centralization of control with authority hierarchically distributed, division of labor based upon differentiated function, rules, and regulations designed to govern operations, a separation of the personal from the official with respect to ownership of property and rights, and an increasing tendency to select personnel on the basis of technical qualifications.[3]   Although Weber argued that as an ideal type, bureaucracy could be the most efficient form of social organization, Benveniste has argued that bureaucracy has served to impede educational progress.[4]

As is well known, bureaucracy is not a new phenomenon in China, and China's ancient imperial system, was very advanced, although it had not developed fully in the Weberian sense. Parsons observes that the classical Chinese administrative system was the mainstay of an imposing socio-political structure, which was without peer in scale, stability, and durability until the modern era.[5]   The Chinese are aware, as are Westerners, that "bureaucracies are powerful institutions which greatly enhance potential capacities for good or for evil, because they are neutral instruments of rational administration on a large scale."[6]

What differentiates Chinese bureaucracy from its western counterpart, however, is the existence of constant political and ideological struggle, waged within Chinese organizations, reflective of external social struggles. An administration's fate often depends upon the political orientation of certain powerful political figures. As a result, administrators tend to form political factions, rallying around powerful leaders. Conflict among the different factions has caused perpetual instability in the Chinese bureaucracy, while western bureaucratic structures appear to be more tolerant of different ideologies, less personalized and more stable.

Administrative Tools

The administrative tools employed by former MOE and other government organizations in China are in many cases similar to those used in state organs in the West. For instance, in our administrative practices, we generally resort to all of the five techniques described by Henri Fayol: general survey, plan of operations, reports of proceedings, minutes of conferences between heads of departments, and organizational charts.[7] In addition, we also employ another three unique mechanisms that are not present in Western central administration: the principles of the mass line, democratic centralism, and collective leadership.

In China, the application of the mass line was Mao's method for developing a form of leadership that does not allocate power to an elite group of party members but converts their power into authority by eliciting the support of the masses. All correct leadership is necessarily "from the masses to the masses."[8] The mass line has not only been an important link between the Party and the masses but also between the higher levels of administration and cadres at the grass-roots levels. Administrators at the grass-roots levels are expected to provide feedback to and exert influence and control over the higher levels through use of the mass line.

A second mechanism is democratic centralism. It is stipulated in the Chinese constitution that the organs of the state must practice democratic centralism. Mao believed that within the popular ranks, democracy is a correlative to centralism and freedom is similarly related to discipline. They are two opposites of a single entity, contradictory as well as united. He promoted a system of democratic centralism whereby people were to enjoy democracy and freedom but within the bounds of socialist discipline.[9]

The third important traditional base for decision-making in China is the principle of collective leadership, which refers to the interaction and the relationship among members within a specific unit. The Party believes, at least in a theoretical sense, that many heads are better than one and that decisions are likely to be more appropriate if they are based upon the experience and wisdom of the collective. In fact, central administration tends to resort to this mechanism during periods after major political crises: the death of a top leader, confusion caused by ideological and factional struggle, pressures from both domestic and external sources, etc. Still, charismatic leaders have always played a more important role than the collective leadership in the history of the People's Republic.

One would think that these three administrative principles assure a certain degree of unity and flexibility in high level state organs, such as the MOE. However, as will be made clear in the following analysis, at times circumstances and conditions have conspired to undermine the application of these as well as other administrative tools, causing dysfunction in China's educational administration.

Function and Dysfunction

We have already seen that the MOE was in a formal sense, a rational and tightly coupled system, established for the purpose of rationalizing China's educational system from the top down. Figure 14.2 illustrates the direction of this rationalization.

Figure 14.2
Educational Administration in China: 1977-1985

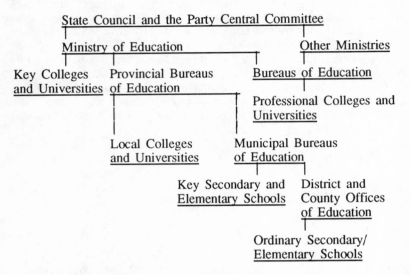

There has always been a tension between centralization and decentralization in China's educational administration.   In a large country like China, local conditions vary greatly from place to place. Although the Chinese constitution vests legislative power in the central authorities, the central state organs should limit themselves to the functions of making general and key policies, coordinating local efforts, and allocating resources, and allowing the local authorities to work out rules and regulations for local practices in light of their own conditions. However, many leaders and staff members in China's central government agencies interpret centralization as taking into their own hands as much administrative power as is possible.   As a result, state organs often waste much time working out the last details for a local unit, while those who work at the lower levels of administration become increasingly reliant upon the flow of authority from above.   Attempting to take care of everything results in taking care of nothing well.   And, simply following orders can lead to terrible consequences.

Mao realized in 1953 that "centralization and decentralization are in constant contradiction with one another."[10]   However, he did not recognize the problem of increasing centralization of control in China, and the fact that as tasks become more complex in modern societies, decentralized nets are usually superior to centralized structures.[11] Nor did he figure out an optimum proportion of centralization versus decentralization for China's unique social system. Although Mao established the principles of the mass line, democratic centralism, and collective leadership, in practice, the state organs have often violated these principles through their emphasis upon centralism to the extreme. The result has been little room for democracy, as orders have been given to the masses, without adequate ideas and feedback being gathered from the masses. In the end, educational administration in China became a linear, top-down, and often times incomplete learning process.

Figure 14.3
An Incomplete Learning Process

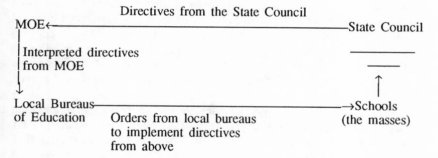

Directives from the State Council

MOE← ————————————————————————————State Council

Interpreted directives
from MOE

Local Bureaus————————————————————————→Schools
of Education   Orders from local bureaus   (the masses)
   to implement directives
   from above

Essentially then, this implies a highly rational model of educational administration; only those who are at the top level posts have the decision-making power, while those at the lower levels are tools for interpreting and transferring directives from the top levels. The majority of the educational administrators in China, therefore, spend much more time interpreting directives from above than innovating policies and methods of educational reform. Both consciously and unconsciously they have helped to remove the decision centers farther away from the masses. Reorganization of the structure of educational administration and decentralization of power to local units thus became an urgent task in China's educational reform.

Overcentralization of power resulted in specific problems within the MOE. The apparatus of the MOE became more bloated and overbureaucratized, and by 1985 the MOE staff had doubled in size since its reestablishment in 1975. As every department and division within the Ministry attempted to increase its size, more personnel were forced to engage in daily office work of a maintenance nature. Not surprisingly, articulation with lower level units became more problematic.

T.C. Schmidt, an American educator, has argued that China has an educational structure more formal, more ordered, and less open to informal influences that of the typical bureaucracy in the United States. [12] I believe this to be a superficial observation, for in China, as is the case in the West, informal relationships may either facilitate or impede purposeful cooperation and communication. [13] To some extent, Chinese organizations encourage a humanistic work environment that may be less impersonal than that of their Western counterparts. However, the existence of factionalism within the Chinese educational bureaucracy has already been noted. The MOE in particular, was one of the oldest ministries in the central government and as a result, complicated informal groupings developed within its formal structure, constantly interfering with its normal functions. By the mid-1980s, it became obvious that there was a need to reorganize this central educational administrative agency in order to break up existing informal ties and bonds that proved so troublesome.

Two decades ago, Charles Perrow observed that apparent leadership problems are often problems of organizational structure. [14] And, the abolition of the former MOE in 1985 can be viewed as a first significant step toward structural reform of China's central educational administration. Although 1985 was relatively prosperous, and a stable political situation was in evidence, efforts to implement educational reform and development lagged behind those in other sectors. The major reorganization of the central educational administration occurred in part, as a strategy to draw the entire country's attention to the importance of education as a key element in facilitating modernization.

Establishment of the State Education Commission: Similarities and Differences

With the abolition of the MOE and the establishment of the State Education Commission (SEC), one would assume that China's central educational administration is now much different from that of the past. However, in reality, the SEC has taken over most of the former structure, personnel as well as work style of the MOE. The abolition of the MOE was not an end to administrative problems, only the beginning of new attempts to solve recurrent problems.

Nevertheless, there are three distinct differences between the SEC and the MOE.[15] First, the SEC has more power and responsibility than the MOE. As Figure 14.2 indicates, in China, professional colleges and universities are under the direct control of their respective ministries. For example, medical colleges are under the jurisdiction of the Ministry of Health, and engineering institutes are under various ministries of industry. Since these ministries occupy the same authority and status as did the MOE, neither they nor their bureaus of education were compelled to listen to orders or recommendations from the MOE or address calls for policy coordination. This lack of coordination is a principal reason why educational reform efforts have not matched those in economic and science and technology areas. The latter two fields are governed by state commissions, their highest policy-making bodies, which are half a level higher than the ministerial unit in China's administrative hierarchy. The establishment of a State Education Commission merely followed their successful example and today, the SEC is directly responsible for the educational work over all of China except for its military schools.

A second difference between the MOE and the SEC pertains to the leadership of the central educational administration. Because of the status differential, for the first time in the history of the People's Republic, those who have assumed direct command of the country's educational system (and are in charge of the SEC) have high positions in the State Council. In addition to politically prominent chairmen, the State Council has appointed several noted educational administrators and scholars as vice-chairmen and consultants to the SEC.

Third, in contrast to the MOE which lacked clear goals and direction, once the SEC was established, it immediately outlined its goals and tasks, and it was expected that the focus of its work would gradually be shifted from stressing micro-management to stressing macro-management.[16]

As one would expect, there were significant organizational changes in the structure of the new central educational administrative body. As Figure 14.4 indicates, the SEC has grown bigger than its predecessor and now includes 1200 staff members.

The Computer Center for the SEC, the National Educational Testing Center, and the Office for World Bank Loan Affairs were created to accommodate new developments in educational technology, testing and international cooperation in education. The Bureau for the Affairs of Retired Cadres was established to take care of the retired senior officials in the Commission. And, the three research centers were established so as to enhance the idea that sound educational policy-making should be based upon solid research.

Figure 14.4

Organization of the State Education Commission: 1985-1988

Chairman and Vice-Chairmen of the SEC

General Affairs Office	Bureau of Planning	Bureau of Foreign Affairs	Department of Student Affairs
First Department of Higher Education (Social Science Education Research Center)	Policy Research Office (National Educational Development and Policy Research Center)	Bureau of Science and Technology (Science and Techology Information and Resources Center)	Department of Elementary and Secondary Ed. (Secondary School Curriculum Research Center)
Second Department of Higher Education	Department of Teacher Education	Department of Physical Education	Department of Vocational Education
Third Department of Higher Education	Department of Education for Minority Nationalities	Department of Graduate Studies	Bureau for the Affairs of Retired Cadres
Computer Center for the SEC	National Educational Testing Center	Office for World Bank Loan Affairs	Department of General Supplies and Construction

However, just as increased size does not always necessitate successful change, new personnel alone do not in guarantee new practice. Newcomers have had little difficulty assimilating established norms and work styles into their normal routines. In fact, it has proven extremely difficult to combat the bureaucratic work style of the former MOE and complaints from lower level educational institutions continue to be heard constantly.

One factor contributing to low bureaucratic efficiency in the SEC is its heavy turnover of personnel. Although no statistics are available, it can be speculated that the turnover rate in the SEC is three or four times higher than that in educational administrative organizations at lower levels in part due to the fact that many SEC staff members are constantly assigned study and work tasks in different regions of China and abroad. As a result, those remaining in the home offices are required to take over their colleagues' sphere of administration, of which they know little.

Prospects for the Future

A number of years have passed since the abolition of the MOE and the establishment of the SEC, and it is time for China's central educational administrators to review their progress and contemplate future prospects. In my opinion, there are at least five areas that urgently need reform.

First, the structure of our organization and work must be changed. Although the establishment of the SEC brought about some structural changes in the central administration, quite a number of existing bureaus, offices, and centers of the SEC are performing tasks not directly related to the SEC's central mission, and they should therefore be removed from its jurisdiction. For instance, the Educational Testing Center, the Secondary School Curriculum Research Center, and the Social Sciences Education Research Center could be separated from the SEC and become independent, non-governmental, and non-profit organizations themselves. The Bureau for the Affairs of Retired Cadres could also be turned into an independent service agency, perhaps in the form of a club or association. In addition, concerted efforts should be made to break up the unhealthy cliques and groupings that originated in the former MOE but still exist in certain sections of the SEC. Incompetent cadres should be removed from their offices and placed in other suitable job positions.

Second, the distribution of power within educational administration should be decentralized. The former MOE exercised too much rigid control over schools, especially over universities and colleges, in the areas of personnel affairs, funding, student enrollment and job assignment, capital construction and academic exchanges with foreign schools. School authorities had little to say in any of these matters and the existence of such tight controls dampened the enthusiasm of local administrators to run their own schools. Although the SEC has made some effort to delegate greater decision-making power to provincial, municipal and autonomous regional governments as well as to major universities across the country, it still holds tremendous power in its own hands. Lessons from American educational reform demonstrate that the necessary reconstruction of schooling must occur from the "bottom up" rather than from "top down."[17] Teachers and educational administrators at grass roots levels rather than policy makers at the top are the key forces in educational reform, and without their active participation, policies, and plans initiated at the top will have little chance of success.

Figure 14.5

A Complete Learning Process

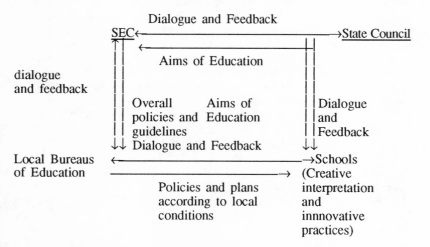

The third area in need of reform concerns the application of the three administrative principles of mass line, democratic centralism and collective leadership. Although these principles have proven to be useful administrative tools in the past, the linear and top-down model of educational administration in China has turned the application of these principles into an incomplete learning process, as demonstrated in

Figure 14.3.   Ideally, a democratic administrative model, where communication "from the masses, to the masses" is expedited, would resemble Figure 14.5.

Such a model ensures a never-ending learning process.   It requires broadly defined but clearly articulated goals for every level in the administration. It demands decentralization of policy-making powers to a considerable degree, the promotion of democracy, and the development of a genuine understanding of the ideas and feedback from lower levels.   Modern research techniques, computers, and various information gathering devices can be used to facilitate this process.   It is important that our leaders and policy-makers learn what the masses really think and feel not just what they would say in official meetings and discussions.   This requires them to go down to the grass-roots levels on a regular basis, visit the masses, listen to their complaints, and show real concern for their welfare.

In a fourth area, the quality of administrative staffing should be improved.   China has had no formal training programs for educational administrators until very recently. Consequently, nearly all of the staff members in the SEC have little familiarity with educational administration theory.   There is an urgent need to establish both pre-service   and   in-service   training   programs   for   our   educational administrators.   They should learn, in addition to decision-making and organizational theory, basic skills in educational research and trends in modern educational technology.   The hope is to socialize our self-disciplined cadres into the role of reflective and creative educational administrators.

The final area of concern focuses upon the supervision of educational administration.   In China, both educational policy making and policy implementation are carried out by the same administrative organs: the SECs at the central and local levels. We need an independent organization or a group of experts whose sole task is to supervise and oversee the work of educational administrators, especially that at the central level, to prevent grave mistakes from being implemented.

Concluding Note

To summarize, educational administration in China has followed a linear, top-down, and rational model, which has had its advantages and disadvantages. The abolition of the MOE signified an answer to the call for structural reform from the Central government and the larger society. And, the establishment of the SEC has created new hopes as well as new challenges to old problems.

To meet the needs of modernization, central educational administrators in China must engage in a continuing process of inquiry and reform. There are at least five areas in need of their immediate attention: the structure of their organization and work, distribution of power, application of the three administrative principles, the quality of staff members, and the supervision of educational administration.

Finally, in studying educational policy, governance and administration, we should recognize that any theoretical model is itself a somewhat arbitrary interpretation imposed on organized social activity, and any model involves trade-offs and unavoidable weaknesses. As long as we keep this in mind, we should feel free to apply models and perspectives from organizational theories in our studies and make recommendations for reform.

Notes

1. Talcott Parsons, "Suggestions for a Sociological Approach to the Theory of Organizations," *Administrative Science Quarterly* no.1 (1956):63-85.

2. Mao Zedong, "The Role of the Chinese Communist Party in the National War," in *Selected Works of Mao Zedong* (Beijing: People's Publishing House, 1969):485-501.

3. Michael B. Katz, *Class, Bureaucracy and Schools* (New York: Praeger, 1971); H.H. Gerth and C.W. Mills, editors, *From Max Weber: Essays in Sociology* (New York: Oxford University, 1946).

4. Guy Benveniste, *Bureaucracy* (San Francisco: Boyd and Fraser, 1977).

5. Talcott Parsons, *Societies* (Englewood Cliffs, New Jersey: Prentice Hall, 1966).

6. Peter M. Blau, *Bureaucracy in Modern Society* (New York: Random House, 1956):4.

7. Henry Fayol, "The Administrative Theory in the State," in Luther Gulick, L. Urwick, James D. Mooney, et al., editors, *Papers on the Science of Administration* (New York: Institute of Public Administration, Columbia University, 1937):99-114.

8. Mao Zedong, "On Several Issues in Our Leadership Style", *Selected Works of Mao Zedong* (Beijing: People's Publishing House, 1969):852-857.

9. Mao Zedong, "On How to Handle Correctly the Contradictions Among the People" in Mao Zedong, *Selected Works*, Vol.V (Beijing: People's Publishing House, 1977):363-402.

10. Mao Zedong, "Fighting Against Bureaucracy, Willful Orders, and Violations of Laws and Disciplines" in *Selected Works of Mao Zedong*, Vol.5, pp.72-74.

11. Richard W. Scott, *Organizations* (Englewood Cliffs, New Jersey:

Prentice Hall, 1981).

12. T.C. Schmidt, "Organization and Structure" in Ronald Montaperto and Jay Henderson, editors, *China's Schools in Flux* (Armonk, New York: M.E. Sharpe, 1979):39-59.

13. See Fritz J. Roethlisberger and W.J. Dickson, *Management and the Worker* (Cambridge: Harvard University, 1939).

14. Charles Perrow, *Organizational Analysis: A Sociological View* (Belmont, Ca.: Wadsworth, 1970).

15. See Jianye Yang, "To Manage Educational Work as We Do With Economy," *Prospects* vol.28 (July 15, 1985):9-13.

16. Yibing Wang, "Updating China's Educational System," *Beijing Review* Vol.28, no.50 (1985):15-22.

17. John Goodlad, *A Place Called School* (New York: McGraw-Hill, 1984).

CHAPTER FIFTEEN

THE INSTITUTIONAL ROOTS OF STUDENT POLITICAL CULTURE: OFFICIAL STUDENT POLITICS AT BEIJING UNIVERSITY

by Corinna-Barbara Francis

Early studies of political culture aimed to explain a society's political institutions, their structures, and modes of operation largely on the basis of the society's dominant culture.[1] Later studies emphasized the role of institutions in shaping the "cultural approach to politics" and the structure of interests in society more broadly.[2] This "institutional approach" has sought to counter the view of formally organized institutions as simply the "arenas within which political behavior, driven by more fundamental factors, occurs."[3] Increased attention to the role of political institutions has been paid in a wide variety of fields, in the structuring of interests in western societies,[4] in analyses of regime transformation,[5] in the study of public policy-making,[6] and more.

This increased attention to the autonomous role of institutions has not, however, had much impact on the study of communist systems. The predominant framework of analysis, strengthened by the collapse of communist regimes in Eastern Europe and communism's fall from grace as a political ideal, is that communism failed to create a new political culture. The behavior structured by communist political institutions is not viewed as generating "real" values. So, the focus of the study of political culture in communist states has centered upon the *dissonance* between beliefs and values on the one hand and behavior imposed by formal structures on the other.[7]

Less attention has been paid to how formal communist institutions have shaped values and defined a particular approach to politics. Communism may have ultimately failed to transform society in the radical, utopian manner for which it aimed. It has, however, had a major impact on attitudes and approaches to politics: the nature of representation, the approach to organization, the methods of political participation, relations between leaders and followers, and the attitudes toward leadership. A distinction must be made between consciously held political beliefs and attachments on the one hand, and embedded attitudes that come from structured patterns of behavior on the other. Institutionally, structured behavior gives rise to attitudes and interests, even if these are in conflict with rationally inspired values.

A rich literature exists that focuses on the opposition role of Chinese students and intellectuals. But much less attention has been paid to the impact of established institutions on student and intellectual culture.[8] This chapter is a study of the institutional characteristics of official student politics in the Chinese university. It takes the Beijing University Student Association (*Beijing Daxue Xueshenghui*), the official student union of Beijing University undergraduate students as a case study. The chapter examines the formal institutions, the organizational set up, power structure, electoral rules and operational norms of the student association with the aim of drawing out the political values, approach to organization, style of leadership, and political participation to which the formal institutions give rise. The chapter highlights the similarities between the *Beida* student government and political institutions in the system at large.

Introduction

Official student organizations in Chinese universities fell increasingly into disrepute as a "new thinking" emerged among Chinese youth throughout the 1980s. Students began the decade with a certain degree of hope in Deng Xiaoping's reforms but by the end of the decade, this hope had been all but extinguished. Profound loss of faith in the socialist model, the Chinese Communist Party, and deepening skepticism toward authority in general had set in.[9] Disillusioned with the system and the possibility of reform from within, students turned to the radical alternative of western style liberal democracy, which embodied values profoundly at odds with those of the existing system: freedom of the press, speech, and association, direct representation, respect for the rule of law, separation of state powers, individual autonomy, and civil rights, etc. While the notion of democracy captured the imagination of Chinese students in the 1980s, it continues to be defined in highly abstract terms, lacking specific institutional content. Institutionalized political activity, on the other hand, is possible only in the context of the official student organizations on campus. These are characterized by an elitist approach to political participation, an indirect and closed system of elections, hierarchical and paternalistic patterns of authority, and operational methods which are based largely upon patron-client relations. As their thinking changed, students became increasingly impatient with the official student organizations. These organizations, nevertheless, continue to represent a dominant political model. In everyday politics, students continue to be exposed to this "traditional" model.

The presence of traditional, authoritarian politics within the university, is significant in light of the long-standing role of the university as a center of resistance to state authority. In a tradition going back to the May Fourth Movement of 1919, Chinese universities have been centers of political resistance, a role which has been strengthened by the growing Chinese democracy movement. It is also significant in light of the overwhelming attachment of university students to democratic ideals and their central role in China's evolving democracy movement, from the Tiananmen Square Incident of 1976, to the Democracy Wall Movement in 1978-79, to the series of student demonstrations throughout the 1980s, culminating in the democracy movement of the spring of 1989. As the democracy movement continues to grow, universities will continue to be a locus of liberal-democratic challenge to authoritarian rule, and the dichotomy between democratic ideals and orthodox communist culture will become more pronounced.

The persistence of this traditional style of politics at *Beida* is particularly significant. *Beida*, more than any other university in China, has been the locus and symbol of resistance to political authority. Since its founding in 1898, *Beida* has been at the heart of political protest. As Lin Xiling, a *Beida* student and outspoken critic of the CCP said during the "Hundred Flowers" campaign in 1956-57, "*Beida*, after all, is *Beida* and inherits the traditions of the May Fourth Movement."[10] This tradition lives on today. Beijing University students continue to view themselves as the political vanguard of the nation, bearing both the prestige and burden of student protest. In the words of a *Beida* classmate who asked during one of the student demonstrations, "if we don't pressure the government, who will?"

Students continue nevertheless, to operate within established political institutions. They are not free to engage in autonomous student politics and are limited in their pursuit of sustained, organized, political activity to participation in official student organizations. Students continue to engage in student government for a broad range of reasons: the appeal of activism, the camaraderie, the sense of purpose, the challenge, the status, etc. Indeed, opportunism is not necessarily the decisive factor drawing students into politics, for the Beijing University Student Association is no longer the avenue of upward mobility that it once was. Student cadres thus include both establishment as well as rebellious types.

The dichotomy between democratic values on the one hand and traditional patterns of politics is not confined to a small group of students but is a more generalized phenomenon. The official student organizations are still the predominant model of politics to which students are exposed and while student political attitudes and ideals have changed rapidly, institutionalized patterns of behavior have not changed as quickly. The enduring political structures continue to impose structured patterns of behavior that shape political values. What might be called the "cultural approach to politics" is as much a *product* of existing institutions as it is their cause, and institutions play a major role in perpetuating deeply rooted political values and behavioral patterns.

Universities, as is true of most institutions in China, are "organizationally saturated." At *Beida* there are three main official student organizations: the Communist Party, the China Youth League (CYL), and student government. At *Beida*, official student politics continued to thrive throughout the 1980s. Elections were heatedly contested, student cadres were busily engaged in political networking; patron-client ties continued to flourish, and "officialdom" continued to be taken very seriously. Within the university, it is not at all unusual for student cadres to be introduced by their official title. Introductions around a dinner table of young college students could spin the head of the uninitiated. One could be seated at a dinner party with the "deputy head of the cultural department of the student association of the Chemistry department," the "secretary of the China Youth League branch of the class of 1987 of the Department of Asian Languages," the "chairman of the Presidium of the Student Association," or the "deputy head of the Academic Affairs department of the Graduate Student Association," almost as though one were seated with a group of old communist officials rather than a group of young college students.

Of the three student organizations on campus, student government provides the most comprehensive look at student political culture. The Beijing University Student Association (BUSA) is the most institutionally complete organization as far as student participation is concerned since all of its cadre positions are held by students, the only exception being the position of Secretary (*mishuzhuang*), which the Student Constitution stipulates is to be held by a "leading cadre" of *Beida's* Communist Youth League (CYL)). BUSA embodies a full range of organizational dynamics, which are conducted virtually entirely within a student context. This includes elections, active electoral campaigning, the formulation of institutional rules and regulations, leadership-follower dynamics, political networking, organizational reform, etc. BUSA is fully elaborated and multi-layered, reaching from the university level at the top to the *ban* or class section level, at the bottom. It has its own constitution. It sets up a full array of institutions including student congresses, executive organs, and "leading organs," and its elections are conducted in relatively autonomous fashion, apart from the school authorities.

This contrasts with both the Party organization and the CYL, which are not composed of or operated exclusively by students, who do not constitute these organizations' leading cadre. Student participation in the Party is limited to rank and file membership and to membership in the lowest organizational level of the Party, the class party branch. The highest rank an undergraduate student generally reaches in the party organization is the head of the party small group. The position of secretary of the class party branch is sometimes held by an undergraduate student but is more often held by a graduate student. Higher positions in the Party are held exclusively by teachers and full-time party cadre.

The school CYL offers students relatively greater opportunities for organizational participation than the Party, although still less than is true of student government. It has a developed hierarchy in which students play a dominant role. The CYL organization reaches from the lowest level, the CYL branch of each *ban*, to the department branches, and finally to the university level organs. Unlike BUSA, the CYL is not an exclusively student organization. Its leading cadres are not students but full-time professional cadres, appointed by the university (although often these are recent graduates who were active in the CYL as students). Unlike student government, the CYL does not elect its leading cadres, and only lower level CYL positions are held by students and the elections for these positions are not as competitive, nor do they involve the student body to the same degree as do elections for cadres in student government. BUSA, in short, while not an autonomous student union, involves a complete range of political activities and is operated and sustained largely by students, beyond the direct management of the school authorities.

The Structure of Student Government

This section examines the formal institutions: the organizational set up, the electoral rules, the operational codes, etc. of student government. Organs of student government are established at three levels: the university level, the department level, and the *ban*, or class section level. At the top level there is the Beijing University Student Association (BUSA), the university-wide organ of student government. Below are the student associations of each department (*xi xuesheng hui*), and at the lowest level are the *ban* committees, the student government in each *ban*. *Bans* are the lowest level student units in the university. They range in size anywhere from five to fifty students, but their average is from 20-25 students.

Chinese terminology relating to student government reflects an institutional ambiguity common to political institutions in the system at large. The term "student association" (*xueshenghu*) is used to refer *both* to the entire structure of student government, including the university, department and *ban* organs and to the university level organs more exclusively. This practice is similar to the way in which the term "party" is used both to refer to the party organization as a whole as well as to its central organs more specifically. The term "student government" will be used here to refer to the entire structure of student government, including the university, department, and *ban* organs. The term BUSA will be used to refer to the university level organs of student government more specifically as well as to the whole of student government in its entirety.

Beida student government has a built-in tension between the role of "representing" a constituency, the students, and the role of subordinate to a higher level authority, the university. This tension not only characterizes student government as a whole but its constituent organs as well. Student government is portrayed as a hierarchical organization that operates according to a top down structure of command, with lower-level organs under the authority of higher level ones. The tension between election by and responsibility to a lower-level constituency and the subordination to a higher-level organ is characteristic of Chinese Communist organization in general as it also marks the organizational structure of the CCP. Party committees are in principle elected by and "representative" of the party members in their unit, yet at the same time, are supposed to operate under the leadership of higher level party organs. Thus, while Party committees are formally elected from below, "leadership" over them is exercised from above.

The student Constitution (*Beijing Daxue Xueshenghui Zhangcheng*) describes BUSA as the "self-governing organization of Beijing University students" and as an organization that is supposed to "accept the leadership of the school party committee and the help and guidance of the school's CYL committee." (Article 1).[11]

The list of the tasks and the nature of the authority stipulated for the student government by its Constitution reflect student government's dual role. Its rights and responsibilities include:

1. To grasp the party's direction of education, to develop a rich array of activities in a spirit of self-education. To carry out education in patriotism, idealism, ethics, and discipline. To promote the construction of spiritual civilization with communist thinking at its core. To encourage all students to become idealistic, moral, cultured and disciplined human resources for the modernization of socialism.

2. To represent and uphold the legitimate interests and demands of the broad mass of students. To enthusiastically serve the students, to be a link between the relevant school authorities and the broad mass of students, and to promote and help the school in its management and education tasks.

3. To develop friendly relations with other schools and academies. To strengthen the ties with students from Taiwan and Hong Kong and Macao, and to promote the unification of the country.

The emphasis on the concept of "self," evident above through expressions of concepts such as "self-education," "self-regulation," etc. is significant. The Chinese term *zi* can be understood both as "auto" and "self," embodying two distinct notions. One idea is that of a "self-governing" organization, of an organization that is autonomous and independent from external interference. The second idea is that of "self-regulation," the idea that an organization should be responsible for educating, regulating, and disciplining its own members. BUSA is called on to "help the school in its management and education tasks." This second idea is a peculiarly Chinese Communist notion and is central to the Chinese Communist approach to social control. The role of student government is characterized by both of these tasks.

The tension between the "representative" and "instrumental" roles of organization, which characterizes student government as a whole, is also reproduced *within* student government. The organs of student government at all levels are in principle democratically elected by and "responsible to" (*duiqi fuze*) the student constituency at that level. Department student associations are in theory elected by and responsible to the students in the departments. Each department at *Beida* has its own student association, which is democratically elected by the entire student body in the department, and the same is true of student government at its lowest level, the *bans*. *Ban* committees are directly elected by and responsible to the All-*Ban* Congress of Students (*Quanban Xuesheng Dahui*), the lowest level student congress.

However, in spite of the principle that the organs of student government encourage election from below, the entire body is supposed to operate as a unified, hierarchically structured organization, under the centralized leadership of BUSA. BUSA, the central organ in theory, exercises "unified leadership" over the lower level organs, the department and *ban* associations, which are called upon to "accept" BUSA leadership. Since department student associations are designated the "basic level organs" (*jiceng danwei*) of BUSA (Article 32), they are expected to operate under its leadership. Similarly, *ban* committees are supposed to "accept the leadership of and be accountable to" their immediate organizational superiors, the department student associations. *Ban* committees are specifically identified as the "most basic level organs" (*zui jicent danwei*) of student government and the "subordinate organs" of the department student associations (*xiashu jigou*). At the same time, BUSA is given authority corresponding to its leadership role. Article 4 explicitly gives BUSA control over the "institutional set-up and division of responsibilities" within the department student associations. No recognition of the conflict in the dual role of organization exists in either the Student Constitution or the Party Constitution, and no formal mechanism or institutional arrangement for resolving conflicting signals coming from below is provided.

The Structure of the Student Congress,
the Executive Committee, the Student Committee

Student government is divided into three types of institutions: representative or legislative organs, executive organs, and "leading organs." This organizational structure mirrors that of the national level.

The University-Wide Congress of Student Representatives (*Quanxiao Xuesheng Daibiao Dahui*) is a body of representatives democratically elected by the entire student population and is stipulated by the Student Constitution to be the "highest organ of power" of student government (*zuigao quanli jigou*) (Article 11). Its functions and responsibilities as detained in the Constitution include:

1. To listen to and appraise the work report of the outgoing Student Committee. To decide the direction of work and overall plan for the current session.

2. To discuss and revise the Student Constitution, and to deliberate on and revise the report on the Constitution.

3. To elect the Student Committee.

4. To carry out other responsibilities that should be handled by the highest decision-making body. (Article 13)

The functions of the Congress of Student Representatives (hereafter termed Student Congress) give it "lawmaking" and "policy-making" authority, certifying its role as the legislative organ of student government. It has the authority to make major policy decisions, which must be passed by a majority of the Congress, and make revisions of the Constitution, which require a two-thirds majority. A Standing Committee is selected from among the members of the Congress to function in its place during the intercession and during the intercession, the Standing Committee functions as the "highest organ of power." A still smaller organ, the Council of the Standing Committee of the Student Congress, is selected from among members of the Standing Committee.

The second leg of student government's institutional triangle is the executive branch. An Executive Committee (*zhexing weiyuanhui*) is designated the "highest executive organ." Its tasks are to implement the policy decisions passed by the Student Congress, and they are described in the Student Constitution as follows:

> 1. To implement the decisions and plans of the the Congress of Student Representatives and the Student Committee.
>
> 2. To guide the daily work of each department and committees (*bu* and weiyuanhui) under its unified leadership.
>
> 3. To determine the institutional set-up of the the departments, committees, and offices and to appoint the deputy department heads and deputy chairmen of offices (of the Executive Committee) and to assign them work.
>
> 4. To carry out other tasks given to it by the Student Committee.

The Executive Committee is in principle elected by and responsible to the Student Congress. During the Congressional intercession, it is to "accept the supervision and inquiries of the Standing Committee of the Congress of Student Representatives." It is responsible for considering the proposals presented to it by the Standing Committee, discussing these with the relevant school authorities and establishing any temporary committees to carry out specific tasks given to it by the Standing Committee.

The Executive Committee consists of a Presidium (*zhuxi tuan*), composed of one chairman from two to four (in practice always four) deputy chairmen, and the heads of seven functional departments (*bu*). The seven departments include the social/life department (*shenghuo bu*); the academic affairs department (*xuexi bu*); the department of culture (*wenhua bu*); the athletic affairs department (*tiyu bu*); the women's department (*funu bu*); the external relations department (*wailian bu*); and the fieldwork department (*shixi bu*). Each department is composed of one department head and one to two deputy heads. These executive departments play a role in student government similar to that of government ministries in national government. The functional departments (*bu*) are responsible for carrying out the routine work of the executive branch. And as is the case with national ministers, department heads of the executive departments are appointed by the central leaders.

The final, and most characteristically Communist institution of student government is the "Student Committee" (*xuesheng weiyuanhui*). It is referred to as the " highest leading organ" (Article 14), whereas the Student Congress is designated the "highest organ of power," and the Executive Committee is the highest executive power of student government.

The functions and responsibilities of the Student Committee as outlined in the Constitution are:

1. To interpret the Student Constitution and oversee its implementation.

2. To draft the "Beijing University Student Association Work Regulations" (*gongzuo tiaoli*) according to the Constitution.

3. To set the work agenda for student government as a whole; to listen to the work reports of the Executive Committee, Council of Congress Representatives, and the student associations of each department; and to lead the work of the student associations of each department.

4. To determine the organizational make-up (*zuzhi jigou*) of the Student Association. To determine the personnel appointments (and dismissals) of leading cadre of the Executive Committee, the Council of the Congress of Representatives.

5. To prepare the convening of the next session of the Congress of Student Representatives; to take charge of the election of the incoming Student Committee, to oversee the convening of the Congress of Representatives.

6. To discuss and decide on other important matters concerning the Student Association.

In its functions, institutional arrangement and role in student government, the Student Committee shares remarkable similarities to the role of the CCP in national government. The Student Committee combines both "legislative" and "executive" functions, mirroring the CCP's role as an institution that carries out both policy decision-making and policy implementation. The Student Committee's formally designated functions overlap with those of both the Student Congress and the Executive Committee. While the Student Congress has the authority "to decide the direction of work and overall plan" of student government, the Student Committee is given the authority to "set the work agenda for student government as a whole." It is given the authority "to interpret the Student Constitution" and "to discuss and decide on other important matters" (clause six), functions that clearly overlap with the decision-making authority of the Student Congress. The result is an ambiguous division of responsibility and authority between the two bodies, an ambiguity that is left unresolved in the Student Constitution.

The functions and responsibilities of the Student Committee also allow it to play an important role in policy implementation, which is in conflict with Executive Committee functions. While the Executive Committee has the responsibility to "implement the decisions and plans of the Student Congress," the Student Committee is given the authority to "oversee the work of all levels of student government, leading the work of the Executive committee, and student associations of each department" (clause 3). These functions clearly fall in the realm of policy implementation. Not only is the Student Committee given the responsibility to "oversee the implementation of the Constitution," but it is furthermore, called upon to "lead the work" of the various organs of student government: the Executive Committee, Student Congress, and the subordinate organs in the departments and the *bans*. Thus, the division of responsibility between the Student Committee and the executive branch within the realm of policy implementation is never clearly articulated.

If the functions of the Student Committee resemble those of the CCP, in the sense that both policy decision-making and policy implementation responsibilities are combined, the similarity both organizations share with respect to the authority they exercise over organizational and personnel matters is even more striking. Authority over these realms is a cornerstone of the CCP's power, embodied in the long standing principle of "the party manages cadres" (*dang guan ganbu*), and the party holds monopoly over organization. The Student Committee is similarly given the authority to "decide the personnel appointments of leading cadres of the Executive Committee and the Council of the Congress of Student Representatives, and to "determine the organizational make-up (*zuzhi jigou*) of student government." The power to appoint top level officials in both the executive and legislative branches extends to department and ban levels within student government, too. Finally, the Student Committee is given the authority to "oversee the preparation of the next session of the Student Congress," giving it effective influence over the selection of successive leaders.

An important characteristic of the CCP, as the leading organ of the State, is to integrate into a single institutional framework the leading cadres of different state organs. Party committees at every level of the state bring together the leading cadre of the executive branches, the legislature, specialized political organs (belonging to the party proper), and the leading cadre of subordinate "local" units. The Central Committee of the CCP, for example, brings together leading cadre of the central party organs such as the Organization Department, the Propaganda Department, the State Council and its ministries, the military and security organs, the National People's Congress as well as the leading cadres at the provincial level.

The Student Committee plays a similar integrative function and is similarly constituted. Its membership is composed of representatives from three groups of student officials: members of the Executive Committee, the Council of the Student Congress, and chairmen of the department student associations. These groups represent the leading cadre of the executive branch, the legislative branch and the "local" or subordinate organs of student government, not unlike those members of the Party Central Committee who come from government (administration), the National People's Congress, and provincial organs.

Reproduction of Structure

When one analyzes formal government structure in China, one recognizes the tendency for subordinate organizations to be constructed on the same institutional model as the whole. The organizational model on which state institutions are based, tends to be reproduced at every level of the state down to basic level units. The result is that institutions of local government tend to organizationally mirror central level organs. The institutional structure of a factory, for example, is similar to the tripartite institutional arrangement discussed above, as it is divided into a congress of representatives of workers and staff, the administration and the party. Each of these institutional branches forms in principle, a vertical system with lower level organs subordinate to their immediate superiors. Organs at the basic level are directly linked and are subject to the jurisdiction of their superior institutional counterparts.

At the same time, there is a tendency for state institutions at all levels to establish the same set of departments. As a result, lower level organs appear as microcosms of higher level ones. This results in what the Chinese refer to as "*maqui suixiao, wuzang juquan*" ("although the sparrow is small, its five internal organs are complete"). The party at the central level, for instance, will establish an organization department, a propaganda department, a discipline-inspection department, a party office, etc. and party organizations at provincial, county, and basic level units, will operate a similar set of departments.

BUSA follows a similar institutional pattern. The same institutional principles which structure student government at the university level are applied at the subordinate, department and *ban* levels. However, while department student associations and *ban* committees may appear as microcosms of BUSA, as one travels to the lower echelons of the organizational hierarchy, there is less organizational articulation.

Department student associations establish student congresses based upon the same principles as the university-wide student Congress. Each department has its own student congress which is in theory, democratically elected by the entire student body of the department. The department student congresses are also given the same functions and powers as the university-wide Student Congress, insofar as they are designated as the "organ of power" of department student government and have the authority to elect the leadership of the department student associations (Article 33). Department student congresses also create standing committees that operate in the place of department congresses during their intercession.

The department student associations have their own executive organs, composed of one chairman, one or two deputy chairmen, and the heads of the functional departments who are, in principle, in charge of policy implementation. The functional departments within department student associations replicate the work of their counterparts at the university level and include a social life department, cultural department, academic affairs department, etc., although they are obviously smaller in size than the departments of BUSA. In fact, what are called "departments," generally consist of only one individual, who, of course is given the title of department head. In some cases, generally at the discretion of the department head himself, a deputy is added.

Department student associations, finally, set up the third leg of the institutional triangle, the "leading organ," called simply the "department student committee" (*xi xueshenghui weiyuan*). The student committees of the departments are modelled after the Student Committee at the center in that they combine both decision-making and policy implementation functions; they bring together the leading cadre within department student government.

Student government at the *ban* level follows the same institutional patterns as that at the department and university levels, even though organizational articulation is much less in evidence because of their small scale of operation. There is an all-*Ban* Congress of Students that plays the role of the legislative organ. In principle, it elects the Committee of *Banwei's* (*Banwei Hui*), the executive organ. Each *ban*, regardless of its size, has a *ban* committee that consists of a minimum of five and up to seven, student officials. These include a *banzhang*, the class president, one or two deputy *ban* heads, and three committee members in charge of functional areas: academic affairs (*xuexi weiyuan*), "life" affairs (*shenghuo weiyuan*), and cultural and athletic affairs (*wenhua tiyu weiyuan*). The three functional areas correspond to the functional departments, established under the executive committees in the university and department level associations, although they are fewer in number. The *banzhang*, is the only elected official of student government within the *ban*. In some cases, the deputy *ban* head may also be elected, but this is the exception, not the rule. The committee members in charge of functional areas are generally appointed by the *banzhang*. Additional *ban* committee members can be added, generally at the discretion of the *banzhang*. Larger *bans* are more likely to have two deputy *ban* heads and four committee members in charge of functional areas, two members being put in charge of cultural and athletic affairs rather than one. In a small *ban* though, with fewer students than there are positions, it would be more likely for students to concurrently hold more than one position, rather than have the positions be eliminated. And, while the idea and institutional framework based upon distinct legislative, executive, and "leading organs" exists in theory at the *ban* level, in practice the distinction is quite "fuzzy," and no real separation between the executive and "leading organ" is made.

The blurring of institutional boundaries at the lower level in fact mirrors the situation in the party/state, a tendency captured by the saying "*shangmian you xitong xiamian dang zongtong*" ("at the top there is a system, at the bottom there is only a boss"). In basic level units, the tendency is for the leading administrative and party positions to be concurrently held by a single individual, and as we have noted, the same tendency exists in student government. The class president, the *banzhang*, functions as both the "head executive" as well as the "leading" cadre in the same way that the positions of party secretary and factory manager are concurrently held by the same individual.

Another characteristic pattern of Communist state institutions, reflected in *Beida* student government, is that of "dual leadership," an approach to institutional control and supervision illustrative of mono-organizational states that have no external or independently autonomous institutions. Dual leadership is the system in which organs of state are simultaneously supervised and controlled both horizontally and vertically. An administrative organ, for example, is controlled by both its superior in the government, and the party organization at the same level. A provincial level industrial bureau, for example, will be supervised by both its superior ministry at the national level as well as the provincial party committee. The system has been adopted by school authorities in their efforts to supervise student government. As a result, each level of BUSA is under the supervision of both the superior level organ of student government as well as the school authorities at the same level. In addition, the system is used within student government so that dual lines of supervision are established which create a criss-crossing matrix within the individual institutions of student government at every level.

The Dynamics of Student Government

The similarities between *Beida* student government and institutions within the political system at large are not limited to their formal structures but extend to their deviation from these structures in practice. This points to the fact that while real structures of authority, through the practice of politics, depart from the terms under which they are formally constituted, they do so in ways which are shaped by formal institutions. Informal authority structures are not simply a distortion of formal institutions but grow out of them.

The divergence between formal and informal forms of authority is a most striking example. The student Constitution stipulates that the Congress of Student Representatives is "the highest organ of power" of student government. In reality, the Student Congress, as is true of the National People's Congress, is more of a rubber-stamp institution than an organ of power. In practice, real power resides with the five man Presidium, which is the locus of decision-making, exerting influence over decisions relating to personnel matters, elections, and institutional reforms. Its relationship to the Student Congress could be compared to that between the Politburo and the National People's Congress, although the Student Congress would probably compare negatively to the NPC because not only does it possess little influence but it barely qualifies as a real, cohesive institution.

The rubber stamp function of the Student Congress can be seen in a number of ways. Major decisions, such as the selection of new set of leaders are generally made by the Presidium prior to the meeting of the Congress. Formally, revisions to the Constitution must be passed by a two-thirds majority of the Student Congress, but the Congress is given no real input into the decision-making process. In 1986, an "extraordinary meeting" of the Student Congress was held to discuss a proposal for institutional reform. By the time the meeting was held, the Presidium had already determined the basic outlines of reform and the meeting only served to rubber stamp its decision. Students have little expectation that the Congress should provide real input from students and serve as a forum for legitimate debate. Indeed, by the time the Congress convened, the agenda and the new set of leaders had already been determined.

The rubber stamp nature of the Student Congress stems in part from its organizational structure. According to the Constitution, it is scheduled to meet only once every two years, for a day. In the interim, student representatives do not meet to exchange ideas and form opinion groups. They have no independent linkages to each other and are unable to constitute a coherent, effective decision-making body, making real participation by student representatives during the time at which the Congress is held, an impossibility.[12]

Representatives of the Student Congress perform a function more closely aligned to that of delegate for a particular student leader than representative of the rank and file. Student representatives are selectively chosen by candidates for the Presidium, as representatives who can be counted upon to support their candidacy. While they are technically *elected* by the student body, the actual process comes closer to their being *selected* by friends to volunteer to "be a representative for a day," so as to support their friend's candidacy. After the election is over and they have carried out their task, they serve no more purpose. Indeed, after the Congress ends, students are unsure as to who their student representatives are. Thus, the Congress is not a body of representatives whose loyalty is to the electorate but is rather a collection of students whose loyalties are attached to particular leaders. This factor mitigates against the Congress asserting any real institutional power and fulfilling its decision-making role.

The Congress Standing Committee, which one might expect to be a more effective organ because of its smaller size, is not much more of a "real" institution. Nominally it is composed of one representative from each class, but the members of the Standing Committee during the intercession of the Congress are no more visible to rank and file students than those who are members of the full Congress. Students seemed at best, to know of a few friends who had been representatives in the last election, but none were currently active.

The one occasion known to this author when the Standing Committee was convened for an extraordinary meeting was in the fall of 1986 for the purpose of discussing the reform proposals mentioned above. Student leaders at the time however, were at a loss to say precisely who and how many people attended this meeting and whether they were the same representatives from the last Congress. The impression given by most student cadres was that the meeting was attended by an imprecise collection of student cadres and activists. The group thus had no cohesion and no identity. Student congresses within the departments appear to be even more loosely structured than that at the university level, for they did not even have a regularly scheduled meeting at the beginning of each session.

The practice of politics diverges from theory in other ways as well. The theoretical separation of powers among specific institutions is compromised as the institutions become thoroughly intertwined with one another. Student congresses, for example, are supposed to exercise autonomy through their power of appointment and supervision over the executive branch. In fact, the leading cadre of the Student Congress in each department, the head of the Standing Committee Small Group (*changdaibiao xiaozu zuzhang*) is actually the deputy chairman of the department student association, the second highest executive officer. Circularity of power is further evident in the fact that the Student Congress is given the authority to elect executive officers, but the latter are given veto power over members of the standing committees.

In practice, BUSA is not the centralized, hierarchical organization it portrays itself to be, since lower-level organs have a significant degree of autonomy from the upper levels, due to the fact that their officers are elected rather than appointed. This is especially true of department officers and the class president, the *banzhang*. The influence of lower level leaders is closely tied to the control they have over their "bailiwicks." In addition, student leaders in the departments have wide social and organizational networks within their departments that serve as a foundation for their organizational power. Leaders at the center cannot have the same degree of influence in each department, and departmental ties give lower level leaders the power to "get out the vote."

As a result of these conflicts, in practice, the role of student organization is one of acting as mediator between subordinate and superior levels. As has been noted, the student Constitution calls upon BUSA to "be a link between the relevant school authorities and the broad mass of students." Organization, and its leadership, neither exclusively "represent," nor are they held accountable to a subordinate constituency. At the same time, they do not exclusively operate under the command of superior organs. The mediation of conflicting roles within student organization is characteristic both of the BUSA and the CCP.

Conclusion

Politically active students at *Beida* are systematically exposed to institutions that emphasize those principles of political organization, leadership and participation that dominate the society at large. Concepts of a "leading" political organ (which maintains control over organization and personnel), the "unified" approach to leadership (which weakens boundaries between theoretically autonomous institutions), dual organizational functions of representation and control, and an indirect, instrumental approach to representation repeatedly find their expression in the operation of student government.

As a result of the complex nature of the institutions, students, who wish to participate in student government, must by necessity, learn the intricacies of its institutional rules and operational procedures. Student activists thus become organizationally sophisticated, and much like party apparatchiks, are kept busy with "organizational matters," focusing their efforts on areas that speak to the internal matters of organization: politicking, networking, building contacts, etc. The complexity of campus political life is not only significant, but it serves to widen the gap between activists and non-activists, making student organizations increasingly inaccessible to outsiders. In addition, participation in student politics absorbs student cadres in organizational processes and hinders their development of a goal-oriented outlook. Student cadres are encouraged to focus their attention inward, toward organizational dynamics, rather than toward the functions of the organization as a whole.

While university students in China turned decisively to democracy as a political ideal in the 1980s, they continue to be enmeshed in established political institutions. Student organizations on campus continue to provide a most systematic exposure to political institutions and offer a real life political model that students assimilate. The spread of democratic ideals on university campuses during the 1980s has and will continue to transform students' political practice, including their participation in opposition politics, but they will continue to be influenced by the old model, too.[13] The tension between democratic principles on the one hand, and authoritarian political institutions, on the other, is not new in China. Educated Chinese have displayed an attachment to democracy for at least a century. The challenge continues to be one of transforming the old political institutions.[14]

Notes

1. A pioneering work in the study of political culture is Gabriel Almond, "Comparative Political Systems," *Journal of Politics* vol.18, no.3 (August 1956):391-409.   See also Gabriel A. Almond and Sidney Verba, *The Civic Culture* (Princeton: Princeton University, 1963); Lucian W. Pye and Sidney Verba, *Political Culture and Political Development* (Princeton: Princeton University, 1965).

2. James G. March and John P. Olsen, "The New Institutionalism: Organizational Factors in Political Life," *American Political Science Review* vol.78, no.3 (September 1984):734-749.   See page 734 for a thorough list of works on "new institutionalism." Also, Kenneth A. Shepsle, "Studying Institutions: Some Lessons from the Rational Choice Approach," *Journal of Theoretical Politics* 1, no.2 (1989):131-147.

3. March and Olsen, "The New Institutionalism," *op. cit.*, p.734.

4. Suzanne Berger, editor, *Organized Interests in Western Europe: Pluralism, Corporatism and the Transformation of Politics* (Cambridge: Cambridge University, 1981).

5. A.L Potter, *Political Institutions, Political Decay and Argentine Crisis of 1930* (Unpublished doctoral dissertation, Stanford University, 1979).

6. F.W. Scharpf, "Does Organization Matter? Task Structure and Interaction in the Ministerial Bureaucracy," in E.H. Burack and A.R. Negandhi, editors, *Organizational Design: Theoretical Perspectives and Empirical Findings* (Kent: Kent State University, 1977):149-167.

7. Archie Brown, "Introduction," in Archie Brown and Jack Gray, editors, *Political Culture and Political Change in Communist States* (New York: Holmes and Meier, 1979): 12.

8. See Andrew Nathan, *Chinese Democracy* (New York: Alfred A. Knopf, 1985); Peter R. Moody, *Opposition and Dissent in Contemporary China* (Stanford: Hoover Institution, 1977); Corinna-Barbara Francis, "The Progress of Protest: The Spring

of 1989," *Asian Survey* vol.XXIX, no.9 (September 1989):898-915.

9. David Ownby, "The Audience: Growing Alienation Among Chinese Youth," in Carol Lee Hamrin and Timothy Cheek, editors, *China's Establishment Intellectuals* (Armonk: M.E. Sharpe, 1986):212-246.

10. *Ta-lu Ching-nien chin hsing chu,* pp.4-11, cited in Dennis Doolin, editor, *Communist China: The Politics of Student Opposition* (Stanford: Hoover Institution, 1964): 18.

11. All references to the student constitution focus upon the Constitution of the 16th Session of the student government, during the 1986-87 academic year.

12. Microphones are not set up so as to allow individual student representatives to speak up during the Student Congress session.

13. For the evolution of student ideology, see Francis, "The Progress of Protest," *op. cit.,* pp.898-915.

14. Peter R. Moody Jr., "The Political Culture of Chinese Students and Intellectuals: An Historical Examination," *Asian Survey* Vol.XXVIII, No.11 (1988):1140-1160. The article points out the historical challenge of institutionalizing democratic principles in China.

CHAPTER SIXTEEN
POLITICAL EDUCATION AND STUDENT RESPONSE:
SOME BACKGROUND FACTORS BEHIND THE 1989
BEIJING DEMONSTRATIONS[1]

by Stanley Rosen

June 4, 1989--the date of the shocking military attack on unarmed student protestors and other citizens in and around Tiananmen Square--may, in time, occupy a place in Chinese history alongside May 4, 1919. The resort to armed suppression by "orthodox Marxist" hardliners who saw their political system and, not coincidentally, their personal power slipping away stunned observers inside and outside China. As the hardliners attempt to consolidate control through a campaign marked by the arrest of large numbers of students and other "counter-revolutionaries," accompanied by the intimidation of the rest of the population, it is useful to examine some of the background to such startling events.

Communist systems used to pride themselves on their ability to socialize their young. Yet the events in Beijing from April-June 1989 indicate that moral and ideological education had become completely ineffective. The Party/state had lost control over the students. Moreover, the continuing ferocity of the response by the aging leadership suggests that party elders may have abandoned their

---

[1] This is a slightly revised version of a paper delivered at the International Conference on Education in Mainland China, sponsored by the Institute of International Relations, Taipei, July 4-7, 1989, published in *Issues and Studies* vol.25, no.10 (October 1989):12-39.

efforts to win the support of the students on moral grounds or to anchor their rule on the basis of authority, opting instead for fear, intimidation, and brute force. How is one to understand such cataclysmic events? As the events are still unfolding, this chapter will concentrate on the recent past rather than the present, offering some preliminary observations rather than firm conclusions. Broadly speaking, answers must be sought in the Communist Party's (CCP) changing relationship to the society it governs. The reform process, with its emphasis on the expansion of the market, has created serious contradictions within the party and in the linkage between the party and society. The CCP has been unable to respond quickly and appropriately to a society in transition, affecting its leadership capability and even its relevance.

More specifically, the 1989 student demonstrations--and the violent response they elicited--represent another act in a continuing drama between those whose interpretation of reform includes the expansion of political participation and those who grudgingly support economic reform measures but fear the side effects of marketization, which include the infiltration of "spiritual pollution" and "bourgeois liberalization," as well as the CCP's loss of social control. This split over the methods and purpose of reform is reflected in the CCP's youth policy. Elsewhere, I have referred to the differences between those who see the need to *accommodate* the changing interests and values of youth and those who stress the necessity of *control* over an unpredictable youth, lest they use their increasing independence to undermine the country's stability and unity.[2]

While some may reasonably object that such a stark dichotomy oversimplifies a far more complex reality, debates over youth policy often seem to pose the question precisely in such dichotomous terms, particularly in times of crisis, as when students have taken to the streets to air their grievances. In this regard, the 1989 demonstrations can best be understood in the context of previous demonstrations. One of the arguments of this paper is that the roots of the 1989 demonstrations can be found in the incomplete resolution of the last major demonstrations, those of 1986-87. Both the students and the elderly orthodox Marxists who continue to influence Deng Xiaoping on non-economic issues were left dissatisfied. The students rejected the suggestion--as China's state-controlled media had put it--that their demonstrations were "a bourgeois liberal attempt to overthrow the Communist leadership." For their part, the elders were upset by General Secretary Zhao Ziyang's success in gaining Deng's ear and short-circuiting the "anti-bourgeois liberalization campaign" after a few months, using the argument that a "leftist" tendency in the party was jeopardizing China's economic reforms. While the students have continued to agitate for political change over the last two years, the massive crackdown apparently represents the aging leadership's final attempt to bury, permanently, "bourgeois liberalization." The removal of Zhao Ziyang--who seems surprisingly to have challenged Deng directly--and many of his reformist allies, along with the anti-Deng thrust of some of the protesters, created an unprecedented opportunity for the hardliners.

This paper is largely about the failure of political-ideological education in China. By the mid-1980s, many of China's university students had become skeptical of both traditional and Communist morality. They were actively searching for new ideas, many imported from the West, to give meaning to their lives. The old methods of political education were no longer effective; indeed, political work cadres had become demoralized, and a majority of those working in universities in Beijing expressed a desire to change their profession. While many reformers sought to adjust ideological work to these new conditions, more orthodox practitioners persisted in the old formulas, with predictably unsatisfactory results.

Much of the evidence presented here derives from survey research conducted by Chinese social scientists. Such attitudinal and behavioral data has become an important new source for the understanding of Chinese society.[2] From the relatively large body of survey and public opinion data now available, we will focus on two recent studies of university students, one conducted in Shanghai and one in Beijing. The studies show, among other things, an independence of thought among Chinese college students and an apparent decline in collectivist values.[3] Students are unwilling to order their belief systems to reflect official values. In the aftermath of the Beijing massacre, it will be interesting to see how--or even whether--the CCP attempts to recover the hearts and minds of the students.

The Crisis in Moral and Political Education

In the past few years, some of China's leading ideological journals have acknowledged the utter failure of the CCP's efforts in political education. One survey of six provinces and municipalities noted that "enterprise workers and staff are universally fed up with traditional ideological and political education efforts"; those who do attend political education classes "just go through the motions."[5] As the country's premier ideological journal asked plaintively, "We have conducted propaganda on the superiority of socialism for so many years, why are the results so meager?"[6]

The variety of answers proposed suggested the great uncertainty among both ordinary citizens and those responsible for political socialization over what to believe and how to instill such beliefs into the population, particularly when confronted by a skeptical younger generation. The uncertainty itself has been well documented in such diverse sources as popular songs, street ballads, and public opinion polls. Contrast the Cultural Revolution when "Chairman Mao quotation songs" contained "truth in every sentence" with the lyrics of a recent popular song:

> There's a sun in the sky and a moon in the water; I do
> not know. I do not know which is the rounder and
> which is the brighter.
>
> There's a big tree on top of the mountain and a big tree
> at the bottom of the mountain; I do not know. I do not
> know which is the bigger and which is the taller.[7]

Among many popular ballads reflecting mass confusion and discontent with government policy, the following example was being widely recited in Beijing several years ago:[8]

> *Dangde luxian xiang taiyang*
> *Zhaodao nali nali liang*
> *Dangde zhengce xiang yueliang*
> *Chuyi shiwu bu yiyang*
>
> The Party line is like the sun
> Wherever it shines will be bright
> The Party's policies are like the moon
> The 15th of the month will be different from the 1st.

Recent public opinion polls show that, aside from inflation, the absence of ideological orientation, leading to confused social values, is the issue of most concern to Chinese citizens. Those conducting the polls argue that the public wants to be "grasped" by a new set of ideas and values, that they are confused over all the new Western ideas and economic reforms of the last ten years, and are finding it difficult to adjust to a relatively free society.[8]

The uncertainty has been fueled by widespread critiques of long established concepts associated with the Communist morality that replaced traditional Chinese morality after 1949. Standard methods--typically used in both traditional and Communist China--to teach appropriate behavior have been called into question. For example, serious questions have been raised regarding the value of model emulation campaigns. In a more or less explicit criticism of Mao's hallowed injunction to "serve the people," critics have noted that morality and individual interests had been erroneously placed in opposition, so that any "individual sacrifice in service to others" was seen as "beneficial to society." Individuals like the model hero Lei Feng may provide a variety of free services to society, but such efforts are actually wasteful since they often do nothing to raise social productivity.[9]

Similarly, one commentator has referred to a "repeatedly-staged farce." For example, it is known that cadres may abuse public office for private interests and take bribes. The media will then give wide publicity to some leader who refuses to abuse public office or take bribes. It is common for primary and secondary school teachers to try to leave the low-paying, low status educational sector. Propaganda organs respond by "hurriedly tracking down an elderly teacher who is committed to educating a new batch of gifted people in the remote mountains, his devotion unchanged for decades." The results of persuading the public to emulate these model personages are "invariably minimal;...unhealthy trends continue despite repeated crackdowns."[10]

Another author, in an article entitled "The Culture of God Suffocates People on All Fronts," objected that the models publicized over the last 30 years were perfect, pure and flawless; hence, they were irrelevant to anyone who had human desires and emotions. He went on to suggest that model emulation campaigns be turned on their head:

> ...youth educators expect all people to behave like one
> or several models, and set a boundary for all people
> with one mode of behavior and thinking. What China
> needs most at present is not millions of duplicates of
> one model, or many in the form of one. Just the

contrary, what China needs now is one in the form of many. That means we need millions of individuals each with his/her own spirit of criticism and creativity, quality and style.[12]

Others extend this argument by calling for the elimination of models entirely, arguing that a prerequisite for successful modernization is the movement away from a reliance on the moral qualities of individual heroes or leaders and their replacement by an institutionalized system based on strict and impartial laws.

The lack of institutionalization is also reflected in the precarious environment in which political theorists toil, stifling any innovation in ideological and political work. A recent report urged that "the phenomenon of leaders acting as indisputable and almighty judges should be ended," that unless the "important person's verdict" is replaced by decisions based on collective scientific confirmation, chaos cannot be eliminated in social science. Lamenting the influence of the political climate on the work of theorists, the report gives examples to show how "normal academic debates may suddenly be charged as indications of political dissidence."[13]

Party-Sponsored Surveys on Student Attitudes

Modern societies cannot govern effectively in the absence of feedback mechanisms. Since the beginning of the 1980s, party and government offices have been conducting surveys on Chinese youth, primarily to gather the information that would enable political workers to perform their tasks more effectively. Some of the critiques cited above, in fact, are reactions to surveys that have revealed the failure of Communist propaganda mechanisms. Of the many surveys conducted on university students, two recent and relatively large-scale studies have been chosen for discussion below.

UNIVERSITY STUDENTS IN SHANGHAI

Under the auspices of the party committee of the Shanghai Education Commission, a survey was conducted among students at 18 Shanghai universities. Tables 16.1-16.8 present excerpts from that survey.[13] Given the standard problems associated with conducting surveys on sensitive political issues in China--respondents tend to be wary of deviating from the official political line--the surveyors deliberately posed some of their questions indirectly, asking about the behavior of others, not just of the respondents. They hypothesized that a new value system--congruent with China's reform program--was in formation and were seeking to discover the extent to which the values of university students had already changed. Since they had no longitudinal data to investigate actual change over time, they were compelled to offer in narrative form an account of student beliefs and traditional values at earlier times, noting, for example, the role the Cultural Revolution and its subsequent repudiation had played in negating an absolutist conception of values and in destroying youthful idealism.

The questions were intended to locate contemporary youth values on a continuum between two extremes, with one pole broadly representative of standard, longstanding officially sanctioned values and the other representative of values the regime had long considered deviant. For example, Tables 16.1 and 16.2 examine the relationship between pragmatism and the "ideal image" with regard to political beliefs. The data show how ineffective political socialization has been. As Table 16.1 reveals, there is a widespread perception that the CCP is attracting opportunists who join to further their personal interests, not because they believe in Communism or desire to serve the people. The surveyors point to the wide gap between the respect still accorded to the CCP's efforts in the pre-1949 period and the current highly negative image of the party, noting that the basic contradiction reflected in these two images "cannot be reconciled" *(wufa tongyi qilaide)*.

Again employing indirect questioning, the surveyors found that 87 per cent of the respondents felt that university students had no interest at all in classes on Marxism or, at best, only a minority of students had some interest. Table 16.2 shows that the objections to political education were equally divided between those who disliked the curriculum and/or teaching methods and, more fundamentally, those who saw no contemporary relevance for Marxism-Leninism.

Table 16.1

Question: Some of your friends have joined the Party, others are striving to do so. What is your observation and understanding of this?

N = 2,063

Responses	Percent
They believe in Communism and want to make a contribution	4%
They think the Party is good and are joining in order to be further educated	10%
In reality they want a "party card" which they can use as capital to receive future benefits	59%
Other responses	Omitted (in original)

Source: Zhao Yicheng, "Jiazhide chongtu" (Value Conflict), *Weidinggao* No. 8 (April 25, 1988): 29.

Table 16.2

Question: As you understand it, if some people are not interested in Marxism, what is the main reason?
N = 2,063

Responses	Percent
The content taught is the same as in middle school, there is nothing new	17%
The teacher's lectures are poor, they provide no fresh meaning	22%
The principles of Marxism-Leninism are good, but it cannot solve practical problems today, so it is useless to study it	29%
They feel that Marxism-Leninism is obsolete and out-of-date, it has no value	10%
I haven't thought about this	20%

Source: Zhao Yicheng, "Jiazhide chongtu" (Value Conflict), *Weidinggao* No. 8 (April 25, 1988): 29.

The surveyors noted that traditional moral concepts were under strong attack, citing the total reversal of familiar maxims. For example, "money is the root of all evil" had become "make a pile of money"; filial piety had been replaced by children turning on their parents. Questions were devised to determine whether moral convictions were seen as absolute or relative concepts, and whether students felt they lacked the ability to distinguish good and bad, or right and wrong. Tables 16.3-16.5 address these questions.

Table 16.3

Statement: It is very difficult today to say clearly what is correct and what is wrong.

N = 2,063

Responses	Percent
Agree	22.90
Partially agree	15.30
It's difficult to say	24.00
Partially disagree	11.46
Disagree	26.10

Source: Zhao Yicheng, "Jiazhide chongtu" (Value Conflict), *Weidinggao* No. 8 (April 25, 1988): 30.

Table 16.4
My Position Regarding Cheating on Exams Is:

N = 2,063

Responses	Percent
It's okay if it can improve your grade a bit	21%
Cheating is never very noble and I couldn't do it, but one should be lenient with others doing it	45%
I wouldn't do it and I oppose others who do it	32%

Source: Zhao Yicheng, "Jiazhide chongtu" (Value Conflict), *Weidinggao* No. 8 (April 25, 1988): 31.

Table 16.5

Question: There are two comrades at a university who fall in love; their ardor develops to the point that they decide to live together. Without giving consideration to whether they will marry in the future, what do you think about this?

N = 2,063

Responses	Percent
This is an example of moral degeneration	9.2%
As long as they have fallen in love, this is understandable and we should be tolerant	28.6%
This is a private matter, I can't say whether it's right or wrong, or good or bad	38.1%
I'm not willing to state my opinion about this	22.9%

Source: Zhao Yicheng, "Jiazhide chongtu" (Value Conflict), *Weidinggao* No. 8(April 25, 1988): 31.

Table 16.3, in which less than 40 percent even partially question the statement that "It is very difficult today to say clearly what is correct and what is wrong," suggests that there is general confusion with regard to belief systems. As the surveyors put it, morality has become relative, not absolute, depending on concrete situations. Moreover, they suggest that not only is there no longer a common standard of right and wrong, but that such a standard is actually unnecessary. This obviously also indicates, as many other surveys have shown, that the party can no longer simply dictate proper attitudes and behavior for China's youth and confidently expect compliance.

Tables 16.4 and 16.5--on exam cheating and unmarried couples living together--extend this notion of the ambiguity of truth by showing the development of a private morality in China, a willingness to understand and accept the behavior of others without interference. Honesty has become situational. Some students report that "If exam questions are easy and I can answer them, or I'm not concerned with high grades, then I won't cheat; otherwise I will."

The fact that less than 10 percent of the respondents would object to unmarried students living together--although official China would find this scandalous in the extreme--further shows the gap between traditional values and the views of the younger generation. The surveyors found this result quite shocking, attributing it to the influence of Western contemporary ethics spread by the pervasiveness of mass communications.

Table 16.6
Question: A student at a conservatory volunteers to join the military. He goes to the front line on the Vietnamese border. He performs meritoriously in a battle, but loses a leg. What is your reaction to this?

N = 2,063

Responses	Percent
We should praise and encourage this patriotic action, what he did was correct	31%
If the country urgently requires it, he should go. But it's unnecessary for him to volunteer	44%
He should not join the military. He can make a greater contribution in his own profession	18%
It is completely worthless	5%

Source: Zhao Yicheng, "Jiazhide chongtu" (Value Conflict), *Weidinggao* No. 8 (April 25, 1988): 32.

Table 16.7

Question: In my class, the majority of students are very concerned about grades. There is one student who studies very hard, but his foundation is poor. Of course, he has many difficulties. People are divided on whether to offer him help. What do you think?
N = 2,063

Responses	Percent
Students with good grades should help him. Even if it interferes with their own time, they should still do it	31%
Students with good grades should help him, but it cannot interfere with their own studies	47%
Students with good grades should not take the initiative to help him. Studies are competitive; those outstanding will be victorious, those inferior will be eliminated	10%
Students with good grades should not help him. Whether one studies well or poorly is an individual matter	9%

Source: Zhao Yicheng, "Jiazhide chongtu" (Value Conflict), *Weidinggao* No. 8 (April 25, 1988): 33.

Table 16.8

Please assess the following sentiments:
N =   2,063

Responses			Percent
	It's reasonable	It's undesirable	Cannot clearly say
Everyone is for me, and I'm for everyone	64%	9%	26%
One should be a rust free screw	26%	28%	45%
The reason one lives is to enable others to live a more beautiful life	39%	17%	42%
Everyone is subjective about themselves and objective about others	56%	11%	36%
After a person dies, all he can leave is his name; after a bird flies away, all that is left is its voice	55%	14%	29%

Source: Zhao Yicheng, "Jiazhide chongtu" (Value Conflict), *Weidinggao* No. 8 (April 25, 1988): 33.

Tables 16.6-16.8 were meant to investigate the relationship between individualism and collectivism. Childhood socialization takes education in collectivist values as one of its most important tasks, with stories in primary school readers, for example, emphasizing the importance of working together and helping others. Patriotism is likewise a core value emphasized throughout one's schooling. In this regard, Table 16.6--which registers reactions to a college student who volunteers to join the military--is interesting. The surveyors were not quite sure how to interpret their findings. They noted, of course, that the students were only giving their opinion about a hypothetical situation; its relationship to actual behavior was unclear. Moreover, they were upset by the concern with individual achievement, even selfishness, exhibited by 23 percent of the respondents. The majority reaction was difficult to gauge. While 31 percent gave unqualified support to the student who volunteered for military service, 44 percent were less definite, suggesting that most students put individual interests ahead of service to the country.

Taken together with other surveys, the results appear to suggest a more sophisticated definition of patriotism and a reaction against blind acceptance of the party's designation of the meaning of patriotism. For example, a survey on Shanghai university students conducted in 1983 asked youth to cite "the proper standards for a good youth in the 1980s." Ranked second among the choices--supported by 46.5 percent of respondents, who could choose two selections--was: "is patriotic and able to preserve national dignity." In the same survey, however, when asked: "What ideological qualities should university students in the 1980s possess?", only 16.5 percent chose "love the country and love the people," while a mere 3% opted for "listen to what the party says and be a revolutionary successor." The majority--58.6 percent--chose "dare to think and be good at thinking."[14]

Table 16.7, on the willingness of students to render academic help to classmates who fall behind, shows an even stronger tendency towards individualism. Only 31 percent were willing to offer help if it interfered with their own studies. As a typical response of the majority, one student was cited as follows: "I feel that each person first has a responsibility to himself, and only then will he have the qualifications to help others."

Finally, Table 16.8 records the responses of students to a series of expressions. Most striking is the lack of support for the two expressions associated with self sacrifice, with the subordination of the individual to the state or the group. The image of the "rust-free screw" *(luosiding)* is of course permanently associated with Lei Feng, the model hero whose greatest desire was to "serve the people" and be a cog in any machine or context in which the party placed him.

The surveyors, it is interesting to note, viewed the data in a positive light. They did not see the current quest for individual achievement and worth as mere selfishness; rather, they saw it as a natural reaction against the "beautiful"--and mindless--slogans of the Cultural Revolution, which had led to the use of individuals as political tools. They also argued that the pursuit of individual interest is beneficial for economic reform and the development of a commodity economy, with society more and more coming to respect the value of the individual.

Students and Political Workers in Beijing in the Aftermath of the 1986-87 Demonstrations

The most ambitious effort to study the effects of political education was a large-scale survey on the state of ideological and political work in Beijing universities from April 1986 to July 1987 under the auspices of the municipal party committee and youth league, various universities, the municipal education union, and other organs. Thirty thousand questionnaires were distributed to students, teachers, and political work cadres. This study is particularly interesting because the student demonstrations of December 1986--January 1987 occurred before the survey was completed, allowing the authorities to incorporate items relating to these events into the survey instrument.[16]

Consistent with previous surveys, the data revealed a student body much more interested in private activities than in overtly political-- or even collectivist--undertakings as Table 16.9 reveals. Authorities particularly lamented the condition of CYL organizations, which were said to be "very weak," offering members few activities. For example, 52 percent of league members felt that the work of their league branch had little influence in promoting collectivism in the classroom, while 75 percent had negative impressions regarding the effectiveness of branch cadres. Many did not even want the league to be more active, with 23 percent hoping for as little activity as possible. In addition, 50 percent of the students would not carry out a league resolution with which they disagreed; 47 percent felt it did not matter whether or not one joined; and 60 percent were not even clear on the nature (*xingzhi*) of the league and its differences with other student organizations. The data on league members' attitudes toward the party and socialism showed a similarly "low" level of consciousness.[17]

Table 16.9

The Interest Expressed by University Students in Beijing
in Participation in Various Kinds of Activities

Activity	Interested	Not Interested	Rank
Sports	92.1%	6.5%	1
Social Practice and Investigation	90.1%	7.7%	2
Various Reports and Lectures	84.7%	13.2%	3
Work-Study Program	81.3%	16.4%	4
Art, Literature, and Entertainment	77.5%	10.2%	5
Work Done for the Public in Addition to One's Job (*shehui gongzuo*)	73.5%	23.5%	6
Public Activities (*shehui huodong*)	67.5%	29.7%	7
Voluntary Labor	63.0%	33.5%	8
Activities of the Party and Youth League	52.3%	44.4%	9
Political Study	35.0%	51.1%	10

Source: Wang Sunyu et al., "Daxueshengzhong dang de jianshe gongzuo chutan" (A Preliminary Exploration of Party Construction Work Among University Students), in Beijing Municipal Party Committee Research Office, ed., *Xin shiqi daxuesheng sixiang zhengzhi jiaoyu yanjiu* (Research on Ideological and Political Education of University Students in the New Period) (Beijing: Beijing Normal University Press, 1988):209.

Table 16.10

University Students in Beijing and Party Membership

	1980	81	82	83	84	85	86
New Members Recruited	318	803	1,420	1,455	3,096	6,072	5,879
Total no. of University Students	83,032*	98,103*	94,864*	90,894*	105,307	125,861	137,282
Total no. of student party members	N/A	N/A	N/A	N/A	8,678	13,562	15,833
% of student party members	N/A	N/A	N/A	N/A	8.25	10.78	11.50
undergraduate student party members	N/A	N/A	N/A	N/A	2,221	4,410	5,678
party members as % of all undergraduates	N/A	N/A	N/A	N/A	2.5	4.4	5.5
graduate student party members	N/A	N/A	N/A	N/A	2,097	4,011	5,507
party members as % of all graduate students	N/A	N/A	N/A	N/A	23.05	27.68	32.00
party members among cadres taking specialized courses	N/A	N/A	N/A	N/A	4,369	5,141	4,648
Party members as % of such cadres	N/A	N/A	N/A	N/A	48.09	45.99	31.30

Source: Wang et al., "Daxueshengzhong dang de jianshe gongzuo chutan," pp.186-187.

* *Achievement of Education in China* (Beijing: People's Education Press, 1984):263. The 1980-83 figures for total number of university students apply only to undergraduates.

Table 16.11

Views of University Students in Beijing About Party Work Style
N = 2,723

Very confident	9.7%
Believe that it will basically improve but not confident the improvement will take place in the next few years	44.6%
As far as the improvement in Party work style, one can only move a step at a time and see the results	26.1%
Lack confidence in any basic improvement	12.2%
No confidence	6.5%

Source: Wang Dianqing et al., "Daxuesheng sixiang zhuangkuang de diaocha fenxi" (An Investigation and Analysis of the Ideology of University Students) in *Xin shiqi daxuesheng sixiang zhengzhi jiaoyu yanjiu*, p.65.

Table 16.12

Views of Graduate Students in Beijing
Regarding the Main Ideas and Thought of Fang Lizhi
N = 1,812

Should be highly praised	11.6%
Should be disdained	0%
Worthy of serious study	79%
Don't know	9.4%

Source: Yu Zerong, Wu Yanxi et al., "Gaijin he jiaqiang yanjiusheng sixiang zhengzhi gongzuode jianyi," in *Xin shiqi daxuesheng sixiang zhengzhi jiaoyu yanjiu*, p.111.

The findings on student party members were better, but still problematic. In the early 1980s, as Table 16.10 shows, there were few student party members being recruited. One internal report from the

Ministry of Education noted in 1983 that in some Beijing universities there were fewer student party members than the number of underground party members that had been there before 1949.[18] By 1986, 5.5 percent of Beijing undergraduates had joined the party but, as the survey showed, some nevertheless held unacceptable political ideas about the party and communism. It was also acknowledged that a minority had joined out of "impure motives." In fact, this was the widespread perception among students in general, as Table 16.1 revealed. Such skepticism over motives appears to be part of a larger suspicion that the party cannot improve its work style in the near future. As Table 16.11 shows, fewer than 10 percent were confident such improvement would occur in the next few years.

In separate chapters on graduate students and young teachers, it was clear that the official party line on the 1986-87 demonstrations had failed to convince a majority. For example, as Table 16.12 shows, despite Fang Lizhi's expulsion from the party on Deng Xiaoping's direct orders in January 1987, and the subsequent vilification of his views in the press, apparently not a single respondent in the sample of more than 1,800 was willing to disdain (*tuoqi*) Fang's ideas. About 50 percent either could not understand the significance of the campaign against bourgeois liberalization, or felt it was unnecessary. In addition, 60 percent of the graduate students saw no improvement in party work style after the three-and-a-half year rectification campaign, with some suggesting it had gotten worse. "A considerable portion" (*xiangdang yi bufen*) were also "strongly dissatisfied" (*qiangliede buman*) with the system of choosing cadres, with about 20 percent suggesting that the result of the reform was to allow the children of cadres to climb up the hierarchy, and a much larger number criticizing the use of *guanxi* (connections) or simple "blindness" (*mangmuxing*) as the main basis for promotions.[19] Given these views, it is not surprising that graduate students played an important leadership role in the 1989 demonstrations.

The responses of young teachers 35 years old and under--who make up about one-third of the teaching staff in Beijing universities--were also worrisome to the leadership. For example, between 30.7-40.7 percent expressed doubt about the necessity for the "Four Basic Principles" (Adherence to Socialism, the Dictatorship of the Proletariat, Rule by the Communist Party, and Marxism-Leninism-Mao Zedong Thought). Those who were either unclear about what constituted bourgeois liberalization felt it had nothing to do with them or that criticism against it was unnecessary constituted over 45 percent of the sample. Perhaps most ominously for the future, "about two-thirds of the young teachers had differing levels of sympathy for the demonstrations," with the majority understanding the feeling that something was needed to speed up reform and democratization, even if they did not necessarily approve of the methods adopted.[19]

Nor did the students absorb the "proper" lessons from the fate of the demonstrations. In surveys done after things had quieted down, 62 percent of the undergraduates and 92 percent of the graduates saw the root cause of the demonstrations as either the corrupt party work style or the lack of democracy; moreover, 76 percent of the undergraduates and 71 percent of the graduates either felt that the demonstrations had promoted democratization or at least had positive aspects as well as negative ones.[20]

Since the survey had been conducted to examine the state of ideological-political work in the universities, a key target group to be investigated was the 3,092 political work cadres--only 37.6 percent of whom were full-time--at the 68 universities. The results, as shown in Tables 16.13 and 16.14, revealed the demoralization of political work cadres. For example, not a single individual engaged in such work at Qinghua University was willing to continue the job over the long term, a situation common at the best universities. At Beijing Normal University, only 7.7 percent, and at Beida, only 12.5 percent, expressed an interest in such work. Among the 9 universities surveyed, the percentage of political work cadres who requested *immediate* transfer to other kinds of work ranged from 17.5 percent to 44.5 percent. Of those seeking a transfer, the most common reason given was the low--and "inaccurate"--evaluation society gave to such work.[21]

The problem was not limited to political work cadres at the university level, however. An extensive survey of middle school political workers conducted from April to June 1987 in Beijing turned up equally discouraging results. Not only was there a shortage of young workers, but those that were there did not really want to work in this field, with many leaving if they could.[22]

Table 16.13

**Desire of Political Work Cadres in Universities
in Beijing to Continue in Their Work**

University (College)	Want to continue in this work over a long period of time	Do not want to continue in this work over a long period of time	Do not want to engage in this work; hope to transfer out of political work
Qinghua University	0%	73.3%	20.0%
Beijing University	12.5%	50.0%	37.5%
Beijing Normal University	7.7%	51.3%	25.6%
Beijing Engineering College	41.2%	23.5%	29.4%
Beijing Teachers' College	37.5%	37.5%	17.5%
Beijing Steel Institute	12.8%	79.5%	23.1%
Capital Medical	50.0%	6.3%	27.6%
Beijing Forestry University	27.8%	55.6%	44.5%
Northern Communications University	37.5%	37.5%	25.0%

Note: Since some respondents opted for two categories, the totals may exceed 100% in some cases.

Source: Li Zhixiang, et al., "Daxuesheng sixiang zhengzhi jiaoyu gongzuo duiwude xianzhuang ji jianyi," *Xin shiqi daxuesheng sixiang zhengzhi jiaoyu yanjiu*, p.138.

Table 16.14

Reasons Why Respondents Do Not Want to Spend Their Lives Engaged in Political Work

University (College)	Does not receive a correct evaluation from society	Fear of future policy change	Cannot develop one's future	Material benefits low	Not suited to this work	Political work is meaningless; one merely is busy wasting time	Fear of making a political mistake	You cannot use what you've studied
Quinghua University	100.0%	53.3%	6.7%	6.7%	26.7%	0.0%	0.0%	0.0%
Beijing University	43.8%	37.5%	31.3%	25.0%	31.3%	6.3%	0.0%	12.5%
Beijing Normal University	60.0%	56.4%	28.2%	10.3%	20.5%	5.1%	0.0%	15.4%
Beijing Engineering	64.7%	52.3%	23.5%	5.8%	29.4%	5.9%	5.8%	0.0%
Beijing Teacher's	55.0%	35.0%	30.0%	15.0%	32.0%	5.0%	10.0%	0.0%
Beijing Steel Institute	15.4%	46.2%	7.7%	15.4%	59.0%	41.0%	7.7%	0.0%
Capital Medical	25.0%	62.5%	25.0%	12.5%	25.0%	0.0%	0.0%	0.0%
Beijing Forestry	22.2%	50.0%	11.1%	11.1%	50.0%	50.0%	5.6%	0.0%
Northern Communications	87.5%	75.0%	25.0%	12.5%	25.0%	0.0%	12.5%	0.0%

Source: Li Zhixiang, et al.

To deal with these problems, a number of policy changes were announced by mid-1987. Political standards were to be reintroduced for university enrollment, labor education was stepped up, and military training time was doubled and made compulsory. The much-maligned and demoralized political work cadres had their status and benefits upgraded. Instructors responsible for political and ideological work, including CYL secretaries, were to be given the same titles, from assistant lecturer to full professor, as their academic counterparts. Moreover, their ranks were to be expanded, with the State Education Commission suggesting that one instructor of ideological and political education would be needed for every 150 college students.[24] Although it is clear that Deng Xiaoping set the tone for the conservative backlash in his remarks to leading officials on December 30, 1986, blaming the student unrest on "weakness in opposing bourgeois liberalization," some of the specific changes may be seen as responses to problems brought out in the Beijing survey.

According to interviewees, official policy toward the students was also shaped by a series of surveys conducted for the State Council by the State Commission for Restructuring the Economic System and its survey arm, the China Social Survey System. They recommended that the authorities improve the democratic atmosphere of the campuses. With more freedom inside, they argued, the students would be less willing to engage in off-campus demonstrations. Moreover, the authorities should seek to prevent the students from leaving the campuses in pursuit of their demands, warning the students that a clear distinction would be made between activities on and off the campus. This distinction should be backed up by a large contingent of off-campus police, when necessary, to discourage demonstrators from leaving the university grounds. These recommendations were largely adopted and, until April 1989, appear to have been reasonably successful. However, given the rising discontent, the pressure to move off campus became increasingly difficult to contain. For example, the number of applications for street demonstrations, mostly from students, swelled in 1988--there were more than 1,000 in the first half of the year alone--but very few were approved. One official admitted at the time that regardless of party efforts, another student movement was probably inevitable.[25]

Despite the conservative backlash, the policy changes of 1987 appear to have had little lasting effect on ideological-political work. For a time, interviewees report, students felt a necessity to attend their politics courses. However, as the campaign against bourgeois liberalization wound down, attendance gradually petered out. Indeed, attendance in all classes began to decline, according to some, right after the 1986-87 demonstrations, with an absentee rate above 30 percent for any course with political content and 20 percent for courses in the student's specialization.[26] "Business fever" and materialism began to "infect" the campuses, with more students typically showing up to hear a lecture on the making of pickled vegetables than to lectures on current events.[27] The "dropout fever," already serious at the primary and high school levels, began to claim graduate students as well. Some students deliberately created the conditions necessary to guarantee their elimination, thus enabling them to pursue business opportunities or study abroad.[27]

Although the "anti-bourgeois liberalization campaign" lasted only from January-May 1987, it had a complex and important effect on both students and ideological hardliners. Students had originally taken to the streets in support of the reform movement but became more critical when the state controlled media began to distort their activities. One Chinese public opinion specialist has cited unpublished surveys to demonstrate that the sense of betrayal the students felt began to transform the movement from a pro- to an anti-government position. Uncommitted students--and even those opposed to the demonstrations--found the official media useless and thus turned to alternative channels. For example, one survey found that 13 percent of the students regularly listened to the Voice of America (VOA) before the demonstrations, but the number had jumped to 30 percent during the demonstrations. While about 70 percent believed the VOA reporting, 75 percent distrusted the official media accounts. Most damning--and a harbinger of things to come--student satisfaction with the political atmosphere decreased by almost 50 percent before and after the demonstrations.[28]

The aging orthodox Marxists came away from the 1986-87 unrest equally frustrated. Although they were able to engineer the removal of Party General Secretary Hu Yaobang, their anti-bourgeois liberalization campaign fizzled out rapidly, with Deng himself fearing a turn toward "leftism" could damage China's economic reforms and the opening to the West. By the Thirteenth Party Congress in October 1987, virtually all the survivors of the founding generation of veteran revolutionaries, including Deng himself, had "retired" or moved to secondary posts.

Despite such highly visible changes, the underlying divisions over the role of political education--not to mention the reform program itself--did not disappear. The crisis in ideology--indeed, the deeper "moral crisis" was a common theme, openly discussed, in the Chinese press throughout 1988, continuing into 1989. When Politburo Standing Committee member Hu Qili met with four university presidents and party secretaries, one told him: "Nowadays, the whole classroom rocks with laughter whenever communism and Marxism-Leninism are mentioned...."[29] Political economy instructors complained that their textbooks "had been the same for 40 years" and were now unrelated to reality.[30] Visitors noted the increasing similarities between the "dens of debauchery" in Hong Kong and Guangzhou and the ineffectiveness of periodic crackdowns.[31] Many reports in the press referred to the "grim" public security situation, with the vice minister of public security warning that things would remain grim for the next few years. The graduate student unions at twelve Beijing universities submitted a petition to the Chinese People's Political Consultative Conference detailing the declining moral climate in the country and asking the authorities to take action.[33] As a partial response, a national meeting on moral education recommended an increase in China's 5.28 million moral educators and, on December 25, 1988, the Party Central Committee issued a "Circular on Reforming and Strengthening Moral Education for Primary and Secondary School Students."[34]

Increasing the ideological workforce and drafting documents was likely to be of little use, however. While everyone agreed that a problem existed, and that a new approach was needed, there was no consensus on how to instill moral and political values that would be appropriate to a developing commodity economy in the primary stage of socialism. The difficulties of such a task--and the clash between old and new concepts of politics and morality--was brought home most forcefully in the wide coverage given to the "Shekou Storm."[35]

In January 1988, invited by the local CYL branch, three well-known "professors" of propaganda from the Research Center on Ideological Education for Chinese Youth addressed seventy young workers in Shekou in the Shenzhen special economic zone (SEZ). What made the symposium newsworthy was the unexpected attack on the content and form of traditional ideological work by members of the audience. Two cultures had collided. Youth in Shekou had no patience with what one called "empty sermons," preferring a discussion of concrete questions. The propagandists were used to neither dialogue nor discourtesy. They could not have expected to be challenged on positions they considered unassailable. For example, one professor had earlier criticized as "gold diggers" those who came to the SEZs to make money; he thought they "should contribute a large portion of their income to the state to be spent on public welfare." This smacked of "leftism" to some youth, who pointed out that making money was fine and, in fact, gold diggers had developed the American west.

Confronted with what they took to be the familiar sanctimonious, self-righteous style of the propagandists, the youth seemed to enjoy flaunting their freedom and Shekou's "foreignness." One reportedly noted that "the central government is far away. Even if I swear at you, no one will come to interfere, and my Hong Kong boss will not fire me because of this." Another stated: "We find newspaper propaganda disgusting. It says Shenzhen takes the socialist road with Chinese characteristics. What Chinese characteristics are actually there? The characteristics of Shenzhen are foreign characteristics!" One propagandist, when challenged, asked whether the troublesome youth dared to reveal his name. To great amusement, he presented his business card.

Between August 15 and September 16, 1988, *People's Daily* published thirty-five letters--out of the thousands received--commenting on the Shekou Storm. The propagandists were given a chance to reiterate and defend their style and their views. They also noted their own personal health and family difficulties and lack of interest in financial remuneration. In comments that could have been made by any political work cadre, one noted that: "When ideological and political work is difficult, we who work on the front line have given so much and yet have not been properly assessed." Most poignantly, he ended with a plea, saying: "We admit that we need to improve. However, even if there are weaknesses and mistakes in our work, shouldn't people help in a positive way and as comrades?"

Conclusion

Among the many casualties of the Beijing massacre is the CCP's youth policy. Even before that event, there was no market for the method and content of the political education that was being dispensed in the classroom. Since the military fired on Chinese citizens ostensibly to defend socialism and the Communist Party, it is reasonable to assume that these basic principles of state power have become further discredited. Nevertheless, many concrete questions remain.

In recent years, relaxed political controls have contributed to creating an environment in which new and unorthodox ideas can be relatively openly discussed, in which membership in the party is not a prerequisite for upward mobility, and in which young people can pursue a variety of options to achieve success. Will the events of June 3-4 and their aftermath drastically change the party's relationship with society and lead to strict new political controls?

What will be the effect, for example, on party recruitment? Over the past five years CCP leaders have sought, with some success, to change the recruitment base of the CCP, appealing to those who are younger and better educated, as well as those who have clearly benefited from the economic reforms. The number of university undergraduates who have joined has steadily increased since 1984. This has reversed a trend that had been clear since the 1950s. An aging CCP had lost touch with an increasingly youthful society. For example, in 1949, when the PRC was established, about 27 percent of party members were 25 years old or younger. By 1983, only about 3 percent of party members fit that age profile. The educational level of CCP members has historically been very low. Within the last five years, two out of every three party members recruited each year have been below the age of 35. Similarly, two-thirds of the new recruits have a senior middle school education or better. This is a significant change because 13 million of the 48 million party members have been recruited since 1982.

Will the young and the educated now shun the party? Will the upward mobility opportunities be tied much more closely to party membership to compensate for the anticipated shortfall and to reward its supporters? This would mark a significant shift from recent years in which party membership was no longer the major route to success for young people. The Chinese press has referred to the "three ways" to pursue a career: the black, the gold, and the red. The black way is to leave China to study abroad, to earn a black graduation cap and gown. The gold way suggests a career in business and the pursuit of wealth. The red way refers to joining the Communist Party and becoming a government official. Some surveys have shown, however, that many youth who seek party membership do so only after success of the black or gold variety. Thus, peasants who have become wealthy seek to enter the party to protect their new riches from extortion by local cadres. Students often hold off applying for party membership until they have attained academic success or have begun a professional career. To maintain its relevance in a rapidly changing society, the party has implicitly acknowledged that attracting the "expert" has become more important than attracting the "Red." Will it continue to do so?

Will there be a major change in the recruitment and job assignment system for university students? Interviewees report that one reason why so many students were willing to defy the authorities and participate in pro-democracy activities was their lack of concern with future job opportunities. The state now has much less control over job assignments and talented students feel confident that they can land positions with the new corporations on the cutting edge of modernization, such as those engaged in foreign trade and joint ventures. Originally, the unified state job assignment system was scheduled to be phased out by 1993. However, the state has moved to restore its control over the students by suspending this plan. Similarly, will political criteria for university enrollment be re-instituted? Can officially-sanctioned youth organizations which have lost their appeal, such as the Communist Youth League, be strengthened in such a way as to compel young people once again to take them seriously? In short, can the CCP turn back the clock and regain control over a society from which it has become increasingly estranged, all the while continuing to pursue the strategies of economic modernization and "openness" that produced much of the estrangement in the first place?

Notes

1. Stanley Rosen, "Prosperity, Privatization and China's Youth," *Problems of Communism* (March, 1985):1-28.

2. For an evaluation of Chinese surveys, see Stanley Rosen and David S.K. Chu, *Survey Research in the People's Republic of China* (Washington, D.C.: United States Information Agency, 1987).

3. I have presented additional evidence of changing youth values in the 1980s in the following papers: "The Impact of Reform Policies on Youth Attitudes," in Deborah Davis and Ezra F. Vogel, editors, *Social Consequences of Chinese Economic Reforms* (Cambridge: Harvard East Asian Studies Publications); "Value Change Among Post-Mao Youth: The Evidence From Survey Data," in Perry Link, Richard Madsen and Paul Pickowicz, editors, *Unofficial China: Popular Culture and Thought in the People's Republic* (Boulder: Westview Press: 1989):193-216; "The Impact of Reform on the Attitudes and Behavior of Chinese Youth: Some Evidence from Survey Research," in Donna Bahry and Joel Moses, editors, *Communist Dialectic: The Political Implications of Economic Reform in Communist Systems* (New York: New York University Press, 1990):264-294.

4. *Sixiang zhengzhi gongzuo yanjiu* (November 1988) translated in the Joint Publications Research Service (JPRS)-CAR-89-015 (February 23, 1989):13-16.

5. *Qiushi* (September 1, 1988) translated in JPRS-CAR-88-065 (October 13, 1988):18-21.

6. *Xin Guancha* January 25, 1988 translated in JPRS-CAR-89-043 (May, 11, 1989):36-37.

7. As reported by a Beijing informant. On this general subject, see Wang Hailun, "Koutou wenxue re yu quanmin laosaochao" (Ballad Fever and the Tide of Mass Discontent) *Jiushi niandai* (February 1989):62-64.

8. South China Morning Post (December 16, 1988) cited in *FBIS*

Daily Report (December 16, 1988):45-46.

9. *Shijie Jingji Daobao* (February 29, 1988) translated in JPRS-CAR-88-024 (May 23, 1988):36-38.

10. *Guangming Ribao* (February 24, 1988) translated in JPRS-CAR-88-029 (June 13, 1988):1-2.

11. *Qiushi* (September 1, 1988 citing *Shekou tongxun bao*) translated in JPRS-CAR-88-065 (October 13, 1988):18-21.

12. *Jiefang Ribao* (June 8, 1988) translated in JPRS-CAR-88-056 (September 19, 1988):18-19.

13. The data presented here derives from Zhao Yicheng, "Jiazhide chongtu," *Weidinggao* no.8 (April 25, 1988):26-33 and *Weidinggao* no.9 (May 10, 1988):18-21.

14. Geng Xiaolin and Zhu Yuejing, "Dangdai qingnian zhuiqiude 'lixiang xingxiang' yu daode bangyang jiaoyu," *Shanghai qingshaonian yanjiu* no.3 (1984):6-7.

15. I have also discussed this survey in "Youth and Social Change in the People's Republic of China" (Paper presented at the 18th Sino-American Conference, Hoover Institution, Stanford, California, June 8-11, 1989).   The results of the survey, covering 375 pages, appear in Beijing Municipal Party Committee Research Office, editor, *Xin shiqi daxuesheng sixiang zhengzhi jiaoyu yanjiu* (Beijing: Beijing Normal University Press, 1988).   Several chapters are translated in Stanley Rosen, editor, "Political Education (I)" and "Political Education (II)," *Chinese Education*, (Fall and Spring, 1990).

16. Stanley Rosen, "Political Education," *op. cit.*, pp.18-19.

17. For additional data, see Rosen, "The Impact of Reform on Attitudes," *op. cit.*

18. *Xin shiqi*, *op. cit.*, pp.84-115.

19. *Ibid.*, pp.170-185.

20. *Ibid.*, p.290.

21. *Ibid.*, pp.134-150.

22. *Gaojiao yanjiu* (Beijing Normal Institute) No.1 (1988):74-80.

23. For more details on the changes, see Rosen, "Students," in Anthony Kane, editor, *China Briefing 1988* (Boulder: Westview, 1988):79-105.

24. *Ming Pao* (October 28, 1988) cited in *Daily Report* (October 31, 1988):33.

25. Zhu Wentao, "Ling ren shenside xiaoyuan 'xin chao': guanyu daxuesheng yanxuede xianzhuang he sikao" (A 'New Tide' on Campus That Causes One to Ponder: Thinking About the New Situation in Which Students Despise Studies), *Shehui*, No. 8 (August, 1988):8-11.

26. *Liaowang Overseas Edition* (November 21, 1988) in *FBIS Daily Report* (December 2, 1988):21-24.

27. Cheng Ying, "Dalu yanjiusheng zhengqu bei 'taotai'" (Mainland Graduate Students Strive to 'Be Eliminated Through Competition), *Jiushi niandai* (January 1989):27-29.

28. J.H. Zhu, "Origins of the Chinese Student Unrest," *The Indianapolis Star* (May 9, 1989).

29. *Zhejiang ribao* (July 31, 1988) cited in *FBIS Daily Report* (August 12, 1988):28-29.

30. *Gongren ribao* (July 15, 1988) cited in *FBIS Daily Report* (November 7, 1988):3.

31. *Hong Kong Standard* (December 5, 1988) cited in *FBIS Daily Report* (December 6, 1988):26-27.

32. *Wen Wei Po* (Hong Kong) (January 26, 1989) cited in *FBIS Daily*

Report (January 27, 1989):13-14; *Zhongguo tongxun she* (April 5, 1989) cited in *Daily Report* (April 10, 1989):33-34.

33. *Renmin Ribao* (January 17, 1989) cited in *FBIS Daily Report*, (January 24, 1989):20-24; *Xinhua* (June 1, 1989) cited in *Daily Report* (June 10, 1988):23.

34. The following discussion draws from *Renmin Ribao* (August 6 and 29, and September 14, 1988) as cited in *FBIS Daily Report* (September 21, 1988):53-60; *Renmin Ribao* (September 3, 1988) cited in *FBIS Daily Report* (September 28, 1988):68-70; *Jingjixue Zhoubao* (October 2, 1988) cited in *FBIS Daily Report* (October 26, 1988):19-21; *China News Analysis*, no.1374 (December 15, 1988); Chang Tianyu, "'Shekou fengbo' shuomingle shenma?" (What Does the 'Shekou Storm' Signify?), *Guangjiaojing* (September 1988):94-95.

BIBLIOGRAPHY

Western Language Serials

Asian Survey
Beijing Review
China Daily
China Exchange News
China News Analysis
China Quarterly
Chinese Education
Chinese Sociology and Anthropology
Comparative Education
Comparative Education Review
Current Background
Eastern Horizon
Foreign Broadcast Information Service Daily Report China [FBIS]
Joint Publications Reference Service, China Political Sociological [JPRS-CPS]
Journal of Asian Studies
Modern China
Survey of China Mainland Press
Xinhua [New China News Agency]

Chinese Language Serials

Beijing Ribao [Beijing Daily]
Beijing Zhengfa Xueyuan Xuebao [Beijing Institute Political Science and Law Journal]
Faxue [Law]
Faxue Yanjiu [Studies in Law]
Faxue Jikan [Law Papers]
Faxue Zazhi [Law Magazine]
Gaojiao Zhanxian [Higher Education Front] (renamed *Zhongguo Gaodeng Jiaoyu* in July, 1986)
Guangming Ribao [Enlightenment Daily]
Jiaogang Yuekan [Education Monthly]
Jiaoshibao [Teacher Newspaper]

449

Jiaoyu Lilun yu Shijian [Educational Theory and Practice]
Jiaoyu Tongxun [Education Newsletter]
Jiaoyu Yanjiu [Educational Research]
Jiaoyu yu Jingji [Education and Economics]
Jingji Yanjiu [Economics Research]
Jiushiniandai [The Nineties]
Minzhu yu Fazhi [Democracy and Legal System]
Ningxia Jiaoyu Xueyuan Xuebao [Ningxia Education Institute Journal]
Qingshaonian Fanzui Yanjiu [Juvenile Delinquency Research]
Renmin Jiaoyu [People's Education]
Renmin Ribao [People's Daily]
Shanghai Jiaoyu [Shanghai Education]
Shanghai Qingshaonian Yanjiu [Shanghai Youth Research]
Shehui [Society]
Shifan Jiaoyu [Teacher Education]
Zhongguo Funu [Chinese Women]
Zhongguo Fazhi Bao [Chinese Law Newspaper]
Zhongguo Gaodeng Jiaoyu [Higher Education]
Zhongguo Jiaoyu Bao [Chinese Education Newspaper]
Zhongguo Shehui Kexue [Chinese Social Sciences]

Selected Books and Articles

A Nation at Risk. Report from the National Commission on Excellence in
    Education, Washington, D.C., 1983.

Achievement of Education in China, Statistics 1949-1983. Beijing:
    People's Education Press, 1985.

Achievement of Education in China 1980-85. Beijing: People's Education
    Press, 1986.

Alford, William. "Of Arsenic and Old Laws: Looking Anew at Criminal
    Justice in Late Imperial China." *California Law Review* vol.72,
    no.6 (December 1984).

_____. "The Inscrutable Occidental? Implications of Roberto
    Unger's Uses and Abuses of the Chinese Past." *Texas Law
    Review* 64, no.5 (1986):915-972.

Allito, Guy. *The Last Confucian: Liang Shu-ming and the Chinese Dilemma of Modernity*. Berkeley: University of California, 1979.

Almond, Gabriel. "Comparative Political Systems." *Journal of Politics* vol.18, no.3 (August 1956):391-409.

Almond, Gabriel, and Sidney Verba. *The Civic Culture*. Princeton: Princeton Unviersity, 1963.

Amnesty International. *China: Violation of Human Rights*. London: Amnesty International Publishing Company, 1984.

_____. *Amnesty International Report on Political Imprisonment*. London: Amnesty International Publishing Company, 1978.

Andors, Phyllis. *The Unfinished Liberation of Chinese Women, 1949-1980*. Bloomington: Indiana University, 1983.

Anhui Provincial Women's Federation, Office of Investigation and Study. "Funu chengcai yinsude tantao." [How Women Can Become Achievers] *Shelian Tonxun* [United Newsletter of Social Sciences] 12 (1985), translated in Chinese Sociology and Anthropology, 20, no.1 (Fall 1987):32-38.

"Annotated Bibliography." *Columbia Journal of Transnational Law* 22 (1983).

Apple, Michael. *Education and Power*. London: Routledge and Kegan Paul, 1982.

Artz, F.B. *The Development of Technical Education in France, 1500 to 1850*. Cambridge, Massachusetts, and London: Society for the History of Technology and M.I.T., 1966.

"Austerity Program Skirts Shenzhen." *Journal of Commerce Special Report* (April 5, 1989).

Ayers, William. *Chang Chih-tung and Educational Reform in China*. Cambridge: Harvard University, 1971.

Ball, Nicole. *Security and Economy in the Third World*. Princeton: Princeton University, 1988.

Banister, Judith. *China's Changing Population*. Stanford: Stanford University, 1987.

Barendsen, Robert. *Half-Work Half-Study Schools in Communist China*. Washington, D.C.: U.S. Department of Health, Education and Welfare, 1964.

_____. "The Agricultural Middle School in Communist China," *China Quarterly*, no.8 (October/December 1961).

Barlow, Tani, and Lowe, Donald. *Teaching China's Lost Generation*. New York: Praeger, 1987.

Beijing Municipal Party Committee Research Office, editors. *Xin shiqi daxuesheng sixiang zhengzhi jiaoyu yanjiu*. Beijing: Beijing Normal University, 1988.

Beijing Normal University Research Group on College Entrance Examination. "Gaige gaokao, gengjia zhunqu youxiaode xuanba renzai" [Reform the University Entrance Exaimination, Select Talented People Correctly and Efficiently] in *Jiaoyu Yanjiu* (Educational Studies) 6 (1985).

Berger, Suzanne editor. *Organized Interests in Western Europe: Pluralism, Corporatism and the Transformation of Politics*. Cambridge: Cambridge University, 1981.

Bernstein, Basil. *Class, Codes and Control* Vol.3. London: Routledge and Kegan Paul, 1975.

Bernstein, Thomas P. *Up to the Mountains and Down to the Villages: The Transfer of Youth from Urban to Rural China*. New Haven: Yale University, 1977.

Biggerstaff, Knight. *The Earliest Modern Government Schools in China*. Ithaca, New York: Cornell University, 1961.

Blau, Peter M. *Bureaucracy in Modern Society*. New York: Random House, 1956.

Borthwick, Sally. *Education and Social Change in China.* Stanford: Hoover Institution Press, 1983.

Bourdieu, Pierre. *Reproduction in Education.* Beverly Hills: Sage, 1977.

Boydston, Jo Ann editor. *The Middle Works of John Dewey (1899-1924), Volume 13: Essays on Philosophy, Education and the Orient: 1921-1922.* Carbondale, Illinois: Southern Illinois University, 1988.

Boyer, Ernest. *High School.* New York: Harper and Row, 1983.

Brown, Archie. "Introduction," in Archie Brown and Jack Gray, editors. *Political Culture and Political Change in Communist States.* New York: Holmes and Meier, 1979, pp. 1-20.

Brown, E. Richard. "Rockefeller Medicine in China: Professionalism and Imperialism," in Robert Arnove editor. *Philanthropy and Cultural Imperialism.* Bloomington: Indiana University, 1980, pp.123-146.

Brown, Hubert O. "Teachers and the Rural Responsibility System in the People's Republic of China," *The Asian Journal of Public Administration* Vol.7, no.1 (1965):2-17.

Broyelle, Claudie. *Women's Liberation in China.* Hassocks: the Harvester Press, 1977.

Bullock, Mary Brown. *An American Transplant: the Rockefeller Foundation and Peking Union Medical College.* Berkeley: University of California, 1980.

Burns, John P., and Stanley Rosen, (eds). *Policy Conflicts in Post-Mao China, A Documentary Survey with Analysis.* Armonk, NY: Sharpe, 1986.

Cang Gong, and Cheng Yunti (eds). *Qingshaonian ziwo baohu* [The Self-protection of Youth]. Shanghai: Shanghai Translation Press, 1988.

Carnoy, Martin, and Henry Levin. *Schooling and Work in the Democratic State.* Stanford: Stanford University Press, 1985.

Castelle, Kay. *In the Child's Best Interest: A Primer on the U.N. Convention on the Rights of the Child.* New York: Foster Parents Plan International and Defense for Children International-USA, 1989.

Central Committee Document Research Section, editors. *Zhishifenzi Wenti Wenxian Xuanbian.* [Selected Documents on the Problems of Intellectuals] Beijing: Renmin chubanshe, 1983.

Central Intelligence Agency. *The World Factbook 1989.* Washington, D.C.: U.S. Government Printing Office, 1989.

Chan, Anita. *Children of Mao.* Seattle: University of Washington, 1985.

Chan, Hugh. "Modern Legal Education in China." *China Law Review* 9 (1936).

Chan, Thomas, Chen, E.K.Y., et al. "China's Special Economic Zones: Ideology, Policy and Practice," in Y.C. Jao and C.K. Leung, editors. *China's Special Economic Zones: Policies, Problems and Prospects.* Hong Kong: Oxford University, 1986, pp.87-104.

Chang Chung-li. *The Chinese Gentry.* Seattle: University of Washington, 1955.

Chang, C.Y. "Bureaucracy and Modernization: A Case Study of Special Economic Zones in China," in Y.C. Jao and C.K. Leung, editors. *China's Special Economic Zones: Policies, Problems and Prospects.* Hong Kong: Oxford University, 1986.

Chang Tianyu. "'Shekou fengbo' shuomingle shenma?" [What does the 'Shekou Storm' Signify?] *Guanjiaojing* (September 1988):94-95.

Chen, C.C. *Medicine in Rural China: A Personal Account.* Berkeley: University of California, 1989.

Chen Chuansheng, and David H. Uttal. "Cultural Values, Parents' Beliefs and Children's Achievement in the United States and China." *Human Development* 31 (1988):351-358.

Chen Qingzhi. *Zhongguo jiaoyu shi.*[History of Chinese Education] Shanghai: Commercial Press, 1936.

Chen, Theodore Hsi-en. *The Maoist Educational Revolution.* New York: Praeger, 1974.

_____. *Academic and Revolutionary Models.* New York: Pergamon, 1981.

Chen Zicheng. "Tansuo jiaoxue guilu tigao jiaoxue zhiliang" [Explore Educational Laws and Raise Educational Quality] in *Jiaoyu keyan lunwenxuan* [A Selection of Educational Research]. Shanghai: Changning District Education Bureau Educational Research Office, 1985.

Chen Ziju. "*Yuanyin zai nar? Chulu he zai?*" [What Is the Reason and Solution for the Disproportionate Enrollment of Male and Female Students at Shanghai's Technical Vocational Schools?] *Qingnian bao* [Youth newspaper] Shanghai, (September 14, 1984):1 translated in *Chinese Sociology and Anthropology* 20, no.1 (Fall, 1987):62-64.

Cheng Wing-chung. "Primary Teacher Education in China: The Case of Harbin." *Canadian and International Education* 16:1 (1987):146-161.

Cheng Ying. "Dalu yanjiusheng zhengqu bei 'taotai'." [Mainland Graduate Students Strive to "Be Eliminated Through Competition"] *Jiushi niandai* (January 1989).

Cheng Yingfan, and Zhao Haiyan. "*Zhongxuesheng weifa fanzui wenti shixi.*" *Beijing Zhengfa Xueyuan Xuebao* no.2 (1982).

Cheng Zifan. "Evolution of Medical Education in China." *Chinese Medical Journal* 97, no.6 (1984).

"Children's Education." *Beijing Review* 31:34 (August 22-28, 1988): 40.

Children's Work Committee of the All-China Women's Federation. *Jiazhang Shouce.* [Parents' Handbook] Beijing: Changzheng Publishing House, 1987.

Chin, Ann-ping. *Children of China.* New York: Alfred Knopf, 1988.

China Education Almanac, translated in *Chinese Education* (Fall, 1986):7-111.

Chow Tse-tsung. *The May Fourth Movement.* Cambridge: Harvard University, 1960.

Chused, Richard H. "The Hiring and Retention of Minorities and Women on American Law School Faculties." *University of Pennsylvania Law Review* vol. 137, no.2 (December 1988):537-569.

Cleverly, John. *The Schooling Of China.* Boston: George Allen and Unwin, 1985.

Cohen, Jerome Alan. *The Criminal Process in the People's Republic of China: 1949-1963.* Cambridge: Harvard University, 1963.

"Colleges Provide Part-time Jobs." 32:4 *Beijing Review* (January 23-29, 1989):11-12.

Colletta, Nat J. "Worker-Peasant Education in the People's Republic of China." Washington, D.C.: World Bank Staff Working Paper no.527, 1982.

Committee on Scholarly Communication with the People's Republic of China. *A Relationship Restored: Trends in U.S.-China Educational Exchanges, 1978-1984.* Washington, D.C.: National Academy Press, 1986.

Connell, R.W. *Teachers' Work.* Boston: Allen and Unwin, 1985.

Connor, Alison. "Legal Education in China: A Look at Nanda." *Singapore Law Review* vol.7 (1986).

Coombs, Philip H. *The World Crisis in Education, the View from the Eighties.* New York: Oxford University Press, 1985.

Copper, John, Franz Michael and Yuan-li Wu. *Human Rights in Post-Mao China.* Boulder: Westview Press, 1985.

Croll, Elizabeth. "The Single-child Family in Beijing," in Elizabeth Croll, Delia Davin and Penny Kane, editors. *China's One Child Family Policy.* London and New York: Macmillan and St. Martins, 1985.

Croll, Elizabeth, Delia Davin, and Penny Kane, editors. *China's One Child Family Policy.* London and New York: Macmillan and St. Martins, 1985.

Crozier, Ralph. *Traditional Medicine in Modern China.* Cambridge: Harvard University, 1968.

Dai Shujun. "Vocational Universities in China." *Canadian and International Education* 16:1 (1987):172-180.

Dangdai Zhongguo Congshu Jiaoyujuan Bianjishi, editors. *Dangdai zhongguo gaodeng shifan jiaoyu ziliaoxuan.* [Selected Materials on Contemporary Chinese University Level Teacher Education] Vol.1 Shanghai: Huadong Shifan Daxue Chubanshe, 1986.

Dangdai Zhongguo Editorial Department. *Dangdai Zhongguo Jundui Qunzhong Gongzuo.*[China Today: The Mass Work of the Chinese Army] Beijing: China Social Science Press, 1988.

Davis, Deborah. "Chinese Social Welfare: Policies and Outcomes." *China Quarterly* no. 119 (1989):557-597.

Deng Yuhong. "New Road for Secondary Education." *China Reconstructs* 36:8 (August 1987):20-25.

Ding Xunxiang. "Chuzhong nan nu sheng zhili chayi chuxi." [A Preliminary Analysis of the Discrepancies in Intelligence Between Male and Female Students at the Junior Middle School Level] *Shanghai qingshaonian yanjiu* [Shanghai youth studies] 10 (1983):21-27, translated in *Chinese Education* 20, no.4 (Winter 1987-88):13-30.

"Discussion on Women and Work." *Beijing Review* 31:33 (August 15-21, 1988):38.

Dittmer, Lowell. "China in 1988: the Continuing Dilemma of Socialist Reform." *Asian Survey* vol.29, no.1 (1989).

Djung Lu-dzai. *A History of Democratic Education in Modern China*. Shanghai: The Commercial Press, 1934.

Dongbei Shifan Daxue Jiaowuchu. *Dongbei Shifan Daxue jiaoxue zhidaoshu (Benke)* .[Northeast Normal University Teaching Guide (Undergraduate Program)]. Changchun, 1985.

Doolin, Dennis, editor. *Communist China: The Politics of Student Opposition*. Stanford: Hoover Institution, 1964.

Doolin, Dennis, and Charles Ridley. *The Making of a Model Citizen in Communist China*. Stanford: Stanford University Hoover Institution, 1968.

"Dropout Rate Alerts Educators." *Beijing Review* 32:3 (January 16-22, 1989):12-13.

"Dropout Rise vs Study Craze." *Beijing Review* 31:52 (December 26-January 1, 1989):12.

Duiker, William. *Ts'ai Yuan-pei: Educator of Modern China*. University Park and London: Pennsylvania State University, 1977.

Editorial Group of the Changsha Military Engineering Academy (Hunan Military District). *Jun Xun Shouce*. [Military Training Handbook] Changsha: Hunan Education Press, 1988.

Education in China. Beijing: Ministry of Education, 1981.

Education and Science: China Handbook Series. Beijing: Foreign Languages Press.

Educational Statistics of the Republic of China. Taipei, Taiwan: Ministry of Education, 1988.

Edwards, R. Randall. "An Overview of Chinese Law and Legal Education." *The Annals of the American Academy of Political and Social Science* vol.476 (November 1984).

Elman, Benjamin. *From Philosophy to Philology: Intellectual and Social Aspects of Change in Late Imperial China*. Cambridge: Harvard University, 1984.

Engels, Fredrick. *The Origin of the Family, Private Property and the State.* New York: International Publishers, 1975.

Epstein, Irving. "Critical Pedagogy and Chinese Education." *Journal of Curriculum Theorizing* 9, no.2 (1990).

_____. "Children's Rights and Juvenile Correctional Institutions in the People's Republic of China." *Comparative Education Review* 30, no.3 (1986):359-372.

_____. "Special Education in Japan and China." *Curriculum and Teaching* 4, no.2 (December 1989):27-38.

_____. "Special Education Provision in the People's Republic of China." *Comparative Education* 24, no.3 (1988):365-375.

Everhart, Robert. *Reading, Writing and Resistance, Adolescence and Labor in a Junior High School.* Boston: Routledge and Kegan Paul, 1983.

Fairbank, John K. editor. *Chinese Thought and Institutions.* Chicago: University of Chicago, 1957.

Fan Gongrong. "Gongtong nuli, banhao Fujian Shida." [Work Hard Together to Run Fujian Normal Well] *Shifan Jiaoyu Yanjiu* 1 (1983):6-10.

Fayol, Henri. "The Administrative Theory in the State," in Gullick, Luther and L. Urwick, James D. Mooney, et al. editors. *Papers on the Science of Administration.* New York: Institute of Public Administration, Columbia University, 1937, pp. 99-114.

Ferdinand, P."Interest Groups in Chinese Politics," in David Goodman, editor. *Groups and Politics in the People's Republic of China.* Cardiff: University of Cardiff, 1984.

Fingar, Thomas and Linda Reed. *An Introduction to Education in the People's Republic of China and U.S.-China Educational Exchanges.* Washington, D.C.: U.S. China Clearinghouse, 1982.

Fitzpatrick, Sheila, editor. *Cultural Revolution in Russia. 1928-1931.* Bloomington: Indiana University, 1978,1984.

_____. *Education and Social Mobility in the Soviet Union.* Cambridge: Cambridge University, 1979.

Francis, Corinna-Barbara. "The Progress of Protest: The Spring of 1989." *Asian Survey* Vol.XXIX no.9 (September 1989):898-915.

Franke, Wolfgang. *The Reform and Abolition of the Traditional Chinese Examination System.* Cambridge: Harvard University, 1972.

Folsom, Ralph H. and John H. Minan. *Law in the People's Republic of China: Text, Readings and Materials.* Dordrecht: Martinus Nijhoff, 1989.

Fraser, Stewart. *Chinese Communist Education: Records of the First Decade.* Nashville: Vanderbilt University, 1965.

Friedman, Deborah Davis. *Long Lives: Chinese Elderly and the Communist Revolution.* Cambridge: Harvard University, 1983.

Gamble, Sidney. *Ting Hsien: A North China Rural Community.* New York: Institute of Pacific Relations, 1954.

Gaojiao Yanjiu no. 1 (Beijing Normal Institute, 1988):74-80.

Gao Xi-Ching. "Today's Legal Thinking and Its Economic Impact in China." *Law and Contemporary Problems* 52, no.2-3 (Spring-Summer 1989).

Gao Yan, and Pu Shanxin. *Zhongguo Renmin Gongheguo Xingzhen Quhua Shouce.* [Handbook of Administrative Regions of the People's Republic of China] Beijing: Guangming Ribao Press, 1986.

Gao Yi. "Banhao shifan jiaoyu tigao shizi shuping wei sihua jianshe peiyang rencai zuochu gongxian." [Run Normal Education Well, Raise the Level of Teachers, Train Talent to Make a Contribution Towards the Construction of the Four Modernizations] *Jiaoyu Yanjiu* 4 (1980):6-12.

Gardner, Howard. *To Open Minds, Chinese Clues to the Dilemma of Contemporary Education*. New York: Basic Books Inc., Publishers, 1989.

Garrett, Shirley S. *Social Reformers in Urban China: the Chinese YMCA, 1895-1926*. Cambridge: Harvard University, 1970.

Gelatt, Timothy A., and Snyder, Frederick E. "Legal Education in China: Training for a New Era." *China Law Reporter* vol.1 (1980).

Geng Xiaolin, and Zhu Yuejing. "Dangdai qingnian zhuiqiude `lixiang xingxiang' yudaode bangyang jiaoyu." *Shanghai qingshaonian yanjiu* no.3 (1984):6-7.

Gerth, H.H., and C.W. Mills, editors. *From Max Weber: Essays in Sociology*. New York: Oxford University, 1946.

Ginsburg, Norton, Bruce Koppel, and Terry McGee, editors. *The Extended Metropolis in Asia: A New Phase of the Settlement Transition*. Honolulu: University of Hawaii, 1990.

Giroux, Henry, and Peter McLaren. "Teacher Education and the Politics of Engagement: The Case for Democratic Schooling" in *Harvard Education Review* 56:3 (August 1986):213-238.

Goldman, Merle, with Timothy Cheek and Carol Lee Hamrin, editors. *China's Intellectuals and the State: In Search of a New Relationship*. Cambridge: Harvard University Contemporary China Series, 1987.

Goodlad, John. *A Place Called School*. New York: McGraw-Hill, 1984.

Grieder, Jerome. *Intellectuals and the State in Modern China*. New York: Free Press, 1981.

Griffin, Patricia Peck. "The Chinese Treatment of Counter-revolutionaries." Unpublished PhD. dissertation, University of Pennsylvania, 1971.

Gu Chunde, and Du Ganjian, "Zhongguo Chuantung Falu Guannian yu Xiandai Shehuizhuyi Fazhi Jianshe," in *Chuantung Wenhua yu Xiandaihua*. Beijing: People's University Press, 1987.

Guy, R. Kent. *The Emperor's Four Treasuries: Scholars and the State in the Late Chien-lung Era*. Cambridge: Harvard University, 1987.

Han Depei, and Stephen Kanter. "Legal Education in China." *The American Journal of Comparative Law* vol.32 (1984).

Han Shizhen. "Bangzhu nusheng saochu chengcai daolushang zhangai de shiyan." [An experiment to help female students remove obstacles to achievement] Shanghai: Changning District Education Bureau Educational Research Office, 1985.

Han Zongli. "The Development of the Economics of Education in China." *Canadian and International Education* 16:1 (1987):23-32.

"Hard to Place University Graduates." *Beijing Review* 31:35 (August 29-September 4, 1988):40-41.

Harriss, J., and M. Moore, editors. *Development and the Rural Urban Divide*. London: Frank Cass, 1984.

Hart, Gillian. *Power, Labor and Livelihood*. Berkeley, University of California: 1986.

Hawkins, John. 1983. *Education and Social Change in the People's Republic of China*. New York: Praeger, 1983.

_____. "The Transformation of Education for Rural Development in China," *Comparative Education Review* no.3 (1988):266-281.

Hayhoe, Ruth. " A Comparative Analysis of the Cultural Dynamics of Sino-Western Educational Cooperation," *China Quarterly* no. 102 (December 1985).

_____. "China's Intellectuals in the World Community." *Higher Education* vol.17, no.1 (1988):121-138.

_____. "China's Scholars Returned from Abroad: A View from Shanghai, Parts I and II." *China Exchange News* vol.17, no. 3 and 4 (September and December 1989).

_____. *China's Universities and the Open Door*. Armonk, N.Y.: M.E. Sharpe, 1989.

_____. "Chinese, European and American Scholarly Values in Interaction." London Association of Comparative Educationalists, Occasional Paper no.13, 1984.

_____. *Contemporary Chinese Education*. Armonk, N.Y.: M.E. Sharpe, 1984.

_____. "Knowledge Categories and Chinese Educational Reform." *Interchange* vol.19 (Autumn/Winter 1988-89).

_____. "Shanghai as a Mediator of the Educational Open Door," *Pacific Affairs* 61 no.2 (1988):253-284.

_____. "Towards the Forging of a Chinese University Ethos: Zhendan and Fudan 1903 to 1919." *China Quarterly* no.94 (June 1983):323-341.

Hayhoe, Ruth, and Mariannne Bastid, editors. *China's Education and the Industrialized World*. Armonk, N.Y. and Toronto: M.E. Sharpe and Ontario Institute for Studies in Education, 1987.

Hayhoe, Ruth, and Zhan Ruiling, editors. "Educational Exchanges and the Open Door." *Chinese Education* vol.XVI, no.1 (Spring, 1988).

Heaton, William. "New Trends in China's Professional Military Education and Training," unpublished paper delivered at the International Studies Association, Anaheim California, March 25-29, 1986.

He Bin. "Dui jiaoshe de kunao yu xuyao de diaocha fenxi." [A Survey and Analysis of Teachers' Troubles and Needs] *Jiaoyu Lilun yu Shijian* no.1 (1985):16-22.

Heitlinger, Alena. *Women and State Socialism: Sex Inequality in the Soviet Union and Czechoslovakia.* London: Macmillan, 1979.

Henderson, Gail. "Issues in the Modernization of Medicine," in Fred Simon and Merle Goldman, editors. *Science and Technology in Post-Mao China.* Cambridge: Harvard University Contemporary China Series, 1989, pp.199-221.

Henley, Lonnie D. "Officer Education in the Chinese PLA." *Problems of Communism* 36:3 (May-June 1987):55-71.

Henze, Jurgen. "Developments in Vocational Education since 1976." *Comparative Education* 20:1 (1984):117-140.

_____. "Educational Modernization as a Search for Higher Efficiency" in Hayhoe and Bastid, *China's Education and the Industrialized World.* Armonk: M.E. Sharpe, 1987 pp. 252-270.

Herman, Richard H. "The Education of China's Lawyers." *Albany Law Review* vol.46 (1982).

Heyzer, Noeleen. *Working Women in Southeast Asia: Subordination and Emancipation.* Philadelphia: Open University Press, 1986.

Highwater, Jamake. *The Primal Mind: Vision and Reality in Indian America.* New York: Meridian Books, 1981.

Ho, David Y.F. "Continuity and Variation in Chinese Patterns of Socialization." *Journal of Marriage and the Family* 51 (February, 1989):149-163.

Ho, Ping-ti. *The Ladder of Success in Imperial China.* New York: Columbia University, 1962.

Ho, Samuel P.S. *The Asian Experience in Rural Nonagricultural Development and its Relevance for China.* Washington, D.C.: The World Bank, 1986.

Hom, Sharon. *American Legal Education Methodology in China: Teaching Notes and Resources.* Englewood New Jersey: Prospect, 1989.

_____. "Legal Education in the People's Republic of China: A Selected Annotated Bibliography of English Language Materials." *China Law Reporter* (Spring, 1990).

Honig, Emily, and Gail Hershatter, (eds). *Personal Voices, Chinese Women in the 1980's.* Stanford: Stanford University Press: 1988.

Hooper, Beverley. "China's Modernization: Are Young Women Going to Lose Out?" *Modern China* 10, no.3 (1984).

_____. *Youth in China.* Harmondsworth and New York: Penguin, 1985.

Hsiao, William. "Transformation of Health Care in China." *The New England Journal of Medicine* 310 (April 5, 1984):932-936.

Hsu, Francis. *Americans and Chinese: Passage to Differences.* Honolulu: University of Hawaii, 1981.

Hu Ruiwen. "A Review and Study of Early-Stage Human Resources Forecasting and Planning Work in Shanghai" 1985 in *Chinese Education* pp. 57-87 (in sociology of education issue)

Hu Shi-ming, and Seifman, Eli (eds). *Education and Socialist Modernization, A Documentary History of Education in the PRC, 1977-1986.* New York: AMS Press, 1987.

Huang Meizhen, Shi Yuanhua, and Zhang Yun, editors. *Shanghai Daxue Shiliao.* [Historical Materials on Shanghai University] Shanghai: Fudan University, 1984.

Huang Shaozeng. "Construction and Education in a Special Zone," *Shenzhen Tequ Jiaoyu Yanjiu* translated in *Chinese Education* no.3 (1988):34-41.

Huang Shiqi. "University Research in China." Paper presented at the International Seminar on Current Policies of Higher Educational Reform, Beijing, June 21-25, 1988.

Huang Weiming (ed). *Huadong liusheng yishi zhongxuesheng zuowen bizai.* [An Essay Competition for Secondary School Students in Six Eastern Provinces] Shanghai: Shanghai Youth Press, 1988.

Huazhong Shifan Xueyuan Jiaoyuxi, Henan Shifan Daxue Jiaoyuxi, Gansu Shifan Daxue Jiaoyuxi, Hunan Shifan Xueyuan Jiaoyuxi, Wuhan Shifan Xueyuan Jiaoyu Jiaoyanshi, eds. Jiaoyuxue [Pedagogy] Beijing: Renmin Jiaoyu Chubanshe, 1982.

Husen, Torsten. *The School in Question.* New York: Oxford University Press, 1979.

Hwa Yol Yung, and Peter Jung, "The Hermeneutics of Poltical Ideology and Cultural Change: Maoism as the Sinicization of Marxism," *Cultural Hermeneutics* vol.3 (August 1975).

Hymes, Robert P. "Not Quite Gentlemen? Doctors in Sung and Yuan." *Chinese Science* 8 (1987):9-76.

Inkeles, Alex, and David Smith. *Becoming Modern.* Cambridge: Harvard University Press, 1974.

"Is Student Business Good for China?" *Beijing Review* 31:50 (December 12-18, 1988):28-29.

Jiang Siyi, editor. *Zhongguo Renmin Jiefangjun Zhengzhi Gongzuo Jiaocheng.* [A Course in PLA Political Work] Beijing: National Defense University Press, 1986.

Jiaoyu gaige zhongyao wenxian xuanbian. [Important Selected Documents on Educational Reform] Beijing: Renmin Jiaoyu Chubanshe, 1986.

Jing Lin. "Rural Dropout Problem: A Dilemma Facing China's Education" (unpublished manuscript) 1987.

Johnson, Kay Ann. *Women, The Family and Peasant Revolution in China*. Chicago: University of Chicago, 1983.

Johnson, Todd. "The Economics of Higher Education Reform in China." *China Exchange News* 17:1 (March, 1989):3-7.

Junshi [Military], Vols. I and II in *Zhongguo Dabaike Quanshu*. [The Great Chinese Encyclopedia] Beijing and Shanghai: The Great China Encyclopedia Press, 1989.

Kailuofu. *Jiaoyuxue*. [Pedagogy] Translated by Shen Ying. Beijing:, Renmin Jiaoyu Chubanshe, 1952.

Kane, Penny. "The Single-child Family Policy in the Cities," in Elizabeth Croll, Delia Davin, and Penny Kane, editors. *China's One Child Family Policy*. London and New York: Macmillan and St. Martins, 1985.

Kao, Frederick. "China, Chinese Medicine, and the Chinese Medical System." *American Journal of Chinese Medicine* 1, no.1 (1973).

Katz, Michael. *Class Bureaucracy and Schools*. New York: Praeger, 1971.

Keenan, Barry. *The Dewey Experiment in China: Educational Reform and Political Power in the Early Republic*. Cambridge: Harvard University, 1977.

Kessen, William, editor. *Childhood in China*. New Haven: Yale University, 1975.

Khan, Azizur Rahman, and Eddy Lee, editors. *Poverty in Rural Asia*. Bangkok: International Labor Organization, 1985.

King, Edmund. *Other Schools and Ours*. New York: Holt, Rinehart and Winston, 1963.

Koppel, Bruce. "Beyond Employment to Work: Asia's Rural Labor Skill Challenge of the 1990's," in Bruce Koppel, editor. *Rural Trnsformation: Issues for Policy, Planning and Project Development.* Tokyo: Asian Productivity Organization, 1989.

Kraus, James. "Legal Education in the People's Republic of China," *Suffolk Transnational Law Journal* vol.13, (1989):75-134.

Kraus, Richard Kurt. "China's Cultural 'Liberalization' and Conflict Over the Social Organization of the Arts." *Modern China* 9, no.2 (April 1983):212-227.

_____. *Class Conflict in Chinese Socialism.* New York: Columbia University, 1981.

_____. *Pianos and Politics in China.* New York: Oxford University, 1989.

Kwok, R.Y.W. "Structure and Policies in Industrial Planning in the Shenzhen Special Economic Zone," in Y.C. Jao and C.K. Leung, editors. *China's Special Economic Zones: Policies, Problems and Prospects.* Hong Kong: Oxford University, 1986.

Kwong, Julia. *Chinese Education in Transition: Prelude to the Cultural Revolution.* Montreal: McGill-Queens University, 1979.

_____. "In Pursuit of Efficiency: Scientific Management in Chinese Higher Education." *Modern China* 13, no.2 (April 1987):226-256.

Labaree, David. *The Making of an American High School.* New Haven: Yale University Press, 1988.

Lamontagne, Jacques. "Educational Development in China: Characteristics and Trends," paper presented at the Comparative and International Education Society annual conference, Atlanta, GA: March, 1988.

Lampton, David. *The Politics of Medicine in China.* Boulder: Westview Press, 1977.

Lapidus, Gail Warshofsky. *Women in Soviet Society: Equality, Development and Social Change.* Berkeley: University of California, 1978.

Lathem, Willoughby. *The Future of Academic Community Medicine in Developing Countries.* New York: Praeger, 1979.

League of Nations' Mission of Educational Experts. *The Reorganization of Education in China.* Paris: League of Nations' Institute of Intellectual Cooperation, 1932.

Leung, Angela Ki Che. "Organized Medicine in Ming Qing China: State and Private Medical Institutions in the Lower Yangzi Region." *Late Imperial China* 8, no.1 (June 1987):134-166.

Leung, Chi Kin. *Industrial Organization and Spatial Economic Relations Between Hong Kong and China: A Linkage Interaction Approach.* Doctoral Dissertation, University of Hawaii, 1989.

_____. "Spatial Redeployment and the Special Economic Zones in China: An Overview," in Y.C. Jao and C.K. Leung. *China's Special Economic Zones: Policies, Problems and Prospects.* Hong Kong: Oxford University, 1986.

Leys, Simon. *The Burning Forest: Essays on Chinese Culture and Politics.* New York: Henry Holt and Company, 1986.

Li Bin. "State Diploma Losing Glamour." *Beijing Review* 31:51 (December 19-25, 1988):11-12.

Li Li. "Enrollment and Job Assignment." *Beijing Review* 31:32 (August 8-14, 1988):12-15.

Li Ning. "Legal Education Surges Ahead." *Beijing Review* (May,6 1985).

Li, Victor. *Law Without Lawyers: A Comparative View of Law in China and the United States.* Boulder: Westview, 1978.

Li Xuemin and Qiu Yangxing. "Youhua Gaodeng Yixue Jiaoyu Cengci Jieguo de Chubu Shexiang." [A Tentative Program for Improving the Administration of Higher Medical Education] *Zhejiang Medical University Higher Medical Education* 4 (1986).

Liang Jun. "Twelve Lectures on Women," Beijing Radio (December, 1988).

Liao Yuangeng. "Jianshe Shenzhen Chengren Jiaoyu Jidi Chuyi." *Shenzhen Tequ Chengren Jiaoyu Wenxuan* (1986).

Liljestrom, Rita et al. *Young Children in China*. London: Multilingual Matters, 1982.

Linden, Allan. "Politics and Education in Nationalist China: The Case of the University Council 1927-28." *Journal of Asian Studies* Vol. XXVIII no.4 (August 1968):763-776.

Liu Bin. "Jiaqiang hongguan guanli tigao jiaoyu zhiliang." [Strengthen Macro-management, Raise the Quality of Education] *Renmin Jiaoyu* 1 (1986):5-8.

Lo, Billie L.C. "Teacher Education in the Eighties," in Ruth Hayhoe, editor. *Contemporary Chinese Education*. Armonk, N.Y.: M.E. Sharpe, 1984.

Lo Fu-Chen, Kamal Smith, and Mike Douglass. "Rural Urban Transformation in Asia," in Fu-Chen Lo, editor. *Rural Urban Relations and Regional Development*. Singapore: Maruzan Asia, 1981, pp.7-43.

Lofstedt, J. *Chinese Educational Policy*. Stockholm: Almquist and Wiksell, 1980.

Lortie, Dan C. *Schoolteacher: A Sociological Study*. Chicago: University of Chicago, 1975.

Lung, Mon Yin. "Annotated Bibliography of Selected English-Language Literature on Chinese Law." *Legal References Services Quarterly* vol.6, no.3-4 (Fall-Winter 1985):95-121.

Luo Yicun and Shen Jiaxian. "Qingshaonian xuesheng lixiang he xingqude diaochao yanjiu." *Jiaoyu Yanjiu* [Educational Research] 8 (1983):58-63, translated in *Chinese Education* 17, no.4 (Winter 1984-85):41-61.

Lu Yun. "New Challenges to Women's Employment." *Beijing Review* 31:44 (October 31-November 6, 1988):18-21.

MacFarquhar, Roderick, editor. *The Hundred Flowers*. London: Atlantic, 1960.

Mao Zedong. *Selected Works*. Beijing: People's Publishing House, 1969.

March, James G., and John P. Olsen. "The New Institutionalism: Organizational Factors in Political Life." *American Political Science Review* vol.78, no.3 (September 1984):734-749.

Martin, Roberta. "The Socialization of Children in China and on Taiwan: An Analysis of Elementary School Textbooks." *China Quarterly* 62 (June 1975):242-262.

Matthews, Mervyn. *Education in the Soviet Union*. London: Allen and Unwin, 1982.

McGough, R.S., et al. "China Technical and Vocational Education Sector Report: Internal Efficiency." Washington,DC: East Asia and Pacific Education Projects, World Bank, 1987.

Mei Renlang. "Qishi Nianlai Wo Guo Gaodeng Yixue Yuanxiao Kecheng Jihua de Fazhan." [Seventy Years of Higher Medical Curriculum Development] *Medical Education and Administration* 3 (1986):45-60.

Mei Renlang, Zhong Shiping, Jin Wentao. "Zhongguo Yixue Jiaoyu de Xianxing Qingkuang." [The Current Status of Chinese Medical Education] Unpublished manuscript, 1987.

Meisner, Maurice. *Li Ta-chao and the Origins of Chinese Marxism*. Cambridge: Harvard University, 1967.

Menzel, Johanna M., editor. *The Chinese Civil Service*. Boston: D.C. Heath, 1963.

Meskill, John. *Academies in Ming China*. Tuscon, Arizona: University of Arizona, 1982.

Meyer, Jeffrey. "Moral Education in Taiwan." *Comparative Education Review* 32:1 (February 1988):20-38.

Mi Zhenyu. *Zhongguode Guofang Gouxing*. [Concepts for China's National Defense] Beijing: PLA Press, 1988.

The Military Balance 1989-1990. London: International Institute for Strategic Studies, 1989.

Min Wei-fang and Tsang Mun Chiu. "Vocational Education and Productivity: A Case Study of the Beijing General Auto Industry Company." Paper presented at the Comparative and International Education Society annual conference, Washington, D.C., March 1987.

Miyazaki, Ichisada. *China's Examination Hell: The Civil Service Examinations of Imperial China*. New Haven: Yale University, 1981.

Molineaux, Maxine. "Women's Emancipation under Socialism: a Model for the Third World?" *World Development* 9:9/10 (1981):1019-1037.

Moody, Peter R. *Opposition and Dissent in Contemporary China*. Stanford: Hoover Institution, 1977.

_____. "The Political Culture of Chinese Students and Intellectuals: An Historical Examination." *Asian Survey* vol. XXVIII, no. 11 (1988):1140-1160.

Naftulin, Lois. "The Legal Status of Women in China," *China Law Reporter* vol.2, no.1 (1982):57-60.

Nathan, Andrew. *Chinese Democracy*. New York: Alfred A. Knopf, 1985.

_____. "Is China Ready for Democracy?" *Journal of Democracy* vol.1, no.2 (Spring, 1990):50-61.

Needham, Joseph. "China and the Origins of Immunology." *Eastern Horizon* 19 (1980):6-12.

Nelson, Harvey. *The Chinese Military System, 2nd edition*. Boulder: Westview Press, 1981.

Noah, Harold, and John Middleton. *China's Vocational and Technical Training*. Washington, CD: World Bank, 1988.

Offer, Daniel, et al. *The Teenage World*. New York: Plenum Medical Book Company, 1988.

"Optimization: Reform or Not?" *Beijing Review* 32:9 (February 27-March 5, 1989):12-13.

Orleans, Leo. *Chinese Students in America*. Washington, D.C.: National Academy Press, 1988.

_____. "The Effects of China's Business Fever on Higher Education at Home and on Chinese Students in the U.S." *China Exchange News* 17:1 (March 1989):8-14.

_____. *Professional Manpower and Education in Communist China*. Washington, D.C.: U.S. Government Printing Office, 1961.

_____. "Soviet Influence on Chinese Higher Education," in Ruth Hayhoe and Marianne Bastid, editors. *China's Education and the Industrialized World: Studies in Cultural Transfer*. Armonk, New York and Toronto: M.E. Sharpe and OISE, 1987.

Oshima, Harry T. *The Significance of Off-Farm Employment and Incomes in Post-War East Asian Growth*. Asian Development Bank Staff Paper number 21. Manila: Asian Development Bank, 1984.

_____. *The Transition to an Industrial Economy in Monsoon Asia*. Asian Development Bank Staff Paper number 20. Manila: Asian Development Bank, 1983.

Ownby, David. "The Audience: Growing Alienation Among Chinese Youth," in Carol Lee Hamrin and Timothy Cheek editors. *China's Establishment Intellectuals*. Armonk, N.Y.: M.E. Sharpe, 1986, pp.212-246.

Paine, Lynn. *Reform and Balance in Chinese Teacher Education*. Doctoral Dissertation, Stanford University, 1986.

_____. "The Teacher as Virtuoso: A Chinese Model for Teaching." *Teachers College Record* vol. 92, no.1 (Fall, 1990).

_____. "Teacher Education in the People's Republic of China," in E.B. Gumbert, editor. *Fit to Teach: Teacher Education in International Perspective*. Lecture Series no.8 (Atlanta: Georgia State University Center for Cross-Cultural Education, 1990):130-142.

Parent Education Committee of the Gulou District, Fuzhou City. *Jiazhang Xuexiao Cankao Ziliao*. [Reference Materials for Parent Craft Classes] Fuzhou: n.d.

Parsons, Talcott. *Societies*. Englewood Cliffs, New Jersey: Prentice Hall, 1966.

_____. "Suggestions for a Sociological Approach to the Theory of Organizations." *Administrative Science Quarterly* no.1 (1956):63-85.

People's Republic of China Yearbook: 1988/89. Hong Kong: Xinhua and NCN L+D Publishing, 1988.

Pepper, Suzanne. "China's Universities: New Experiments in Socialist Democracy and Administrative Reform." *Modern China* 8, no.2 (1982):147-204.

_____. *China's Universities: Post-Mao Enrollment Policies and Their Impact on the Structure of Secondary Education*. Ann Arbor: University of Michigan, 1984.

_____. "Chinese Education After Mao: Two Steps Forward, Two Steps Backward and Begin Again?" *China Quarterly* 81 (1980):1-65.

_____. "Deng Xiaoping's Political and Economic Reforms and the Chinese Student Protests." *Universities Field Staff International Reports No.3* [Asia] (1987).

_____."Education and Revolution: The 'China Model Revisited'." *Asian Survey* 18, no. 9 (1978):847-890.

Perrow, Charles. *Organizational Analysis: A Sociological View*. Belmont, California: Wadsworth, 1970.

Pinard, Jeanette. "The People's Republic of China: A Bibliography of Selected English Language Legal Materials." *China Law Reporter* vol.3 (1985).

Pitney, Henry. "The Role of Legal Practitioners in the People's Republic of China." *Stanford Journal of Interantional Law* vol.24, no.2 (Spring, 1988).

PLA General Political Department. *Zhongguo Jundui: Xin Junxian Zhishi Wenda*. [The Army of China: Questions and Answers about New Military Ranks]. Beijing: Changcheng Press, 1989.

Polyani, Michael. "The Republic of Science: Its Political and Economic Theory," in Edward Shils, editor. *Criteria for Scientific Development: Public Policy and National Goals*. Cambridge: Massachusetts Institute of Technology, 1968.

Potter, A.L. "Political Institutions, Political Decay and the Argentine Crisis of 1930." Unpublished Ph.D. dissertation, Stanford University, 1979.

Pound, Roscoe. "Comparative Law and History as Bases for Chinese Law." *Harvard Law Review* vol.61, no.5 (May 1948).

Price, R.F. "Convergence or Copying: China and the Soviet Union,"in Ruth Hayhoe and Marianne Bastid, editors. *China's Education and the Industrialized World: Studies in Cultural Transfer*. Armonk, N.Y. and Toronto: M.E. Sharpe and OISE, 1987.

_____. *Education in Modern China*. London: Routledge and Kegan Paul, 1979.

_____. *Marx and Education in Russia and China*. London: Croom Helm, 1977.

Project for the Study and Application of Humanistic Education in Law. *Reassessing Law Schooling*. New York: Columbia University, 1980.

Pye, Lucien W., and Sidney Verba. *Political Culture and Political Development*. Princeton: Princeton University, 1965.

Qi Benxun. "Chuantung Wenhua yu Xiandai Yantao Gaishu," [A Summary of Research and Discussions on Traditional Culture and Modernization] *Gaoxiao Shehui Kexue* [University Social Sciences] (June, 1989):73-77.

Qian Jingfang and Huang Kexiao. "On the Contemporary Reform of Secondary Education in the Eighties." *Canadian and International Education* 16:1 (1987):86-102.

"Quanguo nu dangyuan da wubai liushiduowan." [5.6 Million Female Communist Party Members in the Country] *Zhongguo funu* [Chinese Women's Newspaper] (October 2, 1985):1 translated in *Chinese Sociology and Anthropology* 20, no.1 (Fall 1987):13.

Rawski, Evelyn Sakakida. *Education and Popular Literacy in Ch'ing China*. Ann Arbor: University of Michigan, 1978.

Reform of China's Educational Structure--Decision of the CPC Central Committee. Beijing: Foreign Languages Press, 1985.

"Revamping China's Research System - Excerpts from Premier Zhao Ziyang's March 6 Speech at the National Science Conference." *Beijing Review* no.14 (1985):15-21.

Robinson, Jean. "Decentralization, Money and the Case of People-Run Schools in People's China." *Comparative Education Review* vol.30, no.1 (February 1986):73-88.

_____. "State Control and Local Financing of Schools in China," in Mark Bray with Kevin Lillis, editors. *Community Financing of Education: Issues and Policy Implications in Less Developed Countries*. Oxford: Pergamon Press, 1988,pp.181-195.

Roethlisberger, Fritz J., and W.J. Dickson. *Management and the Worker*. Cambridge: Harvard University, 1939.

Rosen, Stanley. "Education and the Political Socialization of Chinese Youths." in John Hawkins. *Education and Social Change in China.* N.Y: Praeger, 1983, pp.97-133.

_____. "Guangzhou's Democracy Movement in Cultural Revolution Perspective." *China Quarterly* no. 101 (March, 1985):1-31.

_____. "The Impact of Educational Reforms on the Attitudes and Behavior of Chinese Youth." *Interchange* vol.19, no.3/4 (Fall-Winter 1988):60-75.

_____. "The Impact of Reform on the Attitudes and Behavior of Chinese Youth: Some Evidence from Survey Research," in Donna Bahry and Joel Moses, editors. *Communist Dialectic: The Political Implications of Economic Reform in Communist Systems.* New York: New York University.

_____. "The Impact of Reform Policies on Youth Attitudes" in Deborah Davis and Ezra F. Vogel, editors. *Social Consequences of Chinese Economic Reforms.* Cambridge: Harvard University East Asian Publications, 1990.

_____. "Introduction." *Chinese Sociology and Anthropology* 22, no.1 (Fall 1987).

_____. "Introduction" to "Women, Education, and Employment." *Chinese Education* 22, no.2 (Summer 1989):3-6.

_____. "New Directions in Secondary Education" in Ruth Hayhoe, editor. *Contemporary Chinese Education.* Armonk: M.E. Sharpe, 1984 pp. 65-92.

_____. "Obstacles to Educational Reform in China." Modern China 8, no.1 (1982):3-40.

_____. editor. "Political Education I;" "Political Education II." *Chinese Education* (Fall, 1989 and Spring, 1990).

_____. "Prosperity, Privatization and China's Youth," *Problems of Communism* (March, 1985):1-28.

_____. "Recentralization, Decentralization and Rationalization: Deng Xiaoping's Bifurcated Educational Policy." *Modern China* 11, no.3 (1985):301-346.

_____. *Red Guard Factionalism and the Cultural Revolution in Guangzhou.* Boulder: Westview, 1982.

_____. "Restoring Key Secondary Schools in Post-Mao China: The Politics of Competition and Educational Quality," in David Lampton, editor. *Policy Implementation in Post-Mao China.* Berkeley: University of California, 1987, pp.321-353.

_____. "Students," in Anthony Kane editor. *China Briefing 1988.* Boulder: Westview, 1988 pp.79-105.

_____. "Value Change Among Post-Mao Youth: the Evidence from Survey Data," in Perry Link, Richard Madsen and Paul Pickowicz editors. *Unofficial China: Popular Culture and Thought in the People's Republic.* Boulder: Westview, 1989, pp.193-216.

_____. "Youth and Social Change in the People's Republic of China." Paper presented at the 18th Sino-American Conference, Hoover Institution, Stanford California, (June 8-11 1989).

Rosen, Stanley and David S.K. *Chu. Survey Research in the People's Republic of China.* Washington, D.C.: United States Information Agency, 1987.

Ross, Heidi. "Making Foreign Things Serve China." Unpublished Ph.D. dissertation, University of Michigan, 1987.

Rowbotham, Sheila. *Woman, Resistance and Revolution.* New York: Vintage Press, 1974.

Ruan Jie. "Shang xiansheng jinxiao zhi shi, jiushi de xiansheng shouhai zhi shi." [The Day Mr. Business Entered the School, Was the Day Mr. Morality Came to Grief] *Shanghai Jiaoyu* [Shanghai Education] (May, 1985):15.

Scharpf, F.W. "Does Organization Matter? Task Structure and Interaction in the Ministerial Bureaucracy," in E.H. Burack and A.R.

Negandhi, editors. *Organizational Design: Theoretical Perspectives and Empirical Findings*. Kent, Ohio: Kent State University, 1977, pp.149-167.

Schell, Orville. *To Get Rich Is Glorious: China in the 1980s*. New York: Pantheon, 1984.

Schmidt, T.C. "Organization and Structure," in Jay Henderson and Ronald Montaperto, editors. *China's Schools in Flux*. Armonk, New York: M.E. Sharpe, 1979, pp.39-59.

"Scholars Discuss Generation Gap." *Beijing Review* 31:34 (August 22-28, 1988):12-13.

"School Dropouts a Major Problem." *Beijing Review* 31:42 (October 17-23, 1988):8.

Scott, Richard W. *Organizations*. Englewood Cliffs, New Jersey: Prentice Hall, 1981.

Selected Stories of Lu Hsun. Peking: Foreign Languages Press, 1972.

Seybolt, Peter. "The Yenan Revolution in Mass Education," *China Quarterly* no.48 (October/December 1971).

Seymour, James D. *The Fifth Modernization: China's Human Rights Movement, 1978-79*. New York: Human Rights Publishing Group, 1980.

Shand, R.T. *Off-Farm Employment in the Development of Rural Asia: Volumes 1 and 2*. Canberra: Australian National University Center for Development Studies, 1986.

Shanghai Educational Examination Center. *Shanghaishi gaokao yingyu shiti pingxi, 1985-1987*. [An Analysis of Questions on the Shanghai English Language College Entrance Examinations, 1985-1987] Shanghai: Shanghai Foreign Language Education Press, 1988.

Shanghai Educational Examination Center. *Shanghaishi gaoxiao zhaosheng kaoshi*. [The Shanghai College Entrance Examination] Shanghai: East China Normal University Press, 1989.

Shanghai Higher Education Student Recruitment Committee Office and Shanghai Education Test Center (eds). *Gaoxiao zhaosheng kaoshi keyan lunwen ji.* [A Collection of Essays on Research on the College Entrance Examination] Shanghai: East China Normal University Press, 1989.

Shanghai Educational Examination Center. *Shanghaishi gaozhong huikao.* [The Shanghai Senior Secondary School Competency Examination] Shanghai: East China Normal University Press, 1989.

Shanghai Number Three Girls' Middle School. "Yanjiu nuzhong jiaoyu de tedian" [Research on the Special Characteristics of Education in a Girls' Middle School] in A Collection of Shanghai Secondary School Work Experiences (Shanghai: Shanghai Education Press, 1983):22-34.

Shanghaishi zhongxue jiaoyu gongzuo jingyan xuanbian, 1981-1982. [A Collection of Shanghai Secondary School Work Experiences, 1981-1982] Shanghai: Shanghai Education Press, 1983.

Shen Baoliang. "Gaibian jinguzhou jiefang ku haizi." [Transform the Incantation of the Golden Hoop and Liberate Exhausted Children] *Shanghai jiaoyu* [Shanghai Education] (May 1989):7.

Shen Zongling, "'Fazhi', 'Fazhi', 'Renzhi' de ciyi Fenxi." [An Analysis of the Meaning of Law, Rule of Law, and the Rule of Man] *Faxue Yanjiu* (August 23, 1989):4-9.

Shenzhen Municipal Education Bureau. "Overview of Educational Development in Shenzhen Special Economic Zone," translated in *Chinese Education* no.3 (1988):7-24.

Shepsle, Kenneth. "Studying Institutions: Some Lessons from the Rational Choice Approach." *Journal of Theoretical Politics* 1, no.2 (1989):131-147.

Shirk, Susan. *Competitive Comrades*. Berkeley: University of California, 1982.

_____. "Educational Political Backlash: Recent Changes in Chinese Educational Policy." *Comparative Education Review* vol.23 (1979):183-217.

Sidel, Ruth. *Women and Child Care in China*. Baltimore: Penguin, 1972.

Sidel, Victor and Sidel, Ruth. *Serve the People*. Boston: Beacon Press, 1973.

Silber, John. *Straight Shooting*. New York: Harper and Row Publishers, 1989.

Smith, Kathlin. "Educational Reform: Toward a New Student Responsibility System?" *China Exchange News* 16:2 (June 1988):25-26.

_____. "Funding China's Education: Will Trickle-up Work?" *China Exchange News* 17:2 (June, 1989):8.

_____. "Red, Black and Yellow Paths: New Choices for Young Scientists" *China Exchange News* 16:4 (December 1988):14-15.

Smith, Patrick. "China's Economic Zones: An Experiment That Failed." *International Herald Tribune* (September 11, 1986).

Song Chongjin. "Guanyu zhongxuesheng qingqunqi jiaoyu de diaocha." [An Investigation into Sex Education for Secondary School Students] Shanghai: Changning District Education Bureau Educational Research Office, 1985, pp. 39-46.

Stacey, Judith. *Patriarchy and Socialist Revolution in China*. Berkeley: University of California, 1983.

State Statistical Bureau. "Education and Reform." *Beijing Review* 31:45 (November 7-13, 1988):31-32.

_____. "Statistics for 1988 Socio-Economic Development" *Beijing Review* 32:10 (March 6-12, 1989):I-VIII.

Statistical Yearbook of China: 1986. New York: Oxford University Press, 1986.

"Students Voice Their Concerns." *Beijing Review* 32:9 (February 27-March 5, 1989):39-40.

"Student Business on Campus." *Beijing Review* 31:33 (August 15-21, 1988):38-39.

"Studies of the Only Child Published." *Beijing Review* 31:42 (October 17-23, 1988):12.

Su Xiaokang. *River Elegy* [1988 Chinese television series].

Sun Lung-Kee. *Zhongguo Wenhua de Shenceng Jiegou* [The Deep Structure of Chinese Culture]. Hong Kong: Ji Hsien Publishing House, 1983.

Sun Peixian. "Air Force Political College." *Bingqi Zhishi*. [Weaponry Knowledge] 2 (May 15, 1987).

Suttmeier, Richard. "China's Science and Technology Reforms: Towards a Post-Socialist Knowledge System." *China Exchange News* vol.16, no.4 (December 1988):7-13.

Sze Szeming. *China's Health Problems*. Washington,D.C.: National Institute of Health, 1972.

Szelenyi, Ivan. "The Intelligentsia in the Class Structure of State-Socialist Societies," in Michael Burawoy and Theda Skocpol, editors. *Marxist Inquiries: Studies of Labor, Class and States*. Chicago: University of Chicago, 1982, pp.287-326.

Tao Kuo-Tai. "Mentally Retarded Persons in the People's Republic of China: Review of Epidemiological Studies and Services." *American Journal on Mental Retardation* 93, no.2 (1988).

"Teaching Pupils Practical Skills." *Beijing Review* 31:30 (July 25-31, 1988):40.

Teng, Ssu-yu and Fairbank, John K. editors. *China's Response to the West: A Documentary Survey, 1839-1923*. New York: Atheneum, 1963.

Thogersen, Stig. "China's Senior Middle Schools in a Social Perspective: A Survey of Yantai District, Shandong Province." *China Quarterly* (March 1987):72-100.

Thompson, James C. Jr. *While China Faced West: American Reformers in Nationalist China, 1928-1937*. Cambridge: Harvard University, 1969.

Tilak, Jandhyala B.G. "Investment in Education in East Asia." presented at the 1989 Symposium on East Asian Educational Reforms, University of Virginia, November 1989.

Tseng Chao-lun. "Higher Education in New China," in Stewart Fraser, editor. *Chinese Communist Education: Records of the First Decade*. Nashville: Vanderbilt University, 1965.

Tsou Tang. *The Cultural Revolution and Post-Mao Reforms*. Chicago: University of Chicago, 1986.

Unger, Jonathan. *Education Under Mao*. New York: Columbia University, 1982.

Unschuld, Paul U. *Medical Ethics in Imperial China*. Berkeley: University of California, 1978.

_____. *Medicine in China: A History of Ideas*. Berkeley: University of California, 1985.

_____. "The Role of Traditional Chinese medicine in Contemporary Health Care," in *Recent Advances in Traditional Medicine in East Asia*. Amsterdam: Excerpta Medica, 1985.

UNICEF. *The State of the World's Children 1989*. New York: Oxford University, 1989.

United States Congress House Committee on Armed Services. *Report of the Panel on Military Education of the One Hundredth Congress*. 101st Congress, First Session. Washington, D.C.: Government Printing Office, April 29, 1989.

Vause, W. Gary. "China's Ideological Retrenchment--Can the Economic and Legal Reforms Survive?" *George Washington Journal of International Law and Economics* vol.11 (1989).

Walder, Andrew. *Communist Neo-traditionalism: Work and Authority in Chinese Society.* Berkeley: University of California, 1986.

Wang Hailun. "Koutou wenxue re yu quanmin laosaochao." [Ballad Fever and the Tide of Mass Discontent] *Jiushi niandai* (February, 1989):62-64.

Wang, Hao and Chen. "On Strengthening Humanities in Higher Education." *Jiaoyu Yanjiu* no.8 (1981) translated in *Chinese Education* vol.19, no.1 (1986).

Wang Hsueh-wen. *Chinese Communist Education: the Yenan Period.* Taiwan: Institute of International Relations, 1978.

Wang, J.L. *Literacy Campaigns in China's Rural Areas.* Paris: IIE, 1982.

Wang Jusheng. *Peiyang Jundui Liangyong Rencai 100 Wen.*[One Hundred Questions on Developing Military Dual-Purpose Personnel] Shanghai: Shanghai Science and Technology Press, 1987.

Wang, Y.C. *Chinese Intellectuals and the West.* 1872-1949. Chapel Hill: University of North Carolina, 1966.

Wang Yibing. "Updating China's Educational System." *Beijing Review* vol.28, no.50 (1985):15-22.

Wei Min. "Reforming Criminals." *Beijing Review* (February 23, 1981).

White, Gordon. *Party and Professionals.* Armonk, New York: M.E. Sharpe, 1981.

White, James J. "Women in the Law." *Michigan Law Review* vol.65 (1966):1051-1122.

Whyte, Martin King, and William L. Parish. *Urban Life in Contemporary China.* Chicago: University of Chicago, 1984.

Wider, Claude editor. *Documents on the Chinese Democratic Movement 1978-89: Unofficial Magazines and Wall Posters*. Hong Kong: Observers Publishers, 1981, 1984.

Williams, Tim, and Robin Brilliant. "Shenzhen Status Report." *The China Business Review* (1986).

Wolf, Diane. *Factory Daughters, Their Families and Rural Industrialization in Center Java*. Doctoral dissertation, Cornell University, 1986.

Wolf, Margery. *Revolution Postponed: Women in Contemporary China*. Stanford: Stanford University, 1985.

"Women, Education and Employment." *Chinese Education* 22, no.2 (Summer, 1989).

World Bank. *China: Issues and Prospects in Education, Annex 1: Long Term Development*. Washington, D.C.: The World Bank, 1985.

Wright, Erik Olin. *Classes*. New York: Schocken, 1985.

_____. *Class, Crisis and the State*. London: Verso, 1979.

Wright, Mary Claubaugh, editor. *China in Revolution: the First Phase, 1900-1913*. New Haven: Yale University, 1968.

_____. "Introduction: the Rising Tide of Change, in *China in Revolution: the First Phase, 1900-1913*. New Haven: Yale University, 1968.

Wu Qingxiang et al. (eds). *Xinli: zice yu xunlian*. [Psychology: Measurment and Training] Shanghai: Shanghai Science and Technology Press, 1989.

Wu Weliang. "A Task of Strategic Importance to the Zhuhai Special Economic Zone--Development of Human Resources," translated in *Chinese Education* no.3 (1988):42-57.

Wu Yenbo. "To Teach or Not to Teach, That is the Question." Paper presented at the Comparative and International Education Society annual conference, Atlanta, GA, March 1988.

Xiang Bo. "Jiefang chu Shanghai liumang gaizao jilue." *Shehui* no.2 (May, 1982):29-32.

Xiao Jing [Classic of Filial Piety] in *Sacred Books of the East*, translated by James Legge. Oxford: Clarendon Press, 1879.

Xi Dihua. "How Education in Shanghai Can Become Internationalized" published in *Chinese Education* pp 112-115.

Xi Xinxiong, et al. (ed). *Shanghaishi zhongdeng zhiye jishu xuexiao minglu*. [A List of Shanghai Secondary Vocational and Technical Schools] Shanghai: Shanghai Secondary Specialized Education Research Publishers, 1986.

Xu Bing, "Renquan Lilun de Chansheng he Lishi Fazhan," [Creation and Historical Development of a Theory of Human Rights] *Faxue Yanjiu* (June, 23, 1989):1-10.

Xu Jian. "Qingshaonian fanzui wenti yanjiu." *Shehui Kexue* (Shanghai) no.11 (1980).

Xu Wenbo. "Zhongguo de Weisheng Renyuan Zhiliang he Yixue Jiaoyu Gaige." [China's Health Personnel Quality and Reforms in Medical Education] Beijing: China Medical Association, 1987.

Xue Daohua. "Shifan yuanxiao zhaosheng tiqian dandu luquhao." [A Separate Early Admissions for Teacher Training Institutions Is Good] *Gaojiao Zhanxian* 5 (1986):34-35.

Yang, Jianye. "To Manage Educational Work As We Do With the Economy." *Prospects* vol.28 (July, 1985):9-13.

Yang Yalin and Li Jinrong. "Chengshi zhigong jiawu laodong yanjiu." [Research into Urban Staff and Workers' Housework] *Zhongguo shehui kexue* [Chinese Social Sciences] 1 (1982):177-190.

Yang Xingnan. "Jushou nu daxueshengde xianxiang yingdang gaibian." [Rejection of female college graduates must be stopped] *Zhongguo funu bao* [Chinese women's newspaper] (February 27, 1985):1 translated in *Chinese Sociology and Anthropology* 20, no.1 (Fall 1987):65-66.

Yang Yinjie. "Guanyu Shenzhen tequ fazhan nongmin jiaoyu de tantao." *Shenzhen tequ chengren jiaoyu luanwenxuan*, 1985,pp.4-9.

Yang Ruisen, "Lun Shehui Zhuyi Minzhu Jianshe," [On the Construction of Socialist Democracy] *Gaoxiao Shehui Kexue* (August, 1989):4-8.

Yao Jiaqun and Liu Lian. "Wei shangpin jingji zhengming." [Justified by a Commodity Economy] *Shanghai jiaoyu* [Shanghai Education] (May, 1989):14-15.

Yao Peikuan, ed. *Qingqunqi changshi duben.* [A Reader on Sexual Development] Shanghai: Shanghai Peoples Press,1987.

Ying Junfeng. "The Structure of Specialized Personnel and the Reform of Vocational-Technical Education." *Canadian and International Education* 16:1 (1987):103-113.

Youmei Tungxue Lu. [Who's Who of American Returned Students]. Peking: Tsing Hua College, 1917 and San Francisco: Chinese Materials Center, Inc. 1987.

Yu, B., and H.Y. Xu. *Adult Higher Education: A Case Study on a Workers' College in the People's Republic of China.* Paris, IIE, 1988.

Yu Daqing, Wang Changlin and Wang Xiaofu. *Junshi Rencaixue Gailun.* [Introduction to the Study of Military Talent]. Hubei: Hubei People's Press and Hubei Science and Technology Press, 1986.

Yu Mengjia. "A General Presentation on China's Endeavor to Establish and Perfect Its Legal System Since 1970." *New York Law School Journal of International and Comparative Law* vol.10 (1989).

Yuan Hui. "Luetan Tequ Chengren Jiaoyu De Chuangkou." *Shenzhen Tequ Chengren* (1986).

___. "On the Development and Management of Shenzhen Adult Education." *Shenzhen Tequ Chengren Jiaoyu Luanwenxuan*, 1985.

Zhang, S.W. "Combatting Illiteracy in China." *Beijing Review* vol.30, no.3 (February 16, 1987).

Zhang Xinxin, and Sang Ye. *Chinese Lives*, edited and translated by W.J.F. Jenner and Delia Davin. New York and London: Pantheon, Macmillan and Penguin, 1987, 1988, 1989.

Zhao Haiyan. "Gaozhong nusheng xuexizhongde xinli zhang'ai ji jiaozheng." [Psychological Barriers of Senior High School Students in Their Studies and Their Remedy] *Qingnian yanjiu* [Youth Studies] 6 (1986):17-19, translated in *Chinese Sociology and Anthropology* 20, no.1 (Fall, 1987):80-85.

Zhao Tian, and Liu Xingwei. "Yao ba shifan jiaoyu wei zhengge jiaoyu de zhanlue zhongdian jia yi zhongshi jiaqiang he fazhan," [Pay Attention to Strengthen and Develop Teacher Education as a Key Point to All of Education] in *Jiaoyu yu Sihua jianshe: Lunwen xuanji*. N.P., Liaoning Provincial Higher Education Association, n.d., pp.28-34.

Zhao Yicheng. "Jiazhide chongtu." *Weidinggao* no.8 (April 25, 1988):26-33; *Weidinggao* no.9 (May 10, 1988):18-21.

Zhao Ziyang, "Advance Along the Road of Socialism with Chinese Characteristics," Report delivered to the Thirteenth Congress of the Communist Party of China (October 25, 1987).

Zhongguo Da Baike Quanshu: Faxue. Beijing and Shanghai: Encyclopedia of China Publishing House, 1984.

Zhongguo Falu Nianjian 1987 . [China Law Yearbook] Beijing: Law Publishing House, 1987.

Zhongguo Falu Nianjian 1989. [China Law Yearbook] Beijing: Law Publishing House, 1989.

"Zhongguo Fazhi Gaige Xueshu Taolunhui Fayan Zhaiyao," [Digest of Speeches on the Reform of the Legal System of China] *Faxue Yanjiu* (April 23, 1989):10-35.

Zhongguo jiaoyu tongji nianjian.[China Educational Statistics Yearbook] Beijing: State Education Commission, 1987.

Zhongguo jiaoyu tongji nianjian. [China Educational Statistics Yearbook] Beijing: State Education Commission, 1988.

Zhongguo Shehui Kexueyuan Qingshaonian Yanjiusuo and the Sichuan Renmin Guangbo Diantai. [Research Institute for Youth and Juvenile Affairs of the Chinese Academy of Social Sciences and the Sichuan Broadcasting Station] *Qingnian Jiuye zhi Lu*. [The Road to Youth Employment] Beijing: Broadcasting Publishing House, 1983.

Zhongguo shehui tongji ziliao 1987. [China Social Statistics Data 1987] Beijing: Zhongguo Tongji Chubanshe, 1987.

Zhonghua Quanguo Funu Lianhehui [All-China Women's Federation], editors. '*Si Da'yilai funu yundong wenxuan, 1979-1983.* [Selections on the Women's Movement Since the Fourth Congress] Beijing: Zhongguo Funu Chubanshe, 1983.

Zhonghua Renmin Gongheguo Zhongyao Falu Xuanbian. [Selected Major Laws of the People's Republic of China] Shanghai: People's Publishing House, 1986.

Zhou Liren. "Dangqian Jiaoxue Gaige de Tedian he qiaoshi," [The Special Aspects and Trends of Educational Reform] *Jiaoyu Yanjiu* no.2 (February 1989).

Zhou Yinjun, Yang Jiezeng and Xue Suzhen. "Xin shehui ba guibien chengren: yi Shaghai gaizao changji shi hua." *Shehui* no.1 (October 1981): 46-51.

Zhu, J.H. "Origins of the Chinese Student Unrest." *Indianapolis Star* (May 9, 1989).

Zhu Wentao. "Ling ren shenside xiaoyuan 'xin chao': guanyu daxuesheng yanxuede xianzhuang he sikao." [A 'New Tide' on Campus That Causes One to Ponder: Thinking About the New Situation in Which Students Despise Studies] *Shehui*, no.8 (August, 1988):8-11.

Zhuang Mingshui."Gaoshi xueshang zhuanye nixiang jiaoyu cuyi." [Some Comments on the Education of Normal College Students' Professional Thinking] *Fujian Shida Xuebao* 1, Part 2 (1983):55-62.

Notes on Contributors

Mary Ann Burris received her Ph.D. in International Development Education from Stanford University. She is the Ford Foundation Program Officer for Reproductive Health in China and has a longstanding interest in gender, health and education issues. She is the author of "Struggle, Criticism, Transformation: Education in the People's Republic of China" in Martin Carnoy and Joel Samoff's *Education and Social Transition in the Third World* (Princeton: Princeton University Press, 1990).

Nat J. Colleta has worked for the World Bank since 1977. He was Team Leader and Senior Education and Training Specialist in the India Population and Human Resources Division until 1989, when he was secunded to United Nations Children's Fund, where he is presently Deputy Executive Secretary of the Inter-Agency Commission on the World Conference on Education for All. Dr. Colletta has authored five books and numerous journal articles on various topics related to education and development.

Delia Davin is a lecturer in East Asian Studies at the University of Leeds. She has written extensively on women, gender and population problems in China. With W.J.F. Jenner, she editied and co-translated *Chinese Lives: An Oral History of Contemporary China* (London: Pantheon, 1987; Macmillan, 1988, Penguin, 1989).

Irving Epstein is an assistant professor and Head of the Education Department at Lafayette College. He is an associate editor of the *Comparative Education Review* and is a member of the editorial advisory committee of *Chinese Education*. His research focuses upon issues of access and equity for children with special needs in China.

Corinna-Barbara Francis is currently a visiting lecturer at the Center for Chinese Studies at the University of Michigan, and is completing her dissertation in the Political Science Department at Columbia University. She spent two years in the People's Republic of China, from 1986-1988, doing research and completing interviews for her dissertation on the question of the changing role of the party in basic level *danweis* (work units). The dissertation looks at the changing

491

relations between state and society in the era of reform. She has published on the Chinese democracy movement in 1989, the *dang-wai* movement on Taiwan, and Chinese foreign policy.

Ruth Hayhoe is a professor in the Higher Education Group, Ontario Institute for Studies in Education. Her research and teaching interests include comparative education, international academic relations and China studies. She has taught Chinese students in Hong Kong and Shanghai for thirteen years and at present is on secondment to the Canadian Embassy in Beijing as cultural attache. She is the author of *Chinese Universities and the Open Door* (New York and Toronto: M.E. Sharpe and OISE Press, 1989).

John N. Hawkins is director of International Studies and Overseas Programs and Professor of Comparative Education at the University of California, Los Angeles.

Sharon K. Hom is an associate professor of law at CUNY Law School at Queens College. She has also taught at the Benjamin N. Cardozo School of Law, Yeshiva University and the China Center for American Law Study, (Beijing, 1990). She was a Fulbright Lecturer at the China University of Politics and Law, (Beijing, 1986-88); a Revson Fellow at the Max E. and Filomen Greenberg Center for Legal Education and Urban Policy (1984-85); and a Root-Tilden Scholar, New York University School of Law, J.D. (1980). She serves on the Committee for Legal Education Exchange With China. Her writings include *American Legal Education Methodology in China: Teaching Notes and Resources* (Chinese and English, 1990) and articles on the American legal profession and legal education.

Beverley Hooper teaches in the History Department of the University of Western Australia. She is the author of *Youth in China* (Penguin, 1985) and has written extensively on gender issues in China.

Bruce Koppel is a research associate with the Resources Systems Institute, East-West Center, Honolulu Hawaii.

Colonel Richard J. Latham is attached to the American Consulate in Hong Kong. He has written extensively about cadre and military affairs in contemporary China.

Lynn Paine, associate professor in Michigan State University's College of Education, teaches and conducts research in sociology of education and comparative education. Her research on China has focused on understanding the relationship between local educational practices and national reform. Her field research has centered on teaching, teacher education, and more recently, on rural schooling.

Suzanne Pepper is a Berkeley Ph.D. (political science, 1972) and long-time Hong Kong resident. Her publications on Chinese education include the relevant chapters in the *Cambridge History of Modern China*, volumes 14 and 15. She was the East Asia associate for the American-based Universities Field Staff International during 1985-87 and correspondent for the *Chronicle of Higher Education* in 1988.

Jean Robinson is associate professor of Political Science at Indiana University-Bloomington. She has published articles on China in *China Quarterly, Asian Survey, Comparative Education Review, Policy Studies Review, Polity*, and in numerous edited volumes. She is currently completing two manuscripts: *The Dynamics of Charismatic Leadership* and *Alienated Families: State, Family and Public Policies in Socialist Societies*.

Stanley Rosen is an associate professor in the Department of Political Science, University of Southern California. His writings focus on political and social change in China. He is currently studying the impact of Chinese reforms on women and youth. He edits the journal *Chinese Education*.

Heidi Ross received her Ph.D. from the University of Michigan Educational Foundations, Policy and Administration program. She has taught at Providence College in Taiwan, the Shanghai Foreign Language School, Indiana University, and is currently assistant professor of education at Colgate University and associate in research with the East Asia Program at Cornell University. Her doctoral study of education in the People's Republic of China will be published by Yale University Press in a forthcoming volume entitled *Making Foreign Things Serve China*. Her most recent research project, for which she was named Paul Garrison Research Fellow at Colgate University, is an historical ethnography of the Shanghai Number Three Middle School for Girls. Funded by the University of Kansas History of Christianity in China Project, the study focuses upon the role of formal schooling in the construction of gender during late imperial, republican and socialist China.

Zhixin Su is an assistant professor of Education at California State University, Northridge. She received her Ph.D. from the University of Washington and holds a Masters degree from the University of Toronto. Professor Su spent a number of years working in China's State Education Commission.

Jianliang Wang is associate professor and director of the Asian Studies Center at Western Kentucky University. He was the founder and executive director of the USA/China Consortium. He received his doctorate from the State University of New York at Albany, and before coming to the United States, he worked for China's Central Institute of Educational Research under the State Education Commission. He also pursued advanced training at the International Institute for Educational Planning, affiliated with UNESCO, in Paris.

Index

Academies, 6-7, 9, 15, 110
Academic Degrees Committee
121-122
Adolescence, 70, 86-90
Adult Education, 109, 145-
151, 152-160
Adult literacy, 146, 147-
152
Adult Higher Education,
152-160
Correspondence Education,
146, 153, 154-155,
154-155
Independent Study
Through Examination,
157-158
Anti-bourgeois Liberalization
Campaign, 417, 440
Autonomy, xiii,xvi,xviii-xxi,
xxiii, 67, 109, 110, 113-
115
Ball, Nicole, 316, 321, 333,
Beida (Beijing University),
111, 395-399, 401, 409,
410, 413, 418, 436
Beijing Foreign Studies
University, 358-359
Beijing University, see also
Beida, xxiv, 15, 111, 338,
356, 395, 396, 400
Beijing University Student
Association, 395, 397-
399, 404
student government, 395,
397-406, 410-412,
413
ban committees, 399, 401,
407
Beijing Normal University, 91,
206
Bernstein, Basil, 118, 208
Brain drain, 190

Burris, Mary Ann, xiii, xix,
xxiv-xxv, 255
Cai Yuanpei, 15, 110-111, 119
Chenbao, 275
see also individual
responsibility system
Central Military Commission,
327, 329, 332, 333, 335
China Communist Youth
League (CYL), 397-399,
400, 431, 432, 438, 444,
China Welfare Fund, 206
Chinese Academy of Sciences,
113, 122
Chinese Academy of Social
Sciences, 122
Chinese Communist Party,
(CCP) xxiv, 1-3, 13, 19-
21, 23, 28, 34, 46, 56, 70,
109-111, 125, 137, 164,
235, 237, 240, 265, 290,
291, 298, 323, 325, 329,
333, 338, 339, 364, 376,
395, 397, 398, 400, 406,
416, 417, 419, 421, 423,
432-435, 440-443
Chinese Medical Ethics
Association, 275
Chinese People's Political
Consultative Congress, 441
Chinese Television University,
153-154
Christianity,
Christian missionaries, 8,
16
missionary schools, 8, 16
Civil service examinations (in
Imperial China), 5, 7, 10,
15, 29, 110, 116, 118
Commodity culture, 87, 113,
129, 133

socialism, xvii-xix, xxv,
  113, 129, 132, 133,
  137-138
Competition, 3, 6, 33, 116,
  130-131, 323-324, 327-
  328
Confucian education, xvi, 45
  learning, 5, 11, 18
  tradition, xvii, 5, 7, 11,
    111, 289, 299
Conscription, 322-324, 340
Cultural Revolution, xiv-xv,
  xviii, xxiii, 25, 26-28, 30-
  31, 46-47, 50, 66, 85-86,
  111, 114, 118, 121-122,
  126-127, 146-148, 155,
  199-201, 204-205, 217,
  221, 234, 266, 268, 270,
  290, 293-294, 297, 355,
  377-379, 419, 422, 430
Curriculum, xx, 24-25, 55-56,
  58, 59-60, 70, 71, 73-74,
  78-79, 88-89, 112, 118,
  123-128, 150, 151, 152,
  157, 165, 203, 219, 224,
  225, 231-233, 260, 263,
  266-272, 277, 296-299,
  332, 422
  Curricular decision
  making, 72, 79, 82, 114-
  115, 121-122, 123-128,
  156, 181, 224, 271-272,
  297, 299
  Fields of Study (Higher
  education), 123-130
  Fundamental subjects, 30,
  54-56, 72-73, 75, 231
  Lesson plans, 70
  Materials, 78, 115, 150-
  151, 159, 297, 302, 335
  Specialization, xvii, 21,
    74, 76, 77-78, 115,

  118-119, 123-128, 156,
  157, 182-187, 205,
  217, 224, 228, 230,
  233, 304
  Textbooks, 68, 73-74, 84,
  89, 115, 219, 224, 296,
  299
Danwei (work unit), 85, 154,
  155, 184-185, 202, 304
Davin, Delia, 42
Decentralization, 77, 79, 149-
  150, 276, 336, 388-389,
  390, 391
Defense Education Campaign,
  338-340
Demobilization (of the
  military), 322, 325, 333-
  337, 340
  dual-purpose training, 334-
  336, 337, 341
Democracy movement, xxii,
  111-113, 128-130, 294,
  300, 396
Deng Xiaoping, xxii, 2, 8, 27,
  29, 66, 68, 163, 164, 176,
  206, 291, 297, 322, 333,
  338, 395, 417, 418, 435,
  439, 440
Dewey, John, 12, 300
Disabled youth, 196-197, 203-
  210, 211
Dual leadership, 409
Early childhood education, 42-
  43
East China Normal University,
  206
Educational Administration,
  375-377, 381-385, 388,
  389-391
Educational equity, equality,
  xiii, xxiv, xvi, xvii, xxiv,
  352, 356, 363, 365, 366

Educational exchange, 115, 135, 137
Educational Reform Document of 1985, 113
  see also *Reform of China's Educational Structure*
Edwards, Randall, 302
Elman, Benjamin, xvi
Fan Shaobao, 66, 68-69, 90
Fang Lizhi, xxii, 137, 434
Filial piety, 45
Financing, 24-31, 67, 71, 90, 115, 135, 149, 150, 164, 165, 181, 184
Foreign models of education, 20, 25, 109-111, 122
Francis, Corinna-Barbara, 394
Fudan University, 110, 111
Gender, xiii, xviii, xix, xxiv, xxv, xvi, 83-85, 86, 132, 149, 222, 272-273, 303-304, 352-366
  and aspiration, 361-363, 365-366
  and Chinese secondary schooling, 83-85
  family, 360-361
  and medical education, 272-273
  and the legal profession, 303-304
  and unemployment, 359-360
  general imbalance, 352-356, 363-366
  obstacles to access to education, 356-357, 360-361, 365-366
Gentry, 5-7, 10, 14
Goldman, Merle and Cheek, Timothy, xvi

Graduate study, 22, 121-122, 128, 129, 131, 133, 135, 137
Great Leap Forward, 23-24, 116
Grieder, Jerome, xvi
Guanxi, 52, 173, 210, 436
Guy, R. Kent, xvi
Hanlin Academy, 110
Hawkins, John, xix, xxiv, 172
Hayhoe, Ruth, xiii, xv-xvi, xviii, 109
Health care, 255-257, 258-270-277
Hershatter, Gail, 364
Hierarchy, 19, 198, 289, 299, 385, 398, 407, 435
Higher Education, 17, 21, 23, 24, 78, 109-144, 147, 148, 152-160, 209, 221, 222, 224, 257, 296, 302, 303, 319, 333, 341, 362, 376-378, 387
Hom, Sharon, xiii, xix, xx, xxv, 287
Hong Kong, xiv, 8, 32, 35, 176-178, 181-182, 188, 190, 400, 440-441
Honig, Emily, 364
Hooper, Beverley, xviii, xxiv, 352
Humanities, xx, 125, 127-128
Hunan Self-Study University, 15
Hu Yaobang, xxii, 131, 440
Illiteracy, xviii, 7, 11, 16-21, 23, 147-149, 149-152, 158-160, 166, 180, 182, 355, 360, 376-377
Imperial university (*taixue*), 110
Individual responsibility system, 30, 281

see also *chenbao*,
  rural responsibility system,
    113, 148, 159
Intellectuals, xvi-xix,xxi-
    xxiii, 3, 5, 8-19, 21, 22-
    24, 26-30, 32, 57, 60, 81,
    82, 86, 112, 136, 137,
    234, 236, 237, 243, 294,
    295, 326, 395
  Intellectual freedom, 110
Jiaotong University, 117, 128
Jiang Zemin, 137
Jiazhang xuexiao (parentcraft
  classes), 47
Jiti jiaoyu (collectivist
  education), 200
Job allocation and job
  assignment, 109, 114, 115,
    126, 129, 130-133
June, 1989, 112, 116, 130,
    132, 133, 135, 136, 137,
    190, 196, 211, 275, 276,
    277, 295, 297, 300, 302,
    338, 340, 416, 442
  see also Tiananmen
    Massacre
Juvenile delinquency, 197-199,
    201-204, 211
K'ao-cheng, xvii
Key schools, xiv, xix, 30, 33,
    67, 72-73, 76, 79, 91,
    164, 165, 219, 228, 231,
    356, 361
Kindergarten, 42-44, 47, 51-
    59
Kraus, Richard, xv
Kwong, Julia, xv
Koppel, Bruce, xix, xxiv, 176

Labor camps, 198-200, 202-
    203
Latham, Richard, 316

Law, 287, 288, 289-295
League of Nations, 18, 119
Legal education, 287-288, 296-
    301, 301-305
Liang Shuming, 15, 18
Li Dazhao, 15
Liu Binyan, xxii
Manual labor, 5, 14, 19, 23,
    28, 30, 35
Mao Zedong, xvii, 2, 3, 15, 19,
    22,23, 24, 25, 26, 28, 70,
    82, 164, 295, 376, 380,
    382, 383, 420, 435
  Maoism, Maoist struggle,
    2, 3, 22, 26, 27, 28,
      33, 34, 35, 46, 163,
      164, 364
  democratic centralism, 380,
    383, 389
  mass line, 383, 389
Market forces, xiii, xv, xvii-
    xviii, xxi, xxiv, 174-179
Marxism, xvii, 13, 62. 117.
    118. 122. 125, 126, 297,
    376, 385, 416, 417, 422,
    423, 435, 440
Mass education, 3, 14, 15-16,
    24, 26, 33, 145
  peasant education, 146,149,
    153, 158, 163, 164,
      168, 169
  worker education, 145, 146,
    147, 148, 149, 150,
      152-153, 155-156, 182,
      184-185, 189-190
May Fourth Movement, xvii,
    13-14, 111, 113, 129
Medical Education, xiii, 16,
    255-257, 258-272, 273-286
Medicine, 255-278
  and the State, 256, 258-
    267, 273, 277

and the family, 256, 258,
    273
Mental labor, 14, 23, 30, 35
Military education, 316-320,
    326-331, 340-341
  combat training, 318, 320,
    336
  officer training school,
    319
  military academies, 319,
    326,327, 328-329,
    330, 331, 332, 333
  military training at civilian
    institutions, 337-338
  professional military
    education, 318, 319,
    330-331, 332
  technical training, 316,
    318, 323, 329-330
Military Service Law, 322,
    337
Military Training Handbook,
    328
Minban schools, xix, xxiii,
    163-169, 218, 238, 240- 241
Ministry of Education, 17, 28,
    118, 125, 146, 155-156,
    227-228, 230, 234, 239,
    242, 243, 297, 337, 375,
    376-378, 436
Modernization (and education),
    xiii, xviii, xxiii, xxv, xxvi,
    29, 35, 67-69, 71-72, 80,
    112, 130, 145, 159, 163,
    164, 196, 200, 211, 218,
    227, 234, 243, 244, 246,
    258, 267, 270-272, 273-
    278, 288, 333, 356, 365,
    377, 384, 391
Moral education, 47, 54-56,
    60-62, 72, 86-90, 91, 198,

    201, 224, 230, 231, 245,
    416, 419-421
  Circular on Reforming and
    Strengthening Moral
    Education for Primary and
    Secondary School Students,
    441
National Defense University,
    331-332
Nei Jing (Canon of Medicine),
    259-260
Noncommissioned officer corps
    (NCO), 322-323, 324, 325,
    336, 340
Non-formal education, xviii, 15-
    16, 21, 109, 145, 152, 153,
    158, 159, 189, 205
Officers, 318, 319, 321-322,
    325-328, 329, 330-332,
    334, 335, 337, 341
  recruitment and selection,
    320, 323, 327, 334,
    337
Only child, see Single child
    policy
Open door, xxv, 116, 133-138,,
    256, 264, 271, 274
Organized dependency, xxi
Overseas study, 12, 133-138
  with Japan, 12, 134
  with the United States, 12,
    135
  with the Soviet Union, 12
  with Western Europe, 12,
    135
Paine, Lynn, xx, xxv, 217
Patronship and clientship, xxi
Pedagogy, xiv, xxiv, 67, 70,
    71, 72, 73,74, 75, 77, 78,
    84, 87, 90, 114, 115, 118,
    181, 182, 203, 206, 209,

230, 232, 299, 300, 301,
302
(see also Teaching
methods)
pedagogic authority, 208
Peking Union Medical
College, 263, 273
People's congresses, 112, 166,
375
National People's
Congress, 166, 291,
292, 406-407, 410
People's Liberation Army
(PLA), 316, 317, 321-330,
330-337, 339, 340-342
People's University, 126, 127
Pepper, Suzanne, xiii, xvii,
xxii, 1
Physical education, 72, 78
PLAAF Engineering College,
329, 330
Political culture, xiii, xxiii,394,
398
Political education, 68, 72, 88-
89, 120, 126-130, 137,
181, 185, 201, 220, 290,
292, 296, 297, 298, 302,
338-340, 416, 418, 419,
422, 431, 432, 439, 440
Post-Mao Era, xiv, xv, xvii,
xviii, xxii, 1, 2, 29, 31,
34, 43, 46, 50, 60, 66,
146-147, 196, 199, 201,
205, 210, 211, 235, 236,
238, 239, 240, 241, 243,
244, 243, 245, 355, 358,
359, 360, 363-365
Prairie Fire Program, 81-82
Primary schools, 43, 51-52,
55, 56-60, 67, 69, 72, 77,
82, 147, 148, 149, 180,

182, 204, 206, 207, 420,
429, 439, 441
Private students, 114, 121
Professions, professionalism,
xiii, xvi, xvii, xx, xxv, 3,
18, 22-28, 84, 87, 90, 115,
121, 122, 123, 124, 128,
130, 132, 134, 136, 149,
150, 164, 209, 217-219,
221-224, 226, 227-230,
232-234, 254, 256, 259,
261, 263, 264, 272-276,
290, 292, 293, 296-304,
304-305, 318, 319, 329,
330-332, 362, 385, 398
Professional standards for
teachers, 232
Provincial universities, 17, 116,
117, 120, 122, 135
Qing dynasty, 6, 10, 12, 118,
289
Qinghua University, 117
Re-education Through Labor,
199
Red Guard factionalism, xiv, 26
Reform (educational) xiii, xv,
xx, 1, 2, 8-10, 12, 15, 17,
19-20, 23-28, 24-29, 31,
33, 66, 67, 69, 72-76, 82,
85, 90, 109, 112-114, 114-
119, 123-124, 127-130,
133, 163, 165, 166, 172,
180-181, 201, 217, 218,
219, 223, 226, 227, 228,
229, 230-232, 236, 238,
240-243, 245-247, 287,
295, 297, 298, 300, 375,
383, 385, 388, 389, 391
*Reform of China's Educational
Structure* (1985), 69
Reform Through Labor, 199
Reformatories, 197-203

work-study schools (for delinquents), 197, 199-203, 208
Republican Era, xvii, 10, 31, 117, 204, 264, 278, 290, 296
Research Institutes 113, 118, 121, 122, 126, 127, 136, 256, 260, 267, 292, 296-298, 297, 303, 332, 385
Retarded children, 204-205, 207-209, 210
Robinson, Jean, xix, xxiii, 163
Rockefeller Foundation, 16, 263
Rosen, Stanley, xxii, xiv, 417
Ross, Heidi, xix, xx, xxiv xxv, 66
Rural-urban disparity, conflicts, xiii, xix, 44, 67, 80-82, 341, 349
Rural responsibility system, xxiv, 113
see also *chenbao*, individual responsibility system
Rural transformation, 173-175, 188, 189
Science, 9, 12-13, 18-20, 21, 29, 57, 74, 75, 76, 113, 114, 117, 125, 126, 128, 153, 156, 157, 159, 166, 176, 188, 230, 255-257, 259-267, 269, 270-272, 273, 274, 276, 277, 300, 356
and technology, 4, 9, 12, 13, 18, 20-21, 29, 114, 159, 188, 256, 267, 271, 273, 277, 300, 303
Scientific cooperation, 166

Secondary education, xxv, 30, 66, 69-77, 90, 147, 148, 149, 170, 180, 181, 182, 185, 186, 187, 189, 218, 221, 223, 224, 232, 233, 234, 239, 241, 242, 317, 318, 323, 326, 328, 329, 341, 353, 354, 355, 357, 359, 359, 360, 364, 366, 376, 377, 378, 382, 387, 388, 396-397
secondary schooling, xix, 18, 21, 23, 33, 66-92, 131, 132, 151, 158, 166, 218, 223, 355, 424, 441
junior secondary (middle) schools, 30, 69-70, 73, 76-77, 78-79, 80, 81, 84, 88, 180, 184-185, 323, 326, 328, 331, 355, 358, 360, 361
senior secondary schools, 21, 29, 30, 69-70, 73-75, 77-82, 83, 84, 88-89, 91-92, 180, 337, 355, 358, 360, 361, 365-366
senior secondary competency examinations (*huikao*), 75
Self-strengthening movement, xvii, 9-10,
Sex education, 84, 88-89
Shanghai, xx, 67, 70, 73, 75-76, 82, 89-91, 110, 119, 128, 131, 133, 134, 136, 137, 156, 157, 197
university students, 422-430

Shantou Supersonic Company,
183
Shensi Institute of Chinese
Medicine, 267
Shenzhen, 172, 174, 176-177,
179-180, 182-189, 442-
443
Shuyuan, 6, 110, 111, 123
Single child policy, 42, 44,
46, 48, 60
Socialization patterns, xxv, 42-
50, 56-62, 86, 88, 149,
208, 316-318, 321, 338-
340, 345, 417, 420, 423,
430
family, 45
school, xxv
moral crisis, 441
Social class, xiii, xiv, xv, xvi,
xix, xxi, 81
background, xv, 327
conflict, xiv-xvii, xxi
consciousness, 432
Social science, xx, xxvi, 115,
122, 126, 127, 130, 137,
271, 387, 388, 422
Soviet education, 20-23, 110,
114, 117-118, 121-123,
126-127, 133, 138, 183,
198, 266, 290, 293, 376
Soviet reforms, 117
Spare-time schools, 147, 149,
151, 155-156
Special economic zones
(SEZs), xxiv, 172-185,
187-191, 442
Special education, 203-211
Spiritual pollution campaign,
32
State, xiii, xv-xviii, xx, xxi,
xxiv, xxvi, 5, 8-10, 11,
18, 21, 23, 24, 29, 31, 43,
45-46, 50, 61, 69, 70, 71,
78, 87, 90, 110, 112, 113,
114, 115, 126, 129, 163,
150, 165, 167-168, 178,
181, 197, 198, 199, 218,
219, 220, 226-227, 229,
232, 234-236, 237-243,
244-245, 256, 258-262,
265, 273, 277, 289, 295,
327, 359, 380-383, 385-
389, 396, 406, 407, 409,
417, 430, 440, 441, 442,
443-444
bureaucracy and the, xxi,
5, 19, 26, 29, 178-179,
218, 226, 233, 237,
241, 242, 379-380,
383-384
State Council, 176, 184, 242,
292, 335, 378, 385, 406,
439
State Education Commission,
xxvi, 67, 73, 75, 77, 80,
82, 87, 88, 120, 125, 126,
131, 135, 137, 149, 152,
154-155, 165, 206, 225,
227, 228, 229. 230, 234,
238, 239, 242, 243, 277,
297, 375, 385-388, 438
Student activism, xiii, 91, 111,
123, 128, 133, 397, 416,
417, 418, 421
student protest, xxii, 295,
397, 416, 417
student demonstrations,
xxiv, 14, 396-397, 416,
417, 418, 431, 436-
437, 440-441
Student attitudes, 422-430, 431-
436
student party members,
437-442

Szelenyi, Ivan, xxi, xxiii
Teachers, xx, xxv, 7, 14, 21,
24, 33, 42, 43, 49, 50,
51-55, 57-60, 67-69, 70-
74, 76-77, 79, 80, 82, 83-
89, 90-92, 117, 120, 133,
135, 147, 149-150, 153,
158, 164, 166-169, 181,
185, 204, 206-209, 217-
245, 263, 270, 274-275,
288, 292-293, 298-305,
353, 355, 356, 361-362,
389, 398, 420, 424, 431,
437, 438
    Teacher roles, 218-219,
        223, 244
    Recruitment of, 227-230,
        235, 237
Teacher education and
    preparation, 127, 218,
    222-225, 227, 231, 232,
    234, 240, 257, 377, 378,
    387
Teaching benefits, 219, 226,
    234-235, 237-243
    salaries, 219, 234, 242
Teaching methods, 54, 71,
    150, 151, 181, 182, 201,
    208, 209, 298, 301, 318,
    431
Television, 45, 47, 62, 68, 89-
    90, 153-154
Tianamen Massacre, xiii, xvii,
    xviii, xx, xxv, 165, 168,
    179, 196, 201, 338, 340,
    396,
    see also June, 1989
United Nations,
    Convention on the Rights
        of the Child, 211
    Unicef, 209

Universities, 15, 16, 17, 23, 27,
51, 76, 82, 91, 112-138,
153, 154, 155, 159, 183,
184, 190, 222, 228-232,
255, 256-258, 260, 262-
263, 265, 266-268, 270-
272, 274-275, 276-278,
296-299, 303, 328, 329,
337, 338, 355, 356, 361,
379, 382, 385, 395-399,
400, 402, 404, 407-408,
411, 413, 418, 422, 427,
431, 432, 435, 436, 437-
438, 441
    entrance examinations, 21,
        72, 73, 74-77, 78, 79,
        83, 84, 87, 130, 154,
        156, 157, 222, 225,
        229, 232, 233, 239,
        358, 361
    linkages with secondary
        schools 76, 130-133
    direct entrance (*zhisheng*)
        system, 76
    enrollments, 114, 115, 121,
        122, 123, 126, 127,
        129, 131, 137
    quotas, 114, 118, 121, 126,
        129, 130, 135
Universal (compulsory)
    schooling, 33-34, 51, 69,
    80, 151, 165-169
    compulsory education law,
        33-34, 81, 165, 166-
        169, 233, 236, 237
Upward mobility, xv, 6, 397,
    443-444
Vocational-technical education,
    5, 18, 24, 30, 33, 68, 70-
    71, 77-80, 82, 84, 90, 116,
    120, 121, 123, 130, 131,
    135, 148, 150, 159, 180-

187, 318, 320, 325, 329,
    330, 334-337, 341, 377
    agricultural schools, 77,
        78, 79-81, 119, 127,
        131, 154, 157
Wei Jingsheng, 294
Western learning, 4, 8-20, 29,
    32, 34, 35, 88, 118, 136,
    200, 262-268, 278, 296,
    300
Wright, Erik Olin, xix
Women's Federation, 364
Work-study, xix, 14, 24-26,
30, 31, 150, 197, 199-203,
207-208
World Bank, 135
Xiao Aiyi ("little auntie"), 48-
    49, 51
Xiao huangdi ("little
    emperors"), 42, 49
Yen, James, 15
Zhao Ziyang, xxii, 112, 136,
    290, 339, 417, 418
Zhongyi (Chinese medicine),
    260, 264, 267-268, 269,
    272, 278